Applications of Spatial Data Structures

Applications of Spatial Data Structures

Computer Graphics, Image Processing, and GIS

Hanan Samet

UNIVERSITY OF MARYLAND

 ADDISON - WESLEY PUBLISHING COMPANY
Reading, Massachusetts • Menlo Park, California • New York
Don Mills, Ontario • Wokingham, England • Amsterdam
Bonn • Sydney • Singapore • Tokyo • Madrid • San Juan

This book is in the Addison-Wesley Series in Computer Science
Michael A. Harrison: Consulting Editor

Many of the designations used by manufacturers and sellers to distinguish their products are claimed as trademarks. Where those designations appear in this book, and Addison-Wesley was aware of a trademark claim, the designations have been printed in initial caps or all caps.

The programs and applications presented in this book have been included for their instructional value. They have been tested with care, but are not guaranteed for any particular purpose. The publisher does not offer any warranties or representations, nor does it accept any liabilities with respect to the programs or applications.

Library of Congress Cataloging-in-Publication Data

Samet, Hanan.
  Applications of spatial data structures: computer graphics, image
processing, and GIS / by Hanan Samet.
    p.   cm.
  Bibliography: p.
  Includes index.
  ISBN 0-201-50300-X
    1. Data structures (Computer science)   2. Computer graphics.
I. Title.
QA76.9.D35S25   1989
006—dc19   89-30365
                                                                CIP

ABCDEFGHIJ-MA-89

Credits:
Thor Bestul created the cover art.
        Figures 1.1, 2.3, 3.1, 4.1, 4.3, and 5.16 are from H. Samet and R. E. Webber, On encoding boundaries with quadtrees, *IEEE Transactions on Pattern Analysis and Machine Intelligence 6*, 3(May 1984), 365–369. © 1984 IEEE. Reprinted by permission of IEEE.
        Figures 1.2, 1.3, 1.17, 6.2, 6.4, 6.5, and 6.12 are from H. Samet and R. E. Webber, Hierarchical data structures and algorithms for computer graphics, Part I. Fundamentals, *IEEE Computer Graphics and Applications 8*, 3(May 1988), 48–68. © 1988 IEEE. Reprinted by permission of IEEE.
        Figures 1.4 through 1.6, 1.9 through 1.14, 1.18, 3.3, 4.16, 4.28, 5.2, 5.17, 5.18, 6.1, 6.3, and 6.10 are from H. Samet, The quadtree and related hierarchical data structures, *ACM Computing Surveys 16*, 2(June 1984), 187–260. Reprinted by permission of ACM.
        Figures 1.15 and 4.24 are from H. Samet and R. E. Webber, Storing a collection of polygons using quadtrees, *ACM Transactions on Graphics 4*, 3(July 1985), 182–222. Reprinted by permission of ACM.
        Figures 2.1, 4.22, 4.23, and 8.1 are from C. R. Dyer, A. Rosenfeld, and H. Samet, Region representation: boundary codes from quadtrees, *Communications of the ACM 23*, 3(March 1980), 171–179. Reprinted by permission of ACM.
        Figures 2.2 and 8.2 through 8.19 are from H. Samet, Data structures for quadtree approximation and compression, *Communications of the ACM 28*, 9(September 1985), 973–993. Reprinted by permission of ACM.
        Figures 2.4 and 4.13 are from C. A. Shaffer and H. Samet, Optimal quadtree construction algorithms, *Computer Vision, Graphics, and Image Processing 37*, 3(March 1987), 402–419. Reprinted by permission of Academic Press.
Continued on p. 507

To my parents, Julius and Lotte

PREFACE

The quadtree and octree are hierarchical data structures used to represent spatial data. They are based on the principle of recursive decomposition (similar to *divide and conquer* methods [Aho74]). This book focuses on the use of quadtree and octree representations of region data (in two and three dimensions, respectively) in applications in computer graphics, image processing, and geographic information systems (GIS), as well as computer vision, robotics, pattern recognition, solid modeling, and other areas. For a comprehensive treatment of related hierarchical representations of spatial data including points, lines, rectangles, regions, and volumes, see [Same90a].

To many people, the terms *quadtree* and *octree* have taken on a generic meaning synonymous with the term *hierarchical data structure*. Hierarchical data structures are useful because of their ability to focus on the interesting subsets of the data. This focusing results in an efficient representation and in improved execution times. Thus they are particularly convenient for performing set operations. Many of the operations described can often be performed as efficiently, or more so, with other data structures. Nevertheless, hierarchical data structures are attractive because of their conceptual clarity and ease of implementation. In addition, the use of some of them provides a spatial index. This is very useful in applications involving spatial databases.

This book is organized as follows. Chapter 1 introduces hierarchical data structures such as the quadtree and octree. It reviews their key properties, traces their history, and gives an overview of their use in representing point and line data, as well as three-dimensional regions. All of these topics are covered in much greater detail in [Same90a].

Most hierarchical data structures are trees. As such they are most often implemented using pointers. Chapter 2 discusses alternative implementations that do not make use of pointers and compares their storage requirements with an implementation that does use pointers. Chapter 3 contains a detailed presentation of how to perform neighbor finding. This is an important technique in the efficient implementation of a number of algorithms that use quadtree and octree-like representations. It is used heavily in their construction (Chapter 4), computing geometric properties (Chapter 5), ray tracing (Chapter 7), and skeletons (Chapter 9). Chapters 2 and 3 may be skipped by readers who are interested only in applications.

The remaining chapters discuss the applications in greater detail. Chapter 4 shows the ease with which conversions can be made between the quadtree representation of two-dimensional regions and more conventional representations such as arrays, rasters, and boundary codes. The extension to three-dimensional regions is straightforward and is discussed only in the context of building an octree from a set of views of an object or a scene of three-dimensional objects. For details on converting between other representations of three-dimensional regions and octrees (e.g., boundary model [BRep], constructive solid geometry [CSG]), see Chapter 5 of [Same90a].

Chapter 5 examines the computation of geometric properties such as connected component labeling. Such operations arise in computer graphics (where it is known as polygon coloring or filling) and as a basic step in the processing of an image.

Chapter 6 discusses the implementation of set-theoretic operations, linear transformations, and other algorithms useful in computer graphics and image processing. Chapter 7 contains a detailed presentation of the use of hierarchical data structures in the display of graphical information. In particular, much attention is given to the problem of ray tracing and some to beam tracing. The radiosity method is covered with considerably less detail. Chapters 6 and 7 may be skipped by readers uninterested in computer graphics.

Chapter 8 treats the problem of image approximation and compression by use of hierarchical representations. This discussion is in the context of two-dimensional binary images. Chapter 9 examines the application of quadtree-like decomposition to the computation of skeletons. In particular, the concept of distance is formulated in the context of a quadtree, and its application is explored. Chapters 8 and 9 are somewhat specialized and may be omitted in the interest of time.

This book is designed to be used as a reference as well as the basis of a course on the implementation of a graphics, image processing, or geographic information system (GIS) based on quadtrees and octrees. It can also be used as a supplement in a general course on these topics.

There are a number of topics for which justice requires considerably more detailed treatment. Due to space limitations, I have omitted a detailed discussion of them and instead refer interested readers to the appropriate literature. The notion of a pyramid is presented only at a cursory level in Chapter 1 so that it can be contrasted with the quadtree. In particular, the pyramid is a multiresolution representation, whereas the quadtree is a variable resolution representation. Readers are referred to Tanimoto and Klinger [Tani80] and the collection of papers edited by Rosenfeld [Rose83a] for a more comprehensive exposition on pyramids. The use of quadtrees in finite element analysis is mentioned in Chapter 1; for more details, see Kela, Perucchio, and Voelcker [Kela86] and the references cited there. Similarly I discuss image compression and coding only in the context of hierarchical data structures. This is done in Chapter 8.

For more details on early results involving these and related topics, consult the surveys by Nagy and Wagle [Nagy79], Peuquet [Peuq84], Requicha [Requ80], Srihari [Srih81], Samet and Rosenfeld [Same80d], Samet [Same84b], and Samet and Webber [Same88c, Same88d]. A number of excellent texts contain material related to the topics that I cover. Rosenfeld and Kak [Rose82a] should be consulted for an encyclopedic treatment of image processing. Mäntylä [Mänt87] has written a comprehensive introduction to solid modeling. Burrough [Burr86] provides a survey of geographic information systems. For a comprehensive view of the literature, see Rosenfeld's annual collection of references in the journal *Computer Vision, Graphics, and Image Processing* (e.g., [Rose88]).

Nevertheless, given the broad and rapidly expanding nature of the field, I am bound to have omitted significant concepts and references. In addition, at times, I devote a disproportionate amount of attention to some concepts at the expense of others. This is principally for expository purposes; I feel that it is better to understand some structures well rather than to give readers a quick runthrough of buzzwords. For these indiscretions, I beg your pardon and hope you nevertheless bear with me.

My approach is an algorithmic one. Whenever possible, I have tried to motivate critical steps in the algorithms by a liberal use of examples. I feel that it is of paramount importance for readers to see the ease with which the representations can be implemented and used. In each chapter, except for the introduction (Chapter 1), I give at least one detailed algorithm using pseudo-code so that readers can see how the ideas can be applied. The pseudo-code is a variant of the ALGOL [Naur60] programming language that has a data structuring facility incorporating pointers and record structures. Recursion is used heavily. This language has similarities to C [Kern78], PASCAL [Jens74], SAIL [Reis76], and ALGOL W [Baue68]. Its basic features are described in the Appendix. However, the actual code is not crucial to understanding the techniques and it may be skipped on a first reading. The index indicates the page numbers where the code for each algorithm is found.

In many cases I also give an analysis of the space and time requirements of different data structures and algorithms. The analysis is usually of an asymptotic nature and is in terms of *big O* and Ω notation [Knut76]. The *big O* notation denotes an upper bound. For example, if an algorithm takes $O(\log_2 N)$ time, then its worst-case behavior is never any worse than $\log_2 N$. The Ω notation denotes a lower bound. As an example of its use, consider the problem of sorting N numbers. When I say that sorting is $\Omega(N \cdot \log_2 N)$, I mean that given any algorithm for sorting, there is some set of N input values for which the algorithm will require at least this much time.

At times I also describe implementations of some of the data structures for the purpose of comparison. In such cases counts such as the number of fields in a record are often given. These numbers are meant only to amplify the discussion. They are not to be taken literally, as improvements are always possible once a specific application is analyzed more carefully.

Each chapter contains a substantial number of exercises. Many of the exercises develop further the material in the text as a means of testing the reader's understanding, as well as suggesting future directions. When the exercise or its solution is not my own, I have preceded it with the name of its originator. The exercises have not been graded by difficulty. They rarely require any mathematical skills beyond the undergraduate level for their solution. However, while some of the exercises are quite straightforward, others require some ingenuity. Solutions, or references to papers that contain the solution, are provided for a substantial number of the exercises that do not require programming. Readers are cautioned to try to solve the exercises before turning to the solutions. It is my belief that much can be learned this way (for the student and, even more so, for the author). The motivation for undertaking this task was my wonderful experience on my first encounter with the rich work on data structures by Knuth [Knut73a, Knut73b].

An extensive bibliography is provided. It contains entries for both this book and the companion text [Same90a]. Not all of the references that appear in the bibliography are cited in the two texts. They are retained for the purpose of giving readers the ability to access the entire body of literature relevant to the topics discussed in them. Each reference is annotated with a key word(s) and a list of the numbers of the sections in which it is cited in either of the texts (including exercises and solutions). In addition, a name and credit index is provided that indicates the page numbers in this book on which each author's work is cited or a credit is made.

ACKNOWLEDGMENTS

Over the years I have received help from many people, and I am extremely grateful to them. In particular, Robert E. Webber, Markku Tamminen, and Michael B. Dillencourt have generously given me much of their time and have gone over critical parts of the book. I have drawn heavily on their knowledge of some of the topics covered here. I have also been extremely fortunate to work with Azriel Rosenfeld over the past ten years. His dedication and scholarship have been a true inspiration to me. I deeply cherish our association.

I was introduced to the field of spatial data structures by Gary D. Knott who asked "how to delete in point quadtrees." Azriel Rosenfeld and Charles R. Dyer provided much interaction in the initial phase of my research. Those discussions led to the discovery of the neighbor-finding principle. It is during that time that many of the basic conversion algorithms between quadtrees and other image representations were developed as well. I learned much about image processing and computer vision from them. Robert E. Webber taught me computer graphics, Markku Tamminen taught me solid modeling and representations for multiattribute data, and Michael B. Dillencourt taught me about computational geometry.

During the time that this book was written, my research was supported, in part, by the National Science Foundation, the Defense Mapping Agency, the Harry Diamond Laboratory, and the Bureau of the Census. In particular, I thank Richard

Antony, Y. T. Chien, Su-shing Chen, Hank Cook, Phil Emmerman, Joe Rastatter, Alan Saalfeld, and Larry Tokarcik. I am appreciative of their support.

Many people helped me in the process of preparing the book for publication. Acknowledgments are due to Rene McDonald for coordinating the day-to-day matters of getting the book out and copyediting; to Scott Carson, Emery Jou, and Jim Purtilo for TROFF assistance beyond the call of duty; to Marisa Antoy and Sergio Antoy for designing and implementing the algorithm formatter used to typeset the algorithms; to Barbara Burnett, Michael B. Dillencourt, and Sandy German for help with the index; to Jay Weber for setting up the TROFF macrofiles so that I can keep track of symbolic names and thus be able to move text around without worrying about the numbering of exercises, sections, and chapters; to Liz Allen for early TROFF help; to Nono Kusuma, Mark Stanley, and Joan Wright Hamilton for drawing the figures; to Richard Muntz and Gerald Estrin for providing temporary office space and computer access at UCLA; to Sandy German, Gwen Nelson, and Janet Salzman for help in initial typing of the manuscript; to S. S. Iyengar, Duane Marble, George Nagy, and Terry Smith who reviewed the book; and to Peter Gordon, John Remington, and Keith Wollman at Addison-Wesley Publishing Company for their encouragement and confidence in this project.

Aside from the individuals already named, I have also benefited from discussions with many people over the past years. They have commented on various parts of the book and include Chuan-Heng Ang, Walid Aref, James Arvo, Thor Bestul, Sharat Chandran, Chiun-Hong Chien, Jiang-Hsing Chu, Leila De Floriani, Roger Eastman, Herbert Edelsbrunner, Christos Faloutsos, George (Gyuri) Fekete, Kikuo Fujimura, John Gannon, John Goldak, Erik Hoel, Liuqing Huang, Frederik W. Jansen, Ajay Kela, David Kirk, Per Åke Larson, Dani Lischinski, Don Meagher, David Mount, Randal C. Nelson, Glenn Pearson, Ron Sacks-Davis, Timos Sellis, Clifford A. Shaffer, Deepak Sherlekar, Li Tong, Brian Von Herzen, Peter Widmayer, and David Wise. I deeply appreciate their help.

CONTENTS

1 INTRODUCTION   **1**
  1.1 Basic Definitions   1
  1.2 Properties of Quadtrees and Octrees   2
  1.3 Variants of Quadtrees and Octrees   9
  1.4 History and the Use of Quadtrees and Octrees   22
  1.5 Implementation   26

2 ALTERNATIVE QUADTREE REPRESENTATIONS   **29**
  2.1 Collection of Leaf Nodes   30
    2.1.1 Linear Quadtrees   30
    2.1.2 Comparison of Pointer Quadtrees and FD Linear Quadtrees   42
    2.1.3 Two-Dimensional Run Encoding   48
    2.1.4 Forests   51
  2.2 Tree Traversals   53

3 NEIGHBOR-FINDING TECHNIQUES   **57**
  3.1 Adjacency and Neighbors in Quadtrees   58
  3.2 Neighbor Finding in Pointer-Based Quadtree Representations   61
    3.2.1 Nearest Common Ancestor Method   61
      3.2.1.1 Algorithms   63
      3.2.1.2 Analysis   70
      3.2.1.3 Empirical Results   78
    3.2.2 Other Methods for Neighbor Finding   81
    3.2.3 Comparison   84
  3.3 Neighbor Finding in Pointer-Based Octree Representations   85

		3.3.1	Definitions and Notation	86
		3.3.2	Algorithms	88
		3.3.3	Analysis	95
		3.3.4	Summary	97
	3.4	Neighbor Finding in Pointerless Representations		98
		3.4.1	FD Linear Quadtree	98
		3.4.2	FL Linear Quadtree	105
		3.4.3	VL Linear Quadtree	108
		3.4.4	DF-Expressions	110

4   **CONVERSION**   **111**

	4.1	Binary Arrays		112
	4.2	Row or Raster Representations		116
		4.2.1	Building a Quadtree from a Raster Representation	117
		4.2.2	Building a Raster Representation from a Quadtree	125
		4.2.3	Building a Pointerless Quadtree from a Raster Representation	135
	4.3	Chain Codes		144
		4.3.1	Building a Quadtree from a Chain Code	144
		4.3.2	Building a Chain Code from a Quadtree	156
	4.4	Quadtrees from Polygons		162
	4.5	Building a PM_1 Quadtree		163
	4.6	Building Octrees from Multiple Views		174

5   **COMPUTING GEOMETRIC PROPERTIES**   **183**

	5.1	Connected Component Labeling		183
		5.1.1	Connection to Graph Theory: Depth First and Predetermined Approaches	184
		5.1.2	Explicit Quadtrees	191
		5.1.3	Pointerless Quadtree Representations	199
	5.2	Perimeter, Area, and Moments		213
	5.3	Component Counting		219

6   **OPERATIONS ON IMAGES**   **225**

	6.1	Point Location		225
	6.2	Neighboring Object Location		228
	6.3	Set-Theoretic Operations		229
		6.3.1	Dithering	229
		6.3.2	Aligned Quadtrees	231
		6.3.3	Unaligned Quadtrees	234
	6.4	Windowing		243
	6.5	Linear Image Transformations		245
		6.5.1	Algorithms Based on Transforming the Source Tree	246
		6.5.2	Algorithms Based on an Inverse Transformation	248
		6.5.3	Algorithms Based on Address Computation	253
	6.6	Region Expansion		260

7 DISPLAY METHODS   **267**
   7.1 Hierarchical Hidden-Surface Algorithms   268
      7.1.1 2.5-Dimensional Hidden-Surface Elimination   270
      7.1.2 Warnock's Algorithm   272
      7.1.3 Weiler-Atherton's Algorithm   275
      7.1.4 Displaying Scenes Represented by Region Octrees   276
      7.1.5 Use of BSP Trees for Hidden-Surface Elimination   283
      7.1.6 Displaying Curved Surfaces   286
   7.2 Ray Tracing   292
      7.2.1 Historical Development   292
      7.2.2 Speeding Up Ray Tracing   296
      7.2.3 How to Trace a Ray   299
      7.2.4 Sample Implementation   305
      7.2.5 Discussion   315
   7.3 Beam Tracing   316
   7.4 Radiosity   321

8 QUADTREE APPROXIMATION AND COMPRESSION   **325**
   8.1 Truncation-Based Approximation Methods   326
   8.2 Forest-Based Approximation Methods   329
      8.2.1 Definitions and Approximation Quality   329
      8.2.2 Compression   346
      8.2.3 Observations   352
   8.3 Progressive Pyramid-Based Approximation Methods   354

9 DISTANCE AND QUADTREE MEDIAL AXIS TRANSFORMS   **357**
   9.1 Distance, Skeletons, and Medial Axis Transforms (MAT)   358
   9.2 Quadtree Distance   361
   9.3 Quadtree Medial Axis Transforms   370
      9.3.1 Definitions   370
      9.3.2 Computing a QMAT from Its Quadtree   375
      9.3.3 Reconstructing a Quadtree from Its QMAT   381
      9.3.4 Using the QMAT as an Image Representation   390

Solutions to Exercises   **399**
Appendix: Description of Pseudo-Code Language   **425**
References   **429**
Name and Credit Index   **479**
Subject Index   **491**

INTRODUCTION 1

There are numerous hierarchical data structuring techniques in use for representing spatial data. One commonly used technique that is based on recursive decomposition is the quadtree. It has evolved from work in different fields. Thus it is natural that a number of adaptations of it exist for each spatial data type. Its development has been motivated to a large extent by a desire to save storage by aggregating data having identical or similar values. However, we will see that this is not always the case. In fact, the savings in execution time that arise from this aggregation are often of equal or greater importance.

This chapter contains a brief overview of hierarchical data structures such as the quadtree and octree. The focus is on the representation of regions. The goal is to define the representations, and their key properties, that are used in the applications described in the remaining chapters. (For more details on these individual representations of spatial data, see [Same90a].)

The rest of this chapter is organized as follows. It starts with some basic definitions followed by an outline of key properties of the quadtree and octree data structures. Next some of the most important quadtree-based representations for point and line data, as well as three-dimensional regions, are reviewed. This is followed by a brief history of the development of the quadtree and octree. Finally, a description is given of an implementation of a quadtree (and octree) as a tree. Much of this chapter is a summary of Chapter 1 of [Same90a].

1.1 BASIC DEFINITIONS

Let us first define a few terms with respect to two-dimensional data. Assume the existence of an array of picture elements (termed *pixels*) in two dimensions. We use the term *image* to refer to the original array of pixels. If its elements are either black or white, it is said to be *binary*. If shades of gray are possible (i.e., gray levels), the image is said to be a *gray-scale* image. In the discussion, we are primarily concerned with binary images. Assume that the image is on an infinite background of white pixels. The *border* of the image is the outer boundary of the square corresponding to the array.

Two pixels are said to be 4-*adjacent* if they are adjacent to each other in the horizontal or vertical direction. If the concept of adjacency also includes adjacency at a corner (i.e., diagonal adjacencies), then the pixels are said to be 8-*adjacent*. A set s is said to be *four-connected* (*eight-connected*) if for any pixels p, q in s there exists a sequence of pixels $p = p_0, p_1, \cdots, p_n = q$ in s, such that p_{i+1} is 4-adjacent (8-adjacent) to p_i, $0 \le i < n$.

A black *region*, or black four-connected *component*, is a maximal four-connected set of black pixels. The process of assigning the same label to all 4-adjacent black pixels is called *connected component labeling* (see Chapter 5). A white *region* is a maximal *eight-connected* set of white pixels defined analogously. The complement of a black region consists of a union of eight-connected white regions. Exactly one of these white regions contains the infinite background of white pixels. All the other white regions, if any, are called *holes* in the black region. The black region, say R, is surrounded by the infinite white region, and R surrounds the other white regions, if any.

A pixel is said to have four edges, each of which is of unit length. The *boundary* of a black region consists of the set of edges of its constituent pixels that also serve as edges of white pixels. Similar definitions can be formulated in terms of rectangular blocks, all of whose pixels are identically colored. For example, two disjoint blocks, P and Q, are said to be 4-*adjacent* if there exists a pixel p in P and a pixel q in Q such that p and q are 4-adjacent. Eight-adjacency for blocks (as well as connected component labeling) is defined analogously.

1.2 PROPERTIES OF QUADTREES AND OCTREES

The term *quadtree* is used to describe a class of hierarchical data structures whose common property is that they are based on the principle of recursive decomposition of space. They can be differentiated on the following bases:

1. The type of data they are used to represent.
2. The principle guiding the decomposition process.
3. The resolution (variable or not).

Currently they are used for point data, areas, curves, surfaces, and volumes. The decomposition may be into equal parts on each level (i.e., regular polygons and termed a *regular decomposition*), or it may be governed by the input. In computer graphics this distinction is often phrased in terms of image-space hierarchies versus object-space hierarchies, respectively [Suth74]. The resolution of the decomposition (i.e., the number of times that the decomposition process is applied) may be fixed beforehand, or it may be governed by properties of the input data. Note that for some applications we can also differentiate the data structures on the basis of whether they specify the boundaries of regions (e.g., curves and surfaces) or organize their interiors (e.g., areas and volumes).

The first example of a quadtree representation of data is concerned with the representation of two-dimensional binary region data. The most studied quadtree approach to region representation, called a *region quadtree* (but often termed a *quadtree* in the rest of this chapter), is based on the successive subdivision of a bounded image array into four equal-sized quadrants. If the array does not consist entirely of 1s or entirely of 0s (i.e., the region does not cover the entire array), it is subdivided into quadrants, subquadrants, and so on, until blocks are obtained that consist entirely of 1s or entirely of 0s; that is, each block is entirely contained in the region or entirely disjoint from it. The region quadtree can be characterized as a variable resolution data structure.

As an example of the region quadtree, consider the region shown in Figure 1.1a represented by the $2^3 \times 2^3$ binary array in Figure 1.1b. Observe that the 1s correspond to picture elements (i.e., pixels) in the region, and the 0s correspond to picture elements outside the region. The resulting blocks for the array of Figure 1.1b are shown in Figure 1.1c. This process is represented by a tree of degree 4 (i.e., each nonleaf node has four sons).

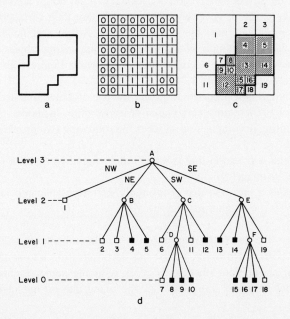

Figure 1.1   An example (a) region, (b) its binary array,
(c) its maximal blocks (blocks in the region are shaded), and
(d) the corresponding quadtree

In the tree representation, the root node corresponds to the entire array. Each son of a node represents a quadrant (labeled in order NW, NE, SW, SE) of the region represented by that node. The leaf nodes of the tree correspond to those blocks for which no further subdivision is necessary. A leaf node is said to be black or white depending on whether its corresponding block is entirely inside (i.e., it contains only 1s) or entirely outside the represented region (i.e., it contains no 1s). All nonleaf nodes are said to be gray (i.e., its block contains 0s and 1s). Given a $2^n \times 2^n$ image, the root node is said to be at level n while a node at level 0 corresponds to a single pixel in the image.[1] The region quadtree representation for Figure 1.1c is shown in Figure 1.1d. The leaf nodes are labeled with numbers, and the nonleaf nodes are labeled with letters. The levels of the tree are also marked.

The region quadtree is easily extended to represent three-dimensional binary region data, and the resulting data structure is called a *region octree* (termed an *octree* in the rest of this chapter). We start with a $2^n \times 2^n \times 2^n$ object array of unit cubes (termed *voxels* or *obels*). The octree is based on the successive subdivision of an object array into octants. If the array does not consist entirely of 1s or entirely of 0s, it is subdivided into octants, suboctants, and so on, until cubes (possibly single voxels) are obtained that consist of 1s or of 0s; that is, they are entirely contained in the region or entirely disjoint from it.

This subdivision process is represented by a tree of degree 8 in which the root node represents the entire object and the leaf nodes correspond to those cubes of the array for which no further subdivision is necessary. Leaf nodes are said to be black or white (alternatively, full or void) depending on whether their corresponding cubes are entirely within or outside the object, respectively. All nonleaf nodes are said to be gray. Figure 1.2a is an example of a simple three-dimensional object, in the form of a staircase, whose octree block decomposition is given in Figure 1.2b and whose tree representation is given in Figure 1.2c.

At this point, it is appropriate to justify the use of a quadtree decomposition into squares. Of course, there are many planar decomposition methods. Squares are used because the resulting decomposition satisfies the following two properties:

1.   It yields a partition that is an infinitely repetitive pattern so that it can be used for images of any size.
2.   It yields a partition that is infinitely decomposable into increasingly finer patterns (i.e., higher resolution).

A quadtree-like decomposition into four equilateral triangles (Figure 1.3a) also satisfies these criteria. However, unlike the decomposition into squares, it does not have a uniform orientation—that is, all tiles with the same orientation cannot be mapped into each other by translations of the plane that do not involve rotation or

---

[1] Alternatively, we can say that the root node is at depth 0 while a node at depth n corresponds to a single pixel in the image. In this book both concepts of level and depth are used to describe the relative position of nodes. The one that is chosen is context dependent.

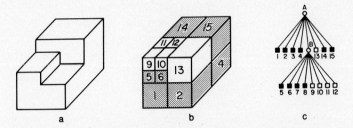

Figure 1.2 (a) Example three-dimensional object, (b) its octree block decomposition, and (c) its tree representation

reflection. In contrast, a decomposition into hexagons (Figure 1.3b) has a uniform orientation, but it does not satisfy property 2. For more details on the properties of decompositions see Bell, Diaz, Holroyd, and Jackson [Bell83] (and Section 1.4 of [Same90a]).

The prime motivation for the development of the quadtree is the desire to reduce the amount of space necessary to store data through the use of aggregation of homogeneous blocks. As we will see in subsequent chapters, an important by-product of this aggregation is the reduction of the execution time of a number of operations (e.g., connected component labeling and component counting). However, a quadtree implementation does have overhead in terms of the nonleaf nodes. For an image with B and W black and white blocks, respectively, $4 \cdot (B + W)/3$ nodes are required. In contrast, a binary array representation of a $2^n \times 2^n$ image requires only 2^{2n} bits; however, this quantity grows quite quickly. Furthermore if the amount of aggregation is minimal (e.g., a checkerboard image), the quadtree is not very efficient.

The worst case for a quadtree of a given depth in terms of storage requirements occurs when the region corresponds to a checkerboard pattern, as in Figure 1.4. The amount of space required is obviously a function of the resolution (i.e., the number of levels in the quadtree), the size of the image (i.e., its perimeter), and its positioning in the grid within which it is embedded. As a simple example, Dyer [Dyer82] has shown

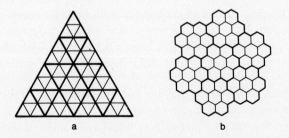

Figure 1.3 Example of nonsquare partitionings of the plane: (a) equilateral triangles and (b) hexagons

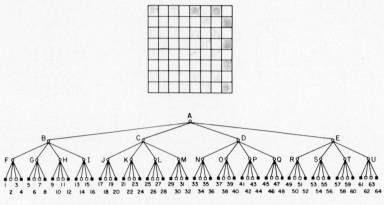

Figure 1.4   A checkerboard and its quadtree

that arbitrarily placing a square of size $2^m \times 2^m$ at any position in a $2^n \times 2^n$ image requires an average of $O(2^{m+2} + n - m)$ quadtree nodes. An alternative characterization of this result is that the amount of space necessary is $O(p + n)$ where p is the perimeter (in pixel widths) of the block.

Dyer's $O(p + n)$ result for a square image is merely an instance of the following theorem due to Hunter and Steiglitz [Hunt78, Hunt79a] who obtained the same result for simple polygons (i.e., polygons with nonintersecting edges and without holes). In fact, this result has been observed to hold in arbitrary images (see [Rose82b] for empirical results in a cartographic environment).

Theorem 1.1   The quadtree corresponding to a polygon with perimeter p embedded in a $2^n \times 2^n$ image has a maximum of $24 \cdot n - 19 + 24 \cdot p$ (i.e., $O(p + n)$) nodes.   □

Hunter and Steiglitz represent a polygon by a three-color variant of the quadtree. It has three types of nodes: interior, boundary, and exterior. A node is said to be of type *boundary* if an edge of the polygon passes through it. Boundary nodes are not subject to merging. *Interior* and *exterior* nodes correspond to areas within, and outside, respectively, the polygon and can be merged to yield larger nodes. The resulting quadtree is analogous to the MX quadtree representation of point data described in Section 1.3, and this term will be used to describe it. In particular, boundary nodes are analogous to black nodes, while interior and exterior nodes are analogous to white nodes.

Figure 1.5 illustrates a sample polygon and its MX quadtree. One disadvantage of the MX quadtree representation for polygonal lines is that a width is associated with them, whereas in a purely technical sense these lines have a width of zero. Also, shifting operations may result in information loss. For more appropriate representations of polygonal lines, see Chapter 4 of [Same90a].

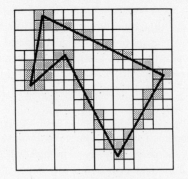

Figure 1.5   Hunter and Steiglitz's quadtree representation of a polygon

Theorem 1.1 can be recast by measuring the perimeter p in terms of the length of a side of the image in which the polygon is embedded—that is, for a $2^n \times 2^n$ image $p = p' \cdot 2^n$. Thus the value of the perimeter no longer depends on the resolution of the image. Restating Theorem 1.1 in terms of p' results in a quadtree having $O(p' \cdot 2^n + n)$ nodes. Therefore we have proved the following important corollary:

Corollary 1.1   The maximum number of nodes in a quadtree corresponding to an image is directly proportional to the resolution of the image.   ☐

The significance of Corollary 1.1 is that when using quadtrees, increasing the image resolution leads to a linear growth in the number of nodes. This is in contrast to the binary array representation where doubling the resolution leads to a quadrupling of the number of pixels.

In most practical cases, the perimeter dominates the resolution. Thus Theorem 1.1 is usually interpreted as stating that the number of nodes in a quadtree is proportional to the perimeter of the regions contained therein. Meagher [Meag80] has shown that this theorem also holds for three-dimensional data (i.e., for polyhedra represented by octrees) when the perimeter is replaced by the surface area. The perimeter and the surface area correspond to the size of the boundary of the polygon and polyhedron—in two and three dimensions, respectively. In fact, this theorem also holds in d dimensions.

Theorem 1.2   The size of a d-dimensional quadtree of a d-dimensional polyhedron is proportional to the sum of the resolution and the size of the boundary of the object.   ☐

Aside from its implication on the storage requirements, Theorem 1.1 also directly affects the analysis of the execution time of algorithms. In particular, most algorithms that execute on a quadtree representation of an image instead of an array representation have an execution time proportional to the number of blocks in the image rather than the number of pixels. In its most general case, this means that the application of a quadtree algorithm to a problem in d-dimensional space executes in time proportional to the analogous array-based algorithm in the $(d-1)$-dimensional space of the surface of the original d-dimensional image. Thus quadtrees are somewhat like dimension-reducing devices.

Theorem 1.2 assumes that the image consists of a polyhedron. Walsh [Wals85] lifts this restriction and obtains a weaker complexity bound. Assuming an image of resolution n and measuring the perimeter, say p, in terms of the number of border pixels, he proves that the total number of nodes in a d-dimensional quadtree is less than or equal to $4 \cdot n \cdot p$. Furthermore he shows that the number of black nodes is less than or equal to $(2^d - 1) \cdot n \cdot p / d$.

The complexity measures discussed do not explicitly reflect the fact that the amount of space occupied by a quadtree corresponding to a region is extremely sensitive to its orientation (i.e., where it is partitioned). For example, in Dyer's experiment, the number of nodes required for the arbitrary placement of a square of size $2^m \times 2^m$ at any position in a $2^n \times 2^n$ image ranged between $4 \cdot (n - m) + 1$ and $4 \cdot p + 16 \cdot (n - m) - 27$, with the average being $O(p + n - m)$. Clearly, shifting the image within the space in which it is embedded can reduce the total number of nodes. The problem of finding the optimal position for a quadtree can be decomposed into two parts. First, we must determine the optimal grid resolution and, second, the partition points.

Grosky and Jain [Gros83] have shown that for a region such that w is the maximum of its horizontal and vertical extent (measured in pixel widths) and $2^{n-1} < w \leq 2^n$, the optimal grid resolution is either n or $n + 1$. In other words, embedding the region in a larger area than 2^{n+1} by 2^{n+1} and shifting it around will not result in fewer nodes. Using similar reasoning, it can be shown that translating a region by 2^k pixels in any direction does not change the number of black or white blocks of size less than $2^k \times 2^k$ [Li82].

Using the above optimal grid resolution, Li, Grosky, and Jain [Li82] report an algorithm that treats the image as a binary array and finds the optimal positioning of a region quadtree corresponding to a $2^n \times 2^n$ image. The algorithm uses $O(2^{2n})$ space and has an execution time of $O(n \cdot 2^{2n})$. Experiments with typical images show that the algorithm has little effect (e.g., [Same84c]).

Exercises

1.1. Given the array representation of a binary image, write an algorithm to construct the corresponding region quadtree.

1.2. Given a quadtree with G nonleaf nodes, prove that the total number of nodes is $4 \cdot G + 1$.

1.3. Given an image represented by a region quadtree with B black and W white nodes, how many additional nodes are necessary for the nonleaf nodes?

1.4. Given an image represented by a region octree with B black and W white nodes, how many additional nodes are necessary for the nonleaf nodes?

1.5. Suppose that an octree is used to represent a collection of disjoint spheres. What would you use as a leaf criterion?

1.6. The quadtree can be generalized to represent data in arbitrary dimensions. As we saw, the octree is its three-dimensional analog. The renowned artist Escher [Coxe86] is noted for etchings of unusual interpretations of geometric objects, such as staircases. How would you represent one of Escher's staircases?

1.7. Consider the arbitrary placement of a square of size $2^m \times 2^m$ at any position in a $2^n \times 2^n$ image. Prove that in the best case $4 \cdot (n-m) + 1$ nodes are required, while the worst case requires $4 \cdot p + 16 \cdot (n-m) - 27$ nodes. How many of these nodes are black and white assuming that the square is black? Prove that on the average, the number of nodes required is $O(p + n - m)$.

1.8. What are the worst-case storage requirements of storing an arbitrary rectangle in a quadtree corresponding to a $2^n \times 2^n$ image? Give an example of the worst case and the number of nodes it requires.

1.9. Assume that the probability of a particular pixel's being black is one-half and likewise for being white. Given a $2^n \times 2^n$ image represented by a quadtree, what is the expected number of nodes, say $E(n)$, in the quadtree? Also compute the expected number of black, white, and gray nodes.

1.10. Suppose that instead of knowing the probability a particular pixel is black or white, we know the percentage of the total pixels in the image that are black. Given a $2^n \times 2^n$ image represented by a quadtree, what is the expected number of nodes in the quadtree?

1.11. Prove Theorem 1.1.

1.12. Can you prove that for an arbitrary quadtree (not necessarily a polygon), the number of nodes doubles as the resolution is doubled?

1.13. Derive a result analogous to Theorem 1.1 for a three-dimensional polyhedron represented as an octree. In this case, the perimeter corresponds to the surface area.

1.14. Prove Theorem 1.2.

1.15. Assuming an image of resolution n and measuring the perimeter, say p, in terms of the number of border pixels, prove that the total number of nodes in a d-dimensional quadtree is less than or equal to $4 \cdot n \cdot p$.

1.16. Assuming an image of resolution n and measuring the perimeter, say p, in terms of the number of border pixels, prove that the total number of black nodes in a d-dimensional quadtree is less than or equal to $(2^d - 1) \cdot n \cdot p / d$.

1.17. Prove that for a region such that w is the maximum of its horizontal and vertical extent (measured in pixel widths) and $2^{n-1} < w \le 2^n$, the optimal grid resolution is either n or $n + 1$.

1.18. Prove that translating a region by 2^k pixels in any direction does not change the number of black or white blocks of size less than $2^k \times 2^k$.

1.3 VARIANTS OF QUADTREES AND OCTREES

The most general definition of an image is as a collection (i.e., set) of image elements. This collection can be represented in a number of different ways, including arrays, lists, and trees. Moreover subcollections of similar image elements may be grouped together into blocks (e.g., quadtrees and octrees) and such a collection of blocks can again be represented using arrays, lists, trees, and so forth. Once a representation is chosen, we must also decide how the individual constituent image elements are ordered with respect to each other. For example, the implementation of a number of image-processing operations such as connected component labeling (see Section 5.1) is greatly facilitated when the ordering captures adjacency information.

The array is the most frequently used image representation. For large images, however, the amount of storage required is often deemed excessive, and a *raster* representation (i.e., a list of image rows) is used. The image is processed one row at a time. The raster representation can be improved upon by decomposing the rows into one-dimensional blocks of identically valued pixels (termed a *run representation* or *runlength endcoding*). The image is then represented as a list of such runs.

The region quadtree is a member of a class of representations characterized as being a collection of maximal (according to an appropriate definition) blocks, each of which is contained in a given region and whose union is the entire region. The simplest such representation is the run representation described above. In this case, the blocks are restricted to $1 \times m$ rectangles [Ruto68]. A more general representation treats the region as a union of maximal square blocks (or blocks of any other desired shape) that may possibly overlap. Usually the blocks are specified by their centers and radii. This representation is called the *medial axis transformation* (MAT) [Blum67, Rose66]. Of course, other approaches are also possible (e.g., rectangular coding [Kim83, Kim86] and TID [Scot85, Scot86]).

The region quadtree is a variant on the maximal block representation. It requires the blocks to be disjoint and to have standard sizes (i.e., sides of lengths that are powers of two) and standard locations. The motivation for its development was a desire to obtain a systematic way to represent homogeneous parts of an image. Thus to transform the data into a region quadtree, a criterion must be chosen for deciding that an image is homogeneous (i.e., uniform).

One such criterion is that the standard deviation of its gray levels is below a given threshold t. Using this criterion, the image array is successively subdivided into quadrants, subquadrants, and so on, until homogeneous blocks are obtained. This process leads to a regular decomposition. If one associates with each leaf node the mean gray level of its block, the resulting region quadtree will then completely specify a piecewise approximation to the image where each homogeneous block is represented by its mean. The case where $t = 0$ (i.e., a block is not homogeneous unless its gray level is constant) is of particular interest since it permits an exact reconstruction of the image from its quadtree.

Note that the blocks of the region quadtree do not necessarily correspond to maximal homogeneous regions in the image. Most likely there exist unions of the blocks that are still homogeneous. To obtain a segmentation of the image into maximal homogeneous regions, we must allow merging of adjacent blocks (or unions of blocks) as long as the resulting region remains homogeneous. This is achieved by a 'split-and-merge' algorithm [Horo76]. However, the resulting partition will no longer be represented by a quadtree; instead the final representation is in the form of an adjacency graph. Thus the region quadtree is used as an initial step in the segmentation process.

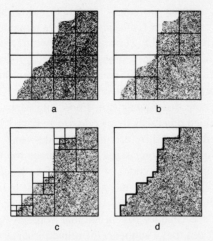

Figure 1.6 Example illustrating the 'split-and-merge' segmentation procedure: (a) start, (b) merge, (c) split, (d) grouping

For example, Figure 1.6b–d demonstrates the results of the application, in sequence, of merging, splitting, and grouping to the initial image decomposition of Figure 1.6a. In this case, the image is initially decomposed into 16 equal-sized square blocks. Next the 'merge' step attempts to form larger blocks by recursively merging groups of four homogeneous 'brothers' (the four blocks in the NW and SE quadrants of Figure 1.6b). The 'split' step recursively decomposes blocks that are not homogeneous (the NE and SW quadrants of Figure 1.6c) until a particular homogeneity criterion is satisfied or a given level is encountered. Finally the 'grouping' step aggregates all homogeneous 4-adjacent black blocks into one region apiece; the 8-adjacent white blocks are likewise aggregated into white regions (Figure 1.6d).

An alternative to the region quadtree representation is to use a decomposition method that is not regular (i.e., rectangles of arbitrary size rather than squares). This alternative has the potential of requiring less space. Its drawback is that the determination of optimal partition points may be a computationally expensive procedure (see Exercise 1.34). A closely related problem, decomposing a region into a minimum number of rectangles, is known to be NP-complete [Gare79] if the region is permitted to contain holes [Ling82].[2]

---

[2] A problem is in NP if it can be solved nondeterministically in polynomial time. A nondeterministic solution process proceeds by 'guessing' a solution and then verifying that the solution is correct. Assume that n is the size of the problem (e.g., for sorting, n is the number of records to be sorted). Intuitively, then, a problem is in NP if there is a polynomial $P(n)$ such that if one guesses a solution, it can be verified in $O(P(n))$ time, whether the guess is indeed a correct solution. Thus the verification process is the key to determining whether a problem is in NP, not the actual solution of the problem.

The homogeneity criterion ultimately chosen to guide the subdivision process depends on the type of region data represented. In the remainder of this chapter we shall assume that the domain is a $2^n \times 2^n$ binary image with 1, or black, corresponding to foreground and 0, or white, corresponding to background (e.g., Figure 1.1). Nevertheless the quadtree and octree can be used to represent multicolored data (e.g., a landuse class map associating colors with crops [Same87a]).

It is interesting to note that Kawaguchi, Endo, and Matsunaga [Kawa83] use a sequence of m binary-valued quadtrees to encode image data of 2^m gray levels, where the various gray levels are encoded by use of Gray codes (see, e.g., [McCl65]). This should lead to compaction (i.e., larger-sized blocks) since the Gray code guarantees that the binary representation of the codes of adjacent gray level values differ by only one binary digit.[3] Note, though, that if the primary interest is in image compression, there exist even better methods (see, e.g., [Prat78]); however, they are beyond the scope of this book (but see Chapter 8). In another context, Kawaguchi, Endo, and Yokota [Kawa80b] point out that a sequence of related images (e.g., in an animation application) can be stored compactly as a sequence of quadtrees such that the ith element is the result of exclusive oring the first i images (see Exercise 1.20).

The quadtree decomposition has the property that at each subdivision stage, the image is subdivided into four equal-sized parts. When the original image is a square, the result is a collection of squares, each of which has a side whose length is a power of 2. The binary image tree (termed *bintree*) [Know80, Tamm84a, Same88b] is an alternative decomposition defined in a manner analogous to the region quadtree except that at each subdivision stage we subdivide the image into two equal-sized parts. In two dimensions, at odd stages, we partition along the x coordinate and at even stages along the y coordinate.

A problem is NP-complete if it is 'at least as hard' as any other problem in NP. Somewhat more formally, a problem P_1 in NP is NP-complete if the following property holds: for all other problems P_i in NP, if P_1 can be solved deterministically in $O(f(n))$ time, then P_i can be solved in $O(P(f(n)))$ time for some polynomial P. It has been conjectured that no NP-complete problem can be solved deterministically in polynomial time, but this is not known for sure. The theory of NP-completeness is discussed in detail in [Gare79].

[3] The Gray code is motivated by a desire to reduce errors in transitions between successive gray level values. Its one bit difference guarantee is achieved by the following encoding. Consider the binary representation of the integers from 0 to 2^m-1. This representation can be obtained by constructing a binary tree, say T, of height m where each left branch is labeled 0 while each right branch is labeled 1. Each leaf node, say P, is given the label formed by concatenating the labels of the branches taken by the path from the root to P. Enumerating the leaf nodes from left to right yields the binary integers 0 to $2^m - 1$. The Gray codes of the integers are obtained by constructing a new binary tree, say T', such that the labels of some of the branches in T' are the reverse of what they were in T. The algorithm is as follows. Initially T' is a copy of T. Next traverse T in preorder (i.e., visit the root node, followed by the left and right subtrees). For each branch in T labeled 1, exchange the labels of the two descendant branches of its corresponding branch in T'. No action is taken for descendants of branches in T labeled 0. Enumerating the leaf nodes in T' from left to right yields the Gray codes of the integers 0 to $2^m - 1$. For example, for 8 gray levels (i.e., $m = 3$), we have 000, 001, 011, 010, 110, 111, 101, 100.

The bintree is equivalent to the region quadtree if we replace all leaf nodes at odd stages of subdivision by two identically colored sons. For example, Figure 1.7 is the bintree representation corresponding to the image of Figure 1.1. We assume that for the x (y) partition, the left subtree corresponds to the west (south) half of the image, and the right subtree corresponds to the east (north) half. Once again, as in Figure 1.1, all leaf nodes are labeled with numbers, and the nonleaf nodes are labeled with letters.

Another variation on the bintree idea, termed *adaptive hierarchical coding* (*AHC*), is proposed by Cohen, Landy, and Pavel [Cohe85b]. In this case, the image is again split into two equal-sized parts at each stage, but there is no need to alternate between the x and y coordinates. The decision as to the coordinate on which to partition depends on the image. This technique may require some work to get the optimal partition from the point of view of a minimum number of nodes (see Exercise 1.23).

An even more general variation on the bintree is the *BSP tree* of Fuchs, Kedem, and Naylor [Fuch80, Fuch83]. Its variants are used in some hidden-surface elimination algorithms (see Section 7.1.5) and in some implementations of beam tracing (see Section 7.3). It is applicable to data of arbitrary dimension, although here it is explained in the context of two-dimensional data. At each subdivision stage, the image is subdivided into two parts that are of arbitrary size. Note that successive subdivision lines need be neither orthogonal nor parallel. Therefore the resulting decomposition consists of arbitrarily shaped convex polygons.

The BSP tree is a binary tree. To be able to assign regions to the left and right subtrees, we associate a direction with each subdivision line. In particular, the sub-

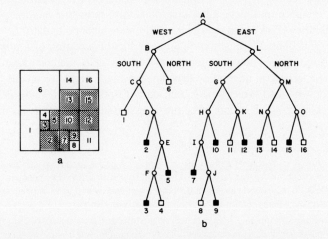

Figure 1.7   The bintree representation corresponding to Figure 1.1: (a) block decomposition and (b) bintree representation corresponding to (a)

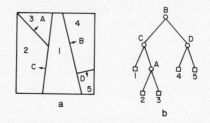

Figure 1.8 (a) An arbitrary space decomposition and (b) its BSP tree. The arrows indicate the direction of the positive halfspaces.

division lines are treated as separators between two halfspaces.[4] Let the line have the equation $a \cdot x + b \cdot y + c = 0$. We say that the right subtree is the 'positive' side and contains all subdivision lines formed by separators that satisfy $a \cdot x + b \cdot y + c \geq 0$. Similarly, we say that the left subtree is 'negative' and contains all subdivision lines formed by separators that satisfy $a \cdot x + b \cdot y + c < 0$. As an example, consider Figure 1.8a, which is an arbitrary space decomposition whose BSP tree is given in Figure 1.8b. Notice the use of arrows to indicate the direction of the positive halfspaces.

Unfortunately the term *quadtree* has taken on more than one meaning. The region quadtree, as described earlier, is a partition of space into a set of squares whose sides are all a power of two long. This formulation is due to Klinger [Klin71] and Klinger and Dyer, who used the term *Q-tree* [Klin76], whereas Hunter [Hunt78] was the first to use the term quadtree in such a context. Actually a more precise term would be *quadtrie*, as it is really a trie structure [Fred60] in two dimensions.[5] A similar partition of space into rectangular quadrants, also termed a *quadtree*, was used by Finkel and Bentley [Fink74] to represent multidimensional point data.

Finkel and Bentley's quadtree is a hierarchical adaptation of a popular method used by cartographers known as the *fixed-grid* (or *cell*) method [Knut73b, p. 554; Bent79b]. The fixed-grid method divides the space into equal-sized cells (i.e., squares and cubes for two- and three-dimensional data, respectively).[6] These cells are often referred to as *buckets*. The data structure is essentially a directory in the form of a

---

[4] A (linear) *halfspace* in d-space is defined by the inequality $\Sigma_{i=0}^{d} a_i \cdot x_i \geq 0$ on the $d+1$ homogeneous coordinates ($x_0 = 1$). The halfspace is represented by a column vector a. In vector notation, the inequality is written as $a \cdot x \geq 0$. In the case of equality, it defines a hyperplane with a as its normal. It is important to note that halfspaces are volume elements; they are not boundary elements.

[5] In a one-dimensional *trie* structure, each data item or key is treated as a sequence of characters where each character has M possible values. A node at depth i in the trie represents an M-way branch depending on the ith character. The data are stored in the leaf nodes, and the shape of the trie is independent of the order in which the data are processed. Such a structure is also known as a *digital tree* [Knut73b].

[6] The size of the cell is usually a function of some property of the data or the operation to be performed on it (e.g., the search radius for a range query). Interestingly this method can also be described as yielding an *adaptive uniform grid* to emphasize that the cell size is a function of the data (e.g., [Fran84, Fran88]).

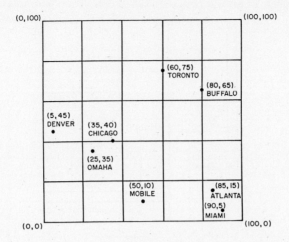

Figure 1.9   Fixed-grid representation with a search radius of 20

k-dimensional array with one element (i.e., point) per cell. Each cell may be imple-mented as a linked list to represent the points within it.

Figure 1.9 is a 5×5 fixed-grid representation for some point data.[7] The conven-tion is that each square is open with respect to its upper and right boundaries and closed with respect to its lower and left boundaries. Therefore Toronto, located at (60,75), is found in the square centered at (70,70). Also all data points located at grid intersection points are said to be contained in the cell for which they serve as the SW corner (e.g., the point (20,20) is contained in the square centered at (30,30)).

The main drawback of the fixed-grid representation is that when the data are not uniformly distributed, many cells will be empty. Finkel and Bentley's quadtree, termed a *point quadtree*, is a marriage of the fixed-grid method and the binary search tree that alleviates this drawback. It results in a tree-like directory with nonuniform-sized cells containing one element apiece. It can be used for multidimensional point data (not just two dimensions). It is referred to as a *point quadtree* where confusion with a region quadtree is possible. As an example of a point quadtree, consider Figure 1.10, which is built for the sequence Chicago, Mobile, Toronto, Buffalo, Denver, Omaha, Atlanta, and Miami in the order in which they are listed here. Note that its shape is highly dependent on the order in which the points are added to it.

The point quadtree that we examined has been for two-dimensional data. The problem with a large number of dimensions is that the branching factor becomes very large (i.e., 2^k for k dimensions), thereby requiring much storage for each node, as well as many NIL pointers for leaf nodes. The *k-d tree* of Bentley [Bent75b] is an improve-ment on the point quadtree that avoids the large branching factor. In principle, it is a

---

[7] The correspondence between coordinate values and city names is not geographically correct. This liberty has been taken so that the same example can be used throughout this section to illustrate a variety of concepts.

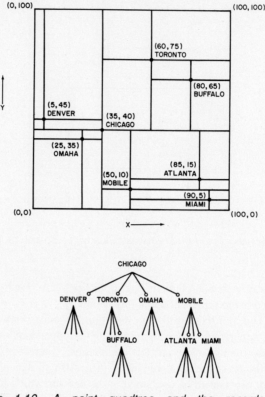

Figure 1.10 A point quadtree and the records it represents

binary search tree with the distinction that at each level of the tree, a different coordinate is tested when determining the direction in which a branch is to be made. Therefore in the two-dimensional case (i.e., a 2–d tree), we compare x coordinates at the root and at even depths (assuming that the root is at depth 0) and y coordinates at odd depths. Each node has two sons. Figure 1.11 is the k-d tree corresponding to the point quadtree of Figure 1.10, where the records have been inserted in the same order.

The k-d tree is related to the point quadtree in the same way as the bintree is related to the region quadtree. The difference is that region quadtrees and bintrees are used to represent region data with fixed subdivision points, while point quadtrees and k-d trees are used to represent point data where the values of the points determine the subdivision. Both the point quadtree and the k-d tree have the property that their shape is dependent on the order in which the points are added to them. This can be avoided by using trie-based representations such as the MX and PR quadtrees.

The *MX quadtree* treats each data point as if it is a black pixel in a region quadtree. An alternative characterization of the MX quadtree is to think of the data points

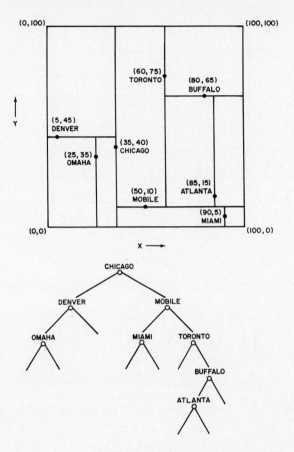

Figure 1.11   A k-d tree and the records it represents

as nonzero elements in a square matrix (hence the qualifier MX), although the term *MX quadtrie* would probably be more appropriate.

The MX quadtree is organized in a similar way to the region quadtree. The difference is that leaf nodes are black or empty (i.e., white) corresponding to the presence or absence, respectively, of a data point in the appropriate position in the matrix. For example, Figure 1.12 is the $2^3 \times 2^3$ MX quadtree corresponding to the point quadtree of Figure 1.10. It is obtained by applying the mapping f such that $f(z) = z$ div 12.5 to both x and y coordinates. The result of the mapping is reflected in the coordinate values in the figure. (For more details, see Section 2.6.1 of [Same90a].)

The MX quadtree is an adequate representation for points as long as the domain of the data points is discrete and finite. If this is not the case, the data points cannot be represented since the minimum separation between the data points is unknown. This leads to an alternative adaptation of the region quadtree to point data that associates data points (that need not be discrete) with quadrants. We call it a *PR quadtree* (P for

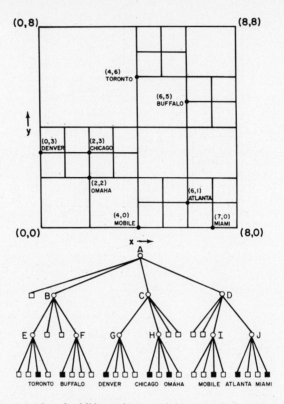

Figure 1.12   An MX quadtree and the records it represents

point and R for region), although again the term *PR quadtrie* is probably more appropriate.

The PR quadtree is organized in the same way as the region quadtree. The difference is that leaf nodes are either empty (i.e., white) or contain a data point (i.e., black) and its coordinates. A quadrant contains, at most, one data point. For example, Figure 1.13 is the PR quadtree corresponding to the point quadtree of Figure 1.10. (For more details, see Section 2.6.2 of [Same90a].) Orenstein [Oren82] describes an analogous data structure using binary trees rather than quadtrees. Such a data structure could be called a *PR k-d tree*, a *PR bintree*, or even a *k-d trie*.

The PR quadtree representation can also be adapted to represent a region that consists of a collection of polygons (termed a *polygonal map*), as in Figure 1.14. The result is a family of representations referred to collectively as a *PM quadtree* [Same85i]. The PM quadtree family represents regions by specifying their boundaries; this is in contrast to the region quadtree, which is based on a description of the region's interior. (It is discussed in great detail in Section 4.2.3.1 of [Same90a].)

As an example of the PM quadtree family, consider the *PM₁ quadtree*. The

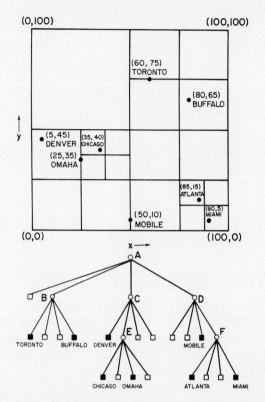

Figure 1.13   *A PR quadtree and the records it represents*

polygonal map is repeatedly subdivided into four equal-sized quadrants until we obtain blocks that do not contain more than one line. To deal with lines that intersect other lines, we say that if a block contains an endpoint *P* of a line, we permit it to contain more than one line provided that *P* is an endpoint of each of the lines it contains. A block can never contain more than one endpoint. For example, Figure 1.15 is the block decomposition of the PM₁ quadtree corresponding to the polygonal map of

Figure 1.14   *Sample polygonal map*

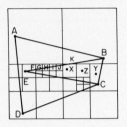

Figure 1.15 PM₁ quadtree corresponding to the polygonal map of Figure 1.14

Figure 1.14, and Figure 1.16 is its tree representation. An algorithm for building and updating a PM₁ quadtree is given in Section 4.5.

The PM₁ quadtree has also been adapted to three-dimensional images [Ayal85, Carl85, Fuji85b, Hunt81, Nava86a, Quin82, Tamm81a, Vand84]. We term the result a *PM octree*. The decomposition criteria are such that no node contains more than one face, edge, or vertex unless all the faces meet at the same vertex or are adjacent to the same edge. For example, Figure 1.17b is a PM octree decomposition of the object in Figure 1.17a. This representation is quite useful since its space requirements for polyhedral objects are significantly smaller than those of a region octree. (For more details, see Section 5.3 of [Same90a].)

Members of the PM quadtree family can be easily adapted to deal with fragments that result from set operations such as union and intersection so that there is no data degradation when fragments of line segments are subsequently recombined. Their use yields an exact representation of the lines, not an approximation. To see how this is achieved, define a *q-edge* to be a segment of a line of the original polygonal map that

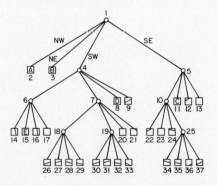

Figure 1.16 Tree representation of the PM₁ quadtree corresponding to the polygonal map of Figure 1.14

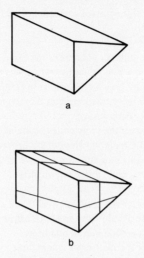

Figure 1.17 (a) Example three-dimensional object and (b) its corresponding PM octree

either spans an entire block in the PM quadtree or extends from a boundary of a block to an endpoint within the block (i.e., when the block contains an endpoint).

Each q-edge is represented by a pointer to a record containing the endpoints of the line of the polygonal map of which the q-edge is a part [Nels86a]. The line segment descriptor stored in a node implies only the presence of the corresponding q-edge; it does not mean that the entire line segment is present as a lineal feature. The result is a consistent representation of line fragments since they are stored exactly, and thus they can be deleted and reinserted without worrying about errors arising from the round-offs induced by approximating their intersection with the borders of the blocks through which they pass (i.e., clipping [Roge85]). The same principles are also applicable to fragments of faces in three dimensions.

The decomposition rules described for building a PR and a PM$_1$ quadtree (and octree) require that each quadrant (octant) contain just one primitive (e.g., point, line, face). The shortcoming of these rules is that if two primitives are very near, we may have to subdivide to a deep level to separate them. This has led to a relaxation of the number of primitives that are permitted to occupy a quadrant (octant). Instead each quadrant (octant) is viewed as a *bucket* with a finite capacity, say c, and the decomposition rule is modified so that decomposition ceases whenever a quadrant (octant) contains no more than c primitive elements. This is the basis of the EXCELL system [Tamm81a]. (For more details, see Section 2.8.2.4 of [Same90a].)

Exercises

1.19. The region quadtree is an alternative to an image representation that is based on the use of an array or even a list. Each of these image representations may be biased in favor of the computation of a particular adjacency relation. Discuss these biases for the array, list, and quadtree representations.

1.20. Let $\oplus$ denote an exclusive or operation. Given a sequence of related images, $<P_n, P_{n-1}, \cdots, P_0>$, define another sequence $<Q_n, Q_{n-1}, \cdots, Q_0>$ such that $Q_0 = P_0$ and $Q_i = P_i \oplus Q_{i-1}$ for $i > 0$. Show that when the sequences P and Q are represented as quadtrees, replacing sequence P by sequence Q results in fewer nodes.

1.21. Prove that in Exercise 1.20 the sequence P can be reconstructed from the sequence Q. In particular, given Q_i and Q_{i-1}, determine P_i.

1.22. Write an algorithm to construct the Gray codes of the integers 0 to 2^m-1.

1.23. Suppose that you use the AHC method. How many different rectangles and positions must be examined in building such a structure for a $2^n \times 2^n$ image?

1.24. Write an algorithm to insert a node in a point quadtree.

1.25. Write an algorithm to delete a node from a point quadtree.

1.26. Write an algorithm to insert a node in an MX quadtree.

1.27. Write an algorithm to delete a node from an MX quadtree.

1.28. Write an algorithm to insert a node in a PR quadtree.

1.29. Write an algorithm to delete a node from a PR quadtree.

1.30. Assume that the minimum Euclidean distance separating two points is d. Given a square region of side length s, what is the maximum depth of the PR quadtree?

1.31. Write an algorithm to insert a line segment in a PM_1 quadtree.

1.32. Write an algorithm to delete a line segment from a PM_1 quadtree.

1.33. Consider a PM_1 quadtree for a polygonal map whose vertices are drawn from a grid (say $2^n \times 2^n$) such that the line segments that comprise it are not permitted to intersect at points other than the grid points (i.e., endpoints). Prove that the maximum depth of any leaf node is bounded from above by $4 \cdot n + 1$. This enables a determination of the maximum amount of storage that will be necessary for each node.

1.34. Find a polynomial-time algorithm to decompose a region optimally so that its quadtree representation uses a minimum amount of space (i.e., a minimum number of nodes). In this case, you can assume that the decomposition lines can be placed in arbitrary positions so that the space requirement is reduced. In other words, the decomposition lines need not split the space into four squares of equal size. Thus the decomposition is similar to that induced by a point quadtree.

1.4 HISTORY OF THE USE OF QUADTREES AND OCTREES

The origin of the principle of recursive decomposition, upon which all quadtrees are based, is difficult to ascertain. Below, to give some indication of the uses of the region quadtree, its applications to geometric data are traced briefly. Most likely it was first seen as a way of aggregating blocks of zeros in sparse matrices. Indeed Hoare [Hoar72] attributes a one-level decomposition of a matrix into square blocks to Dijkstra. Morton [Mort66] used it as a means of indexing into a geographic database (i.e., it acts as a spatial index).

Warnock, in a pair of reports that serve as landmarks in computer graphics [Warn68, Warn69b], described the implementation of hidden-line and hidden-surface elimination algorithms using a recursive decomposition of the picture area. The picture area is repeatedly subdivided into rectangles that are successively smaller while searching for areas that are sufficiently simple to be displayed. Klinger [Klin71] and Klinger and Dyer [Klin76] applied these ideas to pattern recognition and image processing, and Hunter [Hunt78] used them for an animation application.

The SRI robot project [Nils69] used a three-level decomposition of space to represent a map of the robot's world. Eastman [East70] observes that recursive decomposition might be used for space planning in an architectural context and presents a simplified version of the SRI robot representation. A quadtree-like representation in the form of production rules called DF-expressions (denoting depth-first) is discussed by Kawaguchi and Endo [Kawa80a] and Kawaguchi, Endo, and Yokota [Kawa80b]. Tucker [Tuck84a] uses quadtree refinement as a control strategy for an expert vision system.

The three-dimensional variant of the region quadtree—the octree—was developed independently by a number of researchers. Hunter [Hunt78] mentioned it as a natural extension of the quadtree. Reddy and Rubin [Redd78] proposed the octree as one of three representations for solid objects. The second is a three-dimensional generalization of the point quadtree of Finkel and Bentley [Fink74]—that is, a decomposition into rectangular parallelepipeds (as opposed to cubes) with planes perpendicular to the x, y, and z axes. The third breaks the object into rectangular parallelepipeds that are not necessarily aligned with an axis. The parallelepipeds are of arbitrary sizes and orientations. Each parallelepiped is recursively subdivided into parallelepipeds in the coordinate space of the enclosing parallelepiped. Reddy and Rubin prefer the third approach for its ease of display.

Situated between the second and third approaches of Reddy and Rubin is the method of Brooks and Lozano-Perez [Broo83] (see also [Loza81]), who use a recursive decomposition of space into an arbitrary number of rectangular parallelepipeds, with planes perpendicular to the x, y, and z axes, to model space in solving the *findpath* or *piano movers* problem [Schw86] in robotics. This problem arises when planning the motion of a robot in an environment containing known obstacles and the desired solution is a collision-free path obtained by use of a search. Faverjon [Fave84] discusses an approach to this problem that uses an octree, as do Samet and Tamminen [Same85g] and Fujimura and Samet [Fuji89].

Jackins and Tanimoto [Jack80] adapted Hunter and Steiglitz's quadtree translation algorithm [Hunt78, Hunt79b] to objects represented by octrees. Meagher [Meag82a] developed numerous algorithms for performing solid modeling operations in an environment where the octree is the underlying representation. Yau and Srihari [Yau83] extended the octree to arbitrary dimensions in the process of developing algorithms to handle medical images.

Both quadtrees and octrees are frequently used in the construction of meshes for finite element analysis. The use of recursive decomposition for meshes was initially suggested by Rheinboldt and Mesztenyi [Rhei80]. Yerry and Shephard [Yerr83] adapted the quadtree and octree to generate meshes automatically for three-dimensional solids represented by a superquadric surface-based modeler. This has been extended by Kela, Voelcker, and Goldak [Kela84b] (see also [Kela86]) to mesh boundary regions directly rather than through discrete approximations and to facilitate incremental adaptive analysis by exploiting the spatial index nature of the quadtree and octree.

Parallel to the development of the quadtree and octree data structures, there has been related work by researchers in the field of image understanding. Kelly [Kell71] introduced the concept of a *plan*, which is a small picture whose pixels represent gray-scale averages over 8×8 blocks of a larger picture. Needless effort in edge detection is avoided by first determining edges in the plan and then using these edges to search selectively for edges in the larger picture. Generalizations of this idea motivated the development of multiresolution image representations—for example, the recognition cone of Uhr [Uhr72], the preprocessing cone of Riseman and Arbib [Rise77], and the pyramid of Tanimoto and Pavlidis [Tani75]. Of these representations, the pyramid is the closest relative of the region quadtree.

Given a $2^n \times 2^n$ image array, say $A(n)$, a *pyramid* is a sequence of arrays $\{A(i)\}$ such that $A(i-1)$ is a version of $A(i)$ at half the scale of $A(i)$, and so forth. $A(0)$ is a single pixel. For example, Figure 1.18 shows the structure of a pyramid having three levels. It should be clear that a pyramid can also be defined in a more general way by permitting finer scales of resolution than the power of two scale.

At times it is more convenient to define a pyramid in the form of a tree. Again, assuming a $2^n \times 2^n$ image, a recursive decomposition into quadrants is performed, just as in quadtree construction, except that we keep subdividing until we reach the individual pixels. The leaf nodes of the resulting tree represent the pixels, while the nodes immediately above the leaf nodes correspond to the array $A(n-1)$, which is of size $2^{n-1} \times 2^{n-1}$. The nonleaf nodes are assigned a value that is a function of the nodes below them (i.e., their sons), such as the average gray level. Thus we see that a pyramid is a multiresolution representation, whereas the region quadtree is a variable-resolution representation. Another analogy is that the pyramid is a complete quadtree [Knut73a].

Pyramids have been applied to the problems of feature detection and extraction since they can be used to limit the scope of the search. Once a piece of information of interest is found at a coarse level, the finer resolution levels can be searched. This approach was followed by Davis and Roussopoulos [Davi80] in approximate pattern matching. Pyramids can also be used for encoding information about edges, lines, and

Figure 1.18   Structure of a pyramid having three levels

curves in an image [Shne81c, Krop86]. One note of caution: the reduction of resolution has an effect on the visual appearance of edges and small objects [Tani76]. In particular, at a coarser level of resolution, edges tend to get smeared, and region separation may disappear. Pyramids have also been used as the starting point for a 'split-and-merge' segmentation algorithm [Piet82].

Quadtree-like decompositions are also useful as space-ordering methods. The purpose is to optimize the storage and processing sequences for two-dimensional data by mapping them into one dimension (i.e., linearizing them). This mapping should preserve the spatial locality of the original two-dimensional image in one dimension. The result of the mapping is also known as a *space-filling curve* [Gold81, Witt83] because it passes through every point in the image.

Goodchild and Grandfield [Good83] discuss a number of space-ordering methods, two of which are illustrated in Figure 1.19: the Morton [Mort66, Pean90] (Figure 1.19a) and the Peano-Hilbert [Hilb91] (Figure 1.19b) orders. The primary difference is that in the Peano-Hilbert order, every element is a 4-adjacent neighbor of the previous element in the sequence, and thus it has a slightly higher degree of locality than the Morton order. Both the Morton and Peano-Hilbert orders exhaust a quadrant or subquadrant of a square image before exiting it. Both are related to quadtrees; however, as we saw above, the Morton order does not traverse the image in a spatially contiguous manner (the result has the shape of the letter 'N' or 'Z' and is also known as N order [Whit82] and Z order [Oren84]).

For both the Morton and Peano-Hilbert orders, there is no need to know the maximum values of the coordinates. The Morton order is symmetric, while the Peano-Hilbert order is not. One advantage of the Morton order is that the position of each element in the ordering (termed its *key*) can be determined by interleaving the bits of the x and y coordinates of the element; this is not easy for the Peano-Hilbert order. Another advantage of the Morton order is that the recursion necessary for its generation is quite easy to specify.

The Morton and Peano-Hilbert orders can be used to order a space that has been aggregated into squares. Of these two orderings, the Morton order is by far the more frequently used as a result of the simplicity of the conversion process between the key

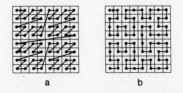

a   b

Figure 1.19 ‹The result of applying a number of different space-ordering methods to an 8 × 8 image whose first element is in the upper left corner of the image: (a) Morton order, (b) Peano-Hilbert order

and its corresponding element in the multidimensional space. In this book we are primarily interested in Morton orderings. (For a further discussion of some of the properties of these two orderings, see [Patr68, Butz71, Alex79, Alex80, Laur85].)

Exercises

1.35. Write an algorithm to extract the x and y coordinates from a Peano-Hilbert order key.

1.36. Write an algorithm to construct the Peano-Hilbert key for a given point (x,y). Try to make it optimal.

1.37. Suppose that you are given a $2^n \times 2^n$ array of points such that the horizontal and vertical distances between 4-adjacent points are 1. What is the average distance between successive points when the points are ordered according to the orders illustrated in Figure 1.19? What about a random order?

1.38. Suppose that you are given a $2^n \times 2^n$ image. Assume that the image is stored on disk in pages of size $2^m \times 2^m$ where n is much larger than m. What is the average cost of retrieving a pixel and its 4-adjacent neighbors when the image is ordered according to the orders illustrated in Figure 1.19?

1.39. The traveling salesman problem [Lawl85] is one where a set of points is given, and it is desired to find the path of minimum distance such that each point is visited only once. This is an NP-complete problem [Gare79], and thus there is a considerable amount of work in formulating approximate solutions to it [Bent82]. For example, consider the following approximate solution. Assume that the points are uniformly distributed in the unit square. Let d be the expected Euclidean distance between two independent points. Now sort the points using the Morton order. Laurini [Laur85] simulated the average Euclidean distance between successive points in this order and found it to be $d/3$ for the Morton order. Can you derive this average analytically? What is the average value for the Peano-Hilbert order? What about a random order?

1.40. Suppose that the traveling salesman problem is solved using a traversal of the points in Morton order as discussed in Exercise 1.39. In particular, assume that the set of points is decomposed in such a way that each square block contains just one point—i.e., a PR quadtree. How close does such a solution come to optimality?

1.5 IMPLEMENTATION

The most common implementation of the quadtree is in the form of a tree, and to distinguish it from other implementations, we call it an *explicit quadtree*. In this case, each node is represented as a record of type *node* containing six fields. The first five fields contain pointers to the node's father and its four sons, which correspond to the four quadrants. If the node is a leaf node, it will have four pointers to the empty record (i.e., NIL). If P is a pointer to a node and I is a quadrant, these fields are referenced as FATHER(P) and SON(P,I), respectively.

We can determine the specific quadrant in which a node, say P, lies relative to its father by use of the function SONTYPE(P), which has a value of I if SON(FATHER(P),I) = P. The sixth field, NODETYPE, describes the contents of the block of the image that the node represents: black, white, or gray. The pointer from a node to its father is not required but is introduced to ease the motion between arbitrary nodes in the quadtree. It is exploited in a number of algorithms to perform basic image-processing operations.

An octree implementation is analogous to that for the quadtree. The only difference is the presence of eight sons instead of four.

ALTERNATIVE QUADTREE REPRESENTATIONS

2

The quadtree[1] is a refinement of the array representation of an image that attempts to save storage by taking advantage of some regularity in the image by decomposing the array into homogeneous disjoint d-dimensional cubes centered at predetermined positions. It is a d-dimensional extension of the run representation. Image elements are now blocks (i.e., d-dimensional cubes) instead of pixels, voxels, and so on. The quadtree can be implemented as a list or as a tree. The list representation facilitates sequential access but is inefficient for random access to specific image elements. The tree representation is an attempt to balance the costs of sequential and random access.

A shortcoming of the tree representation of a region quadtree is that a considerable amount of overhead is associated with it. For example, given an image that can be aggregated to yield B black and W white nodes, $(B + W - 1)/3$ additional nodes are necessary for the nonleaf (i.e., gray) nodes. Moreover, each node requires additional space for the pointers to its sons. This is a problem when dealing with large images that cannot fit into core memory. The bintree can be used to reduce the overhead in part since a node requires space for pointers to only its two sons instead of four sons. Moreover its use generally leads to fewer leaf nodes. Its attractiveness increases further when dealing with higher dimensional data (e.g., three dimensions) since less space is wasted on NIL pointers for leaf nodes. Moreover many algorithms are simpler to formulate using a bintree.

---

[1] In this chapter, the term *quadtree* is used in a general sense to include the octree and any other similarly constructed hierarchical data structure based on regular decomposition for d-dimensional data. In fact, most of the discussion also applies to quadtrees that are not based on a regular decomposition.

Reducing the overhead costs associated with the use of pointers has led to a considerable amount of interest in pointerless quadtree representations in the form of lists. They can be grouped into two categories. The first treats the image as a collection of leaf nodes. The second represents the image in the form of a traversal of the nodes of its quadtree. This chapter contains a detailed discussion of these representations and a brief summary of the type of operations that can be achieved using them. Some of these operations are discussed in greater detail in subsequent chapters, primarily in the context of pointer-based quadtree representations, as well as pointerless representations when the situation warrants it. It also shows under what conditions a pointer-based representation is more efficient spacewise than some of the pointerless representations.

2.1 COLLECTION OF LEAF NODES

There are a number of different ways of representing a quadtree as a collection of the leaf nodes comprising it. The basic idea is that each leaf is encoded by a base 4 or 5 number, termed a *locational code*, corresponding to a sequence of digits whose values are directional codes that locate the leaf along a path from the root of the quadtree. It is analogous to taking the binary representation of the interleaved values of the x and y coordinates of a designated pixel in the block (e.g., the one at the upper left corner when the origin is at the upper left corner of the universe) and interleaving them (i.e., alternating the bits for each coordinate). As we will see, depending on the implementation of the locational code, the level of the leaf must also be recorded. In most of the examples, unless stated otherwise, the locational code data type is operated on as if it is an integer.

The following contains a discussion of the use of locational codes in linear quadtrees, two-dimensional run encodings, and forests. Usually the collection of leaf nodes is kept as a list that is sorted according to the values of the locational codes of the nodes. In many applications this list is implemented using a tree structure so that search and retrieval operations can be speeded up. For very large images, the corresponding quadtrees are too large to fit into internal memory. In such a case, the elements of the list can be stored using a variant of the B-tree [Come79]. Such techniques are used in several applications [Abel84a, Rose83b].

2.1.1 Linear Quadtrees

It is difficult to determine the origin of the concept of a locational code. It was used as an index to a geographic database by Morton [Mort66] and is termed a *Morton matrix*. Klinger and Rhodes [Klin79] presented it as a means of organizing quadtrees on external storage (see also [Klin76, Cook78, Webe78, Garg82a, Garg82b, Wood82a,

Abel83, Burt83, Oliv83a]). In addition, it has also been widely discussed in the literature in the context of multidimensional point data (see Section 2.7 of [Same90a]).

To see how one formulation of the locational code can be computed directly
from an explicit quadtree representation, we make use of the following notation. Let
the quadtree be rooted at node R at level n, and let m ($m < n$) denote the level[2] of the
node, say P, whose locational code is desired. Define a sequence of nodes
$<P_n, P_{n-1}, \cdots, P_m>$ such that $P_n = R$, $P_i = \text{FATHER}(P_{i-1})$ for $m < i \le n$, and $P_m = P$—
that is, corresponding to the path from P_n to P_m. Let the directions NW, NE, SW, and SE
be represented by the function SONTYPE4, which returns 0, 1, 2, and 3, respectively.
For example, node 10 of Figure 2.1 has a SONTYPE4 value of 3. Using the sequence
$<y_n, y_{n-1}, \cdots, y_m>$, given by relation 2.1, the locational code of P is y_m.

$$y_i = \begin{cases} 0 & i = n \\ 4 \cdot y_{i+1} + \text{SONTYPE4}(P_i) & m \le i < n \end{cases} \qquad (2.1)$$

An alternative definition in the form of a procedure called CODE1 is given below.

```
locationalcode procedure CODE1(P);
/* Compute the locational code of the quadtree node pointed at by P. */
begin
  value pointer node P;
  locationalcode C;
  integer I;
  I ← C ← 0;
  while not(null(FATHER(P))) do
    begin
      C ← C+SONTYPE4(P)*4↑I;
      I ← I+1;
      P ← FATHER(P);
    end;
  return(C);
end;
```

For example, node 10 of Figure 2.1, at level 0, has a locational code of 75. In
general, for a $2^n \times 2^n$ image, a locational code C, for a node at level m ($m < n$), can be
decoded into the sequence of $n-m$ digits $<C_{n-1}, C_{n-2}, \cdots, C_m>$, where $C_i = \text{SON-}$
TYPE4(P_i), by use of relation 2.2. For node 10, this yields $<C_3, C_2, C_1, C_0> = <1,0,2,3>$
corresponding to $<$NE,NW,SW,SE$>$.

---

[2] Recall that, unless stated otherwise, the definition of level for a quadtree corresponding to a $2^n \times 2^n$ image
is such that the root is at level n and a pixel is at level 0. On the other hand, the root is at depth 0, while a
pixel is at depth n.

$$C = \sum_{i=0}^{n-m-1} c_i \cdot 4^i \qquad 0 \le c_i \le 3 \quad 0 \le c < 4^{n-m} \qquad (2.2)$$

This definition of a locational code requires a separate number—a in this example—to record the level at which the node is found. The level number is necessary because we need an indicator to mark the end of the decoding process. 0 cannot be used because it is one of the values of the directional codes. We can avoid this

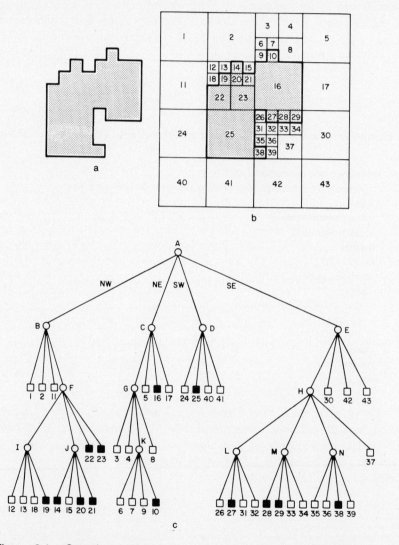

Figure 2.1 Sample quadtree: (a) region, (b) block decomposition, (c) tree representation

problem by making use of the directional codes 1, 2, 3, and 4 to represent the directions NW, NE, SW, and SE, respectively.

In essence, this means that the locational code is now a base 5 number. The only change that needs to be made to the former definition in terms of the sequence $<y_n, y_{n-1}, \cdots, y_m>$ and procedure CODE1 is to modify the multiplicative factor from 4 to 5. Of course, the definition of SONTYPE4 has also changed—SONTYPE5(P)=SONTYPE4(P) + 1. For example, the locational code of node 10 of Figure 2.1 is now 294. Using relation 2.3, it can be decoded into the sequence of four digits $<c_3, c_2, c_1, c_0>$ that has $<2,1,3,4>$ (corresponding to $<$NE,NW,SW,SE$>$) as the value of its directional codes.

$$C = \sum_{i=0}^{n-m-1} c_i \cdot 5^i \qquad 1 \le c_i \le 4 \qquad 5^{n-m-1} \le C < 5^{n-m} \qquad (2.3)$$

Notice that although the level number is no longer stored explicitly, it is still needed to be able to decode the locational code into the necessary sequence of digits with the appropriate directional codes. For a given locational code, say C, the level number is obtained by counting the number of successive divide-by-5 operations necessary before C becomes 0 and subtracting the result from n (e.g., for node 10 in Figure 2.1, 294 must be successively divided by 5 four times before obtaining 0).

The operation of decoding a locational code into the sequence of digits and their directional codes is an important one and should be fast and computationally simple. We want to be able to decode the locational code in such a way that the digits are obtained in the order in which we traverse a path from the root of the quadtree to the node. Unfortunately use of CODE1 results in obtaining the digits in the reverse order when the decoding process consists of a combination of modulo and integer division operations.

For example, for node 10 of Figure 2.1, such a procedure yields the sequence of digits having directional codes corresponding to SE, SW, NW, and NE, in order, whereas it is preferable to obtain them in the order NE, NW, SW, and SE. Thus given a leaf node with locational code C in a quadtree rooted at P, we wish to use procedure ACCESS, given below, to access it. DIR is a function that converts a base 5 directional code into the appropriate quadrant direction—for example, DIR(3)='SW'.

```
pointer node procedure ACCESS(P,C);
/* Locate the leaf node with locational code C in the quadtree rooted at P. */
begin
  value pointer node P;
  value locationalcode C;
  while (C mod 5)≠0 do
    begin
      P ← SON(P,DIR(C mod 5));
      C ← C div 5;
```

```
      end;
   return(P);
end;
```

An encoding satisfying the above decoding requirement can be obtained with the aid of the sequence $<z_n, z_{n-1}, \cdots, z_m>$ $(m < n)$, given by relation 2.4, where z_n corresponds to the locational code of the desired leaf node. The result is termed a *VL locational code* (denoting variable length). Once again we make use of the sequence $<P_n, P_{n-1}, \cdots, P_m>$ such that P_n = root of the quadtree, $P_i = \text{FATHER}(P_{i-1})$ for $m < i \leq n$, and P_m = desired node. The directions NW, NE, SW, SE are represented by the directional codes 1, 2, 3, and 4, respectively, and are accessed by the function SON-TYPE5.

$$z_i = \begin{cases} 0 & i = m \\ 5 \cdot z_{i-1} + \text{SONTYPE5}(P_i) & m < i \leq n \end{cases} \tag{2.4}$$

An alternative definition in the form of a procedure called CODE2 is given below.

```
locationalcode procedure CODE2(P);
/* Compute the VL locational code of the quadtree node pointed at by P. The most
   significant digit corresponds to SONTYPE5 of P. */
begin
  value pointer node P;
  locationalcode C;
  C ← 0;
  while not(null(FATHER(P))) do
    begin
      C ← 5*C+SONTYPE5(P);
      P ← FATHER(P);
    end;
  return(C);
end;
```

For example, node 10 of Figure 2.1, at level 0, has a locational code of 582. In general, for a $2^n \times 2^n$ image, a locational code C, for a node at level m $(m < n)$, can be decoded into a sequence of $n-m$ digits $<C_m, \cdots, C_{n-2}, C_{n-1}>$, where $C_i = \text{SON-TYPE5}(P_i)$, by use of relation 2.3. For node 10, this yields $<C_0, C_1, C_2, C_3> = <4, 3, 1, 2>$ corresponding to $<\text{SE}, \text{SW}, \text{NW}, \text{NE}>$.

Representing the nodes of a quadtree by using locational codes has a potential for saving space when compared with the explicit quadtree representation (but see the discussion at the end of this section). Even further space economies can be achieved by storing only the locational codes for the black nodes and ignoring the gray and white nodes. The resulting list of VL locational codes is termed a *VL linear quadtree*. Using CODE2, we can always reconstruct the explicit quadtree from the VL locational codes of the black nodes by use of procedures BUILD_TREE and ADD_NODE given below.

To facilitate the explanation of the algorithm, we refer to Figure 2.1 as an example and build its tree for the sequence of nodes 25, 16, 22, 23, 28, 14, 27, 29, 20, 38, 19, 21, and 10 in this order, and whose VL locational codes are 13, 17, 96, 121, 184, 196, 284, 309, 446, 459, 546, 571, and 582, respectively. Figure 2.2 shows the intermediate trees obtained during the process of adding nodes 25, 16, 22, and 23.

BUILD_TREE has as its input a list of VL locational codes for the black nodes and invokes ADD_NODE to add each element thereof to the tree. Initially the image is assumed to be white, and thus the root is initialized to be of type white (node A in Figure 2.2a). ADD_NODE decodes the code for the node (i.e., the path to the node from the root of the tree). During this process it may need to expand a node (the transition from Figure 2.2a to Figure 2.2b and 2.2c when adding node 25). In such a case, the node's type is changed to gray, and its four sons take on its previous value (node A in the transition from Figure 2.2a to Figure 2.2b).

When the decoding process is done, the node's type is complemented (node 25 in the transition from Figure 2.2c to Figure 2.2d). Actually there is no need to complement the node's type since it will always be black. However, when the algorithm is expressed in this way, it can be used in other contexts (e.g., see the discussion of quadtree-based approximation methods in Section 8.2.1).

```
pointer node procedure BUILD_TREE(L);
/* Construct the quadtree corresponding to the black nodes whose VL locational codes
   are in the list L. Assume that the image is initially nonempty. Procedure CREATE_-
   QNODE is defined in Section 4.1.   */
begin
  value pointer list L;
  pointer node ROOT;
  ROOT ← CREATE_QNODE(NIL,NIL,'WHITE');
  while not(null(L)) do
    begin
      ADD_NODE(ROOT,DATA(L));
      L ← NEXT(L);
    end;
  return(ROOT);
end;


procedure ADD_NODE(ROOT,C);
/* Add a node with VL locational code C to the quadtree rooted at node ROOT. */
begin
  value pointer node ROOT;
  value locationalcode C;
  quadrant Q;
  while (C mod 5) ≠ 0 do
    begin
      if not(GRAY(ROOT)) then
        begin /* Expand a leaf node */
```

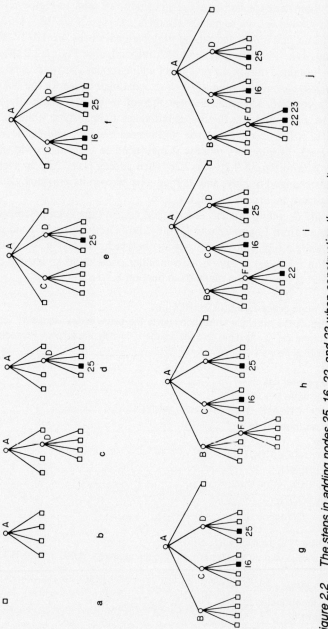
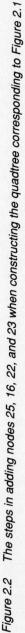

Figure 2.2   The steps in adding nodes 25, 16, 22, and 23 when constructing the quadtree corresponding to Figure 2.1

```
    for Q in {'NW', 'NE', 'SW', 'SE'} do
        SON(ROOT,Q) ← CREATE_QNODE(NIL,NIL,TYPE(ROOT));
        TYPE(ROOT) ← 'GRAY';
    end;
    ROOT ← SON(ROOT,DIR(C mod 5));
    C ← C div 5;
    end;
    TYPE(ROOT) ← COMPLEMENT(TYPE(ROOT));
    /*  The node's type is opposite to the type of the node that was being added or
        expanded—that is, a white (black) node is being replaced by black (white) node */
    end;
```

The representation of a quadtree as a collection of the locational codes of only the black nodes was first reported by Gargantini [Garg82a], where it is termed a *linear quadtree*. However, that encoding makes use of what are termed *quaternary* codes, which are defined in the following manner. Each node in the quadtree is represented by the sequence of n digits $<q_{n-1},q_{n-2}, \cdots ,q_0>$, given by relation 2.5. This sequence forms a number $q = \Sigma_{i=0}^{n-1} q_i \cdot 5^i$. Each digit q_i represents a directional code that can take on a value of 0, 1, 2, 3, 4. Let the quadtree be rooted at node R at level n, and let the node to be encoded be P at level m ($m < n$). Let $<P_n,P_{n-1}, \cdots ,P_m>$ be a sequence of nodes such that $P_n = R$, $P_i = \text{FATHER}(P_{i-1})$ for $m < i \le n$, and $P_m = P$. Let the directions NW, NE, SW, and SE be represented by the directional codes 0, 1, 2, and 3, respectively, and be accessed by the function SONTYPE4.

$$q_i = \begin{cases} 4 & 0 \le i < m \\ \text{SONTYPE4}(P_i) & m \le i < n \end{cases} \qquad (2.5)$$

For example, node 10 of Figure 2.1 ($n = 4$) would be encoded by the sequence $<q_3,q_2,q_1,q_0> = <1,0,2,3>$ or 138 in base 10. Similarly node 25 would be encoded by the sequence $<q_3,q_2,q_1,q_0> = <2,1,4,4>$ or 299 in base 10. The 4 is analogous to a *don't care* directional code in the designated position. Thus in a quadtree corresponding to a $2^n \times 2^n$ image, a leaf corresponding to a $2^k \times 2^k$ block ($k < n$) will have k digits with a *don't care* directional code. Abel and Smith [Abel83, Abel84a] report an almost identical encoding with the only difference being that the roles of 0 and 4 are interchanged—that is, 0 is the *don't care* directional code. They use this encoding to represent a quadtree by a set of codes, organized as a B^+-tree [Come79], corresponding to the black nodes.

The term quaternary is a misnomer since we really have a base 5 code, and thus the term *quinary* is more appropriate. We will refer to it as an FL *locational code* (denoting fixed length). Notice its similarity to CODE1, with the principal difference being that all codes are of fixed length once n has been defined, whereas they are of varying length when using CODE1. The fixed length is achieved by using the *don't care* directional code in the appropriate digit positions. Of course, the codes are longer, but there is no need to store the level at which the node appears, as is necessary when using CODE1.

The FL locational code has the interesting property that when the codes of all the nodes are sorted in increasing order, the resulting sequence is the postorder (also preorder and inorder since the nonleaf nodes are excluded) traversal of the quadtree. When the white nodes are omitted, the result is termed an FL *linear quadtree*. For example, the postorder traversal of the black nodes of Figure 2.1 is 19, 14, 20, 21, 22, 23, 10, 16, 25, 27, 28, 29, 38, with FL locational codes 78, 80, 82, 83, 89, 94, 138, 199, 299, 376, 380, 381, 387, respectively, in base 10.

Gargantini [Garg82a] has demonstrated that the FL locational codes of the white nodes in a quadtree represented as an FL linear quadtree can be obtained by executing a procedure similar to WHITEBLOCKS, as shown below. Given the FL locational codes, say P and Q, of two successive black elements of an FL linear quadtree corresponding to a $2^n \times 2^n$ image, WHITEBLOCKS outputs the FL locational codes of all of the white nodes whose codes are between P and Q. For ease of notation, P and Q are treated as integer arrays that contain the n digits that comprise each of the FL locational codes.

The process is quite simple and consists of three stages once the nearest common ancestor of P and Q (actually its level), say A, has been found. Let P' and Q' be brother ancestors of P and Q, respectively, that are sons of A (assume that neither P nor Q is a son of A). First output the FL locational code of all the white nodes between P and P'. Next output the codes of all the white blocks between P' and Q'. Finally output the codes of all the white blocks between Q' and Q.

As an example, consider nodes 16 and 25 in Figure 2.1 with FL locational codes 1244 and 2144 (expressed as base 5 numbers). Their nearest common ancestor is A at level 4. C is the son of A that is an ancestor of 16. Therefore we first output code 1344 corresponding to node 17. D is the son of A that is an ancestor of 25. Since there are no white brothers of C with codes between C and D, we now proceed to the final step and output code 2044, corresponding to node 24.

```
procedure WHITEBLOCKS(N,P,Q);
/* Given a 2^N × 2^N image represented by an FL linear quadtree, output the FL locational
   codes of all white nodes between P and Q where P and Q are the FL locational codes
   of successive elements (i.e., black) of the FL linear quadtree. P and Q are defined as in
   (5). */
begin
 value integer N;
 value locationalcode P,Q[0:N−1];
 integer I,J,K;
 I ← 0;
 while P[I]=4 do I ← I+1; /* Find the first non–don't care digit in P */
 J ← N−1;
 while P[J]=Q[J] do J ← J−1; /* Find the level of the nearest common ancestor */
 while I<J do /* Output all white blocks between P and the son of the nearest */
   begin        /* common ancestor */
    while P[I]<3 do
```

```
        begin
          P[I] ← P[I]+1;
          output(P);
        end;
        P[I] ← 4;
        I ← I+1;
      end;
  P[J] ← P[J]+1;
  while P[J] < Q[J] do /* Output the white blocks that are sons of the nearest */
    begin                    /* common ancestor */
      output(P);
      P[J] ← P[J]+1;
    end;
  K ← 0;
  while Q[K]=4 do K ← K+1; /* Find the first non–don't care digit in Q */
  while J > K do /* Output all white blocks between Q and the son of the nearest */
    begin          /* common ancestor */
      J ← J–1;
      P[J] ← 0;
      while P[J] < Q[J] do
        begin
          output(P);
          P[J] ← P[J]+1;
        end;
    end;
  end;
end;
```

Using the FL locational code, we can obtain the codes for the white nodes without having to construct the quadtree, as was done in procedure BUILD_TREE for the VL locational code. On the other hand, when the VL locational codes of the black nodes are sorted in increasing order, the resulting sequence is a variant of a breadth-first traversal of the black segment of the quadtree—that is, for $i < j$, nodes at level j appear before nodes at level i. For example, the nodes of Figure 2.1, in increasing order, are 25, 16, 22, 23, 28, 14, 27, 29, 20, 38, 19, 21, and 10 with VL locational codes 13, 17, 96, 121, 184, 196, 284, 309, 446, 459, 546, 571, and 582, respectively.

The breadth-first property of the VL locational code means that the sequence yields a progressive approximation of the image—that is, successive nodes lead to a better approximation (for a discussion of quadtree-based approximation methods, see Chapter 8). An algorithm to obtain the white nodes given the VL locational codes of the black nodes without having to construct the actual quadtree can also be devised. However, it is not as simple as the one obtained as a result of using FL locational codes (see Exercise 2.7).

FL locational codes have several disadvantages when compared to VL locational codes. First, the code words are longer since all contain n base 5 digits for a $2^n \times 2^n$ image, while this is not necessarily so for VL locational codes. Second, increasing the resolution of the image (i.e., from n to $n + 1$) requires recoding of the existing nodes (i.e., multiply the codes of all existing nodes by 5). In contrast, the breadth-first property of the VL locational code ensures that the sequence is unchanged. Third, when attempting to obtain a path from the root of the tree to a particular node, it is easier to decode a VL locational code than the FL locational code, assuming the use of modulo and integer division operations in the decoding procedure. Finally, FL locational codes do not have the progressive approximation property of the VL locational code.

A drawback of both the FL and VL locational codes is the use of base 5 numbers to represent the directional codes. The result is a significant complication of the decoding process by requiring the use of division operations instead of shifts and modulo operations. The *FD locational code* overcomes this drawback. It records the level of the node[3] along with a locational code that represents each directional code with just two bits [Garg82c]. The FD locational code can be implemented using a fixed or a variable number of bits. Using a variable number of bits means that no storage is wasted in the locational code. However, in the following, we assume that the number of bits is fixed because we want each node to be of the same size.

The term *FD linear quadtree* is used to describe a linear quadtree encoding such that each block in the image is represented by a fixed length FD locational code. Such an encoding is used in a quadtree-based geographic information system [Rose83b]. For a $2^n \times 2^n$ image, each $2^k \times 2^k$ block is represented by an FD locational code that is $2 \cdot n + \lceil \log_2 n + 1 \rceil$ binary digits long. The trailing $2 \cdot k$ binary digits of the first $2 \cdot n$

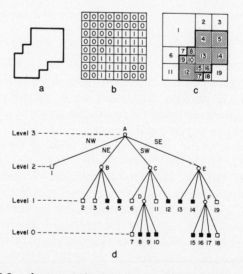

Figure 2.3   *An example (a) region, (b) its binary array, (c) its maximal blocks (blocks in the region are shaded), and (d) the corresponding quadtree*

---

[3] Alternatively, the depth can be recorded instead of the level (see Exercise 2.12).

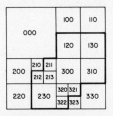

*Figure 2.4   The locational code components of the FD
locational codes corresponding to Figure 2.3*

bits (i.e., the actual locational code of the block) are usually ignored. However, by
always setting them to a constant value (e.g., 0), we find that the locational code component of the FD locational code really corresponds to the interleaved coordinates of a
specific pixel in the block (e.g., the pixel in the block's upper left corner when the origin is in the upper left corner of the image). The $\lceil \log_2 n + 1 \rceil$ factor corresponds to
the level of the block. Figure 2.4 shows the locational code components of the FD
locational codes corresponding to Figure 2.3c.

Exercises
2.1. Toward the computation of which adjacency relation is the linear quadtree biased?
2.2. Is the order in which procedure BUILD_TREE processes the locational codes when building
     the quadtree important?
2.3. Given the locational code using CODE1 for a particular pixel, show how to obtain the loca-
     tional code of its horizontally and vertically adjacent pixel. Repeat for CODE2 and the
     quinary code.
2.4. Does procedure WHITEBLOCKS correctly handle the first and final sequences of white
     blocks (i.e., at the start and at the end of the image)? If not, modify it to do so.
2.5. An FL linear bintree can be defined in an analogous manner to that of the FL linear quad-
     tree. Modify procedure WHITEBLOCKS so that it works for a linear FL bintree.
2.6. How would you adapt the FL linear quadtree and procedure WHITEBLOCKS to deal with
     images of arbitrary dimensions?
2.7. Give an algorithm to obtain the VL locational codes of the white nodes from the VL loca-
     tional codes of the black nodes.
2.8. Given a $2^n \times 2^n$ image represented by a sorted (in increasing order) list of the FL loca-
     tional codes of its black and white blocks, what is the maximum distance in terms of
     nodes between two adjacent pixels in the image? Assume that the locational codes are
     formed in an order so that NW has the smallest directional code followed by NE, SW, and
     SE. Repeat for the general case of a d-dimensional image.
2.9. Consider a square region, say R embedded in the $2^n \times 2^n$ image I, such that P and Q
     represent the minimum and maximum, respectively, FD locational codes of its constituent
     pixels. Assume that R is black and the rest of I is white. Write a procedure to generate
     the FD locational codes of all the black blocks in the quadtree of I.
2.10. Modify the solution to Exercise 2.9 to yield the FD locational codes of the white blocks as
     well.

2.1.2 Comparison of Pointer Quadtrees and FD Linear Quadtrees

One of the motivations for using locational codes instead of pointers is the desire to save space. In this section, the FD linear quadtree is compared with a particular pointer-based representation (defined below) in terms of the number of bits and bytes that they require to store the inherent tree structure of the quadtree. Thus the data fields of the leaf nodes are ignored since they would need the same amount of storage in either encoding. In particular, it is shown that for an image of a given dimension and resolution (i.e., maximum side length), there exists a cutoff value such that if the number of leaf nodes is less than the cutoff value, then the pointer-based quadtree representation is more compact than the FD linear quadtree. This comparison is based on the analysis performed by Samet and Webber [Same89a].

Let I be a d-dimensional image with a maximum side length of 2^h (i.e., the maximum level or depth of a node is h) and whose corresponding quadtree[4] has L leaf nodes. The number of bits required by the FD linear quadtree of I is

$$L \cdot (d \cdot h + \log(h + 1)). \tag{2.6}$$

A *pointer quadtree* has two types of nodes (nonleaf and leaf). Internal nodes consist of 2^d pointers, whereas leaf nodes do not require pointers (see also [Doct81, Meag82d, Yau83, Okaw88]). However, we do need to distinguish between the two node types. This will usually require one bit (but see Exercises 2.14 and 2.16) and is implemented as part of the pointer field that points at the node being described rather than in the node being described. Therefore, in this comparison, no storage is attributed to the leaf nodes; instead all the excess storage attributed to overhead is accounted for in the nonleaf nodes. The number of nonleaf nodes is

$$(L - 1)/(2^d - 1),$$

which is bounded from above by

$$L/(2^d - 1).$$

The following analysis makes use of this upper bound because it makes the manipulation of the equations more tractable. It should be clear that the slight overestimation of the number of nodes in the pointer quadtree will not affect the final results except for small values of L. Thus at times, the derived cutoff values will be lower than they would be had the number of nonleaf nodes (and hence the total as well) in the quadtree not been overestimated. Interestingly this overestimation affects the

---

[4] The term *quadtree* is used here to mean the d-dimensional quadtree.

cutoff value for Figure 2.3 (see Exercise 2.13). However, in general, the effect of this overestimation on the true cutoff value will be seen to be insignificant as the depth of the quadtree is increased because, for small values of L, the pointer quadtree is always superior to the FD linear quadtree when the depth is sufficiently large.

Each pointer field needs to be only wide enough to distinguish among all the possible nodes in a particular tree whose number is

$$L \cdot (1 + 1/(2^d - 1))$$

or

$$L \cdot 2^d/(2^d - 1).$$

Thus the total number of bits needed to store a pointer quadtree is

$$(L/(2^d - 1)) \cdot (2^d \cdot (1 + \log(L \cdot 2^d/(2^d - 1)))). \tag{2.7}$$

Using relations 2.6 and 2.7, we see that in order for the FD linear quadtree to be more compact (i.e., require less bits) than the pointer quadtree, the following relation must hold:

$$L \cdot (d \cdot h + \log(h + 1)) < (L/(2^d - 1)) \cdot (2^d \cdot (1 + \log(L \cdot 2^d/(2^d - 1)))). \tag{2.8}$$

Factoring L out of relation 2.8, letting $m = 2^d$ and $n = 2^d - 1$, and solving for L leads to

$$(n/m) \cdot 2^{(n/m) \cdot (d \cdot h + \log(h + 1)) - 1} < L. \tag{2.9}$$

Letting C denote the left side of relation 2.9, we see that for a given d and h, as long as the number of leaf nodes (i.e., L) is less than or equal to C (i.e., $L \le C$), then the pointer quadtree requires at most as many bits as the FD linear quadtree. Thus C is a cutoff value for the number of leaf nodes.

The cutoff value given in relation 2.9 is not particularly realistic. The problem is that it is based on a continuous model in the sense that the derivation does not restrict the pointer, level, and node type fields to lie on bit boundaries, as would be required in an actual implementation. Letting $\lceil x \rceil$ represent the ceiling of x, we can rewrite relation 2.8 to incorporate a restriction that these fields comprise an integer number of bits by:

$$L \cdot (d \cdot h + \lceil \log(h + 1) \rceil) < (L/(2^d - 1)) \cdot (2^d \cdot (1 + \lceil \log(L \cdot 2^d/(2^d - 1)) \rceil)). \tag{2.10}$$

Factoring L out of relation 2.10, letting $m = 2^d$ and $n = 2^d - 1$, approximating $\lceil \log(L \cdot m/n) \rceil$ by $\log(L \cdot m/n) + 1$, and solving for L yields

$$(n/m) \cdot 2^{(n/m) \cdot (d \cdot h + \lceil \log(h+1) \rceil) - 2} < L. \tag{2.11}$$

Unfortunately bit addressability is awkward on most computer architectures. Therefore typical implementations lead to a further restriction so that the encoding for a given node starts on a byte boundary. Assume 8-bit bytes and let $\{x\}$ denote the quantity $8 \cdot \lceil x/8 \rceil$. In the following, pointers are packed across byte boundaries while still requiring each pointer field to comprise an integer number of bits. Restricting each node to start on a byte boundary results in relation 2.8 being rewritten as

$$L \cdot \{d \cdot h + \lceil \log(h+1) \rceil\} < (L/(2^d - 1)) \cdot \{2^d \cdot (1 + \lceil \log(L \cdot 2^d/(2^d - 1)) \rceil)\}. \tag{2.12}$$

Letting $m = 2^d$ and $n = 2^d - 1$ and expanding $\{\ \}$, we have

$$\{m \cdot (1 + \lceil \log(L \cdot m/n) \rceil)\} \leq 8 \cdot (m \cdot (1 + \lceil \log(L \cdot m/n) \rceil)/8 + 1). \tag{2.13}$$

Factoring L out of relation 2.12, using m, n, and relation 2.13 as done in the derivations of relations 2.9 and 2.11, approximating $\lceil \log(L \cdot m/n) \rceil$ by $\log(L \cdot m/n) + 1$, we solve for the cutoff value

$$(n/m) \cdot 2^{(n/m) \cdot \{d \cdot h + \lceil \log(h+1) \rceil\} - (8/m) - 2} < L. \tag{2.14}$$

Table 2.1 shows the cutoff values of relations 2.9, 2.11, and 2.14 for two-dimensional images whose sizes range from $2^3 \times 2^3$ to $2^{15} \times 2^{15}$.[5] The table assumes 8-bit bytes. For each image, the table also indicates the maximum number of leaf nodes in the corresponding quadtree (i.e., a complete quadtree).

From a practical standpoint, the most realistic of the restrictions on the alignment of the fields and pointer values is the one that forces a node to start on a byte boundary while at the same time forcing all fields to be of integer length (measured in bits). It results in little wasted space because of the multiplicative effect of the 2^d pointers per node. In particular, for a byte size of b, there is no wasted space when-

---

[5] The cutoff values of relations 2.11 and 2.14 are somewhat lower than the actual values indicated by relations 2.10 and 2.12, respectively, because of the approximation of $\lceil \log(L \cdot m/n) \rceil$ by $\log(L \cdot m/n) + 1$, as well as round-off errors in the computation of natural logarithms and noninteger powers of two. However, as the depth increases, these differences become insignificant.

Table 2.1   Minimum leaf node counts for locational codes being better than pointers

Depth (h)	Continuous: Relation 2.9	Each Field on a Bit Boundary: Relation 2.11	Each Node on a Byte Boundary: Relation 2.14	Maximum Number of Nodes
3	24	12	3	64
4	80	57	192	256
5	260	161	192	1,024
6	826	457	192	4,096
7	2,583	1,292	12,288	16,384
8	7,981	6,144	12,288	65,536
9	24,431	17,378	12,288	262,144
10	74,221	49,152	12,288	1,048,576
11	224,085	139,023	786,432	4,194,304
12	673,021	393,216	786,432	16,777,216
13	2,012,390	1,112,183	786,432	67,108,864
14	5,994,178	3,145,728	786,432	268,435,456
15	17,794,925	8,897,462	50,331,648	1,073,741,824

ever $2^d \bmod b = 0$, which is true whenever $d \geq 3$ and $b = 8$. In two dimensions, we waste at most 4 bits when $b = 8$.

For example, using the above restriction, a quadtree of depth 9 must contain at least 12,288 leaf nodes in order for the FD linear quadtree to be more compact than the corresponding pointer quadtree. Since the maximum number of leaf nodes at depth 9 is 262,144 (i.e., 4^9), we see that this means that the number of leaf nodes must be at least 4.7% of the maximum (i.e., the number of leaf nodes in a complete quadtree) in order for the FD linear quadtree to be more compact for images of depth 9. To put this in perspective, consider Figure 2.5, which is an image of depth 9 from a geographic information system that uses quadtrees [Same84d, Same87a, Shaf87c].

Figure 2.5 is an image of a floodplain region whose quadtree requires 5,266 leaf nodes (2.0% of the maximum). Under the byte boundary restriction, its pointer quadtree requires 12,285 8-bit bytes, while its FD linear quadtree requires 15,798 8-bit bytes. Thus Figure 2.5 is more compactly encoded by the pointer quadtree.

From Table 2.1 we see that, at times, the storage requirements of the pointer quadtree are worse than the FD linear quadtree. Table 2.2 contains a more thorough tabulation of the effect of restricting all nodes to start on byte boundaries by varying the dimension of the image, as well as its depth. Again we are using images whose depth ranges from 3 to 15 with a byte size of 8 bits. The images are of two, three, or four dimensions. For each dimension and depth, the table contains the value of the ratio of the log of the cutoff value for this restriction and the log of the maximum number of nodes in the corresponding quadtree.

Figure 2.5   Floodplain image

In three dimensions, for depths of 3, 5, 8, 10, and 15, the storage requirements of the pointer quadtree are never worse than the FD linear quadtree. Similarly, in four dimensions for trees of depth 3, 4, 6, 8, 10, 12, and 14, the same result holds. In fact, in the three- and four-dimensional cases, the cutoff values are so close to the maximum node counts, that in all practical cases the pointer quadtree would still occupy less space than the FD linear quadtree.

The significance of the comparison of the storage requirements of these alternative quadtree implementations lies in addressing the issue of which implementation is

Table 2.2   Log(cutoff leaf node count)/log-
(maximum number of leaf nodes)

depth (h)	2–d	3–d	4–d
3	1.58/6	10.81/9	12.41/12
4	7.58/8	10.81/12	19.91/16
5	7.58/10	17.81/15	19.91/20
6	7.58/12	17.81/18	27.41/24
7	13.58/14	17.81/21	27.41/28
8	13.58/16	24.81/24	34.91/32
9	13.58/18	24.81/27	34.91/36
10	13.58/20	31.81/30	42.41/40
11	19.58/22	31.81/33	42.41/44
12	19.58/24	31.81/36	49.91/48
13	19.58/26	38.81/39	49.91/52
14	19.58/28	38.81/42	57.41/56
15	25.58/30	45.81/45	57.41/60

most likely to permit the storage of the largest number of quadtree nodes in a fixed amount of memory (e.g., the size of a disk or available amount of core) for an image of a given dimension and resolution (i.e., width). It should be clear that at or near the cutoff values, both the FD linear and pointer quadtrees are equally compact. Of course, there are other considerations.

For example, as nodes are inserted and deleted from the quadtree, the storage requirements of the pointer quadtree will change more abruptly than those of the FD linear quadtree. This is because each additional node in the FD linear quadtree requires a fixed amount of extra storage (i.e., $d \cdot h + \lceil \log(h + 1) \rceil$ per node in a d-dimensional image of height h). On the other hand, in the case of the pointer quadtree, the space required for each node in the pointer quadtree is a function of the number of nodes in the tree. Thus additional nodes may result in an increase in the number of bits required for a pointer, thereby resulting in a need to reallocate memory. Therefore the comparison is restricted to files of static size.

Nevertheless the comparison does point out that the greater is the compactness of the quadtree, the smaller is the overhead of the pointer encoding in relation to an encoding that makes use of FD locational codes. Similar statements can be made for other variants of locational codes but not for bintrees (see Exercise 2.26). Furthermore although the asymptotic behavior of the depth of the quadtree is interesting, in practice it is rare for an implementation to have depth values as large as 16 (which corresponds to a $65,536 \times 65,536$ image space).

Exercises

2.11. Prove that all of the cutoff values obtained in the comparisons of the storage requirements of pointer and FD linear quadtrees are unique—that is, that for a given value of L there is only one pair of d and h values.

2.12. The FD locational code is implemented as a triple that contains the path to the node from the root, the level of the node, and its color. However, it could also be implemented by recording the depth of the node instead of its level. Consider a $2^n \times 2^n$ image, and suppose that its quadtree always consists of more than one node (i.e., at least four nodes). In this case, is there an advantage to using the level of the node instead of its depth?

2.13. Compute the space requirements in bits for the pointer and FD linear quadtrees corresponding to the $2^3 \times 2^3$ image in Figure 2.3 when all fields are restricted to lie on integer boundaries. Does your answer agree with the prediction of Table 2.1? If not, explain why.

2.14. The derivations of the space requirements of the pointer quadtree make use of a representation that requires a bit to differentiate between pointers to nonleaf and leaf nodes. How can you avoid using this bit?

2.15. What is the effect on relations 2.9, 2.11, and 2.14 when there is no need for the bit to differentiate between pointers to nonleaf and leaf nodes as in Exercise 2.14?

2.16. [Martin J. Dürst] The pointer quadtree implementation can be improved upon by storing the leaf-type information directly in the tree. In this case, each different leaf node type has a separate address. For example, in a binary image, we have just two leaf node types: black and white. In the general case, if we have W leaf node types, then the total number of possible pointers is reduced from $(2^d \cdot L - 1)/(2^d - 1)$ to $W + (L - 1)/(2^d - 1)$. Moreover, there is no longer a need for the 2^d bits to differentiate between nonleaf and leaf nodes. What is the effect of this implementation on relations 2.9, 2.11, and 2.14?

2.17. Derive relation 2.14 from 2.12 in a step-by-step manner.

2.18. What is the effect on the cutoff value of 2.14 when we waive the requirement that each node of the FD linear quadtree starts on a byte boundary, while still requiring that each node of the pointer quadtree starts on a byte boundary? Assume 8-bit bytes.

2.19. What is the effect on the cutoff value of 2.14 in the worst case when we require that each node of both the FD linear and pointer quadtrees start on a byte boundary?

2.20. Rewrite relation 2.12 to incorporate a further restriction so that each pointer starts on a byte boundary. Derive a cutoff value similar to 2.14. Assume 8-bit bytes.

2.21. What is the effect on the cutoff value of Exercise 2.20 if we waive the requirement that each node of the FD linear quadtree starts on a byte boundary while still requiring that each pointer of the pointer quadtree start on a byte boundary?

2.22. How is the cutoff value of Exercise 2.20 related to that of relation 2.10 in the worst case when we require each node of the FD linear quadtree and each pointer to start on a byte boundary?

2.23. Suppose you want to save k bits per leaf node by using an FD linear quadtree instead of a pointer quadtree. What is the new cutoff value for the continuous case (i.e., the one represented by relation 2.9)? By how much has the old cutoff value increased?

2.24. Rederive relations 2.9, 2.11, and 2.14 using $(L - 1)/(2^d - 1)$ as the number of nonleaf nodes instead of the bound $L/(2^d - 1)$.

2.25. Compare the storage requirements of the pointer quadtree and the FD linear quadtree corresponding to a d-dimensional image when a field for the FATHER pointer is included with the pointer-based representation.

2.26. An FD linear bintree can be defined in an analogous manner to the FD linear quadtree for d-dimensional images. Explain why the FD linear bintree is almost always more efficient spacewise than the pointer bintree.

2.27. Compare the storage requirements of a pointer-based bintree and an FD linear bintree corresponding to a d-dimensional image. Derive the analogs of relations 2.9, 2.11, and 2.14.

2.28. Compare the storage requirements of the FL linear quadtree and the pointer quadtree corresponding to a d-dimensional image. Derive the analogs of relations 2.9, 2.11, and 2.14.

2.29. Compare the storage requirements of the VL linear quadtree and the pointer quadtree corresponding to a d-dimensional image. Derive the analogs of relations 2.9, 2.11, and 2.14. You will need to come up with a probability model for the distribution of the leaf nodes of different sizes.

2.1.3 Two-Dimensional Run Encoding

Section 2.1.1 stressed that, given a node's locational code, we must be able to determine its size. This led us to use base 5 locational codes such as the FL and VL locational codes, or the FD locational code, which records the level explicitly. Lauzon, Mark, Kikuchi, and Guevara [Lauz85] show that when the leaf nodes (i.e., black and white) are represented in a list sorted by the order in which they are visited, starting at the root and visiting the NW, NE, SW, and SE sons in order, there is no need to record the level of a node.

Each leaf node is encoded by use of a locational code, which is the Morton Matrix number of the pixel that occupies its lower right corner—that is, the pixel having the maximum Morton Matrix number in the leaf node.[6] The list of leaf nodes is sorted by their corresponding Morton Matrix numbers. Assuming that the quadtree corresponds to a $2^n \times 2^n$ image, the level of $M[j]$, the jth Morton Matrix number in the list, is given by $\log_4(M[j] - M[j-1])$ where $M[0]$ is initialized to -1.

This method works only when we know the Morton Matrix numbers of all of the leaf nodes, and thus random access is not possible. That is, given the Morton Matrix number of a leaf node, we cannot determine its size without knowing the Morton Matrix number of the next node in the sequence. For example, in a $2^3 \times 2^3$ image, a Morton Matrix number of 47 can correspond to a 1×1, 2×2, or 4×4 block, whereas a Morton Matrix number of 23 can correspond only to a 1×1 or a 2×2 block. For the image of Figure 2.3 the nodes sorted in increasing order of their Morton Matrix numbers are 1, 2, 3, 4, 5, 6, 7, 8, 9, 10, 11, 12, 13, 14, 15, 16, 17, 18, and 19. Assuming a $2^3 \times 2^3$ image, the corresponding Morton Matrix numbers are 15, 19, 23, 27, 31, 35, 36, 37, 38, 39, 43, 47, 51, 55, 56, 57, 58, 59, and 63, respectively.

Lauzon et al. propose to represent the collection of the leaf nodes using a variant of the run-length code [Ruto68] termed a *two-dimensional run encoding* (2DRE). The leaf nodes are represented by their locational codes using the Morton Matrix numbers as defined. Once the codes of the leaf nodes have been sorted in increasing order, the resulting list is viewed as a set of subsequences of codes corresponding to blocks of the same color. The final step in its construction is to discard all but the last element of each subsequence of blocks of the same color. The codes of the intervening blocks can be reconstructed by knowing the codes of two successive blocks in the run encoding. For example, for Figure 2.3, discarding all but the last element of each subsequence of nodes of the same color yields the list of nodes 3, 5, 7, 10, 11, 17, and 19 with Morton Matrix numbers 23, 31, 36, 39, 43, 58, and 63, respectively.

Procedure DECODE_2DRE, given below, shows how the Morton Matrix numbers and levels of the intervening leaf nodes in the two-dimensional run encoding can be reconstructed. Given two consecutive elements of a 2DRE file, say M_1 and M_2 with Morton Matrix numbers C_1 and C_2, respectively, we first determine the Morton Matrix number of the brother block, say N_1, of the largest block having pixel C_1 at its lower right corner. This is done by repeatedly incrementing C_1 by 4^L (L is initially 0) as long as the sum does not exceed C_2. For example, in Figure 2.3, for $C_1 = 43$ and $C_2 = 58$, $N_1 = 47$. Once N_1 has been found, its block is output in the list of nodes, C_1 is set to N_1, and the process is restarted. If C_2 is exceeded prior to finding a brother block of the desired size—that is, $N_2 = C_1 + 4^{L-1}$ such that $N_2 \leq C_2$, and $C_2 < C_1 + 4^L$,

---

[6] This assumes that the origin is at the upper left corner of the universe.

then output the block corresponding to N_2, reset C_1 to N_2, and restart the process. For example, in Figure 2.3, for $C_1 = 31$ and $C_2 = 36$, $N_2 = 35$. The entire process terminates when the block corresponding to C_2 has been output.

```
procedure DECODE_2DRE(C1,C2);
/* Given the 2DRE encoding of a quadtree, determine the Morton Matrix numbers and lev-
   els of all leaf nodes whose Morton Matrix numbers are between locational codes C1 and
   C2. */
begin
  value locationalcode C1,C2;
  integer L;
  while C1 < C2 do
    begin
      L ← 0;
      while C1+4↑L < C2 and ((C1+1) mod 4↑L)=0 do L ← L+1;
      if C1+4↑L > C2 then L ← L−1;
      C1 ← C1+4↑L;
      output(C1,L);
    end;
end;
```

Mark and Lauzon [Mark85b] compare different linear quadtree representations, including two-dimensional run encoding, and a pointer-based representation in terms of bits per pixel for a number of representative binary images. In comparison to linear quadtrees, two-dimensional run encoding is more compact and more efficient for set operations. However, translation and rotation by multiples of 90 degrees are easier with the linear quadtree [Garg83]. Unfortunately the two-dimensional run encoding method, unlike the linear quadtree, does not lend itself to representing other than region data. This is especially true for other data types such as points (see Chapter 2 of [Same90a]) and lines (see Chapter 4 of [Same90a]). The problem is that we use representations with decomposition rules requiring that two entities be separated. Since the entities are of different value, it does not make sense to run encode them. For example, we say that the domain of points (lines) is recursively partitioned until each quadrant contains at most one point (line).

Exercises

2.30. Consider a $2^n \times 2^n$ image whose quadtree's leaf nodes are represented by Morton Matrix numbers and stored in increasing order in the list M. Prove that the level of the jth Morton Matrix number, say $M[j]$, is $n - \log_4(M[j] - M[j-1])$.

2.31. Suppose that each leaf node of the quadtree is encoded by using the Morton Matrix number of the pixel that occupies its upper left corner. How would you compute the level of the jth Morton Matrix number?

2.32. Procedure DECODE_2DRE is written so that its clarity is maximized. Use common subexpression elimination to optimize it so that it does not repeatedly calculate the same quantities.

2.33. Suppose that the two-dimensional run encoding sequence were defined to consist of the first element of each subsequence of blocks of the same color rather than the last element. Give a procedure such as DECODE_2DRE to reconstruct the Morton Matrix numbers of the blocks of the quadtree. If this is not possible, how can you redefine the Morton Matrix number associated with each block so that it will work?

2.34. Adapt the concepts of a Morton Matrix number and the two-dimensional run encoding sequence to an octree. How would you determine the size of a given node?

2.1.4 Forests

Jones and Iyengar [Jone84] (see also [Rama83]) adapt the concept of a forest [Knut73a] to a quadtree. It results in a decomposition of the image into a collection of subquadtrees, each of which corresponds to a maximal square. The maximal squares are identified by storing with each nonleaf node (i.e., a gray node) some information about its subtrees. A nonleaf node is said to be of type *GB* if at least two of its sons are black or of type GB. Otherwise the node is said to be of type *GW*. For example, in Figure 2.1, nodes F, J, and M are of type GB, and nodes A, B, C, D, E, G, H, I, K, L, and N are of type GW. Procedure LABEL_GBGW, given below, results in labeling the nonleaf nodes of a quadtree with GB or GW.

```
procedure LABEL_GBGW(P);
/* Label each nonleaf node of the quadtree rooted at P with GB or GW. */
begin
  value pointer node P;
  integer COUNT;
  quadrant Q;
  if GRAY(P) then
  begin
    COUNT ← 0;
    for Q in {'NW', 'NE', 'SW', 'SE'} do
    begin
      LABEL_GBGW(SON(P,Q));
      if BLACK(SON(P,Q)) or GB(SON(P,Q)) then COUNT ← COUNT+1;
    end;
    NODETYPE(P) ← if COUNT≥2 then 'GB'
                  else 'GW';
  end;
end;
```

Once the nonleaf nodes of the quadtree have been appropriately labeled, we are able to define a forest. Each black node or a nonleaf node with a label of GB is said to be a maximal square. A *black forest* is the minimal set of maximal squares that are not contained in other maximal squares and that spans the black area of the image. Clearly the black forest is unique. For example, the black forest representation of the quadtree of Figure 2.1 is the collection of nodes F, 10, 16, 25, 27, M, and 38 and their corresponding subtrees. Note that the black forest corresponding to an image that is entirely white is the empty set.

The black forest is useful as a storage-saving device because it eliminates the need for a possibly significant number of white and gray nodes. For example, in Figure 2.1 by using a black forest, there is no need for nodes 1, 2, 3, 4, 5, 6, 7, 8, 9, 11, 17, 24, 26, 30, 31, 32, 35, 36, 37, 39, 40, 41, 42, 43, A, B, C, D, E, G, H, K, L, and N.

Creating the black forest from the quadtree is quite straightforward; we simply traverse the quadtree in preorder [Knut73a] looking for the closest nodes to the root that are labeled GB. Procedure FOREST_GB, given below, results in outputting the black forest of nodes corresponding to a quadtree rooted at node P.

```
procedure FOREST_GB(P);
/* Output the black forest corresponding to the quadtree rooted at node P. */
begin
  value pointer node P;
  quadrant Q;
  if GB(P) or BLACK(P) then output(P)
  else if GW(P) then
    begin
      for Q in {'NW', 'NE', 'SW', 'SE'} do FOREST_GB(SON(P,Q));
    end;
end;
```

The elements of a forest are identified by using the locational code of the root of each of its component subquadtrees. Thus the forest representation is a hybrid between the use of locational codes and an explicit quadtree. Using CODE2, procedure FOREST_BLACK, given below, outputs the VL locational codes for the roots of the elements of a forest. It has three parameters: P, C, and I. P is the root of the quadtree with the desired black forest, while C and I are useful for bookkeeping. In particular C represents the VL locational code of the root of the subquadtree currently being processed (P), and I is the node distance of P from the root of the quadtree of the entire image. FOREST_BLACK is initially called with C and I initialized to 0: FOREST_BLACK(ROOT,0,0).

FOREST_BLACK is quite similar to FOREST_GB. It makes use of function QCODE, which maps quadrants into their respective directional codes — such as QCODE(NE)=2. Application of FOREST_BLACK to Figure 2.1 results in the sequence of VL locational codes 21, 582, 17, 13, 284, 59, and 459 corresponding to nodes F, 10, 16, 25, 27, M, and 38, respectively.

```
procedure FOREST_BLACK(P,C,I);
/* Given a 2^N x 2^N image, output the black forest for the quadtree rooted at node P with
   VL locational code C and at level N-I. */
begin
  value pointer node P;
  value locationalcode C;
```

```
    value integer I;
    quadrant Q;
    if GB(P) or BLACK(P) then output(C)
    else if GW(P) then
      begin
        for Q in {'NW', 'NE', 'SW', 'SE'} do
          FOREST_BLACK(SON(P,Q),C+QCODE(Q)*5↑I,I+1);
      end;
    end;
```

It is interesting to observe that when a node is of type GB, the space spanned by it is not necessarily at least 50% black. In fact, for a $2^n \times 2^n$ image array, when the root is of type GB at least $1/2^n$ of the image area (i.e., 2^n pixels) must be black (see Exercise 2.35). Similarly, when the root is of type GW, at most $1-(3/4)^n$ of the image area can be black (see Exercise 2.36). Note the analogy between the concept of labeling nodes with GB or GW and the B-tree [Come79] where nonleaf nodes contain a varying number of records. This number is at least one-half of the node size.

Exercises
2.35. Given a $2^n \times 2^n$ image represented by a quadtree rooted at node P such that node P is of type GB, prove that at least $1/2^n$ of the image must be black.
2.36. Given a $2^n \times 2^n$ image represented by a quadtree rooted at node P such that node P is of type GW, prove that at most $1-(3/4)^n$ of the image area can be black.

2.2 TREE TRAVERSALS

The second pointerless representation is in the form of a preorder tree traversal (i.e., depth-first) of the nodes of the quadtree. The result is a string consisting of the symbols 'G,' 'B,' 'W' corresponding to gray, black, and white nodes, respectively. This representation is due to Kawaguchi and Endo [Kawa80a] and is called a *DF-expression*. For example, assuming that sons are traversed in the order NW, NE, SW, SE, the DF-expression of the image of Figure 2.3 is given by

GWGWWBBGWGWBBBWBGBBGBBBWW.

Procedure BUILD_DF, given below, constructs the DF-expression corresponding to a quadtree rooted at node P. Not surprisingly, it is nothing more than a preorder traversal of the input quadtree.

```
    recursive procedure BUILD_DF(P);
    /* Output the DF-expression for the quadtree rooted at P. */
    begin
      value pointer node P;
      quadrant I;
```

```
if GRAY(P) then
  begin
    output('G');
    for I in {'NW', 'NE', 'SW', 'SE'} do BUILD_DF(SON(P,I));
  end
else output(NODETYPE(P));
end;
```

The original image can be reconstructed from the DF-expression by observing that the degree of each nonleaf (i.e., gray) node is always 4. Procedure DF_TO_QUAD-TREE, given below, reconstructs the quadtree corresponding to the DF-expression represented by the list L. It makes use of procedure DF_TO_QT to perform the task.

```
pointer node procedure DF_TO_QUADTREE(L);
/* Reconstruct the quadtree corresponding to the DF-expression given by list L. */
begin
  value pointer list L;
  return(if null(L) then NIL
         else DF_TO_QT(L,NIL,NIL));
end;


pointer node procedure DF_TO_QT(L,ROOT,T);
/* Use the DF-expression given by list L to reconstruct the quadtree corresponding to son
   T of node ROOT. */
begin
  reference pointer list L;
  value pointer node ROOT;
  value quadrant T;
  pointer node P;
  quadrant I;
  P ← CREATE_QNODE(ROOT,T,DATA(L));
  if DATA(L)='G' then
    begin
      for I in {'NW', 'NE', 'SW', 'SE'} do
        begin
          L ← NEXT(L);
          DF_TO_QT(L,P,I);
        end;
      L ← NEXT(L);
    end;
  return(P);
end;
```

Kawaguchi, Endo, and Matsunaga [Kawa83] show how a number of basic image-processing operations can be performed on an image represented by a DF-expression. In particular, they demonstrate centroid computation, rotation, scaling, shifting, and set operations. Representation of an image using a preorder traversal is also reported by Oliver and Wiseman [Oliv83a]. They show how to perform the operations mentioned above, as well as merging, masking, construction of a quadtree from a polygon, and area filling. Accessing adjacent blocks is also possible when traversal-based representations are used, although it is rather cumbersome and time-consuming. In general, traversal-based representations are best when the entire quadtree must be traversed. Their primary drawbacks arise when attempting a random access of a specified node in the quadtree.

The compression characteristics of DF-expressions in comparison to binary arrays, boundary codes, and run-length codes is discussed by Tamminen [Tamm84c]. Cohen, Landis, and Pavel [Cohe85b] present a detailed analysis of the compression that is attainable for worst-case images (i.e., checkerboards) using encodings that are variants of DF-expressions, such as those discussed in Exercises 2.39 and 2.40. They also compute the expected code length (i.e., in terms of bits) when using such encodings for random images that are constructed by varying the probability of a black pixel, say pB. Their results demonstrate that for each value of pB there is an optimal picture size. For quadtrees, when pB is greater than 0.90, the expected code length is less than 1, yielding superiority over the binary array. Similar results are obtained for the bintree, and when pB is greater than 0.99, the expected code length is lower than that attainable by use of the quadtree.

De Coulon and Johnsen [DeCo76] use a similar scheme to DF-expressions, which they term *auto-adaptive block coding* (also termed *GW coding* by Shaffer and Samet [Shaf87b]). The difference is that the alphabet consists solely of two symbols, '0' and '1.' The '0' corresponds to a block composed of white pixels only. Otherwise a '1' is used, and the block is subdivided into four subblocks. Therefore the '0' is analogous to 'W,' and the '1' is analogous to 'G' and 'B.'

In auto-adaptive coding, only the white pixels are aggregated into blocks; the black pixels are not. Hence the coding is asymmetric, whereas the DF-expression method is symmetric since it aggregates both black and white pixels. Note that in order to be able to decode an image encoded by the auto-adaptive block coding method, the resolution of the image (i.e., the pixel level) must be known a priori, whereas this is not necessary for DF-expressions.

Exercises

2.37. The DF-expression can also be adapted to the bintree. Modify procedures BUILD_DF and DF_TO_QUADTREE to handle the bintree.

2.38. Shaffer and Samet [Shaf87b] devise a quadtree-like encoding for a pyramid, which they term *GL coding*. It is similar to auto-adaptive coding in that it makes use of '0' and '1.' The difference is that in the GL coding a '0' corresponds to a leaf node while a '1' corresponds to a nonleaf (i.e., gray) node. Since it is necessary to determine the actual value of a leaf node (i.e., black or white), this value is stored in all of the descendants of the leaf node (down to the pixel level). How would you determine the color of a node when traversing a pyramid represented by GL coding? In particular, given an arbitrary node in the GL coding, what is its color?

2.39. Tamminen [Tamm84c] defines the following binary tree variant of the DF-expression that also exhibits compression. A nonleaf node is assigned the code '1.' A leaf node at a level other than 0 is given the code '0' followed by its actual color (e.g., 'B' or 'W' for a binary image). Observe that unlike the quadtree, no leaf node has the same color as its brother. In the case of a binary image, this property permits encoding two brother leaf nodes at level 0 with one bit because there are only two combinations (i.e., black and white, and white and black, represented by '1' and '0,' respectively). For example, Figure 1.7 in Chapter 1 has the following encoding:

$$1110\text{W}10\text{B}1110\text{B}0\text{W}11110\text{B}100\text{B}10\text{W}0\text{B}110\text{B}0\text{W}10\text{B}0\text{W}.$$

Notice that nodes 3 and 4 are represented by a '1' while nodes 8 and 9 are represented by a '0.' Of course, we should have also used '0' for 'W' and '1' for 'B.' Write a pair of procedures that convert a bintree to such a representation, and reconstruct the bintree from it.

2.40. How would you apply the compression techniques of Exercise 2.39 to the DF-expression of a quadtree? Again, you must consider what happens at level 0 of a quadtree in terms of the number of bits necessary to encode these blocks and also whether you can infer the values of certain blocks based on what has been seen already. Give a pair of procedures to encode and decode such a representation.

2.41. Assuming a probability of p for a black pixel and a $2^n \times 2^n$ image, compute the expected code length for a DF-expression encoding of a quadtree such that each gray node is represented by one bit and each leaf node is represented by two bits. You should obtain a recurrence relation in terms of p and n.

2.42. Modify the results of Exercise 2.41 to incorporate the encoding of Exercise 2.40.

2.43. Repeat Exercises 2.41 and 2.42 for a random bintree.

NEIGHBOR-FINDING TECHNIQUES 3

A natural by-product of the treelike nature of the quadtree and octree representations is that many basic operations can be implemented as tree traversals. The difference between the operations is in the nature of the computation performed at the node. Often these computations involve the examination of nodes whose corresponding blocks are spatially 'adjacent' to the block corresponding to the node being processed. These adjacent nodes are termed 'neighbors.' Note, however, that adjacency in space does not imply a simple relationship among the nodes in the tree. This relationship is the subject of this chapter. The algorithms given can be used for both quadtrees and octrees, with almost no modification.

This chapter is organized as follows. We first examine the concepts of neighbor and adjacency using the quadtree as an example. Next we see how neighbor finding is achieved in quadtrees implemented by a pointer-based representation (i.e., an explicit quadtree). Several techniques are given. In addition, the various methods are analyzed, and the results of empirical tests are discussed. This is followed by a similar presentation of neighbor finding in octrees implemented by a pointer-based representation. An analysis is also performed. Finally, a description is given of neighbor finding for quadtrees and octrees implemented using a number of different pointerless representations.

The scope of the presentation in the various sections is uneven. There is a strong emphasis on pointer-based methods because they simplify the presentation of a number of different concepts. Moreover, due to their simplicity, many of the subsequent chapters draw heavily on them. This is especially true in the case of the analysis of their computational requirements. The pointerless methods are analogous; the only difference is that they substitute bit manipulation operations for pointer following.

3.1 ADJACENCY AND NEIGHBORS IN QUADTREES

Each node of a quadtree corresponds to a block in the original image. The terms *block* and *node* are used interchangeably. The term used depends on whether the reference is to a decomposition into blocks (Figure 3.1c) or a tree (Figure 3.1d). Each block has four edges, also termed *sides* and *boundaries*, and four vertices, also termed *corners*. At times we speak of edges and vertices collectively as directions. Let the four edges of a node's block be called its N, E, S, and W edges. The four vertices of a node's block are labeled NW, NE, SW, and SE with the obvious meaning. Figure 3.2 illustrates these labelings.

Given two nodes P and Q whose corresponding blocks do not overlap, and a direction I, we define a predicate *adjacent* such that $adjacent(P,Q,I)$ is true if there exist two pixels p and q, contained in P and Q, respectively, such that either q is adjacent to an edge of p in the I direction or q is adjacent to vertex I of p. In such a case we say that nodes P and Q are neighbors (specifically, *edge-neighbors* and *vertex-neighbors*, respectively). For example, nodes 6 and 9 in Figure 3.1[1] are edge-

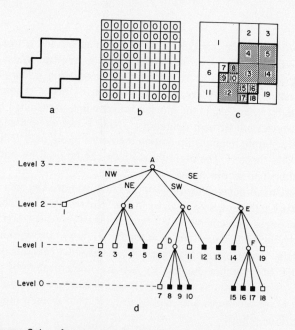

Figure 3.1   An example (a) region, (b) its binary array, (c) its maximal blocks (blocks in the region are shaded), and (d) the corresponding quadtree

---

[1] All examples in this section are taken from Figure 3.1.

neighbors since 6 is to the west of 9, while nodes 8 and 4 are vertex-neighbors since 4 is to the NE of 8. Two blocks may be adjacent both along an edge and along a vertex (e.g., 1 is both to the north and NE of 6; however, 9 is to the east of 6 but not to the SE of 6). Note that the adjacent relation also holds for nonleaf (i.e., gray) as well as leaf nodes.

Unfortunately the neighbor relation is not a function in a mathematical sense. The problem is that given a node, P, and a direction, I, there is often more than one node, say Q, that is adjacent in direction I. For example, nodes 8, 10, D, and C are all western neighbors of node 13. Similarly nodes 10, D, and C are all NW neighbors of node 15. This means that to specify a neighbor, more precise information is necessary about its nature (i.e., leaf or nonleaf), size, and location.

In particular, it is necessary to be able to distinguish between neighbors that are adjacent along an entire edge of a node (e.g., 1 is a northern neighbor of 6) and those that are adjacent along only a segment of a node's edge (e.g., 7 is one of the eastern neighbors of 6). An alternative characterization of the difference is that in the former case we are interested in determining a node Q such that its corresponding block is the smallest block (possibly gray) of size greater than or equal to the block corresponding to P; whereas in the latter case we specify the neighbor in greater detail by, in this case, indicating the vertex of P to which Q must be adjacent. The same distinction can also be made for vertex directions.

Below, functions are defined that express these relations more precisely. The construction of names uses the following correspondence: G for 'greater than or equal,' V for 'vertex,' E for 'edge,' and N for 'neighbor':

1. GEN$(P, I) = Q$: Node Q corresponds to the smallest block (it may be gray) that is adjacent to edge I of node P and is of size greater than or equal to the block corresponding to P.

2. VEN$(P, I, V) = Q$: Node Q corresponds to the smallest block that is adjacent to edge I of the corner formed by vertex V of node P.

3. GVN$(P, V) = Q$: Node Q corresponds to the smallest block (it may be gray) that is diagonally opposite to vertex V of node P and is of size greater than or equal to the block corresponding to P.

4. VVN$(P, V) = Q$: Node Q corresponds to the smallest block that is diagonally opposite to vertex V of node P.

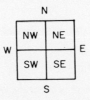

Figure 3.2   The relationship between a block's four quadrants and its boundaries

For example GEN(6,E) = D, GEN(6,S) = 11, VEN(6,E,SE) = 9, GVN(4,NE) = 3, GVN(4,SW) = D, and VVN(4,SW) = 8. From the above we see that GVN is the vertex counterpart of GEN and, likewise, VVN for VEN. The following observations are also in order. First, none of GEN, VEN, GVN, or VVN defines a 1–1 correspondence (i.e., a node may be a neighbor in a given direction of several nodes—for example, GEN(6,N) = 1, GEN(7,N) = 1, and GEN(8,N) = 1). Second, GEN, VEN, GVN and VVN are not necessarily symmetric. For example, GEN(4,W) = 1 but GEN(1,E) = B.

In this book the focus is primarily on GEN and GVN, although VEN and VVN are discussed in Section 3.2. When using the term *neighbor*—P is a neighbor of Q—it is meant that P is a node of size greater than or equal to Q.[2] For example, node 10 in Figure 3.1d (or equivalently block 10 in Figure 3.1c) has neighbors 8, 13, 15, 12, 9, and 7.

A node that is not adjacent to a border of the image has a minimum of five neighbors. This can be seen by observing that a node cannot be adjacent to two nodes of greater size on opposite edges (e.g., Figure 3.3a) or on diagonally opposite vertices (e.g., Figure 3.3b). For a more formal proof, see Exercise 3.1.

A node has a maximum of eight neighbors. In this case, all but one of the vertex-neighbors correspond to blocks of equal size (see Exercise 3.2). For example, for node 13 in Figure 3.1, the neighbors are nodes 4, 5, 14, 19, F, 12, D, and 1. It is interesting to observe that for any black node in the image, its neighbors cannot all be black since otherwise merging would have taken place and the node would not be in the image. The analogous property also holds for white nodes.

Exercises

3.1. Prove that a node that is not adjacent to the border of the image has a minimum of five neighbors.

3.2. Prove that when a node, say P, has eight neighbors, then at least seven of the neighbors must be of the same size as P.

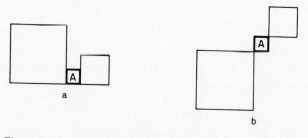

Figure 3.3   Impossible node configurations in a quadtree

---

[2] This convention also applies to the terms edge-neighbor and vertex-neighbor. Whenever the more general definition of a neighbor is used, it is so stated.

3.2 NEIGHBOR FINDING IN POINTER-BASED QUADTREE REPRESENTATIONS

There are a number of different ways of locating neighbors in a quadtree implemented using a pointer based representation. They differ in the type of information used to perform the process. The first method discussed is the most general. It is independent of both position (i.e., coordinates) and size of the node whose neighbor is being sought. It is based on locating a nearest common ancestor. It uses only the structure of the tree—that is, it uses no pointers other than the four links from a node to its four sons and one link to its father for a nonroot node. The second set of methods discussed either uses size and position information or adds explicit links from a node to its neighbors.

3.2.1 Nearest Common Ancestor Method

Understanding the presentation of the algorithms and analysis in this section, as well as in subsequent sections, requires some definitions and an explanation of notation. Assume each quadtree node is stored as a record of type *node* as described in Section 1.5.

The predicate ADJ and the functions REFLECT and COMMON_EDGE aid in the expression of operations involving a block's quadrants and its edges and vertices. Tables 3.1–3.3 contain the definitions of the ADJ, REFLECT, and COMMON_EDGE relationships, respectively. Ω denotes an undefined value.

ADJ(I,O) is true if, and only if, quadrant O is adjacent to the Ith edge or vertex of O's containing block—for example, ADJ('W','SW') is true, as is ADJ('SW','SW'). The

Table 3.1   ADJ(I,O)

I (direction)	O (quadrant)			
	NW	NE	SW	SE
N	T	T	F	F
E	F	T	F	T
S	F	F	T	T
W	T	F	T	F
NW	T	F	F	F
NE	F	T	F	F
SW	F	F	T	F
SE	F	F	F	T

Table 3.2   REFLECT(I,O)

I (direction)	O (quadrant)			
	NW	NE	SW	SE
N	SW	SE	NW	NE
E	NE	NW	SE	SW
S	SW	SE	NW	NE
W	NE	NW	SE	SW
NW	SE	SW	NE	NW
NE	SE	SW	NE	NW
SW	SE	SW	NE	NW
SE	SE	SW	NE	NW

relation can also be described as being true if O is of type I or, equivalently, that I's label is a subset of O's label.

REFLECT(I,O) yields the SONTYPE value of the block of equal size (not necessarily a brother) that shares the Ith edge or vertex of a block having SONTYPE value O—for example, REFLECT('N','SW') = 'NW,' REFLECT('SW','SW') = 'NE', and REFLECT('NW','SW') = 'NE'.

COMMON_EDGE(I,O) yields the type of the edge (i.e., label) of O's containing block that is common to quadrant O and its neighbor in the Ith direction (I is a vertex)—for example, COMMON_EDGE('SW','NW') = 'W'.

For a quadtree corresponding to a $2^n \times 2^n$ image array, we say that the root is at level n and that a node at level i is at a distance of $n-i$ from the root of the tree. In other words, for a node at level i, we must ascend $n-i$ FATHER links to reach the root of the tree. Note that the farthest node from the root of the tree is at level ≥ 0. A node at level 0 corresponds to a single pixel in the image, while a node is of size 2^s if it is found at level s in the tree.

Table 3.3   COMMON_EDGE(I,O)

I (vertex)	O (quadrant)			
	NW	NE	SW	SE
NW	Ω	N	W	Ω
NE	N	Ω	Ω	E
SW	W	Ω	Ω	S
SE	Ω	E	S	Ω

3.2.1.1 ALGORITHMS

Locating edge-neighbors is relatively straightforward [Same82a]. Assume, first, that we are trying to find the equal-sized neighbor of node P in direction I. The basic idea is to ascend the quadtree until a common ancestor is located and then descend back down the quadtree in search of the neighboring node. It is obvious that we can always ascend as far as the root of the quadtree and then start our descent. However, our goal is to find the nearest common ancestor (*nca*) because this minimizes the number of nodes that must be visited. These two steps are described below. They are implemented by procedure QT_EQ_EDGE_NEIGHBOR. This procedure ignores the situation in which the neighbor may not exist (e.g., when the node is on the border of the image).

1. Locate the nearest common ancestor. This is the first ancestor node reached by a son of type O such that ADJ(I,O) is false. In other words, I's label is not a subset of O's label.

2. Retrace the path that was taken to locate the nearest common ancestor by using the function REFLECT to make mirror image moves about the edge shared by the neighboring nodes.

```
recursive pointer node procedure QT_EQ_EDGE_NEIGHBOR(P,I);
/* Locate an equal-sized edge-neighbor of node P in direction I.  */
begin
  value pointer node P;
  value edge I;
  return(SON(if ADJ(I,SONTYPE(P)) then
              QT_EQ_EDGE_NEIGHBOR(FATHER(P),I)
            else FATHER(P),
            REFLECT(I,SONTYPE(P)))));
end;
```

As an example, suppose we wish to find the equal-sized western neighbor of node 13 in Figure 3.1. We first find the nearest common ancestor. This is the first ancestor node reached via its NE or SE son (i.e., the first ancestor node of which 13 is not a western descendant). Node A satisfies this condition, and it is reached by going through a NW link to reach node E and a SE link to reach node A. Now we are ready to descend the tree. We backtrack along the path of the ascent by following a SW link from A to reach node C and then a NE link to reach node D, the desired neighbor. Since we are dealing with the western edge, the mirror images of the SE and NW links are SW and NE, respectively.

Edge-neighbors need not correspond to blocks of the same size. If the neighbor is larger, then only part of the path from the nearest common ancestor is retraced. Otherwise the neighbor corresponds to a block of equal size and a pointer to a black, white, or gray node, as is appropriate, of equal size is returned. If there is no neighbor (i.e., the node whose neighbor is being sought is adjacent to the border of the image in the specified direction), then NIL is returned. This process is encoded below by procedure QT_GTEQ_EDGE_NEIGHBOR (i.e., GEN).

```
recursive pointer node procedure QT_GTEQ_EDGE_NEIGHBOR(P,I);
/* Locate an edge-neighbor of node P, of size greater than or equal to P, in direction I. If
    such a node does not exist, then return NIL. */
begin
  value pointer node P;
  value edge I;
  pointer node Q;
  if not(null(FATHER(P))) and ADJ(I,SONTYPE(P)) then
    /* Find a common ancestor */
    Q ← QT_GTEQ_EDGE_NEIGHBOR(FATHER(P),I)
  else Q ← FATHER(P);
  /* Follow the reflected path to locate the neighbor */
  return(if not(null(Q)) and GRAY(Q) then
          SON(Q,REFLECT(I,SONTYPE(P)))
        else Q);
end;
```

Locating a vertex-neighbor is considerably more complex [Same82a]. Assume that we are trying to find the equal-sized neighbor of node P in direction I. Our initial aim is to locate the nearest common ancestor of P and its neighbor. We need to ascend the tree to do so. We must also account for the situation in which the ancestors of P and its neighbor are adjacent along an edge. Let N denote the node that is being examined in the ascent. There are three cases described below, implemented by procedure QT_EQ_VERTEX_NEIGHBOR. This procedure ignores the situation in which the neighbor may not exist (e.g., when the node is on the border of the image):

1. As long as N is a son of type O such that ADJ(I,O) is true, we continue to ascend the tree. In other words, I's label is a subset of O's label.

2. If the father of N and the ancestor of the desired neighbor, say A, are adjacent along an edge, then calculate A by use of procedure QT_EQ_EDGE_-NEIGHBOR. This situation and the exact direction of A are determined by the function COMMON_EDGE applied to I and the son type of N. Once A has been obtained, the desired neighbor is located by applying the retracing step outlined in step 3.

3. Otherwise N is a son of a type, say O, such that neither of the labels of the edges comprising vertex I is a subset of O's label. Its father, say T, is the nearest common ancestor. The desired neighbor is obtained by simply retracing the path used to locate T except that we now make diagonally opposite moves about the vertex shared by the neighboring nodes. This process is facilitated by use of the function REFLECT.

recursive pointer node procedure QT_EQ_VERTEX_NEIGHBOR(P,I);
/* Locate an equal-sized vertex-neighbor of node P in direction I. */
begin
  value pointer node P;
  value vertex I;
  return(SON(**if** ADJ(I,SONTYPE(P)) **then**
          QT_EQ_VERTEX_NEIGHBOR(FATHER(P),I)
        else if COMMON_EDGE(I,SONTYPE(P)) $\neq \Omega$ **then**
          QT_EQ_EDGE_NEIGHBOR(FATHER(P),
           COMMON_EDGE(I,SONTYPE(P)))
        else FATHER(P),
        REFLECT(I,SONTYPE(P))));
end;

As an example, suppose we wish to locate the equal-sized SE neighbor of node 10 in Figure 3.1. We first ascend the quadtree until reaching a node that is not a son of type SE—that is, node D, a son of type NE. The father of D, C in this case, is adjacent along its eastern edge to an ancestor of the desired neighbor, E in this case, and the neighbor is calculated by using procedure QT_EQ_EDGE_NEIGHBOR. This requires reaching node A via a SW link and descending to E via a SE link. Now we descend one level by retracing the path taken from D to locate C with a diagonally opposite move—that is, we go from node E to F via a SW link. Finally, we retrace the remainder of the path by making diagonally opposite moves—that is, we descend a NW link from F to reach node 15, the desired neighbor.

Note that vertex-neighbors need not correspond to blocks of the same size. If the neighbor is larger, it is handled in the same manner as outlined for an edge-neighbor (i.e., only part of the path from the nearest common ancestor is retraced). This process is encoded below by procedure QT_GTEQ_VERTEX_NEIGHBOR (i.e., GVN).

recursive pointer node procedure QT_GTEQ_VERTEX_NEIGHBOR(P,I);
/* Locate a vertex-neighbor of node P, of size greater than or equal to P, in direction I. If
  such a node does not exist, return NIL. */
begin
  value pointer node P;
  value vertex I;
  pointer node Q;
   /* Find a common ancestor */
  Q ← **if null**(FATHER(P)) **then** NIL
     else if ADJ(I,SONTYPE(P)) **then**
      QT_GTEQ_VERTEX_NEIGHBOR(FATHER(P),I)
     else if COMMON_EDGE(I,SONTYPE(P)) $\neq \Omega$ **then**
      QT_GTEQ_EDGE_NEIGHBOR(FATHER(P),
               COMMON_EDGE(I,SONTYPE(P)))
     else FATHER(P);
  /* Follow opposite path to locate the neighbor */

return(if not(null(Q)) **and** GRAY(Q) **then**
        SON(Q,REFLECT(I,SONTYPE(P)))
     else Q);
end;

If neighbors are of different sizes, we may wish to know the size of the adjacent neighbor. In such a case, we want our neighbor-finding algorithms to return both a pointer to the neighboring node and a value from which the node's size can be easily computed. This is relatively straightforward when we know the level (i.e., height) in the quadtree of the node whose neighbor is being sought. In fact, such an algorithm need only increment the level counter by one for each link that is ascended while locating the common ancestor and then decrement the level counter by one for each link that is descended while locating the appropriate neighbor.

The algorithms for locating edge- and vertex-neighbors of equal or greater size, with their corresponding level positions, are given below using procedures QT_GTEQ_-EDGE_NEIGHBOR2 and QT_GTEQ_VERTEX_NEIGHBOR2, respectively. Note the use of reference parameters to transmit and return results. An alternative is to define a record of type *block* having two fields of type *node* and *integer*, with values that are a pointer to the neighboring node and its level, respectively.

recursive procedure QT_GTEQ_EDGE_NEIGHBOR2(P,I,Q,L);
/* Return in Q the edge-neighbor of node P, of size greater than or equal to P, in direction I. L denotes the level of the tree at which node P is initially found and the level of the tree at which node Q is ultimately found. If such a node does not exist, then return NIL. */
begin
 value pointer node P;
 value edge I;
 reference pointer node Q;
 reference integer L;
 L ← L + 1;
 if not(null(FATHER(P))) **and** ADJ(I,SONTYPE(P)) **then**
  /* Find a common ancestor */
  QT_GTEQ_EDGE_NEIGHBOR2(FATHER(P),I,Q,L)
 else Q ← FATHER(P);
 /* Follow the reflected path to locate the neighbor */
 if not(null(Q)) **and** GRAY(Q) **then**
  begin
   Q ← SON(Q,REFLECT(I,SONTYPE(P)));
   L ← L - 1;
  end;
end;

recursive procedure QT_GTEQ_VERTEX_NEIGHBOR2(P,I,Q,L);
/* Return in Q the vertex-neighbor of node P, of size greater than or equal to P, in direction I. L denotes the level of the tree at which node P is initially found and the level of

the tree at which node Q is ultimately found. If such a node does not exist, then return
NIL. */
begin
  value pointer node P;
  value vertex I;
  reference pointer node Q;
  reference integer L;
  $L \leftarrow L + 1$;
  /* Find a common ancestor */
  if null(FATHER(P)) **then** Q ← NIL
  else if ADJ(I,SONTYPE(P)) **then**
    QT_GTEQ_VERTEX_NEIGHBOR2(FATHER(P),I,Q,L)
  else if COMMON_EDGE(I,SONTYPE(P)) ≠ Ω **then**
    QT_GTEQ_EDGE_NEIGHBOR2(FATHER(P),
                       COMMON_EDGE(I,SONTYPE(P)),Q,L)
  else Q ← FATHER(P);
  /* Follow the opposite path to locate the neighbor */
  if not(null(Q)) **and** GRAY(Q) **then**
    begin
      Q ← SON(Q,REFLECT(I,SONTYPE(P)));
      $L \leftarrow L - 1$;
    end;
end;

At times, we may wish to locate an edge-neighbor regardless of its size (i.e.,
VEN). In such a case, for a given node, say *P*, we specify an edge and a vertex such
that the neighbor is adjacent to the edge of the corner formed by the vertex of *P* (e.g.,
in Figure 3.1, node 10 is adjacent to the northern edge of the corner formed by the NE
vertex of node 12). The algorithm for computing such a neighbor is given below by
procedure QT_VERTEX_EDGE_NEIGHBOR, which makes use of QT_GTEQ_EDGE_NEIGH-
BOR.

  pointer node procedure QT_VERTEX_EDGE_NEIGHBOR(P,I,V);
  /* Locate an edge-neighbor of node P in direction I which is adjacent to edge I of the
    corner formed by vertex V of node P. If such a node does not exist, then return NIL. */
  begin
    value pointer node P;
    value edge I;
    value vertex V;
    P ← QT_GTEQ_EDGE_NEIGHBOR(P,I);
    while GRAY(P) **do** P ← SON(P,REFLECT(I,V));
    /* Descend to the desired corner */
    return(P);
  end;

Similarly, in the case of a vertex-neighbor, we may wish to locate the neighbor
in the given direction regardless of its size (i.e., VVN). For example, node 9 is a NE

neighbor of node 11 in Figure 3.1 that is smaller in size. The algorithm for locating an arbitrary-sized neighbor in the direction of a vertex is given below by procedure QT_VERTEX_VERTEX_NEIGHBOR, which makes use of QT_GTEQ_VERTEX_NEIGHBOR.

```
pointer node procedure QT_VERTEX_VERTEX_NEIGHBOR(P,I);
/* Locate a vertex-neighbor of node P in direction I that touches corner I of node P. If
   such a node does not exist, then return NIL. */
begin
  value pointer node P;
  value vertex I;
  pointer node Q;
  Q ← QT_GTEQ_VERTEX_NEIGHBOR(P,I);
  while GRAY(Q) do Q ← SON(Q,REFLECT(I,I));
    /* Descend to the desired corner */
  return(Q);
end;
```

Procedures similar to QT_VERTEX_EDGE_NEIGHBOR and QT_VERTEX_VERTEX_NEIGHBOR can be constructed that also return the level at which the desired neighboring node is found. This will not be done here.

The procedures outlined above always return NIL when a neighbor in a specified direction does not exist. This situation arises whenever the node whose neighbor is sought is adjacent to the border of the image along the specified direction. At times the NIL pointer is not convenient. Instead we could assume that the image is surrounded by white blocks as in Figure 3.4a or by black blocks as in Figure 3.4b.

The choice of white or black for the surrounding blocks depends on the particular application. For example, white is used in the case of the quadtree-to-chain code construction algorithm (see Section 4.3.2) and the computation of the perimeter of an image represented by a quadtree (see Section 5.2); while black is more useful in the case of the computation of distance (see Section 9.2) and the definition of a quadtree medial axis transform (see Section 9.3.1).

At times it is useful to determine if certain edges of the blocks corresponding to two neighboring nodes extend past each other or are aligned. For example, in Figure

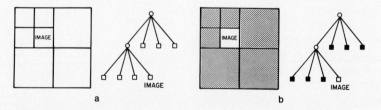

Figure 3.4   Technique to avoid lacking a neighbor in a given direction: (a) image surrounded by white blocks, (b) image surrounded by black blocks

3.1, node 1 extends past node 7 with respect to their eastern boundaries, while the eastern boundaries of nodes 8 and 1 are aligned. We assume that the level of the tree at which each of the two nodes, say P and Q at levels LP and LQ, respectively, reside is known.

It should be clear that determining whether P and Q are aligned requires visiting at most $|LP - LQ|$ nodes. This can be seen by observing that the smaller of the two nodes cannot extend farther than the other because this would imply that the edges of the two nodes overlap partially, which is impossible. At best the smaller node can be aligned with the other node. This occurs if, and only if, the smaller node is adjacent to the extreme side in the designated direction of the nearest common ancestor of the two nodes. The algorithm for computing the aligned relationship is given below by procedure ALIGNED.

Boolean procedure ALIGNED(P,LP,Q,LQ,I);
/* Given two nodes P and Q, at levels LP and LQ, respectively, which are adjacent along the edge counterclockwise (or clockwise) from edge I of node P, determine whether either of P or Q extends farther in the I direction than the other (return FALSE), or their two edges in the I direction are aligned (return TRUE). */
begin
  value pointer node P,Q;
  value integer LP,LQ;
  value edge I;
  pointer node R;
  integer J;
  if LP = LQ **then return**(TRUE)
  else if LP > LQ **then** R ← Q
  else R ← P;
  /* The smaller of the two nodes cannot extend farther than the larger one because this would imply that edges of P and Q overlap partially, which is impossible. At best the smaller node can be aligned with the larger node. This occurs if, and only if, the smaller node is adjacent to the I edge of the nearest common ancestor of nodes P and Q. */
  for J←1 **step** 1 **until** ABS(LP − LQ) **do**
    begin
    if not(ADJ(I,SONTYPE(R))) **then return**(FALSE)
    else R ← FATHER(R);
    end;
  return(TRUE);
end;

Exercises

3.3. It has been suggested that neighbors that are adjacent in the direction of a vertex can be obtained by combining the neighbor-finding operations in the directions of the two edges that make up the vertex. For example, to find a neighbor in the NE direction, we look at the neighbors in the N and E directions. This also involves examining their nearest common ancestor. Show how you would implement QT_EQ_VERTEX_NEIGHBOR and QT_GTEQ_-VERTEX_NEIGHBOR using such a method. If it is not feasible, explain why not.

3.4. Discuss neighbor finding for a two-dimensional image represented as a bintree. Give algorithms for QT_EQ_EDGE_NEIGHBOR and QT_EQ_VERTEX_NEIGHBOR. In addition, define the bintree analogs of QT_GTEQ_EDGE_NEIGHBOR and QT_GTEQ_VERTEX_NEIGHBOR, and give algorithms for their computation in a pointer-based environment. All of your algorithms should proceed by locating a nearest common ancestor.

3.5. Given a line segment whose endpoints are in an image represented by a quadtree, write an algorithm to output all the blocks intersected by the line. Such an algorithm is useful in implementing ray tracing (see Section 7.2).

3.2.1.2 ANALYSIS

The algorithms presented in Section 3.2.1.1 are implementations of the functions GEN, VEN, GVN, and VVN. The analysis of each of these functions differs depending on its implementation and on the assumptions about the underlying random image model. The most natural way to analyze the execution time of these functions is in terms of the number of nodes that must be visited in locating the desired neighbor [Same82a, Same85e]. The analysis of each function is decomposed into two stages: the process of locating the nearest common ancestor and locating the desired neighbor.

The worst-case analysis is trivial. We examine an average case analysis that makes use of a random image model in which each leaf node is assumed to be equally likely to appear at any position and level in the quadtree. Using such a model with a quadtree means that there are 1, 4, 16, 64, $\cdots$, 4^i leaf nodes at levels n, $n-1$, $n-2$, $n-3$, $\cdots$, $n-i$, respectively, or equivalently that $\frac{3}{4} \cdot (\frac{1}{4})^i$ of the nodes are at level i. Of course, this is not a realizable situation, but in practice it does model the image well.

Observe that our notion of a random image differs from the conventional one, which implies that every pixel has an equal probability of being black or white. Such an assumption leads to a very low probability of aggregation—that is, nodes corresponding to blocks of size greater than 1 pixel (see Exercise 1.9). Clearly for such an image the quadtree is the wrong representation (e.g., a checkerboard). The problem with the conventional random image model is that it assumes independence, clearly not the case (i.e., a pixel's value is typically related to that of its neighbors). For a more vivid illustration of the discrepancy between our model and some actual images, consider Table 3.4, which tabulates the distribution of blocks of varying size for four images (described in greater detail in Section 3.2.1.3).

First, we analyze stage 1, locating the nearest common ancestor, as it is common to GEN, GVN, VEN, and VVN. It makes heavy use of the following identities, which can be derived using techniques discussed by Knuth [Knut73a]:

$$\sum_{j=1}^{n} \frac{j}{2^j} = 2 - \frac{n+2}{2^n} \tag{3.1}$$

$$\sum_{j=0}^{n} \frac{1}{2^j} = 2 \cdot \left[1 - \frac{1}{2^{n+1}} \right] \tag{3.2}$$

Table 3.4   Node size (percent) distribution

Leaf Size	Model %	Floodplain	Topography	Landuse	Pebble
1×1	75.00	2,468 (47.4)	14,832 (59.3)	16,112 (56.4)	27,316 (60.8)
2×2	18.75	1,559 (29.9)	7,336 (29.3)	8,484 (29.7)	11,995 (26.7)
4×4	4.69	660 (12.7)	2,175 (8.70)	2,984 (10.5)	4,418 (9.83)
8×8	1.17	263 (5.05)	470 (1.88)	784 (2.62)	1,095 (3.44)
16×16	.293	175 (3.36)	138 (.552)	175 (.613)	108 (.240)
32×32	.073	57 (1.09)	51 (.204)	38 (.133)	18 (.040)
64×64	.018	22 (.423)	8 (.032)	8 (.028)	0 (0.00)
128×128	.005	2 (.038)	2 (.008)	0 (0.00)	0 (0.00)
Total		5,206	25,012	28,549	44,950

$$\sum_{j=0}^{n} \frac{1}{2^{2j}} = \frac{4}{3} \cdot \left[1 - \frac{1}{2^{2n+2}} \right]$$

(3.3)

$$\sum_{j=1}^{n} \frac{j^2}{2^j} = 6 - \frac{n^2 + 4n + 6}{2^n}$$

(3.4)

$$\sum_{j=1}^{n} \frac{j^2}{2^{2j}} = \frac{1}{27} \cdot \left[20 - \frac{9n^2 + 24n + 20}{2^{2n}} \right]$$

(3.5)

Theorem 3.1   The average number of nodes that must be visited in locating the nearest common ancestor when seeking an edge-neighbor is bounded from above by 2.

Proof   Given a node P at level i and direction I (I is an edge), there are $2^{n-i} \cdot (2^{n-i} - 1)$ possible positions where P might be located. The -1 results from the fact that one of the rows (or columns) will not have a neighbor in direction I that is in the image. Of these positions, $2^{n-i} \cdot 2^0$ have their nearest common ancestor at level n, $2^{n-i} \cdot 2^1$ at level $n-1$, $\cdots$, and $2^{n-i} \cdot 2^{n-i-1}$ at level $i + 1$. The same analysis is repeated for each level and all the possible cases are treated as equally likely.

Starting at a node at level i, to reach a nearest common ancestor at level j, $j-i$ nodes must be visited. Therefore, the average is

$$\frac{\displaystyle\sum_{i=0}^{n-1}\sum_{j=i+1}^{n} 2^{n-i} \cdot 2^{n-j} \cdot (j-i)}{\displaystyle\sum_{i=0}^{n-1} 2^{n-i} \cdot (2^{n-i} - 1)}.$$

This can be simplified using Equations 3.1–3.5, and rearranging indexes of summation, to yield

$$2 - \frac{6 \cdot (n-1) \cdot 2^n + 6}{2^{2n+2} - 6 \cdot 2^n + 2}$$

$$\leq 2 \text{ for } n \geq 1. \qquad \square$$

Theorem 3.2   The average number of nodes that must be visited in locating the nearest common ancestor when seeking a vertex-neighbor is bounded from above by 8/3.

Proof   Given a node P at level i and direction I (I is a vertex) there are $(2^{n-i} - 1)^2$ possible positions where P might be located. The -1 results from the fact that one of the rows and one of the columns will not have a neighbor in direction I that is in the image. In [Same82a] it is shown that of these positions $4^0 \cdot (2 \cdot (2^{n-i} - 1) - 1)$ have neighbors in direction I such that the nearest common ancestor is at level n, $4^1 \cdot (2 \cdot (2^{n-i-1} - 1) - 1)$ at level $n-1$, $\cdots$, and $4^{n-i-1} \cdot (2 \cdot (2^{n-i-(n-i-1)} - 1) - 1)$ at level $i + 1$.

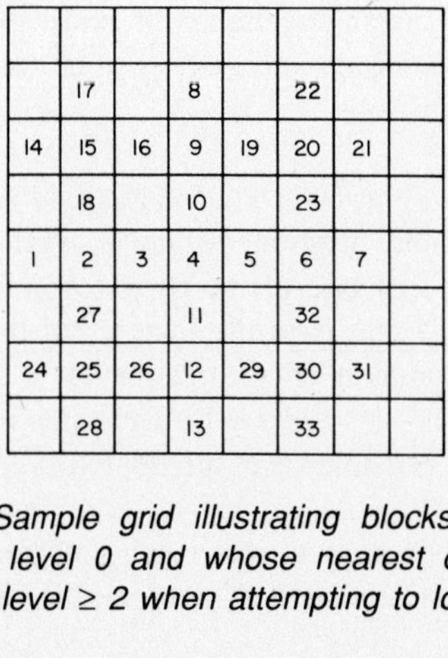

	17		8		22		
14	15	16	9	19	20	21	
	18		10		23		
1	2	3	4	5	6	7	
	27		11		32		
24	25	26	12	29	30	31	
	28		13		33		

Figure 3.5   Sample grid illustrating blocks whose nodes are at level 0 and whose nearest common ancestor is at level ≥ 2 when attempting to locate an NE neighbor

To see this, consider Figure 3.5, where a grid is shown for $n = 3$. If all black and white nodes are at level 0 (i.e., a complete quadtree), then for a neighbor pair in the NE direction we see that nodes along the fifth row (from the top) and fourth column (from the left) have their nearest common ancestor at level 3 (i.e., 13 nodes labeled 1–13).

Continuing the process for the NW, NE, SW, and SE quadrants of Figure 3.5, we find that all neighbor pairs contained exclusively within these quadrants have their nearest common ancestor at level ≤ 2. In particular, for the NW quadrant, nodes along the third row and second column have their nearest common ancestor at level 2 (i.e., 5 nodes labeled 14–18). The NW, SW, and SE quadrants are analyzed in a similar manner. Next, this process is applied to the four subquadrants of each quadrant to obtain the neighbor pairs whose nearest common ancestor is at level 1.

Note that we had to consider every row in the image when analyzing vertex-neighbor pairs, whereas we needed to consider only one row or one column when analyzing edge-neighbor pairs. This is necessary because for vertex-neighbors, each row and column in the image has a different number of neighbor pairs with a common ancestor at a given level. On the other hand, when considering edge-neighbors, each element in a column (row) has the same number of neighbor pairs with a common ancestor at a given level.

Starting at a node at level i, to reach a nearest common ancestor at level j, $j-i$ nodes must be visited. Therefore, the average is

$$\frac{\displaystyle\sum_{i=0}^{n-1} \sum_{j=i+1}^{n} 4^{n-j} \cdot (2 \cdot (2^{n-i-(n-j)} - 1) - 1) \cdot (j-i)}{\displaystyle\sum_{i=0}^{n-1} (2^{n-i} - 1)^2}.$$

This can be simplified using Equations 3.1–3.5, and rearranging indexes of summation, to yield

$$\frac{8}{3} - \frac{(6n-10) \cdot 2^{n+2} - 3n^2 + 5n + 40}{2^{2n+3} - 3 \cdot 2^{n+3} + 6n + 16}$$

$$\leq 8/3 \text{ for } n \geq 1. \qquad \square$$

The results of Theorems 3.1 and 3.2 can be used to analyze the cost of procedures QT_EQ_EDGE_NEIGHBOR and QT_EQ_VERTEX_NEIGHBOR since the neighbor is found at the same level as the starting node. In the case of a checkerboard image, all neighbors are located by use of these procedures. In particular, the average number of nodes visited by the former is 4, while it is 16/3 for the latter. Restricting the above analysis for QT_EQ_EDGE_NEIGHBOR to one row is equivalent to analyzing the average cost of accessing horizontally adjacent elements in a two-dimensional array embedded in a binary tree [DeMi78] (although there it is analyzed by techniques that use recurrence relations).

To analyze the second stage, we must also model the distribution of neighbor pairs (i.e., the possible configurations of adjacent nodes of varying sizes). There are a number of models to choose from. We examine two models and show in detail the results of using one of them that correlates to a reasonable extent with some sample images (see Section 3.2.1.3).

For example, suppose that we wish to determine GEN(17,w) for Figure 3.1 (i.e., 12). In theory, there are three possible neighbors: one each of size 1×1, 2×2, and 4×4 at node distances of 6, 5, and 4, respectively. To compute the average value of GEN, the model employed in [Same82a], termed *model A*, treats each of these cases individually and as equally probable—that is, a node in the same position as 17 makes three contributions to the average value. In contrast, the model employed in [Same85e], termed *model B*, includes only the average contribution of these three cases. In the rest of this section we use model B to model the distribution of neighbor pairs.

Theorems 3.3 and 3.4 analyze the average cost of finding edge-neighbors and vertex-neighbors of greater or equal size (i.e., GEN and GVN, respectively). The resulting cost reflects both the first and second stages. To get the cost of the second stage, we subtract the cost obtained in Theorems 3.1 and 3.2 from the results yielded by Theorems 3.3 and 3.4.

Theorem 3.3   The average number of nodes visited by GEN (i.e., QT_GTEQ_EDGE_NEIGHBOR) is bounded from above by 7/2.

Proof   Using similar reasoning as in Theorem 3.1, given a node P at level i, a direction I, and having a nearest common ancestor at level j, there are $j-i$ possible edge-neighbors of size greater than or equal to that of P. Therefore the average number of nodes that will be visited in the process of locating such a neighbor is $j-i + \sum_{k=i}^{j-1}(j-k)/(j-i)$. This is obtained by observing that the nearest common ancestor is at a distance of $j-i$ from P. In addition, each of the possible neighbors is at level k where k ranges between i and $j-1$ and at a distance of $j-k$ from the nearest common ancestor. Therefore the average number of nodes visited by GEN is

$$\frac{\displaystyle\sum_{i=0}^{n-1} \sum_{j=i+1}^{n} 2^{n-i} \cdot 2^{n-j} \cdot \left(j-i + \frac{1}{j-i} \cdot \sum_{k=i}^{j-1}(j-k)\right)}{\displaystyle\sum_{i=0}^{n-1} 2^{n-i} \cdot (2^{n-i} - 1)}.$$

$$(3.6)$$

This can be simplified using Equations 3.1–3.5 and rearranging indexes of summation, to yield

$$7/2 - \frac{9 \cdot (n-1) \cdot 2^n + 9}{2^{2n+2} - 6 \cdot 2^n + 2}$$

$$\leq 7/2 \text{ for } n \geq 1. \qquad \square$$

Theorem 3.4   The average number of nodes visited by GVN (i.e., QT_-GTEQ_VERTEX_NEIGHBOR) is bounded from above by 9/2.

Proof   Using similar reasoning as in Theorems 3.2 and 3.3, given a node P at level i, a direction I, and having a nearest common ancestor at level j, there are $j-i$ possible vertex-neighbors of size greater than or equal to that of P. These neighbors are at level k where k ranges between i and $j-1$ and at a distance of $j-k$ from the nearest common ancestor. Therefore the average number of nodes visited by GVN is

$$\frac{\sum_{i=0}^{n-1} \sum_{j=i+1}^{n} 4^{n-j} \cdot (2 \cdot (2^{n-i-(n-j)} - 1) - 1) \cdot (j-i + \frac{1}{j-i} \cdot \sum_{k=i}^{j-1}(j-k))}{\sum_{i=0}^{n-1}(2^{n-i} - 1)^2}. \qquad (3.7)$$

This can be simplified using Equations 3.1–3.5, and rearranging indexes of summation, to yield

$$9/2 - \frac{72n \cdot 2^n - 120 \cdot 2^n - 9n^2 + 15n + 120}{16 \cdot 2^{2n} - 48 \cdot 2^n + 12n + 32}$$

$$\leq 9/2 \text{ for } n \geq 1. \qquad \square$$

Theorems 3.5 and 3.6 analyze the cost of finding the smallest neighbor that is adjacent to an edge forming a particular vertex (i.e., VEN), as well as in the direction of a vertex (i.e., VVN). Again, the resulting cost reflects both the first and second stages. To get the cost of the second stage, we subtract the cost obtained in Theorems 3.1 and 3.2 from the results yielded by Theorems 3.5 and 3.6.

Theorem 3.5 The average number of nodes visited by VEN (i.e., QT_-VERTEX_EDGE_NEIGHBOR) is bounded from above by 11/3.

Proof Using similar reasoning as in Theorem 3.3, given a node P at level i, edge I and vertex V, such that the nearest common ancestor is at level j, we see that the only difference from the analysis of GEN is that now the edge-neighbor can be at level k, where k ranges between 0 and $j-1$. Changing the index of summation k in relation 3.6 to run between 0 and $j-1$ and the denominator of the sum's multiplier from $j-i$ to j, we have that the number of nodes visited by VEN is

$$\frac{11}{3} - \frac{9n \cdot 2^n - 7 \cdot 2^n - n + 7}{2^{2n+2} - 6 \cdot 2^n + 2}$$

$$\leq 11/3 \text{ for } n \geq 1. \qquad \square$$

Theorem 3.6 The average number of nodes visited by VVN (i.e., QT_-VERTEX_VERTEX_NEIGHBOR) is bounded from above by 14/3.

Proof Using similar reasoning as in Theorems 3.4 and 3.5, given a node P at level i and vertex I such that the nearest common ancestor is at level j, we see that the only difference from the analysis of GVN is that now the vertex-neighbor can be at level k, where k ranges between 0 and $j-1$. Changing the index of summation k in relation 3.7 to run between 0 and $j-1$ and the denominator of the sum's multiplier from $j-i$ to j, we have that the number of nodes visited by VVN is

$$\frac{14}{3} - \frac{54n \cdot 2^n - 78 \cdot 2^n - 9n^2 + 3n + 78}{12 \cdot 2^{2n} - 36 \cdot 2^n + 9n + 24}$$

$$\leq 14/3 \text{ for } n \geq 1. \qquad \square$$

As mentioned in Section 3.2.1.1 the ALIGNED relationship is closely related to the neighbor-finding process, and it can be analyzed in a similar manner. Let P and Q, at levels LP and LQ, respectively, be the nodes whose alignment is being checked and assume that P is smaller than Q. Starting at P we check if it and its ancestors are in alignment with Q. The process stops when nonalignment is detected or when reaching an ancestor at level LQ. The maximum amount of work expended in this process occurs when LQ is one less than the level of the nearest common ancestor of P and Q. Thus the analysis of ALIGNED, as shown by the following theorem, is analogous to that used for the second stage of GEN (i.e., QT_GTEQ_EDGE_NEIGHBOR), except that we are ascending the quadtree instead of descending it.

Theorem 3.7   The average number of nodes visited by ALIGNED is bounded from above by 1/2.

Proof   We use similar reasoning as in Theorem 3.3. In particular, given node P at level i, a direction I, and P's nearest common ancestor in the direction of the edge counterclockwise from I at level j, then there are $j-i$ possible edge-neighbors in the counterclockwise direction of size greater than or equal to that of P. One of these neighbors is being examined by the ALIGNED predicate. Assuming that each of these neighbors is equally likely, the average of the maximum number of nodes that will be visited in the process of executing ALIGNED is $\sum_{k=i}^{j-1} (k-i)/(j-i)$. This is obtained by observing that for a neighbor at level k, where k ranges between i and $j-1$, we must traverse at most $k-i$ FATHER links to get to P's ancestor at level k while checking alignment. Therefore the average number of nodes visited by ALIGNED is

$$\frac{\sum_{i=0}^{n-1} \sum_{j=i+1}^{n} 2^{n-i} \cdot 2^{n-j} \cdot \frac{1}{j-i} \cdot \sum_{k=i}^{j-1}(k-i)}{\sum_{i=0}^{n-1} 2^{n-i} \cdot (2^{n-i} - 1)}.$$

This can be simplified to yield a result equal to one less than the difference between Theorems 3.1 and 3.3

$$1/2 - \frac{3 \cdot (n-1) \cdot 2^n + 3}{2^{2n+2} - 6 \cdot 2^n + 2}$$

$$\leq 1/2 \text{ for } n \geq 1. \qquad \square$$

Puech and Yahia [Puec85] perform a mathematical analysis of neighbor finding under somewhat different assumptions about the underlying model. Using a branching process model, they assume that there exists a constant β such that the probability of a node's being black is β, the probability of a node's being white is β, and the probability of a node's being gray is $(1 - 2 \cdot \beta)$. Moreover they assume that the distribution in the subtree rooted at a gray node obeys the same rules. At the bottom level of the tree, black and white nodes are assumed to be equally likely—that is, $\beta = 0.5$.

A drawback of this model is that it makes no provision for merging. When either all four sons of a gray node are black or all are white, the node is left as gray instead of changing it to black or white, respectively. This model is used to derive an expected value for the number of nodes that are encountered in locating the nearest common ancestor (i.e., stage 1). Unfortunately no experimental evidence is provided to support the model, nor is there any indication of the reasonable values of β. Thus it is difficult to compare this model with the model described in this section.

Exercises

3.6. The array is a data structure common to most modern programming languages. It is usually implemented as a block of contiguous memory locations with an array descriptor (also known as a *dope vector*) [Knut73a] to enable the determination of the physical address corresponding to a logical element in the array. The problem with using such a scheme is that elements in the array that are logically adjacent are not necessarily physically adjacent. Thus if memory cannot be accessed at random, there may be a high price to be paid for accessing logically adjacent elements. For example, element A[3,3] is logically adjacent to elements A[3,2], A[2,2], A[2,3], A[2,4], A[3,4], A[4,4], A[4,3], and A[4,2]; however, this is not true in a physical sense. To have a bound on the distance between adjacent array elements, the array can be implemented as a binary tree. For an $M \times M$ array the distance between horizontally or vertically adjacent elements is bounded from above by $\lceil \log_2 M \rceil$ and the average distance between two such elements is 4. Show how to derive the average distance using recurrence relations.

3.7. Let $BOUND_i$ denote the bound derived in Theorem 3.i (i.e., 3.1–3.6). Webber [Webb85] observes the following relationships between the results of the various theorems: $BOUND_5 - BOUND_3 = BOUND_6 - BOUND_4$ and $BOUND_4 - BOUND_3 = BOUND_6 - BOUND_5 = 3/2 \cdot (BOUND_2 - BOUND_1)$. Is there any significance to these relationships?

3.8. Can you come up with a better theoretical explanation for the image model used in the analysis? In particular, it should yield a distribution of blocks of varying sizes more like the results tabulated in Table 3.4.

3.2.1.3 EMPIRICAL RESULTS

To test the validity of the image model used in the analysis of Section 3.2.1.2, experiments were conducted with 512×512 images corresponding to a cartographic database, as well as a standard texture. Three of them correspond to a landuse map, a topography map, and a floodplain map of a region in Northern California [Same87a]; the remaining image corresponds to a pebble texture (D23) [Brod66]. All of the images were represented using quadtrees. Each of the neighbor-finding functions described above was applied in all four directions at each leaf node in the images. In the tables that follow, the maps are arranged in ascending order of complexity, where complexity is the number of nodes in the image. All references to model values are for $n = 9$. Table 3.5 summarizes the observed values for the individual images, the average value over all four images, and the predicted value.

We can get a more accurate evaluation of the predicted value by recalling that the neighbor-finding process can be decomposed into two stages. The first stage locates the nearest common ancestor. There are two cases depending on whether we

Table 3.5   Average cost of neighbor-finding operations

Operation	Observed					Predicted
	Floodplain	Topography	Landuse	Pebble	Average	
GEN	3.50	3.60	3.59	3.56	3.57	3.46
VEN	3.66	3.75	3.73	3.71	3.72	3.63
GVN	4.47	4.68	4.63	4.60	4.60	4.44
VVN	4.64	4.83	4.79	4.75	4.76	4.60

are seeking a neighbor in the direction of an edge or a vertex. Table 3.6 shows the empirical results. It is interesting to note how closely the predicted values correlate with the observed values. Table 3.7 gives the cost of the second stage of the neighbor-finding process.

To improve our understanding of the difference between the predicted and observed values of the first and second stages of the neighbor-finding process, Tables 3.8 and 3.9 tabulate the average cost of VEN in all four directions as a function of the distance to and from, respectively, the nearest common ancestor. VEN is used because it provides the greatest range of values for testing the neighbor pair distribution model used in the second stage. Remember that the model used in Section 3.2.1.2 assumes that $\frac{3}{4} \cdot (\frac{1}{4})^i$ of the nodes are at level i.

For each node at level i, its nearest common ancestor is at level j ($n \geq j > i$) with probability $(\frac{1}{2})^{j-i}$. This is relevant to the analysis of the first stage. The average number of nodes visited in locating the neighbor when starting at the nearest common ancestor is $(j + 1)/2$. This is relevant to the analysis of the second stage. The final rows of Tables 3.8 and 3.9 account for the nodes that are adjacent to the border of the image, and thus have no neighbor in the tree (they are labeled as 'on border').

Table 3.8 shows the observed distribution of the nodes that are at a distance i from their nearest common ancestor for the first stage. The observed values are in close agreement with the predicted values. In fact, for a distance of 1, the predicted and observed percentages are exactly the same. This is not surprising because we tabulate VEN in all four directions, and each node has two brothers at a distance of 1.

Table 3.6   Average cost of stage 1 of neighbor finding

Type of Neighbor	Observed					Predicted Upper Bound
	Floodplain	Topography	Landuse	Pebble	Average	
Edge	2.01	2.00	2.00	1.99	2.00	1.98
Vertex	2.69	2.67	2.66	2.65	2.67	2.62

Table 3.7   Average cost of stage 2 of neighbor finding

Operation	Observed					Predicted
	Floodplain	Topography	Landuse	Pebble	Average	
GEN	1.49	1.60	1.59	1.57	1.57	1.48
VEN	1.64	1.74	1.73	1.72	1.71	1.65
GVN	1.79	2.00	1.97	1.95	1.94	1.82
VVN	1.96	2.15	2.13	2.10	2.09	1.98

For all of the images, the average distance to the nearest common ancestor is within 2% of the predicted value.

Table 3.9 shows the average number of nodes that must be descended from a nearest common ancestor at level i in the second stage before encountering the desired neighbor for VEN. It also shows the distribution of the nodes having a nearest common ancestor at level i. Again, the observed values are in close agreement with the predicted values. The observed values are in general slightly higher than the predicted values because there is a greater percentage of nodes with a distance from the nearest common ancestor that exceeds the predicted distance. Thus their contribution is weighted more heavily, thereby increasing the average cost.

Notice that the observed cost of the floodplain image is lower than the predicted cost. The lower cost is not surprising because the floodplain image has a greater

Table 3.8   Node size (%) distribution for stage 1 of neighbor finding

Distance from Node to nca	Model	Observed				
		Floodplain	Topography	Landuse	Pebble	Average
1	50.00	50.00	50.00	50.00	50.00	50.00
2	25.00	25.48	25.17	25.02	24.95	25.12
3	12.50	11.61	12.23	12.42	12.52	12.26
4	6.25	6.08	6.10	6.37	6.43	6.23
5	3.13	2.86	3.00	2.99	3.11	3.01
6	1.56	2.41	1.72	1.62	1.51	1.77
7	0.78	0.69	0.94	0.83	0.82	0.84
8	0.39	0.54	0.56	0.51	0.40	0.50
9	0.20	0.23	0.22	0.20	0.18	0.21
On border	0.20	0.10	0.06	0.04	0.06	0.06
Expected cost	2.00	2.01	2.00	2.00	1.99	2.00

Table 3.9   Node size distribution and average cost of stage 2 of neighbor finding

Depth of nca	Model		Observed									
			Floodplain		Topography		Landuse		Pebble		Average	
	Cost	%	Cost	%	Cost	%	Cost	%	Cost	%	Cost	%
1	1.0	37.5	1.0	23.7	1.0	29.7	1.0	28.2	1.0	30.4	1.0	28.6
2	1.5	28.1	1.3	26.8	1.3	29.5	1.3	29.0	1.3	28.6	1.3	28.4
3	2.0	16.4	1.6	19.6	1.8	19.1	1.7	19.8	1.7	19.2	1.7	19.2
4	2.5	8.79	2.0	12.3	2.5	10.4	2.3	11.3	2.4	10.9	2.3	11.1
5	3.0	4.54	2.3	7.64	3.3	5.33	3.1	5.83	3.3	5.62	3.0	6.02
6	3.5	2.30	2.9	4.39	4.2	2.77	4.0	2.88	4.1	2.67	3.8	3.12
7	4.0	1.16	3.0	2.83	5.1	1.64	5.0	1.56	5.2	1.39	4.7	1.78
8	4.5	0.58	4.5	1.54	5.7	0.95	5.9	0.90	6.3	0.74	5.7	1.00
9	5.0	0.29	6.2	0.76	7.2	0.46	7.3	0.46	7.2	0.37	7.0	0.50
Border		0.30		0.50		0.22		0.23		0.22		0.28
Expected cost	1.65		1.64		1.74		1.73		1.72		1.72	

preponderance of large blocks than the other images (see Table 3.4) and that predicted by the analysis. This preponderance can be seen by noting that the average distances shown in Table 3.9 for the floodplain image are almost always less than those predicted by the model used in the analysis. The remaining images have more smaller blocks, and the average distance to the neighbor from the nearest common ancestor often exceeds the average predicted by the model of the analysis.

3.2.2   Other Methods for Neighbor Finding

Klinger and Rhodes [Klin79] describe a method to move between adjacent brother blocks of equal size that does not make use of the tree structure. Instead coordinate information and knowledge of the size of the image are used to locate an adjacent brother in the direction of a given edge. This is accomplished by a number of primitives termed MOVE_UP, MOVE_DOWN, MOVE_RIGHT, and MOVE_LEFT. Transitions to nonbrother adjacent blocks require the use of approximations through the use of more complex primitives named MORE, LESS, and GAMMA. The disadvantage of these methods is that they require computation (rather than pointer following). They are also awkward when the adjacent block is not a brother or is larger.

Hunter and Steiglitz [Hunt78, Hunt79a, Hunt79b] describe a number of algorithms for operating on images represented by quadtrees by using explicit links from a node to its neighbors. These links connect adjacent nodes in the direction of an edge.

A *rope* is defined to be a link between two adjacent nodes of equal size where at least one of them is a leaf node. For example, there is a rope between nodes D and 13 in Figure 3.1. An *I-adjacency tree* in the direction of edge *I* exists whenever there is a rope between a leaf node, say X, and a gray node, say Y. In such a case, the *I*-adjacency tree of X is said to be the binary tree rooted at Y whose nodes consist of all the descendants of Y (black, white, or gray) that are adjacent to X in direction *I*. For example, Figure 3.6 contains the S-adjacency tree of node 1 corresponding to the rope between nodes 1 and C that crosses the S edge of node 1.

The process of finding a neighbor using a roped quadtree is quite simple. The rope is essentially a way to short-circuit the need to find a nearest common ancestor. Suppose that we want to find the neighbor of node X on edge N using a rope. If a rope from X on edge N exists, it leads to the desired neighbor. Otherwise the desired neighbor is larger, in which case the quadtree is ascended until encountering a node that has a rope on edge N. This rope leads to the desired neighbor. This process is equivalent to ascending the S-adjacency tree of the northern neighbor of node X. For example, to find the northern neighbor of node 8 in Figure 3.1, we ascend through node D to node C, which has a rope along its northern edge leading to node 1 (i.e., 1's S-adjacency tree).

Algorithms for neighbor computation using ropes are easy to formulate. To do this, we must modify the quadtree data structure to include an additional field termed ROPE. For a given leaf node P, ROPE(P,I) yields the rope in the direction of edge I. For example, procedure ROPE_QT_GTEQ_EDGE_NEIGHBOR(P,I), given below, locates a neighbor of node P of greater than or equal size in the direction of edge *I*.

```
pointer node procedure ROPE_QT_GTEQ_EDGE_NEIGHBOR(P,I);
/* Locate the edge-neighbor of leaf node P in direction I. If such a node does not exist,
    then return NIL. */
begin
  value pointer node P;
  value edge I;
  while not(null(P)) and null(ROPE(P,I)) do P ← FATHER(P);
  return(if null(P) then NIL
         else ROPE(P,I));
end;
```

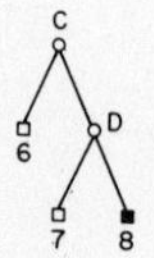

Figure 3.6 Adjacency tree corresponding to the rope between nodes C and 1 in Figure 3.1 (1's S-adjacency tree)

The most natural way to analyze the execution time of neighbor finding in a roped quadtree (i.e., ROPE_QT_GTEQ_EDGE_NEIGHBOR) is in terms of the number of nodes that must be visited in locating the desired neighbor. This is the same technique used in analyzing the cost of the neighbor-finding process for the nearest common ancestor method in Section 3.2.1.2. The only difference is that when using a rope, there is no need to expend any work in locating the nearest common ancestor. In fact, the analysis of ROPE_QT_GTEQ_EDGE_NEIGHBOR yields the same result as that obtained for the second stage of GEN (i.e., QT_GTEQ_EDGE_NEIGHBOR), as is seen by the following theorem. The analysis below closely parallels the analysis of ALIGNED performed in Theorem 3.7.

Theorem 3.8 The average number of nodes visited by ROPE_QT_GTEQ_-EDGE_NEIGHBOR is bounded from above by 3/2.

Proof We use similar reasoning as in Theorem 3.3. In particular, given node P at level i, direction l, and having a nearest common ancestor at level j, there are $j-i$ possible edge-neighbors of size greater than or equal to that of P. Therefore the average number of nodes that will be visited in the process of locating such a neighbor is $1 + \sum_{k=i}^{j-1} (k-i)/(j-i)$. This is obtained by observing that for a neighbor at level k, say Q, where k ranges between i and $j-1$, we must traverse $k-i$ FATHER links to get to P's ancestor at level k, say R, and one more link corresponding to the rope between R and Q. Therefore the average number of nodes visited by ROPE_QT_-GTEQ_EDGE_NEIGHBOR is

$$\frac{\sum_{i=0}^{n-1} \sum_{j=i+1}^{n} 2^{n-i} \cdot 2^{n-j} \cdot (1 + \frac{1}{j-i} \cdot \sum_{k=i}^{j-1}(k-i))}{\sum_{i=0}^{n-1} 2^{n-i} \cdot (2^{n-i} - 1)}.$$

This can be simplified to yield a result equal to the difference between Theorems 3.1 and 3.3:

$$3/2 - \frac{3 \cdot (n-1) \cdot 2^n + 3}{2^{2n+2} - 6 \cdot 2^n + 2}$$

$$\leq 3/2 \text{ for } n \geq 1. \qquad \square$$

At times it is not even desired to ascend nodes in the search for a rope. In those cases, Hunter and Steiglitz make use of a *net*, a linked list whose elements are all the nodes, regardless of their relative size, that are adjacent along a given edge of a node. As an example, in Figure 3.1 there is a net for the southern edge of node 1 consisting of nodes 6, 7, and 8. To implement nets, we augment the quadtree data structure to contain an additional field termed NET. Associated with each leaf node are four NET entries, one for each direction, pointing to lists containing pointers to the adjacent nodes. Using such a representation, an edge-neighbor is located by accessing the appropriate NET field, and it always takes one step (i.e., only one pointer is traversed).

Exercises

3.9.   Generalize the concept of a rope to deal with vertex-neighbors.

3.10. Prove that a quadtree can be roped in time proportional to the number of nodes in the tree.

3.11. Give a procedure, ROPE_QT_GTEQ_VERTEX_NEIGHBOR, analogous to QT_GTEQ_EDGE_NEIGH-BOR, to compute a vertex-neighbor of greater than or equal size.

3.12. Find the average number of nodes visited by procedure ROPE_QT_GTEQ_VERTEX_NEIGHBOR in a manner analogous to that used to analyze ROPE_QT_GTEQ_EDGE_NEIGHBOR in Theorem 3.8.

3.13. Prove that the total number of nodes in all adjacency trees for a given quadtree is bounded from above by four times the number of leaf nodes in the quadtree.

3.14. Generalize the concept of an adjacency tree to a d-dimensional quadtree. What is the upper bound on the number of nodes in all of the adjacency trees?

3.15. Generalize the concept of a net to a vertex-neighbor.

3.16. Prove that a quadtree can be netted in time proportional to the number of nodes in the tree.

3.17. How would you maintain ropes and nets in a Boolean set operation (e.g., union) on two images?

3.2.3   Comparison

The advantage of ropes and nets is that the number of nodes that must be visited in the process of finding neighbors is reduced. The disadvantage is that the storage requirements are increased considerably. In addition, in a dynamic situation, both nets and ropes have the drawback that additional work must be expended to maintain the links properly. In contrast, nearest common ancestor methods [Same82a] make use of only the structure of the tree: four links from a nonleaf node to its sons and a link from a nonroot node to its father (they use a stack). Using a suitably defined model, locating an edge-neighbor of greater than or equal size requires visiting fewer than four nodes, on the average, when using the nearest common ancestor techniques, whereas fewer than two nodes must be visited, on the average, when using ropes. Empirical results reported in [Rose82b, Tuck84b] are similar. Thus, in practice, it is not necessary to add the extra overhead of using a rope and a net because it requires extra storage.

At times the algorithms that perform the basic operations on the image can be reformulated so that they do not require the computation of the neighbors. This is achieved by transmitting, as actual parameters, the neighbors of each node in the principal directions. Such techniques are termed *top-down*, in contrast with the *bottom-up* methods discussed earlier. One such technique is used by Jackins and Tanimoto [Jack83] in the computation of an *n*-dimensional perimeter. Their algorithm requires making *n* passes over the data and works only for edge-neighbors. Independently a similar algorithm was devised that does not require *n* passes but uses just one pass [Rose82b, Same82c]. Another top-down algorithm able to compute edge- and vertex-neighbors with just one pass is reported in [Same85a].

Exercise

3.18. Give an algorithm that traverses a quadtree in a top-down manner so that as each node is visited, all of its neighbors are immediately available.

3.3 NEIGHBOR FINDING IN POINTER-BASED OCTREE REPRESENTATIONS

Neighbor finding in a pointer-based octree representation [Same89a] is quite similar to that in a pointer-based quadtree representation. The difference is that instead of having only edge- and vertex-neighbors, we also have face-neighbors. In particular, in two dimensions, two nodes can be adjacent, and hence neighbors, along an edge (4 possibilities) or along a vertex (4 possibilities). In contrast, in three dimensions, two nodes can be adjacent, and hence neighbors, along a face (6 possibilities), along an edge (12 possibilities), or along a vertex (8 possibilities). These adjacencies are illustrated in Figures 3.7a, 3.7b, and 3.7c, respectively.

The algorithm for locating a face-neighbor in an octree is quite simple (e.g., [Garg82b, Koba87]). In fact, the algorithms for locating face- and edge-neighbors in an octree are virtually identical to the algorithms used to locate edge- and vertex-neighbors, respectively, in a quadtree. The only difference is in the predicates and functions that aid in the expression of the operations involving a block's octants and its faces, edges, and vertices.

This section is organized in the following manner. First key terms are defined and an explanation is given of the notation used to refer to the octants of an octree. Next the algorithms for computing the neighbors are presented. This is followed by

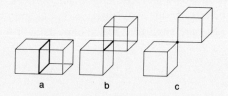

a   b   c

Figure 3.7   Example of (a) a face-neighbor, (b) an edge-neighbor, and (c) a vertex-neighbor

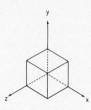

Figure 3.8   Three-dimensional coordinate system

an analysis of their execution time. Finally, a brief comparison is made with neighbor finding in a quadtree and the extension of these methods to higher dimensional data is discussed.

3.3.1   Definitions and Notation

Assume that each octree node is stored as a record of type *node*. Figure 3.8 shows the coordinate system that we are using relative to a cube. It is slightly different from the one used to generate Figure 1.2. Let L and R denote the resulting lower and upper halves, respectively, when the x axis is partitioned. Let D and U denote the resulting lower and upper halves, respectively, when the y axis is partitioned. Let B and F denote the resulting lower and upper halves, respectively, when the z axis is partitioned. Figure 3.9 illustrates the labelings corresponding to the partitions.

The labelings in Figure 3.9 are also used to identify the faces, edges, and vertices of the cube as shown in Figure 3.10. The faces are L (left), R (right), D (down), U (up), B (back), and F (front); however, only R, U, and F are visible. The edges and vertices of the cube are labeled by using an appropriate concatenation of labels of the adjacent faces. Note that vertex LDB and edges LD, LB, and DB are not visible. Similarly the octants are labeled by using a concatenation of these labels as shown in Figure 3.11 (octant LDB is not visible). Figure 3.12 is a numerical labeling for the octants (octant 0 is not visible).

The following predicates and functions aid in the expression of operations involving a block's octants and its faces, edges, and vertices. Tables 3.10–3.13 contain the definitions of the ADJ, REFLECT, COMMON_FACE, and COMMON_EDGE relationships, respectively. They are analogous to the ones defined for a quadtree in Section

Figure 3.9   Three orthogonal partitions of a cube

Figure 3.10   Labeling of faces, edges, and vertices based on the partitioning defined in Figure 3.9

Figure 3.11   Labeling of octants based on the partitioning defined in Figure 3.9 (octant LDB is not visible)

3.2.1. The principal difference is the addition of the function COMMON_FACE. Ω denotes an undefined value.

ADJ(I,O) is true if, and only if, octant O is adjacent to the Ith face, edge, or vertex of O's containing block—for example, ADJ('L','LDB') is true as are ADJ('LD','LDB'), and ADJ('LDB','LDB'). This relation can also be described as true if O is of type I or, equivalently, that I's label is a subset of O's label.

REFLECT(I,O) yields the SONTYPE value of the block of equal size (not necessarily a brother) that shares the Ith face, edge, or vertex of a block having SONTYPE value O—for example, REFLECT('L','RDB') = 'LDB', REFLECT('LD','RDB') = 'LUB', and REFLECT('RDB', 'RDB') = 'LUF'.

COMMON_FACE(I,O) yields the type of the face (i.e., label), of O's containing block, that is common to octant O and its neighbor in the Ith direction (I is an edge or a vertex)—for example, COMMON_FACE('LD','LUF') = 'L' and COMMON_FACE('LDB','LUF') = 'L'.

COMMON_EDGE(I,O) yields the type of the edge (i.e., label), of O's containing block, that is common to octant O and its neighbor in the Ith direction (I is a vertex) —for example, COMMON_EDGE('LDB','LUB') = 'LB'.

Figure 3.12   Numeric labeling of octants based on the partitioning defined in Figure 3.9 (octant 0 is not visible)

Table 3.10   ADJ(I,O)

I (direction)	O (octant)							
	LDB	LDF	LUB	LUF	RDB	RDF	RUB	RUF
L	T	T	T	T	F	F	F	F
R	F	F	F	F	T	T	T	T
D	T	T	F	F	T	T	F	F
U	F	F	T	T	F	F	T	T
B	T	F	T	F	T	F	T	F
F	F	T	F	T	F	T	F	T
LD	T	T	F	F	F	F	F	F
LU	F	F	T	T	F	F	F	F
LB	T	F	T	F	F	F	F	F
LF	F	T	F	T	F	F	F	F
RD	F	F	F	F	T	T	F	F
RU	F	F	F	F	F	F	T	T
RB	F	F	F	F	T	F	T	F
RF	F	F	F	F	F	T	F	T
DB	T	F	F	F	T	F	F	F
DF	F	T	F	F	F	T	F	F
UB	F	F	T	F	F	F	T	F
UF	F	F	F	T	F	F	F	T
LDB	T	F	F	F	F	F	F	F
LDF	F	T	F	F	F	F	F	F
LUB	F	F	T	F	F	F	F	F
LUF	F	F	F	T	F	F	F	F
RDB	F	F	F	F	T	F	F	F
RDF	F	F	F	F	F	T	F	F
RUB	F	F	F	F	F	F	T	F
RUF	F	F	F	F	F	F	F	T

Exercises

3.19. What is the minimum number of neighbors for an octree node that is not adjacent to the border of the image? What about a *d*-dimensional image?

3.20. What is the maximum number of neighbors for an octree node that is not adjacent to the border of the image? What about a *d*-dimensional image?

3.3.2   Algorithms

First let us see how to locate neighbors of equal size. This is relatively straightfor-ward for face-neighbors. Assume that we are trying to find the equal-sized face-

Table 3.11   REFLECT(I,O)

I (direction)	O (octant)							
	LDB	LDF	LUB	LUF	RDB	RDF	RUB	RUF
L	RDB	RDF	RUB	RUF	LDB	LDF	LUB	LUF
R	RDB	RDF	RUB	RUF	LDB	LDF	LUB	LUF
D	LUB	LUF	LDB	LDF	RUB	RUF	RDB	RDF
U	LUB	LUF	LDB	LDF	RUB	RUF	RDB	RDF
B	LDF	LDB	LUF	LUB	RDF	RDB	RUF	RUB
F	LDF	LDB	LUF	LUB	RDF	RDB	RUF	RUB
LD	RUB	RUF	RDB	RDF	LUB	LUF	LDB	LDF
LU	RUB	RUF	RDB	RDF	LUB	LUF	LDB	LDF
LB	RDF	RDB	RUF	RUB	LDF	LDB	LUF	LUB
LF	RDF	RDB	RUF	RUB	LDF	LDB	LUF	LUB
RD	RUB	RUF	RDB	RDF	LUB	LUF	LDB	LDF
RU	RUB	RUF	RDB	RDF	LUB	LUF	LDB	LDF
RB	RDF	RDB	RUF	RUB	LDF	LDB	LUF	LUB
RF	RDF	RDB	RUF	RUB	LDF	LDB	LUF	LUB
DB	LUF	LUB	LDF	LDB	RUF	RUB	RDF	RDB
DF	LUF	LUB	LDF	LDB	RUF	RUB	RDF	RDB
UB	LUF	LUB	LDF	LDB	RUF	RUB	RDF	RDB
UF	LUF	LUB	LDF	LDB	RUF	RUB	RDF	RDB
LDB	RUF	RUB	RDF	RDB	LUF	LUB	LDF	LDB
LDF	RUF	RUB	RDF	RDB	LUF	LUB	LDF	LDB
LUB	RUF	RUB	RDF	RDB	LUF	LUB	LDF	LDB
LUF	RUF	RUB	RDF	RDB	LUF	LUB	LDF	LDB
RDB	RUF	RUB	RDF	RDB	LUF	LUB	LDF	LDB
RDF	RUF	RUB	RDF	RDB	LUF	LUB	LDF	LDB
RUB	RUF	RUB	RDF	RDB	LUF	LUB	LDF	LDB
RUF	RUF	RUB	RDF	RDB	LUF	LUB	LDF	LDB

neighbor of node P in direction I. The basic idea is to ascend the octree until a common ancestor is located and then descend back down the octree in search of the neighboring node. It is obvious that we can always ascend as far as the root of the octree and then start our descent. However, our goal is to find the nearest common ancestor because this minimizes the number of nodes that must be visited. These two steps are described below and implemented by procedure OT_EQ_FACE_NEIGHBOR. It ignores the situation in which the neighbor may not exist (e.g., when the node is on the border of the image).

Table 3.12   COMMON_FACE(I,O)

I (direction)	O (octant)							
	LDB	LDF	LUB	LUF	RDB	RDF	RUB	RUF
LD	Ω	Ω	L	L	D	D	Ω	Ω
LU	L	L	Ω	Ω	Ω	Ω	U	U
LB	Ω	L	Ω	L	B	Ω	B	Ω
LF	L	Ω	L	Ω	Ω	F	Ω	F
RD	D	D	Ω	Ω	Ω	Ω	R	R
RU	Ω	Ω	U	U	R	R	Ω	Ω
RB	B	Ω	B	Ω	Ω	R	Ω	R
RF	Ω	F	Ω	F	R	Ω	R	Ω
DB	Ω	D	B	Ω	Ω	D	B	Ω
DF	D	Ω	Ω	F	D	Ω	Ω	F
UB	B	Ω	Ω	U	B	Ω	Ω	U
UF	Ω	F	U	Ω	Ω	F	U	Ω
LDB	Ω	Ω	Ω	L	Ω	D	B	Ω
LDF	Ω	Ω	L	Ω	D	Ω	Ω	F
LUB	Ω	L	Ω	Ω	B	Ω	Ω	U
LUF	L	Ω	Ω	Ω	Ω	F	U	Ω
RDB	Ω	D	B	Ω	Ω	Ω	Ω	R
RDF	D	Ω	Ω	F	Ω	Ω	R	Ω
RUB	B	Ω	Ω	U	Ω	R	Ω	Ω
RUF	Ω	F	U	Ω	R	Ω	Ω	Ω

Table 3.13   COMMON_EDGE(I,O)

I (direction)	O (octant)							
	LDB	LDF	LUB	LUF	RDB	RDF	RUB	RUF
LDB	Ω	LD	LB	Ω	DB	Ω	Ω	Ω
LDF	LD	Ω	Ω	LF	Ω	DF	Ω	Ω
LUB	LB	Ω	Ω	LU	Ω	Ω	UB	Ω
LUF	Ω	LF	LU	Ω	Ω	Ω	Ω	UF
RDB	DB	Ω	Ω	Ω	Ω	RD	RB	Ω
RDF	Ω	DF	Ω	Ω	RD	Ω	Ω	RF
RUB	Ω	Ω	UB	Ω	RB	Ω	Ω	RU
RUF	Ω	Ω	Ω	UF	Ω	RF	RU	Ω

1. Locate the nearest common ancestor. This is the first ancestor node reached by a son of type O such that ADJ(I,O) is false. In other words, I's label is not a subset of O's label.

2. Retrace the path that was taken to locate the nearest common ancestor by using the function REFLECT to make mirror image moves about the face shared by the neighboring nodes.

```
recursive pointer node procedure OT_EQ_FACE_NEIGHBOR(P,I);
/* Locate an equal-sized face-neighbor of node P in direction I. */
begin
  value pointer node P;
  value face I;
  return(SON(if ADJ(I,SONTYPE(P)) then
               OT_EQ_FACE_NEIGHBOR(FATHER(P),I)
             else FATHER(P),
             REFLECT(I,SONTYPE(P)))));
end;
```

Locating an edge-neighbor is more complex. Assume that we are trying to find the equal-sized edge-neighbor of node P in direction I. Our initial aim is to locate the nearest common ancestor of P and its neighbor. We need to ascend the tree to do so. We must also account for the situation in which the ancestors of P and its neighbor are adjacent along a face. Let N denote the node currently being examined in the ascent. There are three cases described below, implemented by procedure OT_EQ_EDGE_-NEIGHBOR. This procedure ignores the situation in which the neighbor may not exist (e.g., when the node is on the border of the image).

1. As long as N is a son of type O such that ADJ(I,O) is true, we continue to ascend the tree. In other words, I's label is a subset of O's label.

2. If the father of N and the ancestor of the desired neighbor, say A, are adjacent along a face, then calculate A by use of procedure OT_EQ_FACE_NEIGHBOR. This situation and the exact direction of A are determined by the function COMMON_FACE applied to I and the son type of N. Once A has been obtained, the desired neighbor is located by applying the retracing step outlined in step 3.

3. Otherwise N is a son of a type, say O, such that neither of the labels of the faces comprising edge I is a subset of O's label. Its father, say T, is the nearest common ancestor. The desired neighbor is obtained by simply retracing the path used to locate T, except that we now make directly opposite moves about the edge shared by the neighboring nodes. This process is facilitated by use of the function REFLECT.

```
recursive pointer node procedure OT_EQ_EDGE_NEIGHBOR(P,I);
/* Locate an equal-sized edge-neighbor of node P in direction I. */
begin
  value pointer node P;
  value edge I;
  return(SON(if ADJ(I,SONTYPE(P)) then
                OT_EQ_EDGE_NEIGHBOR(FATHER(P),I)
             else if COMMON_FACE(I,SONTYPE(P)) ≠ Ω then
                OT_EQ_FACE_NEIGHBOR(FATHER(P),
                  COMMON_FACE(I,SONTYPE(P)))
             else FATHER(P),
                REFLECT(I,SONTYPE(P)))));
end;
```

Locating a vertex-neighbor is very similar to locating an edge-neighbor. Assume that we are trying to find the equal-sized vertex-neighbor of node P in direction I. Again our initial aim is to locate the nearest common ancestor of P and its neighbor. We need to ascend the tree to do so. We must also account for the situation that the ancestors of P and its neighbor are adjacent along an edge. Let N denote the node currently being examined in the ascent. There are four cases described below. They are implemented by procedure OT_EQ_VERTEX_NEIGHBOR. This procedure ignores the situation that the neighbor may not exist (e.g., when the node is on the border of the image).

1. As long as N is a son of type O such that ADJ(I,O) is true, we continue to ascend the tree. In other words, I's label is a subset of O's label.
2. If the father of N and the ancestor of the desired neighbor, say A, are adjacent along an edge, calculate A by use of procedure OT_EQ_EDGE_NEIGHBOR. This situation and the exact direction of A are determined by the function COMMON_EDGE applied to I and the son type of N. Once A has been obtained, the desired neighbor is located by applying the retracing step outlined in step 4.
3. If the father of N and the ancestor of the desired neighbor, say A, are adjacent along a face, calculate A by use of procedure OT_EQ_FACE_NEIGHBOR. This situation and the exact direction of A are determined by the function COMMON_FACE applied to I and the son type of N. Once A has been obtained, the desired neighbor is located by applying the retracing step outlined in step 4.
4. Otherwise N is a son of a type, say O, such that none of the labels of the faces comprising vertex I is a subset of O's label. Its father, say T, is the nearest common ancestor. The desired neighbor is obtained by simply retracing the path used to locate T except that we now make directly opposite moves about the vertex shared by the neighboring nodes. This process is facilitated by use of the function REFLECT.

recursive pointer node procedure OT_EQ_VERTEX_NEIGHBOR(P,I);
/* Locate an equal-sized vertex-neighbor of node P in direction I. */
begin
  value pointer node P;
  value vertex I;
  return(SON(**If** ADJ(I,SONTYPE(P)) **then**
          OT_EQ_VERTEX_NEIGHBOR(FATHER(P),I)
       else if COMMON_EDGE(I,SONTYPE(P)) $\neq \Omega$ **then**
       OT_EQ_EDGE_NEIGHBOR(FATHER(P),
        COMMON_EDGE(I,SONTYPE(P)))
       else if COMMON_FACE(I,SONTYPE(P)) $\neq \Omega$ **then**
       OT_EQ_FACE_NEIGHBOR(FATHER(P),
        COMMON_FACE(I,SONTYPE(P)))
       else FATHER(P),
       REFLECT(I,SONTYPE(P)))));
end;

In general, neighbors need not correspond to blocks of the same size. If the neighbor is larger, only part of the path from the nearest common ancestor is retraced. Otherwise the neighbor corresponds to a block of equal size, and a pointer to a black, white, or gray node, as is appropriate, of equal size is returned. If there is no neighbor (i.e., the node whose neighbor is being sought is adjacent to the border of the image in the specified direction), NIL is returned. This process is encoded below by procedures OT_GTEQ_FACE_NEIGHBOR, OT_GTEQ_EDGE_NEIGHBOR, and OT_GTEQ_VERTEX_NEIGH-BOR. They replace OT_EQ_FACE_NEIGHBOR, OT_EQ_EDGE_NEIGHBOR, and OT_EQ_VER-TEX_NEIGHBOR, respectively.

recursive pointer node procedure OT_GTEQ_FACE_NEIGHBOR(P,I);
/* Locate a face-neighbor of node P, of size greater than or equal to P, in direction I. If
   such a node does not exist, then return NIL. */
begin
  value pointer node P;
  value face I;
  pointer node Q;
  Q ← **if not**(null(FATHER(P))) **and** ADJ(I,SONTYPE(P)) **then**
     /* Find a common ancestor */
     OT_GTEQ_FACE_NEIGHBOR(FATHER(P),I)
    else FATHER(P);
  /* Follow the reflected path to locate the neighbor */
  return(**if not**(null(Q)) **and** GRAY(Q) **then**
      SON(Q,REFLECT(I,SONTYPE(P)))
     else Q);
end;

recursive pointer node procedure OT_GTEQ_EDGE_NEIGHBOR(P,I);
/* Locate an edge-neighbor of node P, of size greater than or equal to P, in direction I. If
· such a node does not exist, then return NIL. */

```
begin
  value pointer node P;
  value edge I;
  pointer node Q;
   /* Find a common ancestor */
  Q ← if null(FATHER(P)) then NIL
      else if ADJ(I,SONTYPE(P)) then
        OT_GTEQ_EDGE_NEIGHBOR(FATHER(P),I)
      else if COMMON_FACE(I,SONTYPE(P)) ≠ Ω then
        OT_GTEQ_FACE_NEIGHBOR(FATHER(P),
                                COMMON_FACE(I,SONTYPE(P)))
      else FATHER(P);
   /* Follow opposite path to locate the neighbor */
  return(if not(null(Q)) and GRAY(Q) then
          SON(Q,REFLECT(I,SONTYPE(P)))
        else Q);
end;


recursive pointer node procedure OT_GTEQ_VERTEX_NEIGHBOR(P,I);
/* Locate a vertex-neighbor of node P, of size greater than or equal to P, in direction I. If
   such a node does not exist, then return NIL. */
begin
  value pointer node P;
  value vertex I;
  pointer node Q;
   /* Find a common ancestor */
  Q ← if null(FATHER(P)) then NIL
      else if ADJ(I,SONTYPE(P)) then
        OT_GTEQ_VERTEX_NEIGHBOR(FATHER(P),I)
      else if COMMON_EDGE(I,SONTYPE(P)) ≠ Ω then
        OT_GTEQ_EDGE_NEIGHBOR(FATHER(P),
                                COMMON_EDGE(I,SONTYPE(P)))
      else if COMMON_FACE(I,SONTYPE(P)) ≠ Ω then
        OT_GTEQ_FACE_NEIGHBOR(FATHER(P),
                                COMMON_FACE(I,SONTYPE(P)))
      else FATHER(P);
   /* Follow opposite path to locate the neighbor */
  return(if not(null(Q)) and GRAY(Q) then
          SON(Q,REFLECT(I,SONTYPE(P)))
        else Q);
end;
```

At times, we also wish to return the size of the neighbor. This is achieved by procedures OT_GTEQ_FACE_NEIGHBOR2, OT_GTEQ_EDGE_NEIGHBOR2, and OT_GTEQ_-VERTEX_NEIGHBOR2, which are encoded in an analogous manner to that done in Section 3.2.1.1 and will not be given here.

Exercises

3.21. Discuss neighbor finding for a three-dimensional image that is represented as a bintree. Give the analogs of algorithms OT_EQ_FACE_NEIGHBOR, OT_EQ_EDGE_NEIGHBOR, and OT_EQ_VERTEX_NEIGHBOR. In addition, define the bintree analogs of OT_GTEQ_FACE_NEIGHBOR, OT_GTEQ_EDGE_NEIGHBOR, and OT_GTEQ_VERTEX_NEIGHBOR, and give algorithms for their computation in a pointer-based environment. All of your algorithms should proceed by locating a nearest common ancestor.

3.22. Given a line segment with endpoints that are in an image represented by an octree, write an algorithm to output all the blocks intersected by the line. Such an algorithm is useful in implementing ray tracing (see Section 7.2).

3.3.3 Analysis

We analyze the execution time of the algorithms of Section 3.3.2 in terms of the number of nodes that must be visited in locating the desired neighbor. The technique is analogous to that used in Section 3.2.1.2. The analysis of each function is decomposed into two stages: locating the nearest common ancestor and then the desired neighbor. Again we use an average case analysis that makes use of a random image model in which each leaf node is assumed to be equally likely to appear at any position and level in the octree. Applying such a model to an octree means that there are $1, 8, 64, 512, \cdots, 8^i$ leaf nodes at levels $n, n-1, n-2, n-3, \cdots, n-i$, respectively, or equivalently that $\dfrac{7}{8} \cdot (\dfrac{1}{8})^i$ of the nodes are at level i. Although this is not a realizable situation, it does serve our analysis.

The first stage of the analysis is with respect to a node P at level i and a direction I. Depending on the nature of I, there are different positions where P might be located. If I is a face, then there are $(2^{n-i})^2 \cdot (2^{n-i} - 1)$ possible positions where P might be located. The -1 results from the fact that along one of the axial directions, one element will not have a neighbor in direction I that is in the image. Of these positions, $2^{n-i} \cdot 2^{n-i} \cdot 2^0$ have their nearest common ancestor at level n, $2^{n-i} \cdot 2^{n-i} \cdot 2^1$ at level $n-1, \cdots$, and $2^{n-i} \cdot 2^{n-i} \cdot 2^{n-i-1}$ at level $i + 1$. To reach a nearest common ancestor at level j, $j-i$ nodes must be visited. Therefore the average is

$$
\frac{\displaystyle\sum_{i=0}^{n-1} \sum_{j=i+1}^{n} 2^{n-i} \cdot 2^{n-i} \cdot 2^{n-j} \cdot (j-i)}{\displaystyle\sum_{i=0}^{n-1} 2^{n-i} \cdot 2^{n-i} \cdot (2^{n-i} - 1)}.
$$

This can be simplified to yield

$$2 - \frac{(21n - 7) \cdot 2^{2n} + 7}{18 \cdot 2^{3n} - 21 \cdot 2^{2n} + 3}$$

$$\leq 2 \text{ for } n \geq 1.$$

If l is an edge, there are $2^{n-i} \cdot (2^{n-i} - 1)^2$ possible positions where P might be located. The -1 results from the fact that along two of the axial directions, one element will not have a neighbor in direction l that is in the image. Of these positions, $2^{n-i} \cdot 4^0 \cdot (2 \cdot (2^{n-i} - 1) - 1)$ have neighbors in direction l such that the nearest common ancestor is at level n, $2^{n-i} \cdot 4^1 \cdot (2 \cdot (2^{n-i-1} - 1) - 1)$ at level $n-1$, $\cdots$, and $2^{n-i} \cdot 4^{n-i-1} \cdot (2 \cdot (2^{n-i-(n-i-1)} - 1) - 1)$ at level $i + 1$. To reach a nearest common ancestor at level j, $j-i$ nodes must be visited. Therefore the average is

$$\frac{\sum_{i=0}^{n-1} \sum_{j=i+1}^{n} 2^{n-i} \cdot 4^{n-j} \cdot (2 \cdot (2^{n-i-(n-j)} - 1) - 1) \cdot (j-i)}{\sum_{i=0}^{n-1} 2^{n-i} \cdot (2^{n-i} - 1)^2}.$$

This can be simplified to yield

$$\frac{8}{3} - \frac{(28n - 28) \cdot 2^{2n} - (21n - 49) \cdot 2^n - 21}{12 \cdot 2^{3n} - 28 \cdot 2^{2n} + 21 \cdot 2^n - 5}$$

$$\leq 8/3 \text{ for } n \geq 1.$$

If l is a vertex, then there are $(2^{n-i} - 1)^3$ possible positions where P might be located. The -1 results from the fact that along each of the axial directions, one element will not have a neighbor in direction l that is in the image. Of these positions, $8^0 \cdot (3 \cdot (2^{n-i} - 1)^2 - 3 \cdot (2^{n-i} - 1) + 1)$ have neighbors in direction l such that the nearest common ancestor is at level n, $8^1 \cdot (3 \cdot (2^{n-i-1} - 1)^2 - 3 \cdot (2^{n-i-1} - 1) + 1)$ at level $n-1$, $\cdots$, and $8^{n-i-1} \cdot (3 \cdot (2^{n-i-(n-i-1)} - 1)^2 - 3 \cdot (2^{n-i-(n-i-1)} - 1) + 1)$ at level $i + 1$. To reach a nearest common ancestor at level l, $j-i$ nodes must be visited. Therefore the average is

$$\frac{\sum_{i=0}^{n-1} \sum_{j=i+1}^{n} 8^{n-j} \cdot (3 \cdot (2^{n-i-(n-j)} - 1)^2 - 3 \cdot (2^{n-i-(n-j)} - 1) + 1) \cdot (j-i)}{\sum_{i=0}^{n-1} (2^{n-i} - 1)^3}.$$

This can be simplified to yield

$$\frac{22}{7} - \frac{(147n - 217) \cdot 2^{2n+3} - (441n - 1239) \cdot 2^{n+2} + 147 \cdot n^2 - 441n - 3220}{21 \cdot 2^{3n+4} - 147 \cdot 2^{2n+3} + 441 \cdot 2^{n+2} - 294n - 924}$$

$$\leq 22/7 \text{ for } n \geq 1.$$

When the neighbors are of equal size, the analyses for the second stage are the same as for the first stage. The result is that the average number of nodes visited by OT_EQ_FACE_NEIGHBOR, OT_EQ_EDGE_NEIGHBOR, and OT_EQ_VERTEX_NEIGHBOR is bounded by 4, 16/3, and 44/7, respectively.

When the neighbors are not of equal size, then, depending on the position of the node P, a number of different sizes of neighbors are possible. For example, suppose we have a $2^3 \times 2^3 \times 2^3$ image, and we are looking at a node of size 1 voxel (i.e., $1 \times 1 \times 1$). In this case, its position may be such that it can have three possible neighbors: one each of size 1×1, 2×2, and 4×4 at node distances of 3, 2, and 1, respectively, from the nearest common ancestor. We use the average contribution of these three cases as the cost of the second stage. This means that the quantity $(j-i)$ in the analyses of OT_EQ_FACE_NEIGHBOR, OT_EQ_EDGE_NEIGHBOR, and OT_EQ_VERTEX_NEIGHBOR is replaced by

$$\frac{1}{j-i} \cdot \sum_{k=i}^{j-1} (j-k).$$

Using this model, the average number of nodes visited by OT_GTEQ_FACE_NEIGHBOR, OT_GTEQ_EDGE_NEIGHBOR, and OT_GTEQ_VERTEX_NEIGHBOR is bounded by 7/2, 9/2, and 73/14, respectively.

3.3.4 Summary

Neighbor finding in an octree is very similar to neighbor finding in a quadtree. In particular, procedure OT_EQ_FACE_NEIGHBOR is equivalent to procedure QT_EQ_EDGE_NEIGHBOR, and procedure OT_EQ_EDGE_NEIGHBOR is equivalent to procedure QT_EQ_VERTEX_NEIGHBOR. The only difference is in the use of auxiliary function COMMON_EDGE for the quadtree and COMMON_FACE for the octree. Structurally, however, these pairs of procedures are identical.

The techniques that we have used to adapt the quadtree neighbor-finding algorithms to three-dimensional data could also be used for data of higher dimension. The key is that for each additional dimension, we need an additional table to describe the COMMON part. Of course, the existing tables such as ADJ, REFLECT, COMMON_FACE, and COMMON_EDGE will grow considerably larger.

Exercises

3.23. How would you adapt the concepts of ropes and nets to an octree?

3.24. The Ph.D. dissertation of Webber [Webb84] contains a theoretical treatment of the neighbor-finding process in quadtrees that includes proofs of the correctness of a number of primitive operations. Extend this work to octrees using the algorithms of Section 3.3.2.

3.25. Adapt the neighbor-finding techniques developed in this section to four-dimensional images.

3.26. Suppose you have a d-dimensional image. How many different ways are there for nodes to be adjacent?

3.4   NEIGHBOR FINDING IN POINTERLESS REPRESENTATIONS

Chapter 2 contains a discussion of a number of pointerless quadtree (octree) representations. Although their use may lead to significant savings in space, they vary in the ease with which they can be manipulated. In particular, as shown below, performing neighbor finding requires quite a bit of work with some of them, although it is possible. Recall that pointerless quadtree (octree) representations can be grouped into two categories. The first treats the image as a collection of leaf nodes, and the second represents the image in the form of a traversal of the nodes of its tree.

In this section we concentrate on the FD locational code because it is the most efficient. Algorithms are given for finding neighbors in all directions for both quadtrees and octrees that are represented by the FD locational code [Same89a]. Next algorithms are given for a couple of operations using the FL locational code for a quadtree representation that stores only the locational codes of the black nodes (an FL linear quadtree). The result is considerably more complex than that obtained for the FD locational code. We also briefly examine the use of VL locational codes and DF-expressions. Recall that the latter is a traversal of the nodes of the tree. Since this section is somewhat specialized, it may be skipped on an initial reading.

3.4.1   FD Linear Quadtree

When an image is represented as a collection of the leaf nodes comprising it, there are a number of methods of representing the individual leaf nodes. In the FD linear quadtree (octree), each leaf node (black and white) is represented by its FD locational code. Assuming an image of side length 2^n, the FD locational code of each leaf node of side length 2^k is n digits long in which the leading $n-k$ digits contain the directional codes that locate the leaf along a path from the root of the tree. The k trailing digits contain the directional codes that locate the pixel in the block's NW (LDB) corner. The resulting number is the same as that obtained by interleaving the bits that comprise the values of the pixel's x and y (and z) coordinates.

The directional codes are numeric equivalents of the different quadrants (i.e., 0, 1, 2, 3 for NW, NE, SW, SE, respectively) and octants (i.e., 0, 1, 2, 3, 4, 5, 6, 7 for LDB, LDF, LUB, LUF, RDB, RDF, RUB, RUF, respectively). We assume that the origin is in the NW (LDB) corner of the block. Therefore for a block of side length 2^k, the directional codes stored in the k trailing digits are 0.

A node's FD locational code is implemented by a record of type *fd_locationalcode* with three fields PATH, LEV, and COL corresponding to the path from the root to the node, the level of the node, and the color of the node, respectively. For an image of maximum side length 2^n, the path, say P, is implemented as an array of type *fd_path* of n directional codes stored in the order $P[n-1]P[n-2]$ $\cdots P[1]P[0]$.

Neighbor finding when the image is represented as a collection of the FD locational codes of its constituent nodes is similar to the procedure used for a pointer-based tree representation. The key difference is that there is never a need to traverse links since the only operation is one of bit manipulation. This difference is of no consequence when the tree is represented in internal memory. However, when storage requirements are such that the tree is represented in external memory (e.g., using a B-tree as in [Same84d, Same87a, Shaf87c]), this difference is very important. It means that there is no need to traverse links between nodes on different pages, a situation that could cause a page fault. In such a situation, bit manipulation will, in most cases, be considerably faster than link traversal.

Given a node A with FD locational code P, finding its neighbor in direction I of size greater than or equal to A is quite simple. During this process, we first construct T, the path component of the FD locational code of the equal-sized desired neighbor, say Q. The result is analogous to calculating the address of the node's block, except that it is more complex since we are not dealing with the individual values of the x and y (and z) coordinates of the address.

The algorithm is as follows. Starting with the digit position in the path corresponding to the link from A to its father (i.e., PATH(P)[LEV(P)]), reflect each directional code in the designated direction (and assign it to the corresponding entry in T) until encountering the nearest common ancestor of A and Q. The nearest common ancestor is detected by using the function ADJ given in Table 3.2. Note that unlike the algorithm for computing neighbors in a pointer-based quadtree (octree), there is no need to descend the tree since reflection occurs while ascending the tree. As an example, in Figure 3.1, pixel 8 has FD locational code 211, and its adjacent pixel in the eastern direction has FD locational code 300.

Once T has been computed, we must still determine if such a node actually exists, as well as its color. Recall that we are interested in the neighbor of greater than or equal size, while T is the path to a neighboring node of equal size. Assume, without loss of generality, that the collection of FD locational codes, say L, is implemented as a list. Search L for the FD locational code with a path that has the maximum value that is still less than or equal to that of T, say R—that is, PATH(R)$\leq T$. If the level of R is greater than or equal to that of T (i.e., LEV(P)),[3] then R's node contains the node

---

[3] Recall that we use the convention that for a $2^n \times 2^n$ image the root is at level n while a pixel is at level 0.

represented by T, and R is returned as the FD locational code of the neighbor. Otherwise there is no leaf node in the tree that corresponds to the desired neighbor, and the neighbor is gray (see Exercise 3.27). In this case, we return an FD locational code for a gray node at level LEV(P) with T as the path from the root to it.

Given a $2^n \times 2^n$ image whose quadtree contains m leaf nodes, the neighbor computation process described has a worst-case execution time of $O(\log_2 m + n)$. This assumes that the FD locational codes are stored in a list sorted by the numbers formed by the paths to the nodes. As an example of this process, in Figure 3.1, the path to the northern neighbor of node 7 (with FD locational code 210) is 032. However, in the list of FD locational codes for this image, the nearest FD locational code is 000, which corresponds to node 1 which is larger than node 7.

Procedure FD_QT_GTEQ_NEIGHBOR, given below, is used to calculate the FD locational code of the neighbor of a node, say A with FD locational code P, in all directions (i.e., edge and vertex) in an FD linear quadtree. It makes use of procedures FDL_QT_-EQ_EDGE_NEIGHBOR and FDL_QT_EQ_VERTEX_NEIGHBOR to calculate the FD locational code of an equal-sized neighbor of A in the required direction. These procedures are quite general and can be used with locational codes other than the FD locational code. This generality is reflected in the use of the type *path* instead of *fd_path*. Note also the use of arrays as values that can be transmitted as parameters to procedures, as well as returned as the values of procedures. For an explanation of the semantics of the use of such constructs, see the Appendix.

FD_QT_GTEQ_NEIGHBOR uses procedure MAXLEQ (not given here) to find the FD locational code of a node whose path has the maximum value that is still less than or equal to that of the path to A's equal-sized neighbor. If the node is smaller than A, then the FD locational code of an appropriate gray node is returned. The function TYPE aids in the determination of the type of the neighbor's direction (i.e., vertex or edge). To facilitate the bit manipulation operations, the second argument to the functions ADJ, REFLECT, and COMMON_EDGE is now the numeric code of the quadrant. Similarly, the value of the REFLECT function is the numeric code of the quadrant.

```
fd_locationalcode procedure FD_QT_GTEQ_NEIGHBOR(N,L,I,P);
/* Given a 2^N × 2^N image represented by a linear quadtree in the form of a list L, of the
   FD locational codes of its nodes, return the FD locational code of the neighbor in direc-
   tion I of a node with FD locational code P. If no neighbor exists, then NIL is returned.
   Assume N > 0. */
begin
  value integer N;
  value pointer fd_list L;
  value direction I;
  value pointer fd_locationalcode P;
  fd_path array T[0:N–1];
  pointer fd_locationalcode B,Q;
  if LEV(P) ≥ N then return(NIL); /* No neighbor exists in direction I */
  T ← if TYPE(I) = 'EDGE' then
```

```
            FDL_QT_EQ_EDGE_NEIGHBOR(N,I,PATH(P),LEV(P))
          else FDL_QT_EQ_VERTEX_NEIGHBOR(N,I,PATH(P),LEV(P));
    if null(T) then return(NIL) /* No neighbor exists in direction I */
    else B ← MAXLEQ(T,L); /* Find maximum FD locational code in L that is ≤ T */
  if LEV(B) ≥ LEV(P) then return(B)
  else /* The neighbor is smaller; create a new gray node */
    begin
      Q ← create(fd_locationalcode);
      PATH(Q) ← T;
      LEV(Q) ← LEV(P);
      COL(Q) ← 'GRAY';
      return(Q);
    end;
end;
```

```
  path array procedure FDL_QT_EQ_EDGE_NEIGHBOR(N,I,P,LEVEL);
  /* Given a 2^N × 2^N image represented by an FD linear quadtree, return the path from the
     root to the edge-neighbor in direction I of a node at level LEVEL whose path from the
     root is P. */
  begin
    value integer N;
    value edge I;
    value path array P[0:N-1];
    value integer LEVEL;
    do
      begin
        P[LEVEL] ← REFLECT(I,P[LEVEL]);
        LEVEL ← LEVEL+1;
      end
      until LEVEL = N or ADJ(I,P[LEVEL-1]);
    return(if not(ADJ(I,P[LEVEL-1])) then NIL
          else P);
  end;
```

```
  path array procedure FDL_QT_EQ_VERTEX_NEIGHBOR(N,I,P,LEVEL);
  /* Given a 2^N × 2^N image represented by an FD linear quadtree, return the path from the
     root to the vertex-neighbor in direction I of a node at level LEVEL whose path from the
     root is P. */
  begin
    value integer N;
    value vertex I;
    value path array P[0:N-1];
    value integer LEVEL;
    direction_code PREVIOUS;
    do
      begin
        PREVIOUS ← P[LEVEL];
        P[LEVEL] ← REFLECT(I,PREVIOUS);
```

```
        LEVEL ← LEVEL+1;
     end
     until LEVEL = N or not(ADJ(I,PREVIOUS));
    return(if ADJ(I,PREVIOUS) then NIL
            else if COMMON_EDGE(I,PREVIOUS) ≠ Ω then
              FDL_QT_EQ_EDGE_NEIGHBOR(N,COMMON_EDGE(I,PREVIOUS),
              P,LEVEL)
            else P);
  end;
```

Finding a neighbor in an FD linear octree is performed in an analogous manner. We use a procedure FD_OT_GTEQ_NEIGHBOR that differs mainly from procedure FD_-QT_GTEQ_NEIGHBOR in the additional case of a face-neighbor (processed by procedure FDL_OT_EQ_FACE_NEIGHBOR). The remaining modifications are straightforward and are done in the same manner as for the extension of the quadtree neighbor-finding routines to three dimensions in a pointer-based representation. Once again, to facilitate the bit manipulation operations, the second argument to the functions ADJ, REFLECT, COMMON_EDGE, and COMMON_FACE is now the numeric code of the octant. Similarly the value of the REFLECT function is the numeric code of the octant.

```
  fd_locationalcode procedure FD_OT_GTEQ_NEIGHBOR(N,L,I,P);
  /* Given a 2^N × 2^N × 2^N image represented by a linear octree in the form of a list L, of the
     FD locational codes of its nodes, return the FD locational code of the neighbor in direc-
     tion I of a node with FD locational code P. If no neighbor exists, then NIL is returned.
     Assume N>0. */
  begin
   value integer N;
   value pointer fd_list L;
   value direction I;
   value pointer fd_locationalcode P;
   fd_path array T[0:N−1];
   pointer fd_locationalcode B,Q;
   if LEV(P) ≥ N then return(NIL); /* No neighbor exists in direction I */
   T ← if TYPE(I) = 'FACE' then
        FDL_OT_EQ_FACE_NEIGHBOR(N,I,PATH(P),LEV(P))
      else if TYPE(I) = 'EDGE' then
        FDL_OT_EQ_EDGE_NEIGHBOR(N,I,PATH(P),LEV(P))
      else FDL_OT_EQ_VERTEX_NEIGHBOR(N,I,PATH(P),LEV(P));
   if null(T) then return(NIL) /* No neighbor exists in direction I */
   else B ← MAXLEQ(T,L);
     /* Find maximum FD locational code in L that is ≤ T */
   if LEV(B) ≥ LEV(P) then return(B)
   else /* The neighbor is smaller; create a new gray node */
     begin
      Q ← create(fd_locationalcode);
      PATH(Q) ← T;
      LEV(Q) ← LEV(P);
```

```
      COL(Q) ← 'GRAY';
      return(Q);
    end;
end;
```

path array procedure FDL_OT_EQ_FACE_NEIGHBOR(N,I,P,LEVEL);
/* Given a $2^N \times 2^N \times 2^N$ image represented by an FD linear octree, return the path from
  the root to the face-neighbor in direction I of a node at level LEVEL whose path from the
  root is P. */
begin
  value integer N;
  value face I;
  value path array P[0:N−1];
  value integer LEVEL;
  do
    begin
      P[LEVEL] ← REFLECT(I,P[LEVEL]);
      LEVEL ← LEVEL+1;
    end
    until LEVEL = N **or** ADJ(I,P[LEVEL−1]);
  return(if not(ADJ(I,P[LEVEL−1])) **then** NIL
        else P);
end;

path array procedure FDL_OT_EQ_EDGE_NEIGHBOR(N,I,P,LEVEL);
/* Given a $2^N \times 2^N \times 2^N$ image represented by an FD linear octree, return the path from
  the root to the edge-neighbor in direction I of a node at level LEVEL whose path from
  the root is P. */
begin
  value integer N;
  value edge I;
  value path array P[0:N−1];
  value integer LEVEL;
  direction_code PREVIOUS;
  do
    begin
      PREVIOUS ← P[LEVEL];
      P[LEVEL] ← REFLECT(I,PREVIOUS);
      LEVEL ← LEVEL+1;
    end
    until LEVEL = N **or not**(ADJ(I,PREVIOUS));
  return(if ADJ(I,PREVIOUS) **then** NIL
        else if COMMON_FACE(I,PREVIOUS) $\neq \Omega$ **then**
          FDL_OT_EQ_FACE_NEIGHBOR(N,COMMON_FACE(I,PREVIOUS),
          P,LEVEL)
        else P);
end;

```
path array procedure FDL_OT_EQ_VERTEX_NEIGHBOR(N,I,P,LEVEL);
/* Given a 2^N × 2^N × 2^N image represented by an FD linear octree, return the path from
   the root to the vertex-neighbor in direction I of a node at level LEVEL whose path from
   the root is P. */
begin
  value integer N;
  value vertex I;
  value path array P[0:N−1];
  value integer LEVEL;
  direction_code PREVIOUS;
  do
    begin
      PREVIOUS ← P[LEVEL];
      P[LEVEL] ← REFLECT(I,PREVIOUS);
      LEVEL ← LEVEL+1;
    end
  until LEVEL = N or not(ADJ(I,PREVIOUS));
  return(if ADJ(I,PREVIOUS) then NIL
         else if COMMON_EDGE(I,PREVIOUS) ≠ Ω then
           FDL_OT_EQ_EDGE_NEIGHBOR(N,COMMON_EDGE(I,PREVIOUS),
             P,LEVEL)
         else if COMMON_FACE(I,PREVIOUS) ≠ Ω then
           FDL_OT_EQ_FACE_NEIGHBOR(N,COMMON_FACE(I,PREVIOUS),
             P,LEVEL)
         else P);
end;
```

Exercises

3.27. After having calculated the FD locational code of an equal-sized neighbor, say Q with path T, procedures FD_QT_GTEQ_NEIGHBOR and its octree counterpart determine Q's real size by searching the list of FD locational codes for the FD locational code whose path has the maximum value still less than or equal to that of T, say R—that is, PATH(R) $\leq T$. The levels of the codes are compared to determine the size of the neighbor. Prove that this technique works correctly.

3.28. Why can't you find a neighbor of a node by taking the address of one corner of its block and adding an appropriate quantity corresponding to the block's size and neighbor direction?

3.29. Suppose that the FD locational code is implemented in such a way that the trailing k digits of the path of a node at level k are 3 instead of 0. How does this affect the algorithm for computing the neighbors of greater than or equal size?

3.30. The procedures described in this section made use of parameter transmittal by 'value.' Can you make them more efficient by transmitting parameters by 'reference'?

3.31. What features must a programming language provide so that the algorithms discussed in this section can be implemented efficiently? Compare an implementation in ADA, C, PASCAL, and MODULA 2. Which one yields the most efficient encoding?

3.32. Suppose that the FD linear quadtree and octree contain only the FD locational codes of the black nodes. Modify procedures FD_QT_GTEQ_NEIGHBOR and FD_OT_GTEQ_NEIGHBOR, and the procedures that they invoke, to cope with this definition.

3.33. In Section 2.1.3 we discussed the *two-dimensional run encoding* (*2DRE*) [Lauz85]. It first constructs a linear quadtree in which each of the black and white leaf nodes is encoded with the Morton Matrix number of the pixel that occupies its lower right corner—that is, the pixel having the maximum Morton Matrix number in the leaf node. It assumes that the origin is at the upper left corner of the universe. This is a variant of the FD locational code, which uses only the path from the root to the node and does not require recording the level of the node. The list of leaf nodes is sorted by their corresponding Morton Matrix numbers. Show how to compute edge- and vertex-neighbors of greater than or equal size using such a representation. The result should also indicate the color of the neighbor.

3.34. Suppose that you have a list of the Morton Matrix numbers of a quadtree as described in Exercise 3.33. The 2DRE is formed by viewing this list as a set of subsequences of Morton Matrix numbers corresponding to nodes of the same color and discarding all but the last element of each subsequence of blocks of the same color. Show how to compute edge- and vertex-neighbors of greater than or equal size when a quadtree is represented by the 2DRE method. The result should also indicate the color of the neighbor.

3.35. Show how to compute face-, edge-, and vertex-neighbors of greater than or equal size of a face, an edge, and a vertex when an octree is represented by a list of the Morton Matrix numbers of its leaf nodes. The result should also indicate the color of the neighbor.

3.36. Consider the adaptation of 2DRE discussed in Exercise 3.34 scheme to an octree (the result is a *three-dimensional run encoding* (*3DRE*). Show how to compute face-, edge-, and vertex-neighbors of greater than or equal size when an octree is represented by the 3DRE method. The result should also indicate the color of the neighbor.

3.4.2 FL Linear Quadtree

The FL locational code is similar to the FD locational code. It is also a fixed-length code. The difference is that the FD locational code requires an additional field to record the level of a node, while the FL locational code has an additional possible value for the directional code, which is a *don't care*. Assuming an image of side length 2^n, the FL locational code of each leaf node of side length 2^k is n digits long where the k trailing digits contain a *don't care* directional code, and the leading $n-k$ digits contain the directional codes that locate the leaf along a path from the root of the tree.

The FL locational code of a quadtree (octree) node is a base 5 (9) number. However, all arithmetic operations on the FL locational code are performed using base 4 (8). The directional codes are numeric equivalents of the different quadrants and octants (i.e., 0, 1, 2, and 3 for NW, NE, SW, and SE, respectively, for a quadtree), and 4 denotes a *don't care* (see Exercise 3.37 for the ramifications of representing the *don't care* directional code by 0 and the quadrants by 1, 2, 3, and 4).

Each leaf node in the FL linear quadtree (octree) is represented by its FL locational code. In the version used in this section, we store only the FL locational codes of the black nodes, as proposed by Gargantini [Garg82a]. The FL locational codes of the remaining white (as well as gray) nodes can be inferred from the locational codes of the black leaf nodes. A node's FL locational code is implemented by a record of type *fl_locationalcode* with two fields PATH and COL corresponding to the path from the root to the node and the color of the node, respectively. For an image of maximum side length 2^n, the path, say P, is implemented as an array of type *fl_path* of n directional codes stored in the order $P[n-1]P[n-2] \cdots P[1]P[0]$.

Finding the neighbor of a node A with FL locational code P of size greater than or equal to A is achieved in a manner similar to that used for an FD locational code. The difference is that determining the neighbor's color and size (incorporated in the path) is considerably more complex for an FL linear quadtree for which we know only the FL locational codes of the black nodes. We first construct the path of the FL locational code of the equal-sized desired neighbor, say Q. This procedure is the same as that used for the FD locational code (and uses the same auxiliary procedures—that is, FDL_-QT_EQ_EDGE_NEIGHBOR and FDL_QT_EQ_VERTEX_NEIGHBOR in the case of a quadtree) with the exception that the level of the equal-sized neighbor is obtained by finding the first digit position in PATH(P) that does not contain a *don't care* directional code, say at digit position k (i.e., PATH(P)$[i]$ = DONT_CARE for $0 \le i < k$).

Assume that an equal-sized neighbor exists (i.e., we are not at the border of the image), and let T denote the path of its FL locational code. Now search L, using binary search, for B and H, the FL locational codes whose paths have the maximum value that is still less than T and the minimum value that is still greater than or equal to T, respectively—that is, PATH(B) $< T$ and $T \le$ PATH(H).

If PATH(H) $= T$, then H is the FL locational code of the neighbor that is black and of equal size. If T is a descendant of PATH(H) (i.e., there exists m such that $T[j] =$ PATH(H)$[j]$ for $k < m \le j < n$, and PATH(H)$[j]$ = DONT_CARE for $0 \le j < m$), then H is the FL locational code of the neighbor that is black and of side length 2^m. If PATH(B) is a descendant of T (i.e., $T[j] =$ PATH(B)$[j]$ for $k \le j < n$), then T is the path of the neighbor that is gray and of equal size.

Otherwise the neighbor is white, and we must determine its FL locational code and its size. To do this, we must examine both PATH(B) and PATH(H) to see which one has the larger number of consecutive leading digits that match those of T. Without loss of generality, suppose that it is B and that the first digit that mismatches is at position j—that is, PATH(B)$\lfloor j \rfloor$. This means that the neighbor is white, and its side length is 2^j. The path of its FL locational code is $T[i]$ for the digits in position i ($j \le i < n$), and the remaining digits contain a *don't care* directional code. For example, in Figure 3.1, the western neighbor of node 4, with FL locational code 124, is white node 1, with FL locational code 044.

Procedure FL_QT_GTEQ_NEIGHBOR, given below, is used to calculate the FL locational code of the neighbor of a node, say A with FL locational code P, in an FL linear quadtree. It makes use of procedures FDL_QT_EQ_EDGE_NEIGHBOR and FDL_QT_EQ_-VERTEX_NEIGHBOR to calculate the FL locational code of an equal-sized neighbor of A in the required direction. It uses procedures MAXLESS and MINGEQ (not given here) to search the list of FL locational codes that comprises the linear quadtree to find the FL locational codes of the nearest nodes to A's equal-sized neighbor.

```
fl_locationalcode procedure FL_QT_GTEQ_NEIGHBOR(N,L,I,P);
/* Given a 2^N × 2^N image represented by a linear quadtree in the form of a list L, of the FL
   locational codes of its black nodes, return the FL locational code of the neighbor in
   direction I of a node with FL locational code P. If no neighbor exists, then NIL is
   returned. Assume N > 0. */
begin
  value integer N;
  value pointer fl_list L;
  value direction I;
  value pointer fl_locationalcode P;
  fl_path array T[0:N-1];
  pointer fl_locationalcode B,H,Q;
  constant DONT_CARE;
  integer J,K,M;
  M ← 0;
  /* Find first non–don't care digit: */
  while M < N and PATH(P)[M] = DONT_CARE do M ← M+1;
  if M ≥ N then return(NIL); /* No neighbor exists in direction I */
  T ← if TYPE(I) = 'EDGE' then
         FDL_QT_EQ_EDGE_NEIGHBOR(N,I,PATH(P),LEV(P))
         else FDL_QT_EQ_VERTEX_NEIGHBOR(N,I,PATH(P),LEV(P));
  if null(T) then return(NIL); /* No neighbor exists in direction I */
  B ← MAXLESS(T,L); /* Find maximum FL locational code in L that is <T */
H ← MINGEQ(T,L); /* Find minimum FL locational code in L that is ≥ T */
M ← N-1;
if not(null(H)) then
  begin /* The neighbor is not past the last locational code in L */
    while M ≥ 0 and PATH(H)[M] = T[M] do M ← M-1;
    if M < 0 or PATH(H)[M] = DONT_CARE then
      return(H); /* Neighbor is black and of greater than or equal size */
  end;
Q ← create(fl_locationalcode);
J ← N-1;
if not(null(B)) then
  begin /* The neighbor is not before the first locational code in L */
    while PATH(B)[J] = T[J] do J ← J-1;
    if T[J] = DONT_CARE then
      begin /* B is a descendant of T */
        PATH(Q) ← T;
        COL(Q) ← 'GRAY';
        return(Q);
      end;
  end;
for K←0 step 1 until min(M,J)-1 do T[K] ← DONT_CARE;
PATH(Q) ← T;
COL(Q) ← 'WHITE';
return(Q);
end;
```

Calculating the FL locational code of the neighbor in a linear octree is done in an analogous manner to that used in the linear quadtree. It should be clear that when the locational codes of the white nodes are missing, the neighbor-finding process is considerably more complex than when they are present.

In practice, procedure FL_QT_GTEQ_NEIGHBOR is quite difficult to implement. Arrays were used to represent each FL locational code in order to facilitate the expression of the operations necessary to manipulate it. In actuality, arrays cannot be used because they are very wasteful of storage and would defeat the purpose of using a linear quadtree (octree). Moreover, some of the operations, such as procedures MAXLESS and MINGEQ, which search the list of FL locational codes for the nearest value, are cumbersome when using an array representation of an FL locational code. Thus the FL locational code must be represented as a number.

Decoding the individual directional codes of a particular FL locational code is a complicated process, which requires use of division operations. Unfortunately since the directional codes are represented by base 5 (9) numbers, we cannot replace division operations by shifts unless we are willing to waste much of one bit for each digit by using 3 (4) bits to represent each of the directional codes. For this reason, the FD locational code is more popular, and most implementations retain the locational codes of all of the leaf nodes (not just the black ones). In such a case, many of the basic operations on the locational code can be implemented by use of bit manipulation.

Exercises

3.37. Suppose that the *don't care* directional code in the FL locational code is represented by 0 and the quadrants by 1, 2, 3, and 4 (5, 6, 7, and 8 for an octree). How does this affect the algorithms for computing the neighbors of greater than or equal size?

3.38. Procedure FL_QT_GTEQ_NEIGHBOR contains a loop of the form 'while $M \geq 0$ and PATH(H)[M] = T[M] do M ← M-1;' and another loop of the form 'while PATH(B)[J] = T[J] do J ← J-1;'. Why is there no need to check for '$J \geq 0$' in the second loop?

3.39. Write a procedure FL_OT_GTEQ_NEIGHBOR analogous to FL_QT_GTEQ_NEIGHBOR that computes a neighbor of greater than or equal size in an FL linear octree that contains only the FL locational codes of the black nodes.

3.40. Suppose that the FL linear quadtree and octree contain the FL locational codes of all the leaf nodes (i.e., both black and white). Modify procedures FL_QT_GTEQ_NEIGHBOR and FL_OT_GTEQ_NEIGHBOR and the procedures that they invoke to cope with this definition.

3.4.3 VL Linear Quadtree

The VL locational code is similar to the FL locational code with the principal difference being that it is based on using a variable-length locational code. It is of varying length as a result of letting 0 represent the *don't care* directional code, while the values 1, 2,

3, and 4 represent NW, NE, SW, and SE, respectively. Assuming an image of side length 2^n, the VL locational code of each leaf node of side length 2^k is just $n-k$ digits long. It is formed in a manner analogous to that for the FL locational code, which is n digits long, with the exception that the leading k digits contain a *don't care* directional code. Since the leading digits are 0, there is no reason to represent them explicitly in the VL locational code. This is why we have a variable-length code. For example, the VL locational code of node 4 in Figure 3.1 is number 23.

Each leaf node in the VL linear quadtree (octree) is represented by its VL locational code. In the version used in this section, we store only the VL locational codes of the black nodes. The VL locational codes of the remaining white (as well as gray) nodes can be inferred from the locational codes of the black leaf nodes. Finding the neighbor of a node A, of size greater than or equal to A, given A's VL locational code is achieved in a manner similar to that used for an FL locational code. We first construct the path of the VL locational code of the equal-sized desired neighbor, say Q. This procedure is easier than the one used for the FL locational code since we need not look for the first digit position that does not contain a *don't care* directional code. However, we still use the same auxiliary procedures: FDL_QT_EQ_EDGE_NEIGHBOR and FDL_QT_EQ_VERTEX_NEIGHBOR.

Assuming that an equal-sized neighbor exists (i.e., we are not at the border of the image), the remainder of the process is more complex since when the list of VL locational codes is kept in a sorted order, the sequence corresponds to a form of a breadth-first traversal of the tree. This means that VL locational codes do not satisfy the relation that the descendants of a given FL locational code, Q, immediately precede it in a sorted list. This was useful because we can determine the identity of the desired FL locational code, say D, by examining the maximum FL locational code that is less than D and the minimum FL locational code that is greater than or equal to D.

The VL locational code of an equal-sized neighbor is obtained as follows. Calculate the VL locational code of the neighbor, say D. If D does not correspond to a black leaf node, then we may need to search for a containing node in up to n lists—one for each level. This is in contrast to procedures FL_QT_GTEQ_NEIGHBOR and FL_OT_GTEQ_NEIGHBOR that require only a search of the list of FL locational codes of the entire image. Procedures VL_QT_GTEQ_NEIGHBOR and VL_OT_GTEQ_NEIGHBOR could be made more efficient by exploiting the fact that the digits of the locational code can often be manipulated by use of modulo 5 operations.

Exercises

3.41. Write a pair of procedures VL_QT_GTEQ_NEIGHBOR and VL_OT_GTEQ_NEIGHBOR to compute a neighbor of greater than or equal size in a VL linear quadtree and octree that contain only the VL locational codes of the black nodes.

3.42. Suppose that the VL linear quadtree and octree contain the VL locational codes of all the leaf nodes (i.e., both black and white). Rewrite procedures VL_QT_GTEQ_NEIGHBOR and VL_OT_GTEQ_NEIGHBOR, and the procedures that they invoke, to cope with this definition.

3.4.4 DF-Expressions

The second pointerless representation discussed is one that represents the image in the form of a traversal of the nodes of its tree. This is commonly termed a DF-expression [Kawa80a] (see Section 2.2). Neighbor finding is not very convenient using such a representation since there is no notion of random access. For example, a node is identified only by its position in the traversal of the tree and is represented by a code corresponding to its type (i.e., black, white, or gray). We have no explicit information on the path from the root of the tree to it. Thus to perform neighbor finding, it is necessary to start at the root of the tree and locate the node whose neighbor we are seeking, remember the path to it, compute the path to its neighbor, and then sequentially search the list for the neighbor starting at the root of the tree.

This is a cumbersome process, and what usually happens is that algorithms that require neighbor finding are recoded in such a way that neighbor finding is avoided. For example, Samet and Tamminen [Same85f, Same88b] present a method for computing geometric properties of images represented by pointerless quadtree representations that does not require neighbor-finding operations (see Section 5.1.3). Instead they use a data structure termed an *active border*.

Exercise

3.43. Show how to compute face-, edge-, and vertex-neighbors of greater than or equal size in an image represented as a DF-expression. The input is an index into the list representing the DF-expression, and the output should be a pointer to the element in the list corresponding to the neighbor.

CONVERSION 4

The quadtree is proposed as a representation for binary images because its hierarchical nature facilitates the performance of a large number of operations. However, most images are traditionally represented by use of methods such as binary arrays, rasters (i.e., runlength codes), chain codes (i.e., boundaries), or polygons (i.e., vectors), some of which are chosen for hardware reasons (e.g., runlength codes are particularly useful for raster-like devices, such as television). Therefore techniques that can efficiently switch among these various representations are needed. This chapter discusses a number of such techniques and presents algorithms for some of them. Expected execution times are derived for many of the algorithms. The analysis is heavily dependent on the results of Section 3.2.1.2.

The discussion is primarily in the context of a pointer-based representation of a region quadtree. However, an algorithm is presented for building a linear quadtree (i.e., a pointerless representation) from a raster representation. In addition, it is shown how to build a PM_1 quadtree for a polygonal map. This is important for applications where the approximation of a line by a sequence of pixels, as done by the region quadtree, is inadequate. Conversion algorithms involving the bintree and the numerous other variants of pointerless representations discussed in Chapter 2 are left as exercises. Finally, a number of techniques are described to build octrees in applications in computer vision and robotics where the input is a set of views of an object or a scene of three-dimensional objects.

In the algorithms described, it is assumed that each quadtree node is implemented as a record of type *node* as defined in Section 1.5. Heavy use is made of a number of functions that were described in Section 3.1 (e.g., ADJ, REFLECT, COMMON_-EDGE and some neighbor computation algorithms).

The relationships among the various edges are specified by use of the functions OPEDGE, CEDGE, and CCEDGE. Given an edge E, they correspond, respectively, to the edge opposite to E, adjacent to E in the clockwise direction, and adjacent to E in the counterclockwise direction; for example, OPEDGE('N') = 'S', CEDGE('N') = 'E', and

CCEDGE('N') = 'W'. The relationships among the various quadrants are specified by OPQUAD, CQUAD, and CCQUAD with similar meanings. Thus, OPQUAD('NW') = 'SE', CQUAD('NW') = 'NE', and CCQUAD('NW') = 'SW'.

The relationship between edges and quadrants, and edges and vertices, is specified by the functions QUAD and VERTEX, respectively. QUAD(E_1,E_2) yields the quadrant that is adjacent to edges E_1 and E_2 of its parent. Likewise, VERTEX(E_1,E_2) yields the vertex of the block, say B, at which edges E_1 and E_2 of B meet. For example, QUAD('N','W') = 'NW' and VERTEX('N','W') = 'NW'.

4.1 BINARY ARRAYS

The most common image representation is the binary array. There are a number of ways to construct a quadtree from a binary array. The simplest approach is one that converts the array to a complete quadtree (i.e., for a $2^n \times 2^n$ image, a tree of height n with one node per pixel). The resulting quadtree is subsequently reduced in size by repeated attempts at merging groups of four pixels or four blocks of a uniform color that are appropriately aligned. This approach is simple but extremely wasteful of storage since many nodes will be needlessly created. In fact, it is not inconceivable that available memory may be exhausted when an algorithm employing this approach is used, whereas the resulting quadtree fits in the available memory.

We can avoid the needless creation of nodes by visiting the elements of the

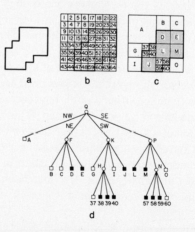

Figure 4.1   An example (a) region, (b) its binary array representation where the pixels are labeled in the order in which they are visited when building the quadtree from the array representation, (c) its maximal blocks (blocks in the region are shaded), and (d) the corresponding quadtree

binary array in a specific order. For example, for a $2^3 \times 2^3$ image array the order is defined by the labels on the array in Figure 4.1b (which corresponds to the image of Figure 4.1a). This order is also known as a Morton order [Mort66] (discussed in Section 1.4). By using such a method, a leaf node is never created until it is known to be maximal. An equivalent statement is that the situation does not arise in which four leaf nodes of the same color require changing the color of their parent from gray to black or white, as is appropriate. For example, we note that since pixels 25, 26, 27, and 28 in Figure 4.1b are all of the same color, no quadtree nodes were created for them; that is, node D in Figure 4.1d corresponds to the part of the image spanned by them.

The binary array-to-quadtree construction algorithm [Same80b] examines each pixel in the binary array only once and in a manner analogous to a postorder tree traversal. The main procedure is termed ARRAY_TO_QUADTREE and is invoked with the values of the log of the image diameter (n for a $2^n \times 2^n$ image array) and the name of the image array. It controls the construction of the quadtree. If the image is all white or all black, it creates the appropriate one-node tree.

The actual construction of the tree is performed by procedure CONSTRUCT, which recursively examines all the pixels and creates nodes whenever all four sons are not of the same type. The tree is built as CONSTRUCT returns from examining its sons. CONSTRUCT makes use of the type *color* to indicate the color of a pixel or the type of a node. Individual nodes are created by procedure CREATE_QNODE. The image is represented as an array of pointers to records of type *pixel*, one of whose fields is COL, denoting its color (i.e., black or white).

As an example of the application of the algorithm, consider the region in Figure 4.1a. Figure 4.1b is a labeling of the pixels that reflects the order in which they are examined by the algorithm. Figure 4.1c is the corresponding maximal block decomposition, while Figure 4.1d is its quadtree representation. Blocks in Figure 4.1c with alphabetic labels correspond to instances where merging has taken place. The alphabetic labels have been assigned according to the order in which the merged nodes were created (i.e., A, B, C, $\cdots$). Figure 4.2 shows the partial quadtrees after pixels 37–40, 33–48, and 17–32 have been examined.

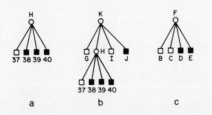

Figure 4.2   Intermediate trees in the process of obtaining a
quadtree corresponding to Figure 4.1a. Partial quadtrees
after processing pixels (a) 37–40, (b) 33–48, and (c) 17–32

```
pointer node procedure ARRAY_TO_QUADTREE(A,LEVEL);
/* Construct a quadtree for the 2^LEVEL × 2^LEVEL image in pixel array A. The origin is
   assumed to be at the NW-most pixel of the image. */
begin
  global pointer pixel array A[1:2↑LEVEL,1:2↑LEVEL];
  value integer LEVEL;
  /* XF and YF contain multiplicative factors to aid in the location of the pixels while des-
     cending the quadtree. */
  preload global integer array XF['NW','NE','SW','SE'] with 1,0,1,0;
  preload global integer array YF['NW','NE','SW','SE'] with 1,1,0,0;
  quadrant I;
  pointer node P;
  color C;
  P ← CONSTRUCT(LEVEL,2↑LEVEL,2↑LEVEL,C);
  /* Create a one-node quadtree if the entire image is black or white: */
  return(if null(P) then  CREATE_QNODE(NIL,NIL,C)
         else P);
end;


recursive pointer node procedure CONSTRUCT(LEVEL,X,Y,C);
/* Construct a quadtree corresponding to the 2^LEVEL × 2^LEVEL portion of the pixel array A
   whose SE-most pixel is A[X,Y].  C is used to indicate whether the portion is all of one
   color. */
begin
  value integer LEVEL,X,Y;
  reference color C;
  pointer node array P['NW'...'SE'];
  color array T['NW'...'SE'];
  quadrant I;
  pointer node Q;
  integer D;
  if LEVEL = 0 then /* At a pixel? */
    begin /* Yes */
      C ← COL(A[X,Y]);
      return(NIL);
    end
  else
    begin
      LEVEL ← LEVEL−1;
      D ← 2↑LEVEL;
      for I in {'NW', 'NE', 'SW', 'SE'} do
        P[I] ← CONSTRUCT(LEVEL,X−XF[I]∗D,Y−YF[I]∗D,T[I]);
      if T['NW'] ≠ 'GRAY' and (T['NW'] = T['NE'] = T['SW'] =T['SE']) then
        begin /* All four brothers are of the same leaf node type */
          C ← T['NW'];
          return(NIL);
        end
      else
```

```
      begin /* Create a nonleaf gray node */
        Q ← CREATE_QNODE(NIL,NIL,'GRAY');
        for I in {'NW', 'NE', 'SW', 'SE'} do
          begin
            /* Create a maximal node for P[I] if there is no son in quadrant I. */
            if null(P[I]) then P[I] ← CREATE_QNODE(Q,I,T[I])
            else
              begin
                SON(Q,I) ← P[I];
                FATHER(P[I]) ← Q;
              end;
          end;
          C ← 'GRAY';
          return(Q);
        end;
      end;
    end;

pointer node procedure CREATE_QNODE(ROOT,T,C);
/* Create a node with color C corresponding to son T of node ROOT and return a pointer
   to it. When ROOT is NIL, the transmitted actual parameter value corresponding to T is
   NIL and is ignored. */
begin
  value pointer node ROOT;
  value quadrant T;
  value color C;
  pointer node P;
  quadrant I;
  P ← create(node);
  if not(null(ROOT)) then SON(ROOT,T) ← P;
  /* Created node has a father */
  FATHER(P) ← ROOT;
  NODETYPE(P) ← C;
  for I in {'NW', 'NE', 'SW', 'SE'} do SON(P,I) ← NIL;
  return(P);
end;
```

The execution time of the binary array-to-quadtree construction algorithm is proportional to four-thirds the number of pixels in the image since this is the number of times procedure CONSTRUCT is invoked (and equal to the number of nodes in a complete quadtree for a $2^n \times 2^n$ image). The algorithm is highly recursive. However, the maximum depth of recursion is equal to the log of the image diameter (i.e., n for a $2^n \times 2^n$ image).

Exercises

4.1. Modify procedures ARRAY_TO_QUADTREE and CONSTRUCT to yield an octree (i.e., a three-dimensional quadtree).

4.2. Modify procedures ARRAY_TO_QUADTREE and CONSTRUCT to yield an FD linear quadtree. In this case, you will need to construct a set of locational codes instead of building a tree.

4.3. Modify procedures ARRAY_TO_QUADTREE and CONSTRUCT to yield a quadtree in the form of a DF-expression. Can you see any problems in performing this task using a one-pass algorithm? Recall that a DF-expression is in essence a preorder traversal of the quadtree, while procedures ARRAY_TO_QUADTREE and CONSTRUCT traverse the quadtree in postorder.

4.4. Modify procedures ARRAY_TO_QUADTREE and CONSTRUCT to yield a VL linear quadtree. Recall that the VL linear quadtree is especially useful when the locational codes for the individual blocks are sorted in increasing order. The sorted list corresponds to a breadth-first traversal of the quadtree. Is there a problem in getting a breadth-first traversal (not necessarily sorted) by using the above procedures?

4.5. Modify procedures ARRAY_TO_QUADTREE and CONSTRUCT to yield a bintree. To do this, you will have to keep track of whether the array is being subdivided along the x or y axes.

4.6. Modify the results of Exercise 4.5 to construct a bintree for an n-dimensional image.

4.7. Procedure CONSTRUCT visits the elements of the binary array in Morton order. Other orders have also been used. For example, Grosky, Li, and Jain [Gros81] suggest using an order based on the Peano-Hilbert [Hilb91] space-filling curve (see Figure 1.19b and the accompanying discussion in Section 1.4). In essence, the elements of the array are visited in such an order that for successive elements the value of either the x coordinate or the y coordinate, but not both, is incremented by one. The key is that as the scanning of one quadrant is finished, only one step in the x or y direction is necessary to reach the starting point of the next quadrant. For example, the pixels in the 8×8 array of Figure 4.1b are visited in the order 1, 2, 4, 3, 9, 11, 12, 10, 13, 15, 16, 14, 8, 7, 5, 6, etc. What is the order in which the remaining elements are visited? Give an algorithm to build a quadtree in such a manner.

4.2 ROW OR RASTER REPRESENTATIONS

An image usually exists as a sequential file where row i precedes row $i + 1$. Recall from Section 1.3 that such a representation is termed a *raster* representation, consisting of a list of the pixels ordered by rows. When the image is large, it is not practical to read it into memory as an array and then convert it to a quadtree. Instead it is preferable to scan the image in a row-by-row manner as the quadtree is constructed.

An image is usually displayed on a raster device, and thus there is also a need for a method to convert a quadtree to a row-by-row representation. In the following, methods are presented for the conversion between quadtrees and raster representations. The raster representation can be improved upon by aggregating the pixels in each row into one-dimensional blocks of identically valued pixels (termed *runs* [Ruto68]). We make use of runs in the algorithm for converting a quadtree to a raster representation.

Empirical tests have shown that in an environment in which images are too large to fit into internal memory, a great part of the execution time is spent in the insertion of nodes and merging them. An algorithm is also presented to build a pointerless quadtree representation (i.e., a linear quadtree) from a raster representation that reduces the number of nodes requiring insertion by a significant amount.

4.2.1   Building a Quadtree from a Raster Representation

The key to the raster-to-quadtree algorithm [Same81a] is that at any instant of time (i.e., after each pixel in a row has been processed), a valid quadtree exists with all unprocessed (also termed *uncolored*) pixels presumed to be white. Thus as the quadtree is built, nodes are merged to yield maximal blocks. This contrasts with an algorithm that first builds a complete quadtree with one node per pixel and then attempts a merge. This is quite wasteful of space, as pointed out in Section 4.1.

The main procedure of the raster-to-quadtree construction algorithm is called RASTER_TO_QUADTREE. It is invoked with a pointer to the first row and the width of the image. Assume that the image has an even number of rows. One of the arguments to RASTER_TO_QUADTREE is the number of pixels in each row. The algorithm will work for any image having at least two rows and two pixels per row. Assume that the

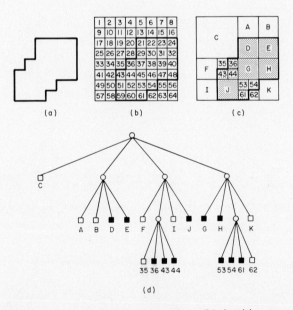

Figure 4.3   *An example (a) region, (b) its binary array representation where the pixels are labeled in the order in which they were visited in the process of constructing the quadtree from the raster representation, (c) its maximal block decomposition (blocks in the region are shaded), and (d) the corresponding quadtree*

image contains an even number of rows. If the image contains an odd number of rows, it is presumed that one extra row of white has been added. The resulting quadtree corresponds to a square image of a side length that is a power of 2. All pixels that are added so that this condition is satisfied are treated as white.

The image is represented as a list of records of type *rowlist*, each of which has two fields, ROW and NEXT. ROW corresponds to an array of records of type *pixel* (see the definition in Section 4.1), and NEXT is a pointer to a record of type *rowlist*, the next element in the list.

As an example of the application of the algorithm, consider the region given in Figure 4.3a. Its decomposition into rows is given in Figure 4.3b. Figure 4.3c is the corresponding block decomposition, and Figure 4.3d is its quadtree representation. It is analogous to Figure 4.1, except that the pixels have been numbered in the order in which the raster-to-quadtree algorithm processes them. All nodes resulting from merging have been labeled with letters (A–K). The alphabetical order corresponds to the order in which the merged nodes were created. Figure 4.4 shows the steps in the construction of the quadtree corresponding to the first four pixels of the first row (pixels 1, 2, 3, and 4). Figures 4.5 and 4.6 show the resulting tree after the first and second rows have been processed.

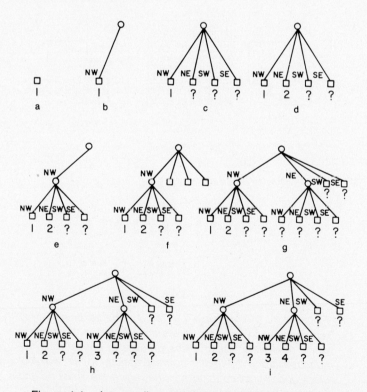

Figure 4.4   Intermediate quadtrees in the process of obtaining a quadtree for the first half of the first row in Figure 4.3

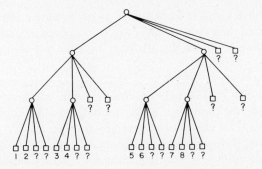

Figure 4.5   The quadtree after processing the first row in Figure 4.3a

Procedures ODDROW and EVENROW are used to add odd-numbered and even-numbered rows, respectively, to the tree. This is achieved by using procedures ADD_EDGE_NEIGHBOR and CREATE_QNODE to locate neighboring nodes and create nodes for pixels that have no corresponding node in the tree. Procedure MERGE is responsible for replacing any gray node having four sons of the same color by a node of the same color.

The amount of work required depends on whether an odd-numbered or even-numbered row is being processed. Clearly no odd-numbered row can lead to a merge of nodes unless it is the last row. Thus odd-numbered rows do not require as much processing as even-numbered rows.

For an odd-numbered row, the tree is constructed by processing the row from left to right, adding a node to the tree for each pixel. As the quadtree is constructed, nonleaf nodes must also be added. Since we wish to have a valid quadtree after processing each pixel, whenever we add a nonleaf node, we also add, as is appropri-

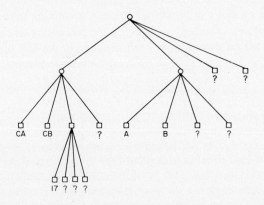

Figure 4.6   The quadtree after processing the second row in Figure 4.3a

ate, three or four nodes said to be uncolored as its remaining sons. These nodes are treated as white until their corresponding pixels have been processed. In our figures, we label them with a '?' to indicate that they have not yet been assigned their final color.

Procedure ADD_EDGE_NEIGHBOR is analogous to QT_EQ_EDGE_NEIGHBOR (see Section 3.2.1.1) in that FATHER links are traversed until encountering a nearest common ancestor. Once the ancestor is found, we descend along a path that is reflected about the axis formed by the common boundary between the two pixels. The difference is that a nearest common ancestor does not exist when the pixel whose neighbor is sought is currently at the extreme right of the row. In such a case, a nonleaf node is added with its three remaining sons being white (e.g., Figure 4.4c and 4.4f).

Once the nearest common ancestor and its three sons are added, we again descend along a path reflected about the axis formed by the boundary of the pixel whose neighbor we seek. During this descent, a white node is converted to a gray node and four uncolored sons are added (e.g., Figure 4.4g). As a final step, the leaf node is colored appropriately (e.g., Figure 4.4d and 4.4h). In the example, Figures 4.4a, 4.4b–d, 4.4e–h, and 4.4i are snapshots of the quadtree construction process for the nodes corresponding to pixels 1, 2, 3, and 4, respectively, of Figure 4.3b.

Even-numbered rows require more work since merging may also take place. In particular, a check for a possible merge must be performed at every even-numbered vertical position (i.e., every even-numbered pixel in an even-numbered row). Once a merge occurs, we may have to check if another merge is possible. In particular, for pixel position $(a \cdot 2^i, b \cdot 2^j)$ where $a \bmod 2 = b \bmod 2 = 1$ and $i, j \geq 1$, a maximum of $k = \min(i, j)$ merges is possible. For example, at pixel 28 of Figure 4.3b (i.e., position (4,4)) a maximum of two merges is possible, and indeed this is how block C Figure 4.3c has been obtained.

The fact that merging does take place necessitates an additional amount of bookkeeping. In particular, we wish to keep track of the position in the tree where the next pixel is to be added, as well as of the next row. Prior to attempting a merge, a node corresponding to the next pixel in the image is added to the quadtree (e.g., node 11 is added to the quadtree in Figure 4.7 prior to attempting to merge nodes 1, 2, 9, and 10 of Figure 4.3b). Similarly we precede the processing of each even-numbered row by adding to the quadtree a node corresponding to the first pixel in the next row (e.g., node 17 in quadtree of Figure 4.7 was added prior to processing row 2 of Figure 4.3b).

pointer node procedure RASTER_TO_QUADTREE(P,WIDTH);
/* Construct a quadtree corresponding to the image whose binary representation is contained in a list of rows, WIDTH pixels wide, pointed at by P. Procedure ADD_EDGE_-NEIGHBOR uses global variable NEWROOT to keep track of the root of the quadtree as it is built in procedures ADD_EDGE_NEIGHBOR and CREATE_QNODE. MAXSIZE is the maximum length of a side of an image for which a quadtree can be built and must be a power of two. It is used to enable merging white nodes at the extreme right and bottom of an image that is not a square and of side length that is a power of two. */

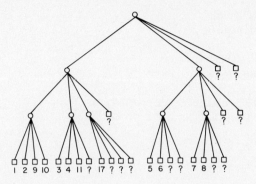

Figure 4.7   The quadtree prior to merging nodes 1, 2, 9,
and 10 in Figure 4.3a

```
begin
  value pointer rowlist P;
  value integer WIDTH;
  global pointer node NEWROOT;
  global integer constant MAXSIZE;
  pixel array Q [1:WIDTH];
  pointer node FIRST;
  integer I;
  Q ← ROW(P);
  FIRST ← CREATE_QNODE(NIL,NIL,Q[1]);
  ODDROW(WIDTH,Q,FIRST);
  P ← NEXT(P);
  I ← 2;
  FIRST ← EVENROW(I,WIDTH,null(NEXT(P)),ROW(P),
                    ADD_EDGE_NEIGHBOR(FIRST,'S','WHITE'));
  while not(null(P←NEXT(P))) do /* Assume an even number of rows */
    begin
      ODDROW(WIDTH,ROW(P),FIRST);
      P ← NEXT(P);
      I ← I+2;
      FIRST ← EVENROW(I,WIDTH,null(NEXT(P)),ROW(P),
                        ADD_EDGE_NEIGHBOR(FIRST,'S','WHITE'));
    end;
  return(NEWROOT); /* Return the root of the quadtree */
end;

  procedure ODDROW(W,Q,R);
  /* Add an odd-numbered row of width W, represented by Q, to a quadtree whose node R
     corresponds to the first pixel in the row. */
  begin
    value integer W;
```

```
value pixel array Q[1:W];
reference pointer node R;
integer I;
NODETYPE(R) ← COL(Q[1]);
for I←2 step 1 until W do
  begin
    R ← ADD_EDGE_NEIGHBOR(R,'E','WHITE');
    NODETYPE(R) ← COL(Q[I]);
  end;
end;
```

node procedure EVENROW(I,W,LASTROW,Q,FIRST);
/* Add row I, an even-numbered row of width W represented by Q, to a quadtree whose node FIRST corresponds to the first pixel in the row. During this process, merges of nodes having four sons of the same color are performed. The value returned is a pointer to the node corresponding to the first pixel in row I+1 unless row I is the last row (denoted by LASTROW), in which case the value returned is irrelevant. For the last column in the row, merging is attempted for the white nodes at the extreme right of the image by setting the column to MAXSIZE. For the last row in the image, merging is attempted for the white nodes at the bottom of the image by setting the row number to MAXSIZE. */

```
begin
  value integer I,W;
  value Boolean LASTROW;
  value pixel array Q[1:W];
  reference pointer node FIRST;
  global integer constant MAXSIZE;
  integer J;
  pointer node P,R;
  P ← FIRST;
  if not(LASTROW) then /* Remember the first node of the next row */
    FIRST ← ADD_EDGE_NEIGHBOR(P,'S','WHITE')
  else I ← MAXSIZE; /* Enable merging white nodes on the bottom of the image */
  for J←1 step 1 until W−1 do
    begin
      R ← ADD_EDGE_NEIGHBOR(P,'E', 'WHITE');
      NODETYPE(P) ← COL(Q[J]);
      if (J mod 2) = 0 then MERGE(I,J,FATHER(P));
      P ← R;
    end; /* Don't invoke ADD_EDGE_NEIGHBOR for the last pixel in a row */
  NODETYPE(P) ← COL(Q[W]);
  /* Merge white nodes at the extreme right of the image: */
  MERGE(I,MAXSIZE,FATHER(P));
  return(FIRST);
end;
```

recursive pointer node procedure ADD_EDGE_NEIGHBOR(Q,E,C);

/* Return a pointer to a node corresponding to the pixel that is adjacent in the direction of edge E to the pixel represented by node Q. This is done by finding the nearest common ancestor of the two nodes and creating one if it does not exist. Whenever a nearest common ancestor or other nodes are created, the color of all created sons is set to C. They are later reset to gray, black, or white, as appropriate. NEWROOT is used to keep track of the root of the quadtree as it is constructed. */

```
begin
  value pointer node Q;
  value edge E;
  value color C;
  global pointer node NEWROOT;
  pointer node P;
  quadrant I,SONTYPEOFQ;
  if null(FATHER(Q)) then /* Nearest common ancestor does not exist */
    begin
      /* Create a nearest common ancestor: */
      NEWROOT ← P ← CREATE_QNODE(NIL,NIL,'GRAY');
      FATHER(Q) ← P;
      SONTYPEOFQ ← QUAD(CCEDGE(E),OPEDGE(E));
      SON(P,SONTYPEOFQ) ← Q;
      /* Create three sons */
      CREATE_QNODE(P,OPQUAD(SONTYPEOFQ),C);
      CREATE_QNODE(P,OPQUAD(REFLECT(E,SONTYPEOFQ)),C);
      return(CREATE_QNODE(P,REFLECT(E,SONTYPEOFQ),C));
    end
  else if ADJ(E,SONTYPE(Q)) then P ← ADD_EDGE_NEIGHBOR(FATHER(Q),E,C)
  else P ← FATHER(Q);
  /* Trace a path from the nearest common ancestor to the adjacent node, creating white
     sons and relabeling nonleaf nodes to gray as necessary: */
  if null(SON(P,REFLECT(E,SONTYPE(Q)))) then
    begin
      NODETYPE(P) ← 'GRAY';
      for I in {'NW', 'NE', 'SW', 'SE'} do CREATE_QNODE(P,I,C);
    end;
  return(SON(P,REFLECT(E,SONTYPE(Q))));
end;
```

procedure MERGE(I,J,P);

/* Attempt to merge a node having four sons of the same color starting with node P at row I and column J. */

```
begin
  value integer I,J;
  value pointer node P;
  while (I mod 2) = 0 and (J mod 2) = 0 and
        NODETYPE(SON(P,'NW')) = NODETYPE(SON(P,'NE')) =
        NODETYPE(SON(P,'SW')) = NODETYPE(SON(P,'SE')) do
```

```
/* Since we start with a pixel-sized node, it is impossible for the four sons to be gray
   nodes. */
begin
   I ← I/2;
   J ← J/2;
   NODETYPE(P) ← NODETYPE(SON(P,'NW'));
   returnsonstoavail(P);
   P ← FATHER(P);
   end;
end;
```

The execution time of the raster-to-quadtree construction process is measured by the number of nodes visited. Thus we only need to analyze the amount of time used by procedures ADD_EDGE_NEIGHBOR and MERGE. Assume a $2^n \times 2^n$ image. Since procedure ADD_EDGE_NEIGHBOR visits each pixel in the image, we can use the part of the analysis of procedure QT_EQ_EDGE_NEIGHBOR (see Theorem 3.1) for a row where all nodes appear at level 0. In particular, the total number of nodes visited by ADD_EDGE_NEIGHBOR is bounded by four times the number of pixels in the image.

The analysis of procedure MERGE is also quite straightforward. Recall that merging is attempted only at specified grid positions. An upper bound on the number of nodes checked for merging is attained when all of the pixels are of the same color. This leads to the following lemma:

Lemma 4.1 The number of nodes examined for merging is bounded by four-thirds times the number of pixels (i.e., 2^{2n}).

Proof Each time a merge is attempted, we are at a node corresponding to a pixel position $(a \cdot 2^i, b \cdot 2^j)$ where $a \bmod 2 = b \bmod 2 = 1$ and $i, j \geq 1$. Let $k = \min(i, j)$. For $k = 1$, three additional nodes must be visited and checked if they are of the same color as the node at pixel position $(a \cdot 2^i, b \cdot 2^j)$. If $k > 1$, and if the node corresponding to pixel position $(a \cdot 2^i, b \cdot 2^j)$ has the same color as the nodes in pixel positions $(a \cdot 2^i, b \cdot 2^j - 1)$, $(a \cdot 2^i - 1, b \cdot 2^j)$, and $(a \cdot 2^i - 1, b \cdot 2^j - 1)$, then we reapply the test to the three nodes that are brothers of the merged node, and so forth. For a $2^n \times 2^n$ image, there are 2^{2n-2} pixels such that $k = 1$, 2^{2n-4} pixels such that $k = 2$, $\cdots$, 2^{2n-2l} pixels such that $k = l$, and 2^0 pixels such that $k = n$. Therefore the maximum number of nodes that can be visited by MERGE is $\sum_{k=1}^{n} 4 \cdot 2^{2n-2k}$, which can be simplified using Equation 3.3 of Section 3.2.1.2 to yield $4 \cdot (2^{2n} - 1)/3$. ☐

Using Lemma 4.1 and the fact that the number of nodes visited by procedure ADD_EDGE_NEIGHBOR is bounded by four times the number of pixels, we have that a quadtree can be constructed from a raster representation in time proportional to the number of pixels.

Exercises

4.8. Modify procedure RASTER_TO_QUADTREE and the procedures it invokes to work for an image that contains an odd number of rows.

4.9. Procedure RASTER_TO_QUADTREE builds a quadtree by processing an image array from left to right and from top to bottom. Modify it so that the image can be processed from right to left and from bottom to top. Will procedure ADD_EDGE_NEIGHBOR need any modification? Generalize your result to cope with the remaining raster-scanning sequences (i.e., left to right and from bottom to top; right to left and from top to bottom).

4.10. Procedure RASTER_TO_QUADTREE constructs the quadtree in a bottom-up manner. The quadtree can also be built in a top-down manner. In this case, once the width of the image is known, the tree can be built by using a recursive algorithm. The advantage over the bottom-up approach is that there is no need for neighbor finding when adding neighbors. Of course, this is achieved at the cost of a stack. The advantage of the top-down approach is not immediately apparent because the cost of neighbor finding is not very high. Write a procedure to construct the quadtree in a top-down manner.

4.11. Modify procedure RASTER_TO_QUADTREE to yield an octree (i.e., a three-dimensional quadtree).

4.12. Prove that the number of nodes visited by procedure ADD_EDGE_NEIGHBOR is bounded by four times the number of pixels in the image. You will have to decompose the analysis into two parts: one for finding neighbors in the horizontal direction and one for the vertical direction.

4.13. Modify procedure RASTER_TO_QUADTREE to yield a bintree. To do this, you will need to change the conditions under which a merge is attempted. You may wish to use the results of Exercise 3.4 to locate neighbors in a bintree.

4.14. Can you modify procedure RASTER_TO_QUADTREE to yield an FD linear quadtree? In this case, you will need to construct a set of locational codes instead of building a tree. If this is not easily done, explain the problems and present an alternative solution. Your solution should not make more than one pass over the data.

4.15. Modify procedures RASTER_TO_QUADTREE to yield a quadtree in the form of a DF-expression. Can you see any problems in performing this task using a one-pass algorithm? Would an alternative method be more efficient? Recall that a DF-expression is in essence a preorder traversal of the quadtree, and it is stored as a list. Thus the repeated need to do neighbor finding may be rather expensive since a sequential search will have to be performed. Analyze the speed of the algorithm in terms of the number of elements of the DF-expression that will have to be visited (how is this related to the number of pixels in the image?).

4.2.2   Building a Raster Representation from a Quadtree

The most obvious method to build a raster representation from a quadtree is to generate an array corresponding to the quadtree, but this method may require more memory than is available and is not considered here. In [Same84a], a number of quadtree-to-raster algorithms are described. All of the algorithms traverse the quadtree by rows from left to right and visit each quadtree node once for each row that intersects it. For example, for pixels 1–8 in the first row of Figure 4.8b, node A of Figure 4.8d is visited first, followed by nodes B, C, D, and E). Each black and white node

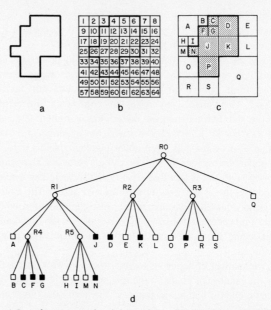

Figure 4.8   An example (a) region, (b) its binary array representation where the blocks and pixels are labeled in the order in which they are output in the process of constructing a raster representation from a quadtree, (c) its maximal decomposition (blocks in the region are shaded), and (d) the corresponding quadtree

at level j in the tree is visited 2^j times (i.e., its height in pixels). Each such visit results in the output of a run of length 2^j (e.g., a run of length 2 for node A of Figure 4.8c).

In the following, we discuss two of the algorithms; one is *top-down* and the other is *bottom-up*. The top-down algorithm, given by ALG1, starts at the root each time it visits a node that participates in a row. In contrast, the bottom-up algorithm, given by ALG2, visits adjacent blocks in a row by use of neighbor-finding techniques. A number of variations of these algorithms are discussed further in the exercises. We distinguish among these variations by using the name ALG*i* instead of QUADTREE_TO_-RASTER.

Both ALG1 and ALG2 make use of procedure FIND_2D_BLOCK to locate the block containing the segment of the row being output. Its parameters are the coordinates of the upper left corner of the leftmost pixel of the segment that is to be output and the coordinates of the lower right corner of a block (may be a nonleaf node) in the image containing the segment. FIND_2D_BLOCK partitions this block repeatedly until the smallest block corresponding to a leaf node is found that contains this segment. Procedure GET_QUADRANT identifies the quadrant of the gray node that contains a block corresponding to the segment to be output.

For example, in locating the block containing the segment starting at row 0 and column 0 in Figure 4.8b, FIND_2D_BLOCK partitions the image successively into blocks having lower right corners at (8,8), (4,4), and (2,2). The result is block A.

The actual output of the runs is done by procedures OUTPUT_RUN and OUTPUT_-END_OF_ROW. In particular, for each black or white node of width W that participates in a row, OUTPUT_RUN outputs a run of length W of the appropriate color (e.g., a black run of length 2 for node A and row 1 of Figure 4.8). OUTPUT_END_OF_ROW outputs a separator symbol to mark the end of the row.

As an example of the application of ALG1, consider the image and quadtree given in Figure 4.8. Nodes Ri correspond to nonleaf nodes. The leaf nodes in Figure 4.8b have been labeled in the order in which they were visited for the first time. For this image, the result of the algorithm is the sequence of strings W332, W242, W242, W152, W224, W224, W8, and W8. There is one string for each row. 'B' and 'W' are used to indicate the color (black and white, respectively) of the first run in the row; the subsequent runs in the row are of alternating colors. For example, the string W332 indicates that the first run is of length 3 and corresponds to white, the second run is of length 3 and corresponds to black, and the third run is of length 2 and corresponds to white.

When outputting the first row, we start at node R0 and successively visit nodes R1 and A; R1,R4,B; R1,R4,C; R2,D; R2,E. For the second row, we visit R1,A; R1,R4,F; R1,R4,G; R2,D; R2,E. For the third row, we visit R1,R5,H; and so on. It is easy to verify that we visit a total of 68 nodes during this process.

ALG1 visits each segment of each row by repeatedly starting at the root of the quadtree. The second algorithm, having ALG2 as its main procedure, attempts to avoid this by using the structure of the tree to locate the successive adjacent blocks. For example, in Figure 4.8, once the run corresponding to block B in the first row has been output, the next block to be visited is C. It can be located by traversing links corresponding to nodes R4 and C. This is in contrast to having to traverse links corresponding to nodes R1, R4, and C, as is necessary when ALG1 is used. This is very much like an inorder traversal of the segment of the tree in which the row participates.

Adjacent nodes are located by use of a combination of procedures QT_GTEQ_-EDGE_NEIGHBOR2 and FIND_2D_BLOCK. Given node P and an edge E, QT_GTEQ_EDGE_-NEIGHBOR2 locates the edge-neighbor (recall the definition of neighbor in Section 3.1) of P, of size greater than or equal to P, in direction E. If P is on the edge of the image and no neighbor exists in the E direction, then NIL is returned. This signals that output for the row is finished (e.g., the eastern neighbor of node E in Figure 4.8).

If the neighboring block does exist, then a pointer to its corresponding node is returned. If it is a gray node (e.g., the eastern neighbor of node A in Figure 4.8), then procedure FIND_2D_BLOCK is used to determine the adjacent black or white block that intersects the row currently being processed (e.g., the eastern adjacent block of A in Figure 4.8 is B for the first row and F for the second row). Note that FIND_2D_BLOCK, in this case, is searching for the appropriate block on the extreme left edge of the gray block that it is currently partitioning. Hence FIND_2D_BLOCK is invoked with a value of 0 for the x coordinate of the desired segment. The actual traversal of the blocks in which each row participates is controlled by procedure OUT_ROW.

Application of ALG2 to the image and quadtree given in Figure 4.8 results in the same output string. However, the order in which nodes are visited is different. When outputting the first row, we start at node R0 and successively visit nodes R1 and A; R1, R4, B; R4, C; R4, R1, R0, R2, D; R2, E; R2, R0. The last pair of nodes results in an indication that no neighbor exists; we have reached the end of the row. For the second row, we visit R1, A; R1, R4, F; R4, G; R4, R1, R0, R2, D; R2, E; R2, R0. For the third row, we visit R1, R5, H; and so on. It is easy to verify that we visit a total of 96 nodes during this process. Although for this particular example, ALG2 visits more nodes than ALG1, we shall later see when ALG2 is superior to ALG1.

```
procedure ALG1(ROOT,LEVEL);
/* Output a raster representation of the 2^LEVEL × 2^LEVEL image corresponding to the
   quadtree rooted at node ROOT. For each row, each block containing a segment of the
   row is located by descending the appropriate links from ROOT. */
begin
  value pointer node ROOT;
  value integer LEVEL;
  pointer node P;
  integer DIAMETER,WIDTH,X,Y;
  DIAMETER ← 2↑LEVEL;
  for Y←0 step 1 until DIAMETER − 1 do
    begin /* Process the blocks in sequence one row at a time */
      X ← 0;
      while X < DIAMETER do
        begin /* Process the blocks in each row from left to right */
          P ← ROOT;
          WIDTH ← DIAMETER;
          FIND_2D_BLOCK(P,X,DIAMETER,Y,DIAMETER,WIDTH);
          OUTPUT_RUN(NODETYPE(P),WIDTH);
          X ← X + WIDTH;
        end;
      OUTPUT_END_OF_ROW();
    end;
end;


procedure FIND_2D_BLOCK(P,X,XFAR,Y,YFAR,W);
/* P points to a node corresponding to a block of width W having its lower right corner at
   (XFAR,YFAR). Find the smallest block in P containing the pixel whose upper left corner
   is at (X,Y). If P is black or white, then return the values of P, W, and FAR; otherwise
   repeat the procedure for the son of P that contains (X,Y). */
begin
  reference pointer node P;
  value integer X,XFAR,Y,YFAR;
  reference integer W;
  preload global integer array XF['NW', 'NE', 'SW', 'SE'] with 1,0,1,0;
```

```
preload global integer array YF['NW', 'NE', 'SW', 'SE'] with 1,1,0,0;
quadrant Q;
while GRAY(P) do
  begin
    W ← W/2;
    Q ← GET_QUADRANT(X,XFAR – W,Y,YFAR – W);
    XFAR ← XFAR – XF[Q]*W;
    YFAR ← YFAR – YF[Q]*W;
    P ← SON(P,Q);
  end;
end;

quadrant procedure GET_QUADRANT(X,XCENTER,Y,YCENTER);
/* Find the quadrant of the block rooted at (XCENTER,YCENTER) that contains (X,Y).
   The origin is assumed to be at the NW-most pixel of the image. */
begin
  value integer X,XCENTER,Y,YCENTER;
  return (if X < XCENTER then
            if Y < YCENTER then 'NW'
            else 'SW'
          else if Y < YCENTER then 'NE'
          else 'SE');
end;

procedure ALG2(ROOT,LEVEL);
/* Output a raster representation of the 2^LEVEL × 2^LEVEL image corresponding to the
   quadtree rooted at node ROOT. For each row, the leftmost block is located by starting
   from ROOT and then visiting in sequence the blocks comprising the row by ascending
   and descending the appropriate links in the tree using neighbor finding. */
begin
  value pointer node ROOT;
  value integer LEVEL;
  pointer node P;
  integer DIAMETER,WIDTH,Y;
  DIAMETER ← 2↑LEVEL;
  for Y←0 step 1 until DIAMETER – 1 do
    begin /* Process the rows in sequence one row at a time */
      P ← ROOT;
      WIDTH ← DIAMETER;
      /* Find the leftmost block containing row Y: */
      FIND_2D_BLOCK(P,0,DIAMETER,Y,DIAMETER,WIDTH);
      OUT_ROW(P,Y,LOG2(WIDTH));
      /* LOG2 returns the log of WIDTH to base 2 */
    end;
end;

procedure OUT_ROW(P,ROW,L);
/* Output a raster corresponding to all of the blocks that have segments in row ROW start-
   ing with node P at level L. */
```

```
begin
  value pointer node P;
  value integer ROW,L;
  pointer node Q;
  integer WIDTH;
  WIDTH ← 2↑L;
  do
    begin
      OUTPUT_RUN(NODETYPE(P),WIDTH);
      /* Find the leftmost adjacent block containing row ROW: */
      QT_GTEQ_EDGE_NEIGHBOR2(P,'E', Q,L);
      WIDTH ← 2↑L;
      if GRAY(Q) then
        FIND_2D_BLOCK(Q,0,WIDTH,ROW,
                      ROW + WIDTH − (ROW mod WIDTH),WIDTH);
      P ← Q;
    end
  until null(P);
end;
```

The analyses of the execution times of ALG1 and ALG2 are in terms of the number of nodes that they visit. Thus we are really only concerned with the time spent by procedures FIND_2D_BLOCK and QT_GTEQ_EDGE_NEIGHBOR2. Recall that in all our analyses we count a visit to node B from node A where there is a link from A to B as a one-node visit.

Theorem 4.1 Given a $2^n \times 2^n$ image, with b_i blocks of size 2^i, the number of nodes visited by ALG1 is $\sum_{i=0}^{n-1} (n - i) \cdot b_i \cdot 2^i$.

Proof Observe that for each block of size 2^i there are 2^i rows, each of which is visited once starting at the root of the quadtree. But each block of size 2^i is at a distance $n - i$ nodes from the root, and our result follows. □

Theorem 4.1 is interesting because it means that for any image, the number of nodes that are visited by ALG1 depends only on the number of blocks comprising it and their respective sizes. The relative position of the blocks is irrelevant. Thus different images are seen to require the same number of node visits. For example, the image in Figure 4.1 requires the same number of node visits as the image in Figure 4.8. Intuitively this is not surprising because ALG1 processes the rows and the segments of blocks comprising them independently of one another.

The analysis of ALG2 is more complex. We first make the following observation. ALG2 (as well as ALG3 and ALG4 discussed in the exercises) visits the various segments of each row by exploiting the tree structure to find neighboring blocks. In doing so, the number of horizontal adjacencies between blocks that are explored is equal to the sum of the heights of the blocks comprising the image. This is true because each block will be visited once for each row in which it is a member. Theorem 4.2 shows that the number of nodes visited by ALG2 is bounded by four times this number. However, we must first prove the following lemma. Assume a $2^n \times 2^n$ image. If the image is a complete quadtree (i.e., all blocks in the image are at level 0), then we have:

Lemma 4.2 In a complete quadtree, the number of nodes visited by ALG2 is bounded by four times the number of blocks in the image (more precisely, it is equal to four times the difference between the area and the diameter for the image, where the diameter is 2^n for a $2^n \times 2^n$ image).

Proof Starting at the root node of the quadtree, for each row in a $2^n \times 2^n$ image, n nodes are visited when locating the node corresponding to the leftmost block. Once this is done, QT_GTEQ_EDGE_NEIGHBOR2 is invoked 2^n times to find neighbors in the eastern direction. Of the nodes corresponding to blocks in the row, 2^0 have their nearest common ancestor at level n, 2^1 at level $n - 1, \ldots,$ 2^i at level $n - i$, and 2^{n-1} at level 1. Once the nearest common ancestor has been found, a path of equal length must be traversed to locate the adjacent neighbors. In addition, the node corresponding to the rightmost block in each row has no eastern neighbor. This is detected by attempting to locate a nonexistent common ancestor, a process that traverses a path of length n (i.e., to the root of the quadtree and including it).

Therefore, for each row, the number of nodes visited is $n + 2 \cdot \Sigma_{i=1}^{n} i \cdot 2^{n-i} + n$, which can be simplified using Equation 3.1 of Section 3.2.1.2 to yield $2^{n+2} - 4$. There are 2^n rows in the image, and thus a total of $2^{2n+2} - 2^{n+2}$ nodes is visited. Since an image that is a complete quadtree contains 2^{2n} blocks, the number of nodes visited is bounded by four times the number of blocks in the image. $\qquad\square$

The result of Lemma 4.2 should not be surprising. It is equivalent to saying that the average distance between two adjacent nodes in a complete quadtree is less than 4. For an alternative derivation of this result using recurrence relations, see [DeMi78]. We are now ready to prove the main theorem.

Theorem 4.2 For any image, the number of nodes visited by ALG2 is bounded by four times the sum of the heights of the blocks in the image, that is, $4 \cdot \Sigma_{i=0}^{n} b_i \cdot 2^i$ for a $2^n \times 2^n$ image with b_i blocks of size 2^i.

Proof By Lemma 4.2, the theorem is true for a complete quadtree. We shall use induction on s, the size of the blocks, to show that the theorem holds for any quadtree.

Let $s = 1$. Consider a 2×2 pixel block in the complete quadtree and assume that the four blocks corresponding to the pixels have been merged to yield one block. Since we are processing the image in a row-by-row manner, the only adjacencies eliminated by the merge are the horizontal ones between the blocks being merged (e.g., between 19 and 20 and 27 and 28 in Figure 4.8b). This means that four fewer nodes will be visited by our algorithm.

In addition, the node corresponding to the merged block (e.g., node J for the blocks corresponding to 19, 20, 27, and 28 in Figures 4.8b and 4.8c) is one node closer to its horizontal neighbors to the left (e.g., blocks 18 and 26 in Figure 4.8b) and right (e.g., blocks 21 and 29 in Figure 4.8b). Thus we find that $4 + 1 + 1 + 1 + 1 = 8$ fewer nodes will be visited. However, the total height of the blocks in the image has decreased by two (initially there were four blocks of size 1 and now there is one block of size 2) and the theorem holds.

More generally, consider a $2^{s+1} \times 2^{s+1}$ block (i.e., we are merging four $2^s \times 2^s$ blocks). Once again, as we are processing the image in a row-by-row manner, the only adjacencies eliminated by the merge are the horizontal ones between the blocks being merged. Since the blocks are of size 2^s, 2^{s+1} adjacencies are eliminated. Moreover, each block of size 2^s is at a distance of 2 from its horizontal neighbor with which it is being merged. Thus the elimination of 2^{s+1} adjacencies results in $2 \cdot 2^{s+1}$ fewer nodes being visited by the algorithm.

In addition, the node corresponding to the merged block is one node closer to each of its horizontal neighbors to the left and right. However, there are 2^{s+1} neighbors in each of the left and right directions. Thus the total number of nodes that will be visited has decreased by $4 \cdot 2^{s+1}$. But the total height of the blocks in the image has decreased by 2^{s+1} (initially there were four blocks of size 2^s and now there is one block of size 2^{s+1}); therefore, the theorem holds. ☐

Theorem 4.2 is useful in comparing ALG1 and ALG2. We see from Theorem 4.2 that for a $2^n \times 2^n$ image with b_i blocks of size 2^i, the number of nodes visited by ALG2 is bounded by $4 \cdot \sum_{i=0}^{n} b_i \cdot 2^i$ in contrast with $\sum_{i=0}^{n} (n - i) \cdot b_i \cdot 2^i$ for ALG1. Thus there is less dependence on the resolution of the image (i.e., n) when ALG2 is used. In particular, for $n \geq 4$, ALG2 is potentially superior to ALG1, as can be seen for a complete quadtree for $n = 4$. In fact, as n gets large, the majority of the nodes appear deeper in the tree (i.e., at a lower level). Since in such a case $(n - i) \cdot b_i \cdot 2^i > 4 \cdot b_i \cdot 2^i$, we find that ALG2 will be more efficient than ALG1.

Also note that a large number of nodes in ALG2 are visited through the use of QT_GTEQ_EDGE_NEIGHBOR2 rather than FIND_2D_BLOCK. This leads to even greater efficiency. In particular, when using QT_GTEQ_EDGE_NEIGHBOR2, a decision as to which node to visit next (i.e., the link to be traversed) depends only on a table lookup operation (using the ADJ and REFLECT relationships). On the other hand, FIND_2D_-BLOCK requires performing arithmetic operations.

In fact, FIND_2D_BLOCK is not necessary in ALG2. Instead we could make use of a procedure that checks only for a NW or SW son. For example, in Figure 4.8, when processing the first row and searching for an eastern neighbor of node A, application of QT_GTEQ_EDGE_NEIGHBOR2 yields node R4. Subsequent application of FIND_2D_-BLOCK yields node B. However, we know that following the NE and SE links is not appropriate. Thus checking for them in FIND_2D_BLOCK and GET_QUADRANT is unnecessary.

The construction used in the proof of Theorem 4.2 is worthy of further attention. It can be used in conjunction with the result of Lemma 4.2 to compute exactly how many nodes will be visited for any image given the number of blocks comprising it and their respective sizes. Thus, as was the case for ALG1, different images will require the same number of node visits when ALG2 is used. We have the following theorem:

Theorem 4.3   Given a $2^n \times 2^n$ image with b_i blocks of size 2^i, the number of nodes visited by ALG2 is

$$2^{2n+2} - 2^{n+2} - \sum_{i=1}^{n} b_i \cdot (2^{2i+2} - 2^{i+2}).$$

Proof   From the proof of Lemma 4.2, we have that traversing a complete quadtree of size 2^i requires $2^{2i+2} - 2^{i+2}$ nodes to be visited. This represents a traversal starting and terminating at a common ancestor. Since the $2^i \times 2^i$ array of pixels has been replaced by one block, $2^{2i+2} - 2^{i+2}$ fewer nodes will be visited for a block of size 2^i. Recall that if the array contains $2^n \times 2^n$ blocks of size 1, then $2^{2n+2} - 2^{n+2}$ nodes will be visited. Subtracting the contribution of b_i blocks of size 2^i yields the desired result.   ☐

Exercises
4.16. Write a pair of procedures GET_OCTANT and FIND_3D_BLOCK to locate the smallest block in an octree that contains a given voxel.
4.17. There are a number of ways in which the performance of ALG2 can be improved, and we shall explore them in this and the following exercises. ALG2 visits the first segment of each row of the leftmost blocks by traversing the links starting at the root of the tree. For example, in Figure 4.8, when outputting the first and second rows, nodes R1 and A are visited twice—once for each row in which block A participates as the initial segment. ALG3 avoids this by only starting the output of the first row in the block at the root. For example, in Figure 4.8, once the first row has been output (i.e., nodes R1, A; R1, R4, B; R4, C; R4, R1, R0, R2, D; R2, E; and R2, R0 have been visited), we output the second row by starting at A and then visit R1, R4, F; R4, G; R4, R1, R0, R2, D; R2, E; R2, R0. For the third row, we start at the root and locate H by going through R1, R5, H; etc. It is easy to verify that we

visit a total of 90 nodes during this process. Modify procedure ALG2 to yield the effect of ALG3.

4.18. When would you use ALG2 instead of ALG3?

4.19. Does Theorem 4.2 hold for ALG3? If yes, why?

4.20. Assume a $2^n \times 2^n$ image with b_i blocks of size 2^i where v_i blocks of size 2^i have segments that include the first column. Find the number of nodes visited by ALG3. The analysis should be analogous to that employed for ALG2. Use the fact that the only difference between ALG2 and ALG3 is that the number of visits to locate the blocks in the first column is reduced.

4.21. ALG3 visits the first segment of the first row of each of the leftmost blocks by repeatedly starting at the root of the quadtree. Thus ALG3 visits the first blocks in each column in a top-down manner just as ALG1 does for the entire image. Devise a procedure ALG4 to be a bottom-up analog of ALG3 in the same way as ALG2 is a bottom-up analog of ALG1. Thus ALG4 uses the structure of the quadtree to locate the immediately adjacent block to the south by invoking QT_GTEQ_EDGE_NEIGHBOR2 in conjunction with FIND_2D_BLOCK. For example in Figure 4.8, once the rows having their first segment in block H have been output (i.e., the third row), the next row to be output has its first segment in block M (i.e., the fourth row). This block is located by traversing links corresponding to nodes R5 and M. This is in contrast to having to traverse links corresponding to nodes R1, R5, and M as is necessary when ALG1, ALG2, or ALG3 are used. It is easy to verify that we visit a total of 94 nodes during this process.

4.22. Assume a $2^n \times 2^n$ image with b_i blocks of size 2^i where v_i blocks of size 2^i have segments that include the first column. Find the number of nodes visited by ALG4. The analysis should be analogous to that employed for ALG2 and ALG3. Use the fact that the only difference between ALG3 and ALG4 is that the number of visits to locate the blocks in the first column is reduced. You may find it convenient to analyze the number of nodes visited in locating the blocks in the first column by using techniques analogous to those used in proving Lemma 4.2.

4.23. Prove that Theorem 4.2 holds for ALG4.

4.24. In general, under what circumstances is ALG4 better than ALG3?

4.25. How does ALG1 compare with ALG3 and ALG4?

4.26. The costs associated with using neighbor-finding methods in ALG2, ALG3, and ALG4 can be avoided by linking neighboring nodes along a row. This is quite similar to the use of ropes (see Section 3.2.2). The disadvantage of such a technique is the amount of extra space required to store the links. However, this does suggest an alternative variation on ALG1, ALG2, ALG3, and ALG4: we can maintain a linked list of all the blocks that participate in a row. As we process each run in a row, we check if the particular run is the last row in which the block participates. If this is the case, then we delink the block from the linked list and replace it with its edge-neighbor to the south. If this neighbor is a gray node, then we replace it with all the northernmost descendants of the gray node (e.g., A in Figure 4.8 has R5 as its southern neighbor and since R5 is gray, A is replaced by H and I). The advantage of this method is that we need not look for neighbors in the eastern direction except when the linked list corresponding to the first row is built. Of course, we now look for neighbors in the southern direction instead. However, this is done once per block rather than for each row in which the block participates. Write an algorithm to implement ALG5.

4.27. Given a $2^n \times 2^n$ image with b_i blocks of size 2^i, use techniques similar to those used in the proof of Theorem 4.2 to show that the execution time of ALG5 is bounded by $\sum_{i=0}^{n} b_i \cdot 2^i + 6 \cdot \sum_{i=0}^{n} b_i$ instead of $4 \cdot \sum_{i=0}^{n} b_i \cdot 2^i$.

4.28. Develop a set of algorithms analogous to ALG1 and ALG2 for a bintree representation of a quadtree. Also obtain the analogs of Theorems 4.1–4.3 and Lemma 4.2 for the bintree. Are the algorithms simplified when the bintree is defined in such a way that the first partition is on the value of the y coordinate rather than on the value of the x coordinate?

4.29. Write a procedure QUADTREE_TO_RASTER to convert a quadtree in the form of an FD linear quadtree to a raster representation.

4.30. Given a $2^n \times 2^n$ image containing b_i blocks of size 2^i, how many FD quadtree blocks are visited by QUADTREE_TO_RASTER as implemented in Exercise 4.29?

4.31. Write an analog of ALG1 to convert a quadtree in the form of a DF-expression to a raster representation. Repeat for an analog of ALG2. Explain the difference in the ease in which the analogs of ALG1 and ALG2 can be implemented.

4.32. Oliver, King, and Wiseman [Oliv84b] modify the quadtree data structure to yield a sextree by adding two fields termed NEXTROW and ENDROW. Given node P in the sextree, NEXTROW(P) points to SON(P,'SW') while ENDROW(P) points to the last element in SON(P,'SE') when the subtree rooted at P is visited in preorder. The result is stored as a linear sextree, which is a DF-expression. In this case, the pointers in the NEXTROW and ENDROW fields are treated as addresses in the form of offsets from the start of the list. Assuming that the fields are ordered NEXTROW, NW, NE, ENDROW, SW, and SE, what is the linear sextree representation of the quadtree of Figure 4.1?

4.33. How do the NEXTROW and ENDROW fields speed up ALG1?

4.34. Implement procedure ALG1 using a linear sextree representation of a quadtree. To do this, assume that the rows of the image are numbered from 0 to N and write a procedure that will extract a particular row (i.e., scan line) from the linear sextree. Notice that each row or scan line corresponds to a binary tree that can be extracted from the sextree by a simple tree traversal facilitated by the NEXTROW and ENDROW fields. Thus the effect is somewhat like a bintree where the y coordinate is partitioned before the x coordinate.

4.2.3 Building a Pointerless Quadtree from a Raster Representation

Often we are dealing with images whose quadtrees are too large to fit into internal memory, which means that they must be stored in external memory. The result is that the nodes of the quadtree are stored over several pages. Following pointers becomes much more costly because a pointer that points to a node on another page usually requires a disk access. Such large images are often represented using a pointerless quadtree representation. This section starts with a raster representation and presents an algorithm for constructing a pointerless representation of a quadtree in the form of a collection of the locational codes of the leaf nodes comprising it. This section is quite complex, but important, and can be omitted on an initial reading.

The basic algorithm described in Section 4.2.1 inserts individually each pixel of the raster image into the quadtree in raster order and performs merging if necessary. In the case of a pointer-based representation, this is a relatively easy process since the pointers facilitate the location of neighboring nodes and candidates for merging. However, when using a pointerless representation, a search must be performed to locate neighbors, as well as the four sons that are candidates for merging.

The natural structure of a pointerless representation is a list. To speed up the searches, the elements of the list are usually reorganized using a tree structure in the form of a B-tree [Come79] with the value of the locational code serving as a key. This approach is used in [Abel84a, Rose83a] where the locational code also reflects the depth of the node (see the discussion of the FD locational code in Section 2.1.1).

When using a pointerless representation, neighbor finding is a two-step process (e.g., see Section 3.4.1). First the address of a neighboring node is computed. Then the list of nodes is searched for the node or a larger node that contains it. The B-tree speeds up the second step; however, the first step is cumbersome because it requires use of bit manipulation techniques. Moreover since we are concerned with large images (such as maps), most of the quadtree resides in secondary storage. This means that the costs of the search through the list (even though it is considerably speeded up by use of a B-tree) and of the insertion of the nodes for the pixels are heavily influenced by the number of page-read operations.

The rest of this section describes an algorithm due to Shaffer and Samet [Shaf86a, Shaf87a] whose execution time is not dominated by the insertion and search operations. The term *optimal* is used (in a loose sense) to describe it because it makes a single insertion for each node in the final quadtree. It is based on processing the image in raster-scan (top to bottom, left to right) order, always inserting the largest node (i.e., block) for which the current pixel is the first (upper leftmost) pixel. Such a policy avoids the necessity of merging since the upper leftmost pixel of any block is inserted before any other pixel of that block. Therefore it is impossible for four sibling nodes to be of the same color. In addition, neighbor finding is not used. Such an algorithm is described below.

At any point during the quadtree building process, there is a processed portion of the image and an unprocessed portion. Both portions of the quadtree have been assigned to nodes. We say that a node is *active* if at least one, but not all, pixel covered by the node has been processed. The optimal quadtree building process must keep track of all of these active nodes. Given a $2^n \times 2^n$ image, it can be shown that the number of active nodes is bounded by $2^n - 1$ (see Exercise 4.35). Using these observations, an optimal quadtree building algorithm, encoded by procedure OPTI-MAL_BUILD, is outlined below.[1]

OPTIMAL_BUILD assumes the existence of a data structure that keeps track of the active quadtree nodes. For each pixel in the raster scan traversal, do the following. If the pixel is the same color as the appropriate active node, do nothing (e.g., when pixel 1 is processed in Figure 4.9, node[2] A is created, whereas nothing is done after processing pixel 2 since it is the same color as pixel 1). Otherwise insert the largest possible node for which this is the first (i.e., upper leftmost) pixel and (if it is not a 1×1 pixel node) add it to the set of active nodes (e.g., after processing pixel 5 in Figure 4.10,

---

[1] The actual code for OPTIMAL_BUILD is difficult to follow. Although it is included here, it may be skipped.

[2] For the sake of uniformity, the discussion uses the term *node* even though, when referring to the figures, the term *block* would be more appropriate.

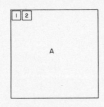

Figure 4.9   Node A is the only active node after processing pixels 1 and 2 of the same color

node B is inserted as well as made active). Remove any active nodes for which this is
the last (lower right) pixel (e.g., in Figure 4.10 node B is removed from the active node
list once pixel 32 has been processed).

To implement OPTIMAL_BUILD we need to keep track of the list of active nodes.
This list is called the *active node table* and is represented by TABLE. TABLE has a row
for each level of the quadtree (except for level 0, which corresponds to the single pixel
level; these nodes cannot be active). Row i of TABLE contains 2^{n-i} entries, with row n
corresponding to the full image. Given a pixel in column j, the color of the active
node (if there is one) at level i is found in entry $j/2^i$ of row i. Note that shift operations can be used instead of divisions if speed is important.

The only remaining problem is how to locate the appropriate active node
corresponding to each pixel. In particular, for a given pixel in a $2^n \times 2^n$ image, as
many as n active nodes could exist (see Exercise 4.36). Multiple active nodes for a
given pixel occur whenever a new node is inserted. For example, when pixel X is
inserted in Figure 4.11, nodes A, E, and I are all active nodes with respect to X, while H
is also an active node. Each pixel will have the color of the smallest of the active
nodes that covers it, since the smallest node is the one that has been inserted most
recently (e.g., I is the smallest active node covering pixel X in Figure 4.11 when building the quadtree corresponding to the image in Figure 4.1a).

Finding the smallest active node that contains a given pixel can be done by
searching from the lowest level in TABLE upward until the first nonempty entry is

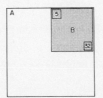

Figure 4.10   Node B becomes active upon processing
pixel 5 and is removed from the active list after processing
pixel 32

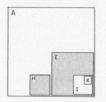

Figure 4.11 Example showing the active nodes when pixel X is processed when building the quadtree corresponding to the image in Figure 4.1

found. However, this is time-consuming, since it might require n steps. Therefore an additional one-dimensional array, called LIST and referred to as the *access array*, is maintained to provide an index into TABLE.

LIST is of size 2^{n-1}, since single-pixel-sized nodes need not be stored. For any pixel in column j, the LIST entry at $j/2$ indicates the row of TABLE corresponding to the smallest active node containing the pixel. At the beginning of the algorithm, each entry of LIST points to the entry of TABLE corresponding to the root (i.e., row n for a $2^n \times 2^n$ image). As active nodes are inserted or completed (and are to be deleted from the active node table), the active node table (TABLE) and the access array (LIST) are updated. Once again, we say that the root of a $2^n \times 2^n$ image is at level n, while a pixel is at level 0.

```
procedure OPTIMAL_BUILD(INPIC,R,C,N,OUTTREE);
/* Build a quadtree in OUTTREE corresponding to input picture INPIC using a quadtree-
   building algorithm that inserts the largest node for which the current pixel is the first (i.e.,
   upper leftmost) pixel. The input picture is a list of R rows with C columns, and the out-
   put quadtree will be of maximum depth N (i.e., a 2^N × 2^N image). Type row is an array
   of type color where color takes on the values NOCOLOR, BLACK, and WHITE. The
   code for procedure INSERT is implementation dependent and thus is not given here. */
begin
  value pointer rowlist INPIC;
  value integer R,C,N;
  reference pointer quadtree OUTTREE;
  row BUFF[0:C–1];
  pointer row array TABLE[1:N];
  integer array LIST[0:2↑(N–1)–1];
  integer ROW,COL,I,J,LEVEL,XT,YT,T;
  /* Allocate space and initialize TABLE for description of active nodes: */
  for I←1 step 1 until N do
    begin
      TABLE[I] ← allocate(row,2↑(N-I));
      for J←0 step 1 until 2↑(N–I)–1 do
        TABLE[I][J] ← 'NOCOLOR';
    end;
```

```
TABLE[N][0] ← 'WHITE';
for J←0 step 1 until 2↑(N–1)–1 do LIST[J] ← N;
/* Process the picture: */
for ROW←0 step 1 until R–1 do
  begin
    BUFF ← ROW(INPIC); /* Process one row at a time */
    INPIC ← NEXT(INPIC);
    for COL←0 step 1 until C–1 do /* Process each pixel in the row */
      begin
        /* Find the smallest active node containing the pixel */
        I ← LIST[COL/2];
        if TABLE[I][COL/2↑I] ≠ BUFF[COL] then
          begin /* The pixel and the node containing it differ in color */
            /* Calculate the level of the largest node for which this is the first pixel: */
            XT ← COL; YT ← ROW; LEVEL ← 0;
            while (XT mod 2) = 0 and (YT mod 2) = 0 and (LEVEL<N) do
              begin
                XT ← XT/2; YT ← YT/2; LEVEL ← LEVEL+1;
              end;
            if LEVEL ≠ 0 then
              begin /* The largest node containing the pixel is > 1×1 */
                /* Update the active node table and the access array */
                TABLE[LEVEL][COL/(2↑LEVEL)] ← BUFF[COL];
                for J←COL/2 step 1 until COL/2+2↑(LEVEL–1)–1 do
                  LIST[J] ← LEVEL;
              end;
            INSERT(OUTTREE,MAKENODE(COL,ROW,LEVEL,BUFF[COL]));
          end;
        if ((ROW+1) mod 2↑I) = 0 and ((COL+1) mod 2↑I) = 0 then
          begin /* The last pixel of one or more active nodes */
            while ((ROW+1) mod 2↑I) = 0 and ((COL+1) mod 2↑I) = 0 do
              begin /* Update the active node table */
                TABLE[I][COL/2↑I] ← 'NOCOLOR'; I ← I+1;
              end;
            T ← I–1;
            while TABLE[I][COL/(2↑I)] = 'NOCOLOR' do
              I ← I+1; /* Get level of next active node */
            for J←COL/2 step –1 until COL/2–2↑(T–1)+1 do
              LIST[J] ← I; /* Update access array */
          end;
      end;
  end;
end;
```

As an example of the optimal quadtree building algorithm, let us consider how the quadtree corresponding to the image in Figure 4.1a is constructed. Table 4.1 is a trace of the values of the active nodes as the pixels that lead to the creation of nodes

Table 4.1   Trace of the active nodes as the quadtree for Figure 4.1a
is built

Pixel	Action	Size	Active Nodes by Level		
			3	2	1
(0,0)	insert white node A	8×8	A		
(2,4)	insert black node B	2×2	A		B
(2,6)	insert black node C	2×2	A		B C
(3,5)	remove B from active		A		C
(3,7)	remove C from active		A		
(4,3)	insert black node D	1×1	A		
(4,4)	insert black node E	4×4	A	E	
(5,2)	insert black node F	1×1	A	E	
(5,3)	insert black node G	1×1	A	E	
(6,2)	insert black node H	2×2	A	E	H
(6,6)	insert white node I	2×2	A	E	H I
(7,3)	remove H from active		A	E I	
(7,5)	insert white node J	1×1	A	E I	
(7,7)	remove I, E, A from active				

(or their removal from the active list of nodes) are processed. Each row in the table indicates the node that has become active (as well as its size), or the nodes that have been removed from the set of active nodes. In addition, the active nodes are tabulated according to their level. The pixel identifier (a,b) means that the pixel is in row a and column b relative to an origin at the upper left corner of the image. Figure 4.12 illustrates some of the nodes created during the building process by using their names to label the pixel that caused their creation. Figure 4.13 indicates in greater detail some of the steps in the construction of the quadtree.

Figure 4.12   Correlation between some of the nodes of the quadtree corresponding to the image in Figure 4.1 and the pixels that led to their creation

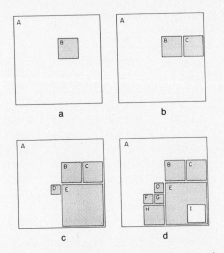

Figure 4.13 Intermediate states of the quadtree as the optimal algorithm is used to build the quadtree corresponding to the image in Figure 4.1: (a) after processing pixel (2,4), (b) after processing pixel (2,6), (c) after processing pixel (4,4), (d) after processing pixel (6,6)

When the first pixel of the array is processed, the entire quadtree is represented by a single white node (node A in Figure 4.13a). No other insertions occur while processing rows 0 and 1. When the first black pixel (2,4) is processed, node B of Figure 4.13a becomes active. The insertion of node B causes node A to be split and its NE son is split again. When black pixel (2,5) is processed, node B will be located in the active node table since it is the smallest active node containing that pixel.

When black pixel (2,6) is processed, node C of Figure 4.13b becomes active, since only active white node A contains it at that point. As row 3 is processed, nodes B and C are deactivated when their lower right pixels are processed (pixels (3,5) and (3,7), respectively). Pixel (4,3) causes the insertion of node D, which resulted in two node-splitting operations. When pixel (4,4) is processed, node E is inserted, as shown in Figure 4.13c. The nodes previously labeled B and C are not active. Similarly pixel-sized node D at (4,3) is not active since it contains no unprocessed pixels. Therefore nodes A and E are the only active nodes.

Pixels (5,2) and (5,3) cause the insertion of nodes F and G. Node H becomes active after processing pixel (6,2). Pixel (6,6) is white, and since the smallest node containing it had been black, white node I has been inserted and made active (Figure 4.13d). When processing pixel (6,7), we find that three active nodes (A, E, and I) contain it, with the smallest being node I. Pixel (7,3) causes node H to be removed from the set of active nodes. Pixel (7,5) results in the insertion of node J. Since pixel (7,7) is the lower rightmost pixel in the image, it causes the removal of all active nodes

Table 4.2   A comparison of the naive and optimal quadtree
building algorithms

Map Name	Number of Nodes	Number of Inserts		Time (secs)	
		Naive	Optimal	Naive	Optimal
Floodplain	5,266	180,000	2,352	413.2	13.8
Topography	24,859	180,000	12,400	429.8	51.2
Landuse	28,447	180,000	14,675	436.7	56.9
Center	4,687	262,144	2,121	603.8	16.1
Pebble	44,950	262,144	20,770	630.1	111.0
Stone	31,969	262,144	14,612	629.5	70.2

from the active node list (nodes I, E, and A). The final result of the quadtree-building process is shown in Figure 4.12.

Table 4.2 contains timing results when the optimal algorithm is applied to some images, including maps from a cartographic database [Same85d]. The first three images are of size 450×400, while the second three images are 512×512. To evaluate the effectiveness of the algorithm, it is compared to an implementation of the procedures given in Section 4.2.1 (the *naive* algorithm).

Both algorithms were encoded in the C programming language and were executed on a VAX11/785 running the 4.3BSD version of UNIX. It is important to note that the execution times of both algorithms are measured in an environment that implements the quadtree as a collection of leaf nodes represented by their FD locational codes. This collection is organized in a B-tree, as described earlier. The naive algorithm inserts each pixel individually. It must make use of neighbor-finding operations that function by computing the address of the neighbor and then searching for it in the list of nodes already processed.

As can be seen from the table, the optimal algorithm often requires far fewer calls to the node insertion routine than the number of nodes in the resulting output tree. This is because some calls to the insertion routine may cause several node splits

Figure 4.14   *Example showing the need to split two nodes upon processing pixel 3 while no nodes need to be split or inserted when processing pixel 5*

to occur, thereby increasing the number of nodes in the tree. For example, in Figure 4.14 when processing pixel 3, we must insert node B into the quadtree containing a single node, say A, which causes two split operations and results in seven nodes. Of course, if the first pixel inserted into the node happens to be the same color as the original node, no insertion is required. This is the case when inserting pixel 5 into node C of Figure 4.14, which is the same color as the node that was originally split—A.

The difference in the execution times between the naive and optimal algorithms can be explained by analyzing their costs in terms of the number of insert operations that they perform. The naive algorithm examines each pixel and inserts it into the quadtree. Assuming a cost of I for each insert operation and a cost of c for the time spent examining a pixel, the total cost of the naive algorithm is $2^{2n} \cdot (c + I)$.

The optimal algorithm must also examine each pixel. However, there will be at most one insert operation for each of the N nodes in the output quadtree. Therefore the cost of the optimal algorithm is $c \cdot 2^{2n} + I \cdot N$ where c is relatively small in comparison to I, and N is usually small in comparison to 2^{2n}. In other words, the quantity $I \cdot N$ dominates the cost of the optimal algorithm.

The result is that using the optimal algorithm reduces the execution time from $O(\text{pixels})$ to $O(\text{nodes})$. Of course, this is achieved at an increase in storage requirements due to the need to keep track of the active nodes (approximately 2^{n+1} for a $2^n \times 2^n$ image). However, when using the optimal algorithm, there is no need for storage for the intermediate quadtree because there is no merging.

Exercises

4.35. Given a $2^n \times 2^n$ image, prove that at any time during a raster-scan building process in which the largest node possible is always inserted, at most $2^n - 1$ nodes will be active.

4.36. Describe a situation that could lead to n nodes being active for a given pixel.

4.37. Give an algorithm for building pointerless octrees that is analogous to OPTIMAL_BUILD.

4.38. Devise an algorithm analogous to OPTIMAL_BUILD for pointer-based quadtrees that uses neighbor finding yet need not perform merging.

4.39. Procedure OPTIMAL_BUILD achieves a speed-up in execution time by use of additional storage for the active nodes. For a $2^n \times 2^n$ image, a maximum of 2^{n+1} nodes is needed. In the case of an octree, the fact that we are dealing with a three-dimensional image means that the additional storage is of the order of 2^{2n} nodes, which may be prohibitive. At each level of the octree, there are many cases in which the elements of the active node table entries corresponding to the level are not being used. A considerable amount of storage can be saved by representing the active nodes and access array by lists. These lists are linked in the order in which their elements will be visited. Revise OPTIMAL_BUILD to make use of linked lists for the active nodes. Such an approach has been used by Samet and Tamminen [Same88b] to enable the efficient computation of connected component labeling for a pointerless quadtree representation of images of arbitrary dimension (see also Section 5.1.3).

4.40. Repeat Exercise 4.39 by representing the list of active nodes for a d-dimensional image by a $(d-1)$-dimensional quadtree. For example, a quadtree can be used when building an octree (e.g., [Yau83]). This approach finds use in plane-sweep algorithms for solving problems involving large collections of rectangles, as discussed in Section 3.3 of [Same90a].

4.3 CHAIN CODES

The chain code representation [Free74] (also known as a boundary or border code) is commonly used in cartographic applications. The chain code of a region can be specified, relative to a given starting point, as a sequence of unit vectors (i.e., 1 pixel wide) in the principal directions so that the interior of the region is always to the right of the vectors. We can represent the directions by numbers; for example, let i, an integer quantity ranging from 0 to 3, represent a unit vector having a direction of $90 \cdot i$ degrees. For example, the chain code for the boundary of the black region in Figure 4.1a, moving clockwise starting from the midpoint of the extreme right boundary, is

$$3^2 2^2 3^1 2^1 3^1 2^3 1^3 0^1 1^1 0^1 1^2 0^4 3^2.$$

This is a four-direction chain code. Generalized chain codes, involving more than four directions, can also be used. Chain codes are not only compact, but they simplify the detection of features of a region boundary, such as sharp turns (i.e., corners) or concavities. On the other hand, chain codes do not facilitate the determination of properties such as elongatedness, and it is difficult to perform set operations such as union and intersection as well. Thus it is useful to be able to convert between chain codes and quadtree representations. Techniques for doing this are presented below.

4.3.1 Building a Quadtree from a Chain Code

There are a number of methods of constructing a quadtree from a chain code [Same80a, Webb84]. This section describes a method derived by Samet [Same80a] that is relatively simple. It has an average execution time proportional to the region's perimeter. It has been improved upon by Webber [Webb84] to obtain an algorithm with a worst-case execution time proportional to the region's perimeter, discussed briefly at the end of this section.

Samet's chain-code-to-quadtree construction algorithm has two phases. The first phase traces the boundary in the clockwise direction and constructs the quadtree. All nodes that correspond to blocks of size 1×1 (i.e., pixels) that are adjacent to the boundary and that are within the region whose boundary is being traced are assigned the color black. They are at level 0 in the quadtree. All remaining nodes are gray nodes or left uncolored. The second phase of the algorithm assigns the appropriate color to the uncolored nodes. In addition, during phase 2, all nonleaf (i.e., gray) nodes with four black sons are converted to black nodes.

Phase 1 starts by choosing a link in the chain code at random and creates a node for it, say P. Next, the following link in the chain code, say NEW, is examined, and its direction is compared with that of the immediately preceding link, say OLD. At this point, three courses of action are possible. If the directions of NEW and OLD are the same, then a node, say Q, may need to be added. Q is a neighbor of P in direction OLD (see Figure 4.15a).

Figure 4.15 Examples of the actions to be taken when the chain code (a) maintains its direction, (b) turns clockwise, and (c) turns counterclockwise

If NEW's direction is to the right of OLD, a new node is unnecessary (Figure 4.15b); but if NEW's direction is to the left of OLD, then we may have to add two nodes. First, a node, say Q, that is a neighbor of P in direction OLD is added (if not already present). Second, a node, say R, that is a neighbor of Q in direction NEW is added (Figure 4.15c).

Nodes are added to the quadtree using the same procedures used for building a quadtree from a raster representation (i.e., ADD_EDGE_NEIGHBOR and CREATE_-QNODE) discussed in Section 4.2.1. The difference is that in the case of a chain code, the nodes whose corresponding blocks are not adjacent to the boundary of the region that is being traced are left uncolored (given the color NOCOLOR), whereas in the case of conversion from rasters to quadtrees, they are treated as black or white, as is appropriate.

Figure 4.16 shows the block decomposition and partial quadtree after the application of phase 1 to the chain code representation corresponding to the region in

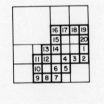

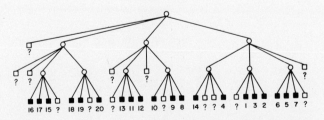

Figure 4.16 Block decomposition and quadtree of the region in Figure 4.1 after application of phase 1 of the chain-code-to-quadtree conversion algorithm

Figure 4.1a. The black nodes have been labeled in the order in which they have been visited, starting at the midpoint of the extreme right boundary of the image and proceeding in a clockwise manner. All uncolored nodes in Figure 4.16b are depicted as white blocks labeled with a '?' to indicate that they have not yet been assigned their final color. Nodes 4, 6, 12, and 14 are shown in the figure as black nodes because they result from an invocation of procedure ADD_EDGE_NEIGHBOR, although they are technically left uncolored.

As the various links in the chain code are processed in phase 1, some nodes may be encountered more than once, thereby indicating that they are adjacent to the boundary on more than one side. We keep track of this information for each node. It is used in phase 2 to assign colors to the uncolored nodes. We associate a code (i.e., a number) with each node created during phase 1 that indicates the part of the boundary, if any, to which it is adjacent on the right.

The code 0 indicates that the node does not have any side adjacent on the right to the boundary in its entirety (such a node is said to be uncolored and given the color NOCOLOR). Nodes that will eventually be assigned the color BLACK, as well as those that will eventually be assigned the color WHITE, may have a code of 0. The codes 1, 2, 4, and 8 correspond to sides of nodes that are entirely to the right of northern, eastern, southern, and western boundaries, respectively. Note that these codes are additive and are stored in the NODETYPE field.

For example, a node whose sides form the southern and western boundaries has 12 as its code. For the sake of completeness, we let gray and white nodes be represented by 16 and 17, respectively. We use GRAY and WHITE to refer to them. The function CODE(B) yields the code corresponding to a boundary of type B (B is N, E, S, or W).

As an example of the encoding process used by phase 1, consider the region represented by the chain code in Figure 4.17. The links are labeled from a to j and the nodes within the region are labeled from A to E. Figure 4.18a–j shows how the corresponding quadtree is constructed where Figure 4.18a shows the quadtree after traversing link α. Figure 4.18d$_1$ has been decomposed into two components 4.18d$_1$ and 4.18d$_2$ in order to reflect the counterclockwise turn between links c and d. Figure 4.18 also indicates how the codes (stored in NODETYPE) are constructed along with the tree.

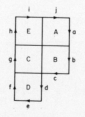

Figure 4.17   Sample region and its chain code

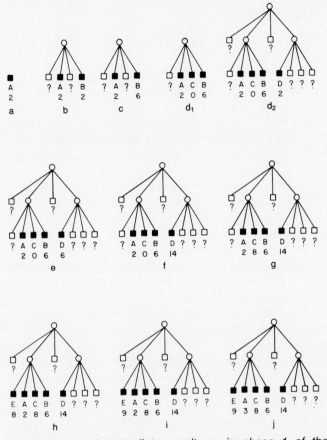

Figure 4.18   Intermediate quadtrees in phase 1 of the chain-code-to-quadtree conversion algorithm when obtaining the quadtree corresponding to Figure 4.17

Note that the resulting quadtree in Figure 4.18j is not minimal in the sense that nodes E, A, B, and C should be merged (see Figure 4.19). This is achieved by phase 2.

Phase 2 has two goals: to assign a color to all uncolored sons of nonleaf nodes and to convert gray nodes that have four black sons to black nodes. This is achieved by a process that moves from the boundary of the region toward the center. Before proceeding further, we make the following observation. For an uncolored son to correspond eventually to a black node, it must be totally surrounded by black nodes since otherwise it would have been adjacent to the boundary and not left uncolored. Therefore if any uncolored son is determined to be black, then all of its remaining uncolored brothers (i.e., the ones that are not gray) must also be black. Similarly if an uncolored son is determined to be white, then all of its remaining uncolored brothers (i.e., the ones that are not gray) must also be white.

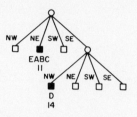

Figure 4.19   The result of the application of phase 2 of the chain-code-to-quadtree conversion algorithm to Figure 4.18

Phase 2 traverses the quadtree in preorder. For each gray node encountered, say P, it performs the following tests. If all of P's sons are uncolored, then P is set to black and its sons are deleted (see Exercise 4.42). If any of P's sons is uncolored, then choose one such son, say R, that is adjacent to a gray or black brother, say Q. Now consider the nodes in the subtree rooted at Q that are adjacent to the side shared by R and Q. If any of these nodes is white or is black with a boundary along the shared side, then R and P's remaining uncolored sons are set to white. Otherwise R and P's remaining uncolored sons are set to black.

If all of P's sons are black, then P is set to black and its sons are deleted. However, in all cases, prior to deleting the four sons, NODETYPE(P) must be set. Its value is obtained by visiting P's four sons so that whenever two 4-adjacent sons both have boundaries along a common side of P, then P also has a boundary along this direction. For example, in Figure 4.18j, nodes E and A have northern boundaries, A and B have eastern boundaries, and C and E have western boundaries. Figure 4.19 contains the resulting tree where the merged node has a NODETYPE value of 11. Figure 4.1 is the result of applying phase 2 to the partial quadtree in Figure 4.16. Since it is impossible for four sons to be white, no check is made for this case (see Exercise 4.42).

Note that the NODETYPE field indicates only whether the entire side of a leaf node, say P, is on the boundary of the region (i.e., to the right of it). If the side is only partially adjacent to the boundary, then P cannot have an uncolored brother with which it shares this side as a boundary. This means that the component of NODETYPE(P) along the given side will not be examined, and thus its value is no longer relevant. For example, in Figure 4.17, the value of the NODETYPE field of the node resulting from the merger of nodes A, B, C, and E does not have a component representing a southern boundary. However, by virtue of the presence of adjacent node D, it can never have an uncolored southern brother.

The following procedures specify the chain-code-to-quadtree algorithm. The chain code is assumed to be stored in a linked list of records of type *cclist*. A record of type *cclist* has two fields named CC and NEXT, which correspond, respectively, to the direction of a code element ('N', 'E', 'S', or 'W') and a link to the record containing the next element of the code.

The main procedure is named CHAINCODE_TO_QUADTREE and is invoked with a pointer to the first element in the chain code. Procedure CHAINCODE_TO_QUADTREE implements phase 1 by constructing the quadtree corresponding to the boundary nodes. Procedures ADD_EDGE_NEIGHBOR and CREATE_QNODE, given in Section 4.2.1, are used to locate neighbors and build the quadtree.

Note that the type *color* has been augmented to encompass NOCOLOR as well as BLACK and WHITE. Once the quadtree has been obtained, recursive procedure AS-SIGN_COLOR implements phase 2. It assigns the correct color to all uncolored nodes (i.e., those nodes that are not adjacent to the right of the boundary of a region in the image). Recursive Boolean procedure INTERIOR aids in this task by determining if a node is totally surrounded by black nodes along a given side of its corresponding block.

The predicate BLACK is used to detect if a node is not gray or white. Given an uncolored node, BLACK returns true. This is not a problem because by the time an uncolored node is tested by the predicate BLACK in procedures ASSIGN_COLOR and IN-TERIOR, its NODETYPE field was already set to WHITE if it did not correspond to a black node. Thus once procedure INTERIOR has been applied and a determination made that the uncolored node is black, there is no need to reset its NODETYPE field.

We also make use of a number of auxiliary functions to aid in the interaction between boundaries and directions. BOUNDARY(E) indicates the type of boundary represented by a code in the direction of edge E (directions E, S, W, and N correspond to northern, eastern, southern, and western boundaries, respectively). The function COM-PARE(E_1, E_2) indicates the relationship of a boundary in the direction of edge E_2 to a boundary in the direction of E_1. It takes on the values SAME, CLOCKWISE, COUNTER-CLOCKWISE, and OPPOSITE. For example, COMPARE('E', 'S') = 'CLOCKWISE'.

```
pointer node procedure CHAINCODE_TO_QUADTREE(P):
/* Construct a quadtree corresponding to the image whose chain code representation is
   contained in a list of chain codes pointed at by P. Global variable NEWROOT keeps
   track of the root of the quadtree as it is built in procedures ADD_EDGE_NEIGHBOR and
   CREATE_QNODE.   */
begin
 value pointer cclist P;
 edge OLD,NEW;
 pointer node Q;
 OLD ← CC(P);
 /* Create the first node in the tree: */
 Q ← CREATE_QNODE(NIL,NIL,'NOCOLOR');
 NODETYPE(Q) ← CODE(BOUNDARY(OLD));
 P ← NEXT(P);
 while not(null(P)) do
  begin /* Traverse the boundary of the region and build the quadtree */
   NEW ← CC(P);
   if COMPARE(OLD,NEW) = 'CLOCKWISE' then /* Figure 4.15b */
    NODETYPE(Q) ← NODETYPE(Q) lor CODE(BOUNDARY(NEW))
   else if COMPARE(OLD,NEW) = 'SAME' then /* Figure 4.15a */
    begin
     Q ← ADD_EDGE_NEIGHBOR(Q,OLD,'NOCOLOR');
```

```
            NODETYPE(Q) ← NODETYPE(Q) lor CODE(BOUNDARY(OLD));
        end
    else if COMPARE(OLD,NEW) = 'COUNTERCLOCKWISE' then
        begin /* Figure 4.15c */
        Q ← ADD_EDGE_NEIGHBOR(Q,OLD,'NOCOLOR');
        Q ← ADD_EDGE_NEIGHBOR(Q,NEW,'NOCOLOR');
            NODETYPE(Q) ← NODETYPE(Q) lor CODE(BOUNDARY(NEW));
        end
    else ERROR('wrong direction');
    OLD ← NEW;
    P ← NEXT(P);
    end;
/* Assign colors to uncolored sons of gray nodes and merge if possible: */
ASSIGN_COLOR(NEWROOT);
return(NEWROOT);
end;


recursive procedure ASSIGN_COLOR(ROOT);
/* Process the quadtree rooted at ROOT by assigning colors to all uncolored sons of gray
   nodes.  Also change every gray node having four black sons to a black node.  */
begin
value pointer node ROOT;
quadrant I,U;
integer NUM_OF_UNCOLORED;
if BLACK(ROOT) then return;  /* A leaf node */
NUM_OF_UNCOLORED ← 0;
for I in {'NW', 'NE', 'SW', 'SE'} do
    begin /* Recursively process the sons of ROOT */
    if UNCOLORED(SON(ROOT,I)) then
        begin /* An uncolored son of a gray node */
        NUM_OF_UNCOLORED ← NUM_OF_UNCOLORED+1;
        U ← I;
        end
    else ASSIGN_COLOR(SON(ROOT,I));
    end;
if NUM_OF_UNCOLORED>0 and NUM_OF_UNCOLORED<4 then
    /*  ROOT is a gray node with at least one uncolored son.  Determine if one of its
        uncolored sons corresponds to a black or white node, and set all of its uncolored
        sons to the same color. */
    begin
    do U ← CQUAD(U) /* Find a colored son adjacent to an uncolored son*/
        until not(UNCOLORED(SON(ROOT,U)));
    if not(INTERIOR(SON(ROOT,U),OPQUAD(U),CCQUAD(U),
                    COMMON_EDGE(OPQUAD(U),CCQUAD(U)))) then
        begin
        /* The uncolored node is white.  Uncolored nodes that are determined to be black
           need not have their NODETYPE field reset since it already correctly reflects the
           fact that they are black and not adjacent to any boundary. */
```

```
    for I in {'NW', 'NE', 'SW', 'SE'} do
      begin
        if UNCOLORED(SON(ROOT,I)) then NODETYPE(SON(ROOT,I)) ← 'WHITE';
      end;
      return; /* A merge is impossible as four white sons are impossible*/
    end;
  end;
if BLACK(SON(ROOT,'NW')) and BLACK(SON(ROOT,'NE')) and
  BLACK(SON(ROOT,'SW')) and BLACK(SON(ROOT,'SE')) then
  /* All four sons of node ROOT are black.  Change ROOT from gray to black, update the
    chain code, and delete ROOT's sons. */
  begin
    NODETYPE(ROOT) ← 'NOCOLOR';
    for I in {'NW', 'NE', 'SW', 'SE'} do
      NODETYPE(ROOT) ← NODETYPE(ROOT) lor
                        (NODETYPE(SON(ROOT,I)) land
                          NODETYPE(SON(ROOT,CQUAD(I)))));
    returnsonstoavail(ROOT);
  end;
end;


recursive Boolean procedure INTERIOR(ROOT,Q1,Q2,T);
/* Determine if the descendants in quadrants Q1 and Q2 of ROOT are black and are not
  adjacent to edge T of ROOT. */
begin
  value pointer node ROOT;
  value quadrant Q1,Q2;
  value edge T;
  return(if GRAY(ROOT) then
          INTERIOR(SON(ROOT,Q1),Q1,Q2,T) and
          INTERIOR(SON(ROOT,Q2),Q1,Q2,T)
        else BLACK(ROOT) and ((CODE(T) land NODETYPE(ROOT)) = 0));
end;
```

The execution time of the chain-code-to-quadtree construction process is measured by the number of nodes visited by its two phases. Phase 1 depends on the speed of procedure ADD_EDGE_NEIGHBOR, which constructs the quadtree by visiting all of the nodes having a side or a corner adjacent to the right part of the boundary. Let LEN be the length of the chain code in terms of the number of unit vectors. This is also the perimeter of the region represented by the chain code. The number of times that ADD_EDGE_NEIGHBOR is invoked is obtained by the following lemma.

Lemma 4.3   ADD_EDGE_NEIGHBOR is invoked LEN−4 times.

Proof   Clearly for any closed connected region, a clockwise chain code requires a minimum of four clockwise turns. Any counterclockwise turn requires an additional clockwise turn in excess of the minimum. To see this, consider a code proceeding in the eastern direction, as in Figure 4.20a. A counterclockwise turn as in Figure 4.20b must eventually be followed by a clockwise turn (north to east) to resume the path in the eastern direction as in Figure 4.20c and 4.20d. Note that every closed, connected nonempty region requires a chain code with at least one link in the E, S, W, and N directions. Moreover, turns in opposite directions are prohibited.

Now, recalling Figure 4.15, we see that ADD_EDGE_NEIGHBOR is invoked once for a link whose direction is unchanged from that of the previous link, never for clockwise turns, and twice for counterclockwise turns. Note that the node resulting from processing the first link in the chain is added by procedure CREATE_QNODE and not by ADD_EDGE_NEIGH-BOR. Since the number of counterclockwise turns is four fewer than the number of clockwise turns, we have the result that ADD_EDGE_NEIGHBOR is invoked LEN−4 times. ☐

Each call to ADD_EDGE_NEIGHBOR for a node P and a direction toward edge E requires time to locate a common ancestor and to retrace the reflected path to the desired node. The average number of nodes visited for each call to ADD_EDGE_NEIGH-BOR is obtained by considering all possible neighbor positions for two nodes at level 0 in a $2^n \times 2^n$ image. This number is bounded by four, as shown by the part of the analysis of procedure QT_EQ_EDGE_NEIGHBOR (see Theorem 3.1) for an image in which all of the nodes appear at level 0. Therefore we have proved

Theorem 4.4   Phase 1 has an average execution time proportional to the region's perimeter. ☐

The execution time of phase 2 depends on the speed of procedure ASSIGN_COL-OR. It traverses the partial quadtree constructed by phase 1, applies procedure INTERI-OR to determine the color of uncolored sons, and attempts to merge four sons of the same color. We first obtain a bound on the number of nodes in the partial quadtree. Assume a $2^n \times 2^n$ image with perimeter LEN.

Lemma 4.4   A quadtree for a region of perimeter LEN embedded in a $2^n \times 2^n$ image has $O(\text{LEN})$ nodes.

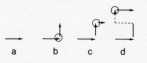

| a | b | c | d |

Figure 4.20   *Sequence of turns illustrating the need for one clockwise turn for each counterclockwise turn*

Proof   Clearly the chain code of the region forms a polygon. Thus Theorem 1.1 is applicable [Hunt78, Hunt79a]. In particular, the number of nodes in a quadtree corresponding to a polygon with perimeter p embedded in a $2^n \times 2^n$ image is $O(p+n)$. The partial quadtree obtained as a result of phase 1 satisfies Theorem 1.1 even though merging has not yet been applied. The reason for the applicability of this theorem is that in the partial quadtree, all black nodes are the same as *boundary* nodes, while those nodes labeled with a '?' are the same as *interior* or *exterior* nodes in Hunter and Steiglitz's formulation (i.e., an MX quadtree) [Hunt78, Hunt79a].

The merging process of phase 2 treats the boundary nodes as interior nodes, but this does not affect the order of the execution time of the algorithm. This $O(p+n)$ bound can be tightened to $O(p)$ because the manner in which the partial quadtree is constructed ensures that $\lceil \log_2 p \rceil - 2 \leq n \leq \lceil \log_2 p \rceil$ (see Exercise 4.47), thereby eliminating the possibility of pathological cases such as the one illustrated by Figure 4.21. Since $p = $ LEN, the desired result follows.   □

Procedure ASSIGN_COLOR visits each gray node in order to assign colors to its uncolored sons and merge the four sons if they are of the same color. Merging requires examining four nodes for each gray node. From Lemma 4.4 it can be shown that there are at most $O(\text{LEN})$ gray nodes in the partial quadtree, and thus at most $O(\text{LEN})$ nodes will be visited while attempting to merge. Coloring uncolored sons requires the traversal of a subtree of a brother of an uncolored son. This subtree is the binary tree that consists of the nodes adjacent to the boundary shared by the two brothers (e.g., the western boundary of node 13 in Figure 4.1d is adjacent to a binary tree consisting of nodes 8 and 10 and their father). The traversal of the subtree is achieved by procedure INTERIOR whose average cost is obtained below.

Lemma 4.5   The average number of nodes visited by INTERIOR is 2.

Proof   Assume a random image in the sense that a node is equally likely to appear at any position and level in the quadtree. The maximum number

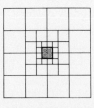

Figure 4.21   Example quadtree with $16 \cdot n - 11$ nodes

of nodes visited by procedure INTERIOR given a gray node at level i is the size of the complete binary tree rooted at level $i-1$—that is, $2^i - 1$. Noting that there are 4^{n-i} possible gray nodes at level i, we obtain the average as follows.

$$\frac{\sum_{i=1}^{n} 4^{n-i} \cdot (2^i - 1)}{\sum_{i=1}^{n} 4^{n-i}} .$$

This can be simplified using equations 3.2 and 3.3 of Section 3.2.1.2 to yield

$$2 - \frac{3 \cdot 2^n - 3}{2^{2n} - 1}$$

≤ 2 as n gets large. ☐

Theorem 4.5   Phase 2 has an average execution time proportional to the region's perimeter.

Proof   From Lemma 4.5 the average cost of assigning a color to an uncolored son is a constant. From the discussion of procedure ASSIGN_COLOR, the cost of merging is also a constant. Coloring and merging are performed for gray nodes. There are at most $O(\text{LEN})$ gray nodes, and our result follows. ☐

Therefore we have proved

Theorem 4.6   The algorithm for converting a chain code to a quadtree has an average execution time proportional to the region's perimeter. ☐

A similar algorithm with the same execution time bounds has been developed by Mark and Abel [Mark85a] to construct an FL linear quadtree from a vector representation of a polygon. Their algorithm has three steps. First they construct a chain code representation of the polygon. Next they obtain a list of the FL locational codes of pixels that are inside the region and adjacent to the boundary. With each pixel a NODETYPE field is associated with the same meaning as used in the algorithm described here. Finally they infer the colors of the absent nodes by using properties of the locational code representation.

Webber [Webb84] has devised a different algorithm for constructing a quadtree from a chain code representation of a region. The analysis of its execution time is in terms of a worst case instead of average behavior—that is, his algorithm's worst-case execution time is proportional to the region's perimeter, which is optimal. However, for a $2^n \times 2^n$ image, its space requirements are $O(2^{2 \cdot n})$.

Webber's algorithm has two phases. The first phase is facilitated by mapping the region onto a two-dimensional array formed by its enclosing rectangle so that each pixel corresponds to an array element. Next it tabulates the number of times each row and column is crossed by a link in the chain code. These frequencies are used to determine the amount by which the image should be shifted in the horizontal and vertical directions so that the average of the number of nodes examined by all of the neighbor-finding operations performed in the first phase is bounded from above by four. This shifting process can be done in time proportional to the region's perimeter. Once the image has been shifted, it is traversed, and a quadtree is built where the nodes on the inside of the border have been colored appropriately.

The second phase traverses the quadtree in a top-down manner by transmitting, as actual parameters, the neighbors of each node in the principal directions (see, e.g., [Same85a]). This traversal is achieved in time proportional to the region's perimeter because the number of nodes is of this order. The technique used is similar to AS-SIGN_COLOR in the sense that a gray node is processed before its uncolored brothers. For more details see [Webb84] in which the algorithm has been somewhat modified to enable it to achieve the same time bounds for an image that contains more than one region as well as holes.

Exercises

4.41. In the process of constructing a quadtree from a chain code, we compare two consecutive chain code segments, NEW and OLD. When the direction of NEW is counterclockwise from OLD, is it true that two nodes are always added?

4.42. In procedure CHAINCODE_TO_QUADTREE when NEW is in the counterclockwise direction with respect to OLD, we may have to add two nodes. In this case, the situation may arise that one of the nodes may have none of its sides adjacent to the boundary (e.g., nodes 4, 6, 12, and 14 in Figure 4.16). Such a node is treated as an uncolored node in phase 1. However, in ASSIGN_COLOR an uncolored node is treated as a black node insofar as the predicate BLACK is concerned. This enables merging four nodes of the same color. Prove that if four uncolored nodes are brothers, they cannot all correspond to white nodes. Can all of them correspond to black nodes?

4.43. Procedure CHAINCODE_TO_QUADTREE converts the chain code of a single region to a quadtree. Modify it to deal with an image that contains several regions.

4.44. Modify procedure CHAINCODE_TO_QUADTREE to deal with an image that contains regions with holes as well.

4.45. Given a region with maximum horizontal and vertical extents h and v, respectively, what is the minimum and maximum size of the side of the quadtree in which it can be embedded? Modify procedure CHAINCODE_TO_QUADTREE so that the resulting quadtree is embedded in a quadtree of minimum side length.

4.46. Suppose that you have found the minimum side length, say m, for the quadtree in which the chain-coded image can be embedded. How would you construct the quadtree so that all images for a given value of m are in a standard position? This ensures that cyclic permutations of the chain code do not result in different quadtrees.

4.47. Assume a region whose chain code has length p, which is embedded in a $2^n \times 2^n$ image. Prove that the relation $\lceil \log_2 p \rceil - 2 \leq n \leq \lceil \log_2 p \rceil$ holds for the partial quadtree resulting from phase 1 of the chain-code-to-quadtree construction process.

4.48. Suppose that the partial quadtree obtained as a result of phase 1 of the chain-code-to-quadtree algorithm contains B black nodes as level 0 (i.e., nodes adjacent to the boundary of the region). Assuming a $2^n \times 2^n$ image, prove that the resulting quadtree has at most $4 \cdot B \cdot n + 1$ nodes.

4.49. The bound obtained in Theorem 4.5 is in terms of an average case. Tighten this bound to be in terms of a worst case by reworking the proof of Lemma 4.5 to use the fact that the total number of nodes in all adjacency trees for a given quadtree is bounded by four times the number of leaf nodes in the quadtree (see Exercise 3.13).

4.50. The quadtree constructed by procedure CHAINCODE_TO_QUADTREE does not necessarily have a minimum number of nodes. For example, we might be able to reduce the number of nodes by choosing a different location to serve as the root of the quadtree. Modify procedure CHAINCODE_TO_QUADTREE so that it locates the root of the quadtree in a position so that the number of nodes will be minimized.

4.51. Procedure CHAINCODE_TO_QUADTREE has an average-case execution time proportional to the region's perimeter. Give a set of procedures to reduce its order of the execution time so that in the worst case it is proportional to the region's perimeter.

4.52. Can you reduce the execution time of the second phase of the chain-code-to-quadtree algorithm described in Exercise 4.51 even further so that the traversal takes time proportional to the number of nodes rather than to the perimeter?

4.53. Modify procedure CHAINCODE_TO_QUADTREE to yield a bintree.

4.54. Modify procedure CHAINCODE_TO_QUADTREE to yield an FD linear quadtree. Can you take advantage of the fact that the list of locational codes for the pixels adjacent to the boundary is sorted in a particular order to implement the analog of procedure ASSIGN_COLOR efficiently? In essence, locational codes of uncolored nodes must be either retained or merged, in the case of black leaf nodes, or ignored, in the case of white leaf nodes. With the exception of sorting the results of phase 1, your solution should try to make only one pass over the data. Analyze the speed of the algorithm in terms of the perimeter of the image and the number of elements in the FD linear quadtree.

4.55. Modify procedure CHAINCODE_TO_QUADTREE to yield a quadtree in the form of a DF-expression. Analyze the speed of the algorithm in terms of the number of elements of the DF-expression that will have to be visited. How is this related to the perimeter of the image?

4.56. Generalize the techniques used in procedure CHAINCODE_TO_QUADTREE to handle three-dimensional data and construct an octree from a three-dimensional boundary representation.

4.3.2 Building a Chain Code from a Quadtree

The quadtree-to-chain-code construction algorithm [Dyer80b] consists of tracing the boundary of a given region in a clockwise direction once an appropriate starting point has been determined. Generally the starting point is not unique. Without loss of generality, the starting point is determined by searching for a pair of nodes, P and Q, such that P is black and Q is white and Q is to the south of P. See Figure 4.22 for some possible configurations involving P and Q.

This process starts at the root of the quadtree and descends in the order SW, SE, NW, and NE, avoiding white nodes until a black node P is reached. This node cannot have a black node adjacent to its southern side because we always descend to southern sons unless both southern sons are white. Assuming that the region does not reach the border of the corresponding image, we see that the node Q that is adjacent to P's southern edge and making contact with the SW vertex of P must be white. The problem that arises when the southern edge of P is on the border of the image is avoided by surrounding the image with white blocks, as in Figure 3.4a. At this point, nodes P and Q form an initial (BLACK,WHITE) node pair.

The boundary consists of a sequence of (BLACK,WHITE) node pairs. Given an arbitrary pair of adjacent black and white nodes, say P and Q, respectively, we assume without loss of generality that the block corresponding to P is to the north of the block corresponding to Q. Boundary tracing is a two-step procedure that is applied to each black-white adjacency. Figures 4.22 and 4.23 illustrate these two steps. First, output the chain link associated with that part of P's boundary adjacent to Q. The length of the chain is equal to the minimum of the sizes of the adjacent blocks.

Second, determine the (BLACK,WHITE) node pair that borders the subsequent link in the chain as the boundary is traversed. This depends on the relative positions of P and Q that define the current link. They are shown in Figure 4.22. In the first case, P extends past Q (Figure 4.22a). In the second case, Q extends past P (Figure 4.22b). In the third case, P and Q meet at the same point (Figures 4.22c and 4.22d).

The identity of the next (BLACK,WHITE) node pair is obtained by examining the node configurations given in Figure 4.23. In particular, the next pair consists of the two blocks that are adjacent to the arrow. The relationship between these node configurations and Figure 4.22 is explained below. Note that at times we may have to examine some adjacent nodes (i.e., X and Y). This is done by using the neighbor-finding techniques discussed in Section 3.2.1.1.

1. Figures 4.23a and 4.23b correspond to Figure 4.22a, with X being WHITE and BLACK, respectively.

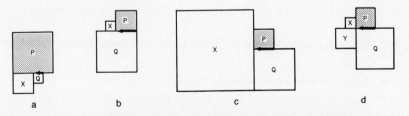

Figure 4.22 Possible overlap relationships between the (BLACK, WHITE) adjacent node pair (P,Q). The arrow indicates the boundary segment just output.

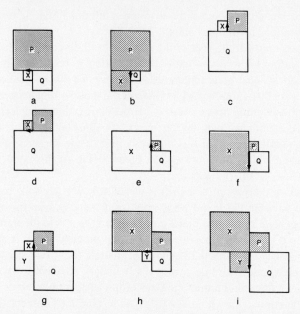

Figure 4.23   Possible configurations of P,Q, and their neighbor blocks in determining the next (BLACK, WHITE) pair. The arrow indicates the next boundary segment to be output.

2. Figures 4.23c and 4.23d correspond to Figure 4.22b, with X being WHITE and BLACK, respectively.

3. Figures 4.23e and 4.23f correspond to Figure 4.22c, with X being WHITE and BLACK, respectively.

4. Figure 4.23g corresponds to Figure 4.22d, with X being WHITE. Note that we assume that the region is 4-connected so that blocks making contact only at a vertex are not adjacent. This is why the pair in Figure 4.23g is (P,X)—that is, the boundary turns right regardless of the type of node Y.

5. Figure 4.23h corresponds to Figure 4.22d, with X being BLACK and Y being WHITE.

6. Figure 4.23i corresponds to Figure 4.22d, with X and Y being BLACK.

The following procedures specify the quadtree-to-chain-code algorithm. The main procedure is termed QUADTREE_TO_CHAINCODE and is invoked with a pointer to the root of the quadtree representing the image and an integer corresponding to the log of the diameter of the image (e.g., n for a $2^n \times 2^n$ image). First it locates the initial (BLACK,WHITE) pair of nodes. Next it invokes procedure NEXT_LINK to trace the boundary and output the appropriate links of the chain code.

The nodes adjacent to the boundary are located by procedure QT_VERTEX_-EDGE_NEIGHBOR2. It is a variant of QT_VERTEX_EDGE_NEIGHBOR, given in Section 3.2.1.1, that also returns the level at which the neighboring node is found. Boolean procedure ALIGNED, given in Section 3.2.1.1, aids in distinguishing between Figures 4.22a and 4.22b and Figures 4.22c and 4.22d for the current (BLACK,WHITE) pair of nodes.

As the chain code is generated, it is placed in a list by procedure ADD_TO_LINK_-LIST (not given here). The function LINK(E) yields the chain code direction associated with edge E of a node. Using the naming convention for chain code directions described in Section 4.3, we have that LINK('N') = 0, LINK('E') = 3, LINK('S') = 2, and LINK('W') = 1. To be able to detect the end of the boundary tracing process, we use procedure MARK to mark each element of an adjacent pair of nodes that has been visited. Procedure MARKED checks if a pair of nodes has been marked and, if so, terminates the boundary tracing process. Application of this procedure to the black region of Figure 4.1a yields

$$2^2 1^3 0^1 1^1 0^1 1^2 0^4 3^4 2^2 3^1 2^1 3^1 2^1.$$

```
procedure QUADTREE_TO_CHAINCODE(ROOT,LEVEL);
/* Construct the chain code corresponding to the quadtree rooted at ROOT representing a
   2^LEVEL × 2^LEVEL image. */
begin
  value pointer node ROOT;
  value integer LEVEL;
  pointer node P,Q;
  integer LP,LQ;
  P ← ROOT;
  LP ← LEVEL; /* LEVEL and LP are used to determine the length of edges of blocks */
while GRAY(P) do
  /* Find a black node P that is on the region boundary and has no black nodes adjacent to
     its southern edge. Q, a white node, is the westernmost of P's southern neighbors. The
     pair (P,Q) defines the initial chain segment. */
  begin
    LP ← LP−1;
    P ← SON(P,if not(WHITE(SON(P,'SW'))) then 'SW'
                else if not(WHITE(SON(P,'SE'))) then 'SE'
                else if not(WHITE(SON(P,'NW'))) then 'NW'
                else 'NE');
  end;
  LQ ← LP;
  QT_VERTEX_EDGE_NEIGHBOR2(P,'S', 'SW', Q,LQ);
  NEXT_LINK(P,LP,Q,LQ,'S'); /* Trace the boundary */
end;
```

recursive procedure NEXT_LINK(P,LP,Q,LQ,E);
/* Black node P at level LP and white node Q at level Q are adjacent along edge E of P.
  Output the corresponding chain code description, and determine the next pair of adjacent black and white nodes. */
begin
 value pointer node P,Q;
 value integer LP,LQ;
 value edge E;
 pointer node X,Y;
 integer I,LX,LY;
 if MARKED(P,Q) **then return** /* Done */
 else MARK(P,Q);
 for I←1 **step** 1 **until** 2↑MIN(LP,LQ) **do** ADD_TO_LINK_LIST(LINK(E));
 /* Determine the next pair of adjacent black and white nodes */
 if ALIGNED(P,LP,Q,LQ,CEDGE(E)) **then**
   /* P and Q are aligned in the direction of CEDGE(E) of P */
   begin
    LX ← LP;
    QT_VERTEX_EDGE_NEIGHBOR2(P,CEDGE(E),
                        VERTEX(CEDGE(E),E),
                        X,LX);
    if WHITE(X) **then** /* Figures 4.23e and 4.23g */
     NEXT_LINK(P,LP,X,LX,CEDGE(E))
    else
     begin
      LY ← LQ;
      QT_VERTEX_EDGE_NEIGHBOR2(Q,CEDGE(E),
                          VERTEX(CEDGE(E),OPEDGE(E)),
                          Y,LY);
      if BLACK(Y) **then**
       NEXT_LINK(Y,LY,Q,LQ,CCEDGE(E)) /* Figures 4.23f and 4.23i */
      else NEXT_LINK(X,LX,Y,LY,E); /* Figure 4.23h */
     end;
   end
 else if LP > LQ **then** /* Black extends farther than white */
   begin
    LX ← LQ;
    QT_VERTEX_EDGE_NEIGHBOR2(Q,CEDGE(E),
                        VERTEX(CEDGE(E),OPEDGE(E)),
                        X,LX);
    if WHITE(X) **then** NEXT_LINK(P,LP,X,LX,E) /* Figure 4.23a */
    else NEXT_LINK(X,LX,Q,LQ,CCEDGE(E)); /* Figure 4.23b */
   end
 else /* White extends farther than black */
   begin
    LX ← LP;
    QT_VERTEX_EDGE_NEIGHBOR2(P,CEDGE(E),
                        VERTEX(CEDGE(E),E),
                        X,LX);

```
      if WHITE(X) then NEXT_LINK(P,LP,X,LX,CEDGE(E)) /* Figure 4.23c */
      else NEXT_LINK(X,LX,Q,LQ,E); /* Figure 4.23d */
   end;
end;
```

The execution time of the quadtree-to-chain-code algorithm is measured by the number of nodes visited. The algorithm has two steps. The first step locates the initial (BLACK, WHITE) node pair, which requires that at most n nodes be visited for a $2^n \times 2^n$ image. The second step traces the boundary using procedure NEXT_LINK. It has two parts that are executed in parallel.

The first part outputs the chain code description for each boundary segment. The time required to output the individual boundary segments is proportional to the region's perimeter, where the perimeter is defined to be the number of unit-square pixels on the region's boundary (not the number of black nodes adjacent to white nodes).

The second part determines the next (BLACK, WHITE) adjacent node pair. This is achieved with the aid of procedures ALIGNED and QT_VERTEX_EDGE_NEIGHBOR2. For each pair (P,Q) of adjacent (BLACK, WHITE) nodes respectively, ALIGNED is called once, and QT_VERTEX_EDGE_NEIGHBOR2 is called at most twice (once in cases corresponding to Figures 4.22a and 4.22b and twice in cases corresponding to Figures 4.22c and 4.22d). From Theorems 3.5 and 3.7, we have that the average number of nodes visited by QT_VERTEX_EDGE_NEIGHBOR2 and ALIGNED is 11/3 and 1/2 respectively. The number of (BLACK, WHITE) adjacency determinations is bounded by the region's perimeter. Therefore we have now proved

Theorem 4.7 The algorithm for obtaining the chain code description of a region of an image represented by a quadtree has an average execution time proportional to the sum of the region's perimeter and the log of the diameter of the image. □

Note that in all but extreme pathological cases, as illustrated by the image in Figure 4.21, the perimeter dominates the cost of the algorithm. If the image has been shifted using methods similar to those described by Webber [Webb84] for the construction of the quadtree from a chain code, then the algorithm can be shown to have a worst-case execution time of order perimeter rather than an average-case bound.

The algorithm described in this section follows the boundary of a single region and uses neighbor finding. This approach is not appropriate when the image is stored on disk using one of the pointerless representations such as the FD linear quadtree. The problem is that neighbor finding may be expensive due to page faults. Dillencourt and Samet [Dill88] give an algorithm to output the boundaries of all regions in a quadtree using one pass over the data. This approach can be used with both pointer and pointerless quadtree representations (see Exercise 4.66).

Exercises

4.57. Procedure NEXT_LINK makes use of MARK and MARKED to determine when the entire boundary of a region has been traversed. Prove that NEXT_LINK does not terminate too early (i.e., without having traversed the entire boundary of the region). In other words, prove that the same pair of nodes cannot be adjacent more than once.

4.58. Is it necessary to dedicate an entire field in each quadtree node for the marking phase?

4.59. Implement QT_VERTEX_EDGE_NEIGHBOR2 by modifying procedure QT_VERTEX_EDGE_NEIGHBOR given in Section 3.2.1.1.

4.60. Procedure NEXT_LINK is written using recursion. However, the recursion is of the type called *tail recursion*, which means that the recursion is the last executable step in the procedure. Thus it can be implemented efficiently by a compiler that performs flow analysis (see [Hech77]). Suppose your compiler is not so smart; recode NEXT_LINK so that it uses a *while* loop instead of recursion.

4.61. By examining Figures 4.22 and 4.23 we see that many of the steps of the various cases are similar. The code given for procedure NEXT_LINK tries to be faithful to the case analysis of the figures. Thus the procedure is longer than it need be. Apply common subexpression elimination techniques to get rid of some of the common code sequences. For example, you could compute X and Y in only one place.

4.62. Extend procedure QUADTREE_TO_CHAINCODE to deal with regions that contain holes.

4.63. Procedure QUADTREE_TO_CHAINCODE could also be used to compute the perimeter of a region. Write an alternative algorithm to compute the perimeter that does not have to trace the boundary of the region sequentially. The algorithm should have an execution time proportional to the number of blocks in the image.

4.64. Procedure QUADTREE_TO_CHAINCODE and Figures 4.22 and 4.23 assume that the region whose boundary is being traced is 4-connected so that blocks touching at a corner are not adjacent. Redefine procedure QUADTREE_TO_CHAINCODE so that it can handle an 8-connected region.

4.65. Develop an algorithm analogous to procedure QUADTREE_TO_CHAINCODE to convert a bintree representation of a quadtree to a chain code.

4.66. Write a procedure QUADTREE_TO_CHAINCODE to convert a quadtree in the form of an FD linear quadtree to a chain code. Assume that the image consists of more than one component. The procedure should make only one pass over the data.

4.67. Write an analog of procedure QUADTREE_TO_CHAINCODE to convert a quadtree in the form of a DF-expression to a chain code. What is the order of the execution time of your algorithm?

4.4 QUADTREES FROM POLYGONS

The chain code can be used as an approximation of a polygon by unit vectors. It is also common to represent polygonal data by an ordered set of vertices or even a point and a sequence of vectors consisting of pairs (i.e., (magnitude, direction)). Recall from Section 1.2 that Hunter and Steiglitz [Hunt78, Hunt79a, Hunt79b] address the problem of representing simple polygons (i.e., polygons with nonintersecting edges and without holes) by using an MX quadtree (e.g., Figure 1.5).

Hunter and Steiglitz present two algorithms for building an MX quadtree from a polygon. The first is a top-down algorithm, which starts at the root and splits the space into four blocks, creating the necessary nodes. Each node whose block (which is not a pixel) intersects the polygonal boundary is recursively split. Given a polygon with v vertices and a perimeter p (in units of pixel width), construction of a quadtree within a $2^n \times 2^n$ space from a polygon has execution time of $O(p+n)$. Unfortunately the quadtree-from-polygon construction algorithm does not distinguish between an interior and an exterior node. This can be done by testing each of the $O(p+n)$ nodes against the polygon, a process that takes $O(v)$ time per node. Thus the total execution time to build the quadtree and label the nodes is $O(v \cdot (p+n))$.

The second algorithm for constructing an MX quadtree from a polygon is termed an *outline-and-color algorithm*. It has two steps, *outline* and *color*. The outline step combines a top-down decomposition of the space in which the polygon is embedded with a traversal of the boundary, resulting in a roped quadtree (see Section 3.2.2). During the construction process, neighbors are computed as a by-product of the top-down decomposition process. The outline algorithm has an execution time of $O(v+p+n)$.

The outline step does not distinguish between an interior and an exterior node. This is achieved by the color step. It propagates the color of the boundary nodes inward, by initially traversing the boundary and stacking all sides that are within the polygon (see Exercise 4.70) for each boundary node. Coloring is propagated by examining stack entries and their adjacent leaf nodes. For stack entry S, if the block corresponding to its adjacent leaf node, say T, is not smaller and is uncolored, then T is colored and all of its sides with the exception of S are placed on the stack. S is removed from the stack and colored.

The key to the color step is that boundary nodes (i.e., pixels) are small and that their neighbors get larger as the center of the polygon is approached. The color step makes use of a netted quadtree (recall Section 3.2.2) to facilitate the calculation of neighboring nodes. It has been shown to have an execution time proportional to the number of nodes in the quadtree being colored. Combining the outline algorithm, a netting process, and the coloring algorithm leads to a quadtree-from-polygon algorithm with execution time of $O(v+p+n)$.

Exercises

4.68. Prove that the outline step has an execution time of $O(v+p+n)$.

4.69. Prove that the color step has an execution time proportional to the number of nodes in the quadtree being colored.

4.70. The color step of the outline-and-color algorithm requires that the boundary be traversed and that all sides within the polygon be stacked. To do this, we must know which sides are within the polygon. How is this done? How much time does it take?

4.5 BUILDING A PM$_1$ QUADTREE

Section 1.3 described the PM$_1$ quadtree, which finds use in representing polygonal maps. It represents regions by specifying their boundaries. This is in contrast to the

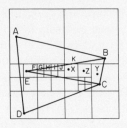

Figure 4.24   PM₁ quadtree corresponding to the polygonal
map of Figure 1.14

region quadtree, which is based on a description of the region's interior. The advantage of the PM₁ quadtree is that it is not an approximation. It is not based on a digitization (as is the MX quadtree). Thus it can be used to represent boundaries of regions (and road networks) exactly. This section gives algorithms to build and update a PM₁ quadtree, as well as discusses its implementation. (For more details on this representation, see Section 4.2.3 of [Same90a].)

The PM₁ quadtree is organized in a similar way to the region and PR quadtrees (recall Section 1.3). A region is repeatedly subdivided into four equal-sized quadrants until we obtain blocks that do not contain more than one line. To deal with lines that intersect other lines, we say that if a block contains a point, say P, then we permit it to contain more than one line provided that P is an endpoint of each of the lines it contains. A block can never contain more than one endpoint. For example, Figure 4.24 is the block decomposition of the PM₁ quadtree corresponding to the polygonal map of Figure 1.14, while Figure 4.25 is its tree representation.

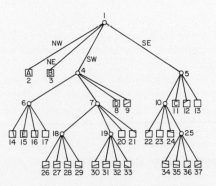

Figure 4.25   Tree representation of the PM₁ quadtree
corresponding to the polygonal map of Figure 1.14

The definition of a PM₁ quadtree can be made more rigorous by viewing the polygonal map as a straight-line planar graph consisting of vertices and edges. The term *q-edge* (denoting a quadtree-decomposition edge) is used to refer to a segment of an edge formed by clipping [Roge85] an edge of the polygonal map against the border of the region represented by a quadtree node (e.g., q-edges FG and GH in Figure 4.24). It should be clear that every edge (i.e., line segment) of the map is covered by a set of q-edges that touch only at their endpoints. For example, edge EB in Figure 4.24 consists of the q-edges EF, FG, GH, HI, IJ, JK, and KB. Note that only B and E are vertices; F, G, H, I, J, and K merely serve as reference points. At this point, the definition of a PM₁ *quadtree* can be restated as satisfying the following conditions:

1. At most, one vertex can lie in a region represented by a quadtree leaf node.
2. If a quadtree leaf node's region contains a vertex, it can contain no q-edge that does not include that vertex.
3. If a quadtree leaf node's region contains no vertices, it can contain, at most, one q-edge.
4. Each region's quadtree leaf node is maximal.

This definition of a PM₁ quadtree is similar to that of a PR quadtree. The difference is that we are representing edges here rather than points. This affects the action to be taken when the decomposition induced by the PM₁ quadtree results in a vertex that lies on the border of a quadtree node (e.g., vertex A in Figure 4.26). We could move the vertices so that this does not happen, but generally this requires global knowledge about the maximum depth of the quadtree prior to its construction.

Alternatively we could establish the convention that some sides of the region represented by a node are closed and other sides are open; that is, the lower and left boundaries of each block are closed, while the right and upper boundaries of each block are open. However, this leads to a problem when at least three edges meet at a vertex on the border of a quadtree node such that two of the edges are in the open quadrant (i.e., the one not containing the vertex). These two edges may have to be

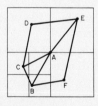

Figure 4.26 *Example polygonal map where vertex A lies on the border of a quadtree node. The decomposition lines are those induced by a PM₁ quadtree definition in which a vertex is inserted in each of the nodes on whose border it lies.*

decomposed to a very deep level in order to separate them (e.g., edges AB and AC in the SW quadrant of Figure 4.26).

Therefore the convention usually adopted is that all quadrants are closed. This means that a vertex that lies on the border between two (or three but never more than four) nodes is inserted in each of the nodes on whose border it lies. Such vertices can be treated as edges of zero length.

Since the PM₁ quadtree is used to implement isolated points and lines as well as polygonal maps, its basic entities are vertices and edges. Each vertex is represented as a record of type *point*, which has two fields, XCOORD and YCOORD, that correspond to the x and y coordinates, respectively, of the point. They can be of type real or integer depending on implementation considerations such as floating point precision.

An edge is implemented as a record of type *line* with four fields: P1, P2, LEFT, and RIGHT. P1 and P2 contain pointers to the records containing the edge's vertices. LEFT and RIGHT are pointers to structures that identify the regions on the two sides of the edge. We shall use the convention that LEFT and RIGHT are with respect to a view of the edge that treats the vertex closest to the origin as the start of the edge. For example, for edge DA in the polygonal map of Figure 1.14, its LEFT and RIGHT fields are marked as being associated with regions 1 and 2, respectively. For a discussion of how such labels are maintained, see Section 4.2.3.6 of [Same90a]. The algorithms given here ignore these two fields.

Each node in a PM₁ quadtree is a collection of q-edges represented as a record of type *node* containing seven fields. The first four fields contain pointers to the node's four sons corresponding to the directions (i.e., quadrants) NW, NE, SW, and SE. If P is a pointer to a node and I is a quadrant, then these fields are referenced as SON(P,I). The fifth field, NODETYPE, indicates whether the node is a leaf node (LEAF) or a nonleaf node (GRAY).

The sixth field, SQUARE, is a pointer to a record of type *square* that indicates the size of the block corresponding to the node. It is defined for both leaf and nonleaf nodes. It has two fields, CENTER and LEN. CENTER points to a record of type point that contains the x and y coordinates of the center of the square. LEN contains the length of a side of the square that is the block corresponding to the node in the PM₁ quadtree.

DICTIONARY is the last field. It is a pointer to a data structure that represents the set of q-edges associated with the node. Initially the universe is empty and consists of no edges or vertices. It is represented by a tree of one node of type LEAF whose DICTIONARY field points to the empty set.

In the implementation given here, the set of q-edges for each LEAF node is a linked list whose elements are records of type *edgelist* containing two fields, DATA and NEXT. DATA points to a record of type line corresponding to the edge of which the q-edge is a member. NEXT points to the record corresponding to the next q-edge in the list of q-edges. Although the set of q-edges is stored as a list here, it should be implemented by a data structure that supports efficient updating and searching, as well as set union and set difference operations.

For example, the set of q-edges could be implemented as a dictionary in the form of a 2-3 tree [Aho74] where the q-edges are ordered by the angle that they form with a ray originating at the vertex and parallel to the positive x axis. Since the number of q-edges passing through a leaf is bounded from above by the number of vertices belonging to the polygonal map, say V, the depth of the dictionary structure is at most $\log_2 V + 1$. However, a linked list is usually sufficient since in empirical tests, described in Section 4.2.4 of [Same90a], the list rarely had as many as five items in it. The set of q-edges corresponding to a gray node is said to be empty. Note that all of the q-edges comprising a given edge point to the same line record.

Lines (or edges) are inserted into a PM$_1$ quadtree by searching for the position they are to occupy. The implementation given below assumes that whenever an edge or an isolated vertex is inserted into the PM$_1$ quadtree, it is not already there or does not intersect an existing edge. However, an endpoint of an edge may intersect an existing vertex provided it is not an isolated vertex (i.e., an edge with length zero). To insert an edge that intersects an isolated vertex, the isolated vertex should be removed beforehand.

An edge is inserted into a PM$_1$ quadtree by traversing the tree in preorder and successively clipping it (using CLIP_LINES) against the blocks corresponding to the nodes. Clipping is important because it enables us to avoid looking at areas where the edge cannot be inserted. The insertion process is controlled by procedure PM_INSERT, which actually inserts a list of edges.

If the edge can be inserted into the node (i.e., the conditions of a PM$_1$ quadtree node are satisfied), say P, then PM_INSERT does so and exits. Otherwise a list, say L, is formed containing the edge and any q-edges already present in the node, P is split using SPLIT_PM_NODE, and PM_INSERT is recursively invoked to attempt to insert the elements of L in the four sons of P. PM_INSERT uses PM1_CHECK and SHARE_PM1_VERTEX to determine if the conditions of the definition of the PM$_1$ quadtree are satisfied. Isolated vertices pose no problems and are handled by PM1_CHECK.

Procedure CLIP_SQUARE is a predicate that indicates if an edge crosses a square. Similarly, procedure PT_IN_SQUARE is a predicate that indicates if a vertex lies in a square. They are responsible for enforcing the conventions with respect to vertices and edges that lie on the boundaries of blocks. Their code is not given here. Equality between records corresponding to vertices is tested by use of the '=' symbol, which requires that its two operands be of the same type (i.e., pointers to records of type point). For example, Figure 4.27 shows how the PM$_1$ quadtree for the polygonal map of Figure 1.14 is constructed in incremental fashion for edges AB, BC, CD, AD, and CE.

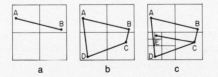

a   b   c

Figure 4.27   Steps in the construction of the PM$_1$ quadtree
for the polygonal map of Figure 1.14 as edges (a) AB, (b)
BC, CD, AD, and (c) CE are processed

```
recursive procedure PM_INSERT(P,R);
/* Insert the list of edges pointed at by P in the PM₁ quadtree rooted at R. */
begin
  value pointer edgelist P;
  value pointer node R;
  pointer edgelist L;
  quadrant I;
  L ← CLIP_LINES(P,SQUARE(R));
  if empty(L) then return; /* No new edges belong in the quadrant */
  if LEAF(R) then /* A leaf node */
    begin
      L ← MERGE_LISTS(L,DICTIONARY(R));
      if PM1_CHECK(L,SQUARE(R)) then
        begin
          DICTIONARY(R) ← L;
          return;
        end
      else SPLIT_PM_NODE(R);
    end;
  for I in {'NW', 'NE', 'SW', 'SE'} do PM_INSERT(L,SON(R,I));
end;


recursive edgelist procedure CLIP_LINES(L,R);
/* Collect all of the edges in the list of edges pointed at by L that intersect the square
   pointed at by R. ADD_TO_LIST(X,S) adds element X to the list S and returns a pointer
   to the resulting list. */
begin
  value pointer edgelist L;
  value pointer square R;
  return(if empty(L) then NIL
          else if CLIP_SQUARE(DATA(L),R) then
            ADD_TO_LIST(DATA(L),CLIP_LINES(NEXT(L),R))
          else CLIP_LINES(NEXT(L),R));
end;


Boolean procedure PM1_CHECK(L,S);
/* Determine if the square pointed at by S and the list of edges pointed at by L form a legal
   PM₁ quadtree node. ONE_ELEMENT(L) is a predicate that indicates if L contains just
   one element. */
begin
  value pointer edgelist L;
  value pointer square S;
  return(if P1(DATA(L)) = P2(DATA(L)) then
            ONE_ELEMENT(L) /* Isolated vertex */
          else if ONE_ELEMENT(L) then /* Both vertices can lie outside the square */
            not(PT_IN_SQUARE(P1(DATA(L)),S) and
                PT_IN_SQUARE(P2(DATA(L)),S))
```

```
        else if PT_IN_SQUARE(P1(DATA(L)),S) and
             PT_IN_SQUARE(P2(DATA(L)),S) then false
        else if PT_IN_SQUARE(P1(DATA(L)),S) then
          SHARE_PM1_VERTEX(P1(DATA(L)),NEXT(L),S)
        else if PT_IN_SQUARE(P2(DATA(L)),S) then
          SHARE_PM1_VERTEX(P2(DATA(L)),NEXT(L),S)
        else false);
end;


recursive Boolean procedure SHARE_PM1_VERTEX(P,L,S);
/* The vertex pointed at by P is in the square pointed at by S. Determine if all the edges in
   the list of edges pointed at by L share P and do not have their other vertex within S. */
begin
  value pointer point P;
  value pointer edgelist L;
  value pointer square S;
  return(if empty(L) then true
        else if P = P1(DATA(L)) then
          not(PT_IN_SQUARE(P2(DATA(L)),S)) and
          SHARE_PM1_VERTEX(P,NEXT(L),S)
        else if P = P2(DATA(L)) then
          not(PT_IN_SQUARE(P1(DATA(L)),S)) and
          SHARE_PM1_VERTEX(P,NEXT(L),S)
        else false);
end;


procedure SPLIT_PM_NODE(P);
/* Add four sons to the node pointed at by P and change P to be of type GRAY. */
begin
  value pointer node P;
  quadrant I,J;
  pointer node Q;
  pointer square S;
  /* XF and YF contain multiplicative factors to aid in the location of the centers of the
     quadrant sons while descending the tree */
  preload real array XF['NW', 'NE', 'SW', 'SE'] with -0.25,0.25,-0.25,0.25;
  preload real array YF['NW', 'NE', 'SW', 'SE'] with 0.25,0.25,-0.25,-0.25;
  for I in {'NW', 'NE', 'SW', 'SE'} do
    begin
      Q ← create(node);
      SON(P,I) ← Q;
      for J in {'NW', 'NE', 'SW', 'SE'} do SON(Q,J) ← NIL;
      NODETYPE(Q) ← 'LEAF';
      S ← create(square);
      SQUARE(Q) ← S;
      CENTER(S) ← create(point);
      XCOORD(CENTER(S)) ← XCOORD(CENTER(SQUARE(P)))+
                          XF[I]*LEN(SQUARE(P));
```

```
        YCOORD(CENTER(S)) ← YCOORD(CENTER(SQUARE(P)))+
                            YF[I]*LEN(SQUARE(P));
        LEN(S) ← 0.5*LEN(SQUARE(P));
        DICTIONARY(Q) ← DICTIONARY(P);
      end;
    DICTIONARY(P) ← NIL;
    NODETYPE(P) ← 'GRAY';
  end;
```

The control structure for deleting an edge from a PM₁ quadtree is identical to that used in the insertion of an edge. Again the tree is traversed in preorder, and the edge is successively clipped (using CLIP_LINES) against the blocks corresponding to the nodes. This process is controlled by procedure PM_DELETE, which actually deletes a list of edges.

Once a leaf node is encountered in which the edge participates, the node's DIC-TIONARY field is updated to show the elimination of the edge. After processing the four sons of a gray node, an attempt is made to merge the four sons by use of procedures POSSIBLE_PM1_MERGE and TRY_TO_MERGE_PM1 to check if the conditions of the PM₁ quadtree are satisfied. These procedures make use of PM1_CHECK. In the case of a merge, storage is reclaimed by RETURN_TREE_TO_AVAIL.

The check for merging is made at each level of the tree in which processing one of the sons of a nonleaf node has resulted in the deletion of a q-edge. In particular, merging can occur if at least one of the sons of a nonleaf node is a leaf node (checked by POSSIBLE_PM1_MERGE). There are two situations where merging must occur. The deletion of edge BE from Figure 1.14 is used as an example to illustrate them. The discussion refers to nodes in Figures 4.24 and 4.25.

The first situation arises when the deletion of an edge has resulted in four brother leaf nodes having zero or one edge pass through them. In the example, removal of q-edges FG and GH from nodes 26 and 27 leaves nonleaf node 18 with only one edge (i.e., CE) passing through it. This means that merging can be applied after processing the remaining sons of nonleaf node 18. Similarly, removal of q-edges HI and IJ from nodes 30 and 31 leaves node 19 with only one edge (i.e., CE) passing through it. Once again merging is applied after processing the remaining sons of nonleaf node 19. In fact, further merging is possible at this point since nonleaf node 7 now has only one edge (i.e., CE) passing through it.

The second situation is somewhat tricky. It arises when deletion causes all of the remaining edges in the descendants of the nonleaf node, say N, to have a common vertex that lies in one of the sons of N (not a descendant of N, which is not a son!). In this case, merging can occur, thereby making N a leaf node. In the example, removal of q-edge JK from node 22 leaves nonleaf node 10 with only two edges (CE and CD) passing through node 25 and having C as a common vertex. Moreover, removal of q-edge JK also leaves nonleaf node 5 with the three edges BC, CD, and CE passing through it and, again, all having C as a common vertex. Thus merging is applied to the sons of nodes 25, 10, and 5 in succession.

In this example, it is very important to note that merging can occur only after processing the sons of nonleaf node 5. The reason it cannot be performed sooner (e.g., in part, after processing the sons of nonleaf nodes 25 or 10) is that the common vertex (C) is not in the node whose sons are being merged.

```
recursive procedure PM_DELETE(P,R);
/* Delete the list of edges pointed at by P from the PM₁ quadtree rooted at R. */
begin
  value pointer edgelist P;
  value pointer node R;
  pointer edgelist L;
  quadrant I;
  L ← CLIP_LINES(P,SQUARE(R));
  if empty(L) then return; /* None of the edges is in the quadrant */
  if GRAY(R) then
    begin
      for I in {'NW', 'NE', 'SW', 'SE'} do PM_DELETE(L,SON(R,I));
      if POSSIBLE_PM1_MERGE(R) then
        begin
          L ← NIL;
          if TRY_TO_MERGE_PM1(R,R,L) then
            begin /* Merge the sons of the gray node */
              RETURN_TREE_TO_AVAIL(R);
              DICTIONARY(R) ← L;
              NODETYPE(R) ← 'LEAF';
            end;
        end;
    end
  else DICTIONARY(R) ← SET_DIFFERENCE(DICTIONARY(R),L);
end;

Boolean procedure POSSIBLE_PM1_MERGE(P);
/* Determine if the subtrees of the four sons of the PM₁ quadtree node pointed at by P
   should be further examined to see if a merger is possible. Such a merger is feasible
   only if at least one of the four sons of P is a LEAF. */
begin
  value pointer node P;
  return(LEAF(SON(P,'NW')) or LEAF(SON(P,'NE')) or
         LEAF(SON(P,'SW')) or LEAF(SON(P,'SE')));
end;

recursive Boolean procedure TRY_TO_MERGE_PM1(P,R,L);
/* Determine if the four sons of the PM₁ quadtree rooted at node P can be merged. Notice
   that the check for the satisfaction of the PM₁ decomposition conditions is with respect to
   the square associated with the original gray node, rooted at R, whose subtrees are
   being explored. Variable L is used to collect all of the edges present in the subtrees. */
begin
  value pointer node P,R;
```

```
reference pointer edgelist L;
if LEAF(P) then
  begin
    L ← SET_UNION(L,DICTIONARY(P));
    return(true);
  end
else return(TRY_TO_MERGE_PM1(SON(P,'NW'),R,L) and
             TRY_TO_MERGE_PM1(SON(P,'NE'),R,L) and
             TRY_TO_MERGE_PM1(SON(P,'SW'),R,L) and
             TRY_TO_MERGE_PM1(SON(P,'SE'),R,L) and
             PM1_CHECK(L,SQUARE(R)));
end;
```

```
recursive procedure RETURN_TREE_TO_AVAIL(P);
/* Return the PM quadtree rooted at P to the free storage list. This process is recursive in
   the case of a PM₁ quadtree. */
begin
  value pointer node P;
  quadrant I;
  if LEAF(P) then return
  else
    begin
      for I in {'NW', 'NE', 'SW', 'SE'} do
        begin
          RETURN_TREE_TO_AVAIL(SON(P,I));
          returntoavail(SON(P,I));
          SON(P,I) ← NIL;
        end;
    end;
end;
```

Analyzing the cost of dynamically inserting or deleting an edge in a PM₁ quad-tree is a process that requires us to look at the whole tree, not just at the particular edge. The worst-case cost is a product of the cost of inserting a q-edge and the number of q-edges that would have to be inserted. The cost of inserting a q-edge is the depth of the PM₁ quadtree plus the cost of accessing the dictionary structure of q-edges associated with each leaf node. The maximum number of q-edges is bounded by the product of the perimeter and the width of the image (i.e., 2^n for a $2^n \times 2^n$ image). The depth of the PM₁ quadtree is bounded by from above $4 \cdot n + 1$. For more details, see Section 4.2.3.1 of [Same90a].

Exercises

4.71. What is the maximum number of entries in the DICTIONARY field of a leaf node in a PM₁ quadtree?

4.72. Why is condition 4 in the definition of the PM₁ quadtree necessary?

4.73. The PM₁ quadtree is defined in a manner analogous to that of the PR quadtree. Consider the following attempt to tighten the analogy by using a definition of the PM₁ quadtree where conditions 2 and 3 are replaced by 2′, which requires only that at most one q-edge can lie in a region represented by a PM$_1$ quadtree leaf. Does condition 2′ imply condition 1? If not, are conditions 1, 2′, and 4 sufficient to handle an arbitrary polygonal map?

4.74. The implementation of the PM$_1$ quadtree does not use the DICTIONARY field of a gray node. Suppose that we use it to record a list of all of the edges that cross its corresponding block or have their endpoints within it. Modify procedures PM_INSERT and PM_DELETE to take advantage of this. Your modification should leave procedures PM1_CHECK and SHARE_PM1_VERTEX unchanged.

4.75. Suppose that, as in Exercise 4.74, you use the DICTIONARY field of a gray node to point to a list of the edges that intersect its corresponding block. Give an upper bound on the number of nodes required to form these lists in a PM$_1$ quadtree. Assume that for a given polygonal map there are m_i edges stored at level i where the root of the quadtree is at level n. Derive a lower bound by considering how many q-edges of an edge can be present in four nodes that are brothers.

4.76. Prove that when PM_DELETE is invoked to delete one edge from a PM$_1$ quadtree, merging is impossible if all of the four sons of a gray node are gray.

4.77. Why is it necessary to examine subtrees at several levels of recursion in procedure TRY_-TO_MERGE_PM1 when deleting an edge from a PM$_1$ subtree?

4.78. One approach to avoid repeatedly invoking procedure PM1_CHECK in TRY_TO_MERGE_PM1 is for PM1_CHECK to use an extra reference parameter to return the name of the vertex that it found to be shared. From now on, all subsequent invocations of PM1_CHECK must share the same vertex or TRY_TO_MERGE_PM1 is false. Modify procedure TRY_TO_MERGE_PM1 to incorporate this change.

4.79. Another approach to avoiding the cost of procedure TRY_TO_MERGE_PM1 is to store a vertex count in each gray node indicating the number of vertices in the subtrees. If this count is 1, merging can be attempted; if it is greater than 1, it cannot. Note that just because the vertex count is less than or equal to 1 does not mean that merging is possible. Modify procedures PM_INSERT and PM_DELETE to incorporate a vertex count.

4.80. Suppose that in addition to keeping a count of the number of vertices in each gray node of a PM$_1$ quadtree, you also keep track of the number of edges that cross the boundaries of each gray node. Crossing means that the endpoints lie outside the block. When is merging possible? Modify procedures PM_INSERT and PM_DELETE to incorporate vertex and crossing counters.

4.81. The implementation of a node has a field called SQUARE that contains information about the size of the block corresponding to the node. This is not necessary. Instead this information can be calculated as the tree is traversed, with the relevant information being passed as parameters to procedures PM_INSERT and PM_DELETE. How many parameters are needed? Modify procedures PM_INSERT and PM_DELETE to accommodate such a representation.

4.82. Procedure PM_INSERT assumes that whenever an edge or an isolated vertex is inserted into the PM$_1$ quadtree, it is not already there or does not intersect an existing edge. For an isolated vertex, this also means that it is not part of an existing edge. Modify PM_INSERT and the associated procedures to indicate when an isolated vertex or an edge cannot be inserted. There is no need to modify procedures PM1_CHECK or SHARE_PM1_VERTEX.

4.83. Modify procedure PM_INSERT to enable the insertion of edges that intersect existing edges. This means that you may have to perform a node-splitting operation and create new edges, as well as delete the edge being intersected and replace it by two edges.

4.84. Assuming that the x and y coordinates of vertices are represented as integers, how would you detect if two edges are colinear? You want an exact answer, and thus you cannot use real arithmetic.

4.85. Modify procedures PM_INSERT and PM_DELETE to deal with the case that two colinear edges meet at a vertex and no other edge is incident at that vertex. In the case of insertion, you are to handle the situation that the inserted edge is colinear and shares a vertex with an existing edge. Prior to the insertion, the shared vertex has degree 1. In the case of deletion, you are to handle the situation that the deletion of an edge results in a vertex whose two incident edges are colinear. This vertex should be deleted and the two edges replaced by one edge.

4.6 BUILDING OCTREES FROM MULTIPLE VIEWS

Constructing a region octree from a three-dimensional array representation of an image is quite costly because of the amount of data that must be examined. In particular, the large number of primitive elements that must be inspected means that the conventional raster-scanning approach used to build quadtrees spends much time detecting the mergibility of nodes. The time and cost of building a region octree from an array can be reduced, in part, by using the predictive technique of Section 4.2.3. It makes use of an auxiliary array whose storage requirements are as large as a cross-section of the image, which may render the algorithm impractical. However, since this array is often quite sparse, this problem can be overcome by representing it by use of a linked list of blocks in a manner similar to that used by Samet and Tamminen [Same88b] for connected component labeling in images of arbitrary dimension (see Section 5.1.3).

The easiest way to speed up the region octree construction process is to reduce the amount of data that needs to be processed. Franklin and Akman [Fran85] show how to build a region octree from a set of rectangular parallelepipeds approximating the object. These data can be acquired, for example, by casting parallel rays along the z axis and perpendicular to the x-y plane [Roth82].

In many applications, an even more fundamental problem than building the octree is acquiring the initial boundary data to form the boundary of the object being represented. One approach is to use a three-dimensional pointing device to create a collection of samples from the surface of the object. After the point data are collected, it is then necessary to interpolate a reasonable surface to join them.

Interpolation can be achieved by triangulation. A surface triangulation in three-dimensional space is a connected set of disjoint triangles that forms a surface with vertices that are points in the original data set. There are many triangulation methods in use—both two-dimensional spaces [Wats84, Saal87] and three-dimensional spaces [Faug84]. They differ in how they determine which points are to be joined. For example, often it is desired to form compact triangles instead of long, narrow ones. However, the problems of minimizing total edge length or maximizing the minimum angle pose difficult combinatorial problems. Posdamer [Posd82] suggests use of the ordering imposed by an octree on a set of points (e.g., by interleaving the bits comprising their coordinate values; see Section 2.7 of [Same90a] for more details) as the basis for determining which points should be connected to form the triangles.

Posdamer's algorithm uses an octree for which the leaf criterion is that no leaf can contain more than three points (similar to a bucket PR quadtree; see Section 1.3). The initial set of triangles is formed by connecting the points in the leaf nodes that contain exactly three points. Whenever a leaf node contains exactly two points, these points are connected to form a line segment associated with the leaf node. This is the starting point for a bottom-up triangulation of the points. It merges disjoint triangulations to form larger triangulations.

The isolated points (i.e., leaf nodes that contain just one point) and isolated line segments are treated as degenerate triangulations. The triangulation associated with a gray node is the result of merging the triangulations associated with each of its sons. By *merging* or *joining* two triangulations, it is meant that a sufficient number of line segments is drawn between vertices of the two triangulations so that we get a new triangulation containing the original two triangulations as subtriangulations.

When merging the triangulations of the eight sibling octants, there are a number of heuristics that can be used to guide the choice of which triangulations are joined first. The order in which we choose the pair of triangulations to be joined is determined, in part, by the following factors. First, and foremost, it is preferred to merge triangulations that are in siblings whose corresponding octree blocks have a common face. If this is impossible, triangulations in nodes that have a common edge are merged. Again if this is not feasible, triangulations in nodes that have a common vertex are merged. For each preference, the triangulations that are closest, according to some distance measure, are merged first.

There are many other methods of building an octree representation of an object. The simplest is to take quadtrees of cross-sectional images of the object and merge them in sequence. This technique is used in medical applications in which the cross-sections are obtained by computed tomography methods [Yau83]. Yau and Srihari [Yau83] discuss this technique in its full generality by showing how to construct a k-dimensional octree-like representation from multiple $(k-1)$-dimensional cross-sectional images.

Yau and Srihari's algorithm proceeds by processing the cross-sections in sequence. Each pair of consecutive cross-sections is merged into a single cross-section. This pairwise merging process is applied recursively until there is one cross-section left for the entire image. For example, assuming a k-dimensional image of side length 2^n, once the initial 2^n cross-sections have been merged, the resulting 2^{n-1} cross-sections are merged into 2^{n-2} cross-sections. In general, when merging 2^m cross-sections into 2^{m-1} cross-sections, only nonleaf nodes at levels m to n are tested for merging. Thus, a cross-section at level m corresponds to a stack of 2^{n-m} volume elements of side length 2^m and is represented by a $(k-1)$-dimensional quadtree whose nodes are at levels m through n.

In other applications, the volume of the available data is not as large. Often a small number of two-dimensional images is used to reconstruct an octree representation of a three-dimensional object or a scene of three-dimensional objects. In this case, projection images (termed *silhouettes*) are taken from different viewpoints. These silhouettes are subsequently swept along the viewing direction, thereby creating a bounding volume, represented by an octree, that serves as an approximation of the object. The octrees of the bounding volumes, corresponding to views from different directions, are intersected to yield successively finer approximations of the object. The rest of this section elaborates on methods based on silhouettes. The discussion is highly specialized for computer vision and can be skipped.

Martin and Aggarwal [Mart83] use this method with volume segments that are parallelepipeds stored in a structure that is not an octree. Chien and Aggarwal [Chie84b, Chie86a] show how to use this method to construct an octree from the quadtrees of the three orthogonal views. Hong and Shneier [Hong85] (see also Chien and Aggarwal [Chie85] and Potmesil [Potm87]) point out that the task of intersecting the octree and the bounding volume can be made more efficient by first projecting the octree onto the image plane of the silhouette and then performing the intersection in the image plane. In contrast, Noborio, Fukuda, and Arimoto [Nobo88] perform the intersection check directly in the three-dimensional space rather than preceding it by a projection. In the rest of this section it is assumed that the silhouettes result from parallel views, although perspective views have also been used (e.g., [Sriv87]).

Generally three orthogonal views are insufficient to obtain an accurate approximation of the object (see Exercise 4.88), and thus more views are needed. Chien and Aggarwal [Chie86b] overcome this problem by constructing what they term a *generalized octree* from three arbitrary views having the requirement that they are not coplanar. The generalized octree differs from the conventional region octree in that each node represents a parallelepiped with faces parallel to the viewing planes. The approximation is refined by intersecting the projection of each object node, say *P*, in the generalized octree with the image plane of the additional view. *P* is relabeled as a nonobject node or a gray node unless its projection lies entirely within the object region in the additional view. Note the similarity of this method with that of Hong and Shneier [Hong85].

A problem with using additional views from arbitrary viewpoints is that intersection operations must be explicitly performed to determine the relationship between the projections of the octants in the octree space and the silhouette of the new view. In the general case, the silhouette can be approximated by a polygon. The intersection of the polygonal projection of an octant with the polygon approximation of a silhouette is a special case of the polygon clipping problem (for more details see [Roge85]).

Chien and Aggarwal [Chie84b] and Veenstra and Ahuja [Veen85, Veen86, Ahuj89] point out that sweeping the silhouette image of an orthographic parallel projection[3] and restricting the views enable the exploitation of a regular relation between

---

[3] An *orthographic* parallel projection is a parallel projection in which the direction of the projection and the normal to the projection plane are the same, while in an *oblique* parallel projection they are not [Fole82]. For more details on projections, see Section 7.1.4.

octants in the octree space and quadrants in the image space. This means that the intersection operation can be replaced by a table-lookup operation. The key idea is to represent the image array by a quadtree and to make use of mappings between the quadrants and the octants so that the octree can be constructed directly from the silhouettes of the digitized image. We thereby avoid the need to perform the sweep operation explicitly.

The image array corresponding to the silhouette is processed as if we are constructing its quadtree. Chien and Aggarwal [Chie84b] use 3 face views, while Veenstra and Ahuja [Veen86, Ahuj89] use 13 views (see Exercise 4.94). The 10 additional views correspond to 6 edge views and 4 vertex views. The face views are taken with the line of sight perpendicular to a different face of the octree space; the faces must be mutually orthogonal. The edge views are taken with the line of sight passing through the center of an edge and the center of the octree space. The vertex views are taken with the line of sight passing through a vertex and the center of the octree space. The vertex views are also known as isometric projections (see Section 7.1.4).

At this point, let us see why these 13 particular views are used. Assume the existence of an octree representation of the scene, and consider which projections of the octree are the most natural. The face views enable us to maintain a quadtree representation of the octree's projection. With rectangular-shaped quadtree blocks (having an aspect ratio of $\sqrt{2}:1$), the edge views also enable the projection of the octree to be maintained as a quadtree. Finally, the projection of the octree as seen from the vertex views can be maintained by a quadtree decomposition based on the use of equilateral triangles [Ahuj83, Yama84].

When the views are taken with the line of sight perpendicular to a face, the result is the same as that described by Chien and Aggarwal [Chie86a]. As an example, using the octant labeling convention of Figure 4.28, when the line of sight is perpendicular to the face shared by octants 0, 2, 4, and 6, we find that pairs of octants are mapped into the same quadrant. Figure 4.29a shows the mapping for this particular view; for example, octants 6 and 7 are mapped into the SE quadrant. By reversing this mapping, we construct the octree directly from the silhouette of the digitized image. The process is recursive. We start with an empty quadtree (octree). We check if the image is homogeneous. If yes, no further processing is necessary. Otherwise the image is decomposed into four quadrants, and the process is repeated.

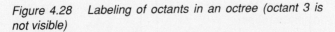

Figure 4.28   Labeling of octants in an octree (octant 3 is not visible)

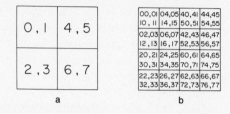

Figure 4.29   *Mapping of octants into quadtrees for a view such that the line of sight is perpendicular to the face shared by octants 0, 2, 4, and 6, using the octant labeling convention of Figure 4.28 at (a) one level of decomposition and (b) two levels of decomposition*

The difference from the conventional quadtree construction process is that each time, instead of adding one node per quadrant into the quadtree, we add a pair of nodes according to the pairing indicated in Figure 4.29a. Each time the level of decomposition increases, there is a doubling of the number of octree nodes mapped into the corresponding quadtree node of the silhouette. For example, Figure 4.29b shows the correspondence of quadtree and octree nodes at depth 2 for the view described in Figure 4.29a. Note the use of concatenation to group the octant labels; for example, 63 denotes suboctant 3 of octant 6.

When the views are taken with the line of sight passing through the center of an edge and the center of the octree space, the situation is more complex [Veen85, Ahuj89]. For such views, the silhouette of a cubelike region is a rectangle such that one of its sides is longer than the other by a factor of $\sqrt{2}$. However, this is not a problem because we apply a scale transformation that replaces the rectangular pixels by

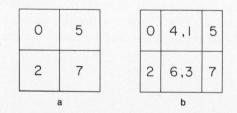

Figure 4.30   *Mapping of octants into quadrants for a view such that the line of sight passes through the center of the edge formed by octants 4 and 6 and the center of the octree space, using the octant labeling convention of Figure 4.28, depending on whether the parts of the silhouette that correspond to octants 1, 3, 4, and 6 in the octree are (a) all empty or (b) not*

square pixels before constructing the octree. As an example, use the view generated by the line of sight perpendicular to the edge formed by octants 4 and 6, according to the octant labeling convention of Figure 4.28.

Depending on its position, each quadrant in the silhouette image can correspond to between one and three octants. There are two possible mappings depending on whether the parts of the silhouette that correspond to octants 1, 3, 4 and 6 in the octree are all empty (e.g., Figure 4.30a) or not (e.g., Figure 4.30b). From Figure 4.30a and 4.30b we see that pixels in the central half (the area in Figure 4.30b labeled 4, 1, 6, 3) of the silhouette can be part of between one and three octants. The construction process is recursive. We start with an empty quadtree (octree). We check if the image is homogeneous. If yes, then no further processing is necessary. If no, then the image is decomposed recursively in two steps:

1. Use the decomposition in Figure 4.30a. For each homogeneous quadrant, add nodes to the octree according to the association indicated in the figure; otherwise recursively apply steps 1 and 2 to the quadrants once step 2 has been completed.
2. Use the decomposition in Figure 4.30b to deal with the central half of the silhouette (i.e., two 'quadrants'). In this case, process the two quadrants in the same way as described above for the case that the line of sight is perpendicular to a face. If the quadrants are homogeneous, add a pair of nodes according to the pairing indicated in the figure; otherwise recursively apply steps 1 and 2 to the two quadrants.

When the views are taken with the line of sight passing through a vertex and the center of the octree space, the silhouette of a cubelike region is a regular hexagon [Veen86, Ahuj89]. The hexagon can be decomposed into six equilateral triangles that are, in turn, treated as triangular quadtrees. The triangular 'quadrants' in the silhouette image can correspond to one, two, or four octants depending on their position. As an example, using the octant labeling convention of Figure 4.28, when the line of sight passes through the exposed vertex of octant 4 and the center of the octree space, we have the mapping given in Figure 4.31.

Veenstra and Ahuja [Veen86, Ahuj89] suggest that instead of directly processing the image array of the silhouette, a set of six disjoint triangular quadtrees be built for the silhouette's hexagon. Each octant of the silhouette's octree is constructed by determining if the six triangles that make up the octant's hexagonal silhouette are homogeneous. If they are, the octant is given the appropriate color; otherwise the process is recursively applied to the octant and the corresponding triangles. A similar technique is used by Yamaguchi, Fujimura, and Toriya [Yama84] to display an isometric view of an object represented by an octree (see Section 7.1.4).

In some situations, even 13 views are inadequate to obtain a sufficiently accurate approximation of the object, particularly when the object has a number of concave regions. Here it is best to use a ranging device to obtain range data. The range data can be viewed as partitioning the scene into three parts: the visible surface of the

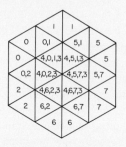

Figure 4.31 Mapping of octants into quadrants of a triangular quadtree for a view such that the line of sight passes through the exposed vertex of octant 4 and the center of the octree space, using the labeling convention of Figure 4.28

scene, the empty space in front of this surface, and the unknown space behind the surface. Connolly [Conn84] constructs an octree representation of the scene that corresponds to the series of such range images. This octree represents a piecewise linear approximation of the surfaces of the scene. A quadtree is used as an intermediate representation of a piecewise linear surface approximating the data comprising a single range image prior to its incorporation into the octree. Connolly [Conn85] derives an octree-based heuristic for selecting the positions from which to take subsequent range images. The issue of determining the next 'best' view is still an open problem.

A drawback of Connolly's use of the quadtree as an intermediate representation is that the quadtree must be transformed into the octree coordinate system when the coordinate axes of the quadtree are not aligned with those of the octree. This is a relatively complex process from a computational standpoint (but see Section 6.3.3). Chien, Sim, and Aggarwal [Chie88] also represent the views by quadtrees. They point out that Connolly's approach can be simplified by exercising control over the configuration of the range sensor. In particular, much of its complexity can be reduced (and avoided) by assuming that the ranging device is aligned with the cube that corresponds to the scene. This enables them to take advantage of the interrelationship between the quadtree and octree structures. They make use of six views to yield six range images—one for each of three pairs of orthogonal viewing directions.

Chien et al. generate a quadtree for each range image using a decomposition criterion so that each block has a constant range value (i.e., each block contains a square surface patch parallel to the image plane). They assume that the observed object occupies the space extending from the visible surfaces to the rear boundary of the scene cube (with respect to the ranging device being at the front for the particular view in question). Based on this assumption, they use a segment tree (a one-dimensional region quadtree; see Section 3.2.1 of [Same90a]) to represent the subpart of the object that is behind the visible surface patch associated with the block. Thus the object corresponding to each view is a quadtree in which each leaf node is, in turn, a segment tree. Whereas the quadtree partitions the two-dimensional image plane into blocks of constant range value, the segment tree decomposes the remaining dimension (i.e., depth) into object and nonobject regions.

The actual octree corresponding to each view (termed a *range octree*) is obtained by recursively merging the segment trees of the quadtree nodes. The rationale for using the combination of quadtrees and segment trees instead of the octree is to reduce the intermediate space requirements. Memory and time can be saved by not merging the six range octrees directly. Instead once a pair of range octrees corresponding to opposite views (e.g., front and rear) is obtained, they are merged. The final step merges these three range octrees to yield the desired octree.

Exercises

4.86. Write an algorithm to build a region octree of side length 2^n, given the quadtrees corresponding to its 2^n cross-sections.

4.87. Write an algorithm to build a region octree from a set of rectangular parallelepipeds.

4.88. Suppose you are given the three orthogonal views of a three-dimensional object with polygonal faces. What conditions must the object satisfy for you to be able to build its region octree?

4.89. Devise an algorithm that will always be able to build a region octree for an object based on views of the object. In case of ambiguity, your algorithm can ask for more views from different viewpoints.

4.90. Write an algorithm to implement Posdamer's [Posd82] method of interpolating a surface of an object for which point data are given.

4.91. Write an algorithm to detect if two polygons intersect.

4.92. Write an algorithm to compute the geometric intersection of the projection of an octree and a silhouette. You may assume that the silhouette is specified as a polygon.

4.93. Write an algorithm to compute the union and intersection of two polygons. Make sure you account for all the degenerate cases such as coincident edges.

4.94. Why don't Veenstra and Ahuja [Veen86, Ahuj89] use 26 views instead of 13 views?

4.95. Write an algorithm to construct the octree corresponding to the silhouette image resulting from a face view—that is, the line of sight is perpendicular to a specific face of the octree space.

4.96. Write an algorithm to construct the octree corresponding to the silhouette image resulting from an edge view—that is, the line of sight passes through the center of a specific edge and the center of the octree space.

4.97. Write an algorithm to construct the octree corresponding to the silhouette image resulting from a vertex view—that is, the line of sight passes through a specific vertex and the center of the octree space.

4.98. Write an algorithm to construct an octree from a range image using the approach of Chien, Sim, and Aggarwal [Chie88]. Build the range octrees first and then the final octree.

COMPUTING GEOMETRIC PROPERTIES

5

The first step in most image-processing applications is to take the raw image and classify its elements by examining the value of one of their properties, such as intensity. This process is known as thresholding. The next step is to group all elements that have identical values for this property (or at least within a given range). When this grouping is based on adjacency, the operation is termed *connected component labeling*. This step is a basic one common to virtually all image-processing applications. It is also known as *polygon coloring* in computer graphics applications.

This chapter presents a number of different methods for connected component labeling. They differ, in part, according to how the quadtree is represented. It also shows how this process can be adapted to compute other geometric properties, such as perimeter and component counting. While discussing the computation of perimeter, it is briefly mentioned how to compute areas and moments. In addition, whenever possible, it is demonstrated how to extend these techniques to images of arbitrary dimension (e.g., octrees).

5.1 CONNECTED COMPONENT LABELING

Prior to discussing connected component labeling, let us see how to extend the definitions of adjacency and connectedness given in Section 1.1 to a d-dimensional image. Assume that the image is represented as an array of d-dimensional pixels termed *image elements*. Each image element has $2 \cdot d$ borders (e.g., an edge in two dimensions and a face in three dimensions), each of which has unit size. Two image elements are said to be *4-adjacent* if they are adjacent in the sense that they share a border in its entirety (i.e., it has a nonzero $(d-1)$-dimensional measure). If they are adjacent without sharing a border (e.g., diagonal adjacencies in two dimensions), they are said to be *8-adjacent*. Black and white regions, as well as 4-adjacency and 8-adjacency for blocks, are defined analogously as in two dimensions.

In essence, connected component labeling is the process of assigning the same label to all 4-adjacent black image elements [Rose66, Park71]. The process of connected component labeling can also be characterized [Lumi83b] as a transformation of a binary input image, say B, into a symbolic image, say S, such that:

1. All image elements that have value white will remain so in S.
2. Every maximally connected subset of black image elements in B is labeled by a distinct positive integer in S.

A similar definition holds for a nonbinary image. In such a case, a set of components is associated with each color. We can define a region of each color, say C, to be a maximal four-connected set of C pixels. Alternatively we can designate one color, say W, to be analogous to white in the binary case so that a W region is a maximal eight-connected set of W pixels; regions of all remaining colors are still maximal four-connected sets of pixels. To simplify the presentation, the rest of this chapter concentrates on binary images and the labeling of black components. The methods can be extended to the gray-scale case with small modifications.

The rest of this section discusses the connected component labeling problem in a general sense by use of an analogy with the related problem for graphs. Next, we examine how the problem is solved when using an explicit quadtree representation (i.e., one that makes use of pointers). We conclude by looking at a solution for pointerless quadtree representations. The solution is a general one that holds for images of arbitrary dimension. The expression of the algorithm for images of arbitrary dimension is facilitated by the use of the bintree representation.

5.1.1 Connection to Graph Theory: Depth-First and Predetermined Approaches

Connected component labeling is also a problem in graph theory. A connection between the image and graph problems is accomplished by conceptualizing the image as an undirected graph (termed the *image graph*) and searching it for connected image elements. Formally we say that a *vertex* corresponds to a black image element and an *edge*[1] corresponds to a $(d-1)$-dimensional adjacency between two black image

---

[1] The terms *edge* and *vertex* are also used to refer to directions when performing neighbor finding. In this chapter, in order to avoid confusion, when dealing with directions, we shall use the equivalent terms *side* and *corner*, respectively.

elements (i.e., they are connected).[2] Finding the connected components of the image graph yields its *connection graph*.

Perhaps the most obvious approach to labeling the connected components of the image graph is to begin by labeling some vertex in some component and then propagating that label via the graph edges in a depth-first fashion to the rest of the component. Having finished labeling this component, we go on to find an as-yet unlabeled vertex in the graph and again label and propagate. We repeat this procedure until there are no more unlabeled vertices remaining.

Given a d-dimensional image with V vertices, represented as an array, at most $2 \cdot d$ edges need to be checked for each vertex. Therefore the algorithm takes $O(d \cdot V)$ time. In the case of a d-dimensional image represented as a quadtree with V leaf nodes, ignoring for the moment the cost of determining the set of all vertices connected to a particular vertex (but see Exercise 5.29), the execution time of the depth-first method is $O(d \cdot V)$ (see Exercise 5.6). The depth-first technique is also known as the *seed-filling* polygon-coloring algorithm in computer graphics [Roge85]. A high-level description of the control structure corresponding to the depth-first approach is given by procedure DEPTH_FIRST.

```
recursive procedure DEPTH_FIRST(E,V,L);
/* Use a depth-first search to label the connected components of an image consisting of
   edges E and vertices V by propagating label L to each of the unlabeled vertices in V.
   Initially L is NIL, in which case a new label is generated.  */
begin
  value edge set E;
  value vertex set V;
  value label L;
  vertex P;
  foreach P in V suchthat not(LABELED(P)) do
    begin
      LABEL(P) ← if null(L) then GENLABEL() /* Generate a unique label */
                 else L;
      DEPTH_FIRST(E,CONNECTED(P,E),LABEL(P));
      /*  CONNECTED(P,E) finds all vertices in V connected to P by an edge in E  */
    end;
end;
```

In the following, we generalize the depth-first approach to obtain what is called a *predetermined approach*. The term *predetermined* reflects the fact that, for efficiency reasons, it is often advantageous to process the image in an order that depends only on the storage scheme and not on the properties of the specific image.

---

[2] In the case of a nonbinary image, it is necessary to redefine the concept of a vertex and an edge to include color information. In particular, all image elements are treated as vertices (not just the black ones), and all $(d-1)$-dimensional adjacencies between nonwhite vertices of the same color are treated as edges. We say that the color of a vertex is the color of its corresponding image element. Similarly an edge is given the color of its constituent vertices.

For example, if the image is represented by a pointerless quadtree or an array stored in raster order, it is more efficient to process it sequentially. Thus the component-labeling strategy is *predetermined* by the storage strategy.

Imagine the depth-first procedure given above not as a traverser of vertices but instead as a traverser of edges that propagates labels across edges from one vertex of the edge to the other. The propagation occurs when the value L, which was assigned to LABEL(P), is transmitted as an argument to a recursive invocation of DEPTH_FIRST, along with the 4-adjacent vertices of P. Notice that when viewed as a traverser of edges, procedure DEPTH_FIRST may traverse some edges twice, but this does not affect the outcome of the label propagation.

It is interesting to observe that the order in which the edges of the image graph are explored is stipulated in the depth-first approach in a manner independent of the way in which the image is stored. That is, once a vertex in a given connected component is chosen, the order in which the edges of that connected component are explored is completely determined by some (fixed) order for processing adjacent vertices. On the other hand, in the predetermined approach, the order in which edges are explored is chosen on the basis of some other criteria, such as optimizing access efficiency by minimizing page faults.

Label propagation is achieved by using a two-stage process known as UNION-FIND [Tarj75] (see also Exercise 5.4). This is a technique for processing equivalence relations (input as pairs) so as to partition the domain into equivalence classes (termed *components* in the application). The equivalence classes are implemented as trees, with the element that is stored at the root serving as the representative of the class. For example, Figures 5.1a and 5.1b show a couple of disjoint equivalence classes with C and E, respectively, as their representative elements.

Initially each element is in a separate equivalence class. These disjoint equivalence classes are formed by a procedure called MAKESET. The UNION of two equivalence classes is the operation of merging their corresponding trees. For example, Figure 5.1c is the result of the UNION of Figures 5.1a and 5.1b with E as the representative element of the merged classes. FIND of an element of an equivalence class determines the root of its corresponding tree (e.g., FIND(A) in Figure 5.1c yields E).

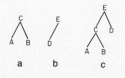

a   b   c

Figure 5.1 Examples of the tree representations of equivalence classes: (a) an equivalence class with C as its representative element, (b) an equivalence class with E as its representative element, (c) the result of the UNION of (a) and (b) with E as the representative element of the merged equivalence classes

The two stages of UNION-FIND are defined as follows. First, use FIND to determine the components associated with each of the vertices that comprise the edge being processed. If they differ, then they are combined using UNION. Given an image with V vertices and E edges, a maximum of V MAKESET, $2 \cdot E$ FIND, and E UNION operations are required. The second stage assigns a final label to each vertex and requires a maximum of V FIND operations.

Assuming that we first perform a MAKESET operation for each vertex (i.e., make a singleton set for it), Tarjan and van Leeuwen [Tarj84b] show that the worst-case execution time of the total (i.e., both stages) task is $\Omega(V + (2 \cdot E + V) \cdot \alpha (V, 2 \cdot V + 2 \cdot E))$ where α is the inverse of the Ackermann function and grows very slowly; it is almost linear. (See [Tarj84b] for more details on the exact formulation.) In most practical cases $\alpha(V, 2 \cdot V + 2 \cdot E) \leq 3$. Samet and Tamminen [Same86c] show that for some image representations, such as the two-dimensional array, the worst-case cost of the total task is in fact linear in V. A high-level description of the control structure corresponding to the predetermined approach is given by procedure PREDETERMINED.

```
procedure PREDETERMINED(E,V);
/* Label the connected components of an image consisting of edges E and vertices V by
   processing the edges in a predetermined order. Labels of components are merged
   using the UNION-FIND algorithm. */
begin
  value edge set E;
  value vertex set V;
  vertex P;
  edge Q;
  foreach Q in E do /* Merge the labels of the vertices of the edges */
    UNION(FIND(START(Q)),FIND(END(Q)));
    /* START(Q) and END(Q) yield the two vertices comprising edge Q */
  foreach P in V do /* Assign a final label to each vertex */
    LABEL(P) ← FIND(LABEL(P));
end;
```

The depth-first approach labels each component in its entirety one by one. Since the extent of a given component in the image is not known a priori, we see that the depth-first approach requires that the entire image always be readily accessible. In contrast, the predetermined approach makes it possible for us to arrange the labeling process so that only part of the image information need be accessible at any particular time. However, it does require that equivalences between labels be stored for processing by the UNION-FIND algorithm. When choosing between the two approaches, we must also take into account the cost of determining the image elements that are adjacent.

At this point, let us examine connected component labeling in the context of the two image representations described in Section 1.3 as forerunners of the quadtree approach (the array and the list). The particular approach chosen to implement connected component labeling is heavily influenced by the ease with which the representation copes with the basic entities (vertices and edges) of the undirected graph corresponding to the image. In particular, the depth-first approach is one that is oriented toward a representation that organizes the data by vertices, making possible the access from each vertex to all of the others with which it shares an edge. On the other hand, the predetermined approach is suitable for any representation that makes possible the processing of all edges in an arbitrary sequence.

Since adjacency information is easily accessible in the array representation (i.e., by address computation), both the depth-first and predetermined approaches are applicable. For either approach, the entire image array will have to be scanned. In the depth-first approach, most adjacencies between black image elements are inspected twice.

When the image is large, the entire array cannot be stored in central memory at once. Consequently the image is represented as a list of rows of runs, and the image is processed one row at a time. This makes the predetermined approach more appropriate because the local edge information that is available is sufficient (i.e., the immediately preceding row and the image elements within the row being processed). For instance, equivalences are detected by examining adjacent image elements in the same row and corresponding image elements in two adjacent rows (i.e., in the same column).

The array adaptation of the predetermined approach was first used by Rosenfeld and Pfaltz [Rose66]. Their implementation uses a table (termed an *equivalence table*) to record all equivalences detected on the first pass. Prior to the second pass, the equivalence pairs are sorted into equivalence classes, and a label is picked to represent each equivalence class. The problem with this method is that the equivalence table may grow quite large. An alternative method proposed by Haralick [Hara81] does not make use of an equivalence table. Instead it makes repeated passes over the image (alternating between the forward and backward directions), propagating equivalent labels until a pass with no label changes occurs.

A compromise between the two methods is reported by Lumia et al. [Lumi83b]. In this case, the equivalence table is limited to the size of one row in the image. After processing each row in the image, the equivalences are determined, and the equivalence class associated with each element in the row is updated to reflect the merges that just took place. A second pass is made over the image using the same process, in the reverse direction. Assuming that the equivalences are processed using UNION-FIND, $4 \cdot E$ FIND and $2 \cdot E$ UNION operations are performed.

Samet and Tamminen [Same86c] restrict the size of the equivalence table by use of the concept of *active* image elements and *active* equivalence classes to derive a general predetermined algorithm that works for an arbitrary image representation. For an image represented as a two-dimensional array, when the image is scanned in a raster-scanning order (i.e., each row is processed from left to right starting at the top row), the active image elements are those that have unscanned borders (i.e., not all of their sides are adjacent to image elements that have already been scanned). The active equivalence classes are those associated with the active image elements.

At any instant, the number of different active equivalence classes is bounded by $N/2$ for an $N \times N$ image. An equivalence class without at least one active image element will never be referenced again, and thus its storage can be reused to represent another component. Components are assigned unique labels by a second pass.

When the equivalences are processed by UNION-FIND, for each black image element, no more than one UNION operation and no more than one FIND operation is performed on the first pass, and one FIND operation is performed on the second pass. Samet and Tamminen show that for a two-dimensional array, in the worst case, the amount of work per black image element done by UNION-FIND (i.e., in terms of the number of links that are manipulated) is constant. Thus the worst-case cost of the algorithm is linear. The concept of active equivalence classes has also been developed by Dinstein, Yen, and Flickner [Dins85], as well as by Fong [Fong84], although in a different context and without the linearity argument.

A linear algorithm has also been obtained by Schwartz, Sharir, and Siegel [Schw85] for images represented by a two-dimensional array. This method makes use of deeper special properties of two-dimensional raster-scanned images by utilizing the nesting behavior of components in a partially scanned image. It also makes use of two passes; however, each successive pair of rows in the image must be processed three times on the first pass and once on the second pass. It is not easy to see how this approach can be applied to other dimensions or even to image representations other than the two-dimensional array (e.g., to quadtrees and octrees).

Most of the above methods have been used primarily for array representations of two-dimensional images. Park and Rosenfeld [Park71] have adapted the algorithm of Rosenfeld and Pfaltz [Rose66] to array representations of three-dimensional images, while Lumia [Lumi83a] has done the same for the algorithm of Lumia et al. [Lumi83b]. In Lumia's approach, the three-dimensional image is decomposed into two-dimensional bands that are labeled separately using two-dimensional connected component labeling methods. Next, voxel adjacencies between bands are propagated using an equivalence table for each band. Thus the problem of too many labels may resurface.

The method of Samet and Tamminen [Same86c] is general and hence applicable to three-dimensional images, as well as to hierarchical representations such as quadtrees, octrees, and bintrees. However, it has been proved to be linear only for the two-dimensional array image representation (see Exercise 5.19).

Both the depth-first and predetermined approaches are applicable to quadtrees. The one used depends on the implementation chosen for the quadtree and the manner in which it handles adjacency information. The next two sections describe in greater detail how to perform connected component labeling for the explicit quadtree and for the pointerless quadtree representations. The discussion is in the general context of d-dimensional images while the implementations described are restricted to two dimensions unless stated otherwise.

Exercises

5.1. How many different types of 8-adjacencies are possible in a d-dimensional image?

5.2. What class of shapes leads to the worst case (i.e., in terms of the number of equivalence classes that are generated) for the binary array method discussed in [Rose66]?

5.3. Modify procedures DEPTH_FIRST and PREDETERMINED to deal with multicolored images.

5.4. The UNION-FIND algorithm works by initially treating each vertex as a member of its own equivalence class. As each edge is added, the equivalence class of each of its constituent vertices is determined by use of a FIND operation. If they are in different classes, the two classes are merged by use of the UNION operation. One implementation is to represent each equivalence class by a tree with one of the vertices as the root and the remaining vertices as sons. Write a pair of procedures to implement FIND and UNION.

5.5. The tree implementation of UNION-FIND used in Exercise 5.4 has been the subject of much research. Various techniques have been proposed to make it more efficient. Ideally we would like each tree to have all of its descendants as sons at the same level (i.e., at a level that is one below the root). This is known as *path compression* [Sedg83]. Modify your implementation of UNION-FIND to make use of path compression.

5.6. Given a d-dimensional image represented as a d-dimensional quadtree with V leaf nodes, prove that the execution time of the depth-first connected component labeling algorithm is $O(d \cdot V)$. In particular, show that the number of edges that must be visited is bounded by $3 \cdot d \cdot V$.

5.7. Haralick's [Hara81] algorithm for labeling a binary array does not use an equivalence table. For a two-dimensional image, it assigns unique labels to different regions. As it encounters equivalences, it continues to use the lower-numbered label in subsequent processing. When it gets to the end of the image (i.e., to the last row), it repeats the process in the reverse direction. This algorithm continues to process the image alternately in the forward and backward directions until a pass occurs such that no pixel's label has changed. Give an example of a 5×5 binary image whose labeling requires more than two passes.

5.8. Can you generalize Exercise 5.7 and give the maximum number of passes necessary to label a $2^n \times 2^n$ binary image? What kind of an image generates this worst case?

5.9. What is the maximum number of different components in a $2^n \times 2^n$ binary image? In other words, how many different labels are generated? What kind of an image has such a property?

5.10. What is an upper bound on the number of components in a binary image represented by a quadtree that has N blocks?

5.11. Consider an array representation of a d-dimensional image of side width N. What is the maximum number of active image elements? What is the maximum number of active equivalence classes?

5.12. There are many ways of scanning the image elements that comprise an image. Given a d-dimensional image, each image element has 4-adjacent neighbors in $2 \cdot d$ directions. These neighbors are adjacent along a border of the image element. We can group the directions into d pairs, each element of which is opposite to the other. A scanning order defines the order in which the image elements are processed. The order is said to be *admissible* if when processing any image element P, all of P's 4-adjacent neighbors in at least one direction of every direction pair have already been processed. For example, the raster-scanning order (i.e., when each row is processed from left to right starting at the top row) is admissible. Why are admissible scanning orders of interest?

5.13.   Prove that the scanning order NW, NE, SW, SE for a quadtree is admissible, while the order NW, SE, NE, SW is not admissible.

5.14.   Is the cyclic scanning order NW, NE, SE, SW for a quadtree admissible?

5.15.   Suppose that a quadtree is scanned in the order NW, NE, SW, SE. What is the maximum number of active image elements? What is the maximum number of active equivalence classes?

5.16.   Suppose that a d-dimensional quadtree is scanned in an admissible scanning order. What is the maximum number of active image elements? What is the maximum number of active equivalence classes?

5.17.   Repeat Exercise 5.16 for a d-dimensional bintree.

5.18.   The correctness of Samet and Tamminen's [Same86c] general algorithm depends on being able to prove that it does not reuse equivalence classes (i.e., labels) while they are still associated with active image elements. This is equivalent to showing that when equivalence class O is encountered as the first representative of component C_1, O will not be reused to represent another component C_2 until the following condition is satisfied. Each equivalence class Y that is subsequently encountered, and also merged with O so that O is retained, no longer is used to represent elements of C_1. Prove that this property is satisfied by the first and second passes of this algorithm.

5.19.   Samet and Tamminen's [Same86c] general algorithm has worst-case linear behavior for the two-dimensional array representation. They show that their particular proof of the linear behavior does not extend to the array representation of a three-dimensional image or to hierarchical representations such as the quadtree. The execution time analysis for the two-dimensional array representation cannot be applied in three dimensions because of the ability of the chains of 4-adjacent elements, which form a connected component, to 'wiggle' their way around each other. For hierarchical representations such as the quadtree and bintree, the analysis is complicated by the fact that image elements do not become inactive in the same relative order that they became active. Can you prove that the algorithm does indeed fail to have this linear behavior for these representations?

5.1.2   Explicit Quadtrees

In general, the quadtree representation does not provide for the direct expression of the adjacency between image elements. Instead it must be determined by techniques such as ropes [Hunt78, Hunt79a] or neighbor finding [Same82a] (see Chapter 3). Assume that the image is a d-dimensional cube with side of length 2^n. In this case, no two connected image elements are more than $2 \cdot n$ nodes apart. However, only a small subset of the possible edges has their constituent vertices at such a distance. Since there is a cost associated with edge following and the depth-first approach generally inspects each black edge twice, in practice the predetermined approach to connected component labeling is preferable for the explicit quadtree. Such an algorithm, for two-dimensional images, that processes each edge exactly once is reported in [Same81b] and is given below.

The connected component labeling algorithm for the explicit quadtree representation of a two-dimensional image has two phases. The first phase is a preorder tree traversal in the admissible scanning order NW, NE, SW, SE (see Exercises 5.12 and

5.13). For each black node that is encountered, say A, all adjacent black nodes on the western and northern sides of A are found and assigned the same label (i.e., equivalence class) as A. The adjacency exploration is done by using the neighbor-finding techniques described in Section 3.2.1.1. At times the adjacent node may have already been assigned a label, in which case the equivalence is noted. This task is accomplished by a combination of the UNION and FIND operations. The second phase performs another traversal of the quadtree and updates the labels on all nodes to reflect the equivalences generated by the first phase of the algorithm. This task is facilitated by use of the FIND operation.

As an example, consider the image of Figure 5.2a, whose quadtree block decomposition is given in Figures 5.2b and 5.2c. All blocks are labeled with a different identifying number in their upper left corner, which indicates the relative order in which they are visited. Their lower right corner contains the label assigned by the first phase of the connected component labeling process. Figure 5.2b shows the status of the image at the conclusion of the first phase of the algorithm. It has four different labels (A, B, C, and D), with B equivalent to C and D. Exploration of the western adjacency of block 31 causes it to be assigned the label D. Subsequent exploration of the

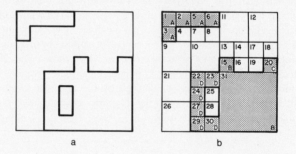

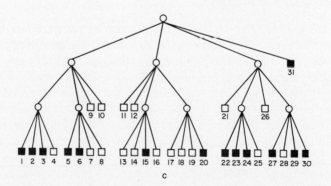

Figure 5.2   (a) An image, (b) the maximal block decomposition of the image in (a), and (c) the quadtree representation of the blocks in (b). Blocks in the image are shaded; background blocks are blank.

northern adjacency of block 31 causes the generation of the equivalence of D with B and of D with C (by use of the UNION step). The result is that block 31 is assigned the label B, and B is used to represent this component. All prior references to C and D are changed to B by the second phase of the algorithm.

The connected component labeling algorithm is specified by the following procedures. As in Section 5.1.1, the equivalence classes are represented by trees. The root of each tree is the representative element of the class. The links between the remaining nodes in the tree reflect equivalences. Each node in the tree corresponds to a record of type *eq_class* with one field called FATHER. To keep track of the label (i.e., equivalence class) associated with each black block, say *P*, the *node* record type is modified to include a field called LABEL, which points to a node in the tree that corresponds to *P*'s label.

The main procedure is termed EXP_CCL and is invoked with a pointer to the root of the quadtree corresponding to the image. Procedure ASSIGN_LABEL implements phase 1 by traversing the tree and controlling the exploration of adjacent black nodes. Procedure UPDATE corresponds to phase 2 and results in the preorder traversal of the tree in order to propagate the equivalences, thus labeling each component uniquely.

Procedure QT_GTEQ_EDGE_NEIGHBOR (given in Section 3.2.1.1) locates a neighboring node of greater or equal size along a specified side of a given node's corresponding block. If the neighbor exists and is black or gray, then procedure LABEL_ADJACENT is invoked to assign labels to the adjacent nodes, if necessary, and attempt to merge their equivalence classes by use of procedures UNION and FIND. When the neighboring node is gray, procedure LABEL_ADJACENT must examine all of the black and white adjacent neighbors of smaller size.

```
procedure EXP_CCL(Q);
/* Label all of the connected components of the quadtree rooted at Q. */
begin
  value pointer node Q;
  ASSIGN_LABEL(Q);
  UPDATE(Q);
end;

recursive procedure ASSIGN_LABEL(P);
/* Assign labels to node P and its sons. */
begin
  value pointer node P;
  pointer node Q;
  quadrant I;
  if GRAY(P) then
    begin
      for I in {'NW', 'NE', 'SW', 'SE '} do ASSIGN_LABEL(SON(P,I));
    end
  else if BLACK(P) then
    begin
      LABEL(P) ← NIL;
```

```
      Q ← QT_GTEQ_EDGE_NEIGHBOR(P,'W');
      if not(null(Q)) and not(WHITE(Q)) then LABEL_ADJACENT(P,Q,'NE', 'SE');
      Q ← QT_GTEQ_EDGE_NEIGHBOR(P,'N');
      if not(null(Q)) and not(WHITE(Q)) then LABEL_ADJACENT(P,Q,'SW', 'SE');
      if null(LABEL(P)) then
        begin
          LABEL(P) ← create(eq_class);
          FATHER(LABEL(P)) ← NIL;
        end;
      end
    else return; /* A white node */
  end;
```

```
recursive procedure LABEL_ADJACENT(P,R,Q1,Q2);
/* Find all descendants of node R that are adjacent to node P (i.e., in quadrants Q1 and
   Q2). */
begin
  value pointer node P,R;
  value quadrant Q1,Q2;
  if GRAY(R) then
    begin
      LABEL_ADJACENT(P,SON(R,Q1),Q1,Q2);
      LABEL_ADJACENT(P,SON(R,Q2),Q1,Q2);
    end
  else if BLACK(R) then LABEL(P) ← UNION(FIND(LABEL(P)),FIND(LABEL(R)))
  else return; /* A white node */
end;
```

```
recursive procedure UPDATE(P);
/* Propagate the equivalences in the quadtree rooted at P. */
begin
  value pointer node P;
  quadrant I;
  if GRAY(P) then
    begin
      for I in {'NW', 'NE', 'SW', 'SE'} do UPDATE(SON(P,I));
    end
  else if BLACK(P) then LABEL(P) ← FIND(LABEL(P))
  else return; /* A white node */
end;
```

```
pointer eq_class procedure UNION(LABEL1,LABEL2);
/* Merge equivalence class LABEL1 with equivalence class LABEL2. If LABEL1 is not NIL
   and if LABEL1 is not equal to LABEL2, then set the FATHER field of LABEL1 to
   LABEL2. */
```

```
begin
  value pointer eq_class LABEL1,LABEL2;
  if not(null(LABEL1)) and LABEL1 ≠ LABEL2 then
    FATHER(LABEL1) ← LABEL2;
  return(LABEL2);
end;

pointer eq_class procedure FIND(LABEL1);
/* Determine the equivalence class containing equivalence class LABEL1. Perform path
   compression at the same time—that is, when an equivalence class requires more than
   one link to reach the head of the class. In this case, the appropriate link is set. */
begin
  value pointer eq_class LABEL1;
  pointer eq_class R,TEMP;
  if null(FATHER(LABEL1)) then return(LABEL1)
  else
    begin
      R ← LABEL1;
      do R ← FATHER(R) until null(FATHER(R));
      do
        begin  /* Short circuit the path by linking LABEL1 to R */
          TEMP ← FATHER(LABEL1);
          FATHER(LABEL1) ← R;
          LABEL1 ← TEMP;
        end
        until null(FATHER(LABEL1));
      return(R);
    end;
end;
```

The execution time of the connected component labeling algorithm for an explicit quadtree is obtained by examining the two phases of the algorithm. Let B be the number of black nodes in the quadtree. Phase 1 is a tree traversal where neighbors are examined as well. Using a random image (in the sense that a node is equally likely to appear at any position and level in the tree), it can be shown [Same81b] that the average number of nodes visited by each invocation of QT_GTEQ_EDGE_NEIGHBOR and LABEL_ADJACENT is $O(1)$. These procedures are invoked for two of the sides of each black node. Thus given a quadtree with B black nodes, the tree traversal component of phase 1 can be computed in $O(B)$ time. However, Samet [Same85a] has shown that the worst case can be as bad as $O(B^2)$, as illustrated by Figure 5.3 for a $2^B \times 2^B$ image (see Exercise 5.21). Phase 2 is also a tree traversal and can be performed in $O(B)$ time.

The work involved in the UNION and FIND operations has a worst case that is almost linear, as discussed in the presentation of the predetermined approach in Section 5.1.1. In general, processing equivalences is not really a problem because in actuality very few equivalence pairs are generated. An example of the worst case, in

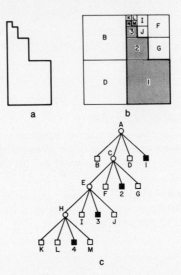

Figure 5.3 A quadtree corresponding to an image that leads to the worst-case behavior of the quadtree connected component labeling algorithm's first phase: (a) region, (b) block decomposition of the region in (a) (blocks in the image are shaded), (c) quadtree representation of the blocks in (b)

terms of the number of equivalence pairs generated, for a $2^3 \times 2^3$ image is given in Figure 5.4. Note the similarity to the result of Exercise 5.2. In fact, it should be clear that some variant of the worst case in terms of configurations leading to the generation of an equivalence pair will arise regardless of the order in which the tree is traversed (the order NW, SW, NE, and SE instead of NW, NE, SW, and SE, as done in the algorithm) or the pair of adjacencies that is explored (i.e., eastern and southern instead of western and northern, as done in the algorithm, but see Exercises 5.26 and 5.27).

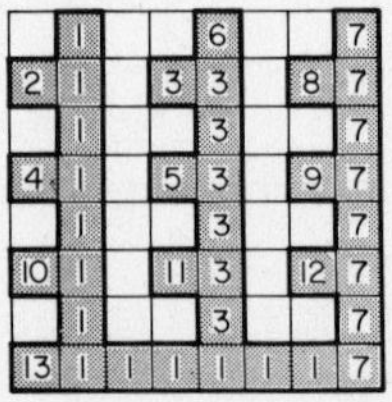

Figure 5.4 Sample image for n = 3, which results in the generation of a maximum number of equivalence pairs

The significance of the result of the analysis is that the execution time of the connected component labeling process is dependent on only the number of black blocks in the image (i.e., connected image elements), not on their size. Our algorithm is analogous to that commonly applied to the binary array representation [Rose66]— that is, the image is scanned one row at a time starting at the top and going from left to right, labeling adjacencies from the right and above. In contrast, the binary array algorithm has an execution time proportional to the number of pixels and hence to the area of the blocks.

Thus we see that by aggregating pixels into blocks, the hierarchical structure of the quadtree saves time and, potentially, space, depending on the representation chosen for the quadtree. The cost associated with neighbor finding can be avoided by using a top-down tree traversal method [Same85a] that transmits the eight neighbors of each node (i.e., one in the direction of each side and corner) as parameters (see also [Jack83]).

Connected component labeling can also be achieved by augmenting the *coloring* algorithm of Hunter and Steiglitz [Hunt78, Hunt79a], as described in Section 4.4. However, the coloring algorithm by itself does not achieve the same effect as the connected component labeling algorithm since for each polygon a point on its border must also be identified.

The coloring algorithm starts with a polygon and traverses its boundary prior to propagating the boundary color inward, and thereby coloring the interior nodes. It does not need to merge equivalence classes since the polygon is itself one equivalence class. The combination of the coloring algorithm with a polygon identification step will, in effect, yield a connected component labeling algorithm. This technique is analogous to the depth-first approach. Using such an approach leads to algorithms having execution times proportional to the number of nodes in the quadtree.

Note that some of the speed of the coloring algorithm is derived from the modification of the explicit quadtree representation by the addition of links (termed *ropes* and *nets*) to store explicitly each adjacency between image elements. The result is that there is no need to perform neighbor computation; however, this speedup is achieved at the expense of extra storage for the added links, as well as the stack. Hunter and Steiglitz also show that a quadtree may be roped in time proportional to the number of nodes in the quadtree. Webber [Webb84] discusses a similar approach with the same computational complexity that does not require a roped quadtree (see Exercise 5.32).

Exercises

5.20. Prove that the average number of nodes visited by each invocation of QT_GTEQ_EDGE_-NEIGHBOR and LABEL_ADJACENT is $O(1)$. Use the concept of a random image discussed in Section 3.2.1.2, and assume that in each case the maximum number of nodes will have to be visited by LABEL_ADJACENT.

5.21. Consider a $2^B \times 2^B$ image with B black nodes of the form of Figure 5.3. Prove that when the image is represented by an explicit quadtree, procedures ASSIGN_LABEL and LABEL_-ADJACENT visit $O(B^2)$ nodes in the worst case.

5.22. Executing procedure LABEL_ADJACENT is similar to visiting the adjacency tree (see Section 3.2.2) of the node. Hunter and Steiglitz [Hunt78, Hunt79a] have shown that the total number of nodes in all adjacency trees for a given quadtree is bounded by four times the number of leaf nodes in the quadtree (see Exercise 3.13). Assuming a quadtree with B black and W white nodes, use this result to find an integer k such that the number of nodes visited by all invocations of LABEL_ADJACENT is bounded by $k \cdot (B + W)$.

5.23. Suppose that procedure EXP_CCL explores the eastern and southern adjacencies of each block instead of the western and northern adjacencies. What changes are necessary in the associated procedures?

5.24. Suppose that procedure EXP_CCL explores the eastern and southern adjacencies of each block instead of the western and northern adjacencies. Given a quadtree with B black nodes, prove that the number of equivalences generated by procedures ASSIGN_LABEL and LABEL_ADJACENT is bounded by $2 \cdot B$.

5.25. Does the result of Exercise 5.24 also hold when procedure EXP_CCL explores the eastern and northern adjacencies? the western and southern adjacencies?

5.26. Construct a $2^3 \times 2^3$ image that results in the generation of a maximum number of equivalence pairs when procedure EXP_CCL explores the eastern and southern adjacencies of each block instead of the western and northern adjacencies.

5.27. Can you prove that the number of equivalence pairs is reduced when procedure EXP_CCL explores the eastern and southern adjacencies of each block instead of the western and northern adjacencies?

5.28. Neighbor finding can be avoided by transmitting the set of eight possible neighbors of the node as parameters. Can you achieve connected component labeling by just transmitting a subset of the eight neighbors? Which ones? Write a procedure to perform connected component labeling by transmitting this subset of eight parameters.

5.29. Can you achieve a connected component labeling algorithm whose execution time is proportional to the number of blocks in the image by transmitting the neighbors as parameters?

5.30. Lumia et al. [Lumi83a, Lumi83b] reduce the size of the equivalence table by making two passes over the image (once in the forward direction and once in reverse) and keeping only an equivalence table for each row in the binary array representation of the image. Can you formulate a similar technique for an image represented by a quadtree? You will have to find an analog for a row.

5.31. Write a set of procedures to implement connected component labeling using Hunter and Steiglitz's augmented coloring algorithm.

5.32. Exercise 4.51 involves an algorithm to convert a chain code to a quadtree that has a worst-case execution time proportional to the region's perimeter. Webber [Webb84] shows that this is feasible when the image is shifted by a quantity determined by the computation of a pathlength balancing transformation. When constructing the quadtree by following the chain code of its regions, this means that the average number of nodes that must be inspected by all of the neighbor-finding operations is bounded from above by four. Use this result to devise an algorithm that labels the connected components by performing a tree traversal where each time it encounters an unlabeled node along the border of a region whose neighbors have also not been labeled before, it follows the border of the region. Prove that the algorithm has an execution time proportional to the perimeter of the regions.

5.1.3   Pointerless Quadtree Representations[3]

Pointerless quadtree representations are linearizations of the explicit quadtree. As such, they render adjacency determination even more difficult. Whereas in the explicit quadtree the physical separation (in terms of quadtree node pointers) between two connected image elements is bounded by $2 \cdot n$, in the pointerless quadtree, for a d-dimensional image, it may be as high as $2^{(n-1) \cdot d}$ (and more; see Exercise 2.8).

Thus for a given image element, traversing a list of quadtree nodes one by one to determine all the image elements connected to it, as would be necessary in a depth-first approach, is not practical. This leads us to conclude that a predetermined approach to connected component labeling is preferable. Nevertheless, the depth-first approach has been used [Garg82c] (although shown to be erroneous in part [Abel84b]) for pointerless representations of two-dimensional images by using neighbor finding, despite the cumbersome search and bit manipulation that are necessary.

Connected component labeling using the predetermined approach for pointerless quadtrees requires us to be able to determine the edges of the graph (i.e., adjacencies between quadtree blocks). We also have the constraint (self-imposed) that the list of the nodes of the quadtree be processed in sequence corresponding to a traversal of the tree. Unfortunately most pointerless quadtree representations do not store edges explicitly, nor do they store them in an order that facilitates the determination of their components.

This problem is resolved by Samet and Tamminen [Same85f] for a two-dimensional image, and in [Same88b] for the general case of a d-dimensional image, by observing that at any instant (i.e., after processing m leaf nodes), the state of the traversal can be visualized as a staircase (recall Exercise 5.30) and termed an *active border*. For example, in two dimensions, given a traversal that visits sons of nonleaf nodes in the order SW, SE, NW, NE, the part of the image described by the m leaf nodes is to the left of and below the staircase.

The active border is said to consist of *active edges*. Actually an *incomplete* or *partial edge* is a more accurate description because for each edge, only one of its two constituent leaf nodes has been processed. For example, for Figure 5.5, a traversal in the above order (without gray nodes) is 1, 2, 3, 4, 5, 6, 7. Figure 5.6 shows the active border before and after processing node 4. A heavy line indicates that the adjacent block is black, and a light line corresponds to an adjacent white block.

Generalizing connected component labeling to d-dimensional data, we see that the active edge, now corresponding to a $(d-1)$-dimensional boundary and termed an *active border element*, must be given the color of the adjacent d-dimensional cube that has already been processed. As each leaf in the list of nodes in the quadtree is processed, its d border elements adjacent to the active border (the southern and western border elements in the two-dimensional case) are examined, and UNION-FIND is applied to any resulting adjacencies between black elements. In addition, the active

---

[3] This section is based on work by Samet and Tamminen [Same88b]. The ideas and techniques it describes are important but complex. The code for the procedures can be skipped on an initial reading.

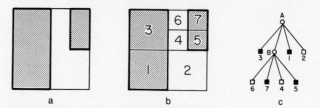

Figure 5.5   An example (a) image, (b) its block decomposition, (c) the corresponding quadtree

border is updated to reflect the new active border elements (i.e., the other d unprocessed border elements of the node—the northern and eastern border elements in the two-dimensional case).

Implementing connected component labeling for a pointerless quadtree representation depends on the data structure chosen for the active border. For a $2^n \times 2^n$ image, at any moment, the active border contains at most 2^n active edges in each direction, although it will usually be considerably fewer. The simplest data structure is a set of one-dimensional arrays of border elements for both the x and y directions containing 2^n entries apiece. This representation is used by Samet and Tamminen [Same85f] in a general framework for computing a number of geometric properties of two-dimensional images represented by pointerless quadtrees (e.g., perimeter, connected component labeling, and genus—i.e., Euler number).

Unfortunately, adapting the array data structure to d-dimensional data requires d arrays of size $2^{n \cdot (d-1)}$ entries apiece. This is clearly a prohibitive amount. Instead Samet and Tamminen [Same88b] represent the active border using a variable-length list whose maximum size is the number of image elements (i.e., d-dimensional cubes of unit side length) participating in one border.

The bintree representation (see Section 1.3) facilitates the generalization of the algorithms to d-dimensional data. In particular, in the following algorithms we use a pointerless representation for the bintree in the form of a preorder traversal of its nodes (i.e., a DF-expression [Kawa80a] as discussed in Section 5.1.1). The traversal

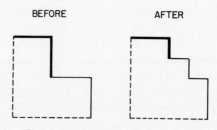

Figure 5.6   The active border before and after processing block 4 in Figure 5.5

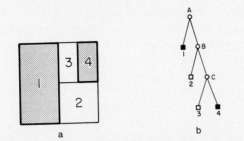

Figure 5.7 The bintree corresponding to Figure 5.5: (a) block decomposition, (b) bintree representation of the blocks in (a)

yields a string over the alphabet 'G', 'B', and 'W' corresponding to the gray (i.e., non-leaf), black, and white nodes, respectively. For example, the DF-expression for the bintree of the two-dimensional image of Figure 5.5, given in Figure 5.7, is GBGWGWB. The algorithms can be easily modified to handle other pointerless quadtree representations (e.g., linear quadtrees in which the locational codes of both black and white nodes are retained).

We label the connected components of an image represented by a pointerless bintree by using the predetermined approach. It requires us to inspect all black border elements. This is done by traversing the bintree and is achieved by inspecting the nodes in the list in sequence. As stated earlier, when $d = 2$, at any instant (i.e., after processing m leaf nodes), the state of the traversal can be visualized as a staircase (termed an active border). The active border can be decomposed into d sets of active border elements. For example, when $d = 2$, in a traversal of the bintree such that the western and southern halves are traversed before the eastern and northern halves, respectively, the m processed leaf nodes describe a portion of the image to the left of and below the staircase. Figure 5.8 shows the active border before and after processing block 3 of Figure 5.7. A heavy line indicates that the adjacent block is black, and a light line corresponds to an adjacent white block.

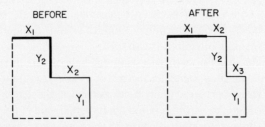

Figure 5.8 The active border before and after processing block 3 of Figure 5.7

We represent the active border as a singly linked list of records of type *border-list*, with fields DATA and NEXT, which contains pointers to records corresponding to the active border elements comprising it. For example, in Figure 5.8, the active x border is the list (X_1, X_2, X_3), and the active y border is the list (Y_1, Y_2). Each active border element is represented as a record of type *borderelement* having three fields, SIZ, COL, and LAB, corresponding, respectively, to the size (length in two dimensions, area in three dimensions, etc.), color, and label (i.e., equivalence class) of the side of the block adjacent to the already processed border element. Initially there are d active border elements all of size $2^{n \cdot (d-1)}$ and color white. As in Section 5.1.1, the equivalence classes are represented by trees, where the root of each tree is the representative element of the class.

Connected component labeling is performed by procedures COMPONENTS, TRAVERSE, and INCREMENT. Procedure COMPONENTS is invoked with the DF-expression encoding of the bintree. First it initializes the active border. Next it invokes procedure TRAVERSE, which controls the traversal of the bintree nodes. During this process each black leaf node is assigned a label (i.e., equivalence class), and a copy is made of the DF-expression (in reverse order). Finally it applies procedure PHASEII to adjust the component labels to their final values. PHASEII reverses the DF-expression while applying FIND once for each black image element.

For each leaf node, procedure TRAVERSE calls procedure INCREMENT d times—once for each of the d borders to perform the actual updating of the active borders and to propagate equivalences among labels. If a black leaf node is not identified with any existing image component, a new label (i.e., equivalence class) is generated.

Procedure TRAVERSE is the key to the algorithm. Using list pointers ACTIVE_BORDER[0], ACTIVE_BORDER[1], $\cdots$, ACTIVE_BORDER[$d-1$], it keeps track of the heads of the lists of the elements of the d active borders. For example, assume that $d = 2$. Let YL and XL correspond to ACTIVE_BORDER[0] and ACTIVE_BORDER[1], the active y and active x borders, respectively, starting at the node currently being processed. Our discussion is illustrated with Figure 5.9, the state of the active borders (XL and YL) before and after each call to TRAVERSE when processing the bintree of Figure 5.7.

First, in the case of a nonleaf node, its block is split in two, and TRAVERSE is applied recursively to the two halves. Parameter CURRENT_COORD indicates the direction along which the block should be partitioned. CURRENT_COORD cycles through all the directions. VOLUME is the DIMENSION-dimensional area of the block, and WIDTH is the width of the block along directions CURRENT_COORD through DIMENSION−1; its width along the remaining directions is WIDTH/2.

After TRAVERSE has finished processing one half, say the first half of a partition on the x (y) coordinate, the pointer to the active y (active x) (note the change in the order of x and y) border is reset to point at the element of the active y (active x) border it pointed at just prior to the partition (although its actual value may have changed during processing). This pointer must be reset because we have swept through its entire range; this is not true for the remaining active borders. For example, after processing node 1 and before processing node B, the value of YL is reset, but the active y border

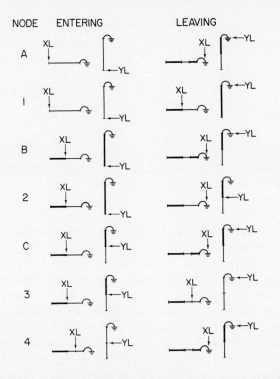

Figure 5.9   State of the active borders (XL) and (YL) before and after each call to TRAVERSE for d = 2

entry is now different from what it was when starting with node 1. The pointer to the active x border retains the value it had at the end of the first half (e.g., XL after processing node 1 and before processing node B).

Second, in the case of a leaf node, TRAVERSE invokes procedure INCREMENT DIMENSION times to process all active border elements bordering on the edge of the new leaf. There are three possible cases depending on whether the entering edge is smaller than its corresponding active border entry, equal in size, or larger. Figure 5.10 illustrates the effect of each of these cases on the active border when $d = 2$. Note that the list comprising the active border will grow in size, stay the same, or shrink, respectively, for the three cases. If the new leaf is black, then the connected component information is also updated if the corresponding active border entry or part thereof is black. This step is analogous to application of procedure LABEL_ADJACENT in the explicit quadtree algorithm.

Once procedure INCREMENT has been applied to all the active borders, TRAVERSE determines if the leaf that has just been processed was black and was only adjacent to white nodes. If this was the case, then a new label (i.e., equivalence class) is generated. Just prior to termination, TRAVERSE advances the list pointers to elements

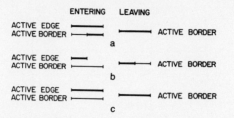

Figure 5.10   The state of the active border in procedure INCREMENT. The comparisons are between the entering edge and its corresponding active border entry.

of the active borders so that they point to the edges corresponding to the block associated with the node to be processed next.

As another example of the application of our algorithm, consider a three-dimensional image (i.e., $d = 3$) in the form of an octree. Assume that octants are labeled in the manner shown in Figure 5.11, and use the coordinate system given in Figure 5.12. Figure 5.13 is an example of the octree corresponding to a staircase-like object. To construct the corresponding three-dimensional bintree, let the first partition be in the x direction, followed by y and z, alternating among the three directions thereafter. Figure 5.14 is the bintree corresponding to Figure 5.13. Using the coordinate system of Figure 5.12, we say that the left subtree corresponds to the negative x,

Figure 5.11   Labeling of the octants in an octree (octant 2 is not visible)

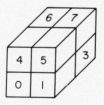

Figure 5.12   Octree coordinate system

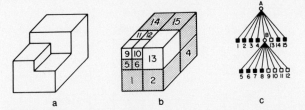

Figure 5.13 *(a) An object, (b) its maximal blocks, and (c) the corresponding octree. Blocks in the object are shaded.*

y, and z directions relative to the origin, and the right subtree to positive values. The bintree for the image of Figure 5.14 has GBGGGBWWB as its DF-expression.

The algorithm for labeling connected components of a three-dimensional bintree is almost identical to that described for the two-dimensional case. The main difference is that now the active border data structure has three different elements instead of two and is a three-dimensional staircase. In particular, we now have an active x-y, active x-z, and active y-z border consisting of active border elements that correspond to faces instead of edges. As an example of the application of the algorithm, let YZL, XZL, and XYL correspond to ACTIVE_BORDER[0], ACTIVE_BORDER[1], and ACTIVE_BORDER[2], the active y-z, active x-z, and active x-y borders, respectively. Figure 5.15 shows the state of the active x-y, active x-z, and active y-z borders before and after each call to TRAVERSE corresponding to the leaf nodes in Figure 5.14.

procedure COMPONENTS(DIMENSION,WIDTH_OF_UNIVERSE,DF);
/* Label the connected components of a WIDTH_OF_UNIVERSE by WIDTH_OF_UNI-
VERSE by ··· by WIDTH_OF_UNIVERSE (WIDTH_OF_UNIVERSE = 2^n) DIMEN-

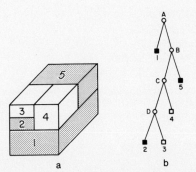

Figure 5.14 *The bintree corresponding to Figure 5.13: (a) block decomposition, (b) bintree representation of the blocks in (a)*

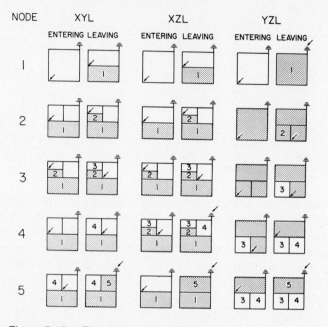

Figure 5.15   The state of the active borders (XYL, XZL, and
YZL) at selected calls to TRAVERSE for d = 3. The arrows
designate the value of XYL, XZL, and YZL as is appropriate.
Black blocks in the image are shaded.

SION-dimensional image represented by DF, a preorder traversal of its bintree.
PHASEII_NODES points to the start of the list of nodes used in the second phase of the
algorithm. Each node is represented by a record of type *node* having two fields, COL and
LAB, corresponding to its color and the equivalence class assigned to it. */
begin
  global value integer DIMENSION;
  value integer WIDTH_OF_UNIVERSE;
  global value pointer dfnodelist DF;
  global pointer nodelist PHASEII_NODES;
  pointer borderlist **array** ACTIVE_BORDER[0:DIMENSION−1];
  integer J;
  /* Initialize each element of ACTIVE_BORDER to represent one active borderelement of
    size WIDTH_OF_UNIVERSE $^{DIMENSION-1}$ and adjacent to white blocks in each of the DI-
    MENSION directions: */
  for J←0 **step** 1 **until** DIMENSION−1 **do**
    begin
      ACTIVE_BORDER[J] ← **create**(borderlist);
      DATA(ACTIVE_BORDER[J]) ← **create**(borderelement);
      SIZ(DATA(ACTIVE_BORDER[J])) ← WIDTH_OF_UNIVERSE↑(DIMENSION−1);

```
      COL(DATA(ACTIVE_BORDER[J])) ← 'WHITE';
      LAB(DATA(ACTIVE_BORDER[J])) ← NIL;
    end;
  if not(empty(DF)) then
    begin
      PHASEII_NODES ← NIL;
      TRAVERSE(WIDTH_OF_UNIVERSE↑DIMENSION, ACTIVE_BORDER,0,
               WIDTH_OF_UNIVERSE);
      PHASEII(PHASEII_NODES);  /* Set the final label of each leaf using FIND */
    end;
  end;


procedure TRAVERSE(VOLUME,ACTIVE_BORDER,CURRENT_COORD,WIDTH);
/* Compute the contribution of a node whose corresponding DIMENSION-dimensional rec-
   tangular parallelepiped has volume VOLUME. CURRENT_COORD of its sides have
   width WIDTH/2, and the remaining DIMENSION-CURRENT_COORD sides are of width
   WIDTH. For each nonleaf node, CURRENT_COORD indicates the direction along
   which the corresponding block should be partitioned and TRAVERSE is recursively
   applied to the two halves. ACTIVE_BORDER contains pointers to the active borders in
   the DIMENSION directions. ACTIVE_BORDER[0], ACTIVE_BORDER[1], · · · , and AC-
   TIVE_BORDER[DIMENSION−1] point to the part of the active border adjacent to the
   parallelepiped currently being processed. */
begin
  value real VOLUME,WIDTH;
  reference pointer borderlist array ACTIVE_BORDER[0:DIMENSION−1];
  value integer CURRENT_COORD;
  global integer DIMENSION;
  global pointer dfnodelist DF;
  global pointer nodelist PHASEII_NODES;
  pointer borderlist TEMP;
  pointer node CURRENT_NODE;
  integer J;
  CURRENT_NODE ← create (node);
  COL(CURRENT_NODE) ← NEXT(DF);
   /* Get the next element in the preorder traversal */
  LAB(CURRENT_NODE) ← NIL;
  if COL(CURRENT_NODE) = 'GRAY' then
    begin /* Nonleaf node */
     /* Add CURRENT_NODE to the front of PHASEII_NODES so that the second phase
        can update the labels to their final equivalence classes. */
      addtolist(PHASEII_NODES,CURRENT_NODE);
      TEMP ← ACTIVE_BORDER[CURRENT_COORD];
       /* Save pointer to start of ACTIVE_BORDER[CURRENT_COORD] */
      if ((CURRENT_COORD+1) mod DIMENSION) = 0 then WIDTH ← WIDTH/2;
      VOLUME ← VOLUME/2;
      TRAVERSE(VOLUME,ACTIVE_BORDER,
```

```
                        (CURRENT_COORD+1) mod DIMENSION,WIDTH);
            /* Partition on CURRENT_COORD */
            ACTIVE_BORDER[CURRENT_COORD] ← TEMP;
            TRAVERSE(VOLUME,ACTIVE_BORDER,
                        (CURRENT_COORD+1) mod DIMENSION,WIDTH);
        end
    else
        begin /* Leaf node */
        /* Compute each border element's contribution to the active border. In computing the
           'size' parameter we must distinguish between active borders 0 ···
           CURRENT_COORD–1 and CURRENT_COORD ··· DIMENSION–1. */
        for J←0 step 1 until DIMENSION–1 do
            INCREMENT(CURRENT_NODE,ACTIVE_BORDER[J],
                        if J ≥ CURRENT_COORD then VOLUME/WIDTH
                        else 2∗VOLUME/WIDTH);
        if COL(CURRENT_NODE) = 'BLACK' then
            begin
            /* Assign CURRENT_NODE's equivalence class to its corresponding active border
               elements */
            if null(LAB(CURRENT_NODE)) then /* New equivalence class */
                begin
                LAB(CURRENT_NODE) ← create (eq_class);
                FATHER(LAB(CURRENT_NODE)) ← NIL;
                end;
            for J←0 step 1 until DIMENSION–1 do
                LAB(DATA(ACTIVE_BORDER[J])) ← LAB(CURRENT_NODE);
            end;
        /* Advance the pointer to the start of the appropriate active border: */
        for J←0 step 1 until DIMENSION–1 do
            ACTIVE_BORDER[J] ← NEXT(ACTIVE_BORDER[J]);
        /* Add CURRENT_NODE to the front of PHASEII_NODES so that the second phase
           can update the labels to their final equivalence classes. */
        addtolist(PHASEII_NODES,CURRENT_NODE);
        end;
    end;


procedure INCREMENT(LEAF,ACTIVE_BORDER,SIZE);
/* Update the active border for a side of leaf node LEAF having size SIZE. SIZE
   corresponds to width in the two-dimensional case and to area in the three-dimensional
   case. ACTIVE_BORDER is a pointer to a list of border elements constituting the active
   border in the present direction. LEAF is adjacent to the first border element in AC-
   TIVE_BORDER. */
begin
    value pointer node LEAF;
    value pointer borderlist ACTIVE_BORDER;
    value integer SIZE;
    pointer borderlist NEIGHBOR,Q; /* Auxiliary variables */
    integer I;
```

if SIZE > SIZ(DATA(ACTIVE_BORDER)) **then**
  begin /* Neighbor is a nonleaf node—case a of Figure 5.10 */
    I ← 0;
    NEIGHBOR ← ACTIVE_BORDER;
    while I ≠ SIZE **do**
      begin
        /* Update the active border for all border elements that are adjacent to the side of
          LEAF that is being processed. */
        if COL(LEAF) = 'BLACK' **and** COL(DATA(NEIGHBOR)) ='BLACK' **then**
         LAB(LEAF) ← UNION(LAB(LEAF), FIND(LAB(DATA(NEIGHBOR))));
        I ← I + SIZ(DATA(NEIGHBOR));
        NEIGHBOR ← NEXT(NEIGHBOR);
      end;
    Q ← NEXT(ACTIVE_BORDER);
    NEXT(ACTIVE_BORDER) ← NEIGHBOR;
    borderlist_dispose (Q,NEIGHBOR);
    /* Reclaim storage for active border elements starting at Q up to but not including
      NEIGHBOR */
  end
else /* Neighbor is a leaf—cases b and c of Figure 5.10 */
  begin
    if COL(LEAF) = 'BLACK' **and** COL(DATA(ACTIVE_BORDER)) = 'BLACK' **then**
     LAB(LEAF) ← UNION(LAB(LEAF), FIND(LAB(DATA(ACTIVE_BORDER))));
    if SIZE < SIZ(DATA(ACTIVE_BORDER)) **then**
      /* Neighbor is larger—case b of Figure 5.10 */
      begin /* Update the active border */
        NEIGHBOR ← **create** (**borderlist**); /* Add a new border element */
        DATA(NEIGHBOR) ← **create** (**borderelement**);
        /* Compute unprocessed portion of the active border: */
        SIZ(DATA(NEIGHBOR)) ← SIZ(DATA(ACTIVE_BORDER))–SIZE;
        COL(DATA(NEIGHBOR)) ← COL(DATA(ACTIVE_BORDER));
        LAB(DATA(NEIGHBOR)) ← LAB(DATA(ACTIVE_BORDER));
        NEXT(NEIGHBOR) ← NEXT(ACTIVE_BORDER);
        /* Update head of active border list: */
        NEXT(ACTIVE_BORDER) ← NEIGHBOR;
      end;
  end;
  /* Update the active border to reflect the new leaf */
  SIZ(DATA(ACTIVE_BORDER)) ← SIZE;
  COL(DATA(ACTIVE_BORDER)) ← COL(LEAF);
end;

pointer nodelist procedure PHASEII(OLD_NODE_LIST);
/* Update the equivalence classes of all elements of list NODES that are leaf nodes (i.e.,

their LAB field) to the correct equivalence class by using FIND. During this process list NODES will be reversed, and the original order of the DF-expression will be restored. *nodelist* has two fields, DATA and NEXT. */

```
begin
  value pointer nodelist OLD_NODE_LIST;
  pointer nodelist NEW_NODE_LIST
  NEW_NODE_LIST ← NIL;
  while not(null(OLD_NODE_LIST)) do
    begin
      if COL(DATA(OLD_NODE_LIST)) ≠ 'GRAY' then
        LAB(DATA(OLD_NODE_LIST)) ← FIND(LAB(DATA(OLD_NODE_LIST)));
      addtolist(NEW_NODE_LIST,DATA(OLD_NODE_LIST));
      OLD_NODE_LIST ← NEXT(OLD_NODE_LIST);
    end;
  return(NEW_NODE_LIST);
end;
```

Ignoring the contribution of UNION-FIND (discussed in Section 5.1.1), the time to traverse a d-dimensional bintree represented by a DF-expression is directly proportional to the number of leaf nodes. This is better than results obtained when using neighbor-finding methods [Same81b] and is comparable to techniques that transmit neighbors as parameters to the traversal algorithm [Jack83, Same85a]. The space requirements of the algorithms reported here are generally better than of those obtained in [Same85f] by virtue of using linked lists instead of arrays. This is heavily dependent on the amount of aggregation present in the image. However, the worst case is still produced by a checkerboard image.

Tables 5.1 and 5.2 from [Same88b] provide additional insight into the performance of the above algorithms by using some 'simple' (i.e., highly aggregated) images. The test images consist of two-dimensional and three-dimensional digital balls of varying diameters (i.e., M). Each ball is generated so that each pixel (voxel) intersecting the boundary is black, as are the elements totally contained in the ball. Programs to perform connected component labeling were written in the C programming language and were executed on a VAX11/750 running the 4.2 BSD version of UNIX.

Table 5.1   2–d connected component labeling (CCL).

M	Leaf Nodes	Black Nodes	Labels	Max Edges	CCL (secs)
512	2,840	1,524	86	157	1.8
1,024	5,840	3,028	178	211	3.4
2,048	11,740	5,916	343	287	6.8
4,096	23,680	11,928	687	382	13.7

Table 5.2   Performance of 3–d connected component labeling (CCL).

M	Leaf Nodes	Black Nodes	Labels	Max Faces	CCL (secs)
32	3,296	1,656	50	571	2.9
64	13,960	6,896	189	1,187	11.3
128	58,712	29,676	755	2,514	46.8

Table 5.1 shows the results for a two-dimensional ball. 'Leaf nodes' denotes the number of black and white leaf nodes in the bintree. 'Labels' corresponds to the number of different equivalence classes that were generated (i.e., the number of nodes that could not be directly labeled from their neighbors that had already been processed). 'Max edges' indicates the maximum number of records of type *border-element* that were required in the active border lists. It is useful for determining the space requirements and comparing to the case when the active border is represented as an array [Same85f].

It is interesting to note that for M = 4,096 the method of [Same85f] required 8,192 edge records, whereas the method of [Same88b], described here, required only a maximum of 382 edge records. The programs implemented were not optimized; subroutine calls alone accounted for about 50% of the processing time. We see that for this class of images, the space requirements are small. Table 5.2 shows the results for a three-dimensional ball.

The data of Tables 5.1 and 5.2 are revealing from several standpoints. First, they illustrate Corollary 1.1 of Section 1.2, which states that as the resolution is doubled, the number of nodes in the quadtree grows linearly. Furthermore, for three-dimensional images, the number of nodes in the octree grows with the second power (i.e., proportionally to the boundary of the image [Meag82a]). In the experiments, these results also hold for the number of labels generated. However, no such easy conclusions can be drawn about the maximum number of edges (faces), whose number seems to grow more slowly. Nevertheless it is interesting to note that in Table 5.2 the maximum number of faces for M=128 is 2,514, whereas, in actuality, were we to apply an array method similar to [Same85f], 49,152 array entries (border elements) would be required to represent the active border. The linked list implementation clearly has a dramatic payoff in this example.

Second, the data show that the execution time of the pointerless bintree-connected component labeling algorithm is approximately linearly related to the number of leaf nodes in the tree.

Third, from the limited data gathered, it seems that for a given image size (i.e., in terms of leaf nodes), the three-dimensional case requires approximately 30% more time than the two-dimensional case. This is not surprising since the active border now has three lists instead of two, and procedure INCREMENT must process each of these lists.

The algorithm encoded in the above procedures requires an equivalence table that may have as many elements as there are black blocks in the entire image. This problem can be easily overcome by using the general connected component labeling algorithm of Samet and Tamminen [Same86c]. It can be used to reduce the number of labels by adapting the concepts of active image elements and active equivalence classes to the active borders and labels, respectively.

In essence, whenever a label is no longer associated with at least one of the active border elements, it can be reused to refer to another component. This is achieved by associating a COUNT field with each label, say L, that records the number of active border elements whose LABEL field refers to L. In addition, a FATHER field is associated with each label to indicate that the label has been merged with another one, via a UNION operation, and that the other label is the surviving label. The key modifications necessary are outlined below.

1. COUNT(L) is incremented whenever elements are inserted into the active border and whenever a UNION operation is performed such that L is the surviving label.

2. COUNT(L) is decremented whenever elements whose LABEL field refers to L are removed from the active border. If COUNT(L) becomes zero (i.e., no elements of the active border refer to it), then L can be reused since it can never again participate in an active border element. In addition, when COUNT(L) becomes zero, the counter of its father field (i.e., COUNT(FATHER(L))) is also decremented. This process is repeated until either encountering a label without a father or the result of the decrement is nonzero.

3. As soon as it is determined that label L can be reused (i.e., when COUNT(L) becomes zero), its previous value (i.e., the contents of its father field FATHER(L)) is stored in nodelist PHASEII_NODES.

4. When assigning final labels in PHASEII, nodelist PHASEII_NODES is scanned in reverse order. Prior to applying FIND to a leaf node in PHASEII, the equivalence potentially stored in the leaf is restored. In this way the equivalence table is reset to its state when the leaf was written to the nodelist. Note that processing PHASEII_NODES in reverse order guarantees that an equivalence in which a label participates will be restored before the first reference to the label in PHASEII.

Exercises

5.33. What class of shapes leads to the worst case in terms of the number of equivalence classes generated for a two-dimensional image when using procedures COMPONENTS, TRAVERSE, and INCREMENT?

5.34. Modify procedures COMPONENTS, TRAVERSE, and INCREMENT to perform connected component labeling for a pointerless quadtree representation in the form of an FD linear quadtree.

5.35. The key to the success of the methods of Lumia et al. [Lumi83a, Lumi83b] is the fact that the equivalence table is stored for only a single row. In contrast, the algorithms of this section require an equivalence table to represent the entire image. Suppose that we use an analogy to the technique of [Lumi83b] by keeping an equivalence table only for the staircase (i.e., the elements adjacent to it) and nothing else. The analogy is to make an additional pass on the list of nodes in the DF-expression in reverse order. Thus there would seemingly be no need for PHASEII. What is the problem with this solution?

5.36. Modify procedures COMPONENTS, TRAVERSE, and INCREMENT to incorporate the method of Samet and Tamminen [Same86c] to reduce the number of labels that need to be generated.

5.37. Lumia et al. [Lumi83b] have a proof for the correctness of their algorithm. Can you apply similar techniques to prove the correctness of procedures COMPONENTS, TRAVERSE, and INCREMENT?

5.38. In Section 2.1.3 we discussed the *two-dimensional run encoding* (*2DRE*) pointerless quadtree representation of Lauzon et al. [Lauz85]. Give an algorithm to do connected component labeling for a two-dimensional binary image represented by this technique.

5.2 PERIMETER, AREA, AND MOMENTS

In many image-processing applications, the ability to compute the length of the boundary of a given region is desired. This quantity is known as the perimeter. Unfortunately it has a number of definitions. The one used is often influenced by the representation chosen for the image. To see that the definition of perimeter is not unique, consider the binary image of Figure 5.16. In particular, we examine its binary array representation. We assume that the border of the image is white and that each pixel represents a square of unit side length. There are at least three definitions for the perimeter.

The first, termed the *inner perimeter*, counts the number of black pixels adjacent to white pixels. This definition is subject to two interpretations depending on whether the pixels must be 4-adjacent to be counted or if 8-adjacency is sufficient. For example, for Figure 5.16, when the 8-adjacencies represented by pixels 10, 15, and the pixels in the NW and SE corners of block 13 are counted, the inner perimeter has a value of 20, while it is 16 if they are not counted.

The second, termed the *outer perimeter*, counts the number of white pixels adjacent to black pixels. Again, this definition is subject to two interpretations depending on whether the pixels must be 4-adjacent to be counted or if 8-adjacency is sufficient. In the former case it is 20, while in the latter case it is 28.

The third, termed the *crack perimeter*, counts the length of the 'cracks' (i.e., boundaries) between black and white pixels. This definition yields 24, which is unique. As can be seen from our example, the crack perimeter is a compromise between the inner and outer perimeters. The difference between the various formulations of the inner and outer perimeters is due, in part, to the definition of connectedness for black and white regions (i.e., 4-connected and 8-connected). (For more details see Rosenfeld and Kak [Rose82a].)

In the case of images represented by quadtrees, the crack perimeter is the most appropriate. One algorithm for its computation is to convert the quadtree representa-

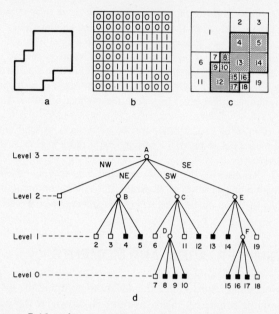

Figure 5.16 *An example (a) region, (b) its binary array,*
(c) its maximal blocks (blocks in the region are shaded), and
(d) the corresponding quadtree

tion to a four-direction chain code (see Section 4.3.2) and then to sum the lengths of the chains. An even simpler solution, as described here, computes the perimeter by traversing the quadtree looking for adjacencies of black and white nodes. The advantage of this solution over the one involving chain codes is that there is no need to visit the elements of the chain code in sequence around the boundary of the region. Instead we need only to make sure that we visit each element of the chain code once.

The solution we employ can be expressed using the terminology of graphs (i.e., edges and vertices) by modifying slightly the analogy between a graph and a quadtree that was set forth in Section 5.1.1. In particular, we say that all blocks in the quadtree, rather than just the black ones, correspond to vertices. We say that a vertex is black (white) if its corresponding block is black (white).

The definition of an edge needs more modification. We say that an edge exists between any two blocks (black or white) that are adjacent along their corresponding sides. For images of more than two dimensions, say d, we say that there is an edge between two nodes whenever there is a nonzero $(d-1)$-dimensional adjacency between them. The size of the edge is the measure of the adjacency. For example, in two (three) dimensions, the size is the minimum of the lengths of the shared sides (faces) of the blocks corresponding to the adjacent nodes.

We say that an edge is black (white) if the adjacent blocks are black (white). If the adjacent blocks are of a different color, the edge is gray. In other words, the color of an edge is the color of its constituent vertices when they are the same color and gray otherwise.

Note that a block may be adjacent to several blocks along a given side (e.g., block 1 in Figure 5.16 is adjacent to blocks 2 and 4 along its eastern side and to blocks 6, 7, and 8 along its southern side). Using these definitions, the perimeter of an image represented by a quadtree is obtained by accumulating the sum of the sizes of all gray edges as shown by procedure PERIMETER below.

```
integer procedure PERIMETER(Q);
/* Compute the perimeter of the image represented by quadtree Q. */
begin
  value pointer quadtree Q;
  edge E;
  integer PER;
  PER ← 0;
  foreach E in {edges(Q)} suchthat GRAY(E) do PER ← PER+SIZE(E);
  return(PER);
end;
```

Note that the formulation of the perimeter algorithm is valid for images of arbitrary dimension. For example, for a three-dimensional image of an object such as a polyhedron, the perimeter corresponds to its surface area. Using the modified analogy between a quadtree and a graph means that we must reformulate the depth-first and predetermined approaches to connected component labeling in terms of black vertices and black edges. This analogy also leads us to observe the close relationship between the process of perimeter computation and connected component labeling. In particular, in the first phase of the connected component labeling process, we search for black edges, while in perimeter computation we search for gray edges.

When an image is represented as an explicit quadtree, there are a number of ways of computing its perimeter. The simplest method traverses the quadtree in preorder, and for each black node it examines the adjacent nodes on all four sides [Same81c]. For each adjacent node that is white, it augments the value of the perimeter by an amount equal to the minimum of the lengths of the shared sides of the blocks corresponding to the two adjacent nodes. This method has the drawback that each black edge is examined twice when neither of these adjacency explorations contributes to the value of the perimeter (e.g., the eastern side of node 13 and the western side of node 14 in Figure 5.16).

A better algorithm follows the analogy to connected component labeling by looking for adjacent nodes only on the western and northern sides of each block. Again the quadtree is traversed in preorder. For each black node encountered, say A, examine all adjacent white nodes on the western and northern sides of A and augment the perimeter by an amount equal to the minimum of the lengths of the shared sides of the blocks corresponding to the two adjacent nodes. Similarly for each white node encountered, say A, examine all adjacent black nodes on the western and northern sides of A and augment the perimeter by an amount equal to the minimum of the lengths of the shared sides of the blocks corresponding to the two adjacent nodes.

The only problem with this algorithm is that the eastern and southern boundaries of an image are never explored. This can be alleviated by embedding the image in a white region, as shown in Figure 3.14. Such an embedding also frees us from having to handle differently the case when the western and northern boundaries of a region coincide with the border of the image.

The algorithm is improved by making use of the observation (due to Shaffer [Shaf85]) that in a digital environment, the contribution of eastern sides of black blocks to the perimeter is identical to the contribution of western sides. Similarly the contribution of southern sides of black blocks is identical to that of northern sides. Thus to compute the perimeter we need only to examine the western and northern sides of each black node and multiply the result by two (see Exercise 5.41). Also there is no need to embed the image totally in a white region. Instead construct a quadtree such that the image is in the SE quadrant and the NW, NE, and SW quadrants are white (e.g., the NW quadrant of Figure 3.14). Such an algorithm is given below by procedures EXP_PERIMETER and SUM_ADJACENT.

EXP_PERIMETER is the main procedure and is invoked with a pointer to the root of the quadtree representing the partially embedded region and an integer corresponding to twice the resolution of the image (e.g., $n + 2$ for a $2^n \times 2^n$ image array embedded in a quadtree corresponding to a $2^{n+1} \times 2^{n+1}$ image). By using twice the resolution, there is no need to double the result to obtain the actual perimeter value.

EXP_PERIMETER traverses the tree and controls the exploration of the adjacencies of each leaf node. For each black node, say A, procedure QT_GTEQ_EDGE_NEIGHBOR (given in Section 3.2.1.1) locates a neighboring node, say B, of greater or equal size along a specified side of A's corresponding block. If B is white, the perimeter is incremented by an amount equal to twice the width of a side of the block corresponding to A (recall that EXP_PERIMETER is invoked with a level corresponding to twice the resolution). If B is gray, then procedure SUM_ADJACENT is invoked to accumulate the contributions of the descendants of B to the value of the perimeter. If B is black, then it is ignored.

The functions OPSIDE, CSIDE, and CCSIDE have the same meaning as OPEDGE, CEDGE, and CCEDGE as defined in the introductory section of Chapter 4. They are used here due to the different meanings assigned to the terms *edge* and *vertex* in this chapter.

```
recursive integer procedure EXP_PERIMETER(P,LEVEL);
/* Find the perimeter of a region represented by a quadtree rooted at node P that spans a
   2^LEVEL-1 × 2^LEVEL-1 space. The image has been embedded in a white region so that it
   is in the SE quadrant. */
begin
  value pointer node P;
  value integer LEVEL;
  pointer node Q;
  integer PER;
  quadrant I;
  direction D;
```

```
PER ← 0;
if GRAY(P) then
  begin
    for I in {'NW', 'NE', 'SW', 'SE'} do
      PER ← PER+EXP_PERIMETER(SON(P,I),LEVEL-1);
  end
else if BLACK(P) then
  begin
    for D in {'W', 'N'} do
      begin
        Q ← QT_GTEQ_EDGE_NEIGHBOR(P,D);
        PER ← PER+if WHITE(Q) then 2↑LEVEL
                  else if GRAY(Q) then
                      SUM_ADJACENT( Q,QUAD(OPSIDE(D),CSIDE(D)),
                          QUAD(OPSIDE(D),CCSIDE(D)),LEVEL)
                  else 0;
      end;
  end; /* No action is needed for a white node. */
  return(PER);
end;



recursive integer procedure SUM_ADJACENT(P,Q1,Q2,LEVEL);
/* Find all white leaf nodes in quadrants Q1 and Q2 of the subquadtree rooted at node P
   corresponding to a 2^LEVEL-1 × 2^LEVEL-1 space. */
begin
  value pointer node P;
  value quadrant Q1,Q2;
  value integer LEVEL;
  return (if GRAY(P) then SUM_ADJACENT(SON(P,Q1),Q1,Q2,LEVEL-1)+
            SUM_ADJACENT(SON(P,Q2),Q1,Q2,LEVEL-1)
          else if WHITE(P) then 2↑LEVEL
          else 0);
end;
```

Using the analogy with phase 1 of the connected component labeling algorithm, we see that for a quadtree containing B black nodes, the execution time of the perimeter algorithm for an explicit quadtree takes $O(B)$ time on the average. Jackins and Tanimoto [Jack83] describe an alternative perimeter computation algorithm for an explicit quadtree that works for an arbitrary number of dimensions. Its worst-case execution time is $O(B)$. This method achieves its efficiency by transmitting the neighbors as parameters rather than having to rely on neighbor exploration, as in the former approach. However, it requires that a separate pass be made over the data for each dimension. Samet [Same85a] obtains a similar result without requiring separate passes for each dimension.

In the case of a pointerless bintree representation, the perimeter can be computed by making two changes to the procedures in Section 5.1.3. First, omit the call to procedure PHASEII from COMPONENTS. Second, modify procedure INCREMENT so that now its goal is to locate gray edges rather than black edges (see Exercise 5.46). In particular, for each black leaf node, look for adjacent white nodes instead of adjacent black nodes.

Areas and moments are image properties that are somewhat related to the perimeter. Their computation is even easier since they do not require the use of any adjacency information. For example, to compute the area requires only that the quadtree be traversed in an arbitrary order and that the sizes of the black blocks be accumulated. In particular, a black block at level k contributes 2^{2k} to the area. Moments of an image represented by a quadtree are obtained by summing the moments of the black blocks. The position of each black block is easy to ascertain because the path that was taken to reach the block is known when processing starts at the root of the quadtree.

Knowledge of the area and the first moments permits the computation of the coordinates of the centroid, and thereupon central moments relative to the centroid can be obtained. It should be noted that all of these algorithms have an execution time proportional to the number of nodes in the quadtree [Shne81b]. Chien and Aggarwal [Chie84a] use a normalized representation of the quadtree with respect to the centroid to match noisy objects against models. Their method also relies on the selection of a principal axis and scaling to a fixed resolution.

Exercises

5.39. Does permitting 8-adjacencies in the definition of the inner perimeter yield the same value as excluding them in the definition of the outer perimeter? If not, explain why.

5.40. Does procedure EXP_PERIMETER work for images that contain holes?

5.41. Prove that the value of the perimeter is equal to twice the result obtained by merely examining the western and northern sides of each black node (i.e., there is no need to embed the image in a white region).

5.42. Write a pair of procedures EXP_PERIMETER2 and SUM_ADJACENT2 to compute the perimeter by visiting the western and northern sides of black nodes looking for adjacent white nodes and the western and northern sides of white nodes looking for black nodes.

5.43. Modify procedures DEPTH_FIRST and PREDETERMINED of Section 5.1.1 to incorporate the association of color with vertices and edges in the analogy between a quadtree and a graph.

5.44. Prove that the average number of nodes visited by each invocation of QT_GTEQ_EDGE_-NEIGHBOR and SUM_ADJACENT is $O(1)$. Use the concept of a random image discussed in Section 3.2.1.2, and assume that in each case the maximum number of nodes will have to be visited by SUM_ADJACENT.

5.45. Executing procedure SUM_ADJACENT is similar to visiting the adjacency tree (see Section 3.2.2) of the node. Hunter and Steiglitz [Hunt78, Hunt79a] have shown that the total number of nodes in all adjacency trees for a given quadtree is bounded by four times the number of leaf nodes in the quadtree (see Exercise 3.13). Assuming a quadtree with B black and W white nodes, use this result to find an integer k such that the number of nodes visited by all invocations of SUM_ADJACENT is bounded by $k \cdot (B + W)$.

5.46. Modify procedures COMPONENTS, TRAVERSE, and INCREMENT of Section 5.1.3 to compute the perimeter of a pointerless bintree representation of an image.

5.47. Write a procedure AREA to compute the area of an image represented by a region quadtree.

5.48. Write a procedure CENTROID to compute the centroid of an image represented by a region quadtree.

5.3 COMPONENT COUNTING

Once the connected components of an image have been labeled, it is easy to count them since the result is the same as the number of different equivalence classes resulting from phase 1 of the connected component labeling algorithm. An alternative quantity is known as the Euler number or genus, say G, which is $V - E + F$ where V, E, and F correspond to the number of vertices, edges, and internal faces, respectively, in a planar graph [Hara69].[4]

In the case of a binary image, the genus is equal to the difference between the number of connected components and the number of holes. In two dimensions, Minsky and Papert [Mins69] have shown that for a binary image represented by a binary array, $G = V - E + F$ where V, E, and F are defined as follows. Assume that a black pixel is represented by 1 and a white pixel by 0. V is the number of 1s in the image, E is the number of horizontally adjacent pairs of 1s (i.e., 11) or vertically adjacent pairs of 1s, and F is the number of 2×2 blocks of 1s.

Dyer [Dyer80a] has obtained the same result for a quadtree representation of a two-dimensional binary image by redefining V, E, and F in the context of a quadtree (for another approach using bintrees see Bieri [Bier87]) . This is accomplished by letting V be the number of black blocks, E be the number of pairs of 4-adjacent black blocks in the horizontal and vertical directions (e.g., Figure 5.17 where YES and NO are used to indicate whether the blocks are 4-adjacent), and F be the number of cases where three or four black blocks touch at a common point (e.g., Figure 5.18). The last

Figure 5.17   Examples of adjacencies for the computation of the genus of an image

---

[4] A *planar graph* separates the plane into regions called *faces*. There is exactly one face that is unbounded (i.e., it contains points that are arbitrarily far apart), and it is called an *external face*. All other faces are called *internal faces*. A graph is *connected* if any two nodes can be joined by a path. Euler's formula states that $G = V - E + F = 1$ for a connected planar graph.

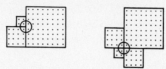

Figure 5.18   Example of three or four blocks meeting at a common point

quantity is equivalent to counting the number of 2×2 blocks of black pixels such that at least three out of the four pixels are in different black blocks. For example, for Figure 5.19, $V = 10$, $E = 10$, and $F = 1$ (contributed by the point labeled A), yielding a genus value of 1.

To cast the process of genus computation in the framework of the analogy between a quadtree and a graph, we add the concept of a cycle. A *cycle* in a quadtree consists of a path of edges of length ≥ 3 from a vertex to itself so that the Boolean intersection of the blocks corresponding to the component vertices is a single point. As was done in Section 5.2, we also associate a color with a cycle by saying that a cycle is black (white) if all of its constituent vertices (or equivalently, its edges) are black (white), and gray otherwise. The computation of the genus involves counting the number of black vertices, black edges, and black cycles of length 3 or 4 as shown by procedure GENUS below.

```
integer procedure GENUS(Q);
/* Compute the genus of the image represented by quadtree Q. */
begin
  value pointer quadtree Q;
  vertex V;
  edge E;
  cycle C;
  integer TV,TE,TC;
  TV ← TE ← TC ← 0;
```

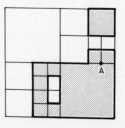

Figure 5.19   Sample image containing two connected components

```
foreach V in {vertices(Q)} suchthat BLACK(V) do TV ← TV+1;
foreach E in {edges(Q)} suchthat BLACK(E) do TE ← TE+1;
foreach C in {cycles(Q)} suchthat BLACK(C) do TC ← TC+1;
return(TV−TE+TC);
end;
```

The value of Dyer's result lies not in the mechanics of the algorithm but in its theoretical implication. It has reinforced our conclusion that for hierarchical representations, such as the quadtree, the most critical measure is the number of blocks and not their size. It also demonstrates another instance of an algorithm originally formulated for the binary array representation being used in an analogous manner for a quadtree representation by treating blocks (of possibly different sizes) as if they were pixels. This technique was used previously in the labeling of connected components.

The genus for a two-dimensional image represented by a quadtree is obtained by a preorder tree traversal. V and E are computed directly by phase 1 of the connected component labeling algorithm (ignoring equivalence classes). To determine F, we augment phase 1 so that for each black node, the leaf nodes surrounding its corner are examined. When the image is represented by an explicit quadtree, the genus is computed by using the algorithms of Section 5.1.2 with the modification that there is no need to deal with equivalence classes. Black cycles are determined by examining the southeastern neighbor of each black node using procedure QT_VERTEX_VERTEX_-NEIGHBOR given in Section 3.2.1.1. The algorithm's expected execution time is proportional to the number of blocks in the image.

In the case of a pointerless quadtree (or bintree) representation of a two-dimensional image, the genus is computed by using the first phase of the connected component labeling algorithm. However, now the active border data structure is not adequate to capture the adjacency information needed to compute the number of cycles. The problem is that in order to determine the presence of a cycle, we must know the colors of three or four nodes that are adjacent at a corner of a black leaf node. Unfortunately the active border data structure keeps track of only the colors of the leaf nodes adjacent to the border along a side and not at a corner.

To see this problem, consider the quadtree of Figure 5.16 and assume that it is traversed in the order SW, SE, NW, and NE. Suppose that we have just processed node 7. Figure 5.20 shows the active border at this point. The next node to be processed is 8. To determine the presence of a cycle, we must be able to examine the color of the block adjacent to its SW corner. This is impossible.

To rectify the situation, we define an additional data structure, termed an *active corner*, which corresponds to a corner on the active border. The set of all such corners is called the *active corners*. It is implemented in the same way as the active border (i.e., an array or list). The information recorded is the color of the block whose NE corner touches the corner. In fact, for a $2^n \times 2^n$ image array, at any one time, there are at most $2^{n+1} - 1$ active corners.

Alternatively the active corner data structure can also be implemented as an additional field in one of the active border data structures, say the active y border, so

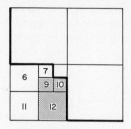

Figure 5.20   The active border after processing node 7 in Figure 5.16

that the color of the block immediately below and to the left of the active border segment is recorded. This yields enough information to detect the presence or absence of a black cycle of the appropriate length. The genus for a two-dimensional image can now be computed by making the appropriate modifications to procedures COMPONENTS, TRAVERSE, and INCREMENT.

Exercises

5.49. In [Same85f], Samet and Tamminen use a slightly different adaptation of the concepts of an edge and vertex to a quadtree corresponding to a two-dimensional image. In particular they refer to a *region graph*, which is defined only for two-dimensional data. It is a variant of the dual of the connection graph described here. In essence, a region graph is a tuple (B,V,E). B is the set of *blocks* that correspond to image elements and can be black or white (e.g., a pointerless quadtree in the form of a DF-expression). V is the set of vertices that are the corners of the blocks. A vertex is colored black (white) if it is completely surrounded by black (white) blocks, and gray otherwise. E is the set of edges that connect the vertices. This definition is useful to describe the computation of the two-dimensional genus but cannot be easily extended to more than two dimensions. Can you explain why?

5.50. Prove Dyer's result that the genus of an image represented by a quadtree is equal to $V - E + F$.

5.51. Can you prove that Dyer's $V - E + F$ result also holds for an image represented by a bintree?

5.52. Prove Euler's formula ($G = V - E + F = 1$) for a connected planar graph.

5.53. Give a set of procedures to compute the genus of an image represented by an explicit quadtree.

5.54. Prove that the expected execution time of the genus computation algorithm is $O(B)$, where B is the number of black nodes in the quadtree.

5.55. When using the explicit quadtree representation in the computation of the genus, the adjacent nodes are examined by a variant of procedure LABEL_ADJACENT of Section 5.1.2. This is similar to visiting the adjacency tree of the node. Hunter and Steiglitz [Hunt78, Hunt79a] have shown that the total number of nodes in all adjacency trees for a given quadtree is bounded by four times the number of leaf nodes in the quadtree (see Exercise 3.13). Does a similar result hold for the number of nodes that must be visited in locating neighbors in the corner direction (i.e., when computing procedure QT_VERTEX_VERTEX_NEIGHBOR for all nodes in the quadtree)? If so, assuming a quadtree with B black and W

white nodes, use these two results to find an integer k such that the number of nodes visited by all invocations of LABEL_ADJACENT and QT_VERTEX_VERTEX_NEIGHBOR is bounded by $k \cdot (B + W)$.

5.56. Show that implementing the active corner data structure as a field in the active y border is sufficient to detect cycles.

5.57. Suppose that the active corner data structure is implemented as a one-dimensional array. Let (x, y) correspond to the x and y coordinates of the northeastern corner of a block participating in the active corner data structure. Prove that $|x - y|$ uniquely identifies each active corner.

5.58. Modify procedures COMPONENTS, TRAVERSE, and INCREMENT of Section 5.1.3 to compute the genus of a pointerless bintree representation of a two-dimensional image.

5.59. Discuss the computation of the genus of an image in three or more dimensions. How would you compute it when the image is represented as an octree? Do the arbitrary dimension pointerless bintree methods used for connected component labeling and perimeter computation generalize for genus as well? If so, show how to do this.

OPERATIONS ON IMAGES

6

This chapter describes how a number of basic image operations useful in computer graphics and image processing can be implemented using quadtrees and octrees. We examine point location, object location, set-theoretic operations, windowing (similar to clipping [Roge85]), linear transformations (e.g., translation, rotation, and scaling), and region expansion. Recall that operations that involve the computation of geometric properties, such as connected component labeling, polygon coloring, perimeter, area, moments, and component counting, were described in Chapter 5. Although most of the examples use quadtrees, they can be extended to octrees in a straightforward manner.

6.1 POINT LOCATION

Probably the simplest task to perform on raster data is to determine the color of a given pixel or voxel. An equivalent statement of this task is that we wish to determine the block associated with a given point. In a traditional array representation, this is achieved by exactly one array access. In the region quadtree (octree), this requires searching the quadtree (octree) structure.

The algorithm starts at the root of the quadtree (octree) and uses the values of the x and y (and z) coordinates of the center of its block to determine which of the four (eight) subtrees contains the pixel (voxel). For example, assuming a search through a quadtree, if both the x and y coordinates of the pixel are less than the x and y coordinates of the center of the root's block, then the pixel belongs in the southwest subtree of the root. This process is performed recursively until a leaf node is reached.

The algorithm requires the transmission of parameters so that the center of the block corresponding to the root of the subtree being processed can be calculated. The

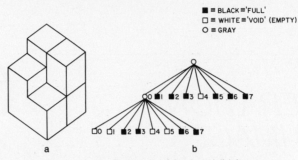

■ ≡ BLACK ≡ 'FULL'
□ ≡ WHITE ≡ 'VOID' (EMPTY)
○ ≡ GRAY

Figure 6.1   (a) Example object and (b) its octree

color of that leaf node is the color of the pixel (voxel). The execution time of the algorithm is proportional to the depth of the leaf node that contains the desired pixel (voxel).

A simple implementation of the point location algorithm for an octree is given below by procedures FIND_3D_BLOCK and GET_OCTANT. They are analogous to procedures FIND_2D_BLOCK and GET_QUADRANT presented in Section 4.2.2 for a quadtree. The parameters to FIND_3D_BLOCK are the point that is to be located, a pointer to the root of the subtree being searched, the width of the block corresponding to the subtree, and the coordinates of the block's farthest corner from the origin. We follow the convention that the left, down, and back faces of a block are closed—if a point lies on one of these faces, then it is in the block bounded by them.

Procedure FIND_3D_BLOCK partitions the block repeatedly until the smallest block corresponding to a leaf node that contains the point is found. It makes use of procedure GET_OCTANT to indicate the particular octant of a gray node that contains the desired point. For example, in locating the block containing the point $(0,2,2)$ in the $4 \times 4 \times 4$ staircase-like object in Figure 6.1, FIND_3D_BLOCK and GET_OCTANT partition the image successively into blocks having furthest corners at $(4,4,4)$, $(2,4,4)$ and $(1,3,3)$.

The function OFFSET, given in Table 6.1, contains multiplicative factors that facilitate the calculation of the coordinate values of the farthest corners of the sons of

Table 6.1   OFFSET (A,O).

A (axis)	O (octant)							
	LDB	LDF	LUB	LUF	RDB	RDF	RUB	RUF
X	1	1	1	1	0	0	0	0
Y	1	1	0	0	1	1	0	0
Z	1	0	1	0	1	0	1	0

each node in procedure FIND_3D_BLOCK. In particular, OFFSET(A,O) is the multiplicative factor for the calculation of the value of coordinate A when descending to the son in octant O.

```
procedure FIND_3D_BLOCK(P,POINT,FAR,W);
/* P points to a node corresponding to a block of width W having its farthest corner from
   the origin at FAR (i.e., FAR['X'], FAR['Y'], and FAR['Z']). Find the smallest block in P
   containing the voxel whose nearest corner to the origin is at POINT. If P is black or
   white, then return the values of P, W, and FAR; otherwise, repeat the procedure for the
   son of P that contains POINT. */
begin
  reference pointer node P;
  value integer array POINT[{'X', 'Y', 'Z'}];
  reference integer array FAR[{'X', 'Y', fH'Z'}];
  reference integer W;
  axis I;
  octant Q;
  while GRAY(P) do
    begin
      W ← W/2;
      Q ← GET_OCTANT(POINT['X'],FAR['X'] – W,
                     POINT['Y'],FAR['Y'] – W,
                     POINT['Z'],FAR['Z'] – W);
      for I in {'X', 'Y', 'Z'} do FAR[I] ← FAR[I] – OFFSET(I,Q)∗W;
      P ← SON(P,Q);
    end;
end;

octant procedure GET_OCTANT(X,XCENTER,Y,YCENTER,Z,ZCENTER);
/* Find the octant of the block rooted at (XCENTER,YCENTER,ZCENTER) that contains
   (X,Y,Z). */
begin
  value integer X,XCENTER,Y,YCENTER,Z,ZCENTER;
  return (if X < XCENTER then
            if Y < YCENTER then
              if Z < ZCENTER then 'LDB'
              else 'LDF'
            else if Z < ZCENTER then 'LUB'
            else 'LUF'
          else if Y < YCENTER then
              if Z < ZCENTER then 'RDB'
              else 'RDF'
            else if Z < ZCENTER then 'RUB'
            else 'RUF');
end;
```

Exercise

6.1. Write an algorithm to implement point location in an FD linear octree.

6.2 NEIGHBORING OBJECT LOCATION

Solving the problem of determining exactly the object at which a user is pointing is useful in many graphics interfaces. At times it is solved by treating it as a point location problem, while at other times it is solved by treating it as a neighboring object location problem. This section discusses the latter. Assuming two-dimensional data, the x and y coordinates of the location of a pointing device (e.g., mouse, graphic tablet, lightpen) must be translated into the name of the appropriate object. To handle this task, we must first determine the leaf that contains the indicated location.

For hierarchical data structures such as the PM quadtree (as well as the PM octree), the leaf node corresponding to the location of the pointing device serves as the starting point of the neighboring object location algorithm. In essence, we wish to report the nearest primitive of the object description stored in the quadtree. If the leaf node is empty, we must investigate other leaf nodes. In fact, even if the leaf node is not empty, unless the location of the pointing device coincides with a primitive, it is possible that a nearer primitive might exist in another leaf node.

Using a pointer-based quadtree representation, finding the nearest primitive (also known as the *nearest neighbor problem*) is achieved by a top-down recursive algorithm. Initially, at each level of the recursion, we explore the subtree that contains the location of the pointing device, say P. Once the leaf node containing P has been found, the distance from P to the nearest primitive in the leaf node is calculated (empty leaf nodes have a value of infinity). Next, we unwind the recursion so that at each level, we search the subtrees that represent regions overlapping a circle centered at P whose radius is the distance to the closest primitive that has been found so far. When more than one subtree must be searched, the subtrees representing regions nearer to P are searched before the subtrees that are farther away (since it is possible that a primitive in them might make it unnecessary to search the subtrees that are farther away).

For example, consider Figure 6.2 and the task of finding the nearest neighbor of P in node 1. We first visit node 1. If we visit nodes in the order NW, NE, SW, SE, then as we unwind for the first time, we visit nodes 2 and 3 and the subtrees of the eastern brother of 1. Once we visit node 4, there is no need to visit node 5 since node 4 contained A. However, we must still visit node 6 containing point B (closer than A), but now there is no need to visit node 7. Unwinding one more level reveals that due to the distance between P and B, there is no need to visit nodes 8, 9, 10, 11, and 12. However, node 13 must still be visited because it could contain a point that is closer to P than B.

Sometimes it is not necessary to calculate the nearest neighbor as long as a 'close' neighbor is found. For example, in a plotting application, it is desired to minimize the amount of wasted pen motions (i.e., motions of the pen that do not involve drawing). In particular, we require an algorithm that minimizes the total time required to preprocess the drawing and to plot it. In such a case, it is helpful to use a quadtree heuristic for calculating the nearest neighbor [Ande83]. For example, in Figure 6.2 such a heuristic might return A as the nearest neighbor of P although B is closer. The heuristic is to use the primitive in the leaf node that contains the location of the

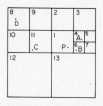

Figure 6.2   Example illustrating the neighboring object problem. P is the location of the pointing device. The nearest object is represented by point B in node 6.

pointing device (unless that leaf node is empty, in which case one of the neighboring nonempty leaf nodes is used).

Exercises

6.2.   Write an algorithm to locate the nearest neighboring edge in a PM_1 quadtree.

6.3.   Write an algorithm to locate the nearest neighboring face in a PM octree.

6.3   SET-THEORETIC OPERATIONS

The basic set-theoretic operations on quadtrees were first described by Hunter and Steiglitz [Hunt78, Hunt79a] for pointer-based quadtrees. Gargantini [Garg83] investigated these operations for linear quadtrees, while Kawaguchi et al. [Kawa83] did the same for DF-expressions. This work dealt with quadtrees that have the same origin, said to be *aligned*. Gargantini also raised the issue of performing these operations on quadtrees that do not have the same origin, said to be *unaligned*. This section shows how to perform set-theoretic operations on both aligned and unaligned quadtrees. The presentation starts with the recoloring operation and then treats the special case of dithering. It continues with a discussion of the different variations of set-theoretic operations. The extension of these techniques to octrees is straightforward.

6.3.1   Dithering

In many applications the entire tree must be traversed. For example, in order to change the color of all the red regions to blue in a region quadtree, the entire tree is traversed in preorder, and the color of each red leaf node is marked blue. In the case of a binary image (i.e., leaf nodes are either black or white), the complement operation is performed in an analogous manner.

A special case of the recoloring algorithm is the dithering (or halftoning) algorithm [Javi76]. The dithering task requires us to convert an image whose pixels are colored with varying intensities of gray into an image whose pixels are either black or white (while maintaining as much similarity to the original image as possible). A simple solution is to associate the colors black or white with each gray value. For example, using a threshold value of 0.5 means that the following 2×2 image

$$\begin{bmatrix} .33 & .33 \\ .33 & .33 \end{bmatrix}$$

would be converted to

$$\begin{bmatrix} 0 & 0 \\ 0 & 0 \end{bmatrix}.$$

The problem with using a single threshold value is that the result bears little similarity to the original image—that is, the entire region is marked as either black or white. In contrast, because their gray value exceeds the threshold, a uniform random distribution of thresholds will cause the number of pixels that are marked black to be proportional to the gray value of the region. In essence, the threshold that differentiates the black gray values from the white gray values is varied in a pseudo-random manner with respect to the location of the pixel in the image.

The process of applying a pseudo-random distribution of thresholds is termed *dithering* and is simulated by a dither matrix. The larger is the size of the matrix chosen, the better is the simulation of a uniform random distribution.[1] Thus, ideally, the dither matrix is the size of the image. However, at times it is more convenient to use a smaller dither matrix and then just replicate it across the image. The dither matrix D is defined recursively as follows:

$$D_0 = 0 \qquad D_n = \begin{bmatrix} D_{n-1} & D_{n-1} + 2/2^{2n} \\ D_{n-1} + 3/2^{2n} & D_{n-1} + 1/2^{2n} \end{bmatrix}.$$

The above formulation shows a scalar term being added to a matrix. In this case, the scalar term is added to each element of the appropriate matrix.

The traditional algorithm, described above, that is used to distribute thresholds across the image can be adapted particularly well to a quadtree image representation because the dither matrix is a square matrix whose width is a power of two. The recursive definition of dither matrix D means that the dithering values can be computed as the block is recursively decomposed into its subblocks. Once a pixel-sized block is encountered, it is thresholded with the appropriate dither value. The dynamic computation of the dithering values takes approximately the same amount of time as that required to access a precomputed dither matrix, hence making the precomputation unnecessary. This means that we can use the largest possible dither matrix—that is, D_n for a quadtree that corresponds to a $2^n \times 2^n$ image.

---

[1] See [Javi76] for a discussion of the significance of using as large a dither matrix as possible.

Exercises

6.4. What is D_1?

6.5. Suppose that the quadtree in Figure 1.1 is a gray quadtree such that when its blocks are listed in depth-first order (NW, NE, SW, SE) with the non-leaf nodes omitted, they have the following gray levels .1, .2, .2, .7, .8, .2, .3, .6, .7, .7, .2, .8, .9, .8, .8, .8, .8, .4, .3. What is the result of dithering it with D_2? Repeat with D_3.

6.6. Write an algorithm to dither a gray quadtree, corresponding to a $2^n \times 2^n$ image, with dither matrix D_m ($m \leq n$).

6.7. Suppose you define a dynamic quadtree ditherer that dithers each block of size $2^m \times 2^m$ by use of the dither matrix D_m. Perform empirical tests to compare it with the standard dithering method that uses a constant dither matrix D_p ($p \leq n$) for a $2^n \times 2^n$ image.

6.8. Write an algorithm that dithers a $2^n \times 2^n$ gray quadtree using the dynamic quadtree dithering technique.

6.3.2   Aligned Quadtrees

Hierarchical data structures (e.g., the region quadtree and octree) are especially useful for performing set-theoretic operations, such as the intersection and union (i.e., overlay) of several aligned images. In the case of the region quadtree, this is described in greater detail by Hunter and Steiglitz [Hunt78, Hunt79a] and by Shneier [Shne81b]. Here, this process is illustrated by showing how to obtain the quadtree corresponding to the intersection of S and T.

The algorithm traverses the two quadtrees in parallel and examines corresponding nodes while it constructs the resulting quadtree, say in U. If either of the two nodes is white, the corresponding node in U is white. If one node is black, say in S, the corresponding node in U is set to the other node, that is, in T. If both nodes are gray, U is set to gray, and the algorithm is applied recursively to the sons of S and T. However, once the sons have been processed, when both nodes are gray, a check must be made if a merger is to take place since all four sons could be white.

For example, consider the intersection of the quadtrees of Figures 6.3a and 6.3b. Both node B in Figure 6.3a and node E in Figure 6.3b are gray. However, the intersection of their corresponding sons yields four white nodes, which must be merged to yield a white node in U, where the corresponding nodes in S and T were gray. Figure 6.3c shows the result of the intersection of Figures 6.3a and 6.3b.

A simple algorithm for achieving the intersection operation for two aligned images that are represented by region quadtrees is given below by procedure INTERSECTION. The representation of the quadtrees is assumed to be pointer based. The parameters to INTERSECTION are pointers to the two quadtrees. It returns a pointer to a new quadtree that represents the result of the operation. The implementation given builds a new quadtree. Thus there is no sharing of subtrees. Therefore at each step, if one of the two subtrees being intersected is black, the output is set to a copy of the other subtree. This copying is achieved by procedure COPY_TREE, which is not given here.

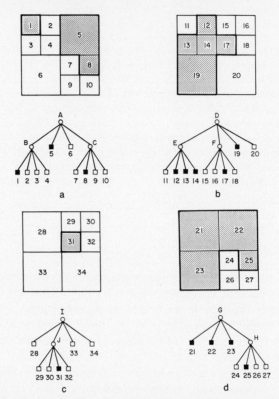

Figure 6.3   Example of set-theoretic operations: (a and b) sample images and their quadtrees, (c) intersection of the images in (a) and (b), (d) union of the images in (a) and (b)

pointer node procedure INTERSECTION(S,T);
/*   Return a pointer to a quadtree that corresponds to the set intersection of the two aligned quadtrees pointed at by S and T. */
begin
  value pointer node S,T;
  pointer node Q;
  pointer node array P['NW' . . . 'SE'];
  quadrant I;
  if WHITE(S) **or** WHITE(T) **then return**(CREATEQNODE(NIL,NIL,'WHITE'))
  else if BLACK(S) **then return**(COPY_TREE(T))
  else if BLACK(T) **then return**(COPY_TREE(S))
  else /* Both subtrees are gray */
    begin
      for I **in** {'NW', 'NE', 'SW', 'SE'} **do**
        P[I] ← INTERSECTION(SON(S,I),SON(T,I));

```
if WHITE(P['NW']) and WHITE(P['NE']) and WHITE(P['SE']) and
   WHITE(P['SW']) then
   begin  /* Four white subtrees cause a merge */
     for I in {'NW', 'NE', 'SW', 'SE'} do returntoavail(P[I]);
     return(CREATEQNODE(NIL,NIL,'WHITE'));
   end
 else
   begin
     Q ← CREATEQNODE(NIL,NIL,'GRAY');
     for I in {'NW', 'NE', 'SW', 'SE'} do
       begin
         SON(Q,I) ← P[I];
         FATHER(P[I]) ← Q;
       end;
     return(Q);
   end;
 end;
end;
```

The union operation is implemented easily by applying De Morgan's law to the above intersection algorithm. In particular, the roles of black and white are interchanged. In addition, when both nodes are gray, a merger occurs only if the four sons are black rather than white, as is the case for set intersection. For example, Figure 6.3d shows the result of the union of Figures 6.3a and 6.3b.

The worst-case execution time and space requirements of the implementations of the intersection and union algorithms are proportional to the sum of the number of nodes in the two input quadtrees. Note that if the implementations did not build a new quadtree for the result (i.e., the sharing of subtrees among the result and input quadtrees would be permitted), then it would be possible for the algorithms to visit fewer nodes than the sum of the nodes in the two input quadtrees. In such a case, the time required for these algorithms would be proportional to the sum of the minimum of the number of nodes at corresponding levels of the two quadtrees.

The ability to perform set-theoretic operations (e.g., overlay) quickly is one of the primary reasons for the popularity of quadtree-like data structures over alternative boundary-based representations such as the chain code. The chain code can be characterized as a local data structure since each segment of the chain code conveys information about only the part of the image to which it is adjacent—that is, that the image is to its right. Therefore performing an overlay operation on two images represented by chain codes requires a considerable amount of work. In contrast, the quadtree is a hierarchical data structure that yields successive refinements at lower depths in the tree. Of course, a hierarchical chain code can be defined, but this is primarily useful in handling extreme cases (e.g., null intersection).

When the set-theoretic operations are interpreted as Boolean operations, union and intersection become 'or' and 'and' operations, respectively. Other operations, such as 'xor' and set-difference, are coded in an analogous manner with linear-time algorithms. Since all of these algorithms are based on preorder tree traversals, they will execute efficiently, regardless of the manner in which the quadtree is represented (e.g., pointers, linear quadtrees, DF-expressions).

Exercises

6.9. Implement procedure COPY_TREE.

6.10. Modify procedure INTERSECTION so that it does not make use of FATHER links.

6.11. Implement procedure INTERSECTION by minimizing the amount of copying. In other words, black and white nodes are shared and, most important, when one of the subtrees is black, the appropriate node in the new subtree is set to the other subtree (i.e., the other subtree is not copied).

6.12. Write a procedure UNION to compute the union of two aligned region quadtrees in a manner analogous to procedure INTERSECTION. The quadtrees are implemented using a pointer-based representation.

6.13. Write a pair of procedures to compute the union and intersection of two aligned region octrees.

6.14. Write a pair of procedures to compute the union and intersection of two aligned region quadtrees that are represented by DF-expressions.

6.15. When a quadtree is represented by a DF-expression, is the order of the execution time of the set-theoretic operations the same as when a pointer-based representation is used?

6.16. Write a pair of procedures to compute the union and intersection of two aligned region quadtrees that are represented by FD locational codes.

6.17. Write an algorithm to compute the chain code of the union of two regions that are represented by chain codes.

6.18. Write an algorithm to compute the chain code of the intersection of two regions that are represented by chain codes.

6.19. Write an algorithm to compute the union of two aligned PM$_1$ quadtrees. The result is also a PM$_1$ quadtree. This is also known as the polygon overlay problem.

6.20. Write an algorithm to compute the union of two aligned PM octrees. The result is also a PM octree.

6.21. Write an algorithm to compute the intersection of two aligned PM octrees. The result is also a PM octree. Be sure that your algorithm detects null objects and yields an empty PM octree in such a case.

6.22. Shamos and Hoey [Sham75] show that the problem of determining whether two simple polygons (possibly nonconvex) intersect can be solved in $O(v \cdot \log_2 v)$ time, where v is the number of vertices in the polygons. Suppose that the polygons are represented using Hunter and Steiglitz's three-color variant of the quadtree described in Section 1.2 (i.e., an MX quadtree). Given an MX quadtree with perimeter p and at resolution n, how would you solve the problem in $O(v + p + n)$ time?

6.3.3 Unaligned Quadtrees

This section discusses the performance of set-theoretic operations on quadtrees that are unaligned. For example, assuming an origin at the lower left corner, consider the two 4×4 quadtrees given in Figures 6.4a and 6.4b whose lower left corners are at locations $(0,2)$ and $(2,0)$, respectively. This alignment information is stored

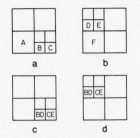

Figure 6.4 Example of rectilinear unaligned-quadtree intersection: (a) a 4 × 4 quadtree with a lower left-hand corner at (0,2), (b) a 4 × 4 quadtree with a lower left-hand corner at (2,0), (c) the intersection of (a) and (b) with (a) as the aligned quadtree, (d) the intersection of (a) and (b) with (b) as the aligned quadtree

separately from the quadtree. Thus, in such a case, to translate or rotate a quadtree, we need only to update the alignment information. However, when two quadtrees of differing alignment must be operated upon simultaneously (e.g., intersected), the algorithm must take the differing alignments into consideration as it traverses the two quadtrees. Two approaches are described; one is designed for a pointer-based representation and the second for a linear quadtree.

The first approach is simplified by the observation [Same88c] that if a square of size $w \times w$ (parallel to the x and y axes) is overlaid on a grid of squares such that each square is of size $w \times w$, then it can overlap at most four of those squares (Figure 6.5a), and those four squares will be neighbors (i.e., they form a $2w \times 2w$ square). We will refer to this case as the *rectilinear unaligned-quadtree* problem. In the case where the $w \times w$ square is not parallel to the x and y axes, we have the *general unaligned-quadtree* problem. In that case, we observe [Same88c] that when an arbitrary square of size $w \times w$ is overlaid at an arbitrary orientation upon a grid of squares such that each square is of size $w \times w$, it can cover at most six grid squares (Figure 6.5b). These six or fewer grid squares will lie within a $3w \times 3w$ square where the center square of the $3w \times 3w$ square is always one of the intersected squares.

To handle the rectilinear unaligned-quadtree intersection problem, we adopt the convention that the output quadtree will be aligned with the first quadtree. We refer to the first quadtree as the *aligned* quadtree and use A to denote it. We refer to the second quadtree as the *unaligned* quadtree and use U to denote it. For example, intersecting the quadtrees in Figures 6.4a and 6.4b so that the quadtree of Figure 6.4a is the aligned quadtree yields the quadtree of Figure 6.4c. On the other hand, if the quadtree of Figure 6.4b is the aligned quadtree, then the result is represented by the quadtree of Figure 6.4d.

When intersecting aligned quadtrees (see Section 6.3.2), we examined pairs of nodes that overlaid identical regions. In contrast, when intersecting rectilinear

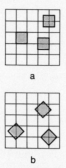

a

b

*Figure 6.5   Examples showing how many squares can be
overlapped when a square of size w × w is overlaid on a
grid of squares such that each square is of size w × w so
that the square and the grid are (a) rectilinearly unaligned,
or (b) generally unaligned*

unaligned quadtrees, upon processing a node in the aligned quadtree, say A, we must
inspect at most four nodes (say U_1, U_2, U_3, U_4) from the unaligned quadtree that overlap the corresponding region. Note that A corresponds to one of the shaded squares in
Figure 6.5a while U_1, U_2, U_3, and U_4 correspond to the overlapped grid cells. For each
i, the block corresponding to node U_i has a width that is greater than or equal to that of
A's block. When A is not white, we may have to process the sons of A further. In this
case, the four nodes from the unaligned quadtree that overlap a given son of A are
chosen from the sons of U_1, U_2, U_3, and U_4. When a pointer-based quadtree representation is used, an efficient recursive top-down algorithm for this version of the quadtree intersection problem can be easily implemented.

The worst-case execution time and space requirements of this algorithm are proportional to the sum of the number of nodes in the two input quadtrees and the output
quadtree after merging (see Exercise 6.23). Note that these bounds are slightly different from the bounds obtained for the aligned quadtree intersection algorithm; in this
case the size of the output quadtree is not bounded from above by the sum of the sizes
of the two input quadtrees. Instead its size depends on the alignment of the input trees
because this will affect the amount of merging that takes place (see Exercise 6.24).

The general unaligned-quadtree algorithm is analogous to the algorithm for rectilinear unaligned quadtrees. The only difference is that each node in the aligned
quadtree can be overlapped by as many as six nodes in the unaligned quadtree (Figure
6.5b). Again, the method is especially well suited for a pointer-based quadtree
representation.

The second approach is designed to work with linear quadtrees [Shaf88c,
Same85d]. Again, an explanation is given only of the algorithm for the rectilinear
unaligned-quadtree problem. The general unaligned-quadtree algorithm is handled in a
similar manner. This discussion is very detailed and may be skipped on an initial
reading.

The nodes in the aligned quadtree are processed in Morton order (see Section 1.4). For each node, say P, in the aligned quadtree, the various nodes of the unaligned quadtree that span P's block are located. The algorithm starts with P's upper left pixel and finds the node, say Q, of the unaligned quadtree that covers it (termed a FIND operation). Next it determines the largest block, say B, that can be covered in both P and Q. Finally it computes the appropriate set operation (intersection in this case) for P and Q, sets B to its result, and transmits B to an output function responsible for creating the nodes in the final quadtree (termed an OUTPUT operation). This sequence of steps is repeated for the remaining unprocessed pixels in P by proceeding in Morton order. The key to making the algorithm efficient is to minimize the number of necessary FIND operations to be performed in the unaligned quadtree, as well as the number of OUTPUT operations.

As an example, consider Figure 6.6a, and let it be the unaligned quadtree. Let the square region within the broken lines, labeled N, be the aligned quadtree, and assume that it is black. The algorithm compares N against each node in the unaligned quadtree that it covers (i.e., E, G, H, I, and J). Figure 6.6b shows the resulting subblocks.

Note that blocks 10, 11, 12, and 13 in Figure 6.6b will form a single white block in the output tree. We say that a block of the output quadtree is *active* if it is possible for it to merge with its siblings to form a larger block. Since our goal is to minimize the number of OUTPUT operations, we do not want to output the active blocks. Instead we take advantage of the fact that the blocks of the output quadtree are generated in Morton order and facilitate the grouping of identically colored blocks by maintaining a table OUT_TAB of the *active* output tree blocks.

Since the blocks in the output quadtree are generated in Morton order (matching the progress made in processing the aligned quadtree), four active blocks that make up a larger block must be adjacent in the list of all active output tree blocks created by the

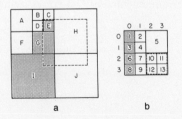

a   b

Figure 6.6 (a) An image (solid lines) serving as the unaligned quadtree in an unaligned quadtree intersection with the square (broken lines and assumed to be black) serving as the aligned quadtree; (b) the result of the unaligned intersection. The broken lines indicate that the constituent blocks will be merged to form a larger block.

intersection algorithm. If these four blocks are identically colored, they are replaced by their parent block.

Once it is certain that active output tree blocks may not combine to form a larger block, then the contents of OUT_TAB can be converted to nodes of the linear quadtree and output by use of the OUTPUT function. This situation is quite easy to detect because it arises whenever the color of an active output tree block is different from the color of the immediately preceding active output tree block. It can be shown that for a $2^n \times 2^n$ image, OUT_TAB contains a maximum of $3 \cdot n$ entries (see Exercise 6.30). Thus the number of OUTPUT operations is bounded by the number of blocks in the final output quadtree.

The number of FIND operations is minimized by keeping track of which blocks in the unaligned quadtree can possibly cover the pixel in the aligned quadtree being processed. We say that a block in the unaligned quadtree is *active* if some, but not all, of its constituent pixels have already been used to cover blocks in the aligned quadtree. The blocks of the aligned quadtree are processed in Morton order. This means that the border of the region consisting of the blocks that have already been processed in the aligned quadtree (termed the *active border*) has the shape of a staircase.

As an example of the active border, consider Figure 6.7, in which the blocks have been assigned labels matching their Morton order. The heavy line represents the state of the active border after processing block 3. The broken line along the southern and eastern border of block 4 shows the change in the active border after processing block 4. The active border of a $2^n \times 2^n$ image consists of sets of horizontal and vertical segments such that the total length of each of these sets is 2^n pixel widths. At any given instant, the active blocks of the unaligned quadtree are those that straddle (i.e., overlap) the active border of the aligned quadtree.

The active border described is related to the active border used by Samet and Tamminen [Same85f] (see also Section 5.1.3). The difference is that Samet and Tamminen's goal is to keep track of the colors of the processed blocks adjacent to the border, whereas in the present application we want to keep track of the blocks in the unaligned quadtree that straddle the active border.

The active border is implemented as two arrays (named X_EDGE and Y_EDGE) of

Figure 6.7 Example of the active border (heavy lines) after processing blocks 1, 2, and 3. The broken lines show the change in the active border after processing block 4. The blocks are processed in Morton order.

nodes such that each array has 2^n elements. Each of these nodes contains a pointer to the block in the unaligned quadtree that covers the segment of the active border that corresponds to it. The arrays are initially empty. Pixel-sized blocks are assumed to be at level 0; a block equal in size to the entire image is at level n.

The algorithm proceeds in the following manner. Assume that we are processing block P in the aligned quadtree. Start with the pixel in the upper left corner of P (at address (cx, cy) with respect to an origin at the extreme NW corner of the image), and find the block, say Q, in the unaligned quadtree that covers the pixel. This is achieved by examining X_EDGE[cx] and Y_EDGE[cy]. There are three possible outcomes.

1. Both X_EDGE[cx] and Y_EDGE[cy] contain Q. Nothing else needs to be done.
2. If one of X_EDGE[cx] and Y_EDGE[cy], but not both, contains Q, then Q is copied into the other.
3. Neither of X_EDGE[cx] and Y_EDGE[cy] contains Q and, thus, we must search (i.e., use the FIND operation) the unaligned quadtree for Q. In such a case, once Q has been found, it is inserted into both X_EDGE[cx] and Y_EDGE[cy].

Once Q has been located, its size and position are compared with that of P to generate the largest block, say B, with an upper left corner at (cx, cy) that is contained in both P and Q. B is added to OUT_TAB, and the OUTPUT function may be invoked. The process continues at the next unprocessed pixel in Morton order until reaching the pixel in the lower right corner of P. Note that no node in the unaligned quadtree will ever be the subject of more than one FIND operation (see Exercise 6.31).

Table 6.2 illustrates the workings of this algorithm for Figure 6.6. Recall that in this case, the image in Figure 6.6a is intersected with the black region corresponding to the square within the broken lines. The image in Figure 6.6a is treated as the unaligned quadtree, while the black square is the aligned quadtree. The table shows the contents of the active border arrays after processing the pixel in the upper left corner of each subblock of the single node comprising the aligned quadtree. These subblocks result from the fact that the node in the aligned quadtree is not totally covered by a node in the unaligned quadtree.

Column 1 of the table indicates the address of the pixel in the aligned quadtree being processed. Columns 2 and 3 correspond to the contents of X_EDGE and Y_EDGE after processing the pixel specified in column 1. The entries in columns 2 and 3 are of the form $p:b$ where b is the block in the unaligned quadtree that is pointed at by the entry at position p. Note that entries adjacent to the border are not shown.

An asterisk (*) next to a block means that it has been located by use of a FIND operation. For example, when processing pixel $(0,0)$ the table is empty. Therefore the record for block E (it contains pixel $(0,0)$) is loaded into X_EDGE[0] and Y_EDGE[0]. A minus (−) next to a block means that the corresponding X_EDGE (or Y_EDGE) entry did not contain a block that covers the current pixel at (cx, cy) and that the block was copied from Y_EDGE (or X_EDGE). A plus (+) appears next to the copied entry.

Table 6.2   Status of the active
nodes for Figure 6.6

Pixel	X_EDGE	Y_EDGE
(0,0)	0: E*	0: E*
(1,0)	0: E 1: H*	0: H*
(0,1)	0: G* 1: H	0: H 1: G*
(1,1)	0: G 1: H+	0: H 1: H–
(2,0)	0: G 1: H 2: H–	0: H+ 1: H
(0,2)	0: G+ 1: H 2: H	0: H 1: H 2: G–
(1,2)	0: G 1: H+ 2: H	0: H 1: H 2: H–
(0,3)	0: I* 1: H 2: H	0: H 1: H 2: H 3: I*
(1,3)	0: I 1: J* 2: H	0: H 1: H 2: H 3: J*
(2,2)	0: I 1: J 2: H	0: H 1: H 2: H 3: J
(3,2)	0: I 1: J 2: H 3: H–	0: H 1: H 2: H+ 3: J
(2,3)	0: I 1: J 2: J– 3: H	0: H 1: H 2: H 3: J+
(3,3)	0: I 1: J 2: J 3: J–	0: H 1: H 2: H 3: J+

As an example, suppose we are processing pixel $(1,2)$ relative to the origin of the aligned quadtree (i.e., block 7 in Figure 6.6b). In this case, we must examine the values of X_EDGE[1] and Y_EDGE[2]. They are given by the entry corresponding to pixels $(0,2)$ in Table 6.2 (i.e., block 6 in Figure 6.6b). X_EDGE[1] contains H, and Y_EDGE[2] contains G. Pixel $(1,2)$ is contained in block H, and we simply copy H from X_EDGE[1] to Y_EDGE[2]. Thus for pixel $(1,2)$, X_EDGE[1] and Y_EDGE[2] are marked with $(+)$ and $(-)$, respectively. Note that upon processing pixel $(0,3)$, block G is still contained in X_EDGE[0], and thus it is replaced by block I obtained using a FIND operation. If G had been a large block covering pixel $(0,3)$, no change would have taken place.

Earlier it was mentioned that the OUTPUT function outputs only blocks that cannot be aggregated to form larger blocks. As described above, OUTPUT is invoked as many times as there are blocks in the final quadtree. It is possible to design an algorithm that makes even fewer calls to OUTPUT. Such an algorithm always inserts the largest block for which the current pixel serves as the upper left corner and keeps track of those nodes that have been inserted and are still active. Thus future pixels of the same color need not cause the insertion of more nodes. This approach has been used in the quadtree construction process (see Section 4.2.3). It is particularly useful when the pixels are processed in a raster-scan order. This is different from the approach discussed in this section, which makes use of the Morton order.

Nevertheless some representations of the quadtree can be constructed most efficiently when the nodes are generated strictly in Morton order. This means that we can afford to have more OUTPUT operations. For example, suppose that the quadtree is represented using a linear quadtree and the locational codes are stored in a B-tree. In such a case, consecutive nodes will be stored in the same page, and the number of OUTPUT operations is not important. For other representations, only the number of OUTPUT operations affects the efficiency.

The algorithm's execution time is $O(N_A + N_U + M + M')$ where N_A and N_U denote the number of nodes in the aligned and unaligned quadtrees, respectively; M and M' are the number of nodes in the output quadtree before and after merging.[2] N_U is the number of FIND operations that must be performed on the unaligned quadtree. N_A is the number of nodes in the aligned quadtree that must be processed. M is the number of times nodes are inserted in OUT_TAB. M is also the total number of subblocks that comprise the set of nodes of the aligned quadtree.

Clearly $N_A \leq M$. M' is the number of calls to procedure OUTPUT. The contribution of the factor M is overshadowed by M' since M represents the number of times that OUT_TAB is updated, while M' represents actual calls to OUTPUT. In particular, if the quadtree resides on disk, then calls to OUTPUT require disk accesses, whereas updates to OUT_TAB are performed in core. Thus we get an asymptotic execution time of $O(N_A + N_U + M')$. For a $2^n \times 2^n$ image, the space requirements are $O(N_A + N_U + M' + n)$.

---

[2] The output quadtree that exists prior to merging is called a *semi-quadtree* [vanL86a].

The cost of a FIND operation depends on the representation of the unaligned quadtree. If the unaligned quadtree is implemented as a sorted list of locational codes, then each FIND operation takes $O(\log_2 N_U)$ time. Therefore a more accurate execution time for the entire algorithm is $O(N_A + N_U \cdot \log_2 N_U + M')$.

If the unaligned quadtree is implemented as a tree structure (i.e., pointers), then the worst-case cost for a FIND operation is $O(n)$ for a $2^n \times 2^n$ image. However, since the node being sought is always a neighbor of the current node in the active border array, neighbor-finding methods (see Chapter 3) can be used. These methods have an average cost of $O(1)$. Use of ropes (see Section 3.2.2) can guarantee an $O(1)$ worst-case cost. The cost of locating the nodes in the aligned quadtree can be analyzed in a similar manner. However, in this case, they are processed in Morton order, and it can be assumed that they are also stored in Morton order. Thus the cost of accessing each node in the aligned quadtree is $O(1)$.

Exercises

6.23. Show that the worst-case execution time and space requirements of the rectilinear unaligned pointer-based quadtree intersection algorithm are proportional to the sum of the number of nodes in the two input quadtrees and the output quadtree after merging.

6.24. Give an example where the intersection of two unaligned quadtrees leads to more nodes than were present in the original trees.

6.25. Implement the algorithm described in the text for the rectilinear unaligned pointer-based quadtree intersection problem.

6.26. Write an algorithm for the general unaligned pointer-based quadtree intersection problem.

6.27. Write an algorithm for the rectilinear unaligned pointer-based octree intersection problem.

6.28. Write an algorithm for the general unaligned pointer-based octree intersection problem.

6.29. How can you modify the unaligned linear quadtree intersection algorithm so that the order of its execution time does not depend on the number of nodes in the output tree before merging (i.e., M)?

6.30. Show that for a $2^n \times 2^n$ image, table OUT_TAB in the unaligned linear quadtree intersection algorithm can contain a maximum of $3 \cdot n$ entries.

6.31. Show that in the rectilinear unaligned linear quadtree intersection algorithm, each block in the unaligned quadtree can be a subject of only one FIND operation.

6.32. Implement the rectilinear unaligned linear quadtree intersection algorithm.

6.33. Implement a rectilinear unaligned linear quadtree intersection algorithm that always inserts the largest block for which the current pixel serves as the upper left corner and keeps track of those nodes that have been inserted that are still active. Thus future pixels of the same color need not cause the insertion of more nodes. Note that only the OUTPUT function in the unaligned linear quadtree intersection algorithm needs modification.

6.34. Extend the rectilinear unaligned linear quadtree intersection algorithm to handle octrees.

6.35. What is the drawback of using the rectilinear unaligned linear quadtree intersection algorithm for images of higher than two dimensions?

6.36. Adapt Samet and Tamminen's generalized linked list representation for the active border [Same88b] (see Section 5.1.3) in an algorithm for rectilinear unaligned intersection for images of arbitrary dimension.

6.37. Write an algorithm for the general unaligned linear quadtree intersection problem.

6.4 WINDOWING

Windowing is the process of extracting a rectangular subsection from an image. It is a special case of clipping [Roge85]. When the original image is represented by a quadtree, we also want the window to be represented by a quadtree, and hence we must build it as the window is extracted. An algorithm designed to achieve this effect for a square window of size $2^k \times 2^k$ at an arbitrary position in a $2^n \times 2^n$ image that is represented by a quadtree is described by Rosenfeld, Samet, Shaffer, and Webber [Rose82b]. In essence, the new quadtree is constructed as the input quadtree is decomposed and relevant blocks are copied into the new quadtree.

The algorithm proceeds in the following manner. Assume that the window is smaller than the image ($k < n$):

1. Find the smallest subtree of the input quadtree that contains the window.
2. If the subtree is a leaf node, we are done. Otherwise subdivide the window into four quadrants and apply steps 1–3 to each quadrant.
3. Attempt to merge the sons of the current node.

The execution time of this windowing algorithm depends on the relative position of the center of the window with respect to the center of the input quadtree and on the sizes of the blocks in the input quadtree that overlap the window. From an asymptotic standpoint, the algorithm takes $O(N + M)$ time where N is the number of nodes in the input quadtree and M is the number of nodes in the window's quadtree prior to merging (see Exercise 6.39). This can be seen by noting that both quadtrees must be traversed. The space requirements are $O(N + M' + n)$ for a $2^n \times 2^n$ image. M' is the number of nodes after merging. This bound assumes that nodes are merged as soon as possible.

For example, consider the 8×8 image of Figure 6.8a, say I, which contains ten leaf nodes, and the 4×4 window, say W, overlaid on Figure 6.8a with broken lines. Initially W is represented by a quadtree of one node. Since W is not contained in a single node of I, we subdivide the window and reapply the algorithm to the four resulting windows, say $W_{NW}, W_{NE}, W_{SW},$ and W_{SE}.

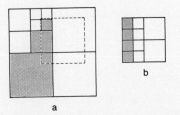

a

b

Figure 6.8   Example of a window operation: (a) 8 × 8 image and the window (shown by broken lines) to be extracted from it, (b) the quadtree of the window

Since W_{NW} is not contained in a single node of I, we must subdivide it again, and now each of its sons is contained in one node of I. W_{NE} is contained in a single node of I (its NE son, which is white), and thus W_{NE} is made white. W_{SW} is not contained in a single node of I, and thus we must subdivide it again; now each of its sons is contained in one node of I. Finally, W_{SE} is also not contained in a single node of I. We subdivide it again, and now each of its sons is contained in one node of I. Since all of the sons of W_{SE} are the same color (white), they are merged to form a larger node. The resulting quadtree corresponding to the window is given in Figure 6.8b.

Windowing can also be achieved by treating the image and the window as two distinct images, say I_1 and I_2, that are not in registration and performing a rectilinear unaligned-quadtree intersection algorithm (see Section 6.3.3). In this case, I_1 is the image from which the window is being extracted, and I_2 is a black image with the same size and origin as the window to be extracted. The quadtree corresponding to the result of the windowing operation has the size and position of I_2, where each pixel of I_2 has the value of the corresponding pixel of I_1. When windowing is implemented in this way, the asymptotic execution time and space requirements depend on which of the two approaches described in Section 6.3.3 is used.

The close relationship between windowing and the unaligned-quadtree intersection operation can also be used to implement a quadtree translation (i.e., shift) algorithm. In particular, translating an image is analogous to extracting a window that is larger than the input image with a different origin from that of the input image. If the image to be translated has an origin at (x,y), then translating it by Δx and Δy means that the window is a black block with an origin at $(x - \Delta x, y - \Delta y)$.

As an example of this analogy, suppose we want to translate the 4×4 image of Figure 6.9a by three and one pixel widths to the right and up, respectively. Assuming an origin at the lower left corner of the image requires that we intersect the image with a 4×4 window having an origin at $(-3,-1)$. The window is overlaid on Figure 6.9a with broken lines. The quadtree of the translated image is shown in Figure 6.9b. The quadtree of the window corresponds to the SW quadrant in Figure 6.9b and is shown by broken lines.

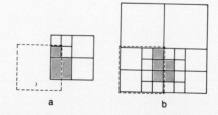

a   b

Figure 6.9   *Example of a translation via windowing: (a) a 4 × 4 image to be translated by 3 pixel widths to the right and 1 pixel width up. The window is shown by broken lines. (b) The quadtree of the shifted image. The quadtree of the window is the SW quadrant and is shown by broken lines.*

When the window is rectangular, a particularly simple implementation of windowing results if we use the *squarecode* representation of Oliver and Wiseman [Oliv83b]. The squarecode is a variant of the locational code, a pointerless quadtree representation technique that represents the image as a collection of disjoint squares of arbitrary side length and at arbitrary positions by recording the length and address of one of the square's corners.

Exercises

6.38. Implement the windowing algorithm of Rosenfeld et al. described in this section.

6.39. Why does the execution time of the windowing algorithm of Rosenfeld et al. described in this section depend on the number of nodes in the window's quadtree prior to merging instead of after merging?

6.5 LINEAR IMAGE TRANSFORMATIONS

Linear image transformations such as translation, rotation, and scaling are important operations in computer graphics and robotics. Their execution on images represented by quadtrees and octrees has been the subject of much research. A common failing of all of the algorithms proposed is that, with the exception of scaling by a power of two, translations by integer multiples of the width of the smallest pixel (voxel), and rotations by multiples of 90 degrees, they result in an approximation. Straight lines (planar faces) are not necessarily transformed into straight lines (planar faces). This failing is often mistakenly attributed to the quadtree and octree representations; in fact, it is a direct result of the underlying digitization process. It manifests itself no matter what underlying representation is used when performing raster graphics. Note that this failing can be avoided by using representations such as the PM quadtree and octree.

This section reviews a number of algorithms that have been proposed to calculate linear image transformations. Frequently, aside from the dimensionality of the space, there is little difference between methods for quadtrees and octrees. Thus the algorithms are described in terms of 'trees,' unless stated otherwise. There are two principal classes of methods. They differ on whether the transformation or its inverse serves as the basis of the operation. The first class proceeds by first transforming the source tree (either the region represented by it or its constituent blocks) and then building the new tree by inserting either the transformed region or its transformed constituent blocks.

The second class performs a tree traversal of the target tree and determines if the nodes overlap any black nodes in the source tree (i.e., an inverse transformation), and colors them as is appropriate. In the case of a transformation that is just a translation (i.e., no rotation or scaling) by integer multiples of the width of the smallest pixel (voxel), there is a third class of methods that calculates the final position in the target tree of the nodes in the source tree and then inserts them. These methods often make use of the locational codes of the nodes that comprise the tree and hence are particularly suitable for pointerless representations such as the linear quadtree (octree).

6.5.1 Algorithms Based on Transforming the Source Tree

The simplest transformations are those in which the translation distance is a power of two and is greater than or equal to the width of the largest block in the image, the rotation is by a multiple of 90 degrees, or the scale factor is a power of two (doubling or halving). To make an image represented by a quadtree (octree) half the size that it was originally, we need only create a new root and give that root three (seven) white sons and one son that corresponds to the original tree. To make the quadtree (octree) twice as big, we choose one of the subtrees to serve as the new root (e.g., the SW subtree), thereby eliminating the remaining three (seven) subtrees. This technique is applied repeatedly for any scale factor that is a power of two.

When the rotation is by a multiple of 90 degrees, the operation can be achieved 'in-place' by simply rearranging pointers. For example, Figure 6.10b is the result of rotating the quadtree of Figure 6.10a by 90 degrees counterclockwise. The algorithm traverses the tree in preorder and rotates the pointers at each node. For this example of a quadtree, it is based on the following observations:

1. All of the pixels in the NW quadrant of the image are in the SW quadrant.
2. All the pixels in the NE quadrant of the image are in the NW quadrant.

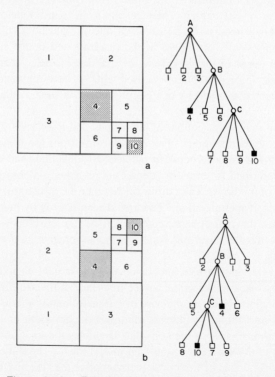

Figure 6.10   Rotating (a) by 90° counterclockwise yields (b)

3. All the pixels in the SE quadrant of the image are in the NE quadrant.
4. All the pixels in the SW quadrant of the image are in the SE quadrant.
5. Each of the quadrants in its new position appears as if it had been locally rotated clockwise by 90 degrees.

When the translation distance is a power of two and is greater than the width of the largest block in the image, then no new blocks need to be created. This situation is equivalent to scaling the image by a scale factor that is a positive power of two.

Usually the transformation is more complex. Hunter and Steiglitz [Hunt78, Hunt79b] implement the transformation for a quadtree by using their polygon-to-quadtree construction algorithm. Each connected black region in the quadtree is treated as a polygon (with orthogonal edges). The edges and vertices are obtained by tracing the boundaries of the black regions using an algorithm such as that described in Section 4.3.2 for deriving a chain code from a quadtree. The images of the vertices that result from the application of the transformation determine the polygons in the target quadtree. The outline-and-color algorithm [Hunt78, Hunt79a] (see Section 4.4) is used to construct the actual target quadtree for each transformed polygon (as well as holes). The final step is the overlay of the polygons, which is performed by using techniques discussed in Section 6.3.2. The outline algorithm saves some work by ignoring the boundaries of the input polygons that will not be visible in the output.

The execution time and space requirements of this algorithm are derived as follows. By assuming that the transformation does not change the resolution (or scale) of the input image, it can be shown that constructing the target quadtree takes time and space of $O(N + p + m \cdot n)$ [Hunt78, Hunt79b], where N is the total number of nodes in the input quadtree, p is the total perimeter of the nonbackground visible portions of the input image, n is the log of the diameter (i.e., resolution), and m is the number of polygons in the input image. Tracing the boundary has an average execution time proportional to p. Overlaying the polygons takes time proportional to N. Thus the average execution time of the entire process is $O(N + p + m \cdot n)$.

Instead of extracting the polygons of the input image, Peters [Pete85] simply applies the transformation to each node in the quadtree. The result is a collection of quadrangles. These quadrangles are inserted into the output quadtree, one by one, by superposing (i.e., a union operation) each quadrangle with the target quadtree. The algorithm takes $O(N + n \cdot M)$ time and uses $O(N + M)$ space, where M is the number of nodes in the output tree prior to merging, while N and n are as defined previously.

Weng and Ahuja [Weng87] describe an algorithm for the transformation of an octree analogous to Peters' algorithm for a quadtree. They traverse the source octree and for each black leaf node encountered, they compute its new position and orientation under the transformation. Next they traverse the target octree (initially one node corresponding to the entire image space) and test each node, say T, for intersection with the transformed node. If the intersection is empty, then T is colored white. If T is entirely within the transformed node, then T is colored black. Otherwise T is decomposed into its eight sons (blocks), and the algorithm is applied recursively to the sons of T. Once this step is completed, if the eight sons are of the same color, then merging will have to be applied. The space and time requirements are the same as in Peters' algorithm.

One of the problems with most transformations is that, in general, the shape of the object is not preserved when the translations are not integer multiples of the voxel size, the scale factors are not integers, or the rotations are not multiples of 90 degrees. An equivalent statement is that the transformations are not invertible. This problem is compounded when the transformations are applied in an incremental manner (as is expected in an application environment). Weng and Ahuja resolve this problem by retaining the original source octree as a reference and maintaining a transformation matrix to keep track of the current position of the octree.

Exercises

6.40. How would you apply Hunter and Steiglitz's algorithm to an image represented by an octree? Can you foresee any problems?

6.41. How would you apply the algorithm of Peters to an octree?

6.42. Show that Peters' algorithm takes $O(N + n \cdot M)$ time and uses $O(N + M)$ space, where N and M are the number of nodes in the input and output (prior to merging) trees, respectively, and n is the resolution of the image.

6.5.2 Algorithms Based on an Inverse Transformation

Jackins and Tanimoto [Jack80] describe a translation algorithm based on the principle that each node in the target octree (quadtree) can correspond to (i.e., be *covered* by) at most 8 (4) nodes of greater than or equal size in the source octree (quadtree). By changing the number of covering nodes from 8 (4) to 18 (6), the algorithm can be used with a linear transformation on an octree (quadtree) that also includes rotation (but not scaling).[3] It traverses the target and source trees in tandem using a control structure similar to that used in the windowing algorithm of Rosenfeld et al. [Rose82b] described in Section 6.4. It maintains a list of the nonwhite nodes in the source tree that cover the node of the target tree being processed. Initially the target tree is assumed to contain one white node.

Each node, say N, in the target tree is examined to see if it is totally contained in a black covering node in the source tree. If yes, then N is black in the target tree. If no, then there are two cases. If all the covering nodes are white, the node is white; otherwise N is decomposed into eight (four) sons, assumed to be white, and the process is applied recursively. The final step tests if the eight (four) sons are of the same color, and, if so, it merges them. Of course, for each son, before we can recursively invoke the algorithm, we must update the list of nodes that cover it. In the case of translation, the containment test is a test for overlapping intervals, and it is applied in

---

[3] It is conjectured that 18 is the maximum number of nodes in the source octree that can cover a node in the target octree (see Exercise 6.47).

each of the three (two) dimensions. It is facilitated by first adding the translation vector, say $T = (T_x, T_y, T_z)$, to the x, y, and z coordinates, respectively, of the node in the source tree being compared.

The algorithm takes $O(N + M)$ time where N and M are the number of nodes in the source and target (prior to merging) trees, respectively, since both must be traversed. The space requirements are $O(N + M' + n)$ for a $2^n \times 2^n$ image. M' is the number of nodes after merging. This bound assumes that nodes are merged as soon as possible.

Van Lierop [vanL86a] describes an algorithm that works for any linear transformation. It is based on the same principle as that of Jackins and Tanimoto. It is applied to a pointerless tree representation in which only the locational codes of the black nodes are retained (i.e., an FD linear quadtree or octree; see Section 2.1.1). The locational codes are stored in a list. It starts with a target tree of one node, say T, corresponding to the entire image space and applies an inverse transformation to T, say $inv(T)$. If $inv(T)$ is contained in a black node in the source tree, then T is black. Otherwise for an octree (quadtree), T is decomposed into eight (four) sons (i.e., blocks), and the algorithm is applied recursively to the sons of T.[4]

The algorithm takes $O(M \cdot (\log_2 N + n))$ time where N and M are the number of nodes in the source and target (prior to merging) trees, respectively, and n is the resolution of the image (see Exercise 6.50). The space requirements are $O(N + M' + n)$ where M' is the number of nodes after merging. This bound assumes that nodes are merged as soon as possible.

A drawback of the two methods is that they check only if a node in the target tree is contained in one of the black covering nodes. They do not check if all of the covering nodes are black.[5] In such a case, an affirmative answer would mean that there is no need for further decomposition. This is the approach used by Meagher [Meag82a] and is analogous to the rectilinear unaligned pointer-based quadtree intersection algorithm described in Section 6.3.3. It results in a considerably faster algorithm; its execution time is proportional to the sum of the number of nodes in the input and output quadtree after merging rather than before merging (see Exercise 6.52). The space requirements are of the same order as the execution time.

In theory the approach discussed works for any linear transformation. However, the number of covering nodes depends on the nature of the transformation. In particular, if the transformation involves translation and rotation (but no scaling), then the number of covering nodes of greater than or equal size in the source quadtree (octree) changes from four (eight) to six (eighteen). When scaling is allowed, the number of covering nodes depends on the magnitude of the scale factor.

---

[4] Actually this decomposition should take place only if $inv(T)$ partially overlaps at least one black node. If it does not, then the node is white and should be ignored (i.e., omitted from the target tree).

[5] For a white node, the method of Jackins and Tanimoto implicitly checks if all of the covering nodes are white. This check is a by-product of the step that assumes that if the target tree node is not partially contained in any black covering node, it is white.

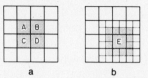

a   b

Figure 6.11   (a) An 8 × 8 image and (b) the result of translating it by one pixel to the right and down

For example, consider the case when the 8 × 8 image in Figure 6.11a is shifted by one pixel to the right and down. The resulting quadtree is given in Figure 6.11b. Although node E in Figure 6.11b is covered by nodes A, B, C, and D in Figure 6.11a, it must nevertheless be decomposed when using the approaches of Jackins and Tanimoto [Jack80] and van Lierop [vanL86a].

As an example of the use of Meagher's method, we describe the rotation of the quadtree of Figure 6.12a, termed A, by 16 degrees in a counterclockwise direction

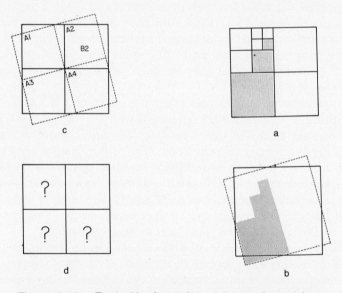

Figure 6.12   Example of rotation: (a) sample quadtree, (b) rotation of (a) by 16° in a counterclockwise direction about its origin, (c) decomposition after the first level of subdivision, (d) rotated quadtree with one level of subdivision, (e) decomposition after the second level of subdivision, (f) rotated quadtree with two levels of subdivision, (g) decomposition after the third level of subdivision, (h) rotated quadtree with three levels of subdivision. Broken lines depict the decomposition of the source quadtree, and solid lines depict the decomposition of the target quadtree.

about its center. The target quadtree, termed B, has been rotated by 16 degrees in the clockwise direction about the center of A (see Figure 6.12b). Broken lines illustrate the decomposition of the source tree, A, and solid lines illustrate the decomposition of the target tree, B.

The algorithm proceeds by first determining if B is a leaf node by checking if the maximum of six nodes of equal size in A that cover it are of the same color. If yes, we are done. Otherwise B is subdivided (it is a gray node), as are the relevant nodes in A. This process is repeated until either all nodes in B's trees are leaf, or we have reached the maximum depth of decomposition.

In the example, the first subdivision is illustrated in Figure 6.12c, and its result is given in Figure 6.12d. Notice the use of the '?' symbol to indicate that the block will be subdivided further. The NE quadrant in Figure 6.12d (corresponding to the block labeled B2 in Figure 6.12c) is white because the blocks in A that cover it (just the two blocks labeled A2 and A4 in Figure 6.12c) are white. Prior to proceeding further, we should check to see if any of the subdivided blocks of B have four identically colored sons, in which case a merge must occur.

Next we subdivide the blocks labeled with a '?' in Figure 6.12d, as well as blocks A1, A2, A3, and A4 in Figure 6.12c to obtain Figure 6.12e. Again we check each of the newly obtained subblocks of B to see if they are covered by subblocks of A that are of the same color. In this case, we find that this is true for block B5 in Figure 6.12e (i.e., by black subblocks A5, A6, and A7), as well as blocks B6, B7, and B8. The result is given in Figure 6.12f where '?' indicates that the block will be decomposed further.

One more level of decomposition is depicted in Figure 6.12g, and the resulting rotated quadtree is shown in Figure 6.12h. Checking if any of the subdivided blocks in B has identically colored sons leads to a merge of the four blocks of the NW son of

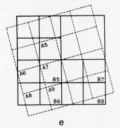

e

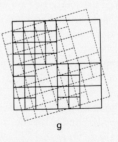

g

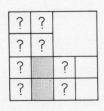

f

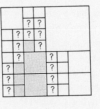

h

the NW quadrant in Figure 6.12h because they are all white. At this point, the maximum depth of the resulting quadtree is the same as the original unrotated quadtree. Nodes labeled with a '?' can be assigned either black or white, as is desired. This may cause more merging.

Exercises

6.43. Given a grid of unit squares, prove that a unit square laid on top of this grid so that its sides are parallel to the sides of the grid squares can overlap no more than four of the grid squares.

6.44. Given a grid of unit cubes, prove that a unit cube laid on top of this grid so that its faces are parallel to the faces of the grid cubes can overlap no more than eight of the grid cubes.

6.45. Given a grid of unit squares, prove that a unit square laid on top of this grid at an arbitrary orientation can overlap no more than six of the grid squares.

6.46. Construct an example where a unit cube is overlaid on a grid of cubes at an arbitrary orientation so that it overlaps eighteen of the grid cubes.

6.47. Given a grid of unit cubes, prove that a unit cube laid on top of this grid at an arbitrary orientation can overlap no more than eighteen of the grid cubes.

6.48. How would you determine if a block in the target tree overlaps a covering block in the source tree for an arbitrary linear transformation (not just a translation)?

6.49. Give an algorithm to determine if a covering block in the source tree contains a block in the target tree for an arbitrary linear transformation (not just a translation).

6.50. Prove that van Lierop's algorithm takes $O(M \cdot (\log_2 N + n))$ time where N and M are the number of nodes in the source and target (prior to merging) trees, respectively, and n is the resolution of the image.

6.51. The text mentions that Meagher's linear transformation algorithm tests if all of the covering nodes in the source tree are of the same color as the node in the target tree. Does this algorithm still need to check for merging—that is, if all four (eight) sons of a node in the target quadtree (octree) are of the same color?

6.52. Give an example two-dimensional image where the algorithms of Meagher and Jackins and Tanimoto are equivalent—that is, they expand the same nodes.

6.53. Implement Meagher's algorithm for applying an arbitrary linear transformation to an image represented by a quadtree. Repeat for an octree.

6.54. Devise an algorithm to rotate a region quadtree about an arbitrary point rather than its center (i.e., the point at the root), as is the case for the algorithm described in this section.

6.55. Write an algorithm to scale an image that is represented by a region quadtree by an arbitrary scale factor f ($0 \leq f \leq 1$).

6.56. Using Meagher's method, write an algorithm to translate a PM_1 quadtree.

6.57. Using Meagher's method, write an algorithm to translate a PM octree.

6.58. Using Meagher's method, write an algorithm to rotate a PM_1 quadtree by θ degrees about its center.

6.59. Using Meagher's method, write an algorithm that applies a general linear transformation to an image represented by a PM_1 quadtree.

6.60. Using Meagher's method, write an algorithm that applies a general linear transformation to an image represented by a PM octree.

6.5.3 Algorithms Based on Address Computation [6]

Restricting the transformation to be a translation by an integer multiple of the width of the smallest pixel (voxel) in the tree leads to simple methods of building the target tree. In particular, no containment or overlapping tests need to be performed. Assume that the translation distance can be expressed as a vector, say $T = (T_x, T_y, T_z)$ where T_x, T_y, and T_z correspond to its components along the x, y, and z axes, respectively. Each of T_i ($i = x$, y, or z) can be rewritten in terms of its binary representation: $T_i = t_{i,n-1} \cdot 2^{n-1} + \cdots + t_{i,1} \cdot 2^1 + t_{i,0} \cdot 2^0$.

There are a number of relevant methods. All make use of the binary representation of the axial components of the translation distance and of the addresses (i.e., locational codes) of the nodes in the source tree to compute the addresses of the resulting nodes in the target tree. Once the entire source tree has been processed in this manner, a merging pass is applied to the nodes in the target tree. When the tree is represented as a collection of the locational codes of the nodes that comprise it, there is no need to insert the new nodes physically in the target tree. Instead the locational codes of the new nodes are inserted into the collection as is appropriate (e.g., by merging into a sorted list).

The simplest method decomposes each black node in the source tree into blocks of unit width, adds the translation distance to their locational code, thereby creating nodes of unit width in the target tree, and then applies a merging pass. For example, block X of size 16×16 in Figure 6.13a would be decomposed into 256 blocks of unit width, shown in Figure 6.13b, prior to the translation. Gargantini [Garg83] uses this method in conjunction with a linear quadtree representation in which only the locational codes of the black nodes are retained. However, it is applicable to octrees as well.

To understand this process, consider Figure 6.14, which shows a labeling for the octants of an octree and a suitable orientation for the coordinate axes. The locational code is a string formed by concatenating the octant labels encountered on the path from the root of the tree to the node. The addition step applies the relations tabulated in Table 6.3 to the corresponding digits of the block's locational code and of the binary representation of the appropriate axial component of the translation vector. Note that when an entry in Table 6.3 has two digits, the leading digit is a 1, and it indicates that a carry is propagated to the next digit (e.g., when translating octant 4 by one unit in the z direction, the result is 10). For example, to translate a block with locational code 345 by three units in the direction of axis z, add 011. From Table 6.3 we find that the result is a block with locational code 741.

Ahuja and Nash [Ahuj84b] observe that it is not always necessary to decompose the blocks to the unit level prior to adding the translation distance. They make use of the fact that a block of width 2^b ($b \geq 0$) is not decomposed by a translation whose axial components (i.e., T_i) have the property that $t_{i,j} = 0$ for all $j \leq b$. In other

---

[6] This section is highly detailed and can be skipped on an initial reading.

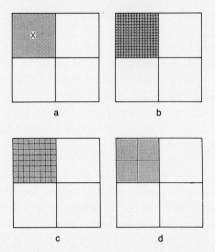

Figure 6.13   (a) A 32 × 32 image and the decomposition required prior to using the translation algorithms of (b) Gargantini [Garg83], (c) Ahuja and Nash [Ahuj84b], and (d) Fujimura et al. [Fuji83b, Yama84], for a translation of six pixels to the right

Figure 6.14   Labeling of octants in an octree and an appropriate orientation for the coordinate axes

Table 6.3   Addition table for unit translations

Initial Label	Final Label after Translation along Direction		
	$+x$	$+y$	$+z$
0	1	2	4
1	10	3	5
2	3	10	6
3	12	11	7
4	5	6	10
5	14	7	11
6	7	14	12
7	16	15	13

words, when the translation distance is a multiple of the block size, no further decomposition is necessary.

They use the following algorithm, which is applicable to octrees and quadtrees. Make three (two) passes over the source octree (quadtree) — one for each of the axial directions, say i. For each black node, say B of width 2^b, compare the base 2 logarithm of its width (i.e., b) with the position of the least significant bit of T_i, which is one, say, $t_{i,j}$. There are two possible actions:

1. If $j \geq b$, then add T_i to the locational code of B.
2. Otherwise replace node B by eight (four) black sons and determine which of actions 1 and 2 is applicable to them.

Once all the nodes have been processed on a given pass, a merging step is applied. For example, for a horizontal translation of six pixels to the right, block X of size 16×16 in Figure 6.13a would be decomposed into 64 blocks of size 2×2, shown in Figure 6.13c.

Ahuja and Nash use a pointer representation of the tree where pointers to white nodes are replaced by pointers to NIL. The locational code of each node is obtained by concatenating the octant labels encountered on the path from the root of the tree to the node. Once a node in the source tree has been translated, it is replaced by a gray node all of whose sons are white (i.e., pointers to NIL). The algorithm executes 'in-place' in the sense that the source and target trees are built in the same space (see Exercise 6.63). The worst-case execution time and space requirements are proportional to the product of the resolution of the image (maximum depth in the tree) and the number of nodes in the target tree prior to the merging step (see Exercise 6.64).

The main bottleneck in the algorithm of Ahuja and Nash is step 2, which forces much decomposition—at times as deep as the resolution of the image. This results in the creation of many nodes. Osse and Ahuja [Osse84] report an improvement. Again their algorithm makes as many passes over the tree as there are nonzero axial components of the translation distance (but see Exercise 6.65). The improvement is that instead of decomposing a black node, say B, to the level of the least significant bit of T_i, which is one, say $t_{i,j}$ (i.e., at level j), they single out two subblocks of B with width 2^j for further processing.

These subblocks are the ones with the minimum and maximum locational codes, say $B_{\min}$ and $B_{\max}$, respectively. They are located at opposite corners of B. For example, in the $2^5 \times 2^5$ two-dimensional image given in Figure 6.13a, the 16×16 black block labeled X has FD locational code 00000. Assume that directional codes 0, 1, 2, 3 correspond to NW, NE, SW, SE, respectively. Translating this block by six pixels to the right means that $T_x = (0, 0, 1, 1, 0)$. Therefore, $j = 1$ (i.e., the least significant bit, which is one), and thus $X_{\min} = 00000$ and $X_{\max} = 03330$.

Osse and Ahuja's algorithm proceeds in the following manner. Let B be the black node that is being processed, 2^b be its width, and $S(T(B))$ be the area spanned by the translation of B. First, calculate the locational codes of the translated positions of $B_{\min}$ and $B_{\max}$ and insert them into the target tree as black nodes, say $T(B_{\min})$ and

$T(B_{max})$, respectively. For example, for block X in Figure 6.13a, blocks Y and Z (in Figure 6.15a) correspond to $T(X_{min}) = 00110$ and $T(X_{max}) = 12320$, respectively.

Next insert black nodes into the target tree corresponding to the locational codes that lie between $T(B_{min})$ and $T(B_{max})$ and that are also within $S(T(B))$. The locational codes of these nodes are calculated by traversing the part of the target tree bounded by the paths to $T(B_{min})$ and $T(B_{max})$. This process (see Exercise 2.9) is similar to procedure WHITEBLOCKS in Section 2.1.1, which calculates the locational codes of all the white nodes between two successive elements (i.e., black) of a linear quadtree. The width of these nodes ranges in size from 2^j to 2^{b-1}. For example, for the image in Figure 6.13a, the result of the translation is shown in Figure 6.15a.

The savings that result from this technique are clear because there is no need to decompose the nodes that are being translated all the way to the maximum depth. Nevertheless the asymptotic cost of the algorithm is the same as that of the algorithm of Ahuja and Nash; it is proportional to the product of the resolution of the image (maximum depth in the tree) and the number of nodes in the target tree prior to the merging step. Of course, once all the passes that insert the nodes have been completed, a final pass is made to merge nodes all of whose sons have the same color.

An approach related to that of Osse and Ahuja is to use the binary representation of the translation vector T to calculate directly the decomposition induced by the translation for each node in the source tree. A final pass merges the nodes in the target tree as necessary. This is the technique described by Walsh [Wals88] and is best illustrated by an example. All nodes are represented by their locational codes.

For the moment, assume a two-dimensional image and that the translation is along only one direction, say in the positive x direction (i.e., east). Thus $T = (T_x, 0)$, where $T_x = t_{x,n-1} \cdot 2^{n-1} + \cdots + t_{x,1} \cdot 2^1 + t_{x,0} \cdot 2^0$. Consider a block, say B, of width 2^b and assume further that $T_x < 2^b$; otherwise use $T_x \bmod 2^b$, and add a multiple of 2^b to the locational code of B. Let $t_{x,j}$ be the least significant bit of T_x, which is one. The resulting decomposition can be partitioned into two sets of blocks, depending on whether they are to the right or to the left of the eastern boundary of B.

To the right of the eastern boundary of B, we have 2^{b-i} blocks of width 2^i for each $t_{x,i} \neq 0$ and $b > i > j$. To the left of the eastern boundary of B, we have 2^{b-i}

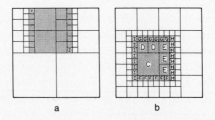

a　　　　　　　b

Figure 6.15　The result of translating block X in Figure 6.13a by (a) six pixels to the right, (b) six pixels to the right and ten pixels down

blocks of width 2^i for each $t_{x,i} = 0$ and $b > i > j$. In addition, there are 2^{b-j} blocks of width 2^j on both the left and right sides of the eastern boundary. As an example, consider the 16×16 black block labeled X in Figure 6.13a, and shift it by six pixels to the right. The resulting decomposition, given in Figure 6.15a, contains two 8×8 blocks and eight 2×2 blocks to the left of the eastern boundary of the block and four 4×4 blocks and eight 2×2 blocks to the right of the eastern boundary of the block. It is easy to compute the locational codes of these blocks since it merely involves the addition of a suffix to the locational code of the node being translated.

When the translation involves just one axial direction, the number and locations of the new blocks are calculated by examining the binary representation of the translation vector. When the translation has nonzero components in more than one of the axial directions, the situation is more complex. Assume a two-dimensional image and that the translation is in the positive x and y directions, defined here to be to the right and downward, respectively. Consider the translation of a block, say B of width 2^b, and assume further that T_x and T_y are both less than 2^b. Let j_x and j_y be the positions of the least significant bits of T_x and T_y, respectively, which are one. There are two cases depending on whether any of j_x or j_y are $b-1$.

If j_x is $b-1$, then the locations of the new blocks are calculated using the procedure for a translation by T_y in the y direction. The only difference is that for each block size, half of the blocks lie to the left of the right boundary of B and the other half lie to the right of the right boundary of B. If j_y is $b-1$, then the locations of the new blocks are calculated using the procedure for a translation by T_x in the x direction. The only difference is that for each block size, half of the blocks lie above the bottom boundary of B and the other half below the bottom boundary of B.

If neither j_x nor j_y are $b-1$, then the algorithm generates the blocks in a spiral-like order starting with the lower right corner of B. The discussion is illustrated with the translation of block X of width 16 in Figure 6.13a by six pixels to the right and ten pixels down. Thus, $T_x = (0, 1, 1, 0)$ and $T_y = (1, 0, 1, 0)$. The result is shown in Figure 6.15b. The idea is to start with an empty region and grow it by adding blocks to it along the appropriate sides as indicated by the binary representation of the components of the translation vector. We first add one block of width 2^{b-1} whose position relative to the lower right corner of B depends on bits $t_{x,b-1}$ and $t_{y,b-1}$ (e.g., on the SW corner if they are 0 and 1, respectively, as is the case for block C relative to X in Figure 6.15b).

The remaining blocks are added in decreasing order of size. The spiral nature of the process is such that all blocks of a given size along one of the axial directions are added before the blocks of the same size are added along the other axial direction. Assume that blocks that are adjacent along the y direction are added before those that are adjacent along the x direction. For example, in Figure 6.15b, we add the two 4×4 blocks labeled D to the north of the upper boundary of the translated region (C at this point) since bit $t_{y,2}$ is 0. Next we add the three 4×4 blocks labeled E to the east of the right boundary of the translated region (the blocks labeled C and D) since bit $t_{x,2}$ is 1. This process continues for the two axial directions in alternating order for all blocks of size 2^l where $l > k$ and k is the maximum of j_x and j_y. When $l \leq k$, there are three cases depending on the relation between j_x and j_y:

1. If $j_x = j_y$, then add $2^{b-k} - 2$ blocks of size 2^k along both the bottom (e.g., in Figure 6.15b, the six 2×2 blocks labeled F) and the top (the six 2×2 blocks labeled G) of the translated region (the blocks labeled C, D, and E). Also add 2^{b-k} blocks of size 2^k along both the right (e.g., the eight 2×2 blocks labeled H) and the left (the eight 2×2 blocks labeled I) of the translated region (the blocks labeled C, D, E, F, and G).

2. If j_x is smaller than j_y, then add $2^{b-k} - 2$ blocks of size 2^k along both the bottom and top of the translated region, and continue the process along the x direction using the technique discussed earlier for a translation in one axial direction. This would be the case in our example for the x direction had we translated by seven pixels to the right instead of six, because now we would have $T_x = (0, 1, 1, 1)$ and j_x would be 0 instead of 1.

3. Otherwise if j_y is smaller than j_x, then add $2^{b-k} - 2$ blocks of size 2^k along both the right and left of the translated region, and continue the process along the y direction using the technique discussed earlier for a translation in one axial direction. This would be the case in our example for the y direction had we translated by eleven pixels down instead of ten, because now we would have $T_y = (1, 0, 1, 1)$ and j_y would be 0 instead of 1.

Extending Walsh's algorithm to images of arbitrary dimension is not difficult. Recall that in two dimensions the algorithm adds rows and columns of blocks in order of decreasing width in a spiral manner. In three dimensions the algorithm adds planes of cubes in order of decreasing width, while in d dimensions it adds $(d-1)$-dimensional hyperplanes of hypercubes in order of decreasing width. The advantage of Walsh's method is that it can be performed using just one pass, and it can be implemented by nonrecursive procedures; it requires only use of nested iteration (i.e., 'for' loops).

When the tree is represented as a collection of the locational codes of the nodes that comprise it, there is no need to insert the new nodes physically in the target tree. Instead the locational codes of the new nodes are inserted into the collection as is appropriate (e.g., by merging into a sorted list). It is in this case that Walsh's method is particularly attractive. For example, for a two-dimensional image, the locational codes of the blocks comprising the translation of a given block, say B, are generated one row or one column at a time. These rows and columns are already in sorted order. Thus their insertion into the list of blocks corresponding to the translation of B can be done in time proportional to the width of B (see Exercise 6.77).

Once all of the nodes have been translated, merging must be applied. However, this must be preceded by the creation of a single sorted list of the locational codes of all of the black nodes that result from the translation. Assuming a source tree with N black nodes, the input to this process consists of N sorted lists—one for each node in the source tree. Assuming a total of M nodes in the N lists, this process takes $O(M \cdot \log_2 N)$ time when merge sorting is used. Merging the M nodes takes $O(M)$ time. Creating a locational code for each of the M translated nodes takes $O(n)$ time for a $2^n \times 2^n$ image. Thus the entire translation process takes $O(M \cdot (n + \log_2 N))$ time. The space requirements are $O(M + N)$. Note that M is the number of nodes in the output prior to merging.

It is interesting to observe that Walsh's algorithm is a generalization of the method of Fujimura et al. [Fuji83b, Yama84], who use table-lookup to precompute the decomposition that would result from the translation of a block of edge length 2^b by distances of 2^{b-2}, 2^{b-1}, and $3 \cdot 2^{b-2}$ pixels in a single given direction, say x. This assumes that the translation, say T_x, is less than 2^b; otherwise use T_x mod 2^b, and add a multiple of 2^b to the locational code of B. When the translation is not one of these three distances, the block is decomposed into four blocks, and the process is repeated. For example, block X of size 16×16 in Figure 6.13a would be decomposed into four 8×8 blocks, shown in Figure 6.13d, prior to a horizontal translation of six pixels. Of course, Walsh's method is superior since it can handle any translation. Nevertheless, the method of Fujimura et al. is an improvement over that of Gargantini since it avoids a decomposition for small translations.

The rectilinear unaligned linear quadtree intersection algorithm [Shaf88c, Same85d] discussed in Section 6.3.3 could also be used to implement an asymptotically faster algorithm for a linear image transformation. It differs from Walsh's approach in that it processes the target tree in Morton order, whereas Walsh's algorithm (and the others discussed in this section) processes the source tree in Morton order. For each block in the source tree, Walsh's algorithm generates the blocks of the target tree in a sorted order. These lists are combined with the remaining blocks by merging the sorted lists with 'merging' of blocks as necessary. In contrast, merging of blocks of the target tree is trivial for the rectilinear linear quadtree algorithm because they are already in Morton order.

The drawback of the rectilinear linear quadtree algorithm is that the blocks of the source tree may be visited more than once. However, this is alleviated by making use of the active border data structures, which also uses more space (2^n for a $2^n \times 2^n$ two-dimensional image). Assuming that the source tree is implemented as a linear quadtree, the rectilinear linear quadtree algorithm takes $O(N \cdot \log_2 N + M)$ time, where N is the number of nodes in the source tree and M is the number of nodes in the target tree prior to merging.

Exercises

6.61. Give a table similar to Table 6.3 for translation in a quadtree. Assume that the NW, NE, SW, and SE quadrants are labeled 0, 1, 2, and 3, respectively.

6.62. Suppose the translation is in a negative direction. What is the effect on relations such as those given in Table 6.3?

6.63. In the text, it is mentioned that Ahuja and Nash's algorithm builds the target tree in the same space as the source tree. Such an algorithm is described as being 'in-place.' How can this be achieved?

6.64. Prove that the execution time of Ahuja and Nash's algorithm is proportional to the product of the resolution of the image (maximum depth in the tree) and the number of nodes in the target tree prior to the merging step.

6.65. Osse and Ahuja apply their algorithm in several passes—one pass for each dimension. Modify the algorithm to use just one pass.

6.66. Let B be a node of width 2^b. Let T be a translation vector such that the minimum of the positions of the least significant bit in all of its axial components with a one is at position j ($j < b$). Let $S(T(B))$ be the area spanned by the translation of B. Let the two subblocks of B of width 2^j with the minimum and maximum locational codes be $B_{\min}$ and $B_{\max}$, respectively. Write an algorithm that generates the FD locational codes of all nodes that lie between $T(B_{\min})$ and $T(B_{\max})$ and that are also within $S(T(B))$.

6.67. Write an algorithm to implement Osse and Ahuja's translation method for a quadtree.

6.68. Write an algorithm to implement Osse and Ahuja's translation method for an octree.

6.69. Although from an asymptotic standpoint the execution times of Ahuja and Nash's algorithm and that of Osse and Ahuja are identical, show why Osse and Ahuja's algorithm is faster.

6.70. Calculate the expected number of black nodes that result from the translation of an arbitrary block in a quadtree. In other words, compute the average cost by trying all possible translations in a given direction of a node of an arbitrary size and position.

6.71. Repeat Exercise 6.70 for an octree.

6.72. Using Walsh's method, write a procedure to translate a block in a quadtree by T_x pixels in the positive x direction.

6.73. Using Walsh's method, write a procedure to translate a block in a quadtree by the translation vector $T = (T_x, T_y)$.

6.74. Using Walsh's method, write a procedure to translate a block in an octree by a translation vector $T = (T_x, T_y, T_z)$.

6.75. Generalize the result of Exercise 6.74 to handle arbitrary translations in d-dimensional images ($d > 0$).

6.76. How many black blocks are created when a black quadtree block of width 2^b is translated by T_x pixels in the x direction?

6.77. Prove that in the worst case, the creation of the sorted list of locational codes for the blocks that comprise the translation of a block of width 2^b takes time proportional to the width of the block.

6.78. In the worst case, how many black blocks are created when a black quadtree block of width 2^b is translated by $T = (T_x, T_y)$ pixels?

6.79. Generalize Exercise 6.78 to a black block of width 2^b in d dimensions where the translation vector is $T = (T_1, T_2, \cdots, T_d)$.

6.80. Prove that prior to the merging step, Walsh's algorithm generates the same number of nodes as the method of van Lierop (and Jackins and Tanimoto) discussed in Section 6.5.2.

6.81. Compare the algorithm of Walsh with that of Osse and Ahuja. In both cases, the region in the target tree that corresponds to the block being translated contains the same set of blocks. Are they equivalent from an algorithmic standpoint?

6.6 REGION EXPANSION

Region expansion (termed EXPAND in this discussion) is an operation that finds use in geographic information systems (where it is known as *polygon expansion*), image processing (where it is known as *image dilation*), and computer graphics. This function generates an image that is black at all pixels within a specified radius of the nonwhite regions of a given image. The result is also known as a *buffer* or a *corridor*.

Region expansion is useful for answering queries such as 'Find all cities within five miles of wheat-growing regions.' In a quadtree environment, such a query would be answered by intersecting the result of applying the EXPAND function to the quadtree corresponding to wheat-growing regions with the quadtree corresponding to the points (e.g., a PR quadtree; see Section 1.3). This section uses a Chessboard distance function (or metric),[7] although other distance functions such as Euclidean and Manhattan (that is, city block) are also possible (see Section 9.1).

A straightforward implementation of the EXPAND function expands each nonwhite block in the input quadtree by R units where R is the radius of expansion, and then inserts all of the nodes making up the expanded square into the output quadtree [Same84c]. This formulation of the algorithm is referred to as EXPAND1. Its execution time increases directly with R since the number of blocks in a quadtree is proportional to the perimeter of the regions that comprise it (see Theorem 1.1 in Section 1.2).

Although EXPAND1 can be implemented so that the blocks are aggregated before inserting them into the output quadtree, it still requires many duplicate insertions and subsequent mergings of black nodes. Note that the execution times for even values of R are generally smaller than those for values of $R - 1$ and $R + 1$ (which are odd) due to the effects of node aggregation, which means that fewer blocks need to be inserted into the output quadtree.

An alternative algorithm, termed EXPAND2 [Shaf88b], tries to avoid the excessive insertion and merging required by EXPAND1 by focusing the work on the white nodes of the quadtree instead of the black nodes. White nodes of width less than or equal to $(R + 1)/2$ are inserted into the output quadtree as black nodes (see Exercise 6.83). White nodes of width greater than $(R + 1)/2$ have their distance from the closest black node determined by use of a modified Chessboard distance function (see Section 9.2).[8] Those portions of these large white nodes that lie within radius R of a nearby black node are output as black nodes.

The problem with EXPAND2 is that many nodes of the input quadtree will be visited more than once while finding the distance from large white nodes to the nearby black nodes. Like EXPAND1, the execution times of EXPAND2 for even values of R are generally lower than those for the adjacent odd values of R.

The execution time of both EXPAND1 and EXPAND2 is dominated by the number of nodes that must be visited and inserted in the output quadtree. Ang, Samet, and Shaffer [Ang88] report an algorithm, termed EXPAND3, that significantly reduces (1) the number of black nodes that must be considered for expansion and (2) the number of nodes that must be inserted as a result of the expansion.

---

[7] The Chessboard distance function for the points (x_1, y_1) and (x_2, y_2) is MAX $(|x_1 - x_2|, |y_1 - y_2|)$.
[8] In this case, given a white block T, its modified Chessboard distance function yields the Chessboard distance from the center of T's block to the border of the nearest nonwhite node.

These reductions are achieved by introducing the concept of a *merging cluster*, which is a nonleaf node of width less than or equal to $R + 1$. Such nonleaf nodes can be replaced automatically by black nodes (see Exercise 6.83) and hence (2) has been achieved. (1) is achieved by only considering a subset of the nodes in each merging cluster, say M, for expansion. This subset, termed the *vertex set of M* and denoted by $VS(M)$, is defined below. For each of the eight expansion directions, only a subset of the elements of $VS(M)$ needs to be expanded. The remaining black nodes (i.e., of size greater than $(R + 1)/2$) are expanded using EXPAND1.

Given merging cluster M, $VS(M)$ is the union of four vertex subsets VS_d where d is in {NW, NE, SW, SE}. For a black node P in M, vertex v of P is in VS_d if v is the d vertex of P and v is not in the closed OPQUAD(d) quadrant of a quadtree-like subdivision rooted at a vertex of any other black node in M (see Exercise 6.88). Recall that OP-QUAD(d) denotes a direction directly opposite to that of d. From this definition, it is easy to see that the vertex subsets are disjoint. It can be shown that the maximum size of a vertex set is proportional to the minimum of the number of black nodes in the quadtree and the radius of expansion (see Exercises 6.92 and 6.93).

Figure 6.16a is an example of a merging cluster with thirteen leaf nodes when $R = 3$. In Figure 6.16a, A, B, C, and D are the black nodes in the merging cluster. The corners of their blocks, termed *vertices*, are designated by using the corresponding lowercase letter with a subscript that designates the vertex. For example, a_{NW} is the NW vertex of node A. A subset of these vertices comprises the vertex set of the merging cluster. The vertex set for the merging cluster of Figure 6.16a is {a_{NW}, b_{NW}, c_{NW}, a_{NE}, d_{NE}, c_{SW}, d_{SE}}. Figure 6.16b shows the result of expanding the merging cluster in Figure 6.16a by three pixels.

Table 6.4 shows a qualitative comparison of the three algorithms for two images. The first, given in Figure 6.17, is a floodplain. The second, given in Figure 6.18, shows the subset of an image of a landuse class map that is called ACC. Each image is of depth nine (i.e., 512×512). The original regions are shown with a solid color (black), and the results of expanding them by seven pixels are shown with a line

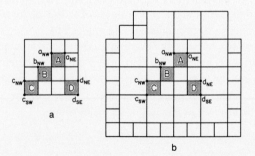

Figure 6.16 (a) Example merging cluster and (b) the result of expanding it by three pixels

Figure 6.17 Floodplain image (black) and the result of expanding it by seven pixels

that is one pixel wide. The quadtrees for the images were implemented as FD linear quadtrees, and execution times were obtained by using the QUILT system [Shaf87c] on a VAX 11/785 running the 4.3 BSD version of UNIX. Notice that the images are of a rather different structure. The execution time of algorithm EXPAND1 is affected by this

Table 6.4 Execution times (secs.) for the EXPAND function

Radius	Floodplain Image			ACC Image		
	1	2	3	1	2	3
1	36.2	16.1	13.6	15.9	11.6	8.2
2	23.7	21.7	16.6	13.2	16.0	10.7
3	55.0	21.1	13.4	29.1	16.1	9.6
4	30.8	25.1	13.9	19.9	19.2	9.1
5	71.9	37.3	18.8	40.6	29.2	14.4
6	51.4	38.5	18.1	31.1	30.1	13.5
7	96.0	31.6	13.0	53.4	28.0	10.6
8	56.2	32.7	12.0	36.6	28.2	9.8
9	107.5	47.6	16.9	64.3	40.5	13.8
10	76.6	44.7	15.6	48.3	39.0	13.2
11	133.0	58.2	19.4	79.2	52.3	16.9
12	80.0	54.9	16.3	54.5	46.8	13.9
13	145.5	73.2	20.9	96.4	64.9	18.0
14	104.9	64.1	18.4	65.9	58.0	15.2
15	169.0	53.3	13.0	104.7	54.9	12.2
16	97.1	46.8	11.2	69.5	47.1	10.7

Figure 6.18   Subset of an image of a landuse class map (black) and the result of expanding it by seven pixels

difference, while the effect on EXPAND2 and EXPAND3 is much smaller. However, the execution time differences between the three algorithms on identical images are more pronounced.

The differences in execution times for the different algorithms can be explained as follows. EXPAND1 is conceptually simple; however, its use results in redundant node insertions. It performs well when the black nodes are sparsely distributed and R is small. EXPAND2 is more efficient than EXPAND1 because only large white nodes require much processing. It performs well for images that contain a small number of large white nodes and when R is small. In addition, it performs very well when R is sufficiently large so that the widths of most of the white nodes are smaller than $(R + 1)/2$. When the images contain large white nodes surrounded by many small black nodes, EXPAND2 performs poorly because it repeatedly inserts portions of these large nodes due to the presence of black nodes within radius R.

EXPAND3 has the best performance of the three algorithms. Its execution time generally increases at a much slower rate and even decreases with increasing R. The key to its efficiency is that it works on a cluster of black nodes rather than on a single black node at a time. As R increases, the performance of EXPAND3 improves further since the merging cluster is bigger and there are fewer of them. In fact, the relative differences in the execution times of EXPAND3 for different radius values are minor when compared to those observed for EXPAND1 and EXPAND2. The differences are primarily due to variations in the size of the merging cluster and to a lesser extent due to the parity (i.e., odd or even) of the values of R.

Exercises

6.82. Given a quadtree corresponding to a binary image and a radius value, write a procedure to compute the EXPAND function as implemented by EXPAND1.

6.83. Assume a region expansion by R. Given a white node T of width W such that $W \le (R + 1)/2$, why can its father be inserted as a black node into the output quadtree?

6.84. Given a quadtree corresponding to a binary image and a radius value, write a procedure to compute the EXPAND function as implemented by EXPAND1.

6.85. Given a quadtree corresponding to a binary image and a radius value, write a procedure to compute the EXPAND function as implemented by EXPAND2. The implementation of EXPAND2 has four cases for each white node of width W. The first case is when $W \le (R+1)/2$ and is discussed in the text. When $W > (R+1)/2$, compute D, the value of the Chessboard distance function from the center of T's block to the border of the nearest nonwhite node. If $D + W/2 \le R$, then insert T as black. On the other hand, if $D - W/2 < R$, then quarter T and recursively apply a slightly more complex procedure to the four resulting nodes. Otherwise insert the node (as white) into the output quadtree.

6.86. Analyze the average number of nodes visited in computing the EXPAND function as implemented by EXPAND2. Use an approach analogous to that used by Dyer [Dyer82] in analyzing the space efficiency of quadtrees (discussed in Section 1.2). In particular, assume a $2^n \times 2^n$ image that consists of just one block of size $2^m \times 2^m$ such that $m \le n$. Now, let the position of the block vary throughout the image and compute the average number of nodes that must be visited in computing the EXPAND function for different radius values. How does the average value depend on the radius?

6.87. Repeat the analysis of Exercise 6.86 for EXPAND1. Also, determine how this value depends on the radius.

6.88. Let P be a black node in merging cluster M. In the definition of a vertex subset VS_d, we say that vertex v of P is in VS_d if v is the d vertex of P and v is not in the closed OPQUAD(d) quadrant of a quadtree-like subdivision rooted at a vertex of any other black node in M. Why must the OPQUAD(d) quadrant be closed?

6.89. Given merging cluster M, suppose you defined the vertex set as the vertices of the black nodes in M that form the polygon of minimal area that covers all of the black nodes in M. Is the resulting polygon equivalent to that formed by joining adjacent elements of the vertex set in the original definition?

6.90. Give an algorithm to compute the vertex set for a merging cluster.

6.91. Prove that no two vertices in VS_d have the same x coordinate value (also y coordinate value).

6.92. Given radius of expansion R, the size of the merging cluster is $w(R)$, which is the largest integer that is a power of 2 and is less than or equal to $R + 1$, i.e., $w(R) = 2^r \le R + 1 < 2^{r+1}$ for $r \ge 0$. Let VS_{d_1} and VS_{d_2} be two adjacent vertex subsets such that vertex d_1 is adjacent to d_2 in the clockwise or counterclockwise directions. Prove that the size of the union of any two adjacent vertex subsets is less than or equal to $w(R) + 1$ and that this bound is attainable.

6.93. Prove that the size of the vertex set of merging cluster M is bounded by the minimum of $2 \cdot w(R) + 2$ and $4 +$ the number of black nodes in M and that the bound is attainable.

6.94. Given a quadtree corresponding to a binary image and a radius value, write a procedure to compute the EXPAND function as implemented by EXPAND3.

6.95. The execution time of EXPAND3 has been observed to be relatively independent of the radius of expansion. Can you give a theoretical explanation for this phenomenon? You should try to formulate an appropriate image model and a measure of complexity—for example, the number of nodes that are expanded.

6.96. Mason [Maso87] proposes yet another algorithm for computing the EXPAND function. It uses an active border data structure (see Section 5.1.3) to keep track of all black nodes that have been seen so far. The algorithm has two passes. On the first pass, for each white node, say P, examine the black nodes within radius R of P that have already been encountered. If there are none, then P is left as white. Otherwise P is either (1) set to black and flagged as not having been black originally or (2) quartered, in which case the process is continued for P's sons in the same order. As the nodes are processed they are added to an output quadtree. The second pass is analogous to the first except that the output quadtree is processed in reverse order. For example, if the first pass traversed the tree in the order NW, NE, SW, and SE, then the second pass traverses it in the order SE, SW, NE, and NW. During the second pass, the white nodes are compared with only the original black nodes—not the nodes that were set to black on the first pass. Implement this algorithm, and compare it with EXPAND1, EXPAND2, and EXPAND3.

6.97. Extend EXPAND3 to handle three-dimensional images.

6.98. Suppose you are given a set of objects in two-dimensional space and their motions (i.e., specified as directions). Calculate the regions through which no object will ever pass.

6.99. Repeat Exercise 6.98 when the motions of the objects are specified using their velocities as well as their directions.

DISPLAY METHODS

7

The most basic operation in computer graphics is the conversion of an internal model of a three-dimensional scene into a two-dimensional scene that lies on the viewplane. The purpose is to generate an image of the scene as it would appear from a given viewpoint and to display it on a two-dimensional screen. Although there are many mappings that are abstractly possible between a three-dimensional space and a two-dimensional space, we are interested in mappings that adhere to the principles of geometric optics.

Conceptually it is easiest to understand the image-generation process by examining how the color of a single pixel of the viewplane is calculated. In this presentation, each pixel of the viewplane determines a pyramid that is formed by the set of all rays originating at the viewpoint and intersecting the viewplane within the boundary of the pixel (see Figure 7.1). We clip away the objects or parts thereof that are outside the viewing pyramid to reduce the number of objects that need to be considered. A color is assigned to each pixel, which, in the simplest case, is the color of the object closest to the viewpoint while also lying within the pixel's pyramid. This is commonly referred to as the *hidden-surface* task [Suth74].

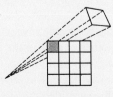

Figure 7.1   The viewing pyramid associated with the black
pixel (shown shaded) in the viewplane

In this chapter, the focus is on the use of hierarchical methods in displaying three-dimensional scenes. The related task of zooming is discussed in conjunction with image scaling in Section 6.3.3. We first examine a number of different hidden-surface algorithms that use hierarchical methods and data structures to determine what is visible. They differ according to whether they make use of hierarchies in the viewplane or in the scene. The situation is more complex when we take into account the position of the light source, the presence of multiple light sources, and the possibility that light is reflected as well as refracted. This requires a calculation of what light falls on the object position represented by a pixel in the viewplane and is known as the *image-rendering* task. We conclude by discussing how hierarchical representations can be used to facilitate the image-rendering task.

We consider three image-rendering techniques: ray tracing, beam tracing, and radiosity. Ray tracing and beam tracing model light as particles moving in the scene. Hierarchical data structures such as the octree speed up the determination of the objects that are intersected by rays emanating from the viewpoint. Ray tracing and beam tracing differ in the manner in which the rays are represented. In contrast, radiosity models light as energy and seeks to determine a point at which its distribution is at equilibrium. This requires the derivation of a large set of linear equations. Using octrees can simplify the process of calculating the geometric coefficients of these equations. This is especially true if rendering is to be done with respect to more than one viewpoint. The efficient solution of these equations is aided by use of heuristics, one of which is the adaptive recursive decomposition of the scene's surface.

7.1 HIERARCHICAL HIDDEN-SURFACE ALGORITHMS

The hidden-surface task can be conceptualized as a two-stage sorting process [Suth74]. The first stage sorts the surfaces into the different viewing pyramids (algorithmically this is similar to bucket sorting). The second stage sorts the surfaces within a given viewing pyramid to determine the closest one to the viewpoint. To execute this task for a given viewpoint in an optimal manner, it is desirable to minimize the number of surfaces that need to be examined. The efficiency of the solutions often depends on the extent to which they exploit coherence (i.e., constancy) in either the three-dimensional scene or the viewplane.

The hidden-surface task is closely related to the hidden-line task, and historically confusion exists with respect to the distinction between them. The source of this confusion is primarily technological. Originally the display of a scene consisted of the production of a line drawing. Thus the objective was to eliminate all line segments of the wireframe representation of the visible objects in the scene that were hidden by other surfaces of the object or other objects in the scene. Note that although the surfaces were not directly displayed, they still influenced what was and was not visible.

As the technology of display devices improved, it became feasible to produce shaded images of the scene. This permitted the rendering of the actual surfaces of the object instead of just the wireframe representation of the object. In this case, not only line segments can be hidden, but some of the surfaces of the scene could also be hidden. Today, in most practical cases, a distinction is no longer being made between these two tasks, and they are lumped together as the *hidden-surface* task.

Traditionally solutions to the hidden-surface task have been differentiated in terms of whether they are image-space algorithms, object-space algorithms, or combinations of the two [Suth74]. This distinction can be best understood by noting that an object-space algorithm seeks to determine if each potentially visible object is indeed visible, whereas an image-space algorithm seeks to determine what is visible within the area corresponding to a pixel on the screen. This is very important in evaluating the cost of the algorithms. In particular, the cost of object-space algorithms increases as the complexity of the scene increases. The cost of image-space algorithms is considerably less dependent on the complexity of the scene.

In this chapter we differentiate between solutions to the hidden-surface task in terms of coherence properties. A coherence property indicates under what conditions entities cohere, or stick together. Image-space coherence means that neighboring pixels on the viewplane tend to have the same value (i.e., be projections of the same object). Object-space coherence means that an object tends to be projected onto neighboring portions of the viewplane.

Image-space coherence focuses on the pixels of the viewplane. These pixels form a uniform discrete sampling of the viewplane. For each of these pixels, the hidden-surface task reduces to a determination of the objects that are closest to it (in the z-dimension). On the other hand, object-space coherence focuses on the objects in the scene. For each object, the hidden-surface task reduces to a determination of the pixels from which the object is visible.

Conceptually the scene is a continuous space, whereas the viewplane is often viewed as a discrete space since the pixels define a discrete sampling on it. Nevertheless, it is often the case that the display process consists of a discrete sampling of the space of the scene (i.e., where the objects are located). Thus it is useful to introduce a concept of 'scene' coherence, which is defined to mean that neighboring points in the scene tend to represent the same object. However, there is really no need to distinguish 'scene' coherence from the concepts of image-space and object-space coherence. It is geometrically obvious that neighboring points in the scene must project onto neighboring points on the viewplane. This means that object-space coherence exists.

Of course, object-space coherence does not necessarily mean that neighboring points in the viewplane are projections of neighboring points in the scene. In particular, for any given scene, there are many viewplanes onto which it can be projected. For image-space coherence to exist in all of these viewplanes, it is necessary for neighboring points in the viewplane to be the projections of neighboring points in the scene. However, by image-space coherence, we know that neighboring points in the viewplane tend to be the projection of the same object. Therefore it must be the case that neighboring points in the scene tend to belong to the same object. Hence, the concept of 'scene' coherence is derivable from the concepts of image-space coherence and object-space coherence.

Six approaches to the hidden-surface task are discussed. They are subdivided into three categories depending on the type of coherence that they exploit. Some of the methods make use of regular decomposition. In particular, regular decomposition in the viewplane is useful in practice because of image-space coherence. Similarly, regular decomposition in the scene is useful because of scene coherence. On the other hand, for object-space coherence to be useful, we must use a decomposition based on the objects themselves (e.g., similar to that used in a point quadtree; see Section 1.3).

The first two approaches are based on image-space coherence. The so-called cel-based approach models the viewplane by a regular decomposition quadtree, and the three-dimensional scene is treated as a sequence of overlays of two-dimensional scenes, each represented by a regular decomposition quadtree. Warnock's algorithm [Warn68, Warn69a], the second approach, models the viewplane by a regular decomposition quadtree, while the three-dimensional scene consists of polygons of arbitrary orientation and placement in the three-dimensional space.

The Weiler-Atherton algorithm [Weil77] is the third approach. It organizes the object space with respect to a specific viewplane orientation, say V. In particular, it treats the scene as a polygonal hierarchy with respect to the projection of its constituent polygons on V. The polygons correspond to faces of the objects in the scene (i.e., it is a boundary model[1]) The Weiler-Atherton algorithm uses object-space coherence in a manner analogous to Warnock's use of image-space coherence. Weiler and Atherton also point out how heuristics based on scene coherence can be used to speed up object-space methods. Both the Warnock and Weiler-Atherton algorithms use an arbitrary representation for the three-dimensional scene.

The next three approaches are based on scene coherence. The situation is at its simplest when the scene is modeled by a region octree (in contrast to other versions of the octree—e.g., the PM octree). In this case we describe the use of projection methods where the viewplane is modeled by regular decomposition quadtrees. The BSP tree [Fuch80] is a representation of the scene as an object hierarchy. Its advantage over the Weiler-Atherton algorithm is that it can cope more easily with a change in the viewpoint (and viewplane). The surface of the scene can also be modeled in a hierarchical manner. In particular, a quadtree can be built for the representation of the surface in parametric space. This technique is useful for the display of curved surfaces. The BSP tree and the curved surface technique use an arbitrary representation for the viewplane.

7.1.1 2.5-Dimensional Hidden-Surface Elimination

2.5-dimensional hidden-surface elimination is a technique devised to handle the display of three-dimensional scenes represented by a forest of quadtrees. It arises

---

[1] The *boundary model* (*BRep*) represents a three-dimensional object by its faces. The result is a graph whose edges correspond to the interconnections between the faces of the object (e.g., the winged-edge representation [Baum72]). For more details, see Section 5.4 of [Same90a].

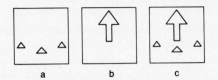

Figure 7.2 *Example of scene creation via cel overlay: (a) plant cel, (b) tree cel, (c) possible overlay of (b) on (a)*

most commonly in applications in cel-based animation. A *cel* is a piece of transparent plastic on which a figure has been drawn. A *scene* can be created by overlaying cels (see Figure 7.2) from 'back-to-front.' A given view of the scene is constructed by first laying down the cel representing the background. On top of the background, cels are placed that represent objects in the foreground. This is also known as a 'painter's' algorithm. When each cel is represented by a quadtree, scenes can be constructed easily. The nodes that correspond to the objects drawn on the cel are marked as opaque, and the remaining nodes are marked as transparent.

Cel-based scene construction is a simplification of the hidden-surface task and is described in greater detail below. It is simpler than the general three-dimensional task because each object is restricted to just one cel. This means that in our domain, occlusion is acyclic, whereas it need not be so in an unrestricted three-dimensional domain (e.g., Figure 7.3). Thus we need not be concerned with problems resulting from situations such as object A occluding object B, object B occluding object C, and object C occluding object A.

2.5-dimensional hidden-surface elimination is equivalent to a sequence of set-union operations and can be implemented in a manner analogous to quadtree intersection as described in Section 6.3.2. In particular, starting with the quadtree corresponding to the backmost cel, while moving toward the front cel, we perform successive overlays of the quadtrees of the cels encountered along the path [Kauf83]. Hunter and Steiglitz [Hunt78, Hunt79a] have shown that the total cost of this process is proportional to the sum of the number of nodes in all of the quadtrees of the cels.

While the algorithm given above is an optimal worst-case method, it can be modified to yield a better average-case performance as follows. We process the cels

Figure 7.3 *Example of a three-dimensional image where occlusion is not transitive*

from 'front to back' and build an *intermediate quadtree*. We mark the blocks in the intermediate quadtree as transparent to indicate that up to now nothing in the sequence of quadtree nodes corresponding to that location has been opaque. Also we mark the nonleaf nodes as opaque if all of their subtrees are opaque, although their subtrees need not be the same color (i.e., correspond to the same object). Thus when traversing the intermediate quadtree and the next cel, say C, if the intermediate quadtree has a nonleaf node marked opaque, then nothing in the corresponding subtree of cel C, say T, is visible, and hence T need not be traversed. Furthermore when the root of the intermediate quadtree is marked opaque, no more cels need be visited.

Such actions have a potential of reducing the execution time of the 2.5-dimensional hidden-surface elimination task because subtrees corresponding to invisible regions need not be traversed. Of course, in a more flexible animation system, it is often desirable to overlay unaligned cels (i.e., unaligned quadtrees). This can be handled by using the techniques described in Section 6.3.3 for computing set operations on unaligned quadtrees.

Exercises

7.1.   Write a 'back-to-front' algorithm to display a 2.5-dimensional scene represented by a forest of quadtrees as described in this section.

7.2.   Write a 'front-to-back' algorithm to display a 2.5-dimensional scene represented by a forest of quadtrees as described in this section.

7.3.   Repeat Exercises 7.1 and 7.2 for a three-dimensional scene represented by a forest of PM_1 quadtrees.

7.4.   The most straightforward view of a cel is as a raster image represented by a two-dimensional array of cells. One of the shortcomings of raster images is that each cell in the array is treated as being entirely full or entirely empty (entirely opaque or entirely transparent). Porter and Duff [Port84] have developed an algebra for describing the compositing (i.e., overlaying) of partially full cells (which could also be thought of as translucent cells). The basic idea is to associate with each cell, say A, a 'gray' value, say $g(A)$, that represents the percentage of fullness of the cell. When two cells, say A and B, are combined (i.e., composited), the percentage of fullness of the new cell, say C, must be calculated. If we assume that the intersection of A and B is empty, then $g(C) = g(A) + g(B)$. It is also possible for A to be a subset of B, or for B to be a subset of A, in which case $g(C) = \max(g(A), g(B))$. Show that regardless of the positioning of the contents of cells A and B, $\max(g(A), g(B)) \leq g(C) \leq g(A) + g(B)$.

7.5.   Continuing Exercise 7.4, Porter and Duff [Port84] adopt the convention that $g(C) = g(A) + g(B) - g(A) * g(B)$. The presentation of Porter and Duff represents the raster image by a two-dimensional array. Describe how to integrate this concept with a quadtree representation of the base images. Instead of treating the pixels in the base images as black and white, assume that the pixels can take on a variety of color values.

7.1.2   Warnock's Algorithm

The usage of the quadtree for modeling the viewplane during the hidden-surface task was first described by Warnock [Warn68]. A variant of the region quadtree is used to represent the parts of the scene currently believed to be visible. This method is an attempt to take advantage of image-space coherence. Warnock was actually interested in two versions of the hidden-surface task: (1) the basic hidden-surface task and (2) the hidden-line task, which is an adaptation of the hidden-surface task to a wireframe representation of a solid. In the process of developing a solution to the hidden-surface task, Warnock also made contributions to light modeling [Warn69b] that are beyond the scope of this book.

For expository purposes, we first examine the hidden-line task and conclude with a description of its adaptation to the hidden-surface task. They differ in how the result of the visibility calculation is displayed. For the hidden-line operation, the viewplane's quadtree consists of polygons formed by the visible edges of the objects in the three-dimensional scene. At most, one edge is associated with each pixel. The edge, if any, that is associated with a pixel corresponds to the one that passes through the pixel's region as part of the border of a polygon that is not occluded by another polygon closer to the viewpoint. In the rest of the discussion of the hidden-line task, we say that a pixel is *colored* if a visible edge passes through it. Thus we use the term *color* to distinguish between pixels that correspond to edges of a polygon and those that do not.

The quadtree is used in the display process to select rapidly the pixels that need to be colored (these are the pixels through which visible edges of the scene pass). The quadtree is not built explicitly. Instead the viewplane is recursively decomposed (traversed as if it were a quadtree) using an appropriate decomposition rule to yield a collection of disjoint square regions (i.e., leaf nodes). At each such region, drawing (i.e., coloring) commands for driving a display are output.

The type of quadtree decomposition rule that is used is analogous to the one devised by Hunter and Steiglitz [Hunt78, Hunt79a] (i.e., an MX quadtree). There are two types of nodes: boundary and empty. A pixel is represented by a boundary node if an edge of a polygon passes through it; otherwise it is represented by an empty node. Empty nodes are merged to yield larger nodes, while boundary nodes are not merged. Using this rule enables us to formulate the actions taken by Warnock's algorithm in terms of the following leaf node types and corresponding output actions:

1. At an empty leaf node, output nothing since no lines pass through this region.
2. At a leaf node corresponding to a pixel, output a point representing the border of the polygon that occludes the upper left-hand corner of the pixel (if no such polygon exists, then output nothing).
3. At a leaf node corresponding to a collection of polygons, output nothing since the existence of such a node means that one of the polygons occludes all the other polygons over this region.

At this point, it is interesting to review briefly the relationship between the hidden-surface and hidden-line tasks. The hidden-line task is closely identified with the usage of vector displays and plotters. This caused Warnock to investigate edge quadtree-like (see [Shne81c] and Section 4.2.1 of [Same90a]) decompositions [Warn69b]. On the other hand, the hidden-surface task is closely identified with the usage of raster devices. Although our treatment of the hidden-line task assumes vector data, it results in the output of line-drawing commands at a raster/pixel level. By doing a bit more calculation, we can often recognize that a line will be visible without having to subdivide all the way down to the pixel level.

The algorithm outlined above for the hidden-line task can be modified to handle the hidden-surface task as well. The only modification that needs to be made here is that empty nodes, which represent regions that are completely spanned by a polygon, must now be colored with the color of that polygon instead of being ignored (as occurs in the hidden-line display process). Of course, the boundary nodes must be assigned one of the colors of their shared polygons.

One problem with building quadtree decompositions of data presented as arbitrary collections of polygons in a three-dimensional space is to determine when there is no need for further subdivision. For example, this situation arises when a node contains a collection of polygons where one polygon completely occludes the other polygons. This requires a sort of all the polygons in the node. Since occlusion in general is not transitive, sorting does not always work (recall Figure 7.3). If sorting fails due to nontransitivity or because the nearest polygon does not occlude the entire region, then further subdivision is needed to determine what is visible in the region corresponding to the node.

It is worthwhile to note that we have been assuming that the closest polygon's color was the most appropriate color for a pixel. However, clearly a pixel could contain small features that this approach would represent falsely. This general problem is referred to as *aliasing* [Roge85], and attempts to resolve it are referred to as *antialiasing*. Warnock handles the situation of a pixel that contains complicated features by pretending that the viewing pyramid for the pixel is a single ray passing through the pixel's upper left-hand corner. If this produces an approximation of the image that is too rough for a particular application, then classical antialiasing techniques [Roge85] (such as computing a weighted average of the visible intensities within a pixel) can be applied without altering the basic algorithm.

Exercises

7.6. Implement Warnock's hidden-line algorithm for a collection of polygons in a three-dimensional space.

7.7. Implement Warnock's hidden-surface algorithm for a collection of polygons in a three-dimensional space.

7.8. Suppose that the surfaces of the objects in the scene radiate light diffusely (i.e., equally in all directions). It is possible that some of the light that falls on a particular cell of the viewplane will actually come from surfaces of the scene that are 'invisible' in the sense that a standard hidden-surface algorithm would fail to find them. This can be visualized by considering a scene that consists of a single cube such that the viewplane is parallel to one of its faces. Only the nearer of the two faces of the cube that are parallel to the viewplane will be visible. However, some of the light will be radiated diffusely onto the viewplane from the faces of the cube that are orthogonal to the viewplane. Ignoring the question of the intensity of the light that reaches the viewplane in this manner, modify Warnock's algorithm so that for each cell, say c, it reports the polygons that can emit some light on c.

7.1.3   Weiler-Atherton's Algorithm

Warnock's hidden-surface algorithm is based on image-space coherence. Weiler and Atherton [Weil77] developed an analogous hidden-surface algorithm based on object-space coherence. The scene consists of a collection of polygons. It is interesting to note that Weiler and Atherton use heuristics based on image-space coherence to speed up their algorithm's use of object-space coherence. Their object-space coherence algorithm has the following structure:

1. Order all the polygons by their smallest z-value (assume that the viewer is located at $z = -\infty$).
2. Find the closest polygon, say P, to the viewer.
3. Form two collections of polygons. The first collection contains those polygons whose projection are totally covered by the projection of P on the viewplane (which we will call the *inner set*). The second collection contains those polygons whose projection is completely outside the projection of P (which we will call the *outer set*). In cases where the projection of polygon Q partially overlaps the projection of P, then we clip Q against P and store the resulting polygons in the appropriate sets.
4. Remove all polygons from the inner set that do not occlude part of P.
5. If no polygons occlude P (i.e., the inner set is empty after applying step 4), then the hidden-surface task has now been solved for P. Proceed to solve the hidden-surface task for the outer set.
6. If there exist polygons that occlude P (i.e., the inner set is nonempty), then recursively go to step 2 and choose a 'nearest' polygon from among the occluding polygons in the inner set of P. Upon return, process the outer set of P.

To reduce the number of polygons that have to be compared in step 4, Weiler and Atherton propose two preprocessing methods relevant to our study. The first method recursively subdivides the viewplane (in the x and y directions) until the number of polygons in a given region, say R, drops below a specified threshold. Within region R, the basic algorithm, described above, is used. Note that in step 4, only the polygons in region R need to be considered.

The second method is based on the observation that besides preprocessing by subdividing in the x and y directions, it might also be useful to subdivide in the z direction. In particular, after subdividing in the z direction, Weiler and Atherton propose to solve the hidden-surface task for the backmost volume elements first and then to use this solution as part of the polygon list for the volume elements in the front. This 'back-to-front' approach is also discussed in Section 7.1.1 in the context of 2.5-dimensional hidden-surface elimination. This last heuristic could be viewed as an octree method and is the basis of projection methods (see Section 7.1.4 for more details).

Exercises

7.9. How can the inner set be empty in step 5 of the Weiler-Atherton algorithm when we assume that polygon *P* is the closest polygon to the viewer?

7.10. Show that mutual occlusion, as illustrated by Figure 7.3, is correctly handled by the Weiler-Atherton algorithm.

7.1.4   Displaying Scenes Represented by Region Octrees

Displaying a three-dimensional object requires us to project it onto a two-dimensional plane. The types of projections that are of interest in computer graphics are such that all the points in the three-dimensional space that project onto the same point in the two-dimensional plane form a straight line in the original three-dimensional space. This line is called a *line of projection*. The two major types of projections are the perspective and parallel projections.

The lines of projection resulting from a *perspective projection* all meet at a common point, called the *viewpoint* (Figure 7.4a). The lines of projection resulting from a *parallel projection* are parallel to each other (Figure 7.4b). A parallel projection can also be viewed as a special case of the perspective projection such that the viewpoint is at infinity. It should be clear that for humans, the parallel projection of an object is easier to read. It is commonly used in engineering drawings.

Until now, the only aspect of projection that was relevant was the related ordering of the projected objects. However, at this point, it becomes necessary to examine the projection itself more closely. The rationale is that the application of a projective transformation to an octree does not produce another octree, whereas the application of a projective transformation to a polygonal scene will produce another polygonal scene (in three dimensions). Thus the presence or absence of projective transformations does not affect the algorithms discussed earlier.

For scenes represented by region octrees, the most common display technique is the parallel projection [Doct81, Gill81]. The parallel projection of a region octree is

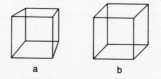

a   b

Figure 7.4   (a)   Perspective   projection   of   a   cube,
(b) parallel projection of a cube

at its simplest when the viewplane is parallel to one of the faces of a node in the tree—that is, a *major axis*. This situation is equivalent to the 2.5-dimensional hidden-surface task discussed in Section 7.1.1. Implicit in the task of displaying a region octree is the solution of the hidden-surface task for the interaction among the objects represented by the octree. Not surprisingly, since the octree imposes a spatial ordering on objects, the hidden-surface task for scenes represented by region octrees can be solved more efficiently than by using general hidden-surface algorithms.

In the special case of a parallel projection in the direction of a major axis, any opaque object in the four front octants of an octree will occlude any opaque object in the back four octants. This property holds recursively within each of the suboctants. In the more general case, when the direction of projection is not parallel to a major axis, this occlusion is weakened. In particular, there exists an ordering of the eight octants such that objects that appear earlier in the ordering never obscure objects that appear later in the ordering.

The process of displaying the scene is facilitated by the construction of a *display quadtree* corresponding to a partial two-dimensional view of the scene. The display quadtree is updated as the nodes of the octree are traversed from 'back to front.' We refer to the nodes of the octree that correspond to the opaque object as *opaque nodes*, while the other nodes of the octree can be thought of as *transparent nodes*. Each opaque node, say P, that is encountered in this traversal 'paints out' (i.e., overwrites) the previous view contained in a portion of the display quadtree that coincides with the projection of P. Of course, as indicated in the discussion of the 2.5-dimensional hidden-surface task in Section 7.1.1, the nodes could also be processed from 'front to back,' thereby allowing for the possibility of visiting fewer nodes.

When contemplating various parallel projections, we observe that parallel line segments of equal length in space project onto parallel line segments of equal length in the plane. However, line segments of equal length that are not parallel will not necessarily project onto line segments of equal length. Nevertheless, we can find a special parallel projection where line segments of equal length that are parallel to any of the principal axes (i.e., the x, y, or z axes) will project onto line segments of equal length in the plane. This special case of the parallel projection is called an *isometric projection*. It is of particular use to engineers because it means that dimensions in the x, y, and z directions can all be measured off a blueprint using the same scale.

Any projection can be represented by a region quadtree. Unfortunately the orthogonal edges of the object that are a by-product of the region octree representation of the object do not usually coincide with the decomposition lines of the quadtree representation of the projection. Thus for most projections, the result is a quadtree that must be decomposed to a very deep level in the vicinity of the edges due to the staircase-like nature of the approximation of the edge. However, for an isometric projection this problem vanishes.

A useful property of the isometric projection is that the silhouette of a cube projects onto a regular hexagon with the edges (visible and invisible) meeting at the centroid and forming six equilateral triangles (e.g., Figure 7.5). Subdividing the cube into eight octants and forming an isometric view of the result (ignoring the distinction

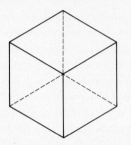

Figure 7.5   Isometric view of a cube

between visible and invisible edges) yields a decomposition into equilateral triangles as shown in Figure 7.6. Notice that each octant is itself a regular hexagon (with each side being one half the size of the original hexagon). One hexagon corresponds to both octants 3 and 4 when octants are labeled using the convention of Figure 4.28. These techniques are similar to those discussed in Section 4.6 in conjunction with the construction of a region octree from silhouettes taken from different viewpoints.

Yamaguchi, Kunii, Fujimura, and Toriya [Yama84] give a 'front-to-back' algorithm to display the isometric view that makes use of this triangular-like decomposition. They generate an isometric view where W (i.e., white) denotes the background and the three colors, say A, B, and C, correspond to the top, left, and right visible faces of the object (e.g., the cube as shown in Figure 7.7). Initially they decompose the projection of the cube corresponding to the space from which the object is drawn into six equilateral triangles.

When the object is more complex than a cube, further decomposition is necessary. In particular, each of the triangles resulting from the initial decomposition is recursively decomposed into four congruent equilateral triangles until each triangle corresponds to one-half of a visible face of a unique cubic block of the region octree decomposition of the object. The decomposition process is based on the use of a

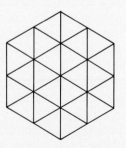

*Figure 7.6   Isometric view of the eight octants of a cube.
No distinction is made between visible and invisible edges.*

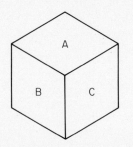

Figure 7.7   Correspondence between colors and faces for the display of an isometric view. A, B, and C correspond to the top, left, and right visible faces of the cube shown.

triangular quadtree as discussed in Section 1.2 (see Figure 1.3a). For example, the staircase-like object of Figure 6.1a, whose region octree decomposition is given by Figure 6.1b, has the triangular decomposition given in Figure 7.8.

In a 'front-to-back' display of the object, each triangle can correspond to faces of several different blocks. The exact one that is displayed depends on its proximity to the viewpoint. Using the octant labeling convention of Figure 4.28, we assume that the object is being viewed from a point incident on the infinite line that joins the two vertices of octants 3 and 4 that do not serve as vertices of the remaining octants. Octant 4 is closer to the viewpoint than octant 3. The result is a priority order of 4, 6, 0, 5, 2, 7, 1, 3. Figure 7.9 illustrates the use of this ordering by labeling the triangles of Figure 7.6 with the numbers of the octants of the cube for which they could serve as faces. The order of the numbers reflects the proximity of the designated octant to the viewpoint.

As an example of this ordering, consider the triangle labeled '4,6,2,3' in Figure 7.9. It is associated with the left face of octant 4 if octant 4 in the original object is nonempty. Otherwise we try, in order, the top face of octant 6, the right face of octant 2, or the left face of octant 3. The one chosen is the first one that is nonempty. If all

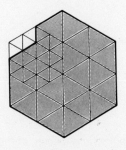

Figure 7.8   Triangular decomposition for the object of Figure 6.1. All triangles in the object are shown shaded.

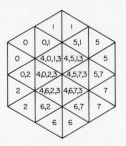

Figure 7.9   Priority order labeling of the faces of the eight octants of a cube. The numbers indicate the octants for which the triangles can serve as faces, with the leftmost octant number having priority over the octant numbers to its right. The octants are labeled using the octant labeling convention of Figure 4.28.

are empty, then no face is associated with the triangle; it is designated as corresponding to an empty or void region (colored white). Figure 7.10 shows the result of the application of this display process to the object whose triangular quadtree is given in Figure 7.8. Each triangle is labeled with A, B, C, or W, thereby indicating if it is a face of type top, left, right, or empty, respectively.

Generalizations of the parallel projection of scenes represented by region octrees onto planes at arbitrary positions and orientations are described by Meagher [Meag82a] and Yau [Yau84]. Generalizations can also be made in a straightforward manner to compute perspective projections onto arbitrary planes as well.

Another approach to the perspective projection task is to transform the three-dimensional scene into a new three-dimensional scene whose parallel projection is the same as the corresponding perspective projection of the original scene. This approach

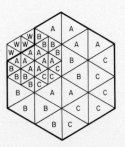

Figure 7.10   Result of the display of the isometric view of the object of Figure 6.1. Triangles labeled A, B, C, and W correspond to the top, left, right, or empty face, respectively.

was used on the constructive solid geometry (CSG) representation[2] by Koistinen et al. [Kois85]. The resulting CSG tree is displayed using parallel projection by traversing the scene in a bintree-like manner, pruning the CSG tree against each bintree block and maintaining a quadtree of the covered area of the image to avoid unnecessary subdivision. Shading[3] is performed by using the surface normals of the primitives in the CSG tree.

One drawback to displaying scenes represented by a region octree is that there is little potential of using lighting models for the shading of the scene since adjacent faces of octree nodes meet at 90 degree angles. One approach at overcoming this drawback is described by Doctor and Torborg [Doct81]. They suggest that the amount of shading applied to each face of a node can be calculated as a function of the number of the transparent neighbors of the node.

Thus since a node on the corner of an object that is surrounded by empty space has fewer transparent neighbors, it will be brighter than another node on the interior of a face of the object. An interesting highlighting effect results. In his octree machine [Meag84], Meagher overcomes this problem for octrees that are formed by conversion from other kinds of geometric models by storing surface normals in the voxels intersecting the surface of the object being viewed. More recently, this problem has been investigated by [Gord85, Chen85a, Brig86, Chie86c].

Exercises

7.11. [David Mount] In the text it is stated that when the viewpoint is along the line joining the extreme vertices of octants 3 and 4 (see Figure 4.28) such that octant 4 is closer to the

---

[2] *Constructive solid geometry* (CSG) [Requ80] methods represent solids by decomposing them into primitive objects that are subsequently combined using variants of Boolean set operations (e.g., union, intersection, and set-difference) and geometric transformations (e.g., translation and rotation). These primitives are often solids such as cubes, parallelepipeds, cylinders, and spheres. A more fundamental primitive is a halfspace with a border that is either linear or nonlinear. CSG methods are usually implemented by a CSG tree, which is a binary tree. The nonleaf nodes correspond to geometric transformations and Boolean set operations, while leaf nodes correspond to the primitive objects. For more details, see Section 5.5 of [Same90a].

[3] *Shading* is a term used to describe the process of displaying an image so that its surface has the proper degree of brightness. Computationally it is the calculation of the intensity of light leaving a particular surface in the direction of the viewer. The simplest approach is to assign each surface an intensity proportional to the cosine of the angle formed by its normal and the direction of the light source (a direct application of Lambert's cosine law for diffuse surfaces [Feyn63]). This approach leads to sharp discontinuities at the borders of adjacent planar surfaces (i.e., they are noticeable). There are two approaches to overcome this discontinuity, *Gouraud shading* [Gour71] and *Phong shading* [Phon75]. Both assign a shading value to each of the vertices of the surface (e.g., a triangle) based on the average of the normals of the surfaces that meet at that vertex. The difference between them is in the shading values assigned to the rest of the points on the surface. With Gouraud shading, the shading values of the remaining points are obtained by linear interpolation of the shading values at the vertices. The drawback of this method is that the value of the cosine is not a linear function of the normal. With Phong shading, the shading values of the remaining points are obtained by applying linear interpolation to the change in the direction of the normal across the surface rather than to the shading values at the vertices. Thus Phong shading uses the interpolated normal to compute the shading value. The observable difference between the two methods is that Phong shading makes highlights sharper than Gouraud shading (which makes them duller). For more details, see [Roge85].

viewpoint than octant 3, the 'front-to-back' priority order is 4, 6, 0, 5, 2, 7, 1, 3. (a) What other orders are allowable 'front-to-back' orders given this viewpoint? (b) Consider the octant labels as 3-bit strings. Give a characterization of all allowable 'front-to-back' orders when viewing the cube along a line that passes through the major diagonal.

7.12. Write a 'back-to-front' algorithm to generate the parallel projection of a region octree when the viewplane is parallel to one of the faces of a node in the tree.

7.13. Write a 'back-to-front' algorithm to generate the parallel projection of a region octree to a plane at an arbitrary position and orientation.

7.14. Write a 'back-to-front' algorithm to generate the perspective projection of a region octree when the viewplane is parallel to one of the faces of a node in the tree.

7.15. Write a 'back-to-front' algorithm to generate the perspective projection of a region octree to a plane at an arbitrary position and orientation.

7.16. Repeat Exercises 7.12–7.15 for a PM octree instead of a region octree.

7.17. Repeat Exercises 7.12–7.16 for a 'front-to-back' algorithm instead of a 'back-to-front' algorithm.

7.18. Crow [Crow77] discusses the use of hidden-surface algorithms to determine what parts of a scene are in the shadow of other portions of the scene. The key is that the parts of the scene that are not in the shadow are those parts 'visible' from the light source. Thus instead of just performing a single hidden-surface calculation from the point of view of the viewer, a better image can be created by performing two hidden-surface calculations: one from the point of view of the viewer and one from the point of view of the light source. Now, display only those portions of the scene that are visible from both viewpoints. The parallel projection of a scene represented by an octree in a direction parallel to one of the faces of a node in the tree is a special case of the hidden-surface task. Assume that the direction of the light source is perpendicular to one of the other faces of the node, and extend this hidden-surface computation to cope with shadows.

7.19. Write an algorithm to generate the isometric view of an object given its region octree representation.

7.20. [Robert E. Webber] The isometric projection is a special case of the parallel projection. The isometric projection display technique of Yamaguchi et al. [Yama84] is based on the observation that a wireframe cubical network isometrically projects into an equilateral triangle network. Can you generalize this approach to handle arbitrary parallel projections? The following two properties of the relation between the cubical and triangular networks should be preserved in the generalization:

    1.   A recursive decomposition in the cubical network results in a recursive decomposition in the triangular network. This is fairly straightforward to see.

    2.   Looking at a finite subregion of the isometric projection of a cubical network, observe that after the cubical network reaches a certain size, further growth (e.g., in a direction away from the viewer) of the cubical network does not add any more edges to its isometric projection.

To build a coherent data structure for an arbitrary parallel projection, one of the following two properties must hold:

    3.   Looking at a finite subregion of an arbitrary parallel projection of a cubical network, it may be observed that after the cubical network reaches a certain size, further growth (e.g., in a direction away from the viewer) of the cubical network does not add any more edges to the given parallel projection.

4. Alternatively, as the cubical network grows, if a finite subregion of its projection becomes infinitely dense, then it must do so in a way that can be described as a recursive decomposition of the triangulation.

7.1.5 Use of BSP Trees for Hidden-Surface Elimination

The Weiler-Atherton algorithm makes use of a decomposition of the scene based on the projections of the polygonal faces of the objects that comprise the scene. Whenever either the scene or the viewpoint changes, the algorithm must be reapplied. Fuchs, Abram, and Grant [Fuch83] observe that the viewpoint changes far more often than the scene (e.g., the case of a moving observer). Thus it is worthwhile to preprocess the scene to remove much of the visible-surface computation overhead. This is done by using an adaptation of the BSP tree of Fuchs, Kedem, and Naylor [Fuch80] (see Section 1.3) to represent the scene.

In the following, we define the adaptation of the BSP tree to the representation of polygons. Although the resulting data structure is slightly different from the one defined in Section 1.3, we shall nevertheless refer to it as a BSP tree. The space spanned by a BSP tree consists of a set of polygons, say $\{p_1, p_2, \cdots, p_n\}$ in three dimensions. The BSP tree is constructed by choosing an arbitrary polygon from this set, say p_k, and splitting the three-dimensional space along the plane in which p_k lies into two subsets, say $P_{k,L}$ and $P_{k,R}$. p_k is associated with the root of the tree.

$P_{k,L}$ and $P_{k,R}$ comprise the two sons of the root and correspond to the two halfspaces separated by this plane. We arbitrarily choose one of the sides of the polygon as the 'front' side and say that $P_{k,L}$ corresponds to it, which means that $P_{k,R}$ corresponds to the 'back' side. We associate $P_{k,L}$ and $P_{k,R}$ with the left and right subtrees, respectively, of the root. Thus $P_{k,L}$ contains all polygons in the left subtree, and $P_{k,R}$ contains all polygons in the right subtree. This decomposition process is applied recursively to $P_{k,L}$ and $P_{k,R}$ and terminates upon encountering empty sets.

Two items are worthy of further note. First, a polygon, say p_i, may be contained in both the left and right subtrees of a node in the BSP tree. Such a situation arises when p_i's plane intersects the plane of one of its ancestor nodes in the BSP tree. Second, a polygon's plane is assumed to extend beyond the boundary of the polygon. For example, the plane of the root's polygon partitions the entire scene. Moreover, for each subtree rooted at T, the polygon associated with T, say p_T, is extended so that p_T partitions the entire space of T.

A problem with the BSP tree is that its shape is heavily dependent on the order in which the polygons are processed and on the polygons selected to serve as the partitioning planes. In the worst case, the BSP tree looks like a chain. Furthermore the decomposition may be such that a polygon is contained in many subtrees. Such a situation arises in complex nonconvex scenes and will lead to large BSP trees. Nevertheless it can be somewhat alleviated by being more careful when choosing the root polygon at each stage of the BSP tree construction process.

For example, one heuristic is to choose the polygon, say M, in the set that splits the minimum number of the remaining polygons in the set (see Exercise 7.26 for another approach). Fuchs, Abram, and Grant [Fuch83] have found that in practice there is no need to try out all possibilities to determine M. Instead they follow a suggestion of Kedem [Fuch83] and select just a small subset of the polygons at random, say S, to serve as candidates and then choose the polygon in S that splits the minimum number of the remaining polygons in the set. An analogous approach was used by Samet [Same80c] in selecting a node to replace the deleted root of a point quadtree (see Section 2.3.2 of [Same90a]).

To illustrate the adaptation of the BSP tree, a collection of line segments is used instead of polygons because it is easier to visualize what is happening. Each line segment has a direction. We say that its 'positive' side is the one to the right of the direction of the line segment. When the line segment is treated as a separator between two halfspaces, we say that the 'positive' side is the one whose equation has the form $a \cdot x + b \cdot y + c \geq 0$, while the 'negative' side is the one whose equation has the form $a \cdot x + b \cdot y + c < 0$.

For example, consider the four line segments labeled A, B, C, and D in Figure 7.11 (they have the same orientation as the partition lines in Figure 1.8 in Section 1.3). Suppose that the BSP tree is constructed by letting B be the root. The positive subset consists of D, while the negative subset consists of A, C, and D. D appears in both subsets because D crosses B when it is extended and thereby serves as a separator between two halfspaces. Now, let us build the BSP tree for the negative subset. Letting C be the root, we find that A is in the positive subset and D in the negative subset. The resulting BSP tree is shown in Figure 7.12a and partitions the plane into six regions as shown in Figure 7.12b.

If, in the first step, we had chosen C instead of B to be the root of the BSP tree, then the positive subset would consist of A, and the negative subset would consist of B and D. Now, let us build the BSP tree for the negative subset. Letting D be the root, we find that the positive subset is empty and B is in the negative subset. The resulting BSP tree is shown in Figure 7.13a and yields a partition of the plane into five regions as shown in Figure 7.13b. Of course, there are many other BSP trees that can be constructed for this set of four line segments.

Using the BSP tree to determine visibility involves a traversal of the tree in an order that is determined by the position of the viewpoint, say V. Each node of the BSP tree partitions the relevant portion of the scene into two parts. They can be identified with respect to whether they contain V. In particular, for each node N in the BSP tree,

Figure 7.11   Example set of four line segments

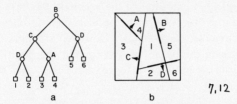

7,12

Figure 7.12 (a) The BSP tree corresponding to Figure 7.11 when B is the root and (b) the partition induced by it

let IN_SON(N,V) correspond to the son of N that contains V, and let OUT_SON(N,V) correspond to the son that does not. There are two basic techniques.

The first technique assigns a visibility number to each polygon in the order in which it has been visited. This order depends on whether we are using a 'back-to-front' or a 'front-to-back' display algorithm. We shall assume a 'back-to-front' algorithm. In such a case, the higher numbers correspond to a higher priority. They are assigned by traversing the BSP tree in such a way that for given node N, all the polygons in IN_SON(N,V) are given a lower number than N's polygon, and all the polygons in OUT_SON(N,V) are given a higher number than N's polygon. It should be clear that this is nothing more than an inorder traversal with respect to the viewpoint. These priorities can be used by conventional hidden-surface algorithms whenever a visibility determination must be made. In fact, we do not even have to assign the visibility numbers.

The second technique does not use the visibility numbers. Instead the traversal is used to control a 'back-to-front' algorithm (i.e., 'painter's' algorithm), which paints each polygon on the screen as it is encountered. If one polygon overlaps another polygon, then the most recently painted polygon determines the color of the overlapped region. Given viewpoint V, BSP tree node N, and the previous definition of IN_SON and OUT_SON, the polygons in OUT_SON(N,V) are visited before the polygon in the root, which in turn is visited before the polygons in IN_SON(N,V). Correctness is assured since polygons that occlude other polygons are closer to the viewpoint and are visited later in the traversal.

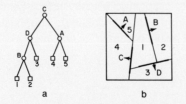

Figure 7.13 (a) The BSP tree corresponding to Figure 7.11 when C is the root and (b) the partition induced by it

The BSP tree yields a partition of the scene on the basis of the polygons in it. However, it is not a true object hierarchy because it chops objects. In fact, it is analogous to a point k-d tree (see Section 1.3). However, it differs from the point k-d tree in that instead of basing the partitioning on points, the partition is based on planes. Interestingly the resulting partition of space is of the same shape but the partition planes are nonorthogonal.

Exercises

7.21. Write a 'back-to-front' algorithm to display a scene represented by a BSP tree.

7.22. Write an algorithm to insert a line (polygon) into a BSP tree.

7.23. Write an algorithm to delete a line (polygon) from a BSP tree.

7.24. Suppose we define a predicate called CONFLICT (P_1,P_2) whose value is true if polygon P_1 intersects the halfspace of polygon P_2, and false otherwise. Is CONFLICT a symmetric relation? In other words, does CONFLICT $(P_1,P_2) =$ CONFLICT (P_2,P_1) always hold?

7.25. [David Mount] What is the physical interpretation when CONFLICT (P_1,P_2) and CONFLICT (P_2,P_1) are both true?

7.26. Fuchs, Kedem, and Naylor [Fuch80] suggest that the number of polygons in a BSP tree for a given polygonal database can be reduced by choosing as the root node of each subtree that node which eliminates the maximum number of future splits. A future split exists between polygons P_1 and P_2 if the value of CONFLICT (P_1,P_2) is true where CONFLICT is defined in Exercise 7.24. Write an algorithm to build a BSP tree that makes use of this method.

7.27. What is the minimum number of regions in the partition of a two (three)-dimensional space that is induced by the BSP tree for n line segments (polygons)?

7.28. Let us use the term *tessellation* to denote the partition of space induced by the construction of the BSP tree. Under what conditions is the tessellation independent of the order in which the BSP tree is built?

7.29. Suppose that the tessellation is independent of the order in which the BSP tree is built. What is the maximum number of polygons (polyhedra) that can be generated by n line segments (polygons) in a two (three)-dimensional space?

7.1.6 Displaying Curved Surfaces

In this book, objects are usually modeled by straight line segments and polygons. However, the quadtree paradigm also has proved useful to researchers interested in the manipulation of curved features, such as surfaces. Curved surfaces are often represented by a collection of parametric bicubic surface patches [Mort85]. The kth coordinate of the point p, i.e., p_k, in the parametric coordinate system measured in terms of u and v is calculated by the equation:

$$p_k(u, v) = \sum_{i=0}^{3}\sum_{j=0}^{3} a_{i,j} \cdot u^i \cdot v^j, \tag{7.1}$$

which can also be written as

$$p_k(u, v) = (1 \ u \ u^2 \ u^3) M_k P_k M_k^T (1 \ v \ v^2 \ v^3)^T, \tag{7.2}$$

where M_k and P_k are 4×4 matrices. M_k is a matrix operator that defines how the control points of the surface are used to create the coefficients of $a_{i,j}$ in Equation 7.1. For example, for a Bezier curve we have the matrix

$$\begin{bmatrix} 1 & 0 & 0 & 0 \\ -3 & 3 & 0 & 0 \\ 3 & -6 & 3 & 0 \\ -1 & 3 & -3 & 1 \end{bmatrix} . \tag{7.3}$$

P_k is a matrix formed from the kth coordinate of the 16 control points of the specific curved surface being modeled. Curved surface representations are important in computer graphics applications because they are often more compact than polygonal representations and also because they enable the stipulation of continuity in the derivative of piecewise surface representations. The latter is important for ray-tracing calculations (see Section 7.2).

One early approach to displaying such surfaces was developed by Catmull [Catm75]. The idea is to decompose the patch recursively into subpatches until the subpatches generated are so small that they span only the center of one pixel (or can be shown to lie outside the display region). The test for how many pixel centers are spanned by the patch (or whether or not the patch lies outside the display area) is based on the approximation of the patch by a polygon connecting the patch's corners. In our examples, patches are denoted by solid lines, and their approximating polygons are denoted by broken lines.

As an example of the recursive decomposition of patches, consider Figure 7.14. Figure 7.14a shows a single patch with corners A, B, C and D on a grid of pixel centers. We observe that quadrilateral ABCD, which approximates the patch ABCD, contains more than one pixel center. Thus the patch must be decomposed. Figure 7.14b shows the decomposition of patch ABCD into quadrilateral patches AFIE, BGIF, CHIG, and DEIH. Since the quadrilateral approximations of each of these patches, again, span more than one pixel center, each must be subdivided further, as shown in Figure 7.14c. This time there is not enough detail in the figure to show the difference between the patch and its quadrilateral approximation.

Note that in Figure 7.14c the quadrilateral approximation for patch JFKN contains only one pixel center and hence will not need to be subdivided further. Also the quadrilateral approximation of patch MNLG contains no pixel centers, and thus it too will not need to be subdivided further. However, the quadrilateral approximation of patch IJNM contains two pixel centers and hence will need to be subdivided further. The final decomposition of the original patch is shown in Figure 7.14d, and the raster image yielded by this decomposition is shown in Figure 7.14e.

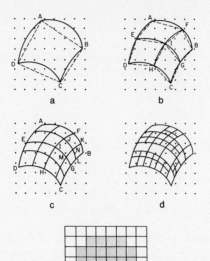

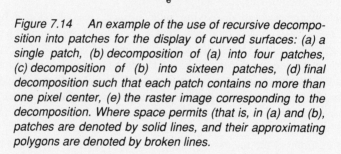

Figure 7.14   An example of the use of recursive decomposition into patches for the display of curved surfaces: (a) a single patch, (b) decomposition of (a) into four patches, (c) decomposition of (b) into sixteen patches, (d) final decomposition such that each patch contains no more than one pixel center, (e) the raster image corresponding to the decomposition. Where space permits (that is, in (a) and (b)), patches are denoted by solid lines, and their approximating polygons are denoted by broken lines.

As was observed by Catmull, the recursive decomposition approach to approximating the location of a patch can be generalized and thereby applied to other patch representations. Patch representations based on characteristic polyhedrons (e.g., Bezier and B-spline patches) [Mort85], allow these test decisions to be based on an approximation of each patch by the convex hull[4] enclosing its control points (which is guaranteed to enclose the entire patch). This yields a more accurate result than Catmull's approximation, which is based only on four corners of a patch.

---

[4] The *convex hull* of an object is the smallest convex set that contains the object. For a finite set s of points, the convex hull is a convex polygon (polyhedron in three dimensions) such that all points of s are on or inside the polygon (polyhedron), and every vertex of the polygon (polyhedron) belongs to s. Hence the problem of computing the convex hull of a finite set of points consists of computing the boundary of this polygon (polyhedron).

As with Warnock's algorithm, Catmull's algorithm is oriented toward the generation of display commands. Thus it does not explicitly generate the quadtree structure,[5] although its processing follows the quadtree decomposition paradigm in the parametric space. Since the patches exist in three-dimensional space, more than one patch can span the same pixel center. Thus the Catmull algorithm makes use of a z-buffer to keep track of the intensity/color of the patch that has most recently been found to be closest to the viewpoint.

Basically a z-buffer is a two-dimensional array that represents the displayed image. Each entry of the array contains a color and a depth. Initially each pixel in the displayed image is black and at an infinite depth. Whenever a new color is to be assigned to a pixel, the depth of the location to which the pixel corresponds is checked. If it is greater than the current depth in the z-buffer, the assignment is ignored; otherwise the color and depth values in the z-buffer are updated. Traditionally the z-buffer has aliasing problems (i.e., it produces jagged borders between neighboring regions), but they can be mitigated by using the rgb-α-z approach [Duff85].

Warnock's algorithm requires that the scene be completely specified at the time the algorithm is initiated. In contrast, the z-buffer enables elements of the scene to be processed in an arbitrary order. This permits elements to be added to the scene without having to reprocess previously processed elements. In other words, at any time during its processing, the z-buffer represents what would be displayed if there were no further elements in the scene.

The z-buffer is usually represented explicitly as a two-dimensional array. Such an array could also be represented by a quadtree. This quadtree z-buffer representation might prove useful for generating line representations of the borders between surfaces but not for generating shaded surfaces [Posd82]. Note that region quadtrees are seldom efficient for representing scenes, including shaded surfaces, since each pixel location on a shaded surface will have a slightly different color. However, if only the borders of the surfaces are represented, then the interior portions of the surfaces can be merged efficiently.

Catmull's subdivision algorithm has been adapted to handle surface intersection for bicubic patches [Carl82]. Instead of subdividing down to the pixel level everywhere, the subdivision is performed only until it has generated subpatches that are mutually disjoint. Two subpatches can be viewed as disjoint when the interiors of the convex hulls of their respective control points are disjoint. While this approach helps to determine the actual intersection between two subpatches, it does not address the problem of choosing which patches should be compared to determine the possible existence of an intersection. A PM octree-like approach to this problem [Nava86b] is mentioned in Section 5.3 of [Same90a].

While quadtrees are a natural way to organize the parametric representation of bicubic patches defined by four corner points plus auxiliary information (e.g., tangents

---

[5] However, Catmull's algorithm can be viewed as performing a postorder traversal of an imaginary quadtree; see also the Lane-Carpenter algorithm [Lane80], which can be viewed as performing a raster-ordered traversal of the same quadtree.

and twist vectors in the case of B-splines [Mort85]), the resulting set of quadrilaterals may be difficult to display. For example, it is difficult to ensure that the resulting four corners of the patches will actually be coplanar. In addition, when one patch is subdivided further than its neighbor, it is almost always the case that the patches will be misaligned (i.e., cracks will arise as shown in Figure 7.15a).

The coplanarity problem can be resolved by triangulating the quadrilaterals determined by the corner values of the leaf nodes. One way to resolve the alignment problem is to adjust the vertices of adjacent blocks of unequal size so that the vertex of the smaller block is on the edge between the vertices of its adjacent block of larger size. This method is used by Tamminen and Jansen [Tamm85b]. For example, the vertex at the NW corner of the SW son of the NE quadrant in Figure 7.15a would be replaced by the midpoint of the eastern boundary of the NW son. The adjacent block can be determined using neighbor-finding techniques as discussed in Chapter 3. Tamminen and Jansen perform the adjustment process by traversing the quadtree of the patch using the active border data structure described in Section 5.1.3.

The alignment problem can also be overcome by combining a nonstandard decomposition rule with triangulation. Von Herzen and Barr [VonH87, VonH88] propose a modification of the quadtree data structure, which they term a *restricted quadtree*. A restricted quadtree is one where all 4–adjacent blocks (i.e., nodes) are either of equal size or of ratio 2:1. Given an arbitrary quadtree decomposition, the restricted quadtree is formed by repeatedly subdividing the larger nodes until the 2:1 ratio

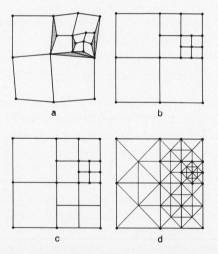

Figure 7.15   (a) The three-dimensional view of the resulting subdivision of a surface using a quadtree-like decomposition rule in parameter space (some of the cracks are shown shaded), (b) the quadtree of (a) in parameter space, (c) the restricted quadtree corresponding to (b), (d) the triangulation of (c)

holds.[6] It results in the quadtree-like decomposition shown in Figure 7.15c, as opposed to the more traditional representation shown in Figure 7.15b. Note that the SE quadrant of Figure 7.15b had to be decomposed once.

A combined solution to the coplanarity and alignment problems [VonH87, VonH88] triangulates the leaf nodes of the restricted quadtree in Figure 7.15c in the manner shown in Figure 7.15d. The rule is that every block is decomposed into eight triangles, or two triangles per edge, unless the edge is shared by a larger block. In that case, only one triangle is formed. This rule is termed the *eight triangle* rule.

An alternative rule decomposes each block into four triangles (instead of eight), or one triangle per edge, unless the edge borders a smaller square. In that case, two triangles are formed along the edge. This rule is termed the *four triangle* rule. Observe that regardless of the rule used, there are no cracks, whereas cracks do arise if we decompose each block into just two triangles (a *two triangle* rule). Nevertheless, it turns out that the eight triangle rule is preferable to the four triangle rule, as can be seen by examining their use in a shading application (see Exercise 7.35).

Exercises

7.30. Why aren't Catmull's quadrilateral patches guaranteed to enclose the patch?

7.31. [David Mount] Prove that the use of the restricted quadtree increases the number of nodes in the quadtree by at most a factor c. What is c?

7.32. Modify Hunter and Steiglitz's quadtree complexity theorem (see Theorem 1.1) to deal with the restricted quadtree of Von Herzen and Barr.

7.33. How would you use the restricted quadtree of Von Herzen and Barr to model terrain elevation data?

7.34. How would you extend the restricted decomposition rule to octrees? Devise a tetrahedralization that would resolve the four-dimensional problem. Can you think of any practical application of this technique?

7.35. [Brian von Herzen] Show why the eight triangle rule is preferable to the four triangle rule in Von Herzen and Barr's triangulation method. To do this, consider a two-dimensional scene of rectangles where we have gray values that are known a priori for each of the vertices of the rectangle. Such a scene might be viewed as the projection of a three-dimensional scene where the vertex values were derived from some standard lighting model. The rectangles are to be represented by a set of triangles. We wish to interpolate linearly the shading across the triangles to obtain the intensity values between the vertices (i.e., Gouraud shading; see Section 7.1.4). As an example, consider a simple horizontal edge 64 pixels wide and 16 pixels long. Assume that the edge starts on a pixel boundary. Assume further that the intensity values at the corners of the pixels, from top to bottom, consist of three rows of intensity 1, one row of intensity 0.8, one row of intensity 0.2, and twelve rows of intensity 0. Model the edge by four 16×16 squares of pixels. Compare the contour maps of the interpolated intensities using the intensity values at the vertices of the squares for the two rules.

7.36. What is the resulting contour pattern when applying the two triangle rule to the example in Exercise 7.35?

---

[6] This method of subdivision is also used in finite element analysis as part of a technique called *h-refinement* by Kela, Perucchio, and Voelcker [Kela86] to refine adaptively a mesh that has already been analyzed, as well as to achieve element compatibility.

7.37. Bicubic patches are often used in computer graphics to represent the surface of an object. Thus we need to have a way of storing these patches in an octree. A bicubic patch can be defined as

$$x(u, v) = \sum_{i=0}^{4} \sum_{j=0}^{4} a_{i,j} u^i v^j \qquad y(u, v) = \sum_{i=0}^{4} \sum_{j=0}^{4} b_{i,j} u^i v^j \qquad z(u, v) = \sum_{i=0}^{4} \sum_{j=0}^{4} c_{i,j} u^i v^j$$

where u and v are restricted to the range between 0 and 1. Give an algorithm to determine whether or not a particular bicubic patch lies within a particular octree node.

7.2 RAY TRACING

Although the parallel and perspective projection display techniques are suitable for computer-aided design, realistic display that incorporates lighting effects generally requires using some variant of ray tracing so that the interaction between visibility and shading can be properly calculated. Ray tracing is an approximate simulation of how the light propagated through a scene lands on the image plane. This simulation is based on the geometric optics approach to reflection (diffuse and specular) and refraction [Whit80]. Although the geometry of the reflection and refraction of 'particles' of light from surfaces is straightforward, the formulation of the equations to model the intensity of the light as it leaves these surfaces is a recent development. The quality of the displayed image is a function of the appropriateness of the model represented by these equations and the precision with which the scene is represented.

The rest of this section expands on the ray-tracing paradigm. It first reviews its historical development. Next, it presents a number of techniques for speeding it up. The emphasis is on the use of hierarchical data structures. This is followed by showing how a ray is traced through an environment that contains cells. Then a detailed implementation is given of ray tracing in a scene represented by an octree. It is based on [Same89b]. This section is quite detailed and may be skipped. Finally, some remaining issues are briefly discussed, and some empirical results are briefly mentioned.

7.2.1 Historical Development

From a procedural point of view, the term *ray tracing* (or *ray casting*) describes the process of casting a ray from the viewpoint through a given pixel on the image plane that appears between the viewpoint and the scene. The pixel is identified with the surface of the nearest object that intersects the ray. This ray is termed the *primary ray*. If an intersection is found, a number of additional rays are often cast. These additional rays are used to calculate shadows when there is another object between the light source and the intersected object and to calculate indirect paths between the light source and the surface.

When the object is opaque (i.e., we cannot see through it), the additional rays are used only for modeling reflection and shadows. On the other hand, when we can see through the object, the additional rays are also used for modeling transparence (i.e., the surface transmits light so that the objects lying beyond it are visible in their entirety) or for modeling translucence (i.e., the surface transmits light so that the objects lying beyond it cannot be seen clearly, as when looking through rose-colored glasses).

In the case of translucence, the ray may undergo refraction, and its direction depends on the nature of the different surfaces that are in contact at the point at which the ray intersects the object. These additional rays are termed *secondary rays*. Figure 7.16 illustrates these terms. Although the distinction between reflected and refracted rays is interesting from a physical standpoint, this distinction has little effect from an algorithmic standpoint. In the following discussion, any reference to reflected rays is actually a reference to both reflected and refracted rays.

Display techniques based on projection can be thought of as first-order approximations to display techniques based on ray tracing [Wegh84]. Recall that projective display is accomplished by executing a hidden-surface elimination algorithm. In essence, we first project the surface of each object into the image plane and then perform a visibility calculation based on a depth sort of all the surface elements of the visible objects. In contrast, ray tracing starts in the image plane and calculates how a ray impinges on the various objects. Ray tracing can be performed from a viewpoint (i.e., an eyeball), in which case it is analogous to perspective projection, or it can be performed in such a manner that all rays are perpendicular to the image plane, which is analogous to parallel projection.

The difference between ray-tracing and projection methods is that projection methods usually ignore the location of the light source and cannot account for the possibility that the light bounces off the object. Alternatively when ray tracing takes only the primary ray into account, it yields the same result as projection methods.

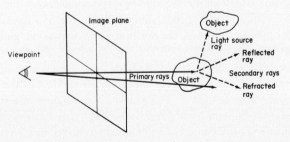

Figure 7.16   Illustration   of   ray   tracing: solid   lines correspond to primary rays while broken lines correspond to secondary and light source rays

Thus it is the ability to deal with secondary rays that accounts for the difference between these two display methods.

The intensity and color of the light associated with the primary ray is a function of the intensity of the light associated with the reflected rays and the intensity of the light associated with the light sources that impinge on the point of intersection of the primary ray with the surface of the object. The reflected ray is a ray emitted from the intersected object into the plane formed by the incident ray and the normal to the tangent plane at the point of intersection of the incident ray with the object. Of course, the angle formed by the reflected ray and the normal is equal to that formed by the incident ray and the normal except that it is on the other side of the normal.

Besides the reflected ray, a light source ray is cast in the direction of each of the light sources. For each of these rays, it is necessary to determine if any object obstructs the path of this ray to the corresponding light source. For each ray that is not obstructed, the light from its corresponding light source contributes to the intensity associated with the primary ray. This contribution is a function of the dot product of the light source ray with the surface normal.

It should be noted that there is a fundamental bias in the way light is handled depending on whether it comes directly from a light source or indirectly as a result of a reflection. Light that comes indirectly is permitted to contribute to the intensity of the primary ray only when it comes from the direction of the reflection, whereas light coming from a light source makes a contribution regardless of the direction from which it comes.

While the above approach is generally adequate because reflected light is usually less intense than light that comes directly from a light source, for more realistic images it is actually necessary to take into account reflected light coming from directions other than that of the reflected ray. There are two applicable techniques: radiosity [Gora84] and distributed ray tracing [Cook84, Kaji86]. Radiosity examines all possible combinations of interaction (see Section 7.4), while distributed ray tracing does a Monte Carlo sampling of the possible interactions.

The quality of the image yielded by ray tracing is heavily dependent on the illumination (shading) model that is used. Below a couple of different illumination models are briefly described, followed by a demonstration of how ray tracing makes use of them. The purpose of an illumination model is to determine the amount of light reflected to the viewpoint from a visible point on the surface as a function of the direction and strength of the light source, the position of the viewpoint, and the orientation and nature of the surface.

A simple shading model is based on Lambert's cosine law. In this case, the intensity of the reflected light is proportional to the dot product of the surface normal and the direction of the light source. The result is a simulation of a perfect diffusing surface (e.g., it scatters light uniformly and is also known as a *Lambertian surface*). It provides a reasonable approximation of an unpolished surface (e.g., a piece of felt).

A more accurate shading model is that of Phong [Phon75]. It accounts for reflection due to ambient light, diffuse reflection, and specular reflection. Specular reflection is a characteristic of shiny objects (e.g., those having a smooth metallic nature) but is present in all objects that have a polished surface (e.g., plastics, paper, wood). In such a case, there appear to be bright, narrow regions (i.e., highlights) on the object, as well as other duller regions. The location of the bright regions moves as the viewing angle is changed. It is modeled as falling off with the nth power of the dot product of the surface normal and a direction halfway between the viewer and each of the light sources. n is referred to as the *specular exponent* and is a function of the glossiness of the surface. This means that the maximum specular contribution of light occurs when the light source ray is coincident with the reflected ray. In particular, as n gets large, the contributions of all other directions become insignificant.

From the above, we see that specular reflection is direction specific. In contrast, in the case of dull (i.e., rough) surfaces, the manner in which the light is reflected is not direction specific; such surfaces are known as *ideal* Lambertian reflectors. Of course, the highlights also exist on the rough surfaces. However, the roughness causes the surface normals to be randomly distributed, thereby softening the effect of specular reflection [Torr67]. In contrast, on a smooth surface, the surface normals over a patch are almost identical, thereby permitting the observation of the effect.

Phong developed equations to model light intensity reflected by a surface as a function of the orientation of the surface, the location of the viewer, and the light source. To make his results useful for realistic scene rendering, it is also necessary to consider phenomena that result from the presence of multiple surfaces in the same scene, such as shadows. Shadows arise when additional objects lie on the path from a light source to an intersected surface of the given object. Also his model assumes that each light source is a point source located at an infinite distance from the objects in the scene. Thus it does not provide for the situation that the objects in the scene can themselves act as light sources, nor does it provide for area light sources such as fluorescent bulbs.

Whitted [Whit80] proposed an extension of Phong's model that accounts for reflections, refractions, and shadows that arise from interactions between the objects in the scene. An additional term accounts for the transmission of refracted light through the surface in a direction that obeys Snell's law.[7] He uses a simpler model of specular reflection than Phong by restricting the specular exponent to $+\infty$. This is equivalent to ignoring specular reflection from any direction other than the direction of the reflected ray. The result is that specular reflection from less glossy surfaces is not handled flexibly since, unlike Phong's model, Whitted's model makes no provision for varying the specular exponent n. Also this model does not handle area light sources (but see [Nish85]). For a more extended discussion of light models see [Cook82].

Whitted's model approximates the reflection from a single surface. Of course, most often light will be reflected from several surfaces before reaching the viewpoint.

---

[7] Let the incident ray be in a medium with index of refraction η_1 and the refracted ray be in a medium with index of refraction η_2. Snell's law states that the refracted and incident rays lie in the same plane, and the angles formed with the normal by the incident (θ_1) and refracted (θ_2) rays obey the relationship $\eta_1 \cdot \sin\theta_1 = \eta_2 \cdot \sin\theta_2$.

Whitted resolves this situation by using a tree, termed a *ray tree*, to represent the various components of light that reach the viewpoint from a particular direction. The ray tree is a tree where the nodes represent surfaces of objects in the scene. The nodes are connected by edges if and only if light reflected (refracted) from one surface passes immediately to the other surface. The root of the tree corresponds to the viewpoint. A ray is transmitted from the viewpoint to the first surface encountered, which is then represented by a child of the root. Edges leaving the child represent the reflected, refracted, and other secondary rays.

These additional secondary rays correspond to light sources that are directly visible from the surface represented by the node. The reflected and refracted rays may in turn affect other surfaces, thereby leading to a tree structure. Once the ray tree has been created, a shader calculates the intensity value of the root by a postorder traversal of the tree. The idea of tracing light backward from the viewer instead of forward from the light source can be traced to some early work on shadow generation by Appel [Appe68], who also formulated a hidden-surface algorithm.

7.2.2 Speeding Up Ray Tracing

A brute force implementation of Whitted's approach checks each ray against each object in the scene. Thus the number of intersection calculations is proportional to the product of the number of rays traced and the number of objects in the entire scene. Clearly a solution that makes use of special-purpose hardware such as multiprocessors or even VLSI implementations of the basic algorithm is preferable. Efficient software solutions are also of interest.

The main task in ray tracing is the search for the surfaces that are to be intersected and the intersection calculation itself [Whit80]. The cost of the search depends on how the items that are being searched are organized. If the items are sorted, the efficiency of the search increases markedly. Moreover, the individual ray-object intersection step can be speeded up considerably by associating with each object a procedure for efficiently intersecting its primitive type with a ray [Newe75].

The most obvious way to speed up the ray-tracing process is to exploit the coherence of the scene. There are several ways in which to proceed. First, image (as well as object) coherence can be used to reduce the number of rays that must be traced. The idea is that adjacent pixels in the viewplane will usually have the same intensity. This approach serves as the basis of *beam tracing* [Dado82, Heck84] where a group of pixels is treated as a thick ray, which is termed a *beam*.

Beam tracing is useful for polygonal objects since the rays will be reflected by them in a uniform manner. However, it is not well suited for curved surfaces (but see cone tracing [Aman84]) nor is it appropriate for complex scenes where the image coherence is too low. Notice that beam tracing can be implemented by modeling the viewplane as a region quadtree and letting the beams correspond to blocks of varying size in the quadtree. (For a further discussion of the geometric problems associated with beam racing, see Dadoun, Kirkpatrick, and Walsh [Dado82, Dado85], as well as Section 7.3.)

Second, scene coherence can be used to reduce the number of objects that are intersected with each ray, as well as the complexity of the ray-object intersection step. In both cases, all rays will be traced (i.e., one ray per pixel). An easy way to simplify the individual ray-object intersection step is to assume that each object (or the collection of objects) is enclosed by a bounding volume. If the ray intersects the bounding volume, then the more expensive ray-object intersection test is performed.

The simplest implementation of bounding volumes uses a rectangular bounding box oriented toward the viewing direction. Brooks et al. [Broo74] permit the box to have an arbitrary orientation. Other shapes such as spheres and cylinders are also used [Wegh84]. Whitted [Whit80] uses spheres because they are direction independent and thus are easier to test with respect to secondary rays (see also [Roth82]).

A logical derivative of the bounding volume approach is to use a hierarchy of bounding volumes as described by Rubin and Whitted [Rubi80]. This is rooted in the work of Clark [Clar76]. In essence, the hierarchy of bounding volumes is represented by a tree. If the ray does not intersect the volume represented by the root, then it does not intersect any object in the space. Otherwise the volumes represented by the subtrees are tested for intersection with the ray. This process is applied recursively.

There are many variations on how the bounding volumes are chosen, on their orientation, and even on the nature of the trees. For example, the tree should be organized so that the overlap between the volumes corresponding to brother subtrees is minimized, as well as balancing the number of objects in brother subtrees. Of course, at times, these goals are not mutually exclusive. When a ray has been found to intersect an object, we can ignore all subtrees with bounding volumes that are behind the intersection point in the direction of the ray.

When the objects that comprise the scene are represented by a boundary model (*BRep*), so that the surface of each object consists of many polygons (i.e., it is modeled by polygons), ray intersection with the object becomes tedious. Rubin and Whitted [Rubi80] address this problem by extending the bounding volume method down to the polygon level. In this case, each polygon is represented by an intersection of bounding rectangles; there is one bounding rectangle for each side of the polygon. Thus the polygons are never explicitly represented in the scene.

Third, the number of objects intersected with each ray can also be reduced by using scene coherence—that is, decomposing the scene into cells and associating with each cell all the objects or polygons contained in the cell. Fujimoto, Tanaka, and Iwata [Fuji86] used this method with a fixed number of cells of equal size. This is identical to the fixed-grid method used to deal with geographic data (see Section 1.3). The individual cells are accessed by use of a three-dimensional array. The adaptive[8] variant of this method has been described by many researchers (e.g., [Glas84, Kapl85, Tamm84e, Wyvi85]), and we shall refer to it as *space tracing*, following Kaplan [Kapl85, Kapl87].

---

[8] By *adaptive* it is meant that the scene is decomposed into cells of different sizes.

The advantage of space tracing can be quickly seen by examining the PM_1 quadtree representation [Same85i] of the five-sided polygon in Figure 7.17. A naive raytracing algorithm would have to test the ray emanating from the viewpoint against each of these sides, sort the resulting intersections, calculate the secondary rays (i.e., the reflected and refracted rays), and finally test the secondary rays to see if they intersect any other portion of the polygon.

For example, consider ray S in Figure 7.17, and assume that the boundary of the polygon is opaque (i.e., no light is transmitted through it). Thus the only secondary ray corresponds to reflection. From Figure 7.17, we see that a quadtree-based algorithm would perform the calculation for ray S by visiting only four cells (cells 1, 7, 8, and 9).

Light-modeling equations rely on the availability of accurate information about the direction of the normal to the surface at the point of its intersection with the ray. Thus the adaptive solutions usually make use of decomposition rules similar to the PM octree described in Section 1.3. This is especially true for PM octrees that represent curved, rather than planar, surfaces using either curved patches [Nava86b] or curved primitives [Wyvi85, Wyvi86].

In most ray-tracing applications, only the surface of the object is of interest. Therefore a subdivision rule is used that associates each object only with the cells through which the object's surface passes. Thus if a cell is totally contained in an object, the object is not associated with it. For planar surfaces, decomposition ceases whenever an octant is intersected either by exactly one face, or by exactly one edge such that all faces that intersect the octant meet at this edge, or by exactly one vertex such that all of the edges that intersect the octant meet at this vertex.

The decomposition rules described above are used in different ways to organize the cells that make up the cell structure. Glassner [Glas84] represents each cell by a variant of its three-dimensional VL locational code and then stores the locational codes in a chained hash table. Tamminen, Karonen, and Mäntylä [Tamm84e] and Kaplan [Kapl87] use a bintree decomposition rule where the cells are like buckets; they decompose until a cell contains no more than a predetermined number of

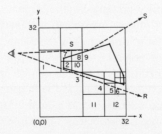

Figure 7.17 The result of tracing rays R and S through a PM_1 quadtree representation of a polygon. The cells intersected by the rays are labeled.

primitives. Kaplan implements the bintree as a tree structure with pointers, while Tamminen et al. use EXCELL, a technique that enables the leaf nodes of the bintree to be accessed directly by use of a directory in the form of an array (for more details, see Section 2.8.2.4 of [Same90a]).

Exercises

7.38. How does space tracing speed up the detection of whether an object is in the shadow of another?

7.39. One possible way of speeding up ray tracing in octrees is to store at each gray node the minimum enclosing sphere or box for the scene consisting of the objects defined by its subtree. Show how to compute the minimum enclosing sphere of an object from its raster octree representation.

7.2.3   How to Trace a Ray

Once the scene has been decomposed into cells, we must trace each ray through it. We adopt the convention that for a ray to pass through a cell (as well as intersect an object), it must enter and exit the cell (or object) at two distinct points. Thus a ray that is tangent to a cell (or object) at just one point does not pass through (intersect) the cell (object). On the other hand, a ray that is tangent to a cell (object) along an edge or a face of a cell (object) is said to pass through (intersect) the cell (object). For example, ray R in Figure 7.17 passes directly from cell 2 to cell 3, without passing through cell 10. This convention is very important; otherwise an error may arise (see Exercise 7.57).

For each cell through which the ray passes, we intersect the ray only with the objects in that cell. If it intersects more than one object, we determine the appropriate object and continue to trace the secondary rays, if necessary. If the ray does not intersect any of the objects in the cell, we project the ray into the next cell and try again. As long as the cost of moving between adjacent cells is relatively low, we will save time over the cost of intersecting the ray with every object in the scene.

There are a number of methods of projecting the ray into succeeding blocks. Jansen [Jans86] discusses these methods in a general manner. They can be best characterized as being either top-down or bottom-up. The top-down method corresponds to a tree traversal, which looks for bounding volumes or cells intersected by the ray. The traversal is guided by the direction of the ray. For example, in a two-dimensional image such that the ray moves from left to right (e.g., Figure 7.17), we visit the western sons before the eastern sons and the northern sons before the southern sons. If the ray does not intersect the space corresponding to a node's block, then no further intersections are attempted with the node's subtrees (e.g., the NE son of the root of Figure 7.17 when tracing ray R).

The bottom-up method has several variants. It follows the ray in the sense that first the closest bounding volume or cell, say C, to the viewpoint that is intersected by the ray is located. Let P be the point at which the ray leaves C. If C does not contain an object that intersects the ray, then locate the smallest cell or bounding volume, say $C\prime$, that contains the point $Q = P + \Delta$.

There are many methods of locating $C\prime$. Glassner's locational code representation requires a search of a hash table. Alternatively, when using a pointer representation, we can perform the point location algorithm (given in Section 6.1). It starts at the root of the tree. Yet another variation is to use the neighbor-finding methods described in Chapter 3. Tamminen et al. [Tamm84e] need one table-lookup operation in EXCELL's directory to find the bucket that contains the point.

The following elaborates on the bottom-up variant that uses neighbor finding. Assume that the ray is defined parametrically by

$$x = m_x \cdot t + b_x \tag{7.4}$$

$$y = m_y \cdot t + b_y \tag{7.5}$$

$$z = m_z \cdot t + b_z \tag{7.6}$$

One way to determine the parameters is to choose two points on the ray and let one correspond to $t = 0$ and the other to $t = 1$, and then to solve the six equations. The ray-tracing computation is simplified when the parameters are integers. This situation is assured when $t = 0$ corresponds to the viewpoint and when the viewpoint and the point corresponding to $t = 1$ both have integer coordinates. Note that $t \geq 0$ for every point on the ray. We also assume that the origin of the three-dimensional space containing the scene is at $(0,0,0)$ and the width of the space is a power of 2. The smallest possible cell is of width 1.

In practice, however, the situation is not so simple. In particular, when the viewplane is in an arbitrary position in space, it is usually not the case that every pixel on the viewplane has integer coordinates relative to the viewpoint. Nevertheless, we do know that (b_x, b_y, b_z) are equal to the coordinate values of the viewpoint. The following describes a more general solution that permits the m_i to be rational numbers while assuming that the viewpoint has integer coordinates.[9]

Let $B = (b_x, b_y, b_z)$ be the viewpoint. Assume that the viewplane is defined by the three points Q, R, and S such that $Q = (q_x, q_y, q_z)$ is the origin of the viewplane. Let $\vec{J}$ and $\vec{K}$ be the base vectors in the viewplane. Assume that $\vec{J} = j_x\vec{\alpha}_x + j_y\vec{\alpha}_y + j_z\vec{\alpha}_z$ and $\vec{K} = k_x\vec{\alpha}_x + k_y\vec{\alpha}_y + k_z\vec{\alpha}_z$, where j_i and k_i are rational numbers, and $\vec{\alpha}_i$ are unit vectors in the x, y, and z directions. Note that $\vec{J}$ and $\vec{K}$ are base vectors, although $j_x^2 + j_y^2 + j_z^2$ and $k_x^2 + k_y^2 + k_z^2$ do not necessarily equal 1. A point $P(u, v)$ on the viewplane (u and v are viewplane coordinates) can be written as:

$$\overrightarrow{P(u,v)} = u\vec{J} + v\vec{K} + \vec{Q}.$$

---

[9] Modifying our solution to permit the viewpoint to have rational coordinates is straightforward.

Ray R from the viewpoint B through point $P(u, v)$ on the viewplane can be expressed as:

$$\vec{R} = (\vec{P} - \vec{B})t + \vec{B}.$$

Expanding this equation yields:

$$x = (j_x \cdot u + k_x \cdot v + q_x - b_x) \cdot t + b_x \qquad (7.7)$$
$$y = (j_y \cdot u + k_y \cdot v + q_y - b_y) \cdot t + b_y \qquad (7.8)$$
$$z = (j_z \cdot u + k_z \cdot v + q_z - b_z) \cdot t + b_z \qquad (7.9)$$

The coefficients of t in Equations 7.7–7.9 correspond to the values of m_i and are rational numbers. In fact, as can be seen below, by redefining the parametric equations for the ray in terms of the lowest common denominator of m_x, m_y, and m_z, say, c, all of the parameters are integers. In the following, $t' = t/c$, and the values of m'_i are the remaining numerators once the denominators have been set to c.

$$x = m'_x \cdot t' + b_x \qquad (7.10)$$
$$y = m'_y \cdot t' + b_y \qquad (7.11)$$
$$z = m'_z \cdot t' + b_z \qquad (7.12)$$

In the remainder of the discussion, we assume that the parametric equations have been manipulated in such a manner. We shall use m_i and t, although we are actually referring to m'_i and t', respectively.

Tracing the ray is achieved by the following three-step process. First, we must show how to compute the points at which the ray enters and exits the cell (i.e., clip the ray). This process is a simplification of the Cyrus-Beck clipping algorithm [Cyru78, Roge85] and is the one used by Glassner [Glas84], as well as by Wyvill and Kunii [Wyvi85]. Glassner does not describe an implementation, while Wyvill and Kunii's implementation can result in errors (see Exercises 7.58–7.60).

The nature of the implementation is very important and requires much care since the computation must be exact. In particular, we cannot use floating point arithmetic. Instead we use rational arithmetic. Next, we process the cell by intersecting the ray with the objects in the cell. Finally, if necessary (i.e., the ray does not intersect any of the objects in the cell), we compute the direction of the next cell intersected by the ray and also locate it.

To determine the points at which a ray enters and exits a three-dimensional cell, each of whose sides is of width W, we test the ray against the bounding planes (i.e., faces) of the volume corresponding to the cell. For example, consider a cell bounded by $x = x_0$ and $x_0 + W$, $y = y_0$ and $y_0 + W$, and $z = z_0$ and $z_0 + W$. We compute a value of t for each of $x = x_0$, $x = x_0 + W$, $y = y_0$, $y = y_0 + W$, $z = z_0$, and $z = z_0 + W$.

Let t_i^{in} and t_i^{out} correspond to the range of values of t taken by coordinate i. In particular, if $m_i < 0$, then t_i^{in} and t_i^{out} correspond to $i = i_0 + \text{W}$ and $i = i_0$, respectively, whereas if $m_i \geq 0$, then t_i^{in} and t_i^{out} correspond to $i = i_0$ and $i = i_0 + \text{W}$, respectively. The intersection of these three ranges of t yields the values that the ray may assume while it is in the cell. In particular, t will range between $\max(t_i^{in})$ and $\min(t_i^{out})$.

To process the next cell $C\prime$, we must locate it. This requires us first to determine its direction, say I, relative to the current cell C. The computation of I is a critical part of the location process and cannot be ignored.[10] The direction depends on the location of the point, say P, at which the ray exits C. We have three possible positions: P is on either a vertex, edge, or face of C. P is on a vertex if t_i^{out} has the same value for each coordinate i. P is on an edge if t_i^{out} has the same value for two of the coordinates i. Otherwise P is on a face (i.e., t_i^{out} has a different value for each coordinate i).

Since the values of t are not necessarily integers and because we need to perform a test involving equality (not within a tolerance!), we represent t as a rational number (i.e., an ordered pair consisting of a numerator and a denominator). Comparisons involving different values of t are made by cross-multiplying the numerators and denominators of the comparands and comparing the results.

Now that we know the direction of $C\prime$ with respect to C, we must locate it. We have two alternatives. The first alternative is to compute a point, say Q, that is guaranteed to be in $C\prime$. Finding the cell containing point Q is easy. We start at the root of the octree, say G, and descend it based on a comparison of Q with the center of the block corresponding to G. The descent ceases once we reach a leaf node. This approach is commonly used [Kapl87, Wyvi85]. Glassner [Glas84] and Tamminen et al. [Tamm84e] do not have a tree structure and thus obtain the node by other means. Glassner uses hashing, while Tamminen et al. perform a table-lookup operation in EXCELL's directory to find the bucket that contains the point.

The computation of Q is relatively straightforward, although its implementation requires us to pay close attention to details. Q depends on the location of P, the point at which the ray exits C. Let $P = (P_x, P_y, P_z)$ and $Q = (Q_x, Q_y, Q_z)$. Let $I = (I_x, I_y, I_z)$ be the direction of the next cell $C\prime$. We follow the convention that the left, down, and back faces of a cell are closed; that is, if a point lies on one of these faces, it is in the cell bounded by them. Using this convention, in order to calculate Q we need to subtract Δ (where Δ is very small) from P_j if I_j is in the negative (i.e., decreasing) direction of j. Δ must be no larger than the width of the smallest possible cell—that is, 1. Δ cannot be smaller than 1 because we are using integer arithmetic in the process of locating the cell containing Q.

For example, if $I = $ 'LUB', then we must subtract 1 from P_x and P_z, with the result that $Q = (P_x-1, P_y, P_z-1)$. On the other hand, when $I = $ 'RD', we need only subtract 1 from P_y while the remaining values remain the same: $Q = (P_x, P_y - 1, P_z)$. Note that the conventions with respect to which faces are closed enable us to use the integer parts of the coordinate values that are not in the I direction. Thus when $I = $ 'RD', we use the

---

[10] For the pitfalls associated with ignoring it, see Exercises 7.58–7.60.

integer parts of P_z. P_x and P_y are already integers by virtue of being on the edge of a cell.

The second alternative makes use of neighbor-finding methods as outlined in Section 3.3. In particular, we find the neighbor of C, say N, in direction I having a width greater than or equal to that of C. If such a neighbor does not exist, we are at the border of the three-dimensional space, and we exit. If N does not correspond to a gray node, we are done (i.e., $C' = N$). Otherwise we now calculate a point Q that is guaranteed to be in C' that is a descendant of N (recall that N's node is gray). We locate C' by applying the point location algorithm described.

The advantage of this approach over just using the point location algorithm is that fewer nodes will be visited since we need not descend from the root of the tree. Also, traversing links in the octree by using neighbor finding is considerably cheaper than the arithmetic operations that are part of the point location algorithm.

When the octree is represented using pointers, then neighbor finding is implemented by using the FATHER links. On the other hand, a pointerless representation can also be used. One example is as a collection of the leaf nodes comprising the octree where each leaf node is represented by its FD locational code. In such a case, a neighboring node is located by first manipulating the bits that comprise the FD locational code of the current node based on the direction of the desired neighbor and then performing a search (recall the discussion in Section 3.4.1).

An advantage of PM-like decomposition methods is that each leaf node refers to just one primitive object. This means that in order to test whether a ray intersects an object, the ray tracer need not do any searching. On the other hand, a disadvantage is that we may have to intersect a ray with a given object more than once. This situation arises whenever an object, say O, occupies a number of cells, say C_i, such that the ray passes through each of C_i yet does not intersect O, or at least not in all of the C_i.

To see this disadvantage, consider the PM_1 quadtree representation of the simple polygon given in Figure 7.17. Ray R does not intersect the polygon, yet while tracing it we must examine six cells (numbered 1–6 in the figure), of which four cells (2, 3, 4, and 6) involve an intersection test with the polygon. As another example, tracing ray S through Figure 7.17 requires an intersection test in cells 1, 7, 8, and 9 when S only intersects the polygon in cell 9.

There are a number of approaches to reduce partially the complexity of the multitude of ray-object intersection tests. One approach is to associate with each ray the result of any prior intersection test with the object or part of it. This result can be in the form of the coordinate values of the intersection point (infinite if the ray does not intersect the object), say N. Once we have tested a ray against an object and found that it does not intersect the object in the current cell, all subsequent tests, say in cell C_i, can be simplified by merely checking if point N is in C_i.

An alternative approach is to try to eliminate the situation that calls for tests. From a theoretical standpoint, whenever a ray passes straight through the scene to the background, there is no need to intersect it with any of the objects in the scene. In such a case, the frequency of ray-object intersections is a direct result of the space subdivision rule being employed.

Wyvill and Kunii [Wyvi85] propose to enforce a minimum level of subdivision. Of course, in some cases, this may lead to a considerable increase in the level of decomposition (e.g., around a vertex in a PM_1 quadtree). The general consequence of such a modification is that instead of having a few large objects that will be tested often for intersection with rays that pass straight through to the background, we have more empty cells that are traversed more quickly (assuming that testing empty cells is considerably cheaper than testing intersections).

An unfortunate consequence of this modification is that too large an increase in the level of decomposition leads to an increase in the number of cells and may cause an increase in the number of ray-object intersection tests. For example, suppose we subdivide cell 2 in Figure 7.17. Prior to the subdivision, ray R had to be tested twice in cell 2 — once for each of the sides of the polygon that intersect cell 2. On the other hand, after the subdivision, ray R must be tested three times—twice against the sides of the polygon in the SW quadrant of cell 2 and once against the side of the polygon in the SE quadrant.

From the previous discussion, it is clear that it is difficult to decide how large to make the largest permissible cell. In fact, as mentioned earlier, Fujimoto, Tanaka, and Iwata [Fuji86] suggest that the space be subdivided into a fixed grid (i.e., cells of equal size). They have found situations where this is preferable to the decomposition induced by an octree. These are generally scenes where the number of distinct objects is large in comparison to the level of decomposition; however, it is not clear what kind of an octree they used.

Not surprisingly, a drawback of using the fixed-grid approach is that it is difficult to decide on the size of the grid. Moreover it results in the usage of more space and means that a large number of ray-object intersection tests will have to be performed. However, since the purpose of using a hierarchical representation is to avoid intersecting the rays with all of the objects, it is not clear if it is justifiable to replace this task with the performance of a very large number of inside/outside point tests. It seems that a judiciously chosen octree variant would remove this bias. Nevertheless this problem is worthy of further study.

Exercises

7.40. Why is $t \geq 0$ for every point that is on a traced ray?

7.41. When calculating the entry and exit points of a ray in a cell, we assume that the points of the ray have t values that range between $\max(t_i^{in})$ and $\min(t_i^{out})$. What happens if $\max(t_i^{in}) > \min(t_i^{out})$? Why isn't this a problem?

7.42. The process of calculating the entry and exit points of the ray in a cell is a simplification of the Cyrus-Beck clipping algorithm [Cyru78, Roge85]. Why can we make these simplifications?

7.43. Give an algorithm to sort a set of n rational numbers. How fast can you do this?

7.44. Develop the parametric representation of a reflected ray given the parametric representation of the incident ray and the plane of reflection. The parameters of the reflected ray must be rational numbers.

7.45. Compare the two alternative methods of locating a neighboring cell when using the bottom-up method of projecting a ray into succeeding blocks. The first method starts at the root of the tree and locates the cell using FIND_3D_BLOCK. The second method makes use of neighbor finding and invokes only FIND_3D_BLOCK if the neighboring cell is smaller than the current node. You must assign a comparative cost to traversing links and performing arithmetic operations in procedure FIND_3D_BLOCK. Try to compute a trade-off point in terms of the level of the tree in a manner analogous to that used in the comparison performed in Section 4.2.2 between the ALG1 and ALG2 algorithms for building a raster representation from a quadtree.

7.46. Give an algorithm to project a ray into succeeding three-dimensional blocks when the blocks are all of equal size. Your algorithm should be as efficient as possible and use integer arithmetic. Try to avoid divisions and multiplications except by powers of two.

7.47. If memory was not a limitation (i.e., everything fits in core) and ray tracing was the application, does it make sense to use a pointerless octree representation (e.g., an FD linear octree) rather than a pointer-based representation?

7.2.4 Sample Implementation

An implementation of the bottom-up process of tracing a ray through a scene, represented by an octree, that uses neighbor finding to locate successive cells is given by the following procedures. The process is controlled by procedure RAY_TRACER. It is invoked with parameters corresponding to the parametric representation of the traced ray, a pointer to the root of the octree, and the width of the scene.

RAY_TRACER's first action is to determine the value of t, if any, for the point, given by POINT, at which the ray first enters the cell corresponding to the entire scene and the direction of the ray relative to the face, edge, or vertex containing POINT. This is achieved by procedure FIRST_POINT. If POINT lies outside the scene, then the process stops since there are no intersections. Otherwise the particular cell containing POINT is located by use of procedure FIND_3D_BLOCK given in Section 6.1.

Once the first cell intersected by the ray has been located, the ray is traced through successive cells. For each cell through which the ray passes, a record of type *cell* is created that has six fields called T_IN, T_OUT, SIZ, PTR, CORNER, and DIRECT. Letting C be a pointer to a record of type *cell*, T_IN(C) and T_OUT(C) indicate the values of t for the points at which the ray enters and exits from C. SIZ(C) is the width of C's cell. PTR(C) is a pointer to C's node in the octree. CORNER(C)[I] is the value of the Ith coordinate of cell C's farthest corner from the origin. DIRECT(C) is the direction of the next cell, relative to cell C, through which the ray must be traced. Procedure RAY_INTERSECTS_OBJECT_IN_CELL, not given here, performs the actual intersection tests of the ray with the objects associated with cell C.

If procedure RAY_INTERSECTS_OBJECT_IN_CELL determines that the ray intersects the object, a reflection or refraction calculation must be made. This is equivalent to tracing a new ray and is not in the code given here, although it is discussed below. Otherwise the ray is traced into the next cell. This cell is determined by use of neighbor finding via a call to procedure OT_GTEQ_NEIGHBOR that returns a pointer P. OT_GTEQ_NEIGHBOR is aided by the function TYPE to determine the type of the neighbor's direction (i.e., face, edge, or vertex) so that it can invoke the appropriate

neighbor-finding method. Procedures OT_GTEQ_FACE_NEIGHBOR2, OT_GTEQ_EDGE_-
NEIGHBOR2, and OT_GTEQ_VERTEX_NEIGHBOR2 are analogous to QT_GTEQ_EDGE_-
NEIGHBOR2 and QT_GTEQ_VERTEX_NEIGHBOR2 in that they return the neighbor as well
as its size (i.e., level). They are not given here.

If the cell pointed at by P does not correspond to a leaf node, the point at which
the ray first enters the next cell is calculated and FIND_3D_BLOCK is used to locate it,
starting at P. The entire process stops when a ray either intersects an object within a
cell or exits the scene (i.e., OT_GTEQ_NEIGHBOR returns a pointer to NIL).

To be able to compare different values of t so that the direction of the next cell
can be determined, we need to compute the minimum and maximum values of t. This
must be done in an exact manner, and thus we represent the values of t as rational
numbers by use of a record of type *rational*, with two fields NUM and DEN, corresponding to the numerator and denominator, respectively.

The actual comparisons are aided by using procedure COMPARE_T to precompute
pairwise comparisons: CYX, CZX, and CZY. These comparisons are used by procedure
NEXT_CELL_DIRECTION to determine the direction of the next cell, relative to the
present cell, that is intersected by the ray. This is facilitated by making use of the sign
of M and functions FACE_DIR, EDGE_DIR, and VERTEX_DIR given in Tables 7.3, 7.4, and
7.5, respectively.

At times, we need to calculate the coordinates of a point in a specific cell. This
situation arises when attempting to locate the first cell that is intersected by the ray,
when attempting to locate a neighboring cell that is smaller than the current cell, and
when setting the CORNER field of a record of type *cell*. The function CHANGE(I,A)
facilitates this task by indicating the smallest amount, with the appropriate sign, by
which the value of coordinate A changes due to motion in direction I. For example,
CHANGE('RB', 'Z') $= -1$ as the value of coordinate z will decrease as a result of motion
in direction 'RB'. On the other hand, CHANGE('RB', 'Y') $= 0$, as the value of coordinate
y is unaffected by motion in direction 'RB'. CHANGE is given in Table 7.2.

To handle reflection and refraction at a surface properly, we need to trace the
appropriate ray anew. This can be done in the same manner starting at the point at
which the primary ray intersects the surface. The secondary (i.e., reflected and
refracted) ray is also defined parametrically. The only difficulty is that the definition
of the secondary ray will require a larger computer word size to cope with the increase
in the number of binary digits necessary to specify the parameters and values of t
correctly. This is a direct result of the use of rational arithmetic. It can be avoided in
part by using parametric equations in the form of 7.7–7.9 instead of 7.10–7.12. However, this requires that m be treated as data of type *rational* in procedure RAY_TRACER
(see Exercise 7.55).

It is difficult to give an example of the algorithm in three dimensions. Thus
instead, we examine below how ray R is traced through the two-dimensional scene
given in Figure 7.17. The algorithm, as encoded by procedure RAY_TRACER and the
associated procedures, is also valid for two-dimensional scenes. The only necessary
modifications are minor and are described briefly below:

1. Replace loops and data structures that cycle through 'X', 'Y', and 'Z' by just 'X' and 'Y'. Thus FIND_3D_BLOCK is replaced by FIND_2D_BLOCK.

2. Remove variables CZX and CZY, as well as all tests involving them. This means that the conclusion of the test (i.e., the action, or actions, to be taken had the test's evaluation yielded a value of true) is also removed.

3. Remove all tests involving 'Z' and the associated actions to be taken had the test's evaluation yielded a value of true.

4. Let the directions W, E, S, N correspond to L, R, D, U, respectively, and simplify Tables 7.2, 7.3, and 7.4. Table 7.5 is no longer necessary.

Continuing with our example, the scene is represented as a PM_1 quadtree in a $2^5 \times 2^5$ space with an origin at the lower left corner. The viewpoint is assumed to be at the point $(8,23)$. Ray R is assumed to pass through the point $(12,16)$. Therefore R is defined parametrically by

$$x = 20 \cdot t - 8$$

$$y = -7 \cdot t + 23.$$

R first enters the scene at the point defined by $t = 2/5$ — $(0,101/5)$. This is obtained by taking the maximum of $t_x^{in} = 2/5$ computed at $x = 0$ and $t_y^{in} = -9/7$ computed at $y = 32$. The point $(0,101/5)$ is contained in cell 1. Cell 1 is exited at the point defined by $t = 4/5$ — $(8,87/5)$ in the easterly direction—and is obtained by taking the minimum of $t_x^{out} = 4/5$ computed at $x = 8$, and $t_y^{out} = 1$ computed at $y = 16$. This process is repeated for the rest of the cells intersected by the ray, and its result is shown in Table 7.1.

Values of t are tabulated as ordered pairs where 'num' and 'den' correspond to t's numerator and denominator, respectively. Notice that $t_x^{out} = t_y^{out}$ for cell 2, which means that CYX=0 and MIN_AXIS is set to 'X' in procedure RAY_TRACER. Procedure

Table 7.1   Result of tracing ray R through Figure 7.17

Cell	Size	t_x^{out}		t_y^{out}		t^{out}		x_{out}	y_{out}	Direction of Next Cell	Neighbor Type
		Num	Den	Num	Den	Num	Den				
1	8	16	20	−7	−7	16	20	8	87/5	R	E
2	4	20	20	−7	−7	20	20	12	16	RD	SE
3	16	24	20	−23	−7	24	20	16	73/5	R	E
4	8	32	20	−15	−7	32	20	24	59/5	R	E
5	4	36	20	−15	−7	36	20	28	52/5	R	E
6	4	40	20	−15	−7	40	20	32	9	R	E

Table 7.2   CHANGE (I, A)

I (direction)	A (axis)		
	X	Y	Z
L	−1	0	0
R	1	0	0
D	0	−1	0
U	0	1	0
B	0	0	−1
F	0	0	1
LD	−1	−1	0
LU	−1	1	0
LB	−1	0	−1
LF	−1	0	1
RD	1	−1	0
RU	1	1	0
RB	1	0	−1
RF	1	0	1
DB	0	−1	−1
DF	0	−1	1
UB	0	1	−1
UF	0	1	1
LDB	−1	−1	−1
LDF	−1	−1	1
LUB	−1	1	−1
LUF	−1	1	1
RDB	1	−1	−1
RDF	1	−1	1
RUB	1	1	−1
RUF	1	1	1

Table 7.3   F = FACE_DIR (A, SIGN_M[A])

A (Normal Axis)	SIGN_M[A]	F (Direction)
X	1	L
X	0	R
Y	1	D
Y	0	U
Z	1	B
Z	0	F

Table 7.4   E = EDGE_DIR(PIJ,SIGN_M[I],SIGN_M[J])

PIJ (Normal Plane)	SIGN_M[I]	SIGN_M[J]	E (Direction)
XY	1	1	LD
XY	1	0	LU
XY	0	1	RD
XY	0	0	RU
XZ	1	1	LB
XZ	1	0	LF
XZ	0	1	RB
XZ	0	0	RF
YZ	1	1	DB
YZ	1	0	DF
YZ	0	1	UB
YZ	0	0	UF

NEXT_CELL_DIRECTION indicates that the direction of the next cell is to be found in EDGE_DIR ('XY',0,1)—that is, 'RD', which is the same as 'SE'. The 'SE' neighbor of cell 2 is cell 3 and is located by use of the two-dimensional analog of procedure OT_GTEQ_NEIGHBOR. Since cell 3 is larger than cell 2, there is no need to make use of procedure FIND_2D_BLOCK to locate it.

procedure RAY_TRACER(M,B,W,R);
/* Trace a ray given parametrically by M and B (i.e., $x = m_x \cdot t + b_x$) through the octree rooted at R that corresponds to the three-dimensional space of width W with origin at (0,0,0). W is a power of 2. Procedure RAY_INTERSECTS_OBJECT_IN_CELL performs object tests in each each cell through which the ray passes. It is not given here. Its argument is a pointer to a record of type *cell* that has fields T_IN, T_OUT, SIZ, PTR, CORNER, and DIRECT corresponding to the value of the parameter *t* for the entry and exit points, the width of the cell, a pointer to its node in the octree, the coordinates of its farthest corner (from the origin), and the direction of the next cell through which the ray must be traced, respectively. */
begin
  global integer array M,B [{'X', 'Y', 'Z'}];
  value integer W;
  value pointer node R;
  global integer array SIGN_M[{'X', 'Y', 'Z'}];
  pointer cell C;
  rational pointer array T[{'X', 'Y', 'Z'}];
  integer array POINT[{'X', 'Y', 'Z'}];
  direction DIR;
  integer CYX,CZX,CZY;
  axis I,MIN_AXIS;
  pointer node P;

Table 7.5   V = VERTEX_DIR(SIGN_M[X],SIGN_M[Y],
                 SIGN_M[Z])

SIGN_M[X]	SIGN_M[Y]	SIGN_M[Z]	V (Direction)
1	1	1	LDB
1	1	0	LDF
1	0	1	LUB
1	0	0	LUF
0	1	1	RDB
0	1	0	RDF
0	0	1	RUB
0	0	0	RUF

```
P ← R;
C ← create(cell);
for I in {'X', 'Y', 'Z'} do /* Keep track of the direction of the ray */
   SIGN_M[I] ← if M[I] > 0 then 0
               else 1;
T_OUT(C) ← FIRST_POINT(W,DIR); /* Find t for the first entry point of the ray: */
for I in {'X', 'Y', 'Z'} do
   begin /* Calculate the first entry point */
      CORNER(C)[I] ← W;
      POINT[I] ← ⌊(M[I]*NUM(T_OUT(C)))/DEN(T_OUT(C))⌋ + B[I]
                + SIGN_M[I]*CHANGE(DIR,I); /* ⌊x⌋ is the floor of x */
   end;
if POINT['X'] < 0 or POINT['Y'] < 0 or POINT['Z'] < 0 or
   POINT['X'] ≥ W or POINT['Y'] ≥ W or POINT['Z'] ≥ W
   then return /* The ray never enters the space */
else /* Locate the closest cell to the entry point */
   FIND_3D_BLOCK(P,POINT,CORNER(C),W);
while true do /* Follow the ray through the space */
   begin
      PTR(C) ← P;
      SIZ(C) ← W;
      T_IN(C) ← T_OUT(C);
      for I in {'X', 'Y', 'Z'} do
         begin /* Compute a t value for the exit point for each plane */
            NUM(T[I]) ← CORNER(C)[I] – SIGN_M[I]*W – B[I];
            DEN(T[I]) ← M[I];
         end;
      COMPARE_T(T,CYX,CZX,CZY);
      /* Find the minimum of the values of t using rational arithmetic: */
      MIN_AXIS ← if CZY < 0 then
```

```
                 if CZX < 0 then 'Z'
                 else 'X'
                 else if CYX < 0 then 'Y'
                 else 'X';
       DIRECT(C) ← NEXT_CELL_DIRECTION(MIN_AXIS,CYX,CZX,CZY);
       T_OUT(C) ← T[MIN_AXIS];
       if RAY_INTERSECTS_OBJECT_IN_CELL(C) then return
       else
         begin
           /* Locate the next cell in direction DIRECT(C) using neighbor finding: */
           OT_GTEQ_NEIGHBOR(PTR(C),DIRECT(C),P,W);
           if null(P) then return; /* Neighbor does not exist */
           for I in {'X', 'Y', 'Z'} do /* Compute location of next cell */
             CORNER(C)[I] ← CORNER(C)[I]
                            + if CHANGE(DIRECT(C),I) = 1 then W
                              else if CHANGE(DIRECT(C),I) = –1 then –SIZ(C)
                              else if (CORNER(C)[I] mod W) = 0 then 0
                              else W – (CORNER(C)[I] mod W);
           if GRAY(P) then /* Neighbor is smaller */
             begin /* Compute a point within the neighbor */
             for I in {'X', 'Y', 'Z'} do /* ⌊x⌋ is the floor of x */
               POINT[I] ← ⌊(M[I]∗NUM(T_OUT(C)))/DEN(T_OUT(C))⌋ +B[I]
                          + SIGN_M[I]∗CHANGE(DIRECT(C),I);
             FIND_3D_BLOCK(P,POINT,CORNER(C),W); /* Locate cell */
             end;
           end;
         end;
end;



pointer rational procedure FIRST_POINT(W,DIR);
/* Return a pointer to a record containing the value of the ray parameter t corresponding to
   the point at which the ray first enters the three-dimensional space of width W through
   which the ray is traced.  DIR is set to the direction of the ray. */
begin
  value integer W;
  reference direction DIR;
  rational pointer array T[{'X', 'Y', 'Z'}];
  global integer array M,B,SIGN_M[{'X', 'Y', 'Z'}];
  integer CYX,CZX,CZY;
  axis I,MAX_AXIS;
  for I in {'X', 'Y', 'Z'} do
    begin /* Compute a t value for the entry point for each plane */
      NUM(T[I]) ← SIGN_M[I]∗W – B[I];
      DEN(T[I]) ← M[I];
    end;
  COMPARE_T(T,CYX,CZX,CZY);
```

```
/* Find the maximum of the values of t using rational arithmetic: */
MAX_AXIS ← if CZY > 0 then
                if CZX > 0 then 'Z'
                else 'X'
                else if CYX > 0 then 'Y'
                else 'X';
DIR ← NEXT_CELL_DIRECTION(MAX_AXIS,CYX,CZX,CZY);
return(T[MAX_AXIS]);
end;


procedure COMPARE_T(T,CYX,CZX,CZY);
/* Compute CYX, CZX, and CZY. CYX is the pairwise comparison of T['Y'] and T['X'],
   CZX is the pairwise comparison of T['Z'] and T['X'], and CZY is the pairwise comparison
   of T['Z'] and T['Y']. */
begin
 value rational pointer array T[{'X', 'Y', 'Z'}];
 reference integer CYX,CZX,CZY;
 CYX ← abs(NUM(T['Y'])*DEN(T['X'])) − abs(NUM(T['X'])*DEN(T['Y']));
 CZX ← abs(NUM(T['Z'])*DEN(T['X'])) − abs(NUM(T['X'])*DEN(T['Z']));
 CZY ← abs(NUM(T['Z'])*DEN(T['Y'])) − abs(NUM(T['Y'])*DEN(T['Z']));
end;


direction procedure NEXT_CELL_DIRECTION(A,CYX,CZX,CZY);
/* Return the direction of the next cell through which the ray must be traced. A is the axis
   corresponding to the value of t. CYX, CZX, and CZY are pairwise comparisons of the
   values of t for the bounding sides of the cell through which the ray is exiting. */
begin
 value axis A;
 value integer CYX,CZX,CZY;
 global integer array SIGN_M[{'X', 'Y', 'Z'}];
 return(if A = 'Z' then FACE_DIR('Z','SIGN_M['Z'])
        else if A = 'Y' then
         if CZY = 0 then EDGE_DIR('YZ','SIGN_M['Y'],SIGN_M['Z'])
         else FACE_DIR('Y','SIGN_M['Y'])
        else if CZX = 0 then
         if CYX=0 then VERTEX_DIR(SIGN_M['X'],SIGN_M['Y'],SIGN_M['Z'])
         else EDGE_DIR('XZ','SIGN_M['X'],SIGN_M['Z'])
        else if CYX = 0 then EDGE_DIR('XY','SIGN_M['X'],SIGN_M['Y'])
        else FACE_DIR('X','SIGN_M['X']));
end;


procedure OT_GTEQ_NEIGHBOR(P,D,Q,W);
/* Determine the type of direction D and invoke the appropriate neighbor-finding pro-
   cedure. Q will contain the neighbor of node P, of size greater than or equal to P, in
   direction D. W denotes the length of a side of node P and the length of a side of node
   Q. If a neighboring node does not exist, then return NIL. LOG2 returns the base 2 log-
   arithm of its argument. */
```

begin
  value pointer node P;
  value direction D;
  reference pointer node Q;
  reference integer W;
  if TYPE(D) = 'FACE' **then** OT_GTEQ_FACE_NEIGHBOR2(P,D,Q,LOG2(W))
  else if TYPE(D)='EDGE' **then** OT_GTEQ_EDGE_NEIGHBOR2(P,D,Q,LOG2(W))
  else OT_GTEQ_VERTEX_NEIGHBOR2(P,D,Q,LOG2(W));
end;

Exercises

7.48. Modify procedure RAY_TRACER and the associated procedures to work for two-dimensional scenes. You must also modify the functions CHANGE, FACE_DIR, and EDGE_-DIR given in Tables 7.2, 7.3, and 7.4, respectively.

7.49. Suppose that ray S in Figure 7.17 passes through the point (16,24). Give a parametric definition of S.

7.50. Tabulate the result of tracing ray S through Figure 7.17 in a manner analogous to Table 7.1.

7.51. Consider the calculation of POINT[I] in procedure RAY_TRACER (i.e., the value of the Ith coordinate of a point that is guaranteed to be in the next cell to be visited in direction D). Can you replace the additive term 'SIGN_M[I]*CHANGE(D,I)' by just 'CHANGE(D,I)'?

7.52. Consider the calculation of the new value of CORNER(C)[I] in procedure RAY_TRACER. When the motion in the direction of coordinate I is negative, can you decrement by 'CORNER(C)[I] mod W' instead of by 'SIZ(C)'?

7.53. Why are the pairwise comparisons in procedure COMPARE_T performed with the aid of the absolute value function?

7.54. In the calculation of POINT in procedure RAY_TRACER, we use a floor operation when we calculate '(M[I] * NUM(T_OUT(C)))/DEN(T_OUT(C))'. Why can't we use integer division in this situation?

7.55. Modify procedure RAY_TRACER to permit m to be a rational number.

7.56. The determination of the direction of the next cell to be visited, as well as MIN_AXIS and MAX_AXIS in procedures RAY_TRACER and FIRST_POINT, can be speeded up somewhat by sorting the three values of t and then deciding if the next cell is in the direction of a vertex, edge, or face. Incorporate this change.

7.57. Let us examine more closely the convention that for a ray to pass through a cell (as well as intersect an object), it must enter and exit the cell (object) at two distinct points. For example, consider Figure 7.17. Assume the existence of a ray that passes from cell 5 to cell 11 through the SW corner of cell 5. What could go wrong if we do not adhere to this convention and say that the ray passes through cell 4 before reaching cell 11?

7.58. Wyvill and Kunii [Wyvi85] identify the next cell by calculating the coordinates of a point (i.e., POINT) that is purportedly guaranteed to be in that cell and then locate it by use of a process similar to that given by FIND_3D_BLOCK. They do not compute a direction as done in RAY_TRACER. Their method of calculating POINT is similar to the method used in RAY_-TRACER with the following minor difference. They subtract SIGN_M[I] from the numerator of the t value corresponding to the Ith coordinate of the exit point; instead we add the term SIGN_M[I] * CHANGE(DIRECT(C),I) in the computation of POINT[I]. Their algorithm is given below:

```
begin
  rational array T[{'X', 'Y', 'Z'}];
  axis I,K;
  for I in {'X', 'Y', 'Z'} do
    begin
      NUM(T[I]) ← CORNER[I] – SIGN_M[I]*W – B[I] – SIGN_M[I];
      DEN(T[I]) ← M[I];
    end;
  K ← 'X';
  for I in {'Y', 'Z'} do
    begin
      if abs(NUM(T[K])*DEN(T[I])) > abs(NUM(T[I])*DEN(T[K])) then K←I;
    end;
  for I in {'X', 'Y', 'Z'} do
    POINT[I] ← M[I]*NUM(T[K])/DEN(T[K])+B[I];
end;
```

Show that this algorithm works for ray R in Figure 7.17.

7.59. Modify Figure 7.17 so that cell 3 is subdivided in the same way as the SE quadrant of the entire quadtree. Show that Wyvill and Kunii's algorithm can yield an erroneous result by tracing ray R through the modified figure.

7.60. One way to fix Wyvill and Kunii's algorithm is to remove the subtraction of SIGN_M[I] from the numerator of the t value corresponding to the Ith coordinate of the exit point. Instead SIGN_M[J] is subtracted in the computation of POINT[J] where J is the coordinate corresponding to the minimum value of t. Wyvill and Kunii claim that it is not necessary to compute the exact direction of motion. In particular, when a ray reaches more than one boundary simultaneously, they arbitrarily pick one of the boundaries and move in a direction perpendicular to it. The fix described above is consistent with this claim. Prove or disprove that the resulting algorithm will function correctly.

7.61. Simplify procedure RAY_TRACER by avoiding the setup of a record of type *cell* to be transmitted to procedure RAY_INTERSECTS_OBJECT_IN_CELL. In addition, speed up the code by removing procedures COMPARE_T and NEXT_CELL_DIRECTION and replacing them with an inline computation of the direction of motion. Note that there is no longer a need to precompute the values of CYX, CZX, and CZY.

7.62. Incorporate reflection into procedure RAY_TRACER.

7.63. The feasibility of procedure RAY_TRACER as implemented here depends on the number of reflections (or refractions) undergone by the ray. What is a reasonable number, and what are the storage requirements in order to perform the intersection and ray-tracing calculations without error?

7.64. Suppose that we want to incorporate the notion of time in our scenes. This means that we add another dimension, say 'T', so that 'P' and 'M' correspond to the past and future, respectively. This is of use in dynamic interference detection [Same85g], path planning among moving obstacles [Fuji89], and even for motion blur. Modify procedure RAY_TRACER and the associated procedures to enable tracing a ray through a four-dimensional scene. You must also modify the functions CHANGE, FACE_DIR, EDGE_DIR, VERTEX_DIR and OT_GTEQ_NEIGHBOR. You will have to create an additional table for the situation that all four values of t are the same.

7.65. Can you generalize procedure RAY_TRACER to handle scenes of arbitrary dimensionality?

7.66. Kaplan [Kapl87] makes use of a bintree instead of an octree. Modify procedure RAY_-
TRACER to handle a bintree representation of a three-dimensional scene. Can you generalize it for a scene of arbitrary dimensionality?

7.67. Why would you want to use a bintree instead of an octree in ray tracing?

7.68. Implement ray tracing by using just a top-down method. The idea is that at each node,
the ray is clipped against the node's block, and if the result is nonempty, the appropriate
link is descended.

7.69. How does the top-down ray-tracing method discussed in Exercise 7.68 compare with the
bottom-up method of procedure RAY_TRACER? In particular, when would you use one
over the other?

7.70. The process of projecting a ray into succeeding blocks is similar to the task of drawing a
rasterized straight line. A simple way of doing this on a two-dimensional grid is the digital differential analyzer (DDA) algorithm [Roge85]. Bresenham [Bres65] has improved
on it by devising an algorithm for drawing lines on a two-dimensional grid that uses only
integer arithmetic, has no division operations, and makes use of only addition, subtraction, and multiplication by two (i.e., a shift). Can you speed up procedure RAY_TRACER
for a two-dimensional scene in an analogous manner by removing division and multiplication operations other than by powers of two?

7.71. Extend the result of Exercise 7.70 to a three-dimensional scene.

7.72. Perform experimental tests comparing the efficiency of ray tracing using the fixed-grid
approach of Fujimoto, Tanaka, and Iwata [Fuji86] with some of the bucket PM octree
variants discussed in this book and in Chapter 5 of [Same90a].

7.2.5 Discussion

The principal benefit of space tracing (i.e., making use of scene coherence) is that the
number of objects that must be intersected with each ray is reduced significantly.
However, in such a case we find ourselves testing a given ray against the same object
several times (recall the discussion of ray R in Figure 7.17); but see [Arna87, Sche87,
Clea88]. As an example of the possible speedup, Glassner [Glas84] reports that tracing 597,245 rays in a particular scene of 1,536 objects required over 42 hours using
nonoctree ray-tracing techniques, while less than 3 hours were required when using
octrees. Another scene that was estimated to require 141 hours using nonoctree
methods was analyzed in slightly over 5 hours using octrees.

In practice, the computation time of space tracing is independent of the number
of objects in the scene. Instead it is dominated by the visible complexity of the
scene—that is, the proportion of the rendered pixels that require shading. This proportion is bounded by the sampling resolution of the image space. An equivalent
justification for this independence is that as the number of objects in the scene
increases, the visible portion of each object decreases. An additional factor in the
speedup of the ray-tracing process is the fact that when one object covers other
smaller objects, we determine the closest ray-object intersection first. Of course,
building the octree of the image does require some time. However, the octree must be
built only once, after which it can be used for a number of different viewpoints.

Note that making use of scene coherence is not the only way to speed up ray tracing. Further speedups are obtained by use of special-purpose hardware [Pull87] and parallel architectures [Dipp84]. In fact, these hardware methods can be augmented to obtain additional speedups by taking advantage of scene coherence.

One of the problems with implementing ray tracing as described here is that for each pixel, only one ray is traced. Thus there is no way to model the interaction between the boundaries of the pixels. The result is an aliased image (i.e., it has jagged edges) and is a direct consequence of undersampling the image. The viewer observes the effects of this phenomenon at regions that exhibit abrupt changes in intensity as well as at locations where small objects that fall between the sampling points have disappeared.

Whitted [Whit80] suggests a quadtree-like solution that has been shown to work well in previewing applications by Jansen and van Wijk [Jans83]. A pixel is defined as a rectangular region, say A, and samples are taken at its four corners. If their intensities are relatively equal and no small object lies between them, the average of the four values is taken as the intensity for the pixel's region. Otherwise A is subdivided into four regions of equal size, and the algorithm is reapplied recursively to these regions. This process is executed until the terminating criteria are satisfied or a predefined maximum level of decomposition is attained. The final intensity value is obtained by weighting the contribution of each subregion by its area.

Distributed ray tracing [Cook84] is an alternative approach to reducing the effects of aliasing. It attempts to ensure a better statistical distribution for the samples within a pixel's region by using Monte Carlo methods. This method can also be used to model motion blur if time is treated as a fourth spatial dimension (see Exercise 7.64).

Exercises

7.73. Implement Whitted's [Whit80] quadtree-like solution to the aliasing problem. How does its use affect the octree corresponding to the space through which the rays are traced?

7.74. Design an algorithm for viewing a CSG representation by using ray tracing.

7.3 BEAM TRACING

Beam tracing is a generalization of ray tracing that uses image-space coherence. A beam is defined as a viewing pyramid with an apex at the viewpoint. Beam tracing treats the ray as a solid angle with a finite polygonal cross-section. This cross-section need not be convex. Also, it need not be connected. In traditional ray tracing, the cross-section of the beam is a single pixel (actually a point). Beam tracing usually assumes that the scene is described using a boundary model (*BRep*) (i.e., polygons). Thus the reflections are linear transformations. Refractions can be approximated in the same way. In particular, the reflection of a beam from a planar surface, unlike from curved surfaces, can be approximated by a pyramidal cone that is a beam. Beams in the shape of cones [Aman84] are a special case of beam tracing.

One criticism of ray tracing is that it does not easily make use of image-space coherence [Dado85]. Beam tracing exploits this coherence by bundling neighboring groups of rays into coherent beams of light (hence the term *beam tracing*) and tracing them in parallel. This use of coherence speeds the rendering algorithm. Moreover, by being able to identify the boundaries between homogeneous regions in the scene with more precision, we can eliminate some of the aliasing problems commonly associated with ray-traced images due to the point sampling nature of ray tracing. This is achieved by applying antialiasing techniques to the resulting regions.

The beam-tracing approach of resolving aliasing problems is to be contrasted with Whitted's [Whit80] technique of adaptive subdivision of pixels in areas of large-intensity changes and casting rays through its corners. Whitted's technique makes use of heuristics, and thus at times, it can result in an inadequate amount of subdivision, in which case aliasing problems persist or, alternatively, in too much subdivision, in which case an unnecessary amount of work has been performed. In particular, the amount of computation necessary can increase markedly, especially in pixels with a large variance of the intensity. Second, small details may fall through the cracks of the sample points and thereby be missed. This is especially true for objects that are reflected or refracted by other objects.

Interestingly, beam tracing originally arose as a solution to the problem of simulating the acoustics of a concert hall. Given the positions of the source and receiver, the goal was to simulate the acoustics encountered at the position of the receiver. A sound beam, emanating from the source position, is modeled as a solid angle with a polygonal cross-section and is traced through the room. The effect of the beam on the receiver depends on factors such as reflection, diffraction, and absorption.

The acoustical task differs from the hidden-surface task in computer graphics in that the problem is dynamic—that is, there are many viewing (receiving) positions. As the beam strikes a surface, it is split into new beams, each of which must be traced, with the surface serving as a new source position. The goal is to preprocess the geometric model of the scene (room) so that the beam/surface intersection task is facilitated.

Generally the scene is assumed to consist of objects having planar polygonal faces. In such a case, the beam-tracing solution of the hidden-surface task reduces to the identification of the visible portions of the planar faces intersected by the beams. The presence of reflection and refraction forces recursive solutions in terms of the newly created beams. This means that we may have an exponential growth in the number of beams, and hence it is useful to preprocess the scene.

Most implementations of beam tracing involve the use of solutions to classical problems in computational geometry. In particular, the hidden-surface task can be decomposed into three subtasks: intersection, sorting, and clipping. First we must determine the surfaces that are intersected by the beam. Next we sort them to find the closest one to the viewpoint. Finally we clip the surfaces to fit the viewing window.

These subtasks are similar to those that comprise a ray-tracing solution. The intersection task is one of intersecting two solids, whereas in ray tracing, we are intersecting a line with a solid. The sorting problem is one of ordering surfaces instead of points. The clipping problem does not arise in ray tracing unless a pixel value involves a number of surfaces (e.g., Whitted's [Whit80] method of using adaptive subdivision to avoid aliasing).

Heckbert and Hanrahan's [Heck84] beam tracer starts with the entire viewing pyramid as the initial beam. They make use of an intermediate data structure termed a *beam tree*, which is analogous to the ray tree of Whitted [Whit80]. The similarity is that the edges in the ray and beam trees correspond to rays and beams, respectively. On the other hand, whereas each node in the ray tree corresponds to a single surface, each node in the beam tree often corresponds to more than one surface. Each surface may give rise to a reflected and a refracted beam.

Once the beam tree has been built, the projection plane is swept through the scene. During this process, beam-surface intersections are computed, and occlusion is determined using a variant of the Weiler-Atherton hidden-surface algorithm [Weil77]. At each intersection, reflected and refracted subbeams are created and recursively traced through the scene.

Dadoun et al. [Dado82, Dado85] take a different approach to the problem. They point out that for a beam-tracing solution to be efficient, it must not test all faces exhaustively for intersection with the beam. Instead it is better to form clusters and test them for intersection. The idea is to do some preprocessing so that the subsequent search time is reduced. This is achieved by using a representation of the scene in the form of a hierarchical approximation of it. Their solutions take reflection into account but do not handle refraction. Initially Dadoun et al. proposed the use of the minimum volume bounding box and convex hull approximations [Dado82].

Each of these methods has advantages and disadvantages. The advantage of the convex hull approximation over the bounding box method is that the convex hull provides a 'tighter' approximation. Thus it is less likely to report false intersections of a beam with the approximation of an object. Also the convex hull approximation is easier to compute than the bounding box (see Exercise 7.86). On the other hand, operations such as the intersection of a beam with a bounding box are faster than its intersection with a convex hull; intersection of a 4-sided window with a bounding box takes a constant amount of time (useful for clipping), while it takes $O(\log_2 n)$ time for a convex hull of n points. Moreover, the storage requirements of a bounding box approximation are smaller.

Nevertheless, the choice between the two methods is not clear-cut. Dadoun et al. feel that the best solution is most likely a hybrid one that uses a bounding box near the root where the space savings would be the largest, although the intersection operations, while more probable, are inexpensive. The convex hull approximation should be used at deeper levels of the tree since its tighter fit reduces the amount of clipping.

More recently, Dadoun et al. [Dado85] propose the use of what they term a *Hierarchical Scene Representation* (HSR). It is a variant of the binary space partition (BSP) tree of Fuchs, Kedem, and Naylor [Fuch80] (see Sections 1.3 and 7.1.5). Recall that the BSP tree induces a partition of the three-dimensional space that consists of multifaceted solids (i.e., polyhedra) that are convex. Generally a BSP tree node at depth n yields an n-faceted convex solid. To form the HSR, each node in the BSP tree contains the approximation of the part of the scene that is in the polyhedron of the node. The approximations are formed by removing bounding halfspaces (i.e., sides). The motivation is that at the shallower depths of the tree (i.e., near the root), the approximations get larger.

Beam tracing with the HSR proceeds in the following manner. The initial beam corresponds to the entire viewing pyramid. The BSP tree is traversed starting at the root, and a determination is made if its HSR convex approximation of the entire scene intersects the beam. If no intersection is detected, then stop. Otherwise if the node is a nonleaf node, then the tree is descended, and the subtree corresponding to the side of the splitting plane that is nearer to the apex of the beam is processed first. The other subtree is processed next. Notice the 'front-to-back' nature of the traversal. When the node is a leaf node (i.e., a polygon in the scene), its polygon is clipped out of the beam and saved for later rendering.

In addition, if reflection is possible, a reflection beam is constructed, and it is recursively traced through the scene by starting at the root of the BSP tree. The actual intersection of the beam with the polygons can also be implemented by approximating the beam in the same manner used to approximate the polygons. In particular, detecting the intersection takes $O(\log_2 b \cdot \log_2 v)$ time for a beam of $b + 1$ points (i.e., the apex and b bounding rays) and an HSR element of v points [Dobk83]. Finding the nearest intersected polygon to the viewpoint is implicit in the order in which the BSP tree and HSR elements are processed. Thus there is no need for a special sorting step. Clipping can be achieved by using techniques such as the Weiler-Atherton hidden surface algorithm [Weil77].

Beam tracing exploits the coherence between similar rays (see also [Spee85]). This coherence is used in a different manner by Arvo and Kirk [Arvo87] in conjunction with recursive decomposition. In particular, they observe that neighboring rays tend to intersect the same objects. This property motivates them to represent the rays as points in a five-dimensional space (called a ray space). A ray is defined by the x, y, and z coordinate values of its origin and the θ and ϕ parameters of its direction as it leaves the origin. Actually θ and ϕ are difficult to work with. Thus Arvo and Kirk use 'uv' rectangular coordinates on the faces of a cube, which they term a *direction cube*.

The space is organized by a bucket variant of a PR bintree (recall Section 1.3). In essence, the space is split by cycling through the dimensions; the first split is on x, then y, z, θ, ϕ, x, and so on. A node is split whenever the number of different objects it intersects exceeds a predetermined value known as its capacity. A node corresponds to a hypercube (i.e., cell) in the five-dimensional space. This hypercube is analogous to a beam in three-dimensional space and corresponds to an unbounded three-dimensional volume formed by rays. The origins of the rays in a specific hypercube are in close proximity to each other; similarly the orientations of the rays are approximately in the same direction.

Ray tracing in this environment requires each cell to contain a list of all the objects in the scene that are intersected by the rays in the cell. Computing this list of objects is a nontrivial task and is done using lazy evaluation (e.g., [Hend80, p. 223]). In particular, it is done when the cell is visited for the first time by a ray if it has not already been done on behalf of a ray that has visited the cell earlier. It is in this step that ray coherence is exploited (see [Arvo87] for the detailed mechanics of this process).

Given a ray, the list of objects intersected by the ray is obtained by executing a point location operation in the five-dimensional space where the ray is the point (see Section 6.1). Once the list of objects is obtained, their intersection with the ray is calculated, and the object that results in the closest intersection to the origin of the ray is identified. This object is used to determine the rays emitted from the object, and the entire process is repeated. Note that the new rays will most likely be in another cell since their origin and orientation will usually be quite different.

Exercises

7.75. How would you compare the efficiency of a beam-tracing solution with a ray-tracing solution?

7.76. Implement beam tracing by modeling the viewplane as a region quadtree and letting the beams correspond to blocks of varying size in the quadtree.

7.77. Implement beam tracing with a representation that partitions the scene into rectangular regions. This means that the partition planes must be orthogonal.

7.78. Repeat Exercise 7.77 with a representation that uses regular decomposition to partition the scene (e.g., an octree).

7.79. Assuming that the BSP tree exists already, prove that the HSR can be built in time proportional to the number of nodes in the BSP tree.

7.80. Consider the construction of the HSR. Suppose that instead of using an approximation that removes bounding halfspaces, you use an approximation that removes vertices. As in the other approximation, the first element is the polyhedron itself. What is the disadvantage of using such an approximation?

7.81. In constructing the BSP tree (see Section 7.1.5), we adopted the convention that whenever a polygon intersects a splitting plane, the polygon is subdivided and the portions placed in the appropriate subtrees. This can be avoided by inserting a pointer to the polygon in both subtrees and incorporating the polygon into both of their convex hulls. What are the ramifications of such a modification on the various tasks in the beam-tracing process?

7.82. Discuss how to incorporate refraction in the HSR solution to beam tracing.

7.83. Most beam-tracing solutions start with the entire viewing pyramid as the initial beam. An alternative is to form the initial beams by first performing a hidden-surface algorithm. Discuss the advantages and disadvantages of such an approach.

7.84. Discuss the geometric problems associated with implementing beam tracing when the initial beams are cones with circular cross-sections whose width is equal to that of a pixel in the viewplane.

7.85. Give an $O(n \cdot \log_2 n)$ time algorithm to construct the convex hull of n points in three dimensions.

7.86. Suppose that you are given a set of n points in three dimensions and the h points that form the convex hull. Explain why standard divide-and-conquer methods cannot be used to construct the minimum volume bounding box approximation of the n points. Be careful on how you define what constitutes a 'minimum volume' bounding box. There are many possible definitions!

7.87. Give an $O(\log_2 k \cdot \log_2 n)$ time algorithm to detect whether a three-dimensional object whose convex hull approximation consists of n points intersects a beam formed by k rays.

7.88.   Give an $O(\log_2 n)$ time algorithm to detect whether a four-sided window intersects a three-dimensional convex hull approximation of n points.

7.89.   Give an $O(\log_2 k)$ time algorithm to detect whether a beam consisting of k rays intersects a bounding box.

7.90.   Implement ray tracing by using Arvo and Kirk's method of representing rays as points in a five-dimensional space.

7.4   RADIOSITY

While for many years ray tracing was the dominant approach to the realistic rendering of images, newer and different techniques have recently emerged. One such method is the radiosity approach [Gora84]. Instead of modeling light as particles bouncing around in a scene (as is done in ray tracing), the radiosity approach models light as energy whose distribution tends toward a stable equilibrium. In other words, the radiosity approach treats light as if it were heat; that is, light sources behave as sources of heat, and surfaces that reflect light behave as surfaces that reflect heat. Below the terms *reflect, radiate,* and *emit* are used interchangeably to denote the light leaving a patch where a *patch* is a portion of a surface of an object in the scene.

Although energy in the form of light and heat is normally viewed as a continuous flow, the radiosity method uses a discrete simulation of the flow so that an approximate rendering can be computed. This section contains only a brief general description of this method and points out how and where hierarchical data structures can be used to improve its performance.

A scene is viewed as a collection of patches (recall Section 7.1.6) where the light emitted by the surface of a given patch, say Q, is either constant (e.g., for a light source) or a linear combination of the light falling on Q from all the other patches. The simplifying assumption is made that the surfaces are Lambertian diffuse reflectors; light is reflected uniformly from the surface in all directions. This restriction can be lifted [Imme86] at the expense of greatly increasing the size of the problem. Of course, many patches do not contribute light to a particular patch because they are occluded by closer patches.

In essence, radiosity converts the image-rendering problem to one of solving a set of simultaneous linear equations. Each equation represents a portion of the discrete simulation of the light flow, that is, the portion of the light from the rest of the scene that is eventually reflected by the patch. Furthermore the equation for patch Q depends on which patches are visible from Q. The approximate form of this equation is $L_i = \sum_{j=1}^{n} HID(i, j) \cdot P(i, j) \cdot L_j$ where L_i is the amount of light emitted from patch i; $P(i, j)$ is the portion of the light emitted from patch j that can reach patch i; and $HID(i, j)$ is a Boolean function indicating whether patch j is hidden from patch i by some obstruction (i.e., whether patches i and j are mutually invisible).

The process of deriving the equations (i.e., the determination of the values of their coefficients) that describe the interactions among the patches was the computational bottleneck in the initial presentation of radiosity [Gora84, Cohe85a]. Deriving the equations is straightforward, although the exact mechanics [Gora84, Cohe85a] are beyond the scope of this book. However, this process can be facilitated, in part, by observing that if two patches, say Q and R, are mutually invisible, the coefficient of the term in the equation of Q (or R) associated with R (or Q) will be zero.

The physical interpretation of the concept of mutual invisibility is that light emitted by one of the patches cannot reach the other patch without first being reflected by yet a third patch. A geometric interpretation of this concept is that two patches, say Q and R, are mutually invisible (i.e., $HID(Q,R) = 0$) only if there does not exist a pair of points p_Q on Q and p_R on R such that a straight line can be drawn between them without intersecting a third patch or passing through the interior of an object in the scene.

The determination of which terms in the equations have zero coefficients corresponds to a hidden-surface task among the patches. It must be solved separately for each patch—that is, if we have M patches, we must solve the hidden-surface interactions among each of the $\binom{M}{2}$ combinations of patches. Worse, we need to solve these tasks not just for a point on a patch but for every point on the surface of the patch. The solution of these tasks could be made easier by using a data structure such as the octree to organize the elements of the scene—that is, the three-dimensional space occupied by the patches. This simplifies the determination of which patches are hidden with respect to the other patches, thereby yielding the zero coefficients.

Unfortunately, the application of radiosity to the rendering of more complicated scenes results in a marked increase in the number of equations necessary to model the scene. This has led to a shift of the computational bottleneck so that it is now associated with the problem of solving the simultaneous equations. Nevertheless, recursive subdivision can still be used.

Instead of recursively subdividing the three-dimensional space occupied by the patches, Cohen et al. [Cohe86] recursively subdivide the surfaces of the patches. This subdivision takes place in the parametric space of the patch in a manner similar to Catmull's algorithm (see Section 7.1.6). As with Catmull's algorithm, recursive subdivision of a patch (described below) does not actually require the construction of a quadtree. Instead the data are simply aggregated in a manner equivalent to the application of a particular leaf criterion to the organization of the surface of a scene.

Observe that to determine the rough flow of light through a scene, the number of patches needed to model the objects in the scene is considerably smaller than the number of patches needed to depict features of the scene caused by the actual flow of light through the scene (e.g., shadow boundaries). For example, suppose we are modeling a scene that corresponds to a room containing boxes. In this case, a rather coarse grid can be used to represent the surface of the room. However, the accurate representation of the shadows that the boxes cast on the walls will usually require a much finer grid. This is especially true for area light sources that cause varying shadow intensities (e.g., fluorescent tubes that cannot be modeled accurately as point light sources).

Of course, the more patches that are used to represent a scene, the more expensive is the solution required to solve the corresponding set of equations since there are more equations with a concomitant increase in terms. In particular, the number of equations is proportional to the number of patches. This can potentially lead to a quadratic number of interpatch relations.

Note that we do not know how many patches will be needed to represent the results of the radiosity calculation until after it has been performed. Early work on radiosity simply guessed the maximum number. However, with more complicated scenes, the guesses are overly pessimistic, thereby resulting in needlessly inefficient algorithms. Recursive subdivision performed in an adaptive manner avoids this problem.

Cohen et al. [Cohe86] propose a two-step algorithm to reduce the number of equations that must be solved simultaneously. The basic approach is first to solve the set of simultaneous equations corresponding to the light flow among the patches used to model the surfaces of the scene. In the second step, patches whose intensity value computed by the first step differs greatly from that of their neighbors are subsequently decomposed into smaller subpatches, termed *elements*, via a regular recursive decomposition (i.e., equal surface area).

The rationale for further subdivision is the assumption that the intensity variance in the scene is a continuous function, meaning that sharp discontinuities are an artifact of undersampling the intensity function (i.e., the grid was too coarse). The result is that the scene consists of a collection of patches (each corresponding to a small portion of the surface of the scene) where each patch is represented by a quadtree whose leaf nodes are elements. The leaf criterion used to construct the quadtree is one based on computing the absolute intensity difference across the portion of the surface approximated by the leaf and checking whether it is below a given threshold.

Now, instead of deriving a new set of equations to represent the interactions among all the elements of each of the patches, the new set of equations assumes that only one patch has been decomposed, and the remaining patches are treated as if they have a constant intensity value, that is, the one computed in the first step. This is equivalent to an assumption that the cumulative effect of elements of patch Q on other patches is approximately the same as that of Q. In other words, for each collection of elements corresponding to a particular patch, a set of simultaneous equations is derived on the basis of the individual variable intensity values of the elements in the collection and the treatment of other patches in the scene as though they have constant intensity. This greatly reduces the number of equations to be solved, with only a modest reduction in the accuracy of the solution.

The approach of Cohen et al. has several advantages. First, by applying adaptive decomposition to the individual patches, it prevents the size of the set of linear equations (i.e., the number of terms) from growing quadratically. Second, it assumes that the decomposition of a particular patch, say Q, into elements does not change the total amount of light that is reflected by Q and that is therefore incident on the other patches.

The second advantage means that after solving the problem of determining the light flow with the initial set of patches, the individual behavior of the light flow within a patch can be solved independently of the individual behavior within the other patches. In fact, the result is an asymmetric relation between the effects of patches and elements of patches. For each element in a patch, we compute the effect of the light from the remaining patches. However, the effect of individual elements of patch Q on patch R is taken collectively; that is, the fact that Q has been decomposed into elements has no effect on the amount of light reflected by R.

As an example, Cohen et al. [Cohe86] report on an application of these techniques to a scene whose objects required 58 patches and whose optical features (e.g., those caused by shadow boundaries) required 1,135 elements. Deriving its radiosity equations took 22.49 minutes, and solving them took 1.10 minutes. However, a simple decomposition of the same scene into 829 patches (instead of using the adaptive approach) required 90.10 minutes to derive the equations and 6.36 minutes to solve them.

Of course, although the solution of the radiosity equations is a major part of the image-rendering process, other issues remain. For example, once the radiosity equations have been solved, we must still render the scene from a particular viewpoint. The scene described in the previous example required 14.67 minutes to render 1,135 elements and 14.16 minutes to render the 829 patches. To improve the rendering time, data structures that facilitate the solution of the standard hidden-surface task are necessary. Earlier it was suggested that the octree is an appropriate data structure for this task.

Exercises

7.91. Given an arbitrary face of a leaf in an octree representation of a scene, show how to find efficiently the set of all faces of leaf nodes that are visible from the face. Note that such a face can be thought of as a patch in terms of the radiosity method. Thus this would be an efficient way to calculate the *HID* function in the equation that relates the amount of light energy that impinges on the patch to the amount of energy emitted from the patch. Does this improvement in the efficiency of the computation of the *HID* function have a significant effect on the speed of deriving these equations?

7.92. For all faces of all leaf nodes in an octree representation of a scene, show how to find efficiently the set of all faces of leaf nodes visible from each of the other faces. Note that you should be able to do this in a more efficient way than just repeatedly applying the solution of Exercise 7.91 to each face in the scene.

7.93. Implement a radiosity solution where the scene is organized using an octree. Try to use the PM octree approach similar to that described by Navazo, Ayala, and Brunet [Nava86b], which makes use of biquadratic patches.

QUADTREE APPROXIMATION AND COMPRESSION

8

Some of the primary motivations for the development of the region quadtree data structure are to save space (in comparison to the binary array representation) and to enable viewing an image at different levels of resolution, thereby yielding a progressive approximation. By progressive, it is meant that as more of the image is transmitted, the receiving device progressively constructs a better approximation. At the end of the transmission, the original image is reconstructed perfectly.

Image representations that are based on progressive approximations contrast with more conventional representations (e.g., runlength encoding, chain code) that yield only a description of a subset of the image before completion of the transmission. Runlength encoding is used when the image is transmitted a line at a time. It serves as the basis of most facsimile transmission methods. A progressive transmission means that a crude picture is received first and the details come later, thereby enabling browsing operations.

In this chapter, we are interested in the quality of the approximations resulting from the use of the region quadtree for binary images and in the amount of compression attainable. Compression here does not mean saving space over that required by the binary array representation. This saving depends on the complexity of the image (e.g., how it is decomposed into blocks) and on the technique used to represent the quadtree (e.g., pointers, locational codes, DF-expressions; for more details see Chapter 2).

Of course, compression can always be achieved by using results from coding theory, such as Huffman coding [Huff52, Lele87], to encode the individual blocks or groups of pixels (e.g., [Know80, Cohe85b]). Instead here we focus on compression in terms of reducing the number of blocks in the quadtree while still reconstructing the image exactly. Note that the quadtree medial axis transform [Same83a] discussed in Section 9.3.1 also exhibits compression, albeit in a different way.

This chapter is organized as follows. First we examine a number of quadtree approximation methods based on a breadth-first traversal of the quadtree that discard all nodes below a given level (i.e., the tree is truncated). This is followed by a definition of a sequence of approximations to quadtrees based on forests (see Section 2.1.4). These methods often lead to compression because the total number of elements in the final representation is bounded by the minimum of the number of black and white nodes in the original quadtree. This presentation is based on work described in [Same85c]. Finally, pyramid-based methods are discussed briefly. These methods are of interest primarily because they are progressive yet do not incur the overhead of additional storage. However, they do not yield compression without the use of coding techniques to encode the values of the pixels or the blocks.

Note that with the exception of the pyramid-based methods, the discussion is restricted to two-dimensional binary images. One way to extend the results to gray-scale images is to use the approach of Kawaguchi et al. [Kawa83] that encodes image data of 2^m gray-scale levels as a sequence of m binary-valued quadtrees as mentioned in Section 1.3. Extension of any of these methods to multidimensional images (i.e., $d \geq 3$) is straightforward.

8.1 TRUNCATION-BASED APPROXIMATION METHODS

By virtue of its hierarchical structure, the region quadtree lends itself to serve as an image approximation device. Truncating the tree (i.e., ignoring all nodes below a certain level) yields a crude approximation. Ranade, Rosenfeld, and Samet [Rana82] define two basic variants, termed an inner and outer approximation. Given an image I, the *inner approximation*, IB(k), is the binary image defined by the black nodes at levels $\geq k$. Figures 8.2a and 8.2b show IB(2) and IB(1), respectively, for Figure 8.1. The *outer approximation*, OB(k), is the binary image defined by the black nodes at levels $\geq k$ and the gray nodes at level k. Figures 8.3a and 8.3b show OB(2) and OB(1), respectively, for Figure 8.1.

Often we find it useful to compare the approximations. We use $\subseteq$ and $\supseteq$ to indicate set inclusion. We say that A $\subseteq$ B and B $\supseteq$ A imply that the space spanned by A is a subset of the space spanned by B. It can be shown that IB(n) $\subseteq$ IB($n-1$) $\subseteq$ $\cdots$ $\subseteq$ IB(0) = I and OB(n) $\supseteq$ OB($n-1$) $\supseteq$ $\cdots$ $\supseteq$ OB(0) = I.

Alternatively we can approximate the image by using its complement, $\bar{I}$ — that is, the white blocks. We define IW(k) and OW(k) in an analogous manner to that of IB(k) and OB(k), respectively, except in terms of white blocks. It can be shown that IW(n) $\subseteq$ IW($n-1$) $\subseteq$ $\cdots$ $\subseteq$ IW(0) = $\bar{I}$, and OW(n) $\supseteq$ OW($n-1$) $\supseteq$ $\cdots$ $\supseteq$ OW(0) = $\bar{I}$. Moreover, Ranade, Rosenfeld, and Samet [Rana82] show that the outer approximations to I are actually the complement of the inner approximations to $\bar{I}$ — that is,

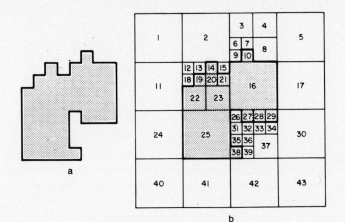

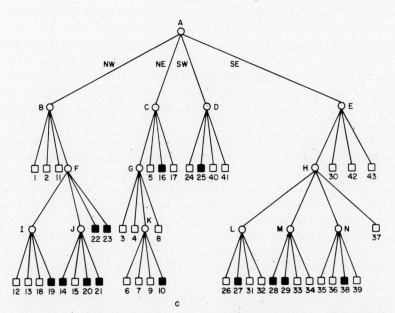

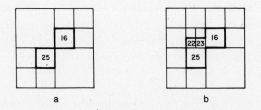

Figure 8.1 (a) A region, (b) its maximal blocks, and (c) the corresponding quadtree. Blocks in the region are shaded, background blocks are blank.

Figure 8.2 (a) IB(2) and (b) IB(1) for Figure 8.1

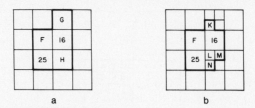

Figure 8.3   (a) OB(2) and (b) OB(1) for Figure 8.1

$OB(k) = \overline{IW(k)}$ (see Exercise 8.1). Similarly it can be shown that the inner approximations to I are actually the complement of the outer approximations to $\bar{I}$ — that is, $IB(k) = \overline{OW(k)}$ (see Exercise 8.2).

The sequences of inner and outer approximations defined above are used by Ranade, Rosenfeld, and Samet [Rana82] for shape approximation. The inner approximation treats gray nodes as white, and the outer approximation treats them as black. This may lead to abrupt transitions at successive levels of approximation. To alleviate this potential problem, Rosenfeld, Samet, Shaffer, and Webber [Rose82a] propose a quadtree truncation technique that treats a gray node as black or white depending on the type of the majority of its constituent pixels. This is shown to lead to a gentler degradation of the image in contrast with the abruptness of the inner and outer approximation methods.

The truncation-based approximation methods described above are breadth-first traversals of the quadtree. They do not yield any compression over the number of leaf nodes in the quadtree. Knowlton [Know80] addresses the same problem by using a variant of the bintree to represent the image and makes use of coding methods to achieve compression. The image is transmitted in order of a breadth-first traversal of the bintree. All nodes are labeled black, white, or mixed. The basic unit of decomposition is a pixel, and these are aggregated into 2×3 rectangles. At this level, all nodes are described using a 7-valued entity corresponding to the number of constituent black pixels. For the nodes at this level, the configuration of the pixels is encoded by a variable-length code.

To obtain a better approximation, Knowlton suggests that mixed nodes be further classified by transmitting a 5-valued number indicating the shade of gray for each block. Whenever a block of size greater than 2×3 is described as black or white, it ceases to participate in the remainder of the transmission process. Knowlton reports compression factors as high as 8:1 (i.e., for a $2^n \times 2^n$ image, instead of transmitting 2^{2n} bits, as few as 2^{2n-3} bits are necessary). It should be noted that these high compression factors do not necessarily result from the use of a bintree over a quadtree. Instead they are due to the uniformity of the image (i.e., blocks of white and black), and when this is not the case, they result from coding groups of pixels.

Exercises

8.1.   Prove that the outer approximations to I are the same as the complement of the inner approximations to $\bar{I}$ — that is, $OB(k) = \overline{IW(k)}$.

8.2. Prove that the inner approximations to I are the same as the complement of the outer approximations to $\bar{\text{I}}$ — that is, IB(k) = $\overline{\text{OW}(k)}$.

8.3. One of the problems associated with inner approximation methods such as IB is that they can lead to a loss of connectivity because some nodes appear at a lower level (i.e., deeper) in the quadtree than the level of approximation. Give an example of this phenomenon. Exactly the opposite problem plagues outer approximation methods such as OB in that they can lead to the creation of holes where there may not be any. Give an example of this phenomenon.

8.2 FOREST-BASED APPROXIMATION METHODS

In Section 2.1.1, while comparing the FL and VL locational codes, it was mentioned that sorting the list of nodes in ascending order of their VL locational codes leads to a useful approximation of the image in the sense that the result is a breadth-first traversal of the quadtree. Although the earlier discussion was in the context of the list of VL locational codes for all of the black nodes in an image represented by a region quadtree, the approximation property also holds for the nodes comprising the black forest (see Section 2.1.4).

For example, the nodes comprising the black forest of Figure 8.1 appear in the order 25, 16, F, M, 27, 38, and 10. This order is a partial ordering $(\text{S}, \geq)$ such that $\text{S}_i \geq \text{S}_{i+1}$ means that the block spanned by S_i is $\geq$ in size than the block spanned by S_{i+1}. In fact, for a breadth-first traversal, we only need to process the nodes in an order that satisfies the above partial ordering. Of course, it is clear that a sorted list is just one of many possible orderings satisfying this partial ordering. Thus the black forest can also yield an approximation to the quadtree when we treat all nodes S_i as black and all remaining nodes as white.

The remainder of this section expands on the use of forests to approximate images. At times, they result in exact representations that also yield image compression. A $2^n \times 2^n$ binary image is assumed, and I denotes the black regions. Unless stated otherwise, when a quadtree is mentioned as a forest or as a list of nodes, each node is represented using its VL locational code.

8.2.1 Definitions and Approximation Quality

The *black forest approximation* is defined as follows. Let FB(P) be the quadtree constructed by coloring black the roots of the subquadtrees comprising the black forest of the quadtree rooted at node P. FB(P) is empty when P is a white leaf node and P when P is a black leaf node. For example, in Figure 8.1, we have FB(A) = {25, 16, F, M, 27, 38, 10}. Note that any node can be approximated by a black forest of quadtrees, not just the root of the quadtree corresponding to the image. Thus we can approximate an image by a sequence of black forests of quadtrees where the sequence is defined by replacing nonleaf node components of a black forest by their black forests. More formally, let FBB(i), $0 \leq i \leq n$, be defined as follows:

$$
\text{FBB}(i) = \begin{cases} \{\text{FB}(root)\} & i = n \\ \{j \mid j \in \text{FBB}(i+1) \text{ and not}(\text{GRAY}(j))\} \\ \quad \cup \ \{\text{FB}(k) \mid j \in \text{FBB}(i+1) \text{ and } \text{GRAY}(j) \\ \qquad \text{and } \text{FATHER}(k) = j\} & 0 \le i < n \end{cases}
$$

For example, in Figure 8.1, we have FBB(4) = {25, 16, F, M, 27, 38, 10}. FBB(3) is obtained by adding the black forests of nodes F (nodes 19, J, 22, and 23) and M (nodes 28 and 29) to yield FBB(3) = {25, 16, J, 22, 23, 28, 27, 29, 38, 19, 10}. FBB(2) is obtained by adding the black forests of node J (nodes 14, 20, and 21) to yield FBB(2) = {25, 16, 22, 23, 28, 14, 27, 29, 20, 38, 19, 21, 10}. No additional nodes are added by FBB(1) and FBB(0) — that is, FBB(2) = FBB(1) = FBB(0) = I. Figures 8.4a and 8.4b show FBB(4) and FBB(3), respectively. Clearly FBB(n) ⊇ FBB($n - 1$) ⊇ ⋯ ⊇ FBB(0) = I.

Approximation FBB provides a closer approximation to the image than OB in the sense that OB(i) ⊇ FBB(i) for all i. This is because the black forest approximation (FBB) includes gray nodes at level i only if they represent $2^i \times 2^i$ blocks that are at least $1/2^i$ black, while OB includes gray nodes at level i if any fraction of their corresponding $2^i \times 2^i$ block is black. Actually the index i in FBB(i) corresponds to an iteration, whereas the index i in OB(i) corresponds to a level. Nevertheless, OB(i) ⊇ FBB(i) because both OB(i) and FBB(i) contain all leaf nodes at levels $k \ge i$, and all nodes of FBB(i) at levels $j < i$ are contained in the gray nodes at level i that are part of OB(i).

We can also define a forest approximation that is made up entirely of nodes corresponding to white blocks. In other words, we approximate the complement of the image, $\overline{\text{I}}$. Such a forest is defined analogously to the one presented earlier using the black blocks—that is, each quadtree is a collection of subquadtrees, each of which corresponds to a maximal square. A *white forest* is the minimal set of maximal

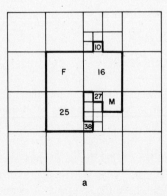

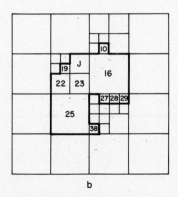

a   b

Figure 8.4   (a) FBB(4) and (b) FBB(3) for Figure 8.1

squares, not contained in other maximal squares, that spans the white area of the image. Now all that remains is to define a maximal square.

As in the case of black forests, maximal squares are defined in terms of nonleaf (i.e., gray) nodes. There are two ways in which we can proceed. First we can retain the definitions of nonleaf nodes in terms of GW and GB. Alternatively we can define a nonleaf node to be of type GW′ if at least two of its sons are white or of type GW′. Otherwise the node is said to be of type GB′. We choose to retain the original definition because it complements the way the nodes are defined to build the black forest. Thus given a tree labeled with GB and GW, both black and white forests can be extracted. On the other hand, when using GW′ and GB′, we must relabel the tree before we can extract the white forest from a tree labeled with GB and GW.

The following notation is used in the discussion of white forests. FW(*P*) is the white forest corresponding to the quadtree rooted at node *P*. FW(*P*) is empty when *P* is a black leaf node and *P* when *P* is a white leaf node. For example, in Figure 8.1, we have FW(A) = {A}; FW(F) = {I, 15}; FW(H) = {H}. We can approximate the complement of the image by a sequence of white forests of quadtrees where the sequence is defined by replacing nonleaf node components by their white forests. The result is termed a *white forest approximation*. More formally, let FWW(*i*), $0 \le i \le n$, be defined as follows:

$$\text{FWW}(i) = \begin{cases} \{\text{FW(root)}\} & i=n \\ \{j \,|\, j \in \text{FWW}(i+1) \text{ and not(GRAY}(j))\} & \\ \quad \cup \{\text{FW}(k) \,|\, j \in \text{FWW}(i+1) \text{ and GRAY}(j) & \\ \quad\quad \text{and FATHER}(k) = j\} & 0 \le i < n \end{cases}$$

For example, in Figure 8.1 we have FWW(4) = {A}. FWW(3) is obtained by adding the white forests of node A (nodes B, C, D, and E) to yield FWW(3) = {B, C, D, E}. FWW(2) is obtained by adding the white forests of node B (nodes 1, 2, 11, I, and 15), C (nodes G, 5, and 17), D (nodes 24, 40, and 41), and E (nodes H, 30, 42, and 43) to yield FWW(2) = {1, 2, 11, I, 15, G, 5, 17, 24, 40, 41, H, 30, 42, 43}. Continuing this procedure we find FWW(1) = {1, 2, 11, 12, 13, 18, 15, 3, 4, K, 8, 5, 17, 24, 40, 41, L, 33, 34, N, 37, 30, 42, 43} and FWW(0) = {1, 2, 11, 12, 13, 18, 15, 3, 4, 6, 7, 9, 8, 5, 17, 24, 40, 41, 26, 31, 32, 33, 34, 35, 36, 39, 37, 30, 42, 43} = Ī. Clearly, FWW(*n*) ⊇ FWW(*n* − 1) ⊇ ⋯ ⊇ FWW(0) = IW(0) = Ī.

Earlier we saw that OB(*i*) ⊇ FBB(*i*) for all *i*. An analogous relationship holds between OW(*i*) and FWW(*i*) — OW(*i*) ⊇ FWW(*i*) and, hence, FWW provides a closer approximation to the inverse image than OW. We can also make use of FWW to approximate I by working with its complement, $\overline{\text{FWW}}$. For example, in Figure 8.1, $\overline{\text{FWW}(4)}$ = { }; $\overline{\text{FWW}(3)}$ = { }; $\overline{\text{FWW}(2)}$ = {22, 23, 14, 20, 21, 16, 25}; $\overline{\text{FWW}(1)}$ = {22, 23, 19, 14, 20, 21, 16, 25, 28, 29}; and $\overline{\text{FWW}(0)}$ = {22, 23, 19, 14, 20, 21, 10, 16, 25, 27, 28, 29, 38}. Clearly, $\overline{\text{FWW}(i)}$ ⊇ $\overline{\text{OW}(i)}$ for all *i*. Recalling that $\overline{\text{OW}(i)}$ = IB(*i*), we have $\text{IB}(i) \subseteq \overline{\text{FWW}(i)}$. Also, $\text{FWW}(i) \supseteq \overline{\text{I}}$ implies that $\overline{\text{FWW}(i)} \subseteq \text{I}$. In fact, we have just shown the existence of better approximations to I (i.e., FBB and $\overline{\text{FWW}}$) than OB and IB and in the process have proved the following theorem:

Theorem 8.1 $\text{IB}(i) \subseteq \overline{\text{FWW}(i)} \subseteq \text{I} \subseteq \text{FBB}(i) \subseteq \text{OB}(i)$ for all i $0 \le i \le n$.   □

Use of approximation FBB results in overestimating the area spanned by the image, while use of $\overline{\text{FWW}}$ results in underestimating the area. In essence, we are approximating the image solely by use of black blocks or solely by use of white blocks. However, we could also approximate the image by a combination of black and white blocks. What we do is use $\text{FBB}(n)$ for the first level of approximation, augment all elements of $\text{FBB}(n)$ that correspond to gray nodes in the original quadtree by use of FWW, and repeat the alternating process until no gray nodes are left. More formally, we define a sequence $\text{FBW}(i)$ as follows:

$$
\text{FBW}(i) = \begin{cases}
\text{empty} & i = n + 1 \\
\text{FBB}(n) & i = n \\
\begin{aligned} &\text{FBW}(i + 1) \\ &\quad \cup \{\text{FW}(j) \mid j \in \text{FBW}(i + 1) \\ &\qquad\qquad \text{and } j \notin \text{FBW}(i + 2)\} \end{aligned} & (n - i) \bmod 2 = 1 \text{ and } i < n \\
\begin{aligned} &\text{FBW}(i + 1) \\ &\quad \cup \{\text{FB}(j) \mid j \in \text{FBW}(i + 1) \\ &\qquad\qquad \text{and } j \notin \text{FBW}(i + 2)\} \end{aligned} & (n - i) \bmod 2 = 0 \text{ and } i < n
\end{cases}
$$

For example, in Figure 8.1 we have $\text{FBW}(4) = \{25, 16, \text{F}, \text{M}, 27, 38, 10\}$. $\text{FBW}(3)$ is obtained by adding the white forests of node F (nodes I and 15) and M (nodes 33 and 34) to yield $\text{FBW}(3) = \{25, 16, \text{F}, \text{M}, 27, 38, 10, \text{I}, 15, 33, 34\}$. $\text{FBW}(2)$ is obtained by adding the black forests of node I (node 19) to yield $\text{FBW}(2) = \{25, 16, \text{F}, \text{M}, 27, 38, 10, \text{I}, 15, 33, 34, 19\} = \text{FBW}(1) = \text{FBW}(0) = \text{I}$. Figures 8.5a and 8.5b show $\text{FBW}(4)$ and $\text{FBW}(3)$.

Procedure ENCODE_FBW, given below, generates the $\text{FBW}(0)$ encoding of an image. It does this by successively generating in order, $\text{FBW}(n), \text{FBW}(n - 1), \cdots$ until $\text{FBW}(i)$ is encountered such that no more gray nodes need to be expanded. In essence, as $\text{FBW}(n)$ (i.e., a black forest) is generated, all of its elements that correspond to gray nodes are output as well as placed on a list termed WLIST (e.g., nodes F and M in Figure 8.1). Next we replace all elements of WLIST by their white forests and thereby generate $\text{FBW}(n - 1)$. During this process all elements of $\text{FBW}(n - 1)$ that correspond to gray nodes are output as well as placed on the BLIST (e.g., node I) to be used in the generation of $\text{FBW}(n - 2)$. This process terminates when encountering an empty BLIST or WLIST.

WLIST is initially empty, and BLIST is initialized to the entire image (e.g., node A in Figure 8.1). BLIST and WLIST are both of type *list*, which is a record having four

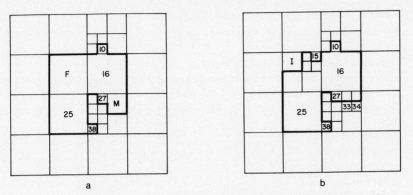

Figure 8.5   (a) FBW(4) and (b) FBW(3) for Figure 8.1

fields PTR, PATH, LEV, NEXT corresponding, respectively, to a pointer to a node, the VL locational code for the path from the root of the quadtree to the node, n minus the level of the node, and a pointer to the next element in the list.

ENCODE_FBW makes use of procedures FOREST_BLACK2 and FOREST_WHITE2 to generate the black and white forests corresponding to elements of BLIST and WLIST, respectively. Note that in addition to outputting a forest of the appropriate color, FOREST_BLACK2 and FOREST_WHITE2 also construct a list of the nonleaf nodes of the forest to serve as input for the next level of encoding.

```
procedure ENCODE_FBW(P);
/* Construct the FBW approximation of a 2^N × 2^N image represented by a quadtree rooted
   at node P. */
begin
  value pointer node P;
  pointer list BLIST, WLIST;
  WLIST ← empty;
  ADDTOLIST(BLIST,P,0,0); /* Initialize BLIST to P */
  while true do
    begin
    if empty(BLIST) then return;
    while not(empty(BLIST)) do
      begin
        FOREST_BLACK2(PTR(BLIST),PATH(BLIST),LEV(BLIST),WLIST);
        BLIST ← NEXT(BLIST);
      end;
    if empty(WLIST) then return;
    while not(empty(WLIST)) do
      begin
        FOREST_WHITE2(PTR(WLIST),PATH(WLIST),LEV(WLIST),BLIST);
        WLIST ← NEXT(WLIST);
      end;
```

```
      end;
   end;


   procedure FOREST_BLACK2(P,B,I,WLIST);
   /* Output the black forest for the subquadtree of a 2^N × 2^N image rooted at P with VL
      locational code B and at level N–I. All elements of the black forest that are nonleaf
      nodes are also added to the list WLIST for subsequent expansion into a white forest. */
   begin
    value pointer node P;
    value integer B,I;
    reference pointer node WLIST;
    quadrant Q;
    if BLACK(P) then output(B)
    else if GB(P) then
      begin
       output(B);
       ADDTOLIST(WLIST,P,B,I);
      end
    else if GW(P) then
      begin
       for Q in {'NW', 'NE', 'SW', 'SE'} do
         FOREST_BLACK2(SON(P,Q),B+QCODE(Q)*5↑I,I+1,WLIST);
         /* QCODE converts a quadrant to a directional code */
      end;
   end;


   procedure FOREST_WHITE2(P,B,I,BLIST);
   /* Output the white forest for the subquadtree of a 2^N × 2^N image rooted at P with VL
      locational code B and at level N–I. All elements of the white forest that are nonleaf
      nodes are also added to the list BLIST for subsequent expansion into a black forest. */
   begin
    value pointer node P;
    value integer B,I;
    reference pointer node BLIST;
    quadrant Q;
    if WHITE(P) then output(B)
    else if GW(P) then
      begin
       output(B);
       ADDTOLIST(BLIST,P,B,I);
      end
    else if GB(P) then
      begin
       for Q in {'NW', 'NE', 'SW', 'SE'} do
         FOREST_WHITE2(SON(P,Q),B+QCODE(Q)*5↑I,I+1,BLIST);
      end;
   end;
```

ENCODE_FBW yields the nodes for FBW(0) in the order of FBW(n), FBW($n-1$), FBW($n-2$), $\cdots$, FBW(0). This is useful because it means that the reverse process of building a quadtree from the transmitted codes yields successive approximations of the image. In fact, procedure BUILD_TREE, given in Section 2.1.1 to construct codes for a quadtree given the set of locational codes for all of its black blocks, can be used to construct the quadtree from the FBW approximation. This is true as long as the order in which the nodes are added to the tree satisfies the following property. For any two nodes P and Q such that P is an ancestor of Q, P is added to the tree before Q.

Procedure ENCODE_FBW yields the nodes in such an order since for each approximation FBW(i), all nodes at level k are output before nodes at level j, where $j < k$. In fact, as will become apparent from the discussion of BUILD_TREE below, if we did not have such an order, then we would have to specify the colors corresponding to the elements of FBW (black, white, GB, or GW). Note that this ordering property can also be satisfied by a sorted sequence, a breadth-first traversal, and even a preorder traversal. In the subsequent discussion, the term *transmit* is used to denote the encoding process.

At this point, let us reexamine the mechanics of BUILD_TREE more closely to see how and why it works correctly. Recall that whenever a node is added, a path (designated by the node's locational code) is traced from the root of the quadtree to the node. In the process, nodes may need to be expanded (e.g., the transition from Figure 2.2a to Figures 2.2b and 2.2c when adding node 25). In such a case the node's type is changed to gray, and its four sons take on its previous value (e.g., node A in the transition from Figure 2.2a to Figure 2.2b). When the decoding process is done, the node's type is complemented (e.g., node 25 changes from white to black in the transition from Figure 2.2c to Figure 2.2d). In the case of an FBW sequence, replacement of a black (white) node by its white (black) forest proceeds in the same way.

For example, Figure 8.6a shows the result of applying BUILD_TREE to FBW(4) = {25, 16, F, M, 27, 38, 10} of Figure 8.1. Next we process FBW(3), which means that we must add nodes I, 15, 33, and 34. Figure 8.6b–h illustrates this process. The presence of node I implies that black node F must be replaced by its white forest. This is accomplished in two steps. First node F is changed to a gray node and gains four black sons (Figure 8.6b). Next, node I is labeled, and in the process it is changed from black to white (Figure 8.6c). Figure 8.6d–e shows how node 15 is added, while Figure 8.6f–h shows the process of adding nodes 33 and 34. The final step is to process FBW(2), which means that we must add node 19. In this case, the presence of node 19 implies that white node I must be replaced by its black forest. Figure 8.6i–j illustrates this process.

Approximation FBW satisfies the following relationships: FBW(n) $\supseteq$ FBW($n-1$), FBW($n-1$) $\subseteq$ FBW($n-2$), FBW($n-2$) $\supseteq$ FBW($n-3$), and, in general, FBW($n-2i$) $\supseteq$ FBW($n-2i-1$) and FBW($n-2i-1$) $\subseteq$ FBW($n-2i-2$). Furthermore it is easy to show that FBW(n) $\supseteq$ FBW($n-2$) $\supseteq \cdots \supseteq$ FBW($n-2i$) $\supseteq \cdots \supseteq$ FBW(0) = I $\supseteq \cdots \supseteq$ FBW($n-2i-1$) $\supseteq \cdots \supseteq$ FBW($n-3$) $\supseteq$ FBW($n-1$). In other words, the approximations FBW spiral in from both sides of I in converging to I.

Note that individually, FBB and $\overline{\text{FWW}}$ may, at times, be better approximations to I than FBW — that is, there exist images for which the amount of black by which FBB

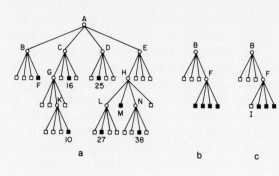

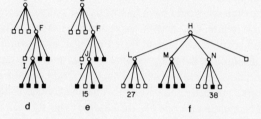

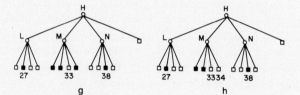

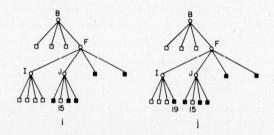

Figure 8.6   The steps in adding nodes I, 15, 33, 34, and 19
when reconstructing the quadtree from the FBW encoding of
Figure 8.1

overestimates I is less than the amount of black by which FBW underestimates I. As an example, suppose that white node 18 in Figure 8.1 is replaced by gray node P and four sons 44, 45, 46, and 47 where nodes 44, 45, and 46 are white and node 47 is black (see Figure 8.7, where the subtree rooted at node F is shown). In such a case FBB(3) = {25, 16, J, 22, 23, 28, 27, 29, 38, 19, 10, 47}, FBW(3) = {25, 16, F, M, 27, 38, 10, I, 15, 33, 34}, and FBB(3) overestimates the black area spanned by node F by four pixels, while FBW(3) underestimates the same black area by five pixels.

Of course, an image can also be constructed where the opposite is true—that is, the amount of black by which FBB overestimates I is greater than the amount of black by which FBW underestimates I. As an example, suppose that black node 20 in Figure 8.1 has been changed to a white node. In this case, FBB(3) = {25, 16, J, 22, 23, 28, 27, 29, 38, 19, 10}, FBW(3) = {25, 16, F, M, 27, 38, 10, I, 15, 33, 34, 20}, and FBW(3) underestimates the black area spanned by node F by 1 pixel, while FBB(3) overestimates the same area by 2 pixels.

FBW is an attractive approximation method because it converges to the image from both sides (i.e., it alternately overestimates and underestimates the black component). Thus it strikes a balance between using all black nodes or all white nodes to approximate the image, as is the case with FBB and FWW.

FBW, by definition, also has the property that the nodes comprising FBW(j) are a subset of the nodes comprising FBW(i) for $0 \le i \le j \le n$. Recall that FBW(0) = I. Thus when we use procedure ENCODE_FBW to encode the image, we can get the successive approximations to I as the elements of FBW(0) are transmitted. Therefore the first elements transmitted make up FBW(n), with the next terms being the ones leading to FBW($n - 1$), and so on. Of course, FBB and FWW could also have been defined in an analogous manner by including gray nodes.

The FBW approximation relies on alternating FBB and FWW approximations. We can also define an approximation, FWB, which alternates between FWW and FBB as follows:

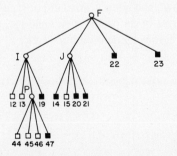

Figure 8.7   Modification to Figure 8.1 showing an example where FBB overestimates the image by less than what FBW underestimates it

$$
\text{FWB}(i) = \begin{cases}
\text{empty} & i = n + 1 \\
\text{FWW}(n) & i = n \\
\text{FWB}(i + 1) \\
\quad \cup \{\text{FB}(j) \,|\, j \in \text{FWB}(i + 1) \\
\qquad\quad \text{and } j \notin \text{FWB}(i + 2)\} & (n - i) \bmod 2 = 1 \text{ and } i < n \\
\text{FWB}(i + 1) \\
\quad \cup \{\text{FW}(j) \,|\, j \in \text{FWB}(i + 1) \\
\qquad\quad \text{and } j \notin \text{FWB}(i + 2)\} & (n - i) \bmod 2 = 0 \text{ and } i < n
\end{cases}
$$

For example, in Figure 8.1 we have $\text{FWB}(4) = \{A\}$. $\text{FWB}(3)$ is obtained by adding the black forests of node A resulting in $\{A, 25, 16, F, M, 27, 38, 10\}$. $\text{FWB}(2)$ is obtained by adding the white forests of node F (nodes I and 15) and M (nodes 33 and 34) to yield $\text{FWB}(2) = \{A, 25, 16, F, M, 27, 38, 10, I, 15, 33, 34\}$. $\text{FWB}(1)$ is obtained by adding the black forests of node I (node 19) to yield $\text{FWB}(1) = \{A, 25, 16, F, M, 27, 38, 10, I, 15, 33, 34, 19\} = \text{FWB}(0) = I$. For our example, $\text{FWB}(3) = \{\text{root}\} + \text{FBW}(4)$. In general, it can be shown (see Exercise 8.8) that when the root of the tree is of type GB, $\{\text{root}\} + \text{FWB}(i) = \text{FBW}(i - 1)$, for $1 \le i \le n$. Also, when the root is of type GW, $\text{FWB}(i - 1) = \{\text{root}\} + \text{FBW}(i)$, for $1 \le i \le n$.

Of course, procedures ENCODE_FBW and BUILD_TREE must be modified slightly to accommodate the FWB approximation. In particular, we create a procedure EN-CODE_FWB whose only difference from ENCODE_FBW is that FOREST_WHITE2 is invoked before FOREST_BLACK2. The only necessary change to procedure BUILD_TREE is that initially the tree is black rather than white.

Earlier when the notion of a white forest was presented, we noted that we could have used an alternative characterization of nonleaf nodes in terms of GW′ and GB′. Recall that a nonleaf node is said to be of type GW′ if at least two of its sons are white or of type GW′; otherwise the node is said to be of type GB′ (i.e., at least three of its sons are black or of type GB′). For example, in Figure 8.1, nodes A, B, C, D, E, G, H, I, K, L, M, and N are of type GW′, and nodes F and J are of type GB′. It is easy to redefine FB, FW, FBB, and FWW in terms of GB′ and GW′ to yield FB′, FW′, FBB′, and FWW′, respectively. This leads to the following definition for FWB′:

$$
\text{FWB}'(i) = \begin{cases}
\text{empty} & i = n + 1 \\
\text{FWW}'(n) & i = n \\
\text{FWB}'(i + 1) \\
\quad \cup \{\text{FB}'(j) \,|\, j \in \text{FWB}'(i + 1) \\
\qquad\quad \text{and } j \notin \text{FWB}'(i + 2)\} & (n - i) \bmod 2 = 1 \text{ and } i < n \\
\text{FWB}'(i + 1) \\
\quad \cup \{\text{FW}'(j) \,|\, j \in \text{FWB}'(i + 1) \\
\qquad\quad \text{and } j \notin \text{FWB}'(i + 2)\} & (n - i) \bmod 2 = 0 \text{ and } i < n
\end{cases}
$$

Similarly, we have FBW':

$$
\text{FBW}'(i) =
\begin{cases}
\text{empty} & i = n + 1 \\
\text{FBB}'(n) & i = n \\
\begin{aligned}
&\text{FBW}'(i + 1) \\
&\quad \cup \; \{\text{FW}'(j) \mid j \in \text{FBW}'(i + 1) \\
&\qquad\qquad \text{and } j \notin \text{FBW}'(i + 2)\}
\end{aligned} & (n - i) \bmod 2 = 1 \text{ and } i < n \\
\begin{aligned}
&\text{FBW}'(i + 1) \\
&\quad \cup \; \{\text{FB}'(j) \mid j \in \text{FBW}'(i + 1) \\
&\qquad\qquad \text{and } j \notin \text{FBW}'(i + 2)\}
\end{aligned} & (n - i) \bmod 2 = 0 \text{ and } i < n
\end{cases}
$$

The various approximation methods discussed above were applied to a 512×512 image (i.e., $n = 9$) consisting of a floodplain (Figure 8.8) used in prior experiments with quadtrees [Same84d, Same87a, Shaf87c]. Its quadtree contains 2,235 black nodes and 2,452 white nodes. Figures 8.9 and 8.10 give an example of what the images corresponding to these approximations look like. Figure 8.9 corresponds to FBW(n), FBW($n - 1$), FBW($n - 2$), and FBW($n - 3$), while Figure 8.10 corresponds to FBW'(n), FBW'($n - 1$), FBW'($n - 2$), and FBW'($n - 3$).

It is interesting to compare approximations when they contain a similar number of nodes, that is, 939 for FBW($n - 1$) and 984 for FBW'(n). No results are shown for the FWB and FWB' approximations because their node counts differ by one from those of FBW and FBW', respectively, and hence the resulting approximations are identical. To see this, recall the statement about the relationship between FBW and FWB (see Exercise 8.8). An analogous relationship holds between FBW' and FWB' (see Exercise 8.9).

Approximations IB, OB, and FBB were also discussed. Table 8.1 contains a summary of these data. Note that entries such as IB(8) = 0 and OW(8) = 4 imply 0 black

Figure 8.8   Floodplain image

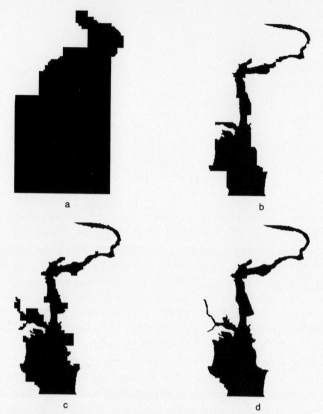

Figure 8.9   FBW approximation: (a) FBW(n) = FBW(9), (b) FBW(n–1) = FBW(8), (c) FBW(n–2) = FBW(7), (d) FBW(n–3) = FBW(6)

Table 8.1   Summary of the IB, OB, and FBB approximations for Figure 8.8 ($n = 9$)

i	IB(i)/OW(i)	OB(i)/IW(i)	FBB(i)
9	0/1	1/0	39
8	0/4	3/1	109
7	0/13	9/4	265
6	1/39	23/17	537
5	8/98	63/43	878
4	27/224	149/122	1,308
3	118/372	372/265	1,745
2	367/1,032	846/553	2,079
1	1,008/1,828	1,625/1,211	2,235
0	2,235/2,452	2,235/2,452	

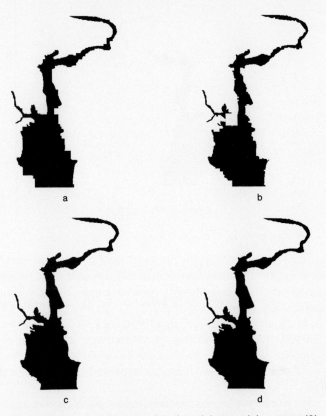

*Figure 8.10   FBW′ approximation: (a) FBW′(n) = FBW′(9),
(b) FBW′(n−1) = FBW′(8), (c) FBW′(n−2) = FBW′(7), (d)
FBW′(n−3) = FBW′(6)*

nodes and 4 white nodes at level 8. Actually if merges had occurred, then we would have had 0 black and 1 white node at level 9. However, our goal is to examine the approximation of level 8, and these nodes are white because some part of the space spanned by them was white in accordance with the definition of OW. Figures 8.11, 8.12, and 8.13 correspond to IB(2), OB(2), and FBB($n - 3$), respectively.

The figures enable us to compare FBB and OB when approximately the same number of nodes are transmitted. This is impossible for IB because it treats a gray node as white if there is any white pixel within it. In this case, we show the IB approximation at the same level as that for OB. The following observations should be apparent. First, as expected, the FBB approximation is less 'blocky' at the edge than OB or IB. Second, IB does not preserve connectivity, whereas OB and FBB do so at the possible expense of creating holes where there may not be any, as is seen in Figure 8.13. These observations are not surprising in the light of the comments made about IB's underestimating the black region.

Figure 8.11   IB(2)

Note that the FBW and FBW′ approximations have connectivity problems similar to IB. In particular, FBW alternates between GB and GW nodes. At iterations that use GW nodes, connectivity may be destroyed. As an example, consider Figure 8.14. Its FBW approximations are shown in Figure 8.15. We see that FBW(3) = {A}, FBW(2) = {A, 9, 13, F, G, D, E}, and FBW(1) = {A, 9, 13, F, G, D, E, 3, 5, 7, 8} = image. Figure 8.15b shows that FBW(2) results in the loss of connectivity. It should be clear that FWB has the same problem with respect to connectivity, while iterations using GW′ cause problems for FBW′ and FWB′ (see the transition between Figures 8.10a and 8.10b, and Exercise 8.10).

On the other hand, FWB′ approximations lead to the creation of spurious holes in the same way as does OB. In particular, FWB′ alternates between GW′ and GB′ nodes. At iterations that use GB′ nodes, spurious holes may result. One example of this phenomenon can be seen in the small hole in Figure 8.10c. For a clearer example,

Figure 8.12   OB(2)

Figure 8.13 FBB(n–3) = FBB(6)

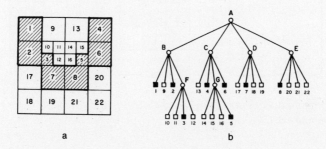

a   b

Figure 8.14 (a) Sample image and (b) its quadtree that demonstrates loss of connectivity by using the FBW approximation

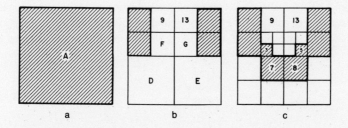

a   b   c

Figure 8.15 (a) FBW(3), (b) FBW(2), and (c) FBW(1) for Figure 8.1

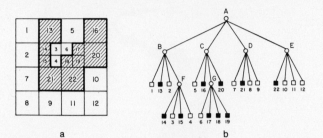

a   b

Figure 8.16   (a) Sample image and (b) its quadtree that demonstrates spurious holes by using the FWB′ approximation

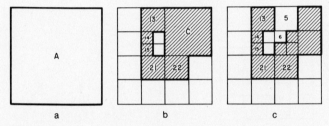

a   b   c

Figure 8.17   (a) FWB′(3), (b) FWB′(2), and (c) FWB′(1) for Figure 8.16

consider Figure 8.16. Its FWB′ approximations are shown in Figure 8.17. We see that FWB′(3) = {A}, FWB′(2) = {A, 13, 14, 15, 21, 22, C}, and FWB′(1) = {A, 13, 14, 15, 21, 22, C, 5, 6} = image. Figure 8.17b shows that FWB′(2) results in the creation of a spurious hole. It should be clear that FBW′ has the same problem with respect to the creation of a spurious hole. However, it can be shown that FBW and FWB cannot create spurious holes (see Exercise 8.11).

It would be useful to make an objective comparison among the approximation methods discussed in this section. Unfortunately the problem is that the result of any comparison would be subjective and heavily influenced by factors such as aesthetics

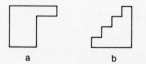

a   b

Figure 8.18   Sample images illustrating the biases of the FBW approximation: (a) panhandle, (b) staircase

and how closely the approximation resembles the shape of the approximated object. One measure would use criteria such as those mentioned in Theorem 8.1. In such a case, we can claim that use of FBW and its variants as an approximation method is superior to the inner and outer approximations of [Rana82].

Another criterion is to examine what types of features are highlighted by the approximation. In this case, we find that FBW and its variants are biased in favor of objects with so-called panhandles rather than staircases, as shown in Figure 8.18. This is in marked contrast with the inner and outer approximations that neglect all features below a certain depth in the tree, regardless of their significance. Another possible approach to evaluating the effectiveness of different approximation methods is by defining a measure such as 'nodes'/'area in the approximation' or, even better, some measure that reflects the amount of area by which members of the sequence of approximations underestimate or overestimate the true area.

Exercises

8.4. Can you define FWW(i) in a manner similar to that used to define FWW (i.e., in terms of FWW($i + 1$) instead of merely placing a complement symbol on the definition of FWW)?

8.5. Why is it not necessary to specify the node types (i.e., gray, black, or white) in the FBW approximation?

8.6. Modify procedures ENCODE_FBW, FOREST_BLACK2, and FOREST_WHITE2 by combining procedures FOREST_BLACK2 and FOREST_WHITE2 into a single procedure SUBFOREST that has an additional parameter to indicate whether a black or a white forest is to be constructed.

8.7. The FBW approximation requires storing gray nodes as well as black and white nodes. Can we do without the gray nodes? In other words, suppose we construct an approximation, say SBW as defined below, similar to FBW with the exceptions that gray nodes are omitted and that the color of each node is stipulated in the approximation. Can you define an encoding and decoding scheme such that the entire quadtree can be reconstructed?

$$\text{SBW}(i) = \begin{cases} \text{FBB}(n) & i = n \\ \{\,j\,|\,j\in \text{SBW}(i+1) \text{ and not}(\text{GRAY}(j))\} \\ \quad \cup\, \{\text{FW}(j)\,|\,j\in \text{SBW}(i+1) \text{ and GRAY}(j)\} & (n-i)\bmod 2 = 1 \text{ and } i < n \\ \{\,j\,|\,j\in \text{SBW}(i+1) \text{ and not}(\text{GRAY}(j))\} \\ \quad \cup\, \{\text{FB}(j)\,|\,j\in \text{SBW}(i+1) \text{ and GRAY}(j)\} & (n-i)\bmod 2 = 0 \text{ and } i < n \end{cases}$$

8.8. Prove that when the root of a quadtree is of type GB, then $\{\text{root}\} + \text{FWB}(i) = \text{FBW}(i-1)$ for $1 \le i \le n$, and when the root is of type GW, $\text{FWB}(i-1) = \{\text{root}\} + \text{FBW}(i)$ for $1 \le i \le n$.

8.9. Prove that when the root of a quadtree is of type GW′, then $\{\text{root}\} + \text{FBW}'(i) = \text{FWB}'(i-1)$ for $1 \le i \le n$, and when the root is of type GB′, $\text{FBW}'(i-1) = \{\text{root}\} + \text{FWB}'(i)$ for $1 \le i \le n$.

8.10. Using a DF-expression representation, give an example quadtree showing that the FBW′ and FWB′ approximations can lead to a loss of connectivity.

8.11. Prove that the FBW and FWB approximations cannot create spurious holes.

8.12. Consider the issue of evaluating the effectiveness and quality of different approximation methods such as FBW, its variants, and the inner and outer approximation methods of

[Rana82]. Are there other shapes besides panhandles where use of FBW is superior? Construct some sample images and compute the measure 'nodes'/'area in the approximation' for them using these approximation methods.

8.2.2 Compression

The FBW approximation (as well as its variants FWB, FBW′, and FWB′) has the interesting property that its use will often lead to compression in the sense that it reduces the amount of data needed to encode the image (and transmit it). Recall that we can represent a quadtree by merely specifying all of the black blocks or all of the white blocks. Of course, depending on the image, we would use the color with the smaller cardinality in order to save storage. The FBW approximation consists of a combination of gray, black, and white nodes, thereby striking a balance between using all black or all white. For example, encoding Figure 8.1 with FBW requires 12 nodes, whereas the image contains 13 black and 30 white nodes.

Aside from its superiority with respect to the quality of the resulting approximation, use of FBW or its variants can also lead to compression. Let F, B, and W denote the number of nodes when encoding the quadtree using FBW (or one of its variants), black, and white nodes, respectively. Compression is said to exist whenever $F < \text{MIN}(B,W)$. As we shall see below, we can choose from the variants of FBW so that $F \leq \text{MIN}(B,W)$ always. Thus we can guarantee that our approximation methods are always at least as good as or better than encoding the quadtree by listing its black nodes (or its white nodes).

To see the type of compression that is achievable, let $C = F/\text{MIN}(B,W)$ be a compression factor. Below, we see that C can be made as close to zero as desired. Figure 8.19a demonstrates the empty tree with $F = 0$ (i.e., a white node at the root), which we exclude. Figure 8.19b illustrates a tree with $F = 1$ but $C = 1$. Figure 8.19c is an example of the type of tree that yields much compression—that is, a small C value although it is by no means the minimum C for a $2^n \times 2^n$ image. In this case, $F = 3$ (nodes 1, D, and 19) while $B = 10$, $W = 9$, and $C = 1/3$. For a $2^n \times 2^n$ image, a tree having depth $n = 2 \cdot m$ can be constructed such that $F = 3$ and $C = 3/(3 \cdot m) = 1/m$. Figure 8.19c is such a tree with $n = 6$. Note that such a tree has $3 \cdot m - 1$ white nodes at levels $n - 1$ to $n/2$, one black node at level $n - 1$, $3 \cdot (m - 1)$ black nodes at levels $n/2 - 1$ to 1, one white node at level 0, and three black nodes at level 0.

In the following, we derive an upper bound on the number of nodes comprising FBW (i.e., F), as well as FWB. The derivation makes use of the following definitions. Let $\text{NBW}(r)$ be the maximum number of nodes in an FBW approximation of a quadtree with root r. $\text{NWB}(r)$ is defined similarly for an FWB approximation. Let W_r be the number of white nodes in a quadtree rooted at r. For the purpose of this discussion, we let type GW include leaf white nodes as well, and type GB include leaf black nodes. Theorem 8.2 gives the upper bound with the aid of Lemmas 8.1 and 8.2, which are proved below.

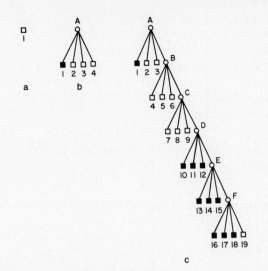

Figure 8.19   Examples illustrating the compression factors available through the use of FBW

Lemma 8.1   For a quadtree whose root is of type GB, {root} + FWB(i) = FBW($i - 1$) for $1 \le i \le n$.

Proof   Since the root is of type GB, FWB(n) ignores it and proceeds to collect all of the root's descendants of type GW that do not have an ancestor of type GW. But these are precisely the nodes that comprise FBW($n - 1$). In other words, {root} + FWB(n) = FBW($n - 1$). The rest of the sequence is constructed in an analogous manner—that is, {root} + FWB(i) = FBW($i - 1$) for $1 \le i \le n$.   □

Lemma 8.2   For a quadtree whose root is of type GW, FWB($i - 1$) = {root} + FBW(i) for $1 \le i \le n$.

Proof   Since the root is of type GW, FWB(n) includes it. FWB($n - 1$) consists of the root and all its descendants of type GB that do not have an ancestor of type GB. But these are precisely the nodes that comprise FBW(n). In other words, FWB($n - 1$) = {root} + FBW(n). The rest of the sequence is constructed in an analogous manner—that is, FWB($i - 1$) = {root} + FBW(i) for $1 \le i \le n$.   □

Theorem 8.2   The number of nodes in the FBW and FWB approximation of a quadtree rooted at r is given by the following relations:

1. $\text{NBW}(r) \leq \text{w}_r + 1$, if r is of type GB.
2. $\text{NWB}(r) \leq \text{w}_r$, if r is of type GB.
3. $\text{NBW}(r) \leq \text{w}_r - 1$, if r is of type GW.
4. $\text{NWB}(r) \leq \text{w}_r$, if r is of type GW.

Proof   The proof makes use of induction on the level at which the root of the quadtree is found.[1]

Base Step   When the root of the quadtree is at level 0, then the quadtree consists of a single node.

Case a   The node is black. Therefore the root is of type GB and $\text{w}_r = 0$.

(i)   Relation 1:

$$\text{NBW}(r) = 1 \leq \text{w}_r + 1.$$

(ii)   Relation 2:

$$\text{NWB}(r) = 0 \leq \text{w}_r.$$

Case b   The node is white. Therefore the root is of type GW and $\text{w}_r = 1$.

(i)   Relation 3:

$$\text{NBW}(r) = 0 \leq \text{w}_r - 1.$$

(ii)   Relation 4:

$$\text{NWB}(r) = 1 \leq \text{w}_r.$$

Inductive Step   Assume that relations 1, 2, 3, and 4 hold for all quadtrees having roots at a level $\leq n - 1$. We now show that the relations also hold for quadtrees whose root is at level n. Consider a quadtree with a root r at level n. The four sons of this quadtree are quadtrees with roots s_1, s_2, s_3, and s_4, respectively, each at level $n - 1$. It is easy to see that $\text{w}_r = \text{w}_{s_1} + \text{w}_{s_2} + \text{w}_{s_3} + \text{w}_{s_4}$. Let NB be the number of sons of node r of type GB, and let NW = 4−NB be the number of sons of node r of type GW. If r is of type GB, then $2 \leq \text{NB} \leq 4$; otherwise $0 \leq \text{NB} \leq 1$.

Case a   The root is of type GB.

(i)   Relation 1:

---

[1] This proof is due to Jiang-Hsing Chu and is a simplification of the proof in [Same85c]. It is terse and can be skipped.

$NBW(r) = NWB(s_1) + NWB(s_2) + NWB(s_3) + NWB(s_4) + 1$ by Lemma 8.1

$\leq W_{s_1} + W_{s_2} + W_{s_3} + W_{s_4} + 1$ by the inductive hypothesis

$= W_r + 1.$

(ii) Relation 2:

$$NWB(r) = \sum_{i=1}^{4} \begin{cases} NWB(s_i) & \text{if } s_i \text{ is of type GB} \\ NBW(s_i) + 1 & \text{otherwise} \end{cases} \quad \text{by Lemma 8.1}$$

$\leq W_{s_1} + W_{s_2} + W_{s_3} + W_{s_4}$ by the inductive hypothesis

$= W_r.$

Case b The root is of type GW.

(i) Relation 3:

$$NBW(r) = \sum_{i=1}^{4} \begin{cases} NWB(s_i) + 1 & \text{if } s_i \text{ is of type GB} \\ NBW(s_i) & \text{otherwise} \end{cases} \quad \text{by Lemma 8.2}$$

$\leq W_{s_1} + W_{s_2} + W_{s_3} + W_{s_4} + NB - NW$ by the inductive hypothesis

$\leq W_r - 2$ since $0 \leq NB \leq 1.$

$\leq W_r - 1$ since $0 \leq NB \leq 1.$

(ii) Relation 4:

$NWB(r) = NBW(s_1) + NBW(s_2) + NBW(s_3) + NBW(s_4) + 1$ by Lemma 8.2

$\leq W_{s_1} + W_{s_2} + W_{s_3} + W_{s_4} + NB - NW + 1$ by the inductive hypothesis

$\leq W_r - 1$ since $0 \leq NB \leq 1.$

$= W_r.$

Therefore, by use of induction, we have shown that relations 1, 2, 3, and 4 hold for all quadtrees. □

Figure 8.19c demonstrates how the lower bound on the compression factor can be approached. A checkerboard image is an example of the upper bound on F. Its

FBW approximation has FBW(n) = {root} and FBW($n - 1$) = {root} + {all leaf white nodes}. Thus F = W + 1 = B + 1. Note that by Theorem 8.2 the upper bound on F is solely in terms of the white nodes. This is better than the weaker upper bound of MAX(B,W) + 1 because W ≤ MAX(B,W). Of course, the upper bound of W + 1 can be tightened to be W by using the FWB approximation—that is, alternating between FWW and FBB instead of FBB and FWW.

As we see from Theorem 8.2, there really is not a big difference between using FBW and FWB. If we want to have the lowest upper bounds, then we can use FBW when the root is of type GW and FWB when the root is of type GB. In fact, we can also obtain upper bounds in terms of B, the number of black nodes. To do this, we use approximation sequences FWB′ and FBW′ as defined in Section 8.2.1. Recall that in such a case, the quadtree is labeled in terms of GB′ and GW′.

Approximations FWB′ and FBW′ are formed in the same manner as approximations FBW and FWB, respectively, except that the roles of black and white (GB and GW) are interchanged. Therefore we obtain the following upper bounds. Let NBW′(r) be the maximum number of nodes in an FBW′ approximation of a quadtree with root r. NWB′(r) is defined similarly for an FWB′ approximation. Let B_r be the number of black nodes in a quadtree rooted at r.

Theorem 8.3 The number of nodes in the FWB′ and FBW′ approximation of a quadtree rooted at r is given by the following relations:

1. NWB′(r) ≤ B_r + 1, if r is of type GW′.
2. NBW′(r) ≤ B_r, if r is of type GW′.
3. NWB′(r) ≤ B_r − 1, if r is of type GB′.
4. NBW′(r) ≤ B_r, if r is of type GB′.

Theorem 8.3 is interesting because it brings us back a full circle to our starting point. Recall that a quadtree can be encoded just by listing its black blocks, but this method did not lead to a useful approximation. Subsequently we looked at sequences of approximations based on the notion of a forest that also have the property that they never require more nodes than merely listing the black nodes. Of course, the analogous result holds were we to use white blocks to encode the quadtree. A summary of these results is given in Table 8.2.

To evaluate the compression results described above, we use the floodplain image of Figure 8.8. Its quadtree contains 2,235 black nodes and 2,452 white nodes. Table 8.3 is a summary of the results for the FBW and FBW′ approximations. No results are tabulated for the FWB and FWB′ approximations because their node counts differ by one according to Lemmas 8.1 and 8.2. Since the approximations alternate between black and white nodes, Table 8.3 specifies the counts for them, as well as the total number of nodes.

Table 8.3 correlates with our theoretical results with respect to upper bounds on the number of necessary nodes. In particular, we find that FBW′ requires 1,704 nodes to encode the image while FBW requires 1,796 nodes. Thus comparing these counts

Table 8.2   Upper bounds for the various
             approximations

Approximation	Root Type	
	GB (GB′)	GW (GW′)
FBW	W+1	W−1
FWB	W	W
FBW′	B	B
FWB′	B−1	B+1

with the minimum of the black and white nodes in the quadtree (i.e., 2,235 black nodes), we find that FBW′ leads to 23.8% fewer nodes, while FBW leads to 19.6% fewer nodes. These compression factors increase considerably as larger images are used (i.e., greater than $2^9 \times 2^9$, as in this example).

From Table 8.3 we also observe that FBW(n) and FBW′(n) have different numbers of nodes. This is because of the different definition of GB. Recall that for FBW, a nonleaf node is of type GB if at least two of its sons are black or of type GB, whereas for FBW′, we use GB′, which requires that at least three of its sons are black or of type GB′. Thus it should be clear that the GB′ criterion of FBW′ is harder to satisfy than the GB criterion of FBW, thereby causing the initial approximation FBW′(n) to contain nodes from lower levels in the tree (and, hence, more of them!).

The compression that is attainable as a result of using FBW and its variants reinforces our definition of a white forest in terms of GB and GW in Section 8.2.1. Recall that we could have defined a white forest to be analogous to a black forest—that is, a nonleaf node is of type GW′ if at least two of its sons are white or of type GW′ rather than GW, which requires that at least three of its sons are white or of type GW. If we define FBW in terms of GB and GW′, then we need to label the tree twice: once in terms

Table 8.3   Summary of FBW and FBW′ approximations
             for Figure 8.8 ($n = 9$)

i	FBW(i)			FBW′(i)		
	Black	White	Total	Black	White	Total
9	39	0	39	984	0	984
8	39	900	939	984	242	1,226
7	255	900	1,155	1,376	242	1,618
6	255	1,422	1,677	1,376	294	1,670
5	325	1,422	1,747	1,405	294	1,699
4	325	1,468	1,793	1,405	297	1,702
3	328	1,468	1,796	1,407	297	1,704

of GB and once in terms of GW' (see Exercise 8.17). More important, we cannot obtain limits such as those of Theorems 8.2 and 8.3 on the number of nodes in the approximation (e.g., consider a checkerboard image as in Exercise 8.18).

Exercises

8.13. What combinations of colors of sons of a node lead to compression when using approximations based on FBW and its variants?

8.14. The construction of Figure 8.19 shows how a lower bound on the compression factor C can be approached—that is, $2/n$ for a $2^n \times 2^n$ image. Is it a minimum? If not, what is it as a function of n?

8.15. Formulate an appropriate image model and determine the average amount of compression for a $2^n \times 2^n$ image as a function of n. This is hard because a random image will tend to be like a checkerboard. One possibility is to use Dyer's [Dyer82] (see also Section 1.2) approach of arbitrarily placing a square of size $2^m \times 2^m$ at any position in a $2^n \times 2^n$ image and calculating the average number of nodes required in the FBW and FBW' approximations.

8.16. Why does the FBW' encoding of Figure 8.8 (see Table 8.3) take up less storage than its FBW encoding?

8.17. Suppose that we define the FBW'' sequence in terms of GB and GW'. Why do we need to label the tree twice: once in terms of GB and once in terms of GW'?

8.18. Suppose that we define the FBW'' sequence in terms of GB and GW'. Give the FBW'' encoding of a 4×4 checkerboard image.

8.2.3 Observations

FBW and its variants lead to approximations that are superior to merely listing the black nodes (or just the white nodes). Furthermore these approximations also lead to compression in the sense that the number of nodes required is always less than or equal to MIN(B,W). There are a number of reasons for the success of the FBW approximation. In the following, the term FBW is used to mean FBW and its variants FWB, FBW', and FWB'.

First, FBW yields a saving of space whenever the situation arises that three out of four sons are the same type (black or white). The amount of space saved increases with the frequency of the occurrence of this state at different levels of the quadtree (e.g., Figure 8.19c). This, coupled with the alternation between black and white forests, enables the approximation to zoom in on the final goal.

Second, the encoding and decoding procedures ENCODE_FBW and BUILD_TREE give rise to an encoding that makes use of black, white, and gray nodes without needing to specify their type. In addition, these procedures are very efficient. ENCODE_FBW takes time proportional to the size of the quadtree being encoded since it is nothing but a tree traversal. BUILD_TREE takes time proportional to the product of the number of nodes in the FBW encoding and the resolution of the image (i.e., n for a $2^n \times 2^n$ image) because the node is represented by an n digit base 5 code indicating the path from the root.

It is desirable to compare FBW with other representations, such as runlength codes, chain codes, arrays, and quadtrees. How hard is it to perform basic image-processing operations given an FBW encoding? For many operations, it will be difficult to do anything without first decoding the FBW representation into its corresponding quadtree. However, some operations, such as set union and set inter-section, can be performed directly on the FBW representation, although this requires some work. Operations that use neighbor finding require a considerable amount of work.

Labeling nonleaf nodes of a quadtree with GB and GW to indicate information about the subtrees may find application in using quadtrees for matching of images. There is no need for extra storage since a type field already exists for each node. Internal nodes can be distinguished from leaf nodes by the fact that the latter have four empty sons. Thus nonleaf nodes can also be labeled black or white, corresponding to GB and GW, respectively.

Ismail and Steele [Isma80] make use of an approximation method, termed *aplc*, that is similar in spirit to the forest method. They treat each $M \times M$ block in the image as black if at least $M^2 - 1$ of its constituent pixels are black. Similarly a $M \times M$ block is treated as white if at least $M^2 - 1$ of its pixels are white. Otherwise the block is decomposed into four blocks, and the same coding process is recursively attempted. The principal difference between the two methods is that the forest method is hierarchical, whereas the aplc approximation is not. For example, when four brother blocks of size 2×2 each contain one white pixel, aplc treats them as four 2×2 black blocks, not as one 4×4 black block. Also the aplc method does not lead to an exact reconstruction of the image, whereas the forest method does.

Exercises

8.19. Give an algorithm to perform the set union and set intersection of two images whose quadtrees are represented by the FBW representation. You are to perform the operations directly on the FBW representation and not convert it to a pointer-based quadtree. Assume that the nodes in the FBW representation are sorted in increasing order of their VL loca-tional codes. You may also assume that you know the type of each node in the FBW representation (i.e., whether it is B, W, GB, or GW). As a hint, consider the effect of the set operation on nodes of different types. For example, GB union GB yields GB, and then the algorithm is applied recursively to the four sons. However, the type of the father is already known. In contrast, GW union GW forces you to descend the tree and examine the four sons. The final type of the father depends on the types of the sons. In both cases, depending on the type of the father node, absent sons will have a particular type.

8.20. Section 4.2.3 contains an algorithm for constructing a pointerless quadtree from a raster representation. Recall that this algorithm examined each pixel but inserted a block only if the color of the pixel differed from that of the block containing it. In case of insertion, it created the largest block for which the current pixel was the first (i.e., upper leftmost) pixel. Shaffer [Shaf86a] suggests using this sequence of blocks to describe the image and terms it *LBR*, denoting *largest block representation*. What are the nodes comprising the LBR encoding of the image in Figure 1.1?

8.21. The LBR encoding can be specified using locational codes. Do you need to specify the color of each member of the encoding?

8.22. Give an algorithm to reconstruct a quadtree from its LBR encoding.

8.23. How is the LBR encoding related to the FBW approximation? Can you prove that the FBW approximation never requires more nodes than the LBR encoding?

8.3 PROGRESSIVE PYRAMID-BASED APPROXIMATION METHODS

Sloan and Tanimoto [Sloa79] (see also [Tani79]) treat the problem of transmitting a gray-scale image by successively approximating it by use of pyramid-based approaches [Tani75]. They discuss a number of methods; however, none features any compression. Recall from Section 1.4 that a *pyramid* is a sequence of arrays $\{A(i)\}$ such that $A(i - 1)$ is a version of $A(i)$ at half the resolution; $A(0)$ is said to be a single element. Given a $2^n \times 2^n$ image, the pyramid can be considered as a complete quadtree with $A(n)$ corresponding to the image.

The simplest transmission technique presented by Sloan and Tanimoto is analogous to a breadth-first traversal of the complete quadtree. The shortcoming of this approach is that redundant information must be transmitted (i.e., one-third more information), and thus no compression exists. Sloan and Tanimoto propose a number of refinements to this method. In this description the term *node* is used to refer to both a block or a pixel, as is appropriate. The first refinement includes a level number and a pair of coordinate values for each node. However, they are transmitted only if the intensity value differs from the value of the node's predecessor. In this case, the amount of information transmitted depends heavily on the complexity of the image.

The second refinement requires the receiver to deduce one node's value from those of its predecessor and its three siblings. Using such a method, there is no need for redundant node information to be transmitted; however, there is no compression since the amount of information transmitted is equal to the number of pixels in the image. The predecessor's value can be a sum of the values of the four sons (like an average). In such a case, each level of the pyramid requires two more bits per node than the level of its sons (see Exercise 8.24). An even better method, in the sense of requiring less storage and computational overhead, is simply to use one of the values of the sons. This method is best when images do not contain periodic high-frequency variations such as regular textures. In contrast, the averaging method is less sensitive to aliasing (i.e., the creation of jagged edges due to sharp changes in intensity).

Knowlton [Know80] describes the use of a binary pyramid to achieve an averaging effect without the additional storage cost (i.e., extra bits) at successive levels in the tree. He makes use of a bintree such that the image is repeatedly split into two halves alternating between vertical and horizontal splits. Given a $2^n \times 2^n$ gray-scale image,[2] each two-pixel group (hence, the binary subdivision) is described by two

---

[2] For an analogous treatment of 3-dimensional images, see Hardas and Srihari [Hard84].

numbers that enable the computation of their corresponding gray-scale values. The first number is analogous to an average, termed a *composite value* and referred to as v_c, while the second is like a difference, termed a *differentiator* and referred to as v_d. These two-pixel groups are recursively aggregated in groups of two to form a complete bintree (analogous to a binary pyramid). In other words, at each successive level of the tree, a new composite value and a new differentiator are formed based on the composite values of its two sons.

For example, suppose that an image has four gray-scale levels. Figure 8.20 shows one possible way of determining a composite value and a differentiator given the gray-scale values of two pixels, v_1 and v_2. In the figure, composite values are circled, and differentiator values are in squares. Notice that there are four bands, each corresponding to a different composite value, with the leftmost band being the smallest. The differentiator enables disambiguating within each band.

Of course, there are many ways that the sixteen combinations of gray-scale levels could have been divided into four groups (see Exercise 8.27). The one depicted in the figure has the effect of yielding a composite value that is a good approximation to the average for the high probability cases (i.e., when v_1 is equal to or close to v_2). This is seen by observing that $v_1 = v_2 = v_c$ along the main diagonal of Figure 8.20.

Given the above definitions of v_c and v_d, it is easy to define a sequence of approximations to the image. Each pair of pixels is represented by a composite value and a differentiator. This process is repeated at each level of the binary pyramid. Thus for a $2^n \times 2^n$ image, a total of $2^{2n} - 1$ composite values and $2^{2n} - 1$ differentiators would be needed. However, only the composite value for the root of the binary pyramid and the successive sets of differentiators (i.e., $1 + 2^{2n} - 1 = 2^{2n}$ data items) need to be transmitted to reconstruct the image.

Progressive approximation results from a transmission in the form of a breadth-first traversal of the binary tree of differentiator values. The result is that the image has been transmitted progressively with no additional storage overhead—an image of p pixels of 2^b gray levels is transmitted and reformatted by using $p \cdot b$ bits. Compression can be achieved by using techniques such as Huffman codes [Huff52] to encode the differentiator values. Note that use of the composite values leads to successively

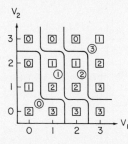

Figure 8.20   *One possible way of determining a composite value (circled) and a differentiator (square) given the grayscale values of two pixels, v_1 and v_2*

better approximations to the image until an exact reconstruction is obtained at the end of the transmission. Moreover, the manner in which v_c is defined ensures that large monotone areas will appear as monotone areas with the right gray-scale value early in the transmission process.

A comparison of Knowlton's use of the binary pyramid with the method of Sloan and Tanimoto reveals that Knowlton achieves the effect of an average without requiring extra bits at successive levels of the pyramid. Of course, Sloan and Tanimoto can avoid this extra cost but at the sacrifice of obtaining an average-like value at successive levels. Nevertheless, their approach does have an advantage over that of Knowlton in that it does not have the computational overhead of precomputing differentiator values and can be achieved by a simple traversal of the image array.

Exercises

8.24. Suppose that you use the second refinement to the pyramid approach of Sloan and Tanimoto. In particular, let the predecessor's value be the sum of the values of the four sons. Prove that each level of the pyramid requires two more bits per pixel than the previous level.

8.25. Augment Figure 8.20 to show how composite values and differentiators would be defined for an image having 16 gray-scale levels.

8.26. What is the maximum deviation from the average value when using the definition of a composite value as shown in Figure 8.20 for an image with 2^v gray-scale levels? Make a two-dimensional plot of the deviation as a function of the gray-scale levels of the pixels that are aggregated (v_1 and v_2).

8.27. Knowlton uses table-lookup methods to compute the appropriate v_c and v_d values for pixel pairs. Can you give a pair of functions $v_c(v_1, v_2)$ and $v_d(v_1, v_2)$ so that there is no need for table-lookup?

8.28. Can you adapt Knowlton's definition of a composite value and a differentiator to the pyramid of Sloan and Tanimoto? The idea is to be able to transmit a value more closely related to the average without requiring extra bits. If this is impossible, show why.

DISTANCE AND QUADTREE MEDIAL AXIS TRANSFORMS

9

The region quadtree is a member of a class of region representations characterized as being a collection of 'maximal blocks' that partition a given region. Recall from Section 1.3 that the simplest such representation is the runlength code, where the blocks are restricted to $1 \times m$ rectangles [Ruto68]. A more general representation treats the region as a union of maximal square blocks (or blocks of any desired shape), which may possibly overlap. Usually the blocks are specified by their centers and radii. This representation is called the *medial axis transformation* (MAT) [Blum67, Rose66].

The region quadtree is a variant on the maximal block representation. It requires the blocks to be disjoint, to have standard sizes (i.e., have sides of lengths that are powers of two), and to be at standard locations. This chapter discusses the effects of relaxing the first two requirements so that the blocks need not be disjoint or of a fixed size. This is achieved by adapting the concepts of a distance, a skeleton, and a medial axis transformation to an image that is represented by a quadtree to yield a quadtree medial axis transform (QMAT).

This chapter is organized as follows. We first review the concept of a distance and see how it can be formulated in a way that is meaningful for an image represented by a quadtree. Next a quadtree skeleton and a quadtree medial axis transform (QMAT) are defined. Algorithms are also presented for converting between a quadtree and a QMAT. Note that the primary motivation of this chapter is not to study skeletons and medial axis transformations for the usual purpose of obtaining an approximation to an image, although it is discussed briefly. Instead the QMAT is an exact representation of the image, and the focus is on its storage requirements. In particular, the QMAT is shown to be less sensitive to shifts than the quadtree.

The algorithms presented make heavy use of the neighbor computation functions described in Section 3.2.1. In addition, in order to express the relationships among the edges, vertices, and quadrants, use is made of the functions OPEDGE, CEDGE, CCEDGE, OPQUAD, QUAD, and VERTEX, which are described in the introductory section of Chapter 4.

9.1 DISTANCE, SKELETONS, AND MEDIAL AXIS TRANSFORMS

Given an image represented by a binary array, let d be a function that maps pairs of points (i.e., pixels) into nonnegative numbers. It is called a *metric* or a *distance function* if for all points p, q, and r the following relations are satisfied:

1. $d(p, q) \geq 0$ and $d(p, q) = 0$ if and only if $p = q$ (positive definiteness).
2. $d(p, q) = d(q, p)$ (symmetry).
3. $d(p, r) \leq d(p, q) + d(q, r)$ (triangle inequality).

Some of the more common metrics are examined below in the context of the points $p = (p_x, p_y)$ and $q = (q_x, q_y)$. By far the most popular metric is the *Euclidean* metric

$$d_E(p, q) = \sqrt{(p_x - q_x)^2 + (p_y - q_y)^2}.$$

Two other metrics used in image processing are the absolute value metric, also known as the *city block* metric (or *Manhattan* metric)

$$d_A(p, q) = |p_x - q_x| + |p_y - q_y|$$

and the maximum value metric, also known as the *Chessboard* metric

$$d_M(p, q) = \max \{ |p_x - q_x|, |p_y - q_y| \}.$$

The set of points with $d_E(p, q) \leq T$ are those points contained in a circle centered at p having radius T. The set $d_A(p, q) \leq T$ is a diamond, centered at p, with side length $T \cdot \sqrt{2}$. The set $d_M(p, q) \leq T$ is a square, centered at p, with side length $2 \cdot T$.

Consider an image where the set of points in a certain region is labeled s and the set of points outside of the region is labeled $\bar{s}$ (analogous to black and white respectively in a binary image). We say that for a point x and a set V, the distance, d, from x to the nearest point of V is $d(x, V) = \min \{d(x, y) | y \in V\}$. The set of elements in s

having a distance from $\bar{S}$ that is greater than or equal to that of all of its 'neighbors' in S constitutes a skeletal description of S and is called a *skeleton*. The meaning of 'neighbors' depends on the metric chosen. If we use the City Block metric, i.e., d_A, then the 4-*adjacent* neighbors are considered to be the 'neighbors.' If we use the Chessboard metric, i.e., d_M, then the 8-*adjacent* neighbors are considered to be the 'neighbors.'

For example, consider the 7×10 rectangle array in Figure 9.1a. The values of d_A and d_M for this rectangle are given by Figure 9.1b. The corresponding skeletons are given by Figures 9.1c and 9.1d, respectively. The Euclidean metric (i.e., d_E) is more appropriate for the continuous case. As an example of the use of d_E, consider the rectangle in Figure 9.2 whose skeleton, using d_E, consists of line segments labeled a, b, c, d, and e. In this case, an alternative characterization of a skeleton is that it corresponds to what is left when the boundary of the object is set on fire.

If we know the points of the skeleton and their associated distance values, then we can reconstruct region S exactly. The set of points comprising the skeleton and their associated distance values is termed the *medial axis transformation* (*MAT*).

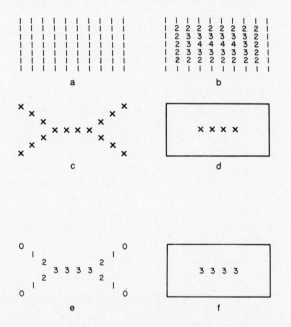

Figure 9.1   *A binary array representation of an image, its distance values, its skeleton, and its MAT: (a) image, (b) d_A and d_M for the image in (a), (c) skeleton of the image in (a) using d_A, (d) skeleton of the image in (a) using d_M, (e) MAT of the image in (a) using d_A, (f) MAT of the image in (a) using d_M*

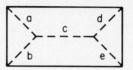

Figure 9.2   A rectangle and its skeleton using d_E

The part of the image that is spanned by each skeleton point and its associated distance value is termed a *maximal block*. The MAT of s provides a concise method of defining and representing s. For example, using d_E, the MAT corresponding to a circle is a point at its center having a distance value equal to the circle's radius. Note that the MAT determines the entire image, although it is true that a point in the image may lie in more than one maximal block.

Figures 9.1e and 9.1f show the MATs of the rectangle of Figure 9.1a using d_A and d_M, respectively. Figure 9.1b shows d_A and d_M for the rectangle, which in this example are identical. Note that the MATs in Figures 9.1e and 9.1f have distance values one less than the values in Figure 9.1b. This is due to defining the MAT as extending to the last pixel within the image rather than to the first pixel outside the image [Rose82a].

Exercises

9.1. Borgefors [Borg84] discusses four different families of metrics for binary images. The most popular is the city block / Chessboard metric family. Other families are the Chamfer metric, Octagonal metric, and D-Euclidean metric. Their *raison d'être* is to enable a reasonable approximation of the Euclidean metric that is also easy and fast to implement. It should be clear that the city block and Chessboard metrics are analogous to inner and outer approximations, respectively, to the Euclidean metric. The Chamfer, Octagonal, and D-Euclidean metrics are so-called closer approximations. Given a pair of points $p = (p_x, p_y)$ and $q = (q_x, q_y)$, arbitrary integers a and b, the (a, b) Chamfer metric, $d_{c(a, b)}(p, q)$, is defined as follows:

$$e = ||p_x - q_x| - |p_y - q_y||$$
$$f = \min \{ |p_x - q_x|, |p_y - q_y| \}$$
$$d_{c(a, b)}(p, q) = a \cdot e + b \cdot f.$$

The pair of values (3,4) are used as a close approximation of the Euclidean metric. Compute $d_{c(3,4)}$ and the MAT for the rectangle of Figure 9.1a.

9.2. What is the locus of points having $d_{c(a, b)}(p, q) \leq T$?

9.3. Find the values of (a, b) that yield the Chessboard metric. Do the same for the city block metric.

9.2   QUADTREE DISTANCE

For an image represented by a quadtree, the concept of points is not so relevant. Thus a definition of distance in terms of blocks is more appropriate. Let us identify blocks by their center points. We define the *distance transform* for a quadtree as a function, DIST, which yields for each black block in the quadtree the distance (in the chosen metric) from the center of the block to the nearest point that is on a black-white boundary. More formally, letting x be the center of a black block b, W be the set of white blocks, and z be a point on the boundary of white block w (say BOUNDARY(w)), we have:

$$\text{DIST}(b) = \min \{ d(x, z) \mid center(b) = x, \ z \in \text{BOUNDARY}(w), \ w \in W \}.$$

To be able to define DIST for all blocks, we say that DIST of a white or gray block is zero and that the border of the image is black. Notice that the distance transform is not defined in terms of a center-to-center distance. This is done in order to avoid a bias against large-sized adjacent blocks that are white. Moreover, this definition will be seen to restrict the number of nodes that need to be visited while computing it.

In Section 3.1, we observed that for any black node in the image, its neighbors (of greater than or equal size) cannot all be black, since otherwise merging would have taken place, and the node would not be in the image. This makes the Chessboard metric especially attractive. It means that for a black block of size 2^s, say P, the center of the white block whose boundary is nearest to P (hereafter referred to as the nearest white block) must be found at a distance of $< 3 \cdot 2^{s-1}$ (i.e., within a square centered at P of side length $3 \cdot 2^s$). In fact, the worst case arises when the nearest white block is a block of minimum size (i.e., a single pixel) adjacent to the furthest boundary of P's neighboring gray block (e.g., the white blocks adjacent to black blocks 14–49 with respect to black block 1 in Figure 9.3a).

Notice that none of P's neighboring black blocks (i.e., of size ≥ to that of P) need to be taken into consideration in computing P's Chessboard distance transform since the value would have to be at least $3 \cdot 2^{s-1}$ (e.g., black blocks 1, 2, and 12 with respect to black block 13 in Figure 9.3a). This observation means that when computing the Chessboard distance transform of a quadtree, for each node corresponding to a black block we need to consider only its gray neighboring nodes. Figure 9.3a illustrates the worst case in terms of the number of blocks that need to be examined; that is, black block 1 is surrounded by rings of black blocks of decreasing size. Figure 9.3b is the Chessboard distance transform of the image in Figure 9.3a.

Our observation can also be used to constrain the amount of work needed to compute other distance transforms. For example, in the case of the Euclidean distance transform, given black node P of size 2^s, the nearest white block is at distance $< 3 \cdot 2^{s-1} \cdot \sqrt{2}$. Similarly, when a city block distance transform is used, the maximum distance is $< 3 \cdot 2^s$. These values are all derived in a manner analogous to that used for the Chessboard distance transform.

Unfortunately we cannot say that larger-sized neighbors need not be taken into consideration when computing the Euclidean and city block distance transforms. That this is true can be seen by examining Figure 9.4, which illustrates the regions within which the nearest white block must be found. For example, given black block A of size 2^s, in the case of both the Euclidean and city block distance transforms, block B may be the nearest white block to block A. This may require visiting a gray northern or northeastern neighbor of block A of size 2^{s+1}. On the other hand, when the Chessboard distance transform is used, block C is the nearest to block A, and in fact no neighboring blocks of greater size ever need to be visited. Thus we see that use of the Euclidean and city block distance transform may lead to more than eight neighboring blocks of equal size being visited or even to blocks of greater size.

Note that our definition of a distance transform treats nonexistent neighbors (i.e., on the other side of the border of the space represented by the quadtree) as black and

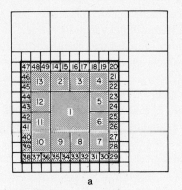

a

b

Figure 9.3   An (a) image illustrating the maximum number of nodes that need to be visited when computing the (b) Chessboard distance transform of the image in (a)

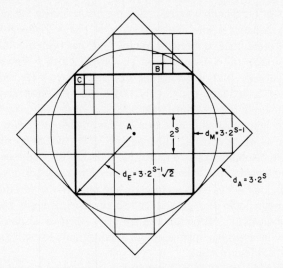

Figure 9.4   Regions within which the closest white node to black node A must lie for several metrics

of equal size. This is consistent with the definition of the Chessboard distance transform as yielding, for each black node in the quadtree, the distance from the center of the block to the nearest point that is on the boundary between a black and a white node.

Although it is possible to use the Euclidean and the city block metrics with quadtrees, in the following, we focus on the Chessboard distance transform because of its computational simplicity [Same82b]. This simplicity arises from the property of the Chessboard metric that the set of points q such that $d(p,q) \le t$ is a square, rather than a circle or a diamond as is true for the Euclidean and city block metrics, respectively. Shneier [Shne81a] uses a variant of the Chessboard metric to define a distance transform that associates with each black node P the minimum of the lengths of the horizontal or vertical paths from P's center to the boundary of the closest white node (not diagonally closest). This distance is termed a *path-length* distance transform (see Exercise 9.7).

The Chessboard distance transform is computed by traversing the quadtree in preorder where for each black block of size 2^s, the 8 edge- and vertex-neighbors are examined to determine the closest white block. If any of the neighbors is white, then the minimum distance is 2^{s-1} and we cease processing. Neighboring black nodes do not affect the value of the Chessboard distance transform since they result in a minimum Chessboard distance transform value of $3 \cdot 2^{s-1}$, which exceeds the theoretical maximum. Thus the heart of the algorithm lies in processing neighboring gray nodes.

The following procedures specify the computation of the Chessboard distance transform. The main procedure is termed CHESSBOARD_DIST and is invoked with a pointer to the root of the quadtree representing the image and an integer corresponding to the log of the diameter of the image (e.g., n for a $2^n \times 2^n$ image). Note that the definition of a quadtree node as a record of type *node* has been modified to include an additional field, DIST, to contain the value of its block's Chessboard distance transform. CHESSBOARD_DIST traverses the tree and controls the exploration of the eight neighbors of each black node. QT_GTEQ_EDGE_NEIGHBOR and QT_GTEQ_VERTEX_NEIGHBOR are used to locate the neighbors.

If an edge-neighbor, say G in direction E, is gray, then procedure DIST_EDGE continues the search by examining the subquadrants of G. We first examine the nodes corresponding to the subquadrants of G that are adjacent to edge E of the node being processed (e.g., subquadrants NW and SW of the eastern neighbor of node 1 in Figure 9.3a). If either node is white, then a closest white node in the specified direction has been found. If both nodes are gray, then we recursively apply DIST_EDGE to the corresponding subquadrants. If both nodes are black, then we examine the remaining two subquadrants in a similar manner (e.g., subquadrants NE and SE of the eastern neighbor of node 1 in Figure 9.3a).

If a vertex-neighbor, say G in direction V, is gray, then procedure DIST_VERTEX continues the search by examining the subquadrants of G. We first examine the node corresponding to the subquadrant of G that is adjacent to vertex V of the node being processed (e.g., subquadrant SW of the NE neighbor of node 1 in Figure 9.3a). If the node is white, then a closest node in the specified direction has been found. If the node is gray, then we recursively apply DIST_VERTEX to the subquadrant. If the node is black, say B, then we recursively examine the three remaining subquadrants in the following manner. We apply DIST_EDGE to the sibling subquadrants of B that share an edge with B (e.g., DIST_EDGE is applied to the NW and SE subquadrants of the NE neighbor of node 1 in Figure 9.3a). We also apply DIST_VERTEX to the remaining sibling subquadrant of B (e.g., the NE subquadrant of the NE neighbor of node 1 in Figure 9.3a).

```
recursive procedure CHESSBOARD_DIST(P,LEVEL);
/* Given a quadtree rooted at node P for a 2^LEVEL × 2^LEVEL image, find the Chessboard
   distance of each black node to its closest white node. White nodes are assigned dis-
   tance 0. */
begin
  value pointer node P;
  value integer LEVEL;
  pointer node Q;
  integer C;
  quadrant I;
  edge E;
  if GRAY(P) then
    begin
      for I in {'NW', 'NE', 'SW', 'SE'} do
        CHESSBOARD_DIST(SON(P,I),LEVEL−1);
    end
```

```
else if BLACK(P) then
  begin /* Examine P's eight neighbors */
    E ← 'N';
    C ← 2↑LEVEL;
    do
      begin
        Q ← QT_GTEQ_EDGE_NEIGHBOR(P,E);
        C ← if null(Q) or BLACK(Q) then C
            else if WHITE(Q) then 0
            else DIST_EDGE(Q,QUAD(OPEDGE(E),CCEDGE(E)),
                           QUAD(OPEDGE(E),CEDGE(E)),
                           2↑(LEVEL−1),0,C);
        if C ≠ 0 then
          begin
            Q ← QT_GTEQ_VERTEX_NEIGHBOR(P,VERTEX(E,CEDGE(E)));
            C ← if null(Q) or BLACK(Q) then C
                else if WHITE(Q) then 0
                else DIST_VERTEX(Q,OPEDGE(E),CCEDGE(E), 2↑(LEVEL−1),0,C);
            E ← CEDGE(E);
          end;
        end
      until C = 0 or E = 'N';
    DIST(P) ← C+2↑(LEVEL−1);
  end
else DIST(P) ← 0; /* A white node */
end;
```

recursive integer procedure DIST_EDGE(P,Q1,Q2,W,B,C);
/* Given a subquadtree rooted at node P whose block is 2 · W wide, determine the distance of the closest white node to the edge that borders quadrants Q1 and Q2 of P. B is a lower bound for the distance. C is an upper bound for the distance. */
```
begin
  value pointer node P;
  value quadrant Q1,Q2;
  value integer B,C,W;
  return(if B ≥ C then C /* The minimum has already been found */
         else if WHITE(P) then B
         else if BLACK(P) then C
         else if BLACK(SON(P,Q1)) and BLACK (SON(P,Q2)) then
             DIST_EDGE(SON(P,OPQUAD(Q1)),Q1,Q2,W/2,B+W,
                     DIST_EDGE(SON(P,OPQUAD(Q2)),
                             Q1,Q2,W/2,B+W,C))
         else DIST_EDGE(SON(P,Q2),Q1,Q2,W/2,B,
                     DIST_EDGE(SON(P,Q1),Q1,Q2,W/2,B,C)));
end;
```

```
recursive integer procedure DIST_VERTEX(P,E1,E2,W,B,C);
/* Given a subquadtree rooted at node P whose block is 2 · W wide, determine the dis-
   tance of the closest white node to the vertex of P formed by edges E1 and E2 of its
   block.  B is a lower bound for the distance.  C is an upper bound for the distance. */
begin
  value pointer node P;
  value edge E1,E2;
  value integer B,C,W;
  integer TEMP;
  if B ≥ C then return(C) /* The minimum has already been found */
  else if WHITE(P) then return(B)
  else if BLACK(P) then return(C)
  else
    begin
      TEMP ← DIST_VERTEX(SON(P,QUAD(E1,E2)),E1,E2,W/2,B,C);
      TEMP ← DIST_EDGE(SON(P,QUAD(OPEDGE(E1),E2)),
                       QUAD(E1,E2),
                       QUAD(E1,OPEDGE(E2)),W/2,B+W,TEMP);
      TEMP ← DIST_EDGE(SON(P,QUAD(E1,OPEDGE(E2))),
                       QUAD(OPEDGE(E1),E2),
                       QUAD(E1,E2),W/2,B+W,TEMP);
      TEMP ← DIST_VERTEX(SON(P,QUAD(OPEDGE(E1),OPEDGE(E2))),
                       E1,E2,W/2,B+W,TEMP);
      return(TEMP);
    end;
end;
```

The execution time of the Chessboard distance transform computation algorithm is measured by the number of nodes visited. Using a random image in the sense that a node is equally likely to appear at any position and level in the tree, it can be shown [Same82b] that the average number of nodes visited by each invocation of QT_GTEQ_-EDGE_NEIGHBOR and DIST_EDGE is $O(1)$. The same result holds for each invocation of QT_GTEQ_VERTEX_NEIGHBOR and DIST_VERTEX. These procedures are invoked once for each edge and vertex of a black node. Thus given a quadtree with B black nodes, the Chessboard distance transform can be computed in $O(B)$ time.

The algorithm and the analysis are quite similar to those employed in the computation of the total perimeter [Same81c] (see Section 5.2) and also for the first phase of a connected component labeling algorithm [Same81b] (see Section 5.1.2) for an image represented by the quadtree. The difference is, in part, due to the analysis of QT_GTEQ_VERTEX_NEIGHBOR. The similarity should not be surprising because in the former we are searching for adjacencies involving black and white nodes, while in the latter we are searching for adjacencies involving black and black nodes. In the case of the Chessboard distance transform, we are also searching for black and white adjacencies except that, unlike in the computation of the perimeter, we do not cease the search when an adjacent black node is found.

An asymptotically faster algorithm traverses the quadtree using the top-down neighbor transmitting method of Samet [Same85a] and processes smaller black blocks before their larger-sized black neighbors [Shaf89]. A variant of it is described below, and it is called TOP_DOWN_NEIGHBOR_DIST. Assume that the image is surrounded by black blocks as in Figure 3.4b. Assume further that the Chessboard distance transform value of each of these surrounding blocks is initialized to 0.5 of its width.

TOP_DOWN_NEIGHBOR_DIST is best understood by looking at a variant that traverses the quadtree nine times. In the first traversal, all eight neighbors of each node P are transmitted. In this traversal, each black block of size 2^s that is adjacent to a white block is assigned a Chessboard distance transform value of 2^{s-1}. The remaining black blocks (with the exception of those blocks that surround the image) are initialized with a large Chessboard distance transform value—for example, 2^{2n} for a $2^n \times 2^n$ image.

The second through ninth traversals propagate the distance values obtained in the first traversal toward the center of the image where the larger black blocks are located. There is one traversal for each of the N, E, S, W, NW, NE, SE, and SW directions.[1] To each black node, the traversal assigns the minimum Chessboard distance transform value obtained so far. These traversals require only a small subset of the neighbors to be transmitted as parameters.

For example, the N traversal transmits the S neighbor. For each node P at level L_P that is visited, if P and its S neighbor, say Q at level L_Q, are both black, then the distance transform of Q is set to the minimum of its previous value and that of P plus the sum of $2\uparrow(L_P - 1)$ and $2\uparrow(L_Q - 1)$. If P is gray, then the traversal is continued in such a manner that the NW and NE sons of P are visited first. All other cases of node color combinations are ignored. Other directions are treated in a similar manner (see Exercise 9.13).

The execution time of TOP_DOWN_NEIGHBOR_DIST is proportional to the number of blocks in the image, since no neighbor finding is necessary. Note that this procedure is analogous to depth-first connected component labeling as implemented by using the outline-and-color algorithm of Hunter and Steiglitz [Hunt78, Hunt79a] (see Section 4.4).

Interestingly the top-down method can also be implemented without transmitting neighbors. In particular, an equivalent (see Exercise 9.18) two-pass algorithm traverses the quadtree in preorder and makes use of a data structure termed an *active border* that contains all of the blocks that still have neighbors not yet examined [Shaf89]. This technique has been used in the computation of geometric properties, such as connected component labeling for pointerless quadtree representations [Same88b] (see Section 5.1.3). However, it is also applicable to pointer-based quadtree representations. We call this algorithm TOP_DOWN_ACTIVE_BORDER_DIST.

TOP_DOWN_ACTIVE_BORDER_DIST makes two passes over the quadtree. In essence, the first pass computes partial distance transform values for each node based on the distance transform values of its neighbors as found in the active border. The

---

[1] The actual implementation makes only two traversals by combining the first traversal with a traversal that is equivalent to the traversals in the N, W, SW, and SE directions, while the new second traversal is equivalent to the traversals in the N, E, NW, and NE directions plus the old first traversal [Shaf89] (see Exercise 9.15).

second pass repeats this process in reverse. Assume that the first pass performs the traversal in the order NW, NE, SW, SE, and that black node P at level L_p is currently being processed.

The partial distance transform value of P is computed by examining each of P's neighbors that have already been processed and computing a minimum using their partial distance transform values. On the first pass, these neighbors are a subset of those to the SW, W, NW, N, and NE of P. On the second pass, the traversal is performed in reverse order (SE, SW, NE, NW), and these neighbors are a subset of those to the NE, E, SE, S, and SW of P. The final distance transform value is the minimum value obtained after the second pass.

If any neighbor is white, then the distance transform value of P is set to $2\uparrow(L_p - 1)$, and the next node in the preorder traversal is processed. Otherwise (i.e., all neighbors are black) for each such neighbor Q at level L_Q, the new value of the distance transform of P is the minimum of P's current distance transform value (initialized to $3 \cdot 2\uparrow(L_p - 1)$ and that of the sum of $2\uparrow(L_p - 1)$, DIST(Q), and $2\uparrow(L_Q - 1)$).

Exercises

9.4. Given a $2^n \times 2^n$ image, what is the maximum value of the Chessboard distance transform? Give a sample image illustrating this case.

9.5. Extend the concept of distance and distance transform to three-dimensional images represented by octrees. Which of the distance metrics is most appropriate?

9.6. Show how to adapt the concept of a Chamfer distance to an image represented by a quadtree.

9.7. Show that the Chessboard distance transform is always less than or equal to the path-length distance transform.

9.8. Prove that the average number of nodes visited by each invocation of QT_GTEQ_EDGE_-NEIGHBOR and DIST_EDGE is $O(1)$. Do the same for each invocation of QT_GTEQ_VERTEX_-NEIGHBOR and DIST_VERTEX. Use the concept of a random image discussed in Section 3.2.1.2, and assume that in each case the maximum number of nodes will have to be visited by DIST_EDGE and DIST_VERTEX. This analysis should be similar to that performed for perimeter computation and the first stage of connected component labeling (see Exercises 5.20 and 5.44).

9.9. Executing procedure DIST_EDGE is similar to visiting the adjacency tree (see Section 3.2.2) of the node. Hunter and Steiglitz [Hunt78, Hunt79a] have shown that the total number of nodes in all adjacency trees for a given quadtree is bounded by four times the number of leaf nodes in the quadtree (see Exercise 3.13). Using this result, find an integer k such that for a quadtree with B and W black and white nodes, respectively, the number of nodes visited by all invocations of DIST_EDGE is bounded by $k \cdot (B + W)$.

9.10. Repeat Exercise 9.9 for procedure DIST_VERTEX. In other words, find an integer k such that for a quadtree with B and W black and white nodes, respectively, the number of nodes visited by all invocations of DIST_VERTEX is bounded by $k \cdot (B + W)$.

9.11. Procedure CHESSBOARD_DIST computes the Chessboard distance transform by use of a bottom-up tree traversal. An alternative is to use a top-down method (e.g., [Shne81a] for a path-length distance). In this case, more storage is required since with each gray node we must store the distance to its various sides. Write a procedure, TOP_DOWN_CHESSBOARD_DIST, to implement this technique.

9.12. Analyze the execution time of TOP_DOWN_CHESSBOARD_DIST and compare it to that of CHESSBOARD_DIST.

9.13. Write a set of procedures to implement the top-down Chessboard distance transform computation algorithm that transmits neighbors [Shaf89] (i.e., TOP_DOWN_NEIGHBOR_DIST). You will need to handle the four traversals for the directions NW, NE, SW, and SE in a slightly different manner from that described for the N, E, S, and W directions.

9.14. Prove that TOP_DOWN_NEIGHBOR_DIST is correct.

9.15. Suppose that you implement TOP_DOWN_NEIGHBOR_DIST with two traversals instead of nine. In essence, the new first traversal is equivalent to the traversals in the S, W, SW, and SE directions, while the new second traversal is equivalent to the traversals in the N, E, NW, and NE directions. Which neighbors must be transmitted for these two traversals?

9.16. Write a set of procedures to implement the top-down Chessboard distance transform computation algorithm that makes use of an active border [Shaf89] (i.e., TOP_DOWN_ACTIVE_BORDER_DIST). Recall that this algorithm makes two passes over the data and that you must define a data structure to represent the active border.

9.17. Prove that TOP_DOWN_ACTIVE_BORDER_DIST is correct.

9.18. Prove that TOP_DOWN_NEIGHBOR_DIST and TOP_DOWN_ACTIVE_BORDER_DIST are equivalent.

9.19. An intermediate approach to computing the Chessboard distance transform visits the adjacencies of a black node in a breadth-first fashion rather than depth-first as is done by procedure CHESSBOARD_DIST. In such a case, the neighbors of a black node are explored in a ringlike manner. For example, given node P of size 2^s, all of the sons of P's neighbors that are adjacent to the boundary of P are visited first. If all are black and of the same size, then the next ring is visited. For example, in the image given in Figure 9.3a, this would mean that to obtain the distance transform for node 1, nodes 2 through 13 would have to be visited first. If they are all black, then nodes 14 through 49 would have to be visited next, and so on. Write a procedure, BREADTH_FIRST_CHESSBOARD_DIST, to implement this technique.

9.20. Analyze the execution time of BREADTH_FIRST_CHESSBOARD_DIST and compare it to that of CHESSBOARD_DIST.

9.21. Procedure CHESSBOARD_DIST attempts to locate all eight neighbors of each black node. This is not necessary. Write a procedure CHESSBOARD_DIST2 that checks if any of the neighbors overlap and thereby avoids invoking QT_GTEQ_EDGE_NEIGHBOR or QT_GTEQ_VERTEX_NEIGHBOR for the overlapping neighbor (e.g., in Figure 9.3a the eastern neighbor of node 12 is 1, which overlaps with the SE neighbor of 1). Compare the execution time of CHESSBOARD_DIST2 with that of CHESSBOARD_DIST.

9.22. For each black node, procedure CHESSBOARD_DIST explores all of its neighbors. Borgefors [Borg84] discusses the distance computation process for binary images. She gives two-pass algorithms that make use of masks to compute the distance. Can you design similar methods to compute the Chessboard distance transform for an image represented by a quadtree? The idea is to start at the top left corner of the image and scan forward in the southern and eastern directions. This process is repeated starting in the lower right corner of the image and scanning backward in the northern and western directions. You will probably have to redefine the meaning of distance to be able to compute it in two passes.

9.23. Suppose that you were trying to solve a path planning problem for a robot. The idea is to represent space in such a way that the distance to the nearest obstacle is easy to ascertain. How would you adapt the concept of quadtree distance to this task?

9.24. In this section, we have adapted the concept of distance to an image represented by a quadtree by measuring distance in terms of the widths of the blocks. Since a quadtree represents a hierarchical aggregation of homogeneous regions, perhaps there exist more appropriate distance measures. For example, node distance could be used. Such a distance measure would reflect the number of nodes that must be visited when attempting to locate a black node's 'nearest' neighbor. Another alternative is to measure distance in terms of the log of the block sizes. Discuss the advantages and disadvantages of these alternative distance measures. Can you propose other distance measures?

9.25. Adapt the concept of distance to an image represented by a bintree. What are the shapes of the maximal blocks? Discuss the various metrics in terms of a diagram similar to Figure 9.4. Is the Chessboard metric still the most appropriate?

9.3 QUADTREE MEDIAL AXIS TRANSFORMS

In Section 9.1, the medial axis transformation was defined for an image as consisting of a set of maximal blocks. The maximal blocks can be of any size and at any position. Thus they are somewhat unwieldy as primitive elements for representation purposes since the process of determining them may be complex. Recall that the quadtree approach to image representation is an attempt to exploit the maximal block concept in a more systematic manner by constraining the sizes of the blocks and the positions of their centers. The quadtree medial axis transform (QMAT) [Same83a] is a combination of the concepts of MAT and quadtree that constrains only the positions of the centers of the maximal blocks, not their sizes.

The rest of this section is organized as follows. First, the QMAT is defined. Second, we see how the QMAT can be constructed from a quadtree. Next, an algorithm is presented to reconstruct a quadtree from its QMAT. This algorithm can be skipped on an initial reading. We conclude by discussing the use of the QMAT as an image representation.

9.3.1 Definitions

First, let us define a quadtree skeleton. Let the set of black blocks in the quadtree of the image be denoted by B. For each black block, b_i, let $S(b_i)$ be the part of the image spanned by a square with side width $2 \cdot \mathrm{DIST}(b_i)$ centered about b_i — that is, we use the Chessboard distance transform defined in Section 9.2. The *quadtree skeleton* consists of the set, T, of black blocks satisfying the following properties:

1. the set of pixels in $B = \bigcup_{t \in T} S(t)$,

2. for any t in T there does not exist b in B ($b \neq t$) such that $S(t) \subseteq S(b)$, and

3. for each b in B there exists t in T such that $S(b) \subseteq S(t)$.

For example, for the quadtree of Figure 9.5, the quadtree skeleton consists of nodes 1, 11, and 15 with Chessboard distance transform values of 6, 2, and 4,

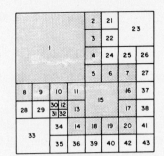

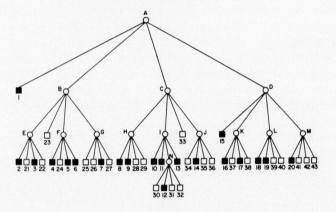

Figure 9.5   Sample quadtree

respectively. Property 1 ensures that the entire image is spanned by the quadtree skeleton. Property 2 is termed the *subsumption property* wherein b_j is *subsumed* by b_k when $S(b_j) \subseteq S(b_k)$. Property 2 means that the elements of the quadtree skeleton are the blocks with the largest Chessboard distance transform values. Property 3 ensures that no block in B requires more than one element of T for its subsumption—for example, the case that one-half of the block is subsumed by one element of T and the other half is subsumed by another element of T is not permitted.

Theorem 9.1   The quadtree skeleton of an image is unique.

Proof   Assume that the quadtree skeleton is not unique. Let T_1 and T_2 both be quadtree skeletons of the same image, $B = \bigcup_{t \in T_1} S(t)$ and $B = \bigcup_{t \in T_2} S(t)$. Assume, without loss of generality, that there exists $t_1 \in T_1$ such that $t_1 \notin T_2$. Therefore, by property 3, treating t_1 as an element of B, there exists $t_2 \in T_2$ ($t_2 \neq t_1$) such that $S(t_1) \subseteq S(t_2)$. However, this contradicts property 2 that stipulates that for any $t \in T_1$ there does not exist

$b \in B$ $(b \neq t)$ such that $S(t) \subseteq S(b)$. Hence the quadtree skeleton of an image is unique. ☐

Theorem 9.1 follows from the fact that the definition of a quadtree skeleton is derived directly from the definition of a quadtree. Thus since the quadtree for a particular orientation of an image is unique, the same will be true for its quadtree skeleton. An alternative interpretation of Theorem 9.1 is that although the quadtree skeleton is a collection of squares that span the image and whose centers are constrained to be centers of quadtree blocks, the converse is not true. This is not surprising because the squares that comprise the quadtree skeleton are maximal blocks in the quadtree sense—that is, four elements of the quadtree skeleton cannot be merged to form a larger element.

The QMAT of an image is the quadtree whose black nodes correspond to the black blocks comprising the quadtree skeleton and their associated Chessboard distance transform values. All remaining nodes in the QMAT are white and gray with Chessboard distance transform values of zero. For example, Figure 9.6 contains the block and tree representations of the QMAT of Figure 9.5.

We now make the following observations with the aid of Figures 9.5 and 9.6. The squares spanned by the Chessboard distance transform of the blocks of the QMAT have sides whose lengths are sums of powers of 2 and are not necessarily disjoint. This is in contrast with the quadtree, which is a partition of an image into a set of

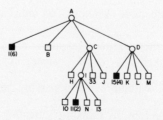

Figure 9.6   QMAT corresponding to the quadtree of Figure 9.5

disjoint squares having sides whose lengths are powers of 2. For example, block 11 is subsumed by both blocks 1 and 15.

Recall that the subsumption property (property 2) means that the elements of the QMAT are the blocks with the largest distance transform values. For example, for Figure 9.5, the quadtree skeleton consists of blocks 1, 11, and 15 rather than blocks 1, 12, and 15 since block 12 is subsumed by block 11. The latter result would have been permitted had we modified property 2 as in 2′:

2′. For any t in T there does not exist u in T $(u \neq t)$ such that $S(t) \subseteq S(u)$.

Property 2′ only ensures that there are no extraneous elements with respect to subsumption of the image in a given quadtree skeleton. In other words, the quadtree skeleton can contain only one of blocks 11 and 12 — not both of them. Replacing property 2 with 2′ yields a definition of a quadtree skeleton with several undesirable implications. First, it means that the quadtree skeleton of an image is no longer unique; for example, for Figure 9.5 both {1, 11, 15} and {1, 12, 15} would be legal quadtree skeletons. Second, it leads to a QMAT that contains more nodes; for example, white node N in Figure 9.6 would be replaced by a gray node having black son 12 and white sons 30, 31, and 32.

The fact that the border of the image is assumed to be black results in reducing the number of nodes in the QMAT. Without this assumption, block 1 would be of radius 4 and would not lead to subsumption of blocks 2, 3, 4, 8, 9, and 10. Note that blocks 5 and 11 are subsumed by block 15 anyway, so their subsumption is not dependent on our assumption.

Before proceeding any further, it is appropriate to make a few additional comments about property 3 of the quadtree skeleton definition. This property does not yield a minimal set of blocks. For example, in the image of Figure 9.7a, property 3 requires that the quadtree skeleton contain blocks 5, 14, and 15, while in actuality blocks 5 and 15 are sufficient since together they subsume block 14. Thus if we were interested in a minimal set of blocks, we would modify property 3 as in 3′:

3′. There does not exist u in T such that $S(u) \subseteq \bigcup_{t \in T \wedge t \neq u} S(t)$.

We do not use the definition of a quadtree skeleton that yields the minimal set of blocks for two reasons. First, by virtue of the definition of the QMAT, the tree size of the QMAT would be unaffected by using property 3′ instead of property 3 since the only difference is that the additional blocks are represented by black nodes rather than white nodes—for example, node 14 in Figures 9.7b and 9.7c. To see that this is always true, observe that for a node to be extraneous by virtue of property 3′, it must be subsumed by its neighbors, which must themselves be black. Thus the extraneous node, when represented by a white node, cannot be merged with its neighbors to yield a larger node and must remain part of the QMAT. Second, as will be seen in Section 9.3.2, the QMAT creation algorithm is considerably simpler when property 3 is used.

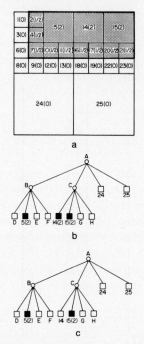

Figure 9.7 *(a) An image and its corresponding QMATs using (b) property 3 and (c) property 3′*

Exercises

9.26. Suppose that we relax the definition of the quadtree skeleton so that the blocks need not be maximal quadtree blocks. In particular, we remove property 2 of the definition. Instead we say that the blocks must be maximal quadtree skeleton blocks, where a *maximal quadtree skeleton block* is defined to be a quadtree block, say q, and its distance transform value such that the four quadrants of q do not have the same color and distance transform values. This means that the quadtree skeleton would be permitted to contain blocks that would normally be merged into larger blocks. Prove that using such a definition means that the quadtree skeleton of an image is not unique.

9.27. In the definition of the distance transform, we assumed that the border of the image is always black. Prove that assuming a black border can never lead to a QMAT with more nodes than that obtained by assuming a white border.

9.28. Section 3.4 of [Same90a] discusses the following three methods of representing a rectangle by a representative point in a four-dimensional space.

   1. The x and y coordinates of two diagonally opposite corners of the rectangle (e.g., the lower left and upper right).

   2. The x and y coordinates of a corner of the rectangle, together with its horizontal and vertical extents.

   3. The x and y coordinates of the centroid of the rectangle, together with its

horizontal and vertical extents (i.e., the horizontal and vertical distances from the centroid to the relevant sides).

Which of these methods is most closely related to the QMAT?

9.29. The definition of the QMAT given in this section is primarily oriented toward binary images. How would you adapt the concept of a QMAT to multicolored images (i.e., more than two values)?

9.30. The definition of a quadtree makes no distinction between black and white nodes in terms of merging criteria. On the other hand, the QMAT does make a distinction between black and white in the sense that the QMAT is defined in terms of the foreground color (i.e., black) because of the distance transform. For certain images, the QMAT could require fewer nodes if it were defined in terms of the distance transform values of white nodes (as was done in the formulation of the region expansion function EXPAND2 given in Section 6.6). In essence, the issue is whether black or white should be treated as the foreground color. Give some criteria for deciding whether black or white should be the foreground color. Back up your choice with some quantitative and qualitative data.

9.31. Can you extend the definition of a QMAT to three dimensions? an arbitrary number of dimensions?

9.32. Suppose you use a bintree representation of a quadtree. Define a bintree medial axis transform (BMAT)? Does it make sense? What is its physical interpretation?

9.3.2 Computing a QMAT from Its Quadtree

Properties 2 and 3 of the quadtree skeleton definition of Section 9.3.1 suggest the following simple two-step algorithm (termed *Algorithm A*) for determining the QMAT. At the end of the algorithm, the set T contains the black blocks comprising the QMAT.

Algorithm A

1. Sort the black blocks in increasing order by value of their Chessboard distance transform forming the set T such that for each $t_i \in T$, $\text{DIST}(t_i) \le \text{DIST}(t_{i+1})$.

2. Starting with $i = 1$, remove each t_i from T when there exists t_j in T such that $i < j$ and $S(t_i) \subseteq S(t_j)$.

From a computation complexity standpoint, Algorithm A is quite costly since it involves sorting the black blocks and examining whether a block is subsumed by the remaining blocks. Instead we use the following algorithm (termed *Algorithm B*), which traverses the quadtree in postorder (that is, the sons of a node are visited first) and determines for each node corresponding to a black block, say P, whether $S(P) \subseteq S(Q)$ where Q is one of P's eight neighbors in the N, NE, E, SE, S, SW, W, and NW directions.

Algorithm B

1. Sort the black nodes in postorder, forming the set T.

2. Starting with $i = 1$, remove each t_i from T when there exists t_j in T such that $i \neq j$, t_j is a neighbor of t_i in one of the directions N, NE, E, SE, S, SW, W, NW, and $S(t_i) \subseteq S(t_j)$.

The remainder of the discussion elaborates on properties of Algorithm B. In general, whenever a black block is subsumed by one of its neighbors, it appears in the QMAT as a white block. Once all the sons of a gray node have been processed and if in the QMAT they all correspond to white blocks, then the gray node is changed to correspond to a white block (e.g., gray node N of Figure 9.5 having sons 30, 12, 31, and 32 is changed to correspond to a white block in Figure 9.6).

At this point, it is appropriate to examine the notion of subsumption in a more rigorous manner. Let P and Q be adjacent nodes (along an edge or a vertex) corresponding to black blocks appearing at levels L_P and L_Q, respectively, in the quadtree such that $L_Q > L_P$. Also let $D(P,Q) = \text{DIST}(Q) - 2\uparrow(L_Q - 1) - 2\uparrow(L_P - 1)$. P is said to be *subsumed* by Q if $D(P,Q) = \text{DIST}(P)$. It should be clear that $D(P,Q)$ cannot be greater than $\text{DIST}(P)$ since this would contradict the definition of the Chessboard distance transform. In such a case, P would have a closer black-white border point than does Q, although P is constrained by the value of $D(P,Q)$ to be entirely contained in the square of the side width $2 \cdot \text{DIST}(Q)$ centered at Q. Clearly when $D(P,Q) < \text{DIST}(P)$, P is not subsumed by Q.

When $D(P,Q) = \text{DIST}(P)$, there are two cases to consider. If $\text{DIST}(P) = 2\uparrow(L_P - 1)$, then P is adjacent to the outer border of $S(Q)$, and thus no black blocks can be subsumed by P (e.g., black block 9 in Figure 9.5 is adjacent to the outer border of the square of width 6 centered at block 1). Thus changing block P from black to white will not affect the detection of subsumption of other nodes.

However, if $\text{DIST}(P) > 2\uparrow(L_P - 1)$, the second case to be considered when $D(P,Q) = \text{DIST}(P)$, then P is not adjacent to the outer border of $S(Q)$. This means that some blocks subsumed by Q can be detected only by virtue of being subsumed by P since they are not adjacent to Q. Define $U(P,Q)$ to be a subset of these blocks having the following properties:

1. Q is larger than P.
2. Each element of $U(P,Q)$ is smaller than P.
3. If Q is adjacent to P along edge R of the black block corresponding to P, then $U(P,Q)$ is equal to the blocks subsumed in the direction of the opposite edge, denoted by $\text{OPEDGE}(R)$, of P's block.
4. If P touches the vertex V formed by edges R and T of the block corresponding to Q, then $U(P,Q)$ is equal to the blocks subsumed in the direction of edges R and T of P's block and the blocks subsumed in the direction of vertex V.

It can be shown that for a block Q, the sets of blocks formed by the various blocks $P — U(P,Q)$ — are disjoint. Furthermore their union is the set of the blocks that are not adjacent to Q and are subsumed by Q. Properties 1–4 imply that all elements of $U(P,Q)$ are in the block corresponding to $\text{FATHER}(P)$; that is, they are in the blocks corresponding to the brothers of P. This means that an algorithm that processes a gray son prior to its black or white brothers ensures that the QMAT is formed by examining blocks for subsumption according to increasing size—that is, smaller size first. As soon as a black block is determined to be subsumed by its neighbors, its Chessboard distance transform value and type are changed to zero and white, respectively. This leads to the following result.

Lemma 9.1   Both Algorithms A and B compute a result that satisfies the definition of a quadtree skeleton, given in Section 9.3.1, and the QMAT of an image.

Proof   Algorithm A clearly satisfies properties 1–3 of the definition since its steps are equivalent to the definition. To show that Algorithm B meets our requirements is slightly more complex. Properties 1 and 3 of the definition are satisfied since Algorithm B starts with the QMAT and the quadtree as identical and then systematically removes nodes whose corresponding blocks are subsumed by others. Satisfaction of property 2 of the definition is shown below.

   Algorithm B is based on the principle that as black block P is determined to be subsumed by neighboring black block Q (i.e., one that has not yet been removed by virtue of being subsumed by yet another larger adjacent block), P is removed from the quadtree (i.e., its color is changed to white). This is achieved by examining each adjacency. Properties 1–4 of the case when $D(P,Q) = \text{DIST}(P)$ and $\text{DIST}(P) > 2\uparrow(L_p - 1)$, plus the fact that a gray node is processed before its black and white brothers, ensure that no block is removed from the quadtree before blocks that are subsumed by it. Thus we see that no block in the QMAT is subsumed by another block in the quadtree. Recall from Section 9.3.1 that this is a stronger statement than stating that no block in the QMAT is subsumed by another block in the QMAT.   ☐

Theorem 9.2   Algorithms A and B are equivalent.

Proof   By Lemma 9.1, both Algorithms A and B compute the quadtree skeleton. Theorem 9.1 indicates that the quadtree skeleton of an image is unique, and our result follows.   ☐

   The equivalence of Algorithms A and B can also be seen by observing that both start with smaller black blocks and attempt to determine if they are subsumed by other larger black blocks. Algorithm B is superior because no sorting is required. Moreover, blocks that cannot possibly subsume one another are not checked for subsumption; that is, Algorithm B examines only a maximum of eight neighboring blocks, while Algorithm A examines all possible larger-sized black blocks. Also note the simplicity of Algorithm B that results from using property 3 rather than 3′ in the definition of a quadtree skeleton, since each block in the original image can only be subsumed in its entirety. Thus there is no need to examine whether a node is subsumed by a set of other nodes, for example, node 14 of Figure 9.7a is subsumed by nodes 5 and 15.

The main procedure for computing the quadtree medial axis transform is termed QUADTREE_TO_QMAT and is given below. It is invoked with a pointer to the root of the quadtree representing the image and an integer corresponding to the log of the diameter of the image (e.g., n for a $2^n \times 2^n$ image array). We assume that the value of each block's Chessboard distance transform has already been computed by procedure CHESSBOARD_DIST described in Section 9.2. QUADTREE_TO_QMAT traverses the tree and controls the examination of the eight neighbors of each black node. QT_GTEQ_-EDGE_NEIGHBOR2 and QT_GTEQ_VERTEX_NEIGHBOR2 are used to locate the neighbors.

Procedure QUADTREE_TO_QMAT is different from Algorithm B in that it has been modified so it can achieve step 2 by performing a postorder traversal of the quadtree. There is no longer a need to process the gray sons before processing their black and white brothers. Instead whenever a black block, say P, has been found to be subsumed by an adjacent black block, say Q, then P's NODETYPE field is changed to white, but its DIST field is left alone. This ensures that application of QUADTREE_TO_QMAT to any of P's yet unprocessed gray brothers will result in subsumption of their descendants by P (actually Q), if appropriate.

Note that when P is a genuine white block and R is one of the descendants of a gray brother of P, then $D(R,P)$ is negative since DIST(P) is zero. Thus R cannot be subsumed by P; for example, $D(R,P) <$ DIST(R). Once all of a gray node's sons have been processed, a check is made if they all correspond to white blocks. If yes, then they and their father are replaced by a node having NODETYPE and DIST field values of white and zero, respectively. Otherwise the DIST field of any son corresponding to a white block is set to zero.

As an example of the application of the algorithm, consider the quadtree in Figure 9.5 whose QMAT is in Figure 9.6. All of the black nodes have labels ranging from 1 to 20, while the white nodes have labels ranging from 21 to 43. The gray nodes have labels ranging between A and N. The black nodes have been labeled in the order in which their subsuming adjacencies were explored by procedure QMAT.

```
recursive procedure QUADTREE_TO_QMAT(P,LEVEL);
/*  Given a quadtree rooted at node P for a 2^LEVEL × 2^LEVEL image, determine its
    corresponding quadtree medial axis transform.  */
begin
  value pointer node P;
  value integer LEVEL;
  integer L;
  quadrant I;
  edge E;
  if BLACK(P) then
```

```
      begin /* Determine if P is subsumed by any of its neighbors */
        for E in {'N', 'E', 'S', 'W'} do
          begin
            L ← LEVEL;
            QT_GTEQ_EDGE_NEIGHBOR2(P,E,Q,L);
            if not(null(Q)) and DIST(Q)-2↑(L-1)-2↑(LEVEL-1) = DIST(P) then
              begin /* P is subsumed by its neighbor Q */
                NODETYPE(P) ← 'WHITE';
                return;
              end;
            L ← LEVEL;
            QT_GTEQ_VERTEX_NEIGHBOR2(P,VERTEX(E,CEDGE(E)),Q,L);
            if not(null(Q)) and DIST(Q)-2↑(L-1)-2↑(LEVEL-1) = DIST(P) then
              begin /* P is subsumed by its neighbor Q */
                NODETYPE(P) ← 'WHITE';
                return;
              end;
          end;
      end
    else if GRAY(P) then
      begin
        for I in {'NW', 'NE', 'SW', 'SE'} do
          QUADTREE_TO_QMAT(SON(P,I),LEVEL-1);
        if WHITE(SON(P,'NW')) and WHITE(SON(P,'NE')) and
          WHITE(SON(P,'SE')) and WHITE(SON(P,'SW')) then
          begin /* Merge the four sons */
            NODETYPE(P) ← 'WHITE';
            returnsonstoavail(P);
          end
        else /* All four sons are not white or subsumed */
          begin
            for I in {'NW', 'NE', 'SW', 'SE'} do
              begin
                if WHITE(SON(P,I)) then DIST(SON(P,I)) ← 0;
              end;
          end;
      end;
  end; /* White nodes are left alone */
```

The execution time of the QMAT construction algorithm is measured by the number of nodes that are visited and by the size of the quadtree. To determine whether a black node's corresponding block is subsumed, between one and eight neighbors must be visited. This means that procedures QT_GTEQ_EDGE_NEIGHBOR2 and QT_GTEQ_VERTEX_NEIGHBOR2 are invoked a maximum of four times for each black node. From Theorems 3.3 and 3.4, we have that the average number of nodes visited by each invocation of these procedures is bounded from above by 7/2 and 9/2, respectively. Since for a quadtree with B and W black and white nodes, respectively, the number of nodes is $O(B + W)$, we have now proved:

Theorem 9.3 The average execution time of constructing a QMAT from a quadtree is $O(B)$. □

Exercises

9.33. Procedure QUADTREE_TO_QMAT is an 'in-place' algorithm since it overwrites the quadtree in the process of constructing the corresponding QMAT. Modify it so that the quadtree is left intact.

9.34. Analyze the execution time of a direct implementation of Algorithm A. Can you implement it in such a way that the algorithm would be $O(B)$ where B is the number of black blocks in the quadtree?

9.35. Can you combine procedures CHESSBOARD_DIST and QUADTREE_TO_QMAT in their present forms to yield a one-pass algorithm to compute the QMAT?

9.36. Procedure QUADTREE_TO_QMAT attempts to locate all eight neighbors of each black node when subsumption does not occur. This is not necessary. Write a procedure QUADTREE_TO_QMAT2 that checks if any of the neighbors overlap and thereby avoids invoking QT_GTEQ_EDGE_NEIGHBOR or QT_GTEQ_VERTEX_NEIGHBOR for the overlapping neighbor (see Exercise 9.21).

9.37. How would you compute the QMAT from any of the pointerless quadtree representations?

9.38. Are any of the pointerless quadtree representations more suitable for the computation of the QMAT than others? Would Algorithm A be more appropriate than Algorithm B for the computation of the QMAT when using pointerless quadtree representations?

9.39. The QMAT is defined as a collection of blocks whose centers are at predetermined positions. Suppose that we relax this restriction by defining a new structure, called QCAT, that permits the centers to be at arbitrary positions within the block. This means that we no longer need to resort to the fiction that an image is surrounded by black in order to enable blocks adjacent to the border of an image to subsume their neighbors. Thus an element of the quadtree skeleton would be identified by a center point and a Chessboard distance transform value. Assume that properties 1–3 of the quadtree skeleton still hold. Can you come up with a reasonable algorithm for the computation of the QCAT from its corresponding quadtree. By 'reasonable' it is meant that the algorithm does not search the entire universe! Is the QCAT of a quadtree unique? If not, can you modify some of the properties of its definition so that it is unique? Is the quadtree skeleton corresponding to the QCAT minimal?

9.40. Suppose that we further relax the restrictions on elements of a QMAT by yet defining another new structure, called QRAT, for which we remove the stipulation that the blocks be square. Repeat Exercise 9.39 for the QRAT.

9.41. Suppose that we bend the definition of a QMAT in another direction by removing the restriction that the blocks be rectangular in shape. One variation is to use a decomposition into cross-shapes. When the cross consists of five squares of equal size, we have a QMAT constructed with the path-length distance transform. Of course, we can also vary the shapes of the crosses by using different values for the lengths of the horizontal and vertical segments of the crosses. Another more general variation is not to require the horizontal and vertical segments to cross at their midpoints. Discuss how crosslike quadtree medial axis transforms can be defined and efficiently computed from their quadtrees. Is it reasonable to expect any of these representations to be unique? Are they minimal in terms of the amount of storage that they require?

9.42.   Define a QMAT in terms of a Chamfer distance transform (see Exercise 9.1). Recall that the shapes of the blocks depend on the values of the parameters a and b and that the Chamfer distance is an attempt to approximate a Euclidean metric. Is the computation of the QMAT facilitated by choosing certain values of a and b over others (besides the obvious ones)? Modify your definition of the QMAT to permit different values of a and b to be used with different blocks.

9.3.3   Reconstructing a Quadtree from Its QMAT [1]

The process of reconstructing a quadtree from its QMAT, although somewhat tedious, is relatively straightforward [Same85b]. It demonstrates the type of techniques that must be used in algorithms to manipulate images represented by QMATs. We perform a postorder traversal of the QMAT, and for each element of the quadtree skeleton (i.e., a black node in the QMAT), say t, we add all elements of $S(t)$ to the quadtree. This is done by examining the neighbors of t. Recall that there are at most eight such neighbors.

Once a neighbor, say u, is found to be subsumed by an element of the QMAT, the same process of neighbor examination is performed for the neighbors of u in the specified direction. For example, in Figure 9.8, when processing the eastern edge of node 1 of the QMAT, we add nodes 3 and 6 by expanding node F. Next, we add nodes 4 and 5, and nodes 7 and 8 by expanding nodes P and Q, respectively, because they are the eastern neighbors of 3 and 6.

The main procedure is termed QMAT_TO_QUADTREE and is invoked with a pointer to the QMAT representing the image and an integer corresponding to the log of the diameter of the image (e.g., n for a $2^n \times 2^n$ image array). QMAT_TO_QUADTREE traverses the QMAT and controls the examination of the eight neighbors of each black node that is an element of the QMAT. Our algorithm requires that the neighbors along each of the directions be of equal size. If the neighbor is of larger size, then use ADD_FOUR_WHITE_SONS to decompose it into four white sons as many times as is required to get the appropriate size.

For example, in the QMAT of Figure 9.8, the western neighbor of node 2 is D and is larger than 2. Therefore we replace it by a gray node with four white sons (62, K, 63, and L) and return K as the appropriate neighbor. Of course, if the node is on the edge of the image in the desired direction, then no neighbor exists and NIL is returned (e.g., the northern neighbor of node 1 in Figure 9.8). Neighbors of equal size in directions N, E, S, and W are located by MAKE_EQ_EDGE_NEIGHBOR, while neighbors of equal size in directions NE, SE, SW, and NW are located by MAKE_EQ_VERTEX_NEIGHBOR.

Once a neighboring node of equal size has been located, we propagate the subsumption and add black nodes as necessary. This may require changing white nodes

---

[1] This section can be skipped.

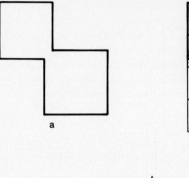

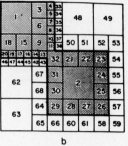

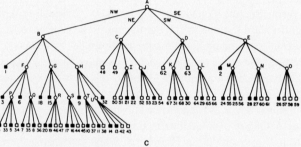

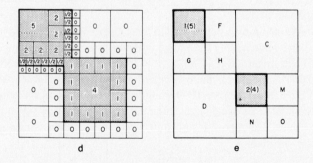

Figure 9.8 (a) An image, (b) its block decomposition, (c) its quadtree, (d) its distance transform, (e) the block decomposition of its QMAT, and (f) its QMAT

to black or decomposing them into smaller nodes. Procedure PROPAGATE_EDGE propagates subsumption in the direction of an edge. It checks if the neighboring node, say Y, is subsumed entirely by the node currently being processed, say X. If Y is not, then there are three cases depending on Y's type:

1. If Y is black, then Y is left alone (e.g., when propagating subsumption in the northern direction for node 11 in Figure 9.6 and encountering black node 1).

2. If Y is white, then Y is decomposed into four white sons, and PROPAGATE_-EDGE is reapplied recursively to the two sons closest to the node whose subsumption is being propagated, i.e., X. For example, node F of the QMAT in Figure 9.8 is an eastern neighbor of node 1, but it is not totally subsumed by node 1, and thus it is decomposed into white sons 3, 6, P, and Q. PROPA-GATE_EDGE is now reapplied to nodes 3 and 6.

3. If Y is gray, then recursively reapply PROPAGATE_EDGE to the two adjacent sons as was done for a white node.

When the neighboring node, Y, is subsumed entirely, perform the following two steps:

1. Convert Y to a black node if it is white or gray.
2. Determine if there is further subsumption in the direction being processed. For example, while processing node 1 of the QMAT in Figure 9.8, node 3 is subsumed by node 1, but so is part of node P. This forces the recursive reapplication of PROPAGATE_EDGE to the eastern neighbor of 3 — that is, P.

Procedure PROPAGATE_VERTEX is analogous in spirit to PROPAGATE_EDGE. It propagates subsumption in the direction of a vertex (NE, SE, SW, and NW). It checks if the neighboring node, say Y, is subsumed entirely by the node being processed, say X. If Y is not, then there are three cases depending on Y's type.

1. If Y is black, then Y is left alone.
2. If Y is white, then Y is decomposed into four white sons, and PROPAGATE_-VERTEX is reapplied recursively to the son closest to the node whose subsumption is being propagated, that is, X. For example, node H of the QMAT in Figure 9.8 is a southeastern neighbor of node 1, but it is not totally subsumed by node 1. Thus it is decomposed into white sons 9, T, U, and V (labeled 32 in Figure 9.8). PROPAGATE_VERTEX is now reapplied to node 9.

3. If Y is gray, then recursively reapply PROPAGATE_VERTEX to the nearest son, as was done for a white node.

When the neighboring node, Y, is subsumed entirely, perform the following two steps:

1. Convert Y to a black node if it is white or gray.
2. Determine if there is further subsumption in the direction of the vertex being processed, as well as its two adjacent directions. For example, while

processing node 1 of the QMAT in Figure 9.8, node 9 is subsumed by node 1, but so are parts of nodes T, U, and V. This forces the recursive reapplication of PROPAGATE_VERTEX to the southeastern neighbor of 9—that is, V—and PROPAGATE_EDGE to the eastern and southern neighbors of 9—that is, T and U, respectively.

Figures 9.9a and 9.9b provide a snapshot of the QMAT-to-quadtree construction process by showing the intermediate quadtree immediately after finishing processing node 1. Note that node V is a gray node having sons 12, 39, 40, and 41, of which 12 is black, while 39, 40, and 41 are white. In contrast, in the quadtree of Figure 9.8, node V is black (and is termed 32). This is because when processing node 2 and checking its northeastern neighbor (i.e., H) for subsumption, we are compelled to reapply PROPAGATE_VERTEX to node V, which is a gray node. However, as far as node 2 is concerned, the entire block corresponding to node V is subsumed by node 2, and hence it is converted to a black node. A similar situation can arise when PROPAGATE_EDGE encounters a gray node.

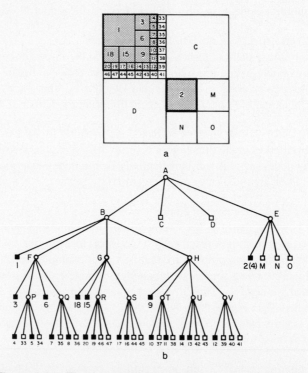

Figure 9.9   The intermediate quadtree immediately after propagating the subsumption of node 1 when reconstructing the quadtree corresponding to the QMAT of Figure 9.8(f): (a) block decomposition and (b) tree representation

The process of recursive application of procedures PROPAGATE_EDGE and PROP-AGATE_VERTEX is guaranteed to terminate by virtue of the observation made in Section 9.2 that a QMAT black block of size $2^s \times 2^s$ has an upper bound of $3 \cdot 2^{(s-1)}$ for its Chessboard distance transform value. Practically, this means that in Figure 9.8e, when checking the space subsumed by node 1, we need not examine nodes to the east, south, and southeast of nodes F, G, and H, respectively.

As an example of the application of the algorithm, consider the $2^4 \times 2^4$ region given in Figure 9.8a. Figure 9.8b is the corresponding block decomposition, while Figure 9.8c is its quadtree representation. Figure 9.8d contains the Chessboard distance transform corresponding to Figure 9.8b. Figures 9.8e and 9.8f contain the block decomposition of the QMAT and the tree representation of the QMAT corresponding to Figure 9.8b, respectively. Figure 9.9 shows the quadtree resulting after propagating the subsumption of node 1.

The black nodes have labels ranging from 1 to 32, while the white nodes have labels ranging from 33 to 68. The gray nodes have labels ranging between A and V. Nodes 1 and 2 are the elements of the quadtree skeleton (i.e., the black nodes comprising the QMAT). The remainder of the black nodes have been labeled in the order in which they were visited (and thereby created) by procedures PROPAGATE_EDGE and PROPAGATE_VERTEX. Note the presence of gray node V, black node 12, and white nodes 39, 40, and 41 in Figure 9.9 and their replacement by black node 32 in Figure 9.8. This was explained earlier to be a result of checking the subsumption of node 2.

```
recursive procedure QMAT_TO_QUADTREE(P,LEVEL);
/* Given a QMAT rooted at node P for a 2^LEVEL × 2^LEVEL image, find its corresponding
   quadtree. */
begin
 value pointer node P;
 value integer LEVEL;
 pointer node Q;
 edge E;
 quadrant I;
 if BLACK(P) then
  begin
   if DIST(P) > 2↑(LEVEL−1) then
    begin /* Node P subsumes some of its neighbors */
     for E in {'N', 'E', 'S', 'W'} do
      begin
       Q ← MAKE_EQ_EDGE_NEIGHBOR(P,E);
       if not(null(Q)) then
        PROPAGATE_EDGE(Q,LEVEL,DIST(P)−2↑(LEVEL−1),E);
       Q ← MAKE_EQ_VERTEX_NEIGHBOR(P,VERTEX(E,CEDGE(E)));
       if not(null(Q)) then
        PROPAGATE_VERTEX(Q,LEVEL,DIST(P)−2↑(LEVEL−1),E);
      end;
    end;
```

```
      DIST(P) ← 0;
    end
  else if GRAY(P) then
    begin
      for I in {'NW', 'NE', 'SW', 'SE'} do
        QMAT_TO_QUADTREE(SON(P,I),LEVEL−1);
      end;
end; /* White nodes are left alone */
```

recursive pointer node procedure MAKE_EQ_EDGE_NEIGHBOR(P,E);
/* Return the neighbor of node P in the direction of edge E that is equal in size to P. If P is
   adjacent to the border of the image along the specified direction, then NIL is returned. If
   the neighbor is of size greater than P and is white, then it is broken up into four white
   quadrants in order to obtain the desired neighbor. If the neighbor is black, then it is not
   broken up further. */
begin
  value pointer node P;
  value edge E;
  pointer node Q;
  Q ← **if not**(null(FATHER(P))) **and** ADJ(E,SONTYPE(P)) **then**
      /* Find a common ancestor */
      MAKE_EQ_EDGE_NEIGHBOR(FATHER(P),E)
      else FATHER(P);
  /* Follow the reflected path to locate the neighbor */
  return(**if not**(null(Q)) **and not**(BLACK(Q)) **then**
      SON(**if** GRAY(Q) **then** Q
          else ADD_FOUR_WHITE_SONS(Q),
          REFLECT(E,SONTYPE(P)))
      else Q);
end;

recursive pointer node procedure MAKE_EQ_VERTEX_NEIGHBOR(P,V);
/* Return the vertex-neighbor of node P in direction V that is equal in size to P. If P is
   adjacent to the border of the image along the specified direction, then NIL is returned. If
   the neighbor is of size greater than P and is white, then it is broken up into four white
   quadrants in order to obtain the desired neighbor. If the neighbor is black, it is not broken up further. */
begin
  value pointer node P;
  value vertex V;
  pointer node Q;
  Q ← **if** null(FATHER(P)) **then** NIL
    else if ADJ(V,SONTYPE(P)) **then**
    MAKE_EQ_VERTEX_NEIGHBOR(FATHER(P),V)
    else if COMMON_EDGE(V,SONTYPE(P)) $\neq \Omega$ **then**
    MAKE_EQ_EDGE_NEIGHBOR(FATHER(P),
                  COMMON_EDGE(V,SONTYPE(P)))
    else FATHER(P);

```
/* Follow the opposite path to locate the neighbor */
return(if not(null(Q)) and not(BLACK(Q)) then
        SON(if GRAY(Q) then Q
              else ADD_FOUR_WHITE_SONS(Q),
              REFLECT(V,SONTYPE(P)))
        else Q);
end;


pointer node procedure ADD_FOUR_WHITE_SONS(P);
/* Return node P after converting it to a gray node and adding four white sons. Make use
   of procedure CREATE_QNODE from Section 4.2.1.   */
begin
 value pointer node P;
 pointer node Q;
 quadrant I;
 NODETYPE(P) ← 'GRAY';
 for I in {'NW', 'NE', 'SW', 'SE'} do
   begin
    Q ← CREATE_QNODE(P,I,'WHITE');
    DIST(Q) ← 0;
   end;
 return(P);
end;


recursive procedure PROPAGATE_EDGE(P,L,T,E);
/* Node P at level L is adjacent to edge E of a QMAT node whose span exceeds its width
   by T — that is, P is subsumed or partially subsumed by that node. P or its appropriate
   sons are converted to black nodes if they are not already black. */
begin
 value pointer node P;
 value integer L,T;
 value edge E;
 if 2↑L > T then
   begin /* P is too large to be totally subsumed by its adjacent QMAT node */
    if BLACK(P) then return;
    if WHITE(P) then ADD_FOUR_WHITE_SONS(P);
    PROPAGATE_EDGE(SON(P,QUAD(OPEDGE(E),CCEDGE(E))),L−1,T,E);
    PROPAGATE_EDGE(SON(P,QUAD(OPEDGE(E),CEDGE(E))),L−1,T,E);
   end
 else
   begin /* P is subsumed by its adjacent QMAT node */
    if GRAY(P) then
      /* Account for nondisjointness of the QMAT; see Figure 9.9 */
      returnsonstoavail(P); /* May need to return entire subtree rooted at P */
    NODETYPE(P) ← 'BLACK'; /* Change P to black if not already so */
    if 2↑L < T then /* Propagate subsumption to P's neighbors on edge E */
      PROPAGATE_EDGE(SON(FATHER(P),REFLECT(E,SONTYPE(P))),L,
                         T−2↑L,E);
```

```
      end;
  end;


  recursive procedure PROPAGATE_VERTEX(P,L,T,E);
  /* Node P at level L is adjacent to the vertex formed by edges E and CEDGE(E) of a
     QMAT node whose span exceeds its width by T — that is, P is subsumed or partially
     subsumed by that node. P or its appropriate sons are converted to black nodes if they
     are not already black. */
  begin
   value pointer node P;
   value integer L,T;
   value edge E;
   if 2↑L > T then
     begin /* P is too large to be totally subsumed by its vertex adjacent QMAT node */
       if BLACK(P) then return;
       if WHITE(P) then ADD_FOUR_WHITE_SONS(P);
       PROPAGATE_VERTEX(SON(P,QUAD(OPEDGE(E),CCEDGE(E))), L–1,T,E);
     end
   else
     begin /* P is subsumed by its adjacent QMAT node */
       if GRAY(P) then
         /* Account for nondisjointness of the QMAT; see Figure 9.9 */
         returnsonstoavail(P); /* May need to return entire subtree at P */
       NODETYPE(P) ← 'BLACK'; /* Change P to black if not already so */
       if 2↑L < T then
         begin
           /* Propagate subsumption to neighbors of P In the direction of edges E and
              CEDGE(E) and the vertex formed by them */
           PROPAGATE_EDGE(SON(FATHER(P),QUAD(E,CCEDGE(E))), L,T–2↑L,E);
           PROPAGATE_VERTEX(SON(FATHER(P),QUAD(E,CEDGE(E))), L,T–2↑L,E);
           PROPAGATE_EDGE(SON(FATHER(P),QUAD(OPEDGE(E),CEDGE(E))),
     L,T–2↑L,CEDGE(E));
         end;
     end;
  end;
```

The execution time of the quadtree-from-QMAT reconstruction algorithm, measured by the number of nodes visited, depends on the ultimate size of the quadtree and the number of elements in the quadtree skeleton (i.e., black nodes in the QMAT). The analysis of the execution time is the same as that performed for the Chessboard distance transform computation algorithm in Section 9.2. In essence, we propagate subsumption for each black element of the QMAT by use of procedures MAKE_EQ_EDGE_-NEIGHBOR, PROPAGATE_EDGE, MAKE_EQ_VERTEX_NEIGHBOR, and PROPAGATE_VER-

TEX. Actually we need to do this work only for those elements of size 2^s whose Chessboard distance transform value is $> 2^{(s-1)}$. Elements of the QMAT satisfying this criterion are termed *subsuming elements*.

Using the model of a random image of Section 3.2.1.2, it can be shown that the average number of nodes visited by each invocation of MAKE_EQ_EDGE_NEIGHBOR and PROPAGATE_EDGE (analogous to QT_GTEQ_EDGE_NEIGHBOR and DIST_EDGE) is $O(1)$. The same result holds for each invocation of MAKE_EQ_VERTEX_NEIGHBOR and PROPAGATE_VERTEX (analogous to QT_GTEQ_VERTEX_NEIGHBOR and DIST_VERTEX). These procedures are invoked once for each edge and vertex of a subsuming element. Thus given a QMAT with B black elements in the original quadtree, the average execution time of reconstructing the corresponding quadtree is $O(B)$.

Exercises

9.43. The amount of work performed by procedures MAKE_EQ_EDGE_NEIGHBOR, PROPAGATE_-EDGE, MAKE_EQ_VERTEX_NEIGHBOR, and PROPAGATE_VERTEX depends on the value of the Chessboard distance transform of the subsuming element. Given a $2^n \times 2^n$ image, what is the maximum number of nodes that will be visited when propagating subsumption in the direction of an edge (e.g., east)? of a vertex (e.g., northeast)?

9.44. Procedure QMAT_TO_QUADTREE is an 'in-place' algorithm since it overwrites the current tree (the QMAT) in the process of constructing the corresponding quadtree. Modify it so that the QMAT is left intact.

9.45. Whenever a black node is generated by procedures PROPAGATE_EDGE or PROPAGATE_VERTEX, its DIST field is set to zero. Why?

9.46. Defining a quadtree skeleton in terms of properties 1, 2, and 3 means that each block in the quadtree must be subsumed in its entirety by a block in the quadtree skeleton. This situation can be remedied by replacing property 3 in the definition by property 3′ (see Section 9.3.1). Modify procedure QMAT_TO_QUADTREE to handle this refinement.

9.47. Procedure QMAT_TO_QUADTREE adopts an approach similar to that used in the computation of the perimeter of an image represented by a quadtree [Same81c]—that is, for each black node, its neighbors in the four directions N, E, S, and W are examined to see if they are gray or white; if yes, then the appropriate values are added to the perimeter. In the discussion of the perimeter computation algorithm, it was proposed that instead of examining the four neighbors of each black node, the perimeter could also be obtained by traversing the quadtree and examining only the S and E edges of black and white nodes. In the case of the black nodes, white adjacent nodes are examined, and in the case of white nodes, black adjacent nodes are examined. This removed redundant checks since each edge has a node on each side. Construct an analogous algorithm for the reconstruction of the quadtree from its QMAT that always examines E, SE, S, and SW neighbors in the propagation of subsumption.

9.48. Procedure QMAT_TO_QUADTREE makes use of bottom-up neighbor-finding techniques. Modify it to use a neighbor vector containing the eight neighbors of each node as an actual parameter to the tree traversal.

9.3.4 Using the QMAT as an Image Representation

The QMAT representation can be used as an alternative data structure for the representation of an image. In particular, it has the property that for any image, it requires, at most, as many nodes as the quadtree. This is obvious when we recall that each node in the QMAT corresponds to one or more nodes of the quadtree and that each member of the quadtree skeleton is a node in the quadtree. Of course, the QMAT does require that the value of the Chessboard distance transform of the block be stored with each node. As an example of the savings in storage, consider the quadtree in Figure 9.5. The QMAT, shown in Figure 9.6, requires 17 nodes, and the quadtree requires 57 nodes.

An interesting property of the QMAT is that there is a class of images for which it requires a minimum number of nodes regardless of the image resolution. Clearly if the image is all white or all black, then both the quadtree and the QMAT require a single node. However, when a $2^n \times 2^n$ image consists of a black square of side length $2^n - 1$ (recall Exercise 9.4), then the advantage of the QMAT over the quadtree in terms of space utilization is at a maximum. Of course, in order to attain this minimum for this example, we have made use of the property that the image is assumed to be surrounded by black. For example, given a 7×7 black block in an 8×8 image, the quadtree requires 45 nodes, while the QMAT requires only 5 nodes. On the other hand, it should be clear that for a given image, the optimal position of its QMAT, in terms of the minimum number of nodes required, need not be the same as that of its quadtree (see Exercise 9.53).

The QMAT representation also has the property that the number of nodes necessary to represent an image is not as shift sensitive as it is for the quadtree. This is a direct result of the fact that the QMAT always requires a number of nodes less than or equal to the quadtree. It is also quite apparent when we realize that the QMAT is most economical in storage, *vis-à-vis* the quadtree, when large blocks are surrounded by smaller blocks, which is normally the situation when a shift operation takes place. For example, when the image of Figure 9.10 is shifted by one unit to the right, yielding Figure 9.11, its quadtree gets considerably larger. In particular, the quadtree in Figure 9.10b contains 17 nodes, while the quadtree corresponding to the shifted image in Figure 9.11b contains 49 nodes.

The QMAT, however, is not as sensitive to shifts since it always requires a number of nodes less than or equal to those contained in the quadtree. In Figure 9.10, the QMAT is identical to the quadtree. Interestingly the QMAT of the shifted image, given in Figure 9.11c, is considerably smaller than its corresponding quadtree, as well as the QMAT of the image prior to the shift—i.e., 9 nodes versus 17 nodes.

Of course, shifting does not always lead to a smaller QMAT. As another example, consider the image of Figure 9.12, which has a minimal nontrivial QMAT in terms of the number of nodes—i.e., 5 nodes. Figure 9.13 is the result of shifting the image of Figure 9.12 by one unit to the right. Note that the new QMAT given in Figure 9.13c requires more nodes than the one corresponding to the unshifted image given in Figure 9.12c—i.e., 21 nodes versus 5 nodes. However, this number is less than the

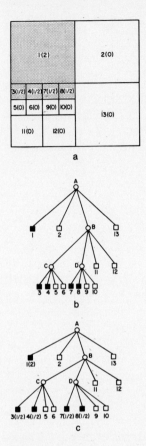

Figure 9.10   Sample quadtree: (a) block decomposition,
(b) tree representation, (c) QMAT

number of nodes in the shifted quadtree as shown in Figure 9.13b — i.e., 21 nodes for the shifted QMAT versus 41 nodes for the shifted quadtree. Thus we see that the compactness of the QMAT is also preserved when the image is subjected to shifts.

The fact that a QMAT node can subsume other nodes means that it is much harder to analyze the effects of shifting the image. In particular, for a quadtree, we know that horizontal and vertical shifts of an image are independent in the sense that each causes a different amount of decomposition. For example, when a shift in the horizontal direction is applied, a subsequent shift in the vertical direction can cause only a further decomposition. It will not result in merging of blocks.

In fact, when an image represented by a region quadtree is shifted by s pixels such that $s = i \cdot 2^m$, all blocks whose side length is less than 2^m are unaffected by the shift (they are neither split nor merged). This was the basis of an algorithm for determining the optimal positioning of the region quadtree [Li82] (see Section 1.2).

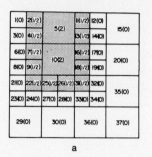

a

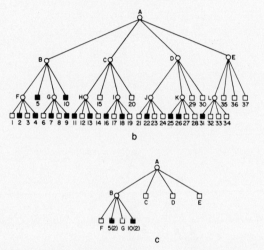

b

c

Figure 9.11   The result of shifting the image in Figure 9.10 by one pixel to the right: (a) block decomposition, (b) tree representation, (c) QMAT

On the other hand, in the case of a QMAT, these shifts will interact so that merges do in fact occur [Shaf86a]. The reason is that the subblocks resulting from shifting a given block are remerged with neighboring blocks due to subsumption, and thus the number of nodes will tend to vary less for the QMAT than for the quadtree. As an example, consider the image and QMAT of Figure 9.14a and the result of shifting it down by two pixels, as shown in Figure 9.14b. Note that this shift has affected nodes whose side length is less than two (the amount of shift).

Of course, the shift sensitivity of the quadtree and the QMAT derives from the fact that the positions of the maximal blocks are not explicitly represented in the data structure. Instead their positions are determined by the paths leading to them from the root of the tree. Thus when the image is shifted, the maximal blocks are formed in a different way. A shift-invariant maximal block data structure can be devised by representing the maximal blocks by triples containing the size of the block (assuming

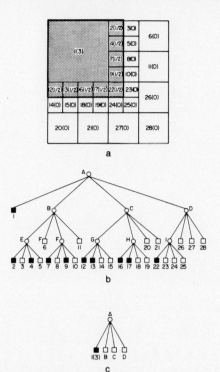

Figure 9.12   Sample quadtree: (a) block decomposition, (b) tree representation, (c) QMAT

that they are square) and the coordinates of its centroid or another known point (e.g., its upper left-hand corner).

Scott and Iyengar [Scot85, Scot86] propose such a representation which they term *TZD* (see also the squarecode of Oliver and Wiseman [Oliv83b] and Exercise 9.39). They start by identifying the largest black square for which each pixel serves as a center. These squares are the maximal blocks, and a procedure is applied to remove redundant ones (i.e., those subsumed by others). They do not obtain the minimal set of blocks because this involves an inordinate amount of search. This is avoided by restricting the configuration of blocks that will be examined. The rectangular coding of Kim and Aggarwal [Kim83, Kim86] also has similar shift-invariant properties.

The QMAT can be used as an image representation in a way similar to quadtrees. However, at times, some operations may require more work. For example, the medial axis transformation often serves as an alternative to a border representation because of its amenability to the determination of whether a given point lies within a particular region. This is not a problem when the quadtree representation is used. However, in the case of a QMAT this is slightly more complex since a white node, say W, does not necessarily imply that the block corresponding to W is completely white.

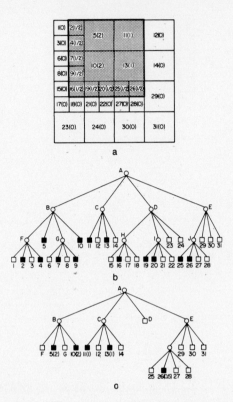

Figure 9.13   The result of shifting the image in Figure 9.12 by one pixel to the right: (a) block decomposition, (b) tree representation, (c) QMAT

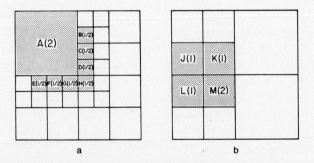

Figure 9.14   Example of how a shift of 2^m pixels of an image can affect blocks of the QMAT of size less than 2^m: (a) QMAT of the original image, (b) QMAT of the image of (a) after a downward shift by two pixels

Figure 9.15   Example of a white block, C, whose points can be spanned by QMAT blocks A and B

In such a case, the nodes that surround *W* must be examined to see if any of them is black and subsumes *W*. These nodes are always adjacent to *W* (along a side or a corner) or adjacent to ancestors of *W*. The reason that these nodes are not always adjacent to *W* is that *W* can be partially subsumed by several nodes of the QMAT. For example, consider Figure 9.15 where we see that points in white block C can be subsumed by black QMAT block A or B. The number of nodes that must be visited in this process is constrained by the position of the point relative to the sides of its enclosing white block and by geometric properties of the Chessboard distance transform (see Exercise 9.59).

An interesting observation about the QMAT is that it lends itself to parallel processing. In particular, the process of examining a white node's neighbors to determine its true color (or the color of a subarea of its corresponding block) can be done in parallel by assigning one processor to each of the nodes that must be examined at each level (a maximum of nine). Note that unlike other parallel processing applications, here the number of necessary processors is bounded. To reduce memory contention, it is best to distribute the nodes of the QMAT among the memory modules so that for a node, say *N*, at level *m* assigned to module *A*, neither *N*'s level *m* neighbors, *N*'s father, or *N*'s sons are in module *A*.

Such a scheme, making use of nine processors, is described by Shaffer [Shaf86a] and works as follows. Assume a complete quadtree. The nodes at even levels of the tree are grouped into repeated 3×3 aggregates as shown in Figure 9.16a. Each node is assigned to a module according to the number associated with its position in the aggregate. On the other hand, for nodes at odd levels of the tree, the 3×3 aggregates are formed by reversing the order of the module numbers (Figure 9.16b).

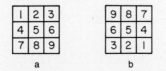

Figure 9.16   The assignment of nodes of a QMAT to memory modules for (a) even levels and (b) odd levels

Again, each node is assigned to a module according to the number associated with its position in the aggregate. An example of such an assignment to an 8×8 image is given in Figure 9.17.

As stated in the opening remarks of this chapter, the motivation for the development of the QMAT is its decreased sensitivity to shift operations, not the usual purpose of obtaining skeleton-like approximations of the image. Nevertheless algorithms such as those presented for converting between a quadtree and a QMAT should be useful when the QMAT is used to facilitate operations such as thinning [Rose82a] and it is desired to have the quadtree representation of the thinned image. To see this, we note that traditional thinning requires examination of the image pixel by pixel. In contrast, using a quadtree representation, we can take advantage of its hierarchical nature and perform thinning by traversing the image block by block and possibly replacing a block by a smaller block.

The QMAT representation stores the radius of the area spanned by the QMAT block, thereby facilitating the detection of stopping points for thinning (i.e., when connectivity is lost). Now, thinning may be implemented by traversing the image block by block and, at times, just changing the value of the radius. Since the QMAT is often even more compact than the quadtree, thinning is speeded up as well since there are fewer elements (i.e., blocks) to examine. The appropriateness of the QMAT as a skeleton-like approximation of an image to aid in shape recognition remains to be investigated.

Exercises

9.49 Given a $2^n - 1 \times 2^n - 1$ black block embedded within a $2^n \times 2^n$ image, determine the number of nodes that can be saved by using a QMAT instead of a quadtree, as a function of n.

9.50. Consider the problem of embedding a square of size $2^m \times 2^m$ in a $2^n \times 2^n$ image. Assume that the image is surrounded by black. At what position would its QMAT require the largest number of black nodes, and how many? How many white nodes are required at this position?

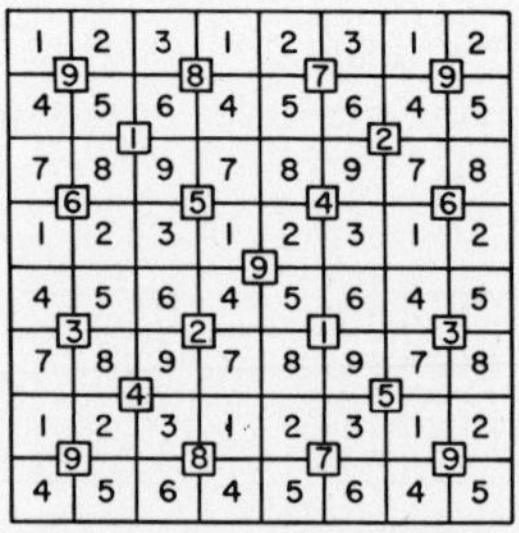

Figure 9.17 The assignment of nine memory modules to nodes of a QMAT at all levels. No node appears in the same module as one of its neighbors of equal size, its father, or any of its children.

9.51. Repeat Dyer's [Dyer82] experiment of arbitrarily placing a square of size $2^m \times 2^m$ at any position in a $2^n \times 2^n$ image. How many QMAT nodes are required on the average?

9.52. Consider a $2^n \times 2^n$ image containing a black block of size $2^{n-1} \times 2^{n-1}$ in its upper left corner that has been shifted by one unit in the vertical and horizontal directions (one unit to the right and one unit down). Compare the number of nodes in the QMAT of the shifted image with the quadtree of the shifted image. In particular, compute the number of gray, black, and white nodes for each of the representations of the shifted image as a function of n.

9.53. Give an example image for which the optimal position, in terms of the minimum number of nodes required, of its QMAT is different from that of its quadtree.

9.54. Write a procedure AREA_QMAT to compute the area of an image represented by a QMAT.

9.55. Write a procedure UNION_QMAT to compute the QMAT corresponding to the union of two images represented by QMATs.

9.56. Write a procedure INTERSECTION_QMAT to compute the QMAT corresponding to the intersection of two images represented by QMATs.

9.57. Write a procedure PERIMETER_QMAT to compute the total perimeter of an image represented by a QMAT. Which of the variants described in Section 5.2 is most efficient?

9.58. Write a procedure CCL_QMAT to perform connected component labeling on an image represented by a QMAT. Analyze the execution time of the algorithm in terms of the number of nodes in the QMAT. When examining a QMAT node's neighbor in a given direction and finding that it is white, you may have to examine other neighbors in the same direction in order to determine its real color and label.

9.59. Given a $2^n \times 2^n$ image represented by a QMAT, what is the maximum number of blocks that must be examined when determining the region in which point P lies? Recall that for the maximum to arise, the QMAT node containing P is white.

9.60. Write a procedure POINT_IN_QMAT to determine the region in which a given point lies when an image is represented by a QMAT. You may assume that connected component labeling has already been applied to the image.

9.61. Prove that Shaffer's [Shaf86a] scheme for assigning memory modules to nodes in the determination of the true color of a white QMAT node satisfies the property that for node N at level m assigned to module A, neither N's level m neighbors, N's father, nor N's sons is in module A.

9.62. Suppose that we tighten the requirement of Exercise 9.61 so that memory modules must be assigned to nodes such that for a node, say N at level m, neither N's level m neighbors, N's father, nor N's sons is in the same module. In other words, if N is assigned to module A, then none of these nodes is in A nor is any of them in the same module. Does the assignment of Figure 9.17 satisfy these constraints? Can you devise a general assignment of nine modules to satisfy them? If nine modules are inadequate, what is a minimum number of modules?

9.63. Image expansion is the opposite of image thinning. In this case, we are given an integer value, and all black blocks are expanded in all directions by this number of pixels (see Section 6.6). Construct an algorithm, EXPAND_QMAT, to perform expansion of a binary image represented by a QMAT. Can you implement EXPAND_QMAT by merely incrementing the radius value stored with each block of the QMAT?

9.64. In Section 9.1, the medial axis transformation was defined in terms of maximal blocks. The QMAT is a decomposition of an image into blocks that may not necessarily coincide with the maximal blocks of the medial axis transformation since the centers of the QMAT's blocks are constrained by the quadtree decomposition. Prove that for a given image, say I, the convex hull formed from its medial axis transformation points (i.e., the centers of the maximal blocks comprising it) is a subset of the convex hull formed by the centers of the black blocks of the QMAT of I.

9.65. Investigate the appropriateness of the QMAT as a method of describing shape. As a sample task, take the quadtree skeleton of a polygonal region and form the convex hull of the centers of its elements. Shift the original image by small amounts in the horizontal and vertical directions and reconstruct their quadtree skeletons and the corresponding convex hulls. Are the shapes of the new convex hulls very different from the original ones?

SOLUTIONS TO EXERCISES

CHAPTER 1

1.1. See Section 4.1.

1.2. Each nonleaf node has out degree 4. The quadtree has $4 \cdot G$ edges. An acyclic graph (e.g., a tree) with $4 \cdot G$ edges has $4 \cdot G + 1$ nodes, and the result follows.

1.3. $(B + W - 1)/3$.

1.4. $(B + W - 1)/7$.

1.5. No two spheres can occupy the same leaf node. In other words, each leaf node contains a part of just one sphere.

1.6. Since the staircases are usually infinite, a tree is inadequate and a graph is necessary. Use an octgraph.

1.7. See [Dyer82].

1.8. $O(2^n)$. The worst case is a rectangle of width $2^n \times 2$ that straddles the x axis (i.e., one pixel on each side). It needs $5 + 16 \cdot 2^{n-2}$ nodes.

1.9. The probability that the entire image is black is $P_b(n) = (\frac{1}{2})^{2n}$, and similarly the probability that the entire image is white is $P_w(n) = (\frac{1}{2})^{2n}$. To find $E(n)$, solve the recurrence relation $E(n) = 4 \cdot E(n-1) + 1 - 4 \cdot (P_b(n) + P_w(n))$ with the initial condition $E(0) = 1$. The result is approximately $(29/24) \cdot 2^{2n}$. The expected number of black nodes, $B(n)$, is obtained by solving the recurrence relation $B(n) = 4 \cdot B(n-1) - 3 \cdot P_b(n)$ with the initial condition $B(0) = \frac{1}{2}$. The result is approximately $(29/64) \cdot 2^{2n}$. The expected number of white nodes is the same as $B(n)$, while the expected number of gray nodes is approximately $(29/96) \cdot 2^{2n} - 1/3$. For more details, see [Chu88a].

1.10. See [Chu88a].

1.11. See Section 1.5 of [Same90a].

1.13. See [Meag80] for a proof that the size of the octree is bounded by four times the surface area.

1.15. See [Wals85].

1.16. See [Wals85].

1.17. See Grosky and Jain [Gros83]. Intuitively, shifting the region may require fewer nodes as long as the region's maximum extent is such that the region occupies at least one block of side 1 in three horizontally (or vertically) adjacent blocks of size $2^m \times 2^m$. For the given value of w, the value of m is $n - 1$, and hence the $n + 1$ result follows.

1.18. See [Li82]. The proof is analogous to that used to obtain the optimal grid resolution.

1.19. The array, not surprisingly, has no such bias. The list is ordered by adjacency in one dimension. The region quadtree is ordered by adjacency in a hierarchical sense (i.e., by use of a parent relation).

1.20. Compression is a result of the property of the exclusive or operation that $0 \oplus 0 = 0$ and $1 \oplus 1 = 0$.

1.21. $Q_i \oplus Q_{i-1} = (P_i \oplus Q_{i-1}) \oplus Q_{i-1} = P_i \oplus (Q_{i-1} \oplus Q_{i-1}) = P_i \oplus 0 = P_i$.

1.23. For a $2^n \times 2^n$ image there are $(n + 1) \cdot (n + 1)$ different sizes of rectangles. For a given rectangle of size $2^i \times 2^j$ there are $(2^n/2^i) \cdot (2^n/2^j)$ positions where it can be placed when using the AHC method.

1.24. See Section 2.3.1 of [Same90a].

1.25. See Section 2.3.2 of [Same90a].

1.26. See Section 2.6.1 of [Same90a].

1.27. See Section 2.6.1 of [Same90a].

1.28. See Section 2.6.2 of [Same90a].

1.29. See Section 2.6.2 of [Same90a].

1.30. $\lceil \log_2((s/d) \cdot \sqrt{2}) \rceil$. The $\sqrt{2}$ term arises from the fact that the points may be at opposite corners of the smallest square of side width s/d.

1.31. See Section 4.2.3.1 of [Same90a].

1.32. See Section 4.2.3.1 of [Same90a].

1.33. See Section 4.2.3.1 of [Same90a] and [Same86b, Same87b].

1.34. Dillencourt and Mount [Dill87] propose the following solution. An optimal hierarchical decomposition of a binary image can be obtained by using a method based on dynamic programming [Hill67]. Dynamic programming is a general technique in which a problem is solved by storing the solution to all subproblems and combining them appropriately. Assume an $M \times N$ image. The subproblems consist of the possible positions of the rectangles that correspond to the quadrants. There are at most $O(M^2 \cdot N^2)$ subproblems as there are $M \cdot N$ possible positions for the upper leftmost corner of the rectangles, and, for each of these rectangles, there are at most $M \cdot N$ positions for the lower rightmost corner. Thus the total is $O(M^2 \cdot N^2)$.

    The algorithm stores with each subproblem (i.e., rectangle) the best decomposition into quadrants, along with the number of rectangles in the decomposition. If the image is a single pixel (i.e., if $M = N = 1$), there is only one way to subdivide the image: not to subdivide it at all. Otherwise the image may be subdivided into quadrants in $M \cdot N$ ways, as any grid point splits the image into four quadrants. For an $M \times N$ rectangle, this information is computed by examining all $(M - 1) \cdot (N - 1)$ possibilities, provided the information is known for all smaller rectangles.

    The heart of the algorithm is the computation of the solutions of the subproblems. The execution time of the algorithm is $O(M^3 \cdot N^3)$. This is obtained by noting that for each rectangle of size $i \times j$, there are $i \cdot j$ possible partitions, and all must be examined. There are $(M - i + 1) \cdot (N - j + 1)$ rectangles of size $i \times j$. Since i and j vary from 1 to M

and 1 to N, respectively, the result follows. Therefore for an $N \times N$ image, the optimal quadtree can be computed in $O(N^6)$ time using $O(N^4)$ space.

1.35. See [Good83].

1.37. For the Peano-Hilbert order it is 1. For the Morton order it is:

$$\frac{1}{2^{2 \cdot n} - 1} \cdot (2^{2 \cdot n - 1} + \sqrt{1 + (2^n - 1)^2} + 3 \cdot 2^{2 \cdot n - 1} \cdot \sum_{i=1}^{n-1} \frac{\sqrt{1 + (2^i - 1)^2}}{2^{2 \cdot i}}).$$

1.38. For the Morton and Peano-Hilbert orders it is $1 + 2^{2-m}$, as each page represents a $2^m \times 2^m$ block. The four corner pixels require that three pages be accessed; the remaining $4 \cdot (2^m - 2)$ pixels along the edges require that two pages be accessed; the neighbors of all other pixels are on the same page, and thus only one page need be accessed.

CHAPTER 2

2.1. The linear quadtree is ordered by the traversal that it represents (e.g., preorder, inorder, or postorder are all equivalent when the nonleaf nodes are ignored).

2.2. No.

2.8. For two dimensions, the maximum distance is at least $2^{2n} \cdot \sum_{i=1}^{n} (\frac{1}{4})^i$. In d dimensions we have at least $2^{2n \cdot d} \cdot \sum_{i=1}^{n} (2^{d-1} - 1)/(2^{d \cdot i})$.

2.9. Use a technique analogous to procedure WHITEBLOCKS.

2.11. C can be written as a function of d and h, which is monotonically increasing in both d and h as long as each of them is greater than or equal to 2.

2.12. Yes. The actual maximum level of a node in an FD linear quadtree is $n - 1$, and now we need only $\lceil \log_2 n \rceil + 2 \cdot n$ binary digits to represent each FD locational code instead of $\lceil \log_2 n + 1 \rceil + 2 \cdot n$. In other words, we insist that the nodes are at level m where $m < n$.

2.13. 150 bits are required for the pointer quadtree and 152 bits are required for the FD linear quadtree. For such an image, Table 2.1 indicates that the FD linear quadtree is more efficient spacewise than the pointer quadtree when the number of leaf nodes is more than 12. In fact, the true cutoff value for depth 3 is somewhere between 22 and 25 (there cannot be a quadtree with 23 or 24 leaf nodes since the number of leaf nodes modulo 3 is always 1). The reason for the discrepancy is easy to see by recalling the derivation of relation 2.7. Its consequence is that all of our cutoff values are really lower bounds since they are based on an overestimation of the number of nonleaf nodes (and hence the total as well) in the quadtree.

2.14. If we knew that all leaf nodes were stored at higher memory locations than the nonleaf nodes and if we knew the value of the boundary, there would be no need for the bit.

2.15. The cutoff values are doubled.

2.17. After factoring L out of relation 2.12, using m and n as in relation 2.8, multiplying both sides by n, and using relation 2.13 we have:

$$(n \cdot \{d \cdot h + \lceil \log(h + 1) \rceil \} - 8)/m < 1 + \lceil \log(L \cdot m/n) \rceil$$

$$(n/m) \cdot \{d \cdot h + \lceil \log(h + 1) \rceil \} - (8/m) < 1 + \lceil \log(L \cdot m/n) \rceil$$

$$(n/m) \cdot \{ d \cdot h + \lceil \log(h + 1) \rceil \} - (8/m) - 1 < \lceil \log(L \cdot m/n) \rceil$$

$$(n/m) \cdot \{ d \cdot h + \lceil \log(h + 1) \rceil \} - (8/m) - 2 < \log(L \cdot m/n)$$

$$(n/m) \cdot 2^{(n/m) \cdot \{ d \cdot h + \lceil \log(h + 1) \rceil \} - (8/m) - 2} < L.$$

2.18. This means that no bits are wasted in the case of the FD linear quadtree. The result is a cutoff value that is $2^{-8/m}$ times the cutoff value of relation 2.10:

$$(n/m) \cdot 2^{(n/m) \cdot (d \cdot h + \lceil \log(h + 1) \rceil) - (8/m) - 2} < L.$$

2.19. This means that a maximum of 7 bits is wasted in the case of the FD linear quadtree since the maximum difference between $\{ x \}$ and x is 7 when x is an integer. Thus, seven-eighths of one byte is wasted for each locational code. The resulting cutoff value is $2^{7 - 8/m}$ times the cutoff value of relation 2.10:

$$(n/m) \cdot 2^{(n/m) \cdot (d \cdot h + \lceil \log(h + 1) \rceil) + 5 - (8/m)} < L.$$

2.20.

$$L \cdot \{ d \cdot h + \lceil \log(h + 1) \rceil \} < (L/(2^d - 1)) \cdot 2^d \cdot (1 + \{ \log(L \cdot 2^d/(2^d - 1)) \}).$$

After factoring L out, letting $m = 2^d$ and $n = 2^d - 1$, expanding $\{ \}$, we solve for L and get

$$\{ d \cdot h + \lceil \log(h + 1) \rceil \} < (m/n) \cdot (1 + \{ \log(L \cdot m/n) \})$$

$$(n/m) \cdot \{ d \cdot h + \lceil \log(h + 1) \rceil \} - 1 < \{ \log(L \cdot m/n) \}$$

$$(n/m) \cdot \{ d \cdot h + \lceil \log(h + 1) \rceil \} - 1 - 8 < \log(L \cdot m/n)$$

$$(n/m) \cdot 2^{(n/m) \cdot \{ d \cdot h + \lceil \log(h + 1) \rceil \} - 1 - 8} < L.$$

2.21. This means that no bits are wasted in the case of the FD linear quadtree. The result is a cutoff value that is 2^{-7} times the cutoff value of relation 2.10:

$$(n/m) \cdot 2^{(n/m) \cdot (d \cdot h + \lceil \log(h + 1) \rceil) - 7 - 2} < L.$$

2.22. The two cutoff values would tend to be the same as n/m approaches 1 since the maximum difference between $\{ x \}$ and x is 7 when x is an integer. This means that seven-eighths of one byte is wasted for each locational code.

2.23. To save k bits per node, the following relation must hold:

$$L \cdot (d \cdot h + \log(h + 1)) + k \cdot L < (L/n) \cdot (m \cdot (1 + \log(L \cdot m/n))).$$

Solving for L yields

$$(n/m) \cdot 2^{(n/m) \cdot (d \cdot h + \log(h + 1) + k) - 1} < L.$$

Therefore the old cutoff value has increased by a multiplicative factor of $2^{(n/m) \cdot k}$ (recall that n/m is $1 - 2^{-d}$).

2.25. The analysis needs some modification due to the use of $2^d + 1$ pointers in nonleaf nodes and one pointer in leaf nodes.

2.26. For quadtree-like data structures, as the dimension of the space increases, the majority of the nodes are leaf nodes, while the proportion of nonleaf nodes is considerably smaller. On the other hand, for the bintree, the number of nonleaf nodes is always one less than the number of leaf nodes regardless of the dimension of the space. Thus the fact that for quadtrees the proportion of nonleaf nodes is lower means that the FD linear quadtree requires proportionally more space than the FD linear bintree when compared to their pointer counterparts.

2.27. The analysis is performed in the same manner, with the exception that the maximum depth of the bintree is $n \cdot d$. In the case of a two-dimensional image, the maximum depth of the bintree is twice that of the quadtree and thus requires one extra bit for its specification. In general the extra bits required to distinguish the level of the bintree are insignificant in comparison to the reduction in the number of leaf nodes [Tamm84a]. For the continuous case with L leaf nodes, the following relation must hold for the FD linear bintree to be more compact than the pointer bintree:

$$L \cdot (d \cdot h + \log(h + 1)) < 2 \cdot L \cdot (1 + \log(2 \cdot L)).$$

It can be solved for L so that the FD linear bintree will require fewer bits than the pointer bintree as long as

$$\sqrt{(h + 1) \cdot 2^{d \cdot h - 4}} < L.$$

2.31. $n - \log_4(M[j + 1] - M[j])$.

2.33. Such a definition leads to ambiguity in the sense that it is impossible to determine the sizes of the blocks. For example, for Figure 2.3, such a sequence yields 1, 4, 6, 8, 11, 12, and 18 with Morton Matrix numbers of 15, 27, 35, 37, 43, 47, and 59. We cannot tell if 4 corresponds to a block of size 1×1 or 2×2. This problem can be fixed by encoding each leaf node by using the Morton Matrix number of the pixel that occupies its upper left corner.

2.35. Let b_i denote the minimum number of pixels that must be black for a node at level i to be of type GB. $b_1 = 2$ while $b_i = 2 \cdot b_{i-1}$ for $i > 1$. Solving for b_n yields the desired result.

2.36. Let w_i denote the maximum number of pixels that can be black for a node at level i to still be of type GW. $w_1 = 1$ while $w_i = 2^{i-1} \cdot 2^{i-1} + 3 \cdot w_{i-1}$ for $i > 1$. Solving for w_n yields the desired result.

2.38. If the node's code is 0, then its color is white when its parent is 0 and the color of one of its sons otherwise. If the node's code is 1, then multiple ancestors may have to be visited by moving up the pyramid until encountering either a node with code 0 or the root. If a node with code 0 is encountered first, the node's color is black; otherwise the node's color is gray.

2.40. Cohen, Landy, and Pavel [Cohe85b] observe that for a binary image there is only a need to use one bit for each of the blocks at level 0. Moreover, if it is known that the first three blocks at level 0 are of one color, there is no need to code the remaining block because it must be of the opposite color.

2.41. See [Cohe85b].

2.42. See [Cohe85b].

2.43. See [Cohe85b].

CHAPTER 3

3.1. Observe that a split of a block creates four subblocks of equal size. Each subblock is 4-adjacent to two other subblocks (one horizontally adjacent neighbor and one vertically adjacent neighbor) at two of its edges and 8-adjacent to the remaining subblock at one of its vertices. As an example, given node P such that nodes Q and R are adjacent to its eastern and western edges, respectively, then at most one of nodes Q and R can be of greater size than P. Thus a node can have at most two larger-sized neighbors, adjacent to nonopposite edges. One of these neighbors can overlap three neighboring directions, while the other can overlap two neighboring directions. The remaining three neighbors must be of equal size. For example, for node 7 in Figure 3.1, node 1 overlaps the NW, N, and NE neighboring directions, node 6 overlaps the W and SW directions, while the remaining neighbors are nodes 8, 10, and 9 in the E, SE, and S directions, respectively.

3.2. A node cannot be adjacent to two nodes of greater size on opposite edges or on diagonally opposite vertices. Thus the larger node can be adjacent at only one of the vertices.

3.3. [Robert E. Webber] When the neighbor in the direction of one of the edges is larger and extends past the other edge, then the algorithm obtains the wrong neighbor. For example, to find the NE neighbor of node 15 in Figure 3.1, the algorithm first obtains the N neighbor 13 and then its E neighbor, which is 14. However, 13 is the NE neighbor of 15.

3.5. Locate the blocks containing the endpoints of the line segment, determine its direction, and then use neighbor-finding operations to locate the blocks (see Section 7.2.4).

3.6. See [DeMi78].

3.10. Perform a top-down tree traversal and keep track of the neighbors in the four directions. This process executes in time proportional to the number of nodes in the tree.

3.13. Each leaf node appears in two adjacency trees. The adjacency tree is an extended binary tree. The number of nonleaf nodes in an extended binary tree is one fewer than the total number of leaf nodes. For a quadtree with L leaf nodes, the adjacency trees contain a maximum of $2 \cdot L - 2$ nonleaf nodes and $2 \cdot L$ leaf nodes. The resulting upper bound of $4 \cdot L$ follows [Hunt78, Hunt79a].

3.14. Each adjacency tree represents a $(d - 1)$-dimensional adjacency. Each leaf node can appear as a leaf node in d adjacency trees that are $(d - 1)$-dimensional quadtrees. A $(d - 1)$-dimensional quadtree with D leaf nodes has $(D - 1)/(2^{d-1} - 1)$ nonleaf nodes. Therefore for a d-dimensional quadtree with L leaf nodes, the adjacency trees contain a maximum of $d \cdot (L - 1)/(2^{d-1} - 1)$ nonleaf nodes and $d \cdot L$ leaf nodes.

3.16. Traverse the quadtree in a top-down manner and visit the adjacency tree of each node that has a gray edge-neighbor. From Exercise 3.13, we know that the total number of nodes in all adjacency trees for a given quadtree is bounded from above by four times the number of leaf nodes in the quadtree.

3.18. See [Same85a].

3.19. 10. In d dimensions, it is $2^d - 1 + d$.

3.20. 26. In d dimensions, it is $3^d - 1$.

3.22. Locate the blocks containing the endpoints of the line segment, determine its direction, and then use neighbor-finding operations to locate the blocks (see Section 7.2.4).

3.27. The comparison between the values of the paths is feasible because the trailing k digits of the path of a node at level k are 0. Recall that the FD locational code corresponds to the coordinates of a specific pixel (or voxel) in the block (e.g., for an octree, it is the voxel in the LDB corner of the block when the origin is in the LDB corner of the image).

3.28. If the neighboring block is larger, we need some way of organizing the blocks so that we can find it. This organization is provided by the FD locational code, which is a unique number based on interleaving the bits that comprise the values of the x, y, and z coordinates.

3.29. In procedures FD_QT_GTEQ_NEIGHBOR and FD_OT_GTEQ_NEIGHBOR we would have to find the minimum FD locational code in L that is $\geq$ P instead of the maximum FD locational code in L that is $\leq$ P. Thus we need to replace 'MAXLEQ(P,L)' by 'MINGEQ(P,L)'.

3.30. You must be careful not to overwrite the locational code of the node whose neighbor is being sought.

3.31. It should have bit manipulation. Implementing a locational code as an array is very inefficient.

3.33. You must first determine the size (i.e., level) of the node, which requires looking up the next element in the sequence.

3.37. In procedures such as FL_QT_GTEQ_NEIGHBOR and FL_OT_GTEQ_NEIGHBOR, we would have to find the maximum FL locational code in L that is $\leq$ T and the minimum FL locational code in L that is $>$ T, instead of the minimum FL locational code in L that is $\geq$ T and the maximum FL locational code in L that is $<$ T, respectively. This also means that the logic of the code must be changed. The problem is that now if a node A is contained in another node B, then the FL locational code of B will be smaller in magnitude than that of A, whereas the situation was reversed when the *don't care* directional code was represented by 4 (8).

3.38. Because PATH(B) $<$ T.

3.40. The only change from procedures FD_QT_GTEQ_NEIGHBOR and FD_OT_GTEQ_NEIGHBOR is that the new procedures start by determining the first digit that does not contain a *don't care* directional code.

CHAPTER 4

4.3. There are no problems once the output of the gray node indicator is delayed.

4.4. The VL locational codes are obtained in a depth-first order, and a second pass is needed to obtain a breadth-first traversal.

4.7. The remaining elements are visited in the order 17, 19, 20, 18, 21, 22, 24, 23, 29, 30, 32, 31, 28, 26, 25, 27, 49, 51, 52, 50, 53, 54, 56, 55, 61, 62, 64, 63, 60, 58, 57, 59, 48, 47, 45, 46, 40, 38, 37, 39, 36, 34, 33, 35, 41, 42, 44, 43.

4.14. See [Unni84].

4.16. See Section 6.1 for code that is analogous to GET_QUADRANT and FIND_2D_BLOCK.

4.18. Never, because ALG3 is always superior to ALG2.

4.19. Yes, because ALG3 is always superior to ALG2.

4.20. $2^{2n+2} - 2^{n+2} - \sum_{i=1}^{n} b_i \cdot (2^{2i+2} - 2^{i+2}) - \sum_{i=1}^{n} (n-i) \cdot v_i \cdot (2^i - 1)$.

4.22. $2^{2n+2} - (n+4) \cdot 2^n - 4 - \Sigma_{i=1}^{n} b_i \cdot (2^{2i+2} - 2^{i+2}) + \Sigma_{i=1}^{n} v_i \cdot (i \cdot 2^i + 4)$.

4.23. The proof is analogous to that for Theorem 4.2. Start with a complete quadtree for which the number of nodes that are visited is $2^{2n+2} - n \cdot 2^n - 4$. This is obtained by subtracting $n \cdot 2^n$ from the number of nodes visited when using ALG2 and adding $2^{n-2} - 4$. This accounts for the difference in accessing the first elements of each row. Use induction on the block size for the remainder of the proof.

4.24. ALG4 is potentially superior to ALG3 when the resolution increases and there is a relatively large number of blocks in the first column at the lower levels of the tree.

4.25. ALG1 may be superior to ALG3 and ALG4 for small values of n (e.g., $n \le 4$).

4.27. $\Sigma_{i=0}^{n} b_i \cdot 2^i$ results from the fact that each block is visited once for each row in which the block participates. $4 \cdot \Sigma_{i=0}^{n} b_i$ results from the neighbor computation in the southern direction. Another $2 \cdot \Sigma_{i=0}^{n} b_i$ results from the fact that the neighbor in the southern direction, say P, may be gray. In this case, we visit all of the nodes in the N-adjacency tree of P. Since each leaf node can participate in only one N-adjacency tree, the total number of nodes in all of the N-adjacency trees is bounded by $2 \cdot \Sigma_{i=0}^{n} b_i$. This bound makes use of the fact that the adjacency tree is an extended binary tree.

4.31. ALG1 is trivial because it is a top-down algorithm, and in the DF-expression, all nodes are ordered in such a manner that the algorithm is the same as that used for the pointer-based representation. ALG2 is much more complicated because of the need to do neighbor finding.

4.32. Letting '(' denote a gray node, we have (11 A (9 B C 10 D E 37 (23 G (20 37 38 21 39 40 24 I J (30 L M 37 (35 57 58 36 59 60 O.

4.33. There is no longer a need to execute procedure FIND_2D_BLOCK.

4.34. Replace the part of ALG1 that invokes procedure FIND_2D_BLOCK by the following method to output a scan line. Decompose the row number into a sequence of binary digits, and use it to traverse the sextree, starting with the most significant bit. Bit i indicates the sons that are to be visited at level i. If bit i is zero, then visit the NW and NE sons of the tree and use the ENDROW field to locate the part of the tree to be visited at level $i + 1$. If bit i is one, then use the NEXTROW field to skip past the NW and NE sons of the tree and visit the SW and SE sons.

4.35. Any pixel can be covered by at most n active nodes—that is, a node at each level from 1 to n (corresponding to the root). At any given instant, there can be at most 2^{n-1} active nodes at level 1 (i.e., nodes of size 2×2). This is true because, for any given column, only one node at level 1 will be active, giving at most a solid line of 2×2 active nodes along a row just processed. In a like manner, there will be at most 2^{n-2} active nodes at level 2, and so on with 2^{n-i} active nodes at level i, up to a single active node at level n (the root). Summing across all levels yields $\Sigma_{i=0}^{n-1} 2^i = 2^n - 1$ as the maximum number of active nodes.

4.36. Consider an image defined in such a way that its NW, NE, and SW nodes are black. Its SE son has its NW, NE, and SW sons as white. The SE son of the SE son has its NW, NE, and SW sons as black. This alternating process is repeated up to the desired level. The DF-expression of such a tree for odd values of n is of the form BBBGWWWG-BBBGWWW $\cdots$ BBBW.

4.38. Process each pixel in raster scan order. After processing the first pixel, the quadtree is represented by a leaf node of color c corresponding to the root. As subsequent pixels are processed, if a pixel of a different color, say C', is encountered, then the color of the current node is set to gray and given four sons with the previous color of the current node (c). The son containing the current pixel becomes the current node. If the current pixel is the first (i.e., upper leftmost) pixel of the node, then the node's color is changed to C'. Otherwise the split step is repeated until the current pixel becomes the upper leftmost corner of the current node. If the next pixel to be processed is beyond the eastern edge of the current node, then that node's eastern neighbor is located by use of neighbor finding.

4.41. No. There are occasions when no nodes, or only one node, need to be added. This is the case when there is a long sliver in the form of the letter J and the turn is made at the lip. For example, consider the chain code sequence $21^2030\cdots$ and let (OLD,NEW) be the pair (3,0). In this case only one node is added.

4.42. Yes! Consider a crosslike object with a nonempty cross-section.

4.45. Grosky and Jain [Gros83] (see also Section 1.2) show that if $m = \max(h,v)$, then the side of the quadtree is either $2^{\lceil \log_2 m \rceil}$ or $2^{\lceil \log_2 m \rceil + 1}$. Michener [Mich80] suggests that procedure CHAINCODE_TO_QUADTREE be modified to achieve this effect.

4.46. Michener [Mich80] suggests using the far NW corner as the standard position (i.e., origin). It is not difficult to modify procedure CHAINCODE_TO_QUADTREE to achieve this effect. First, make a pass over the list of chain codes to determine the maximum displacements in the north, say ND, and west, say WD, directions from the start of the chain code. The tree is initialized as follows:

```
pointer node Q,R,T;
integer ND,WD;
Q ← CREATE_QNODE(NIL,NIL,'NOCOLOR');
R ← Q;
while (ND ≠ 0) or (WD ≠ 0) do
  begin /* Initialize the quadtree in a bottom-up manner. */
    T ← CREATE_QNODE(NIL,NIL,'GRAY');
    SON(T,QUAD(if (ND mod 2) = 0 then 'N'
              else 'S',
              if (WD mod 2) = 0 then 'W'
              else 'E')) ← R;
    R ← T;
    ND ← ND / 2;
    WD ← WD / 2;
  end;
```

4.47. The minimum value of n arises when the region is a square of side length $p/4$. The maximum value arises when the region is a long, narrow rectangle of width $p/2$. This takes into account the optimal grid resolution result [Gros83] mentioned in Section 1.2.

4.48. Given B black nodes at level 0, there is a maximum of $3 \cdot B$ white nodes at level 0. At worst, for each black node at level 0, there are one gray node at level 1 and three white nodes at level 0. Furthermore for each gray node at level i ($i > 0$), there are, at worst, three additional white nodes at level i. Thus at most $4 \cdot B$ nodes exist at level 1. Repeating the same argument for levels 2 through $n - 1$, we have a total of $4 \cdot B \cdot n$ nodes at these levels. At level n there is only one node. Therefore the maximum number of nodes is $4 \cdot B \cdot n + 1$.

4.50. See [Webb84]. [Li82] approaches the problem in a different way as discussed in Section 1.2.

4.51. See [Webb84] for a technique to shift the image so that the traversal can be done in order perimeter time.

4.52. See [Webb84] for an alternative method to shift the image to achieve this effect. However, the calculation of the shift still requires time proportional to the perimeter.

4.57. The proof is trivial if we use an analogy to a graph.

4.58. No. Use global pointers FIRSTP and FIRSTQ to store the pointers to the first pair of nodes marked.

4.66. Traverse the linear quadtree sequentially. The basic data structure keeps track of *active regions*. These are the regions for which part (but not all) of the boundary has been encountered. Associated with each active region is a list of the segments known to belong to the (partial) boundary. As new quadtree nodes are processed, new boundary segments are encountered and added to the partial boundary of appropriate regions. Distinct regions may be merged (just as in the component labeling problem; see Section 5.1), in which case the partial boundaries of the regions are merged. When the boundary of a region is complete, it is written to the output file, and the region is removed from the list of active regions. For more details, see [Dill88].

4.69. Each node is visited at most four times as it can only be a neighbor of four nodes.

4.70. Hunter and Steiglitz [Hunt78, Hunt79a] suggest the following method. Assume that we know the adjacency of edges but not necessarily the clockwise ordering of the edges. First, find the leftmost point in the polygon, say A. Clearly anything to the left of A is outside. Now, examine the angle formed by the two line segments that meet at A. Points along its angle bisector are candidates for points inside the polygon. Clearly those points that are infinitesimally close to A but along the angle bisector are inside A. Now we must determine how far down the angle bisector it is safe to go and still remain within the polygon. This is achieved by finding the leftmost vertex that is to the right of A, say B. Draw a vertical line through B, say L, and notice that, to its left, is a simple triangle, all of whose interior points are also interior to the polygon. Choose the point that is halfway down the angle bisector of A toward L, say C. The rest of the process is easy. In particular, now we can determine which of the sides of the edges that are adjacent at A are inside the polygon and then traverse the edges in a clockwise order so that the inside of the polygon is to the right. Given v vertices, this process takes $O(v)$ time.

4.71. The maximum degree of a vertex.

4.72. It ensures that the decomposition stops as soon as possible. An alternative formulation is that if a leaf node contains a vertex, say V, then at least one of its brothers must contain a vertex or a q-edge that is a segment of an edge not incident at V. For example, it precludes the further subdivision of the node containing D in Figure 4.24.

4.73. Condition $2'$ does not imply condition 1 due to the possible presence of isolated vertices. Conditions 1, $2'$, and 4 are insufficient because polygonal maps exist that would require a PM_1 quadtree of infinite depth to satisfy condition $2'$. For example, consider vertex E in Figure 4.24. We observe that the node containing vertex E does not satisfy condition $2'$ because of the two q-edges incident at it. Assume that the x and y coordinates of E cannot be expressed (without error) as a rational number whose denominator is a power of two (e.g., let both coordinates be one-third). This means that E can never lie on the boundary between two quadrants. Thus by virtue of the continuity of the q-edges, no matter how many times we subdivide the quadrant containing vertex E, there will always exist a pair of (possibly infinitesimally small) q-edges incident at E that will occupy the same quadtree leaf.

4.74. PM_INSERT requires only that the DICTIONARY field be set immediately after the call to CLIP_LINES in PM_INSERT and that DICTIONARY(P) be left unmodified in SPLIT_PM_NODE. The revised PM_DELETE is considerably simpler, as shown below.

recursive procedure PM_DELETE(P,R)

/* Delete the list of edges pointed at by P in the PM (i.e., PM_1, PM_2, and PM_3) quadtree rooted at R. It is assumed that the DICTIONARY field of all gray nodes indicates the edges in the subtrees below. PM_CHECK is generic. It is replaced by its appropriate analog for the PM_1, PM_2, and PM_3 quadtrees. */

begin

  value pointer edgelist P;

  value pointer node R;

  pointer edgelist L;

  quadrant I;

  L ← CLIP_LINES(P,SQUARE(R));

  if empty(L) **then return**; /* None of the edges is in the quadrant */

  DICTIONARY(R) ← SET_DIFFERENCE(DICTIONARY(R),L);

  if GRAY(R) **then**

    begin

      if PM_CHECK(DICTIONARY(R),SQUARE(R)) **then** PM_MERGE(R)

      else

        begin

          for I **in** {'NW', 'NE', 'SW', 'SE'} **do** PM_DELETE(L,SON(R,I));

        end;

    end;

end;

recursive procedure PM_MERGE(P)

/* Merge the four sons of the quadtree rooted at node P. The storage taken up by the four sons is reclaimed by use of returntoavail. This process is recursive in the case of a PM_1 quadtree. */

begin

  value pointer node P;

  quadrant I;

  for I **in** {'NW', 'NE', 'SW', 'SE'} **do**

    begin

      if GRAY(SON(P,I)) **then** PM_MERGE(SON(P,I))

      else

        begin

          returntoavail(SON(P,I));

          SON(P,I) ← NIL;

        end;

    end;

end;

4.75. An upper bound when leaf and gray nodes are counted is $\Sigma_{i=0}^{n} (n - i) \cdot m_i$. This is the same as the total path length of the tree (ignoring nonleaf nodes) if there is only one edge stored with each leaf node. A lower bound can be estimated by assuming that for each gray node, at most three of its sons are intersected by a given edge. Actually a better estimate can be achieved by noting that if three sons are intersected at one level, then only one son is intersected at the next level. See the discussion of space requirements in

Section 1.2 and the analysis of the dynamic insertion of an edge in a PM_1 quadtree in Section 4.2.3.1 of [Same90a].

4.76. If all four sons of a node are gray, then at least one son contains a vertex, say v, and an edge that does not intersect v.

4.77. A subtree containing two edges cannot be merged until it is large enough to include their common vertex without including any other vertices or nonsharing edges.

4.80. Merging is possible when the number of vertices is 1 and the crossing count is zero, or when the number of vertices is 0 and the crossing count is 1.

4.84. Compute the slopes of the two edges as ratios, say a/b and c/d, and then determine if $a \cdot d = b \cdot c$, as well as whether the edges overlap.

4.86. See [Yau83].

4.87. See [Fran85].

4.88. It is not always possible if the views are silhouettes. Even convex objects can cause problems. However, there are no problems if the views are like engineering drawings (e.g., hidden lines and other auxiliary lines are present).

4.91. See [Roge85].

4.93. See [Marg88].

4.94. Silhouettes from two opposite directions convey the same information.

4.95. See [Chie86a].

4.96. See [Veen86, Ahuj89].

4.97. See [Veen86, Ahuj89].

4.98. See [Chie88].

CHAPTER 5

5.1. $d - 1$.

5.2. An image composed of 'U' shapes or a horizontal sequence of them (e.g., a 'w').

5.4. See procedures UNION and FIND in Section 5.1.2.

5.5. See procedure FIND in Section 5.1.2.

5.6. For each leaf node (i.e., vertex), we must examine adjacencies on its $2 \cdot d$ edges for a total of $2 \cdot d \cdot v$. When a leaf node, say L, is adjacent to a set of leaf nodes along an edge, say E, then we visit L's adjacency tree along edge E. We know that a leaf node cannot be adjacent to two nodes of greater size on opposite sides (recall Figure 3.3a in Section 3.1). Therefore each leaf node cannot appear in more than d adjacency trees. Since the leaf nodes in the adjacency trees represent the edges that must be visited when a leaf node is adjacent to more than one node along an edge, the total number of adjacencies (i.e., edges) contributed by such situations is bounded by $d \cdot v$. Therefore the total number of edges is bounded by $3 \cdot d \cdot v$, and the algorithm takes $O(d \cdot v)$ time.

5.7. Row 1: BWBWB. Row 2: BWBWB. Row 3: BWBBB. Row 4: BBBWB. Row 5: BWBWB.

5.9. 2^{2n-1} labels. An example image is a checkerboard.

5.10. $N/2$ when all the blocks are of equal size and they form a checkerboard.

5.11. The number of active image elements is N^{d-1}, and the maximum number of active equivalence classes is $N^{d-1}/2$.

5.12. They ensure that a transition has been made through all adjacencies between image elements. Thus each image element will be visited just once on each pass of the connected component labeling algorithm. Also regardless of the position of the current image element, we always know which of its adjacent elements have already been visited.

5.13. The order NW, NE, SW, SE is admissible because as each block is processed, its northern and western 4-adjacent neighbors have already been processed. To see that the order NW, SE, NE, SW is not admissible, we note that when a NW son of a SE son is processed, none of its 4-adjacent neighbors will have been processed already.

5.14. No. Consider the NW son of the SE son. When this node is processed, only one of its 4-adjacent neighbors (i.e., the northern one) will have been processed already.

5.15. The number of active image elements is bounded by $2^n + 2^{n-1} - n$, and the number of active equivalence classes is bounded by $3 \cdot 2^{n-2}$.

5.18. See [Same86c].

5.21. Computing the western neighbor of the black nodes requires $\sum_{i=1}^{B} (i + 1) = B \cdot (B + 3)/2$ nodes to be visited. Computing the northern neighbor of black nodes requires $2 + \sum_{i=1}^{B-1} (2 + 2) = 4 \cdot B - 2$ nodes to be visited.

5.23. The interaction of LABEL_ADJACENT with UNION and FIND must be modified to deal with the situation that both the node being processed and its neighbor are black, yet there is no label associated with them (e.g., when processing the southern neighbor of node 15 — node 31, in Figure 5.2). In this case, a new label must be generated and assigned to them.

5.24. For each eastern and southern adjacency explored, at most one new equivalence pair can be generated.

5.25. It does not hold for either case. In the case that explores the eastern and northern adjacencies, the northern adjacency can result in the generation of more than one new equivalence pair. In the case that explores the western and southern adjacencies, the western adjacency can result in the generation of more than one new equivalence pair.

5.27. This seems to be true at least for a $2^3 \times 2^3$ image.

5.28. There is only a need to transmit the eastern and southern neighbors as parameters.

5.29. Yes. This process can be used to construct a netted quadtree [Hunt78, Hunt79a] (see Section 3.2.2), and now the depth-first approach is applicable [Same88b].

5.30. At any instant the boundary of the set of nodes that have already been processed by the tree traversal forms a staircase (the analog of the row). To complete the analogy, the nodes in the quadtree would be traversed in preorder and in reverse of preorder. To implement this solution, you need to devise a way to access the elements of the staircase one more time in order to update their labels.

5.32. See [Webb84].

5.35. Once we have processed a leaf node in the DF-expression, there is no easy way to access it again in order to update its label (unless we keep pointers from the active border to the elements in the DF-expression that comprise it). In contrast, when using the methods of [Lumi83b], each element of an image row is accessible.

5.39. The presence of holes causes problems. Also, consider a region consisting of just one pixel.

5.40. Yes.

5.42. **recursive integer procedure** EXP_PERIMETER2(P,LEVEL);
/* Find the perimeter of a region represented by a quadtree rooted at node P that spans a $2^{\text{LEVEL}} \times 2^{\text{LEVEL}}$ space. Assume that the image has already been embedded in a white region. */

```
begin
  value pointer node P;
  value integer LEVEL;
  pointer node Q;
  integer PER;
  quadrant I;
  direction D;
  PER ← 0;
  if GRAY(P) then
    begin
      for I in {'NW', 'NE', 'SW', 'SE'} do
        PER ← PER+EXP_PERIMETER2(SON(P,I),LEVEL−1);
    end
  else
    begin
      for D in {'W', 'N'} do
        begin
          Q ← QT_GTEQ_EDGE_NEIGHBOR(P,D);
          if not(null(Q)) and NODETYPE(P) ≠ NODETYPE(Q) then
            PER ← PER+SUM_ADJACENT2(Q,QUAD(OPSIDE(D),CSIDE(D)),
                                      QUAD(OPSIDE(D),CCSIDE(D)),
                                      LEVEL,NODETYPE(P));
        end;
    end;
  return(PER);
end;
```

```
recursive integer procedure SUM_ADJACENT2(P,Q1,Q2,LEVEL,C);
/* Find all leaf nodes of color different from C in quadrants Q1 and Q2 of the subquadtree
   rooted at node P corresponding to a 2^LEVEL × 2^LEVEL space. */
begin
  value pointer node P;
  value quadrant Q1,Q2;
  value integer LEVEL;
  value color C;
  return (if GRAY(P) then SUM_ADJACENT2(SON(P,Q1),Q1,Q2,LEVEL−1,C)+
                          SUM_ADJACENT2(SON(P,Q2),Q1,Q2,LEVEL−1,C)
          else if NODETYPE(P) ≠ C then 2↑LEVEL
          else 0);
end;
```

5.49. The problem is that the definition of edge reflects a one-dimensional adjacency, whereas for data of more than two dimensions, we need a $(d-1)$-dimensional adjacency.

5.57. The line $K = x - y$ can intersect the active border at only one position. Thus no two active corners may have the same $|\,x - y\,|$ value.

CHAPTER 6

6.1. Construct an address, say κ, for a hypothetical leaf node corresponding to the pixel. This hypothetical leaf node is located by performing a binary search on the sorted list of FD locational codes for the leaf nodes of the octree and returning the leaf node with the largest locational code value that is less than or equal to κ. The execution time for the algorithm is proportional to the log of the number of leaf nodes in the tree (assuming key comparisons can be made in constant time).

6.4.

$$D_1 = \begin{bmatrix} 0.0 & .5 \\ .75 & .25 \end{bmatrix}$$

6.15. No. For example, when computing the union, we may have to jump around the list when one node is black and another node is gray. In particular, we need to skip some elements in the subtree that contains the gray node. Thus every element in the two DF-expressions must be visited. In contrast, using a pointer-based representation in such a case results in fewer nodes being visited.

6.22. Hunter [Hunt78] suggests constructing the MX quadtrees for the polygons, intersecting them, and then checking the result to see if it is the empty quadtree. Of course, the $O(v + p + n)$ time bound is a function of the accuracy required and is subject to errors due to limitations imposed by the digitization process. However, the fact that the representations are so different makes it difficult to compare the two algorithms (i.e., the constants and quantities are dissimilar).

6.23. Assume that the node in the aligned quadtree is a leaf node. If the four covering nodes are identically colored and are leaf nodes, then the node in the output quadtree is colored appropriately. Otherwise there are two cases:

    1. The covering nodes are leaf nodes of different colors. The covering nodes must be decomposed, as must be the node in the aligned quadtree. However, these nodes will never be merged so the cost of this work is reflected in the size of the output tree.

    2. Some of the covering nodes are gray. Thus some of the covering nodes must be decomposed, as well as the node in the aligned quadtree. This extra decomposition in the aligned quadtree is bounded by four times the number of nodes in the unaligned quadtree. The cost of this work is reflected in the size of the unaligned tree.

6.24. Consider two trees such that their NW and SW quadrants are black and their NE and SE quadrants are white. Assume that they are out of alignment by one pixel.

6.29. The problem is that a node in the aligned quadtree is decomposed when it is not covered by (totally contained in) a node in the unaligned quadtree. To get rid of the factor M, we need to check if the node in the aligned quadtree is covered by several nodes in the unaligned quadtree, in which case it is not decomposed. This is the approach taken by the rectilinear unaligned pointer-based quadtree intersection algorithm. However, the extra FIND operations required will make this approach not worthwhile.

6.30. Four siblings of the same color are immediately replaced by their parent block when the fourth sibling is created. The worst possible case occurs when the NW, NE, and SW quadrants of the image are all of color c, the first three subquadrants of the SE quadrant are also of color c, and so forth. This situation can continue for at most n levels for a $2^n \times 2^n$ image, and the result follows.

6.31. This follows from the fact that the pixels of each block in the aligned quadtree are processed in Morton order. Consider the side of the active border of the aligned quadtree that corresponds to the unprocessed image. At any instant, the next pixel to be processed can only be one of the pixels in the vertex of one of the convex angles formed by the segments on this side (e.g., the upper leftmost corners of blocks 4 and 8 in Figure 6.7). Assume that after processing pixel (cx, cy), both X_EDGE[cx] and Y_EDGE[cy] contain a pointer to node Q in the unaligned quadtree and that the block that has been generated is of width w. The new active border of the aligned quadtree will have at most two new convex angles: one at $(cx + w, cy)$ and one at $(cx, cy + w)$. When pixel $(cx + w, cy)$ is processed, Y_EDGE[cy] still points at Q since no other pixel with y coordinate value cy was processed in the meantime. Similar reasoning applies to pixel $(cx, cy + w)$ and X_EDGE[cx].

6.32. See [Shaf88c].

6.33. See [Shaf86a, Shaf87a].

6.35. For a d-dimensional image, the active border tables are $(d - 1)$-dimensional arrays of width 2^n. There are d such arrays.

6.39. Step 2 requires that the containing subtree in the input quadtree be a leaf node. In other words, even if a node in the window's quadtree is covered by four nodes in the input quadtree, we must still decompose it.

6.40. It is difficult to trace the boundary of a three-dimensional image because the concept of a three-dimensional chain code does not exist. Thus you will need an algorithm to obtain the boundary of the regions (i.e., polyhedra) in the image (see Section 5.4 of [Same90a]).

6.42. The time requirements follow from the fact that each node in the input tree must be visited. In the worst case, for each node added to the output tree, n levels will be descended. Merging takes $O(M)$ time. The space requirements follow from the fact that the input and output trees are disjoint. The factor n results from the number of levels of recursion.

6.48. You need to determine the polygon (polyhedron) that is the inverse transformation of the block in the target tree and then perform a polygon (polyhedron) intersection with the covering block in the source tree.

6.50. Finding the smallest enclosing quadrant for the inverse transformation of each node in the target tree takes $O(n)$ time, and searching for this node in the list of nodes in the source tree takes $O(\log_2 N)$ time. There are M nodes in the target tree, and the result follows. Merging takes $O(M)$ time.

6.51. Yes. This is necessary when some of the covering nodes are gray.

6.52. This situation arises when some nodes in the output tree can be merged only once the maximum depth of the tree has been reached. Consider a $2^n \times 2^n$ image containing one black block of size $(2^{n-1} + 1) \times (2^{n-1} + 1)$ that is adjacent to the upper left corner of the image. Suppose that it is shifted by $2^{n-1} - 1$ to the right and downward. The result is that the SE quadrant will be black. However, it will have to be decomposed to depth n before merging. The number of extra nodes created will be $4 \cdot (n - 1)$, and they will disappear by virtue of merging.

6.55. Use the property that when a square, say S, of size $f \cdot w \times f \cdot w$ $(0 \le f \le 1)$ is placed on a grid of squares such that each square is of size w, then S can overlap no more than four grid squares.

6.62. The technique is the same with the exception that the 2s complement representation of T is used. The final carry, if any, is lost.

6.63. Reverse the order in which the nodes are processed (in the sense that it is exactly opposite to the direction of the translation). For example, if the translation is from left to right, then the nodes are processed from right to left. Thus the space occupied by the destination of a node has already been processed by the time blocks are moved into it.

6.64. The translation step requires an addition operation in which the maximum number of elements that must be added is equal to the resolution of the image.

6.65. Given translation vector T, let j be the minimum of the positions of the least significant bit in all of its axial components with a one. All blocks of width $\le 2^j$ are inserted into the target tree by simply adjusting their locational code. Each remaining block, say B, is processed by inserting all blocks with locational codes between $T(B_{\min})$ and $T(B_{\max})$ inclusive. These are the translated positions of $B_{\min}$ and $B_{\max}$, B's subblocks of width 2^j with the minimum and maximum locational codes, respectively.

6.66. See Exercise 2.9.

6.69. Let the minimum of the positions of the least significant bit of all the axial components of the translation vector with a one be at position j. Assume a d-dimensional image. For each leaf node of width 2^w such that $j < w$, Ahuja and Nash's algorithm must create $2^{(w-j) \cdot d}$ nodes of width 2^j, whereas Osse and Ahuja's algorithm must create far fewer nodes.

6.70. See [Dyer82, Shaf88a].

6.72. See [Wals88].

6.73. See [Wals88].

6.74. See [Wals88].

6.75. See [Wals88].

6.76. Assume that the least significant bit of T_x, which is one, occurs at position j. Therefore we have $\sum_{i=j}^{b-1} 2^i + 2^{b-j}$ blocks, which simplifies to $3 \cdot 2^{b-j} - 2$ [Wals88].

6.77. Consider a translation in just one of the axial directions, say x. In the worst case, the translation distance is odd. Measure the complexity in terms of the number of comparisons. Each column is sorted. Merging of two sorted lists can be done in time proportional to the sum of their lengths. The result is bounded by $\sum_{i=2}^{b+1} (\sum_{j=1}^{i} 2^j) - 2^b$ $= 7 \cdot 2^b - 2 \cdot b - 8$.

6.78. Assuming that both T_x and T_y are odd (i.e., for both of them the least significant bit, which is one, occurs at position 0), we have $1 + \sum_{i=2}^{b-1} (2^i - 2 + 2^i - 1) + 4 \cdot (2^b - 1)$ blocks, which simplifies to $6 \cdot 2^b - (3 \cdot b + 5)$ [Dyer82, Wals88].

6.79. There is one node of width 2^{b-1}. There are $2^{d-1} + 3 \cdot 2^{d-2} + \cdots + 3^{d-1}$ nodes of width 2^{b-2}. Walsh [Wals88] bounds this number by $d \cdot 4^{d-1}$ and makes a similar approximation for the remaining widths to get the bound $1 + d \cdot (\sum_{i=2}^{b} 2^{i \cdot (d-1)}) + d \cdot 2^{b \cdot (d-1)}$. Letting b get large, this is bounded by $2 \cdot d \cdot 2^{b \cdot (d-1)} \cdot (1 + (2^d - 2)^{-1})$. Can you obtain a tighter bound?

6.80. van Lierop, as well as Jackins and Tanimoto, checks the inverse image of each node in the target tree for intersection or inclusion with a single node in the source tree instead of a union of nodes as done by Meagher [Meag82a].

6.81. The algorithm of Osse and Ahuja generates the blocks corresponding to the translated region by starting with the node with the smallest locational code (also the smallest node) and continues with larger and larger nodes until the largest nodes have been generated. It concludes by generating smaller and smaller nodes until it generates the smallest node with the largest locational code. This is equivalent to a depth-first, bottom-up tree traversal. The algorithm of Walsh proceeds in a spiral manner by starting with the largest block in the translated region and then generating smaller and smaller blocks. This is equivalent to a breadth-first, top-down tree traversal.

6.83. If $w \leq (R+1)/2$, then one of T's brothers will have a nonwhite descendant, say U, so that all of T is within R of U's border. In such a case, after the expansion, T and its brothers are all black and the father of T can be inserted into the output quadtree as a black node.

6.88. In this way, vertices that lie on the axis lines are said to be in the quadrant. For example, the vertex at the SE corner of C in Figure 6.16a is not in the vertex set because it is in the NW quadrant of quadtree rooted at the SE vertex of D.

6.89. No. Consider Figure 6.16a. Such a definition means that the vertex set may include all of the vertices. Moreover, the polygon may not necessarily be unique if we restrict ourselves to simple polygons (i.e., a polygon that does not intersect itself).

6.90. See [Ang88]

6.91. Use contradiction.

6.92. Assume that the elements of vs_{d_1} and vs_{d_2} are arranged in ascending order of the values of their x coordinates. Since no two vertices in vs_d have the same x coordinate value, the number of vertices in vs_d is at most $w(R)$. Consider vs_{NW} and vs_{NE}. All vertices of blocks in the SW quadrant with respect to the last vertex v in vs_{NW} cannot be in vs_{NE}. Therefore, vertices in vs_{NE} can only be taken from the region with x coordinate values greater than that of v. Thus, all vertices in vs_{NW} and vs_{NE} have different x coordinate values and there are at most $w(R)+1$ such values. See [Ang88].

6.93. If node P is the only black node in M that is closest to the boundary of M in a given direction, then P contributes two vertices to the vertex set; otherwise a node contributes at most one vertex. There are at most four nodes in M that can contribute two vertices because there are only four directions. $2 \cdot w(R) + 2$ is the maximum size of the two disjoint pairs of adjacent vertex subsets by Exercise 6.92. See [Ang88].

6.94. See [Ang88]

6.95. As the radius of expansion increases, the size of the merging cluster increases, and there are fewer merging clusters. However, the complexity of the vertex set usually increases as the size of the merging cluster increases.

6.96. See [Ang88].

6.98. Use a variant of the EXPAND function.

6.99. See [Fuji89].

CHAPTER 7

7.4. Interpret $g(A)$ as the size of cell A (generally denoted as $|A|$) and now $|C| = |A \cup B| = |A| + |B| - |A \cap B|$.

7.5. Store in each leaf node a 'gray' value between 0 and 1. Whenever $g(A)$ or $g(B)$ is equal to 1, then $g(C) = g(A) + g(B) - g(A) * g(B) = 1$. Thus, overlaying a subtree A such that its leaf nodes all have a 'gray' value 1 with another subtree will yield subtree A as the result. Hence it is useful to mark the nonleaf nodes of the quadtree with a flag indicating whether all of the leaf nodes in the subtree rooted at that node have value 1. Of course, if four sibling leaf nodes have value 1, they would normally be merged. Porter and Duff [Port84] deal with color images where the color is represented as a vector of three values indicating intensity values of the three primary colors, red, green, and blue. The 'gray' value then becomes a fourth component of this vector (termed the *alpha* component), which is manipulated in the manner described in the exercise. Such a color application could have four sibling leaf nodes whose alpha values were all 1 but which are still distinct because their red, green, or blue intensities are different.

7.9. Consider the situation illustrated in Figure 7.3 without polygon B. In this case, the minimum z value for polygon C could be smaller than the minimum z value for polygon A, even though parts of polygon C are in the inner set of A.

7.10. It is handled implicitly.

7.11. (a) 4 followed by any permutation of {6,0,5} followed by any permutation of {2,7,1} followed by 3. (b) Let σ denote the index of the first octant. The second through the fourth octants are those bit strings that differ from σ in exactly one bit position. The fifth through the seventh octants are those bit strings that differ from σ in exactly two bit positions. The eighth octant differs from σ in all bit positions.

7.13. See [Meag82a, Yau84].

7.18. There are three kinds of faces: transparent, lit object, and unlit object. Initially the faces of the nodes in the octree are marked as being either unlit or transparent. First, mark as lit all faces that are visible from the light source initially marked unlit. This is achieved by a parallel projection algorithm in the direction of the light source, although we will not need the display quadtree once done. Next, perform the parallel projection in the direction of the viewer painting the unlit visible faces as shadows and the lit visible faces with the color of the object.

7.19. See [Yama84].

7.24. No. See the two-dimensional example in Figure 7.11 where line segment B does not intersect the halfspace of line segment D, whereas line segment D does intersect the halfspace of line segment B.

7.25. In two dimensions, P_1 and P_2 must intersect. In three dimensions, either P_1 and P_2 are coplanar, or else both P_1 and P_2 intersect the line along which their planes intersect (it does not imply that P_1 and P_2 intersect).

7.27. $n + 1$.

7.28. When all line segments (polygons) span the entire two (three)-dimensional space from which they are drawn. Alternatively, referring to Exercise 7.24, CONFLICT $(P_1, P_2) =$ CONFLICT (P_2, P_1) for every pair of line segments (polygons).

7.29. $\Sigma_{i=0}^{d} \binom{n}{i}$ in a d-dimensional space.

7.30. Because we are just using the quadrilateral approximation of the base of the surface patch. If we were to view the patch from a direction normal to the base, then the patch would most probably lie inside the base. However, if the patch were viewed at an acute angle, then it is quite possible that the patch would curve far enough off the base so that the projection of the surface would extend beyond the border of the projection of the base.

7.35. Consider the corners of the pixels, and refer to them as rows and columns. Let us number the rows from 1 to 17 starting from the top, and the columns from 1 to 65 starting from the left. The four triangle rule produces a shading pattern with a contour map having a value of 1 for all positions in column 1 and two scalloped edges (one for 0 and one for 0.5). The problem is that interpolation means that there are values of 0.5 in columns 5, 13, 21, 29, 37, 45, 53, and 61 of row 5 and in columns 1, 17, 33, 49, and 65 of row 9. At the same time, there are values of 0 in columns 9, 25, 41, and 57 in row 9 and in columns 1, 17, 33, 49, and 65 of row 17. On the other hand, the eight triangle rule produces a shading pattern with a contour map having no scalloped edges. In particular, the interpolated values in each row are the same and equal to that of the vertices that are in the row, if any. Row 1 has a value of 1, row 5 has a value of 0.5, rows 9, 13, and 17 have a value of 0.

In this example, the four triangle rule is inferior because the maximum gradient of the shading variation is along a vertical line (because the edge is horizontal). In particular, the four triangle rule yields a shading pattern with a 'speckled' effect resulting from rapidly moving back and forth between values of 0.5 and 1.0, which the eye is quick to notice. Using the eight triangle rule yields an edge that is colinear with the original one, if displaced somewhat. In contrast, the eight triangle rule is inferior when the maximum gradient of the shading variation is along a 45 degree angle. This discussion is applicable to the shading of parametric surfaces because it is common for the maximum curvature of the surface (and, hence, the largest change in the derivative) to occur parallel to the border of the parametric patch (i.e., one of the parametric contours or axes). Thus even for smooth surfaces, the effects are similar to those described for a triangulated surface. The difference is that unlike the parameter space, the grid in the 'real' space need not be 'regular.'

7.36. The edge is colinear with the original edge; there is no scalloping effect. However, there may be cracks along the edges of the triangles.

7.38. A ray is cast from the surface of the object, say A, toward the light source, say S. If the ray intersects another object before encountering S, then A lies in the shadow. Ray-tracing methods that do not use scene coherence must generate a list of all intersections of the ray in order to find the closest intersection, a computationally costly process.

7.40. Because of the manner in which the parametric representation of the ray was formed. In particular, the ray is being traced starting from the viewpoint in the direction of increasing values of t.

7.41. The ray does not intersect the cell. This is not a problem in the implementation described for procedure RAY_TRACER because, except for the cell corresponding to the initial three-dimensional space, we never examine a cell that is not intersected by the ray. For the initial entry into the cell corresponding to the entire three-dimensional space, say E, we merely test if the point that has been calculated to be in E is really in E.

7.42. There is no need to worry about whether a ray is totally visible or totally invisible (except for the initial cell corresponding to the entire three-dimensional space).

7.43. One possible way is to take the floors of each of the numbers, sort them, and then repeatedly sort them according to their integer remainders. This could be achieved by a combination of a bucket sort and a radix sort.

7.44. In two dimensions, the plane of reflection is a line. Let (i,j) be the point of intersection of the ray with the plane of reflection. Assume that the plane of reflection passes through $(0,0)$ and (a,b), and that the incident ray passes through (α,β). The normal to the plane of reflection is represented by $(i,j) + s \cdot (b,-a)$. A line through (α,β) that is parallel to the plane of reflection is represented by $(\alpha,\beta) + t \cdot (a,b)$. Solving for the point of intersection of the normal with the line parallel to the plane of intersection by eliminating s leads to $t = (a(i - \alpha) + b(j - \beta)) / (a^2 + b^2)$. The point at which the reflected ray intersects the line through (α,β) that is parallel to the plane of reflection is simply $(\alpha,\beta) + 2 \cdot t \cdot (a,b)$. To derive the result in three dimensions, use vector notation.

7.46. See [Fuji86] for a description of 3DDDA, a three-dimensional digital differential analyzer algorithm closely related to Bresenham's algorithm [Bres65] (see also Exercise 7.70).

7.47. No. The problem is that we need to execute some form of a search (e.g., a binary search) to locate the neighboring node once its address has been calculated.

7.49. $x = 24 \cdot t - 8$ and $y = t + 23$.

7.51. No. The problem is that when the motion is in the positive direction of the Ith coordinate, the assumptions with respect to open and closed regions mean that no increment is to be made, yet CHANGE(D,I) has a value of 1.

7.52. No. It yields the wrong answer when the current cell and the neighboring cell are of equal size.

7.53. Otherwise a value of t with a negative numerator and a negative denominator will cause the comparison to be erroneous. For example, compare $t_x = 16/7$ with $t_y = -14/-7$. Remember, that the values of t are rational numbers that may not necessarily have been reduced via removal of their greatest common divisor.

7.54. Depending on the compiler, integer division of a positive number by a negative number may be rounded off instead of being truncated. This could cause a problem when all three terms are negative, as is the case in two dimensions where M['X'] and M['Y'] are both negative. This is despite the fact that NUM(T_OUT(C)) and DEN(T_OUT(C)) always have the same sign since $t \geq 0$ for every point on each ray.

7.55. Instead of using M[I] in the computations of T[I] and POINT[I], use NUM(M[I]) and DEN(M[I]). Also, SIGN_M[I] becomes the sign of NUM(M[I]).

7.57. Let (a_x,a_y) denote the point at which cells 5 and 11 touch. Cell 4 is the next cell intersected by the ray if we apply procedure FIND_2D_BLOCK to the point $(a_x - 1,a_y)$. Suppose cell 4 is completely occupied by an object such that the object's southern and eastern boundaries coincide with the southern and eastern boundaries of the cell. This means that a false object intersection will be reported. On the other hand, cell 12 is the next cell intersected by the ray if we apply FIND_2D_BLOCK to the point $(a_x, a_y - 1)$, in which case no false object intersection is reported.

7.59. Procedure RAY_TRACER goes to cell 3 after cell 2, whereas Wyvill and Kunii calculate POINT = (12,16), which FIND_2D_BLOCK determines to be in cell 10. From cell 10, they compute POINT = (14,15) instead of the correct value of POINT = (12,15). Although in the case of the original Figure 7.17, FIND_2D_BLOCK determines both of these points to be in cell 3, this is not the case in the modified figure, and a transition is made to the wrong cell.

7.60. This will not always yield the correct result. For example, in two dimensions, a motion in the SW direction is decomposed into two motions—one each in the S and W directions. This can lead to an error, as described in the solution to Exercise 7.57. Thus the only way to ensure the correctness of Wyvill and Kunii's algorithm is to make it identical to procedure RAY_TRACER (i.e., to compute the exact direction of the neighboring cell relative to the current cell).

7.67. The number of cells in the bintree is usually lower than in the octree. However, the total number of nodes in the bintree may be higher since the number of nonleaf nodes in the bintree is much larger than that in the octree.

7.73. Whitted's solution requires that a pixel's region may have to be subdivided. When determining the minimum cell width of the space through which the rays are traced (i.e., Δ), we must take into consideration the maximum level of decomposition for the pixel subdivision process.

7.74. See [Gold71] and the improvements in [Roth82].

7.75. Heckbert and Hanrahan [Heck84] suggest comparing the size of the average ray tree with the total beam tree size. The lower is this value, the more fragmented is the beam tree and hence there is less homogeneity. As the homogeneity increases, so does the efficiency of beam tracing.

7.80. As long as the polyhedra are complex, the elements of successive approximations become smaller and smaller. Thus just because a beam does not intersect an element of the new approximation does not mean that it does not intersect any polygon in the space corresponding to the node of the BSP tree. On the other hand, when the beam fails to intersect an element of the approximation based on removing bounding halfspaces, then we know that it cannot intersect any of the polygons in the space corresponding to the node of the BSP tree.

7.81. Before we clip a duplicated polygon from a beam, we must first clip it by the splitting plane(s).

7.84. See [Aman84].

7.85. See [Prep77].

7.86. 'Divide-and-conquer'–like methods that are used for constructing a convex hull are inapplicable to the construction of minimum bounding boxes because the problem cannot be decomposed into combinable subproblems. In particular, the minimum bounding box of a given set of points may not necessarily contain the minimum bounding boxes of all of its subsets. Of course, if the faces of the bounding boxes are restricted to be parallel to the coordinate axes, then the problem is indeed decomposable; however, the result is no longer a minimum bounding box.

7.87. See [Dado82] and also [Dobk83].

7.88. See [Dobk83]. This is a special case of Exercise 7.87, where $k = 4$.

7.89. Project the bounding box onto a cross-section of the beam. The projection is a convex polygon with at most six sides. A cross-section of the beam is a convex polygon with k sides. Hence their intersection can be detected in $O(\log_2 k)$ time since the intersection of two convex polygons with p and q sides can be detected in $O(\log_2 p \cdot \log_2 q)$ time [Dado82]. Note that improvements on the $O(\log_2 p \cdot \log_2 q)$ time bound are possible [Dobk83, Chaz87].

7.91. Given a face F of a node N, if a face C' of a node N' is visible from F, then C' is visible from some face of some transparent node that is a neighbor of N.

7.92. The control flow of this solution is very similar to a relaxation (i.e., iterative) [Rose82a] solution of a system of simultaneous equations.

CHAPTER 8

8.1. See [Rana82].

8.2. See [Rana82].

8.3. See Figure 8.11 for a connectivity problem and Figure 8.13 for a spurious hole.

8.5. Because of the encoding and decoding schemes embodied by procedures ENCODE_FBW and BUILD_TREE.

8.7. Unfortunately, no encoding and decoding scheme exists that can be used with SBW. To see this, we observe that a given forest is not sufficient to describe uniquely an image, or a portion thereof, in the sense that we must also know its parent node. As an example, consider the white forest consisting of nodes I and 15 in Figure 8.1. It is the white forest corresponding to node F. However, suppose that nodes 1, 2, and 11 are black rather than white. We now find that the white forest {I, 15} corresponds to both nodes B and F. In other words, SBW for Figure 8.1 with nodes 1, 2, 11 being black is the same as SBW when these three nodes are white. In particular when nodes 1, 2, 11 are black, SBW(4) = {B, 25, 16, M, 27, 38, 10}, SBW(3) = {25, 16, 27, 38, 10, I, 15, 33, 34}, SBW(2) = {25, 16, 27, 38, 10, 15, 33, 34, 19} = SBW(1) = SBW(0); when nodes 1, 2, 11 are white, SBW(4) = {25, 16, F, M, 27, 38, 10}, SBW(3) = {25, 16, 27, 38, 10, I, 15, 33, 34}, SBW(2) = {25, 16, 27, 38, 10, 15, 33, 34, 19} = SBW(1) = SBW(0). Thus we see that since nodes B and F have identical white forests, after SBW(4) we cannot tell them apart no matter what encoding scheme we use.

8.8. See Lemmas 8.1 and 8.2 in Section 8.2.2.
8.9. See Lemmas 8.1 and 8.2 in Section 8.2.2.
8.10. GGBWBBGGBBWBBWBGBBBWGGBBWWBWW.
8.11. Use contradiction. Assume that a spurious hole, say H, is created. Consider the smallest square, say S, containing the hole in its entirety. Two of the brothers of S must be of type GB, and thus the father of S is of type GB; therefore the hole cannot exist.
8.13. Whenever three out of four sons have the same color (i.e., black or white).
8.16. Because most of the background is white.
8.17. Because a node can be labeled with GB and GW′ at the same time.
8.18. FBW″(2) is the root node. FBW″(1) is the root node plus its four sons. FBW″(0) is the root node, its four sons, plus two sons from each of the four subtrees of the root.
8.20. A, 4, 5, 8, E, 9, 10, 12, 18, 19.
8.21. No. Just specify the color of the first node.
8.22. The algorithm is analogous to procedure BUILD_TREE given in Section 2.1.1.
8.23. They are related in the sense that they alternate between black and white nodes.
8.24. The sum of four numbers is at most four times the largest one, leading to a requirement of at most two more bits.
8.26. The maximum deviation occurs at a maximum distance from the diagonals.
8.27. Hardas and Srihari [Hard84] give a solution that works for an odd number of gray-scale levels (i.e., $0 \cdots r$ where r is even).

CHAPTER 9

9.2. It resembles a sawtooth approximation to a circle.
9.3. The Chessboard metric is represented by the pair (1,1) since $d_M(p, q) = e + f$. The city block metric is represented by the pair (1,2) since $d_A(p, q) = e + 2 \cdot f$.
9.4. For a $2^n \times 2^n$ image, the maximum value of the Chessboard distance transform value is $2^{(n-1)} + 2^{(n-2)} - 1$. As an example, consider a square black region of size $2^n - 1 \times 2^n - 1$.
9.7. For example, in Figure 1.1, node 13 has a Chessboard distance transform value of 1, whereas its path-length distance transform value is 2 because neighbors in the direction of a vertex such as white node 1 are not taken into account.
9.10. It is conceivable that a good answer does not exist since the concept of an adjacency tree does not exist for a vertex-neighbor. Of course, the bound can still exist.
9.13. For the NW, NE, SW, and SE traversals, you have to transmit two additional neighbors instead of one. For example, the NW traversal transmits the S and E neighbors, as well as

the SE neighbor. Also, when processing gray node P, the traversal is continued in such a manner that P's NW son is visited first, followed by P's NE and SW sons in arbitrary order, and then P's SE son.

9.15. The first traversal transmits neighbors in the directions W, NW, N, NE, and E, while the second traversal transmits neighbors in the directions W, SW, S, SE, and E.

9.16. Use a data structure similar to that used for the active border in Section 5.1.3. You will also have to deal with vertex-neighbors for which you may wish to define an additional separate data structure termed an *active corner* (see the discussion of component counting in Section 5.3).

9.17. Decompose the proof into two parts. First, show that no black node's distance transform value is too large. Second, show that no black node's distance transform value is too small. The key is that the second pass processes the nodes of the tree in reverse order.

9.18. The forward pass of TOP_DOWN_ACTIVE_BORDER_DIST is equivalent to the pass of TOP_-DOWN_NEIGHBOR_DIST that processes neighbors in directions E, SE, S, and SW, while the reverse pass of TOP_DOWN_ACTIVE_BORDER_DIST is equivalent to the pass of TOP_DOWN_-NEIGHBOR_DIST that processes neighbors in directions W, NW, N, and NE.

9.21. The effect of such an improvement is limited since the number of neighbors ranges between five and eight.

9.23. Andresen et al. [Andr85] address this problem by computing the Chessboard distance transform of the white blocks. This yields the minimum distance between the center of each white block and the boundary of the nearest obstacle.

9.24. A disadvantage of a distance measure in terms of the number of links that must be traversed is that the distance becomes a function of the positioning of the image (i.e., it is shift sensitive).

9.26. Shaffer [Shaf86a] gives an example of the nonuniqueness whose DF-expression is given below. We use W to refer to the white nodes, the letters A–Q to refer to the black nodes, and '(' to refer to the gray nodes. The DF expression assumes a traversal in the order NW, NE, SW, and SE.

$$((WWW(WWWA(WW(WWBC(WW(WWDWW(W(WEWFW(W(WGWWWW$$

$$(H((IWJWW(KWLWW((MNWW(OPWWWW((QWWWWWW.$$

The quadtree skeleton is given by listing the blocks with their distance transform values in parentheses. The distance transform value assumes a $2^4 \times 2^4$ image. The quadtree skeleton using property 2 consists of blocks A(1), B(1), C(1), E(1), F(1), and H(3). When property 2 need not be satisfied, we can obtain a smaller quadtree skeleton (in terms of the number of elements) by decomposing block H into four blocks $H_{NW}(3)$, $H_{NE}(2)$, $H_{SW}(2)$, $H_{SE}(2)$, where the subscript indicates the quadrant.

9.27. If the border is white, then no block that is adjacent to the border could be subsumed by another block nor can it subsume other blocks. However, when the border is black, then only blocks adjacent to the border can possibly have an increase in the value of their distance transform. Hence they can subsume previously unsubsumed blocks, resulting in a smaller QMAT.

9.28. Representation 3 since the QMAT can be conceptualized as a set of representative points that are restricted to be centers of quadtree blocks. The extents of these blocks are bounded by three times their length. Although the QMAT is defined in terms of squares, it could also be defined in terms of rectangles.

9.29. There is a problem in deciding what is a background color (i.e., what does it mean for a block to subsume another block?). What is the analog of white? One possibility is to use a quadtree decomposition rule that quarters an image until obtaining blocks of two colors. Then compute the QMAT for this block, treating one color as black and the other as white. Another alternative is to choose one color to serve as the background color (i.e., white) and then compute the distance transform for each block b_i of color c_i (not white) in terms of the distance to the border of the nearest block to b_i with a color different from c_i.

9.30. See [Shaf86a] for a brief, but inconclusive, discussion of this problem.

9.33. Create a copy of the nodes while forming the QMAT. The only modification to QUAD-TREE_TO_QMAT that is necessary is to create a copy of each node prior to examining its neighbors.

9.34. The execution time of Algorithm A is $O(B^2)$ since sorting is required (an $O(B \cdot \log B)$ operation), as well as checking every black block against every other black block for subsumption. To reduce the execution time of the entire algorithm to $O(B \cdot \log B)$, a $B \cdot \log B$ procedure to check subsumption is necessary.

9.35. No. The computation of the QMAT relies on knowledge of the values of the Chessboard distance transform of a node's neighbors.

9.43. In the worst case, the subsuming element is found at level $n - 1$ and has a Chessboard distance transform value of $2^{(n-1)} + 2^{(n-2)} - 1$ (see Exercise 9.4). In such a case, a maximum of $2^{(n+1)} - 2$ nodes must be visited for an edge-neighbor and $2^{(n+2)} - 2 \cdot (2n + 1)$ nodes for a vertex-neighbor.

9.44. Create a copy of the QMAT as the quadtree is constructed, thereby processing the two trees in parallel.

9.45. In this way, procedure QMAT_TO_QUADTREE need not waste its time trying to propagate subsumption for it.

9.46. Procedure QMAT_TO_QUADTREE requires an additional step to check for merging. This would be performed at the conclusion of processing a gray node. Since property 3 does not permit a node to require more than one element of the quadtree skeleton for its subsumption, this merger is impossible, and it need not be checked.

9.47. In the case of black elements of the QMAT, the result is identical to procedure QMAT_TO_-QUADTREE. However, white nodes are considerably more cumbersome to process. For example, when processing the eastern edge of white QMAT node D of Figure 9.8f, it must be determined if there are any black nodes (of any size) adjacent to D's eastern side and then propagate their subsumption back to node D. This requires the examination of all of the adjacent black nodes. The result is a QMAT reconstruction algorithm that is considerably more complex.

9.49. The exact number of nodes required for such a quadtree of level n can be obtained by use of the following recurrence relations. Assume, without loss of generality, an image such that the largest block is in the NW quadrant. Let t_i denote the number of nodes in a quadtree of level i, and r_{i-1} be the contribution made by the NE and SW quadrants of a quadtree of level i:

$$t_i = \begin{cases} 1 & i = 0 \\ 1 + 1 + 2 \cdot r_{i-1} + t_{i-1} & i \geq 1 \end{cases} \qquad r_i = \begin{cases} 1 & i = 0 \\ 1 + 2 + 2 \cdot r_{i-1} & i \geq 1 \end{cases}$$

It can easily be shown that these relations have the solutions $r_i = 2^{i+2} - 3$ and

$t_i = 2^{i+3} - 4 \cdot i - 7$. To see this, we observe that $r_i = 3 \cdot \Sigma_{j=0}^{i-1} 2^j + 2^i = 3 \cdot (2^i - 1) + 2^i = 2^{i+2} - 3$, and substituting into t_i yields $t_i = 2 + 2 \cdot (2^{i+1} - 3) + t_{i-1} = 4 \cdot (2^i - 1) + t_{i-1}$. Solving for t_i we get $t_i = 4 \cdot \Sigma_{j=1}^{i} (2^j - 1) + 1 = 4 \cdot (2^{i+1} - 2 - i) + 1 = 2^{i+3} - 4 \cdot i - 7$. Thus for a quadtree of level n, the number of nodes that can be saved by using the QMAT representation is $2^{n+3} - 4 \cdot n - 12$. For example, for $n = 3$, the difference is 40 nodes, a reduction by a factor of 15.

9.50. Shaffer [Shaf86a] shows that the worst-case position arises when the block is shifted by one pixel from its best-case position (see Exercise 9.49) in the direction of one axis and any nonzero multiple of 2^{m-1} pixels in the direction of the other axis. This is the worst-case position because in order for a black QMAT node to subsume other nodes, it must be surrounded on all four sides by black nodes. In this case, only two black nodes (of size $2^{m-2} \times 2^{m-2}$) subsume other nodes. In the worst case, for $m \geq 2$ we need $2^m + 2 \cdot (m + 1)$ black nodes. When the nonzero multiple of 2^{m-1} is such that the shifted block overlaps the center of the image, the number of white nodes is at a maximum of $3 \cdot 2^m + 3 \cdot (n - m + 1)$ white nodes.

9.52. The shifted QMAT has $2 \cdot n - 2$, $4 \cdot n - 6$, and $2 \cdot n - 3$ black, white, and gray nodes, respectively, while the shifted quadtree has $3 \cdot (2^n - n) - 2$, $3 \cdot (2^n + n - 2)$, and $2^{n+1} - 3$ black, white, and gray nodes respectively [Scot86].

9.53. The following example is from [Shaf86a] and is specified by DF-expressions traversed in the order NW, NE, SW, SE. No distance transform values for the QMAT nodes are given. W corresponds to white nodes, the letters A–M denote black quadtree and QMAT nodes, and '(' refers to gray nodes. The $2^3 \times 2^3$ image whose quadtree is

((A(WWBC(WDWEF((WWGWW(HWIWW((WJWW(KLWWWW((MWWWWWW

has an optimal QMAT of

((AWWFWWW.

The optimal quadtree for this image, obtained by shifting it three pixels to the right and three pixels down, is

((WWW(WWWA(WW(WWBWW(W(WCWWWWD.

and has a QMAT consisting of the same black nodes.

9.59. We must visit the root, its four sons, and a maximum of nine nodes at each of the remaining levels for a total of $5 + 9 \cdot (n - 1)$ nodes.

9.62. No, as can be seen by the presence of module 9 in the root and in one son of each of the quadrants of the root node.

9.63. No, because the result of the increment is not necessarily a QMAT. You will also have to perform merging.

9.64. If the squares spanned by the black nodes of the QMAT are identical to the maximal blocks, then the convex hulls are identical. If not, then some of the maximal blocks require more than one black QMAT node to cover their constituent pixels. Let M be such a maximal block with medial axis transformation point C_M and let Q_i be the black QMAT nodes with centers c_i that cover M. In such a case, some of the points c_i will lie on opposite sides of C_M and, thus, the convex hull formed from c_i and other relevant points will contain C_M. For more details, see [Shaf86a].

APPENDIX
DESCRIPTION OF
PSEUDO-CODE
LANGUAGE

The algorithms are given using pseudo-code. This pseudo-code is a variant of the ALGOL [Naur60] programming language, which has a data structuring facility that incorporates pointers and record structures. We make heavy use of recursion. This language has similarities to C [Kern78], PASCAL [Jens74], SAIL [Reis76], and ALGOLW [Baue68]. Its basic features are described below. All reserved words are designated in boldface. This also includes the names (i.e., types) of predefined record structures.

A program is defined as a collection of functions and procedures. Functions are distinguished from procedures by the fact that they return values via the use of the **return** construct. Also the function header declaration specifies the types of the data that it returns as its value. In the following the term *procedure* is used to refer to both procedures and functions.

All formal parameters to procedures must be declared along with the manner in which they have been transmitted (**value** or **reference**). All local variables are declared. Global variables are declared and are specified by use of the reserved word **global** before the declaration. Variables and arrays may be initialized to prespecified values by prefacing the declaration with the reserved word **preload** and appending the reserved word **with** and the initialization values to the declaration.

'Short-circuit' evaluation techniques are used for Boolean operators that combine relational expressions. In other words, as soon as any parts of a Boolean **or** (**and**) are true (false), the remaining parts are not tested. This is similar to what is used in LISP [McCa60] but is different from PASCAL, where the order of the evaluation is deemed to be immaterial.

Record structures are available. An instance of a record structure of type **rec** is created by use of the command **create(rec)**. The result of this operation is a pointer to a record structure of the appropriate type. Pointers to record structures are declared by use of the reserved word **pointer**, which is followed by the name of the type of the record structure. Instances of record structures are referred by using functional notation where the field name is in the position of the function and pointer is its argument. For example, if variable L points to an instance of a record structure of type **list**, then we use 'NEXT(L)' to refer to the NEXT field of this instance. Of course, L must be declared to be a pointer to a record structure of type L by using a declaration of the form '**pointer list** L'. Note the use of bold face for the specification of the type of the record structure since we assume that it has been predefined.

The fields of a record structure may be of any type, including an array. For example, suppose that a record of type has a field called ARR, which is a one-dimensional array. Moreover, assume that L has been declared as a pointer to a record of type **rec**. We use ARR(L)[I] to refer to the Ith element of the ARR field of the **rec** record pointed at by L.

The procedures are usually recursive and make heavy use of the 'if-then-else' mechanism. The value of an 'if-then-else' can be a statement or an expression. They are frequently used like a select statement in BLISS [Wulf71] and are similar to a COND in LISP. They are often nested. Observance of the placement of semicolons ensures a proper understanding of their semantics. In other words, they must nest. A procedure is a block of statements separated by semicolons. A block is delimited by **begin** and **end**. An 'if-then-else' constitutes a statement. Blocks must be used after a **then** and an **else** when there is more than one statement in this position.

There is a rich set of types. These types are defined as they are used. In particular, enumerated types in the sense of PASCAL are used heavily. For example, the type **quadrant** is an enumerated type whose values are NW, NE, SW, SE.

The array data type is treated as a special type of a record; however, there are some differences. Although an identifier that has been declared to be a record type is usually only used as a parameter to a function that allocates storage for an instance of the record type or to qualify the declaration of a pointer variable, when an identifier that has been declared to be an array appears by itself (i.e., without a suffix to indicate a particular array element—e.g., ARR instead of ARR[I]), then the identifier is treated as a pointer to an instance of the data type associated with the array declaration. This is useful when it is desired to pass an array as a parameter to a procedure or to return an entire array as the value of a procedure. Thus, in such cases, the array identifier is analogous to a pointer to a record having a type equal to that of the array declaration.

Storage for an array is allocated from a heap rather than a stack. This means that there is a need for some form of garbage collection for array elements that are not pointed at by any of the currently accessible pointers (i.e., pointer variables). If an array is local to a procedure, then its storage is allocated upon entering the block in which the array is declared. If the array is transmitted as a formal 'value' parameter to a procedure, then its storage is allocated upon entry to the procedure, and its elements are set to the value they had in the corresponding array in the calling procedure. If the array is transmitted as a formal 'reference' parameter to a procedure, then the array occupies the same storage in both the calling and called procedures. It is the user's responsibility to make sure that the type declarations in the calling and called procedure match.

Two subtle points about memory management for arrays are worth noting. The first is that while storage for an array is usually deallocated when exiting from a procedure in which it has been declared or transmitted as a 'value' parameter, deallocation should not take place for an array returned as the value of a procedure. The second is that if an array name, say A, appears on the left-hand side of an assignment statement and the right-hand side is an expression whose value is an array of the same type, then A is overwritten and the original instance of the array that was bound to A is inaccessible once the assignment has taken place.

As an example of the first point, let us examine the situation that a procedure returns as its value an array that has been transmitted to it as a 'value' parameter. In such a case, once the called procedure has exited, there are two instances of the array, one of which is the value returned by the procedure and which is a (possibly modified) copy of the array that was transmitted as a parameter.

One shortcoming with the array data type is the absence of a true analogy with record structures. The problem is that the process of allocating storage for an array should be decoupled from its declaration (which is more like setting up a template). This is a shortcoming of many implementations, including the one described here. It could be overcome easily by replacing the keyword **array** by the keyword **array_pointer** whenever it is desired only to set up the template for the array rather than also allocating the storage. For example, the declaration '**integer array_pointer** ARR[0:N]'; would set up the template for array ARR without actually allocating the space for it, while '**integer array** ARR[0:N]' retains its original meaning of template declaration and storage allocation.

Note that the C language allows for either array declaration with allocation or without (i.e., template declaration). However, in C, for the case of the array template, the actual size of the array cannot be specified. In other words, the template is really a pointer to an element of the type of the members of the array but cannot indicate how many elements are in the array.

REFERENCES

1. [Abda88] S. K. Abdali and D. S. Wise, Experiments with quadtree representation of matrices, *Proceedings of the International Symposium on Symbolic and Algebraic Computation*, Rome, July 1988 (also University of Indiana Computer Science Technical Report No. 241). [matrices] D.2.6.1

2. [Abel84a] D. J. Abel, A B^+-tree structure for large quadtrees, *Computer Vision, Graphics, and Image Processing 27*, 1(July 1984), 19–31. [regions] A.2.1 A.2.1.1 A.4.2.3

3. [Abel84b] D. J. Abel, Comments on "detection of connectivity for regions represented by linear quadtrees," *Computers and Mathematics with Applications 10*, 2(1984), 167–170. [regions] A.5.1.3

4. [Abel85] D. J. Abel, Some elemental operations on linear quadtrees for geographic information systems, *Computer Journal 28*, 1(February 1985), 73–77. [regions] D.3.5.2

5. [Abel83] D. J. Abel and J. L. Smith, A data structure and algorithm based on a linear key for a rectangle retrieval problem, *Computer Vision, Graphics, and Image Processing 24*, 1(October 1983), 1–13. [rectangles] D.3.5 D.3.5.1 A.2.1.1

6. [Abel84c] D. J. Abel and J. L. Smith, A simple approach to the nearest-neighbor problem, *Australian Computer Journal 16*, 4(November 1984), 140–146. [points]

7. [Abel84d] D. J. Abel and J. L. Smith, A data structure and query algorithm for a database of areal entities, *Australian Computer Journal 16*, 4(November 1984), 147–154. [points]

8. [Adam49] O. Adams, Latitude developments connected with geodesy and cartography, US Coast and Geodetic Survey Special Publication No. 67, US Government Printing Office, Washington, DC, 1949. [cartography] D.1.4.1

9. [Adel62] G. M. Adel'son-Velskii and Y. M. Landis, An algorithm for the organization of information, *Doklady Akademii Nauk SSSR 146*, (1962), 263–266 (English translation in *Soviet Math. Doklady 3* (1962), 1259–1262). [general] D.2.4.1 D.2.7

Each reference is followed by a key word(s). It is also followed by a list of the sections in which it is referenced. The format is D or A followed by the section number. D corresponds to [Same90a] while A corresponds to this book. D.P and A.P denote the appropriate preface, and L denotes the appendix describing the pseudo code language. All references that are cited in the solutions to exercises are associated with the section in which the exercise is found.

10. [Aho74] A. V. Aho, J. E. Hopcroft, and J. D. Ullman, *The Design and Analysis of Computer Algorithms*, Addison-Wesley, Reading, MA, 1974. [general] D.P D.2.4.1 D.2.7 D.4.2.3.1 D.4.2.3.6 A.P A.4.5

11. [Ahuj83] N. Ahuja, On approaches to polygonal decomposition for hierarchical image representation, *Computer Vision, Graphics, and Image Processing 24*, 2(November 1983), 200–214. [regions] D.1.4.1 D.5.2 A.4.6

12. [Ahuj84a] N. Ahuja, Efficient planar embedding of trees for VLSI layouts, *Proceedings of the Seventh International Conference on Pattern Recognition*, Montreal, August 1984, 460–464. [hardware]

13. [Ahuj84b] N. Ahuja and C. Nash, Octree representations of moving objects, *Computer Vision, Graphics, and Image Processing 26*, 2(May 1984), 207–216. [volumes] A.6.5.3

14. [Ahuj89] N. Ahuja and J. Veenstra, Generating octrees from object silhouettes in orthographic views, *IEEE Transactions on Pattern Analysis and Machine Intelligence 11*, 2(February 1989), 137–149. [volumes] D.5.2 A.4.6

15. [Alan84a] J. Alander, Interval arithmetic methods in the processing of curves and sculptured surfaces, *Proceedings of the Sixth International Symposium on CAD/CAM*, Zagreb, Yugoslavia, 1984. [surfaces] D.5.5.1.3

16. [Alan84b] J. Alander, K. Hyytia, J. Hamalainen, A. Jaatinen, O. Karonen, P. Rekola, and M. Tikkanen, Programmer's manual of interval package IP, Report-HTKK-TKO-B59, Laboratory of Information Processing, Helsinki University of Technology, Espoo, Finland, 1984. [surfaces] D.5.5.1.3

17. [Alex78] N. Alexandridis and A. Klinger, Picture decomposition, tree data-structures, and identifying directional symmetries as node combinations, *Computer Graphics, and Image Processing 8*, 1(August 1978), 43–77. [regions]

18. [Alex80] V. V. Alexandrov and N. D. Grosky, Recursive approach to associative storage and search of information in data bases, *Proceedings of the Finnish-Soviet Symposium on Design and Application of Data Base Systems*, Turku, Finland, 1980, 271–284. [regions] D.1.3 A.1.4

19. [Alex79] V. V. Alexandrov, N. D. Grosky, and A. O. Polyakov, Recursive algorithms of data representation and processing, Academy of Sciences of the USSR, Leningrad Research Center, Leningrad, 1979. [regions] D.1.3 A.1.4

20. [Alte88] M. Altenhofen and R. Diehl, Conversion of boundary representations to bintrees, in *Proceedings of the EUROGRAPHICS'88 Conference*, D. Duce, ed., North-Holland, Amsterdam, 1988, 117–127. [volumes]

21. [Aman84] J. Amanatides, Ray tracing with cones, *Computer Graphics 18*, 3(July 1984), 129–135 (also *Proceedings of the SIGGRAPH'84 Conference*, Minneapolis, July 1984). [volumes] A.7.2.2 A.7.3

22. [Ande83] D. P. Anderson, Techniques for reducing pen plotting time, *ACM Transactions on Graphics 2*, 3(July 1983), 197–212. [points] D.2.6.2 A.6.2

23. [Andr85] F. P. Andresen, L. S. Davis, R. D. Eastman, and S. Kambhampati, Visual algorithms for autonomous navigation, *Proceedings of the International Conference on Robotics*, St. Louis, March 1985, 856–861. [regions] A.9.2

24. [Ang88] C. H. Ang, H. Samet, and C. A. Shaffer, Fast region expansion for quadtrees, *Proceedings of the Third International Symposium on Spatial Data Handling*, Sydney, Australia, August 1988, 19–37 (also *IEEE Transactions on Pattern Analysis and Machine Intelligence*). [regions] A.6.6

25. [Ansa85] S. Ansaldi, L. De Floriani, and B. Falcidieno, Geometric modeling of solid objects by using a face adjacency graph representation, *Computer Graphics 19*, 3(July

1985), 131–139 (also *Proceedings of the SIGGRAPH'85 Conference*, San Francisco, July 1985). [volumes] D.5.4

26. [Anto86] R. Antony and P. J. Emmerman, Spatial reasoning and knowledge representation, in *Geographic Information Systems in Government*, vol. 2, B. K. Opitz, ed., A. Deepak Publishing, Hampton, VA, 795–813. [regions]

27. [Appe68] A. A. Appel, Some techniques for shading machine renderings of solids, *Proceedings of the Spring Joint Computer Conference 32*, Atlantic City, NJ, April 1968, 37–45. [ray tracing] A.7.2.1

28. [Arna87] B. Arnaldi, T. Priol, and K. Bouatouch, A new space subdivision method for ray tracing CSG modelled scenes, *Visual Computer 3*, 2(August 1987), 98–108. [volumes] A.7.2.5

29. [Artz81] E. Artzy, G. Frieder, and G. T. Herman, The theory, design, implementation, and evaluation of a surface detection algorithm, *Computer Graphics and Image Processing 15*, 1(January 1981), 1–24. [volumes]

30. [Arvo87] J. Arvo and D. Kirk, Fast ray tracing by ray classification, *Computer Graphics 21*, 4(July 1987), 55–64 (also *Proceedings of the SIGGRAPH'87 Conference*, Anaheim, July 1987). [volumes] D.2.1 A.7.3

31. [Athe83] P. R. Atherton, A scan-line hidden surface removal procedure for constructive solid geometry, *Computer Graphics 17*, 3(July 1983), 73–82 (also *Proceedings of the SIGGRAPH'83 Conference*, Boston, July 1983). [volumes] D.5.5

32. [Atki84] H. H. Atkinson, I. Gargantini, and M. V. S. Ramanath, Determination of the 3d border by repeated elimination of internal surfaces, *Computing 32*, 4(October 1984), 279–295. [volumes]

33. [Atki85a] H. H. Atkinson, I. Gargantini, and M. V. S. Ramanath, Improvements to a recent 3d-border algorithm, *Pattern Recognition 18*, 3/4(1985), 215–226. [volumes]

34. [Atki85b] H. H. Atkinson, I. Gargantini, and T. R. S. Walsh, Counting regions, holes, and their nesting level in time proportional to their border, *Computer Vision, Graphics, and Image Processing 29*, 2(February 1985), 196–215. [regions] D.1.5

35. [Avis83] D. Avis, A survey of heuristics for the weighted matching problem, *Networks 13*, 4(Winter 1983), 475–493. [points] D.2.9

36. [Ayal85] D. Ayala, P. Brunet, R. Juan, and I. Navazo, Object representation by means of nonminimal division quadtrees and octrees, *ACM Transactions on Graphics 4*, 1(January 1985), 41–59. [volumes] D.5.3 A.1.3

37. [Aziz88] N. M. Aziz, A hierarchical model for spatial stacking, in *New Trends in Computer Graphics: Proceedings of CG International '88*, N. Magnenat-Thalmann and D. Thalmann, eds., Springer-Verlag, Tokyo, 1988, 267–274. [volumes]

38. [Ball81] D. H. Ballard, Strip trees: A hierarchical representation for curves, *Communications of the ACM 24*, 5(May 1981), 310–321 (see also corrigendum, *Communications of the ACM 25*, 3(March 1982), 213). [lines] D.4 D.4.1 D.5.7

39. [Barn86] J. Barnes and P. Hut, A hierarchical $O(N\log N)$ force-calculation algorithm, *Nature 324*, 4(December 1986), 446–449. [regions]

40. [Barr87] R. Barrera and A. Hinojosa, Compression methods for terrain relief, CINEVESTAV-IPN, Engineering Projects Section, Department of Electrical Engineering, Polytechnic University of Mexico, Mexico City, 1987. [surfaces] D.5.6

41. [Barr84] R. Barrera and A. M. Vazquez, A hierarchical method for representing terrain relief, *Proceedings of the Pecora 9 Symposium on Spatial Information Technologies for Remote Sensing Today and Tomorrow*, Sioux Falls, SD, October 1984, 87–92. [surfaces] D.5.6

42. [Bart83] J. J. Bartholdi III and L. K. Platzman, A fast heuristic based on spacefilling curves for minimum-weight matching in the plane, *Information Processing Letters 17*, 4(November 1983), 177–180. [points] D.2.9

43. [Baue68] H. Bauer, S. Becker, S. Graham, and E. Satterthwaite, ALGOL W (Revised), Computer Science Department Report No. STAN-CS-68–114, Stanford University, Stanford, CA, October 1968. [general] D.P A.P L

44. [Baue85] M. A. Bauer, Set operations in linear quadtrees, *Computer Vision, Graphics, and Image Processing 29*, 2(February 1985), 248–258. [regions]

45. [Baum72] B. G. Baumgart, Winged-edge polyhedron representation, STAN-CS-320, Computer Science Department, Stanford University, Stanford, CA, 1972. [volumes] D.5.4 A.7.1

46. [Baum74] B. G. Baumgart, Geometric modeling for computer vision, Ph.D. dissertation, STAN-CS-463, Computer Science Department, Stanford University, Stanford, CA, 1974. [volumes] D.5.4

47. [Baum75] B. G. Baumgart, A polyhedron representation for computer vision, *Proceedings of the National Computer Conference 44*, Anaheim, CA, May 1975, 589–596. [volumes] D.5.4

48. [Beau89] J. M. Beaulieu and M. Goldberg, Hierarchy in picture segmentation: a stepwise optimization approach, *IEEE Transactions on Pattern Analysis and Machine Intelligence 11*, 2(February 1989), 150–163. [regions]

49. [Beck85] D. A. Beckley, M. W. Evens, and V. K. Raman, Multikey retrieval from k-d trees and quad-trees, *Proceedings of the SIGMOD Conference*, Austin, TX, May 1985, 291–301. [points]

50. [Beer84] M. Beer, Interactive editing of cartographic raster images, *Photogrammetria 39*, (1984), 263–275. [regions]

51. [Bell83] S. B. M. Bell, B. M. Diaz, F. Holroyd, and M. J. Jackson, Spatially referenced methods of processing raster and vector data, *Image and Vision Computing 1*, 4(November 1983), 211–220. [regions] D.1.4.1 A.1.2

52. [Bent80a] S. W. Bent, D. D. Sleator, and R. E. Tarjan, Biased 2–3 trees, *Proceedings of the Twenty-first Annual Symposium on Foundations of Computer Science*, Syracuse, NY, October 1980, 248–254. [general] D.2.8.2.1 D.4.2.3.1

53. [Bent75a] J. L. Bentley, A survey of techniques for fixed radius near neighbor searching, SLAC Report No. 186, Stanford Linear Accelerator Center, Stanford University, Stanford, CA, August 1975. [points] D.2.1

54. [Bent75b] J. L. Bentley, Multidimensional binary search trees used for associative searching, *Communications of the ACM 18*, 9(September 1975), 509–517. [points] D.1.4.1 D.2.3 D.2.4 D.2.4.1 D.2.4.2 D.2.4.3 D.2.7 A.1.3

55. [Bent77a] J. L. Bentley, Algorithms for Klee's rectangle problems, unpublished, Computer Science Department, Carnegie-Mellon University, Pittsburgh, 1977. [rectangles] D.3.2.1 D.3.3

56. [Bent79a] J. L. Bentley, Decomposable searching problems, *Information Processing Letters 8*, 5(June 1979), 244–251. [points] D.2.3 D.2.5

57. [Bent80b] J. L. Bentley, Multi-dimensional divide-and-conquer, *Communications of the ACM 23*, 4(April 1980), 214–229. [points]

58. [Bent82] J. L. Bentley, *Writing Efficient Programs*, Prentice-Hall, Englewood Cliffs, NJ, 1982. [general] D.1.3 A.1.4

59. [Bent79b] J. L. Bentley and J. H. Friedman, Data structures for range searching, *ACM Computing Surveys 11*, 4(December 1979), 397–409. [points] D.P D.2.1 D.2.2 A.1.3

60. [Bent80c] J. L. Bentley, D. Haken, and R. W. Hon, Statistics on VLSI designs, CMU-CS-80-111, Computer Science Department, Carnegie-Mellon University, Pittsburgh, April 1980. [rectangles] D.3.2.4

61. [Bent79c] J. L. Bentley and H. A. Maurer, A note on Euclidean near neighbor searching in the plane, *Information Processing Letters 8*, 3(March 1979), 133–136. [points]

62. [Bent80d] J. L. Bentley and H. A. Maurer, Efficient worst-case data structures for range searching, *Acta Informatica 13*, 2(1980), 155–168. [rectangles] D.2.3 D.2.5

63. [Bent79d] J. L. Bentley and T. A. Ottmann, Algorithms for reporting and counting geometric intersections, *IEEE Transactions on Computers 28*, 9(September 1979), 643–647. [rectangles] D.3.2 D.3.2.4

64. [Bent81] J. L. Bentley and T. Ottmann, The complexity of manipulating hierarchically defined sets of rectangles, CMU-CS-81-109, Computer Science Department, Carnegie-Mellon University, Pittsburgh, April 1981. [rectangles] D.3.2.4

65. [Bent80e] J. L. Bentley and J. Saxe, Decomposable searching problems I: static to dynamic transformations, *Journal of Algorithms 1*, 4(December 1980), 301–358. [points] D.2.9

66. [Bent75c] J. L. Bentley and D. F. Stanat, Analysis of range searches in quad trees, *Information Processing Letters 3*, 6(July 1975), 170–173. [points] D.2.3.3

67. [Bent77b] J. L. Bentley, D. F. Stanat, and E. H. Williams Jr., The complexity of fixed radius near neighbor searching, *Information Processing Letters 6*, 6(December 1977), 209–212. [points] D.2.2 D.2.3.2 D.2.3.3

68. [Bent80f] J. L. Bentley and D. Wood, An optimal worst-case algorithm for reporting intersections of rectangles, *IEEE Transactions on Computers 29*, 7(July 1980), 571–577. [rectangles] D.3.2.1 D.3.2.4

69. [Bern88] M. Bern, Hidden surface removal for rectangles, *Proceedings of the Fourth Symposium on Computational Geometry*, Urbana-Champaign, IL, June 1988, 183–192. [rectangles]

70. [Bess82] P. W. Besslich, Quadtree construction of binary images by dyadic array transformations, *Proceedings of the IEEE Conference on Pattern Recognition and Image Processing*, Las Vegas, June 1982, 550–554. [regions]

71. [Bhas88] S. K. Bhaskar, A. Rosenfeld, and A. Y. Wu, Parallel processing of regions represented by linear quadtrees, *Computer Vision, Graphics, and Image Processing 42*, 3(June 1988), 371–380. [regions]

72. [Bier87] H. Bieri, Computing the Euler characteristic and related additive functionals of digital objects from their bintree representation, *Computer Vision, Graphics, and Image Processing 40*, 1(October 1987), 115–126. [regions] A.5.3

73. [Bloo87] J. Bloomenthal, Polygonalization of implicit surfaces, Xerox Palo Alto Research Center Technical Report, Palo Alto, CA, May 1987. [surfaces]

74. [Blum67] H. Blum, A transformation for extracting new descriptors of shape, in *Models for the Perception of Speech and Visual Form*, W. Wathen-Dunn, ed., MIT Press, Cambridge, MA, 1967, 362–380. [regions] D.1.2 A.1.3 A.9

75. [Bolo79] A. Bolour, Optimality properties of multiple-key hashing functions, *Journal of the ACM 26*, 2(April 1979), 196–210. [points]

76. [Bonf88] F. Bonfatti and L. Cavazza, SECT: an effective coding technique for polygonal geographic data, *Computers & Graphics 12*, 3/4(1988), 503–513. [regions]

77. [Borg84] G. Borgefors, Distance transformations in arbitrary dimensions, *Computer Vision, Graphics, and Image Processing 27*, 3(September 1984), 321–345. [regions] A.9.1 A.9.2

78. [Bowy81] A. Bowyer, P. J. Willis, and J. R. Woodwark, A multiprocessor architecture for solving spatial problems, *Computer Journal 24*, 4(November 1981), 353–357. [hardware]

79. [Brai80] I. C. Braid, R. C. Hillyard, and I. A. Stroud, Stepwise construction of polyhedra in geometrical modeling, in *Mathematical Models in Computer Graphics and Design*, K. W. Brodlie, ed., Academic Press, New York, 1980, 123–141. [volumes] D.5.4

80. [Bres65] J. E. Bresenham, Algorithm for computer control of a digital plotter, *IBM Systems Journal 4*, 1(1965), 25–30. [lines] A.7.2.3 A.7.2.4

81. [Brig86] S. Bright and S. Laflin, Shading of solid voxel models, *Computer Graphics Forum 5*, 2(June 1986), 131–137. [volumes] A.7.1.4

82. [Brod66] P. Brodatz, *Textures*, Dover, New York, 1966. [general] A.3.2.1.3

83. [Broo74] J. Brooks, R. Muraka, D. Onuoha, F. Rahn, and H. A. Steinberg, An extension of the combinatorial geometry technique for modeling vegetation and terrain features, Mathematical Applications Group Inc., NTIS AD-782–883, June 1974. [volumes] A.7.2.2

84. [Broo83] R. A. Brooks and T. Lozano-Perez, A subdivision algorithm in configuration space for findpath with rotation, *Proceedings of the Eighth International Joint Conference on Artificial Intelligence*, Karlsruhe, West Germany, August 1983, 799–806. [regions] D.1.3 A.1.4

85. [Brow86] R. L. Brown, Multiple storage quad trees: a simpler faster alternative to bisector list quad trees, *IEEE Transactions on Computer-Aided Design 5*, 3(July 1986), 413–419. [rectangles]

86. [Brun87] P. Brunet and D. Ayala, Extended octtree representation of free form surfaces, *Computer-Aided Geometric Design 4*, 1–2(July 1987), 141–154. [surfaces]

87. [Brun89] P. Brunet and I. Navazo, Solid representation and operation using extended octrees, *ACM Transactions on Graphics 8*, 1989. [volumes]

88. [Buch83] W. Bucher and H. Edelsbrunner, On expected and worst-case segment trees, in *Advances in Computing Research*, vol. 1, *Computational Geometry*, F. P. Preparata, ed., JAI Press, Greenwich, CT, 1983, 109–125. [rectangles] D.3.2.1

89. [Burk83] W. A. Burkhard, Interpolation-based index maintenance, *BIT 23*, 3(1983), 274–294. [points] D.2.7 D.2.8.2.1

90. [Burr86] P. A. Burrough, *Principles of Geographical Information Systems for Land Resources Assessment*, Clarendon Press, Oxford, Great Britain, 1986. [general] D.P A.P

91. [Burt80] P. J. Burt, Tree and pyramid structures for coding hexagonally sampled binary images, *Computer Graphics and Image Processing 14*, 3(November 1980), 271–280. [regions] D.1.4.1

92. [Burt81] P. J. Burt, T. H. Hong, and A. Rosenfeld, Segmentation and estimation of image region properties through cooperative hierarchical computation, *IEEE Transactions on Systems, Man, and Cybernetics 11*, 12(December 1981), 802–809. [regions] D.1.3

93. [Burt83] F. W. Burton and J. G. Kollias, Comment on the explicit quadtree as a structure for computer graphics, *Computer Journal 26*, 2(May 1983), 188. [regions] A.2.1.1

94. [Burt84] F. W. Burton, J. G. Kollias, and N. A. Alexandridis, Implementation of the exponential pyramid data structure with application to determination of symmetries in pictures, *Computer Vision, Graphics, and Image Processing 25*, 2(February 1984), 218–225. [regions]

95. [Burt85] F. W. Burton, V. J. Kollias, and J. G. Kollias, Expected and worst-case storage requirements for quadtrees, *Pattern Recognition Letters 3*, 2(March 1985), 131–135. [regions]

96. [Burt86] F. W. Burton, V. J. Kollias, and J. G. Kollias, Real-time raster to quadtree and quadtree to raster conversion algorithms with modest storage requirements, *Angewandte Informatik 28*, 4(April 1986), 169–174. [regions]

97. [Burt87] F. W. Burton, V. J. Kollias, and J. G. Kollias, A general PASCAL program for map overlay of quadtrees and related problems, *Computer Journal 30*, 4(August 1987), 355–361. [regions]

98. [Burt77] W. Burton, Representation of many-sided polygons and polygonal lines for rapid processing, *Communications of the ACM 20*, 3(March 1977), 166–171. [lines] D.4.1

99. [Butz71] A. R. Butz, Alternative algorithm for Hilbert's space-filling curve, *IEEE Transactions on Computers 20*, 4(April 1971), 424–426. [regions] D.1.3 A.1.4

100. [Came84] S. A. Cameron, Modelling solids in motion, Ph.D. dissertation, University of Edinburgh, Edinburgh, Scotland, 1984. [volumes] D.5.5.1.3

101. [Carl87] I. Carlbom, An algorithm for geometric set operations using cellular subdivision techniques, *IEEE Computer Graphics and Applications 7*, 5(May 1987), 44–55. [volumes] D.5.3

102. [Carl85] I. Carlbom, I. Chakravarty, and D. Vanderschel, A hierarchical data structure for representing the spatial decomposition of 3–D objects, *IEEE Computer Graphics and Applications 5*, 4(April 1985), 24–31. [volumes] D.5.3 A.1.3

103. [Carl82] W. E. Carlson, An algorithm and data structure for 3D object synthesis using surface patch intersections, *Computer Graphics 16*, 3(July 1982), 255–264 (also *Proceedings of the SIGGRAPH'82 Conference*, Boston, July 1982). [surfaces] D.5.6 A.7.1.6

104. [Casp88] E. Caspary, Sequential and parallel algorithms for ray tracing complex scenes, Ph.D. dissertation, Electrical and Computer Engineering Department, University of California at Santa Barbara, Santa Barbara, CA, June 1988. [volumes]

105. [Catm75] E. Catmull, Computer display of curved surfaces, *Proceedings of the Conference on Computer Graphics, Pattern Recognition, and Data Structure*, Los Angeles, May 1975, 11–17. [surfaces] A.7.1.6

106. [Chan86] K. C. Chan, I. A. Gargantini, and T. R. Walsh, Double connectivity filling for 3d modeling, Computer Science Report 155, University of Western Ontario, London, Ontario, December 1986. [volumes]

107. [Chan81] J. M. Chang and K. S. Fu, Extended k-d tree database organization: a dynamic multiattribute clustering method, *IEEE Transactions on Software Engineering 7*, 3(May 1981), 284–290. [points]

108. [Chau85] B. B. Chaudhuri, Applications of quadtree, octree, and binary tree decomposition techniques to shape analysis and pattern recognition, *IEEE Transactions on Pattern Analysis and Machine Intelligence 7*, 6(November 1985), 652–661. [regions]

109. [Chaz88] B. Chazelle, A functional approach to data structures and its use in multidimensional searching, *SIAM Journal on Computing 17*, 3(June 1988), 427–462. [rectangles]

110. [Chaz87] B. Chazelle and D. Dobkin, Intersection of convex objects in two and three dimensions, *Journal of the ACM 34*, 1(January 1987), 1–27. [volumes] A.7.3

111. [Chaz86a] B. Chazelle and L. J. Guibas, Fractional cascading: I. A data structuring technique, *Algorithmica 1*, 2(1986), 133–162. [general] D.3.2.2 D.4.3.2

112. [Chaz86b] B. Chazelle and L. J. Guibas, Fractional cascading: II. Applications, *Algorithmica 1*, 2(1986), 163–191. [general] D.3.2.2 D.4.3.2

113. [Chen88a] C. Chen and H. Zou, Linear binary tree, *Proceedings of the Ninth International Conference on Pattern Recognition*, Rome, November 1988, 576–578. [regions]

114. [Chen88b] H. H. Chen and T. S. Huang, A survey of construction and manipulation of octrees, *Computer Vision, Graphics, and Image Processing 43*, 3(September 1988), 409–431. [volumes]

115. [Chen85a] L. S. Chen, G. T. Herman, R. A. Reynolds, and J. K. Udupa, Surface shading in the cuberille environment, *IEEE Computer Graphics and Applications 5*, 12(December 1985), 33–41. [volumes] A.7.1.4

116. [Chen85b] Y. C. Chen, An introduction to hierarchical probe model, Department of Mathematical Sciences, Purdue University Calumet, Hammond, IN, 1985. [regions] D.1.4.2 D.5.8

117. [Chen86] Z. T. Chen and W. R. Tobler, Quadtree representations of digital terrain, *Proceedings of Auto-Carto London*, vol. 1, London, September 1986, 475–484. [surfaces] D.5.6

118. [Ches85] R. Chestek, H. Muller, and D. Chelberg, Knowledge-based terrain analysis, *SPIE 548 Applications of Artificial Intelligence II*, 1985, 46–56. [regions]

119. [Chie84a] C. H. Chien and J. K. Aggarwal, A normalized quadtree representation, *Computer Vision, Graphics, and Image Processing 26*, 3(June 1984), 331–346. [regions] A.5.2

120. [Chie84b] C. H. Chien and J. K. Aggarwal, A volume/surface octree representation, *Proceedings of the Seventh International Conference on Pattern Recognition*, Montreal, August 1984, 817–820. [volumes] D.5.2 A.4.6

121. [Chie85] C. H. Chien and J. K. Aggarwal, Reconstruction and matching of 3–d objects using quadtrees/octrees, *Proceedings of the Third Workshop on Computer Vision: Representation and Control*, Bellaire, MI, October 1985, 49–54. [volumes] D.5.2 A.4.6

122. [Chie86a] C. H. Chien and J. K. Aggarwal, Volume/surface octrees for the representation of three-dimensional objects, *Computer Vision, Graphics, and Image Processing 36*, 1(October 1986), 100–113. [volumes] D.5.2 A.4.6

123. [Chie86b] C. H. Chien and J. K. Aggarwal, Identification of 3–d objects from multiple silhouettes using quadtrees/octrees, *Computer Vision, Graphics, and Image Processing 36*, 2/3(November/December 1986), 256–273. [volumes] D.5.2 A.4.6

124. [Chie86c] C. H. Chien and J. K. Aggarwal, Computation of volume/surface octrees from contours and silhouettes of multiple views, *Proceedings of Computer Vision and Pattern Recognition 86*, Miami Beach, June 1986, 250–255. [volumes] D.5.3 A.7.1.4

125. [Chie87] C. H. Chien and J. K. Aggarwal, Shape recognition from single silhouettes, *Proceedings of the First International Conference on Computer Vision*, London, June 1987, 481–490. [volumes]

126. [Chie88] C. H. Chien, Y. B. Sim, and J. K. Aggarwal, Generation of volume/surface octree from range data, *Proceedings of Computer Vision and Pattern Recognition 88*, Ann Arbor, MI, June 1988, 254–260. [volumes] D.5.2 A.4.6

127. [Chu88a] J. H. Chu, Notes on expected numbers of nodes in a quadtree, Computer Science Department, University of Maryland, College Park, MD, January 1988. [regions] D.1.5 A.1.2

128. [Chu88b] J. H. Chu and G. D. Knott, An analysis of spiral hashing, Computer Science TR-2107, University of Maryland, College Park, MD, September 1988. [points] D.2.8.2.2

129. [Clar76] J. H. Clark, Hierarchical geometric models for visible surface algorithms, *Communications of the ACM 19*, 10(October 1976), 547–554. [surfaces] A.7.2.2

130. [Clay88] R. D. Clay and H. P. Moreton, Efficient adaptive subdivision of Bézier surfaces, in *Proceedings of the EUROGRAPHICS' 88 Conference*, D. A. Duce and P. Jancene, eds., North-Holland, Amsterdam, 1988, 357–371. [surfaces]

131. [Clea88] J. G. Cleary and G. Wyvill, Analysis of an algorithm for fast ray tracing using uniform space subdivision, *Visual Computer 4*, 2(July 1988), 65–83. [volumes] A.7.2.5

132. [Clem83] M. Clemmesen, Interval arithmetic implementations using floating point arithmetic, Institute of Datalogy Report 83/9, University of Copenhagen, Copenhagen, 1983. [general] D.5.5.1.3

133. [Cohe80] E. Cohen, T. Lyche, and R. Riesenfeld, Discrete B-splines and subdivision techniques in computer-aided geometric design and computer graphics, *Computer Graphics and Image Processing 14*, 3(October 1980), 87–111. [surfaces] D.4 D.5.6

134. [Cohe79] J. Cohen and T. Hickey, Two algorithms for detecting volumes of convex polyhedra, *Journal of the ACM 26*, 3(July 1979), 401–414. [volumes] D.5.5

135. [Cohe85a] M. F. Cohen and D. P. Greenberg, The hemi-cube, *Computer Graphics 19*, 3(July 1985), 31–40 (also *Proceedings of the SIGGRAPH'85 Conference*, San Francisco, July 1985). [surfaces] A.7.4

136. [Cohe86] M. F. Cohen, D. P. Greenberg, D. S. Immel, and P. J. Brock, An efficient radiosity approach for realistic image synthesis, *IEEE Computer Graphics and Applications 6*, 3(March 1986), 26–35. [surfaces] A.7.4

137. [Cohe85b] Y. Cohen, M. S. Landy, and M. Pavel, Hierarchical coding of binary images, *IEEE Transactions on Pattern Analysis and Machine Intelligence 7*, 3(May 1985), 284–298. [regions] D.1.4.1 A.1.3 A.2.2 A.8

138. [Cole87] A. J. Cole, Compaction techniques for raster scan graphics using space-filling curves, *Computer Journal 30*, 1(February 1987), 87–96. [regions]

139. [Cole82] A. J. Cole and R. Morrison, Triplex: A system for interval arithmetic, *Software Practice and Experience 12*, 4(April 1982), 341–350. [general] D.5.5.1.3

140. [Come79] D. Comer, The ubiquitous B-tree, *ACM Computing Surveys 11*, 2(June 1979), 121–137. [general] D.2.7 D.3.5.3 D.4.2.3.6 A.2.1 A.2.1.1 A.2.1.4 A.4.2.3

141. [Conn84] C. I. Connolly, Cumulative generation of octree models from range data, *Proceedings of the International Conference on Robotics*, Atlanta, March 1984, 25–32. [volumes] D.5.2 A.4.6

142. [Conn85] C. I. Connolly, The determination of next best views, *Proceedings of the International Conference on Robotics*, St. Louis, March 1985, 432–435. [volumes] D.5.2 A.4.6

143. [Cook78] B. G. Cook, The structural and algorithmic basis of a geographic data base, in *Proceedings of the First International Advanced Study Symposium on Topological Data Structures for Geographic Information Systems*, G. Dutton, ed., Harvard Papers on Geographic Information Systems, 1978. [regions] A.2.1.1

144. [Cook84] R. L. Cook, T. Porter, and L. Carpenter, Distributed ray tracing, *Computer Graphics 18*, 3(July 1984), 137–145 (also *Proceedings of the SIGGRAPH'84 Conference*, Minneapolis, July 1984). [ray tracing] A.7.2.1 A.7.2.5

145. [Cook82] R. L. Cook and K. E. Torrance, A reflectance model for computer graphics, *ACM Transactions on Graphics 1*, 1(January 1982), 7–24. [general] A.7.2.1

146. [Cott85] M. S. Cottingham, A compressed data structure for surface representation, *Computer Graphics Forum 4*, 3(September 1985), 217–228. [surfaces]

147. [Coxe86] H. S. M. Coxeter, M. Emmer, R. Penrose, and M. L. Teuber (eds.), *M. C. Escher, art and science: Proceedings of the International Congress on M. C. Escher*, Elsevier North-Holland, New York, 1986. [general] D.1.2 A.1.2

148. [Creu81] E. Creutzburg, Complexities of quadtrees and the structure of pictures, Friedrich-Schiller University Technical Report N/81/74, Jena, East Germany, 1981. [regions]

149. [Crow77] F. C. Crow, Shadow algorithms for computer graphics, *Computer Graphics 11*, 2(Summer 1977), 242–248 (also *Proceedings of the SIGGRAPH'77 Conference*, San Jose, CA, July 1977). [general] A.7.1.4

150. [Cutl86] M. W. Cutlip, Verification of numerically controlled machine tool programs for 2.5–d parts using Z-tree solid modeling techniques, M.Sc. dissertation, School of Engineering and Applied Science, George Washington University, Washington, DC, 1986. [surfaces]

151. [Cyru78] M. Cyrus and J. Beck, Generalized two- and three-dimensional clipping, *Computers & Graphics 3*, 1(1978), 23–28. [general] A.7.2.3

152. [Dado82] N. Dadoun, D. G. Kirkpatrick, and J. P. Walsh, Hierarchical approaches to hidden surface intersection testing, *Proceedings of Graphics Interface '82*, Toronto, May 1982, 49–56. [volumes] A.7.2.2 A.7.3

153. [Dado85] N. Dadoun, D. G. Kirkpatrick, and J. P. Walsh, The geometry of beam tracing, *Proceedings of the Symposium on Computational Geometry*, Baltimore, June 1985, 55–61. [volumes] A.7.2.2 A.7.3

154. [Dand84] S. P. Dandamudi and P. G. Sorenson, Performance of a modified k-tree, Department of Computational Science Report 84–10, University of Saskatchewan, Saskatoon, Canada, 1984. [points]

155. [Dand85] S. P. Dandamudi and P. G. Sorenson, An empirical performance comparison of some variations of the k-d tree and BD tree, *International Journal of Computer and Information Sciences 14*, 3(June 1985), 135–159. [points] D.2.6.2

156. [Dand86] S. P. Dandamudi and P. G. Sorenson, Algorithms for BD trees, *Software— Practice and Experience 16*, 12(December 1986), 1077–1096. [points] D.2.6.2 D.2.8.1

157. [Davi84] E. Davis, Representing and acquiring geographic knowledge, Ph.D. dissertation, Department of Computer Science, Yale University, New Haven, CT, 1984. [artificial intelligence]

158. [Davi80] L. S. Davis and N. Roussopoulos, Approximate pattern matching in a pattern database system, *Information Systems 5*, 2(1980), 107–119. [regions] D.1.3 A.1.4

159. [Davi86] W. A. Davis, Hybrid use of hashing techniques for spatial data, *Proceedings of Auto-Carto London*, vol. 1, London, September 1986, 127–135. [regions]

160. [Davi85] W. A. Davis and X. Wang, A new approach to linear quadtrees, *Proceedings of Graphics Interface '85*, Montreal, May 1985, 195–202. [regions]

161. [DeCo76] F. De Coulon and O. Johnsen, Adaptive block schemes for source coding of black-and-white facsimile, *Electronics Letters 12*, 3(February 5, 1976), 61–62 (also erratum, *Electronics Letters 12*, 6(March 18, 1976), 152). [regions] D.2.6.1 A.2.2

162. [DeFl87] L. De Floriani, Surface representations based on triangular grids, *Visual Computer 3*, 1(February 1987), 27–50. [surfaces] D.5.6

163. [DeFl84] L. De Floriani, B. Falcidieno, G. Nagy, and C. Pienovi, A hierarchical structure for surface approximation, *Computers & Graphics 8*, 2(1984), 183–193. [surfaces] D.5.6

164. [DeFl85] L. De Floriani, B. Falcidieno, G. Nagy, and C. Pienovi, Efficient selection, storage and retrieval of irregularly distributed elevation data, *Computers and Geosciences 11*, 6(1985), 667–673. [surfaces] D.5.6

165. [Dela34] B. Delaunay, Sur la sphere vide, *Izvestiya Akademii Nauk SSSR, VII Seria, Otdelenie Matematicheskii i Estestvennyka Nauk 7*, 6(October 1934), 793–800. [surfaces] D.5.6

166. [DeMi78] R. A. DeMillo, S. C. Eisenstat, and R. J. Lipton, Preserving average proximity in arrays, *Communications of the ACM 21*, 3(March 1978), 228–231. [general] A.3.2.1.2 A.4.2.2

167. [Dew85] P. M. Dew, J. Dodsworth, and D. T. Morris, Systolic array architectures for high performance CAD/CAM workstations, in *Fundamental Algorithms for Computer Graphics*, R. A. Earnshaw, ed., Springer-Verlag, Berlin, 1985, 659–694. [hardware]

168. [Dill87] M. B. Dillencourt and D. Mount, personal communication, 1987. [regions] D.1.2 A.1.3

169. [Dill88] M. B. Dillencourt and H. Samet, Extracting region boundaries from maps stored as linear quadtrees, *Proceedings of the Third International Symposium on Spatial Data Handling*, Sydney, Australia, August 1988, 65–77. [regions] A.4.3.2

170. [Dins85] I. Dinstein, D. W. L. Yen, and M. D. Flickner, Handling memory overflow in connected component labeling applications, *IEEE Transactions on Pattern Analysis and Machine Intelligence 7*, 1(January 1985), 116–121. [regions] A.5.1.1

171. [Dipp84] M. Dippe and J. Swensen, An adaptive subdivision algorithm and parallel architecture for realistic image synthesis, *Computer Graphics 18*, 3(July 1984), 149–158 (also *Proceedings of the SIGGRAPH'84 Conference*, Minneapolis, July 1984) [hardware] A.7.2.5

172. [Dobk83] D. P. Dobkin and D. G. Kirkpatrick, Fast detection of polyhedral intersections, *Theoretical Computer Science 27*, 3(December 1983), 241–253. [volumes] A.7.3

173. [Dobk74] D. Dobkin and R. J. Lipton, Some generalizations of binary search, *Proceedings of the Sixth Annual ACM Symposium on the Theory of Computing*, Seattle, April 1974, 310–316. [points]

174. [Dobk76] D. Dobkin and R. J. Lipton, Multidimensional searching problems, *SIAM Journal on Computing 5*, 2(June 1976), 181–186. [points]

175. [Doct81] L. J. Doctor and J. G. Torborg, Display techniques for octree-encoded objects, *IEEE Computer Graphics and Applications 1*, 1(July 1981), 29–38. [volumes] A.2.1.2 A.7.1.4

176. [Dors84a] L. Dorst and R. P. W. Duin, Spirograph theory: a framework for calculations on digitized straight lines, *IEEE Transactions on Pattern Analysis and Machine Intelligence 6*, 5(September 1984), 632–639. [lines]

177. [Dors84b] L. Dorst and A. W. M. Smeulders, Discrete representation of straight lines, *IEEE Transactions on Pattern Analysis and Machine Intelligence 6*, 4(July 1984), 450–463. [lines]

178. [Dris89] J. R. Driscoll, N. Sarnak, D. D. Sleator, and R. E. Tarjan, Making data structures persistent, *Journal of Computer and System Sciences 38*, 1(February 1989), 86–124. [general] D.3.2.4

179. [Dubi81] T. Dubitzki, A. Wu, and A. Rosenfeld, Parallel region property computation by active quadtree networks, *IEEE Transactions on Pattern Analysis and Machine Intelligence 3*, 6(November 1981), 626–633. [regions]

180. [Duda73] R. O. Duda and P. E. Hart, *Pattern Classification and Scene Analysis*, Wiley Interscience, New York, 1973. [general]

181. [Duff85] T. Duff, Compositing 3–d rendered images, *Computer Graphics 19*, 3(July 1985), 41–44 (also *Proceedings of the SIGGRAPH'85 Conference*, San Francisco, July 1985). [general] A.7.1.6

182. [Dürs88] M. J. Dürst and T. L. Kunii, Integrated polytrees: a generalized model for integrating spatial decomposition and boundary representation, Department of Information Science Technical Report 88–002, University of Tokyo, Tokyo, January 1988. [volumes]

183. [Dutt84] G. Dutton, Geodesic modelling of planetary relief, *Cartographica 21*, 2&3(Summer & Autumn 1984), 188–207. [surfaces] D.1.4.1 D.5.6

184. [Dyer80a] C. R. Dyer, Computing the Euler number of an image from its quadtree, *Computer Graphics and Image Processing 13*, 3(July 1980), 270–276. [regions] A.5.3

185. [Dyer81] C. R. Dyer, A VLSI pyramid machine for hierarchical parallel image processing, *Proceedings of the IEEE Conference on Pattern Recognition and Image Processing*, Dallas, August 1981, 381–386. [hardware]

186. [Dyer82] C. R. Dyer, The space efficiency of quadtrees, *Computer Graphics and Image Processing 19*, 4(August 1982), 335–348. [regions] D.1.5 A.1.2 A.6.5.3 A.6.6 A.8.2.2 A.9.3.4

187. [Dyer80b] C. R. Dyer, A. Rosenfeld, and H. Samet, Region representation: boundary codes from quadtrees, *Communications of the ACM 23*, 3(March 1980), 171–179. [regions] A.4.3.2

188. [East70] C. M. Eastman, Representations for space planning, *Communications of the ACM 13*, 4(April 1970), 242–250. [regions] D.1.3 A.1.4

189. [East81] C. M. Eastman, Optimal bucket size for nearest neighbor searching in k-d trees, *Information Processing Letters 12*, 4(August 1981), 165–167. [points]

190. [East79] C. M. Eastman and K. Weiler, Geometric modeling using Euler operators, *Proceedings of the First Conference on Computer Graphics in CAD/CAM Systems*, Cambridge, MA, May 1979, 248–259. [volumes] D.5.4

191. [East82] C. M. Eastman and M. Zemankova, Partially specified nearest neighbor searches using k-d trees, *Information Processing Letters 15*, 2(September 1982), 53–56. [points]

192. [Edah84] M. Edahiro, I. Kokubo, and T. Asano, A new point-location algorithm and its practical efficiency — comparison with existing algorithms, *ACM Transactions on Graphics 3*, 2(April 1984), 86–109. [points]

193. [Edel85a] S. Edelman and E. Shapiro, Quadtrees in concurrent Prolog, *Proceedings of the IEEE International Conference on Parallel Processing*, St. Charles, IL, August 1985, 544–551. [regions]

194. [Edel80a] H. Edelsbrunner, Dynamic rectangle intersection searching, Institute for Information Processing Report 47, Technical University of Graz, Graz, Austria, February 1980. [rectangles] D.3.2.2 D.4.3.2

195. [Edel80b] H. Edelsbrunner, Dynamic data structures for orthogonal intersection queries, Institute for Information Processing Report 59, Technical University of Graz, Graz, Austria, October 1980. [rectangles]

196. [Edel81a] H. Edelsbrunner, A note on dynamic range searching, *Bulletin of the EATCS*, 15(October 1981), 34–40. [rectangles] D.2.5

197. [Edel82] H. Edelsbrunner, Intersection problems in computational geometry, Institute for Information Processing Report 93, Technical University of Graz, Graz, Austria, June 1982. [rectangles] D.3.2.4

198. [Edel83a] H. Edelsbrunner, A new approach to rectangle intersections: Part I, *International Journal of Computer Mathematics 13*, 3–4(1983), 209–219. [rectangles] D.3.2.2 D.4.3.2

199. [Edel83b] H. Edelsbrunner, A new approach to rectangle intersections: Part II, *International Journal of Computer Mathematics 13*, 3–4(1983), 221–229. [rectangles] D.3.2.2 D.4.3.2

200. [Edel84] H. Edelsbrunner, Key-problems and key-methods in computational geometry, *Proceedings of the Symposium of Theoretical Aspects of Computer Science*, Paris, 1984, 1–13 (Lecture Notes in Computer Science 166, Springer-Verlag, New York, 1984). [general] D.P D.4 D.4.2.3.6 D.4.3

201. [Edel87] H. Edelsbrunner, *Algorithms in Combinatorial Geometry*, EATCS Monographs on Theoretical Computer Science, Springer-Verlag, Berlin, 1987. [general] D.P D.4.3

202. [Edel88] H. Edelsbrunner (ed.), A bibliography in computational geometry, Department of Computer Science, University of Illinois at Urbana-Champaign, Urbana, IL, 1988. [general] D.P

203. [Edel86a] H. Edelsbrunner, L. J. Guibas, and J. Stolfi, Optimal point location in a monotone subdivision, *SIAM Journal on Computing 15*, 2(May 1986), 317–340. [regions] D.P D.3.2.2 D.4.3 D.4.3.2

204. [Edel81b] H. Edelsbrunner and H. A. Maurer, On the intersection of orthogonal objects, *Information Processing Letters 13*, 4,5(End 1981), 177–181. [rectangles] D.3.2.4

205. [Edel86b] H. Edelsbrunner, J. O'Rourke, and R. Seidel, Constructing arrangements of lines and hyperplanes with applications, *SIAM Journal on Computing 15*, 2(May 1986), 341–363. [rectangles] D.3.3

206. [Edel85b] H. Edelsbrunner and M. H. Overmars, Batched dynamic solutions to decomposable searching problems, *Journal of Algorithms 6*, 4(December 1985), 515–542. [rectangles] D.3.2 D.3.3

207. [Edel83c] H. Edelsbrunner and J. van Leeuwen, Multidimensional data structures and algorithms: a bibliography, Institute for Information Processing Report F104, Technical University of Graz, Graz, Austria, January 1983. [general] D.P

208. [Egen88] M. J. Egenhofer and A. U. Frank, Towards a spatial query language: user interface considerations, *Proceedings of the Fourteenth International Conference on Very Large Data Bases*, F. Bachillon and D. J. DeWitt, eds., Los Angeles, August 1988, 124–133. [general]

209. [Elbe88] G. Elber and M. Shpitalni, Octree creation via C. S. G. definition, *Visual Computer 4*, 2(July 1988), 53–64. [volumes]

210. [Elco87] E. W. Elcock, I. Gargantini, and T. R. Walsh, Triangular decomposition, *Image and Vision Computing 5*, 3(August 1987), 225–231. [regions]

211. [Elme87] G. A. Elmes, Data Structures for quadtree-addressed entities on a spatial relational database, *Proceedings of the International Symposium on Geographic Information Systems*, vol. 2, Arlington, VA, November 1987, 177–179. [regions]

212. [Enbo88] R. J. Enbody and H. C. Du, Dynamic hashing schemes, *ACM Computing Surveys 20*, 2(June 1988), 85–113. [points]

213. [Este83] D. M. Esterling and J. Van Rosedale, An intersection algorithm for moving parts, *Proceedings of the NASA Symposium on Computer-Aided Geometry Modeling*, Hampton, VA, April 1983, 119–123. [surfaces]

214. [Fabb86] F. Fabbrini and C. Montani, Autumnal quadtrees, *Computer Journal 29*, 5(October 1986), 472–474. [regions]

215. [Fadd59] V. N. Faddeeva, *Computational Methods of Linear Algebra*, Dover, New York, 1959. [general] D.2.6.1

216. [Fagi79] R. Fagin, J. Nievergelt, N. Pippenger, and H. R. Strong, Extendible hashing — a fast access method for dynamic files, *ACM Transactions on Database Systems 4*, 3(September 1979), 315–344. [points] D.2.7 D.2.8.1 D.2.8.2.1 D.2.8.2.3 D.2.8.2.4

217. [Falo86] C. Faloutsos, Multiattribute hashing using Gray codes, *Proceedings of the SIGMOD Conference*, Washington, DC, May 1986, 227–238. [points] D.2.7

218. [Falo88] C. Faloutsos, Gray codes for partial match and range queries, *IEEE Transactions on Software Engineering 14*, 10(October 1988), 1381–1393. [points] D.2.7

219. [Falo87] C. Faloutsos, T. Sellis, and N. Roussopoulos, Analysis of object oriented spatial access methods, *Proceedings of the SIGMOD Conference*, San Francisco, May 1987, 426–439. [rectangles] D.3.5.3

220. [Fan88] N. P. Fan and C. C. Li, Computing quadtree medial axis transform by a multi-layered pyramid of LISP-processor arrays, *Proceedings of Computer Vision and Pattern Recognition 88*, Ann Arbor, MI, June 1988, 628–634. [hardware]

221. [Faug84] O. D. Faugeras, M. Hebert, P. Mussi, and J. D. Boissonnat, Polyhedral approximation of 3–d objects without holes, *Computer Vision, Graphics, and Image Processing 25*, 2(February 1984), 169–183. [surfaces] D.4.1 D.5.2 D.5.6 D.5.7 A.4.6

222. [Faug83] O. D. Faugeras and J. Ponce, Prism trees: a hierarchical representation for 3–d objects, *Proceedings of the Eighth International Joint Conference on Artificial Intelligence*, Karlsruhe, West Germany, August 1983, 982–988. [surfaces] D.4.1 D.5.6

223. [Fave84] B. Faverjon, Obstacle avoidance using an octree in the configuration space of a manipulator, *Proceedings of the International Conference on Robotics*, Atlanta, March 1984, 504–512. [volumes] D.1.3 A.1.4

224. [Fave86] B. Faverjon, Object level programming of industrial robots, *Proceedings of the IEEE International Conference on Robotics and Automation*, San Francisco, April 1986, 1406–1412. [volumes]

225. [Feke84] G. Fekete and L. S. Davis, property spheres: A new representation for 3–d object recognition, *Proceedings of the Workshop on Computer Vision: Representation and Control*, Annapolis, MD, April 1984, 192–201 (also University of Maryland Computer Science TR-1355). [surfaces] D.1.4.1 D.5.6

226. [Feyn63] R. P. Feynman, R. B. Leighton, and M. Sands, *The Feynman Lectures on Physics*, Addison-Wesley, Reading, MA, 1963. [general] A.7.1.4

227. [Fink74] R. A. Finkel and J. L. Bentley, Quad trees: a data structure for retrieval on composite keys, *Acta Informatica 4*, 1(1974), 1–9. [points] D.1.2 D.1.3 D.1.4.1 D.2.1 D.2.3 D.2.3.1 D.2.3.2 D.2.3.3 A.1.3 A.1.4

228. [Flaj83] P. Flajolet and C. Puech, Tree structures for partial match retrieval, *Proceedings of the Twenty-fourth Annual IEEE Symposium on the Foundations of Computer Science*, Tucson, November 1983, 282–288. [points] D.2.6.3 D.2.8.1

229. [Folc82] J. D. Foley and A. van Dam, *Fundamentals of Interactive Computer Graphics*, Addison-Wesley, Reading, MA, 1982. [general] D.5.2 A.4.6

230. [Fong84] A. C. Fong, A scheme for reusing label locations in real time component labeling of images, *Proceedings of the Seventh International Conference on Pattern Recognition*, Montreal, August 1984, 243–245. [regions] A.5.1.1

231. [Forr85] A. R. Forrest, Computational geometry in practice, in *Fundamental Algorithms for Computer Graphics*, R. A. Earnshaw, ed., Springer-Verlag, Berlin, 1985, 707–724. [general]

232. [Fran81] A. Frank, Applications of dbms to land information systems, *Proceedings of the Seventh International Conference on Very Large Data Bases*, C. Zaniolo and C. Delobel, eds., Cannes, France, September 1981, 448–453. [general]

233. [Fran83] A. Frank, Problems of realizing LIS: storage methods for space related data: the field tree, Technical Report 71, Institut für Geodasie und Photogrammetrie, ETH, Zurich, Switzerland, June 1983. [rectangles]

234. [Fran84] W. R. Franklin, Adaptive grids for geometric operations, *Cartographica 21*, 2&3(Summer & Autumn 1984), 160–167. [regions] D.2.2 A.1.3

235. [Fran85] W. R. Franklin and V. Akman, Building an octree from a set of parallelepipeds, *IEEE Computer Graphics and Applications 5*, 10(October 1985), 58–64. [volumes] D.5.2 A.4.6

236. [Fran88] W. R. Franklin and V. Akman, An adaptive grid for polyhedral visibility in object space: an implementation, *Computer Journal 31*, 1(February 1988), 56–60. [regions] D.2.2 A.1.3

237. [Fred60] E. Fredkin, Trie memory, *Communications of the ACM 3*, 9(September 1960), 490–499. [general] D.1.2 D.2.1 D.2.6 A.1.3

238. [Fred78] M. L. Fredman and B. Weide, The complexity of computing the measure of $\cup [a_i, b_i]$, *Communications of the ACM 21*, 7(July 1978), 540–544. [general] D.3.3

239. [Free74] H. Freeman, Computer processing of line-drawing images, *ACM Computing Surveys 6*, 1(March 1974), 57–97. [lines] D.P D.4 D.4.4 A.4.3

240. [Free75] H. Freeman and R. Shapira, Determining the minimum area encasing rectangles for an arbitrary closed curve, *Communications of the ACM 18*, 7(July 1975), 409–413. [regions] D.4.1

241. [Free87] M. Freeston, The BANG file: a new kind of grid file, *Proceedings of the SIG-MOD Conference*, San Francisco, May 1987, 260–269. [points] D.2.6.2

242. [Frie75] J. H. Friedman, F. Baskett, and L. J. Shustek, An algorithm for finding nearest neighbors, *IEEE Transactions on Computers 24*, 10(October 1975), 1000–1006. [points] D.2.2

243. [Frie77] J. H. Friedman, J. L. Bentley, and R. A. Finkel, An algorithm for finding best matches in logarithmic expected time, *ACM Transactions on Mathematical Software 3*, 3(September 1977), 209–226. [points] D.1.4.2 D.2.4.1

244. [Fuch83] H. Fuchs, G. D. Abram, and E. D. Grant, Near real-time shaded display of rigid objects, *Computer Graphics 17*, 3(July 1983), 65–72 (also *Proceedings of the SIG-GRAPH'83 Conference*, Boston, July 1983). [volumes] D.1.4.1 A.1.3 A.7.1.5

245. [Fuch80] H. Fuchs, Z. M. Kedem, and B. F. Naylor, On visible surface generation by a priori tree structures, *Computer Graphics 14*, 3(July 1980), 124–133 (also *Proceedings of the SIGGRAPH'80 Conference*, Seattle, July 1980). [volumes] D.1.4.1 D.2.4 D.3.5.3 A.1.3 A.7.1 A.7.1.5 A.7.3

246. [Fuhr88] D. R. Fuhrmann, Quadtree traversal algorithms for pointer-based and depth-first representations, *IEEE Transactions on Pattern Analysis and Machine Intelligence 10*, 6(November 1988), 955–960. [regions]

247. [Fuji85a] A. Fujimoto and K. Iwata, Accelerated ray tracing, *Proceedings of Computer Graphics'85*, Tokyo, 1985, T1–2, 1–26. [volumes]

248. [Fuji86] A. Fujimoto, T. Tanaka, and K. Iwata, ARTS: accelerated ray-tracing system, *IEEE Computer Graphics and Applications 6*, 4(April 1986), 16–26. [volumes] D.5.3 A.7.2.2 A.7.2.3 A.7.2.4

249. [Fuji85b] K. Fujimura and T. L. Kunii, A hierarchical space indexing method, *Proceedings of Computer Graphics'85*, Tokyo, 1985, T1–4, 1–14. [volumes] D.5.3 A.1.3

250. [Fuji89] K. Fujimura and H. Samet, A hierarchical strategy for path planning among moving obstacles, *IEEE Transactions on Robotics and Automation 5*, 1(February 1989), 61–69. [volumes] D.1.3 D.5.3 A.1.4 A.6.6 A.7.2.4

251. [Fuji83a] K. Fujimura, H. Toriya, K. Yamaguchi, and T. L. Kunii, An enhanced oct-tree data structure and operations for solid modeling, *Proceedings of the NASA Symposium on Computer-Aided Geometry Modeling*, Hampton, VA, April 1983, 269–277. [volumes]

252. [Fuji83b] K. Fujimura, H. Toriya, K. Yamaguchi, and T. L. Kunii, Oct-tree algorithms for solid modeling, *Computer Graphics: Theory and Applications*, T. L. Kunii, ed., Springer-Verlag, Tokyo, 1983, 96–110. [volumes] A.6.5.3

253. [Gao87] P. Gao and T. Smith, Space efficient hierarchical structures: relatively addressed compact quadtrees for GIS, *Proceedings of the International Symposium on Geographic Information Systems*, vol. 2, Arlington, VA, November 1987, 405–414. [regions]

254. [Garc87] G. Garcia and J. F. Le Corre, Geometrical transformations on binary images represented by quadtrees, *Proceedings of MARI' 87 (Intelligent Networks and Machines)*, Paris, May 1987, 203–210. [regions]

255. [Gare79] M. R. Garey and D. S. Johnson, *Computers and Intractability, A Guide to the Theory of NP-Completeness*, W. H. Freeman and Co., San Francisco, 1979. [general] D.1.2 D.1.3 A.1.3 A.1.4

256. [Garg82a] I. Gargantini, An effective way to represent quadtrees, *Communications of the ACM 25*, 12(December 1982), 905–910. [regions] D.1.5 D.2.6.2 A.2.1.1 A.3.4.2

257. [Garg82b] I. Gargantini, Linear octtrees for fast processing of three dimensional objects, *Computer Graphics and Image Processing 20*, 4(December 1982), 365–374. [volumes] A.2.1.1 A.3.3

258. [Garg82c] I. Gargantini, Detection of connectivity for regions represented by linear quadtrees, *Computers and Mathematics with Applications 8*, 4(1982), 319–327. [regions] D.1.5 A.2.1.1 A.5.1.3

259. [Garg83] I. Gargantini, Translation, rotation, and superposition of linear quadtrees, *International Journal of Man-Machine Studies 18*, 3(March 1983), 253–263. [regions] A.2.1.3 A.6.3 A.6.5.3

260. [Garg86a] I. Gargantini, M. V. S. Ramanath, and T. R. S. Walsh, Linear octtrees: from data acquisition or creation to display, *Proceedings of Computer Graphics '86*, vol. 3, Anaheim, CA, May 1986, 615–621. [volumes]

261. [Garg82d] I. Gargantini and Z. Tabakman, Linear quad- and oct-trees: their use in generating simple algorithms for image processing, *Proceedings of Graphics Interface '82*, Toronto, May 1982, 123–127. [regions]

262. [Garg86b] I. Gargantini, T. R. Walsh, and O. L. Wu, Viewing transformations of voxel-based objects via linear octrees, *IEEE Computer Graphics and Applications 6*, 10(October 1986), 24–31. [volumes]

263. [Gast84] P. C. Gaston and T. Lozano Perez, Tactile recognition and localization using object models: the case of polyhedra on a plane, *IEEE Transactions on Pattern Analysis and Machine Intelligence 6*, 3(May 1984), 257–266. [volumes] D.4.1

264. [Gaut85] N. K. Gautier, S. S. Iyengar, N. B. Lakhani, and M. Manohar, Space and time efficiency of the forest-of-quadtrees representation, *Image and Vision Computing 3*, 2(May 1985), 63–70. [regions]

265. [Gerv86] M. Gervautz, Three improvements of the ray tracing algorithm for CSG trees, *Computers and Graphics 10*, 4(1986), 333–339. [volumes]

266. [Gibs82] L. Gibson and D. Lucas, Vectorization of raster images using hierarchical methods, *Computer Graphics and Image Processing 20*, 1(September 1982), 82–89. [regions] D.1.4.1

267. [Gill81] R. Gillespie and W. A. Davis, Tree data structures for graphics and image processing, *Proceedings of the Seventh Conference of the Canadian Man-Computer Communications Society*, Waterloo, Canada, June 1981, 155–161. [regions] D.5.3 A.7.1.4

268. [Glas84] A. S. Glassner, Space subdivision for fast ray tracing, *IEEE Computer Graphics and Applications 4*, 10(October 1984), 15–22. [volumes] A.7.2.2 A.7.2.3 A.7.2.5

269. [Glas88] A. S. Glassner, Spacetime ray tracing for animation, *IEEE Computer Graphics and Applications 8*, 2(March 1988), 60–70. [volumes] D.5.3

270. [Gold81] L. M. Goldschlager, Short algorithms for space-filling curves, *Software—Practice and Experience 11*, 1(January 1981), 99. [regions] D.1.3 D.2.7 A.1.4

271. [Gold71] R. A. Goldstein and R. Nagel, 3–D visual simulation, *Simulation 16*, 1(January 1971), 25–31. [volumes] A.7.2.5

272. [Gome79] D. Gomez and A. Guzman, Digital model for three-dimensional surface representation, *Geo-Processing 1*, 1979, 53–70. [surfaces] D.5.6

273. [Good83] M. F. Goodchild and A. W. Grandfield, Optimizing raster storage: an examination of four alternatives, *Proceedings of Auto-Carto 6*, vol. 1, Ottawa, October 1983, 400–407. [regions] D.1.3 D.2.7 A.1.4

274. [Gora84] C. M. Goral, K. E. Torrance, D. P. Greenberg, and B. Battaile, Modeling the interaction of light between diffuse surfaces, *Computer Graphics 18*, 3(July 1984), 213–222 (also *Proceedings of the SIGGRAPH'84 Conference*, Minneapolis, July 1984). [surfaces] A.7.2.1 A.7.4

275. [Gord85] D. Gordon and R. A. Reynolds, Image space shading of three-dimensional objects, *Computer Vision, Graphics, and Image Processing 29*, 3(March 1985), 361–376. [volumes] A.7.1.4

276. [Gors88] N. D. Gorsky, On the complexity of the quadtree and 2d-tree representations for binary pictures, *Proceedings of the COST-13 Workshop on From the Pixels to the Features*, Bonas, France, August 1988. [regions]

277. [Gour71] H. Gouraud, Continuous shading of curved surfaces, *IEEE Transactions on Computers 20*, 6(June 1971), 623–629. [general] A.7.1.4

278. [Gouz84] L. Gouzènes, Strategies for solving collision-free trajectories problems for mobile and manipulator robots, *The International Journal of Robotics Research 3*, 4(Winter 1984), 51–65. [volumes]

279. [Gowd83] I. G. Gowda, D. G. Kirkpatrick, D. T. Lee, A. Naamad, Dynamic Voronoi diagrams, *IEEE Transactions on Information Theory 29*, 5(September 1983), 724–731. [regions]

280. [Gree89] D. Greene, An implementation and performance analysis of spatial data access methods, *Proceedings of the Fifth IEEE International Conference on Data Engineering*, Los Angeles, February 1989, 606–615. [regions]

281. [Gros83] W. I. Grosky and R. Jain, Optimal quadtrees for image segments, *IEEE Transactions on Pattern Analysis and Machine Intelligence 5*, 1(January 1983), 77–83. [regions] D.1.5 A.1.2 A.4.3.1

282. [Gros81] W. I. Grosky, M. Li, and R. Jain, A bottom-up approach to constructing quadtrees from binary arrays, Computer Science Report CSC-81–011, Wayne State University, Detroit, MI, 1981. [regions] A.4.1

283. [Gros89] W. I. Grosky and R. Mehrotra, A pictorial index mechanism for model-based matching, *Proceedings of the Fifth IEEE International Conference on Data Engineering*, Los Angeles, February 1989, 180–187. [general]

284. [Grün77] B. Grünbaum and G. C. Shephard, The eighty-one types of isohedral tilings in the plane, *Mathematical Proceedings of the Cambridge Philosophical Society 82*, 2(September 1977), 177–196. [regions] D.1.4.1

285. [Grün87] B. Grünbaum and G. C. Shephard, *Tilings and Patterns*, W. H. Freeman and Co., New York, 1987. [regions] D.1.4.1

286. [Guib78] L. J. Guibas and R. Sedgewick, A dichromatic framework for balanced trees, *Proceedings of the Nineteenth Annual IEEE Symposium on the Foundations of Computer Science*, Ann Arbor, MI, October 1978, 8–21. [general] D.3.2.3

287. [Günt87] O. Günther, Efficient structures for geometric data management, Ph.D. dissertation, UCB/ERL M87/77, Electronics Research Laboratory, College of Engineering, University of California at Berkeley, Berkeley, CA, 1987 (Lecture Notes in Computer Science 337, Springer-Verlag, Berlin, 1988). [regions] D.3.5.3 D.4.1

288. [Günt89] O. Günther, The design of the cell tree: an object-oriented index structure for geometric databases, *Proceedings of the Fifth IEEE International Conference on Data Engineering*, Los Angeles, February 1989, 598–605. [regions]

289. [Günt88] O. Günther and J. Bilmes, The implementation of the cell tree: design alternatives and performance evaluation, Department of Computer Science TRCS88–23, University of California at Santa Barbara, Santa Barbara, CA, October 1988. [regions] D.3.5.3

290. [Güti80] H. Güting and H. P. Kriegel, Multidimensional B-tree: an efficient dynamic file structure for exact match queries, *Proceedings of the Tenth Gesellschaft für Informatik Conference*, R. Wilhelm, ed., Saarbrücken, West Germany, September 1980, 375–388. [points] D.2.8.2.3

291. [Güti81] H. Güting and H. P. Kriegel, Dynamic k-dimensional multiway search under time-varying access frequencies, *Proceedings of the Fifth Gesellschaft für Informatik Conference on Theoretical Computer Science*, P. Deussen, ed., Karlsruhe, West Germany, March 1981, 135–145 (Lecture Notes in Computer Science 104, Springer-Verlag, Berlin, 1981). [points] D.2.8.2.3

292. [Güti84] R. H. Güting, An optimal contour algorithm for iso-oriented rectangles, *Journal of Algorithms 5*, 3(September 1984), 303–326. [rectangles]

293. [Güti87] R. H. Güting and W. Schilling, A practical divide-and-conquer algorithm for the rectangle intersection problem, *Information Sciences 42*, 2(July 1987), 95–112. [rectangles]

294. [Gutt84] A. Guttman, R-trees: a dynamic index structure for spatial searching, *Proceedings of the SIGMOD Conference*, Boston, June 1984, 47–57. [rectangles] D.2.8.1 D.3.5 D.3.5.3

295. [Hach89] N. I. Hachem and P. B. Berra, Key-sequential access methods for very large files derived from linear hashing, *Proceedings of the Fifth IEEE International Conference on Data Engineering*, Los Angeles, February 1989, 305–312. [points]

296. [Hanr86] P. Hanrahan, Using caching and breadth-first search to speed up ray-tracing, *Proceedings of Graphics Interface '86*, Vancouver, May 1986, 56–61. [volumes]

297. [Hara81] R. M. Haralick, Some neighborhood operations, in *Real Time/Parallel Computing Image Analysis*, M. Onoe, K. Preston, and A. Rosenfeld, eds., Plenum Press, New York, 1981. [regions] A.5.1.1

298. [Hara69] F. Harary, *Graph Theory*, Addison-Wesley, Reading, MA, 1969. [general] D.3.3 D.3.5.2 D.4.2.3.3 D.4.3 D.4.3.1 D.4.3.2 A.5.3

299. [Hard84] D. M. Hardas and S. N. Srihari, Progressive refinement of 3–d images using coded binary trees: algorithms and architecture, *IEEE Transactions on Pattern Analysis and Machine Intelligence 6*, 6(November 1984), 748–757. [volumes] A.8.3

300. [Hayw86] V. Hayward, Fast collision detection scheme by recursive decomposition of a manipulator workspace, *Proceedings of the IEEE International Conference on Robotics and Automation*, San Francisco, April 1986, 1044–1049. [volumes]

301. [Hech77] M. S. Hecht, *Flow Analysis of Computer Programs*, Elsevier North-Holland, New York, 1977. [general] A.4.3.2

302. [Heck84] P. S. Heckbert and P. Hanrahan, Beam tracing polygonal objects, *Computer Graphics 18*, 3(July 1984), 119–127 (also *Proceedings of the SIGGRAPH'84 Conference*, Minneapolis, July 1984). [volumes] A.7.2.2 A.7.3

303. [Hend80] P. Henderson, *Functional Programming: Application and Implementation*, Prentice-Hall International, Englewood Cliffs, NJ, 1980. [general] A.7.3

304. [Hend82] T. C. Henderson and E. Triendl, Storing feature descriptions as 2–d trees, *Proceedings of the IEEE Conference on Pattern Recognition and Image Processing 82*, Las Vegas, June 1982, 555–556. [regions]

305. [Herb85] F. Herbert, Solid modeling for architectural design using octpaths, *Computers & Graphics 9*, 2(1985), 107–116. [volumes]

306. [Herm86a] M. Herman, Fast, three-dimensional, collision-free motion planning, *Proceedings of the IEEE International Conference on Robotics and Automation*, San Francisco, April 1986, 1056–1063. [volumes]

307. [Herm86b] M. Herman, Fast path planning in unstructured, dynamic, 3–d worlds, *Proceedings of SPIE—Applications of Artificial Intelligence 3*, Orlando, April 1986, 505–512. [volumes]

308. [Hert83] S. Hertel and K. Mehlhorn, Fast triangulation of simple polygons, *Proceedings of the 1983 International FCT Conference*, Borgholm, Sweden, August 1983, 207–218 (Lecture Notes in Computer Science 158, Springer-Verlag, New York, 1983). [regions] D.4.3.1

309. [Hilb91] D. Hilbert, Ueber stetige Abbildung einer Linie auf ein Flächenstück, *Mathematische Annalen 38*, 1891, 459–460. [regions] D.1.3 A.1.4 A.4.1

310. [Hill67] F. S. Hillier and G. J. Lieberman, *Introduction to Operations Research*, Holden-Day, San Francisco, 1967. [general] D.1.2 A.1.3

311. [Hinr85a] K. Hinrichs, The grid file system: implementation and case studies of applications, Ph.D. dissertation, Institut für Informatik, ETH, Zurich, Switzerland, 1985. [rectangles] D.2.8.2.3 D.3.1 D.3.4

312. [Hinr85b] K. Hinrichs, Implementation of the grid file: design concepts and experience, *BIT 25*, 4(1985), 569–592. [rectangles] D.2.8.2.3 D.3.4

313. [Hinr83] K. Hinrichs and J. Nievergelt, The grid file: a data structure designed to support proximity queries on spatial objects, *Proceedings of the WG'83 (International Workshop on Graphtheoretic Concepts in Computer Science)*, M. Nagl and J. Perl, eds., Trauner Verlag, Linz, Austria, 1983, 100–113. [rectangles] D.3.1 D.3.4

314. [Hirs80] D. S. Hirschberg, On the complexity of searching a set of vectors, *SIAM Journal on Computing 9*, 1(February 1980), 126–129. [points]

315. [Hoar72] C. A. R. Hoare, Notes on data structuring, in *Structured Programming*, O. J. Dahl, E. W. Dijkstra, and C. A. R. Hoare, eds., Academic Press, London, 1972, 154. [matrices] D.1.3 A.1.4

316. [Hong85] T. H. Hong and M. Shneier, Describing a robot's workspace using a sequence of views from a moving camera, *IEEE Transactions on Pattern Analysis and Machine Intelligence 7*, 6(November 1985), 721–726. [volumes] D.5.2 A.4.6

317. [Hong87] T. H. Hong and M. Shneier, Rotation and translation of objects represented by octrees, *Proceedings of the IEEE International Conference on Robotics and Automation*, Raleigh, NC, March 1987, 947–950. [volumes]

318. [Horo76] S. L. Horowitz and T. Pavlidis, Picture segmentation by a tree traversal algorithm, *Journal of the ACM 23*, 2(April 1976), 368–388. [regions] D.1.2 A.1.3

319. [Hosh82] M. Hoshi and T. Yuba, A counter example to a monotonicity property of k-d trees, *Information Processing Letters 15*, 4(October 1982), 169–173. [points]

320. [Hout87] P. Houthuys, Box sort, a multidimensional method for rectangular boxes, used for quick range searching, *Visual Computer 3*, 4(December 1987), 236–249. [rectangles]

321. [Huff52] D. A. Huffman, A method for the construction of minimum-redundancy codes, *Proceedings of the IRE 40*, 9(September 1952), 1098–1101. [general] A.8 A.8.3

322. [Hunt78] G. M. Hunter, Efficient computation and data structures for graphics, Ph.D. dissertation, Department of Electrical Engineering and Computer Science, Princeton University, Princeton, NJ, 1978. [regions] D.1.2 D.1.3 D.1.5 D.2.6.1 D.3.5.1.3 D.4.2.1 D.4.2.4 D.5.5.1.2 A.1.2 A.1.3 A.1.4 A.3.2.2 A.4.3.1 A.4.4 A.5.1.2 A.5.2 A.5.3 A.6.3 A.6.3.2 A.6.5.1 A.7.1.1 A.7.1.2 A.9.2

323. [Hunt81] G. M. Hunter, Geometrees for interactive visualization of geology: an evaluation, System Science Department, Schlumberger-Doll Research, Ridgefield, CT, 1981. [volumes] D.2.6.2 D.5.3 A.1.3

324. [Hunt86] G. M. Hunter Three-dimensional frame buffers for interactive analysis of three-dimensional data, *Optical Engineering 25*, 2(February 1986), 292–295. [hardware]

325. [Hunt79a] G. M. Hunter and K. Steiglitz, Operations on images using quad trees, *IEEE Transactions on Pattern Analysis and Machine Intelligence 1*, 2(April 1979), 145–153. [regions] D.1.5 D.2.6.1 D.3.5.1.3 D.4.2.1 D.4.2.4 D.5.5.1.2 A.1.2 A.3.2.2 A.4.3.1 A.4.4 A.5.1.2 A.5.2 A.5.3 A.6.3 A.6.3.2 A.6.5.1 A.7.1.1 A.7.1.2 A.9.2

326. [Hunt79b] G. M. Hunter and K. Steiglitz, Linear transformation of pictures represented by quad trees, *Computer Graphics and Image Processing 10*, 3(July 1979), 289–296. [regions] D.1.3 A.1.4 A.3.2.2 A.4.4 A.6.5.1

327. [Hutf88a] A. Hutflesz, H. W. Six, and P. Widmayer, Globally order preserving multidimensional linear hashing, *Proceedings of the Fourth IEEE International Conference on Data Engineering*, Los Angeles, February 1988, 572–579. [points]

328. [Hutf88b] A. Hutflesz, H. W. Six, and P. Widmayer, The twin grid file: a nearly space optimal index structure, *Proceedings of the International Conference Extending Database Technology*, Venice, Italy, March 1988, 352–363. [points]

329. [Hutf88c] A. Hutflesz, H. W. Six, and P. Widmayer, Twin grid files: space optimizing access schemes, *Proceedings of the SIGMOD Conference*, Chicago, June 1988, 183–190. [points]

330. [Ibbs88] T. J. Ibbs and A. Stevens, Quadtree storage of vector data, *International Journal of Geographical Information Systems 2*, 1(January–March 1988), 43–56. [lines]

331. [Ibra84] H. A. H. Ibrahim, The connected component labeling algorithm on the NON-VON supercomputer, *Proceedings of the Workshop on Computer Vision: Representation and Control*, Annapolis, MD, April 1984, 37–45. [regions]

332. [Ichi81] T. Ichikawa, A pyramidal representation of images and its feature extraction facility, *IEEE Transactions on Pattern Analysis and Machine Intelligence 3*, 3(May 1981), 257–264. [regions]

333. [Imme86] D. S. Immel, M. F. Cohen, and D. P. Greenberg, A radiosity method for non-diffuse environments, *Computer Graphics 20*, 4(August 1986), 133–142 (also *Proceedings of the SIGGRAPH'86 Conference*, Dallas, August 1986). [surfaces] A.7.4

334. [Iri81] M. Iri, K. Murota, and S. Matsui, Linear-time approximation algorithms for finding the minimum-weight perfect matching on a plane, *Information Processing Letters 12*, 4(August 1981), 206–209. [points] D.2.9

335. [Isma80] M. G. B. Ismail and R. Steele, Adaptive pel location coding for bilevel facsimile signals, *Electronics Letters 16*, 10(May 8, 1980), 361–363. [regions] A.8.2.3

336. [Jack80] C. L. Jackins and S. L. Tanimoto, Oct-trees and their use in representing three-dimensional objects, *Computer Graphics and Image Processing 14*, 3(November 1980), 249–270. [volumes] D.1.3 A.1.4 A.6.5.2

337. [Jack83] C. L. Jackins and S. L. Tanimoto, Quad-trees, oct-trees, and k-trees — a generalized approach to recursive decomposition of Euclidean space, *IEEE Transactions on Pattern Analysis and Machine Intelligence 5*, 5(September 1983), 533–539. [regions] D.5.3 A.3.2.3 A.5.1.2 A.5.1.3 A.5.2

338. [Jans86] F. W. Jansen, Data structures for ray tracing, *Data Structures for Raster Graphics*, F. J. Peters, L. R. A. Kessener, and M. L. P. van Lierop, eds., Springer Verlag, Berlin, 1986, 57–73. [volumes] A.7.2.3

339. [Jans87a] F. W. Jansen, Solid modelling with faceted primitives, Ph.D. dissertation, Department of Industrial Design, Delft University of Technology, Delft, The Netherlands, September 1987. [volumes] D.5.5

340. [Jans87b] F. W. Jansen and R. J. Sutherland, Display of solid models with a multiprocessor system, *Proceedings of the EUROGRAPHICS'87 Conference*, G. Marechal, ed., North-Holland, Amsterdam, 1987, 377–387. [hardware] D.5.5

341. [Jans83] F. W. Jansen and J. J. van Wijk, Fast previewing techniques in raster graphics, in *Proceedings of the EUROGRAPHICS'83 Conference*, P. J. W. ten Hagen, ed., North-Holland, Amsterdam, 1983, 195–202. [volumes] A.7.2.5

342. [Jare84] G. E. M. Jared and T. Varady, Synthesis of volume modelling and sculptured surfaces in BUILD, *Proceedings of CAD'84*, Brighton, Great Britain, 1984, 481–495. [surfaces]

343. [Javi76] J. F. Javis, C. N. Judice, and W. H. Ninke, A survey of techniques for the image display of continuous tone images on a bilevel display, *Computer Graphics and Image Processing 5*, 1(March 1976), 13–40. [regions] A.6.3.1

344. [Jens74] K. Jensen and N. Wirth, *PASCAL User Manual and Report*, Second Edition, Springer-Verlag, New York, 1974. [general] D.P A.P L

345. [Jone84] L. Jones and S. S. Iyengar, Space and time efficient virtual quadtrees, *IEEE Transactions on Pattern Analysis and Machine Intelligence 6*, 2(March 1984), 244–247. [regions] A.2.1.4

346. [Josh88] R. C. Joshi, H. Darbari, S. Goel, and S. Sasikumaran, A hierarchical hex-tree representational technique for solid modelling, *Computers & Graphics 12*, 2(1988), 235–238. [volumes]

347. [Joy86] K. I. Joy and M. N. Bhetanabhotla, Ray tracing parametric surface patches utilizing numerical techniques and ray coherence, *Computer Graphics 20*, 4(August 1986), 279–285 (also *Proceedings of the SIGGRAPH'86 Conference*, Dallas, August 1986). [surfaces]

348. [Kaji86] J. T. Kajia, The rendering equation, *Computer Graphics 20*, 4(August 1986), 143–150 (also *Proceedings of the SIGGRAPH'86 Conference*, Dallas, August 1986). [general] A.7.2.1

349. [Kamb86] S. Kambhampati and L. S. Davis, Multiresolution path planning for mobile robots, *IEEE Journal of Robotics and Automation 2*, 3(September 1986), 135–145. [regions]

350. [Kana85] K. Kanatani, personal communication, 1985. [regions] D.1.4.1

351. [Kapl85] M. R. Kaplan, Space-tracing: a constant time ray-tracer, SIGGRAPH'85 Tutorial on the Uses of Spatial Coherence in Ray-Tracing, San Francisco, ACM, July 1985. [volumes] A.7.2.2

352. [Kapl87] M. R. Kaplan, The use of spatial coherence in ray tracing, in *Techniques for Computer Graphics*, D. F. Rogers and R. A. Earnshaw, eds., Springer-Verlag, New York, 1987, 173–193. [volumes] A.7.2.2 A.7.2.3 A.7.2.4

353. [Karl88] R. G. Karlsson, Greedy matching on a grid, *BIT 28*, 1(1988), 19–26. [points]

354. [Karo83] O. Karonen, M. Tamminen, P. Kerola, M. Mitjonen, and E. Orivouri, A geometric mine modeling system, *Proceedings of Auto-Carto 6*, vol. 1, Ottawa, October 1983, 374–383. [volumes]

355. [Kasi88] S. Kasif, Optimal parallel algorithms for quadtree problems, *Proceedings of the Fifth Israeli Symposium on Artificial Intelligence, Vision, and Pattern Recognition*, Tel Aviv, Israel, December 1988, 353–363. [regions]

356. [Kata88] J. Katajainen and M. Koppinen, Constructing Delaunay triangulations by merging buckets in quadtree order, *Fundamenta Informaticae 11*, 3(September 1988), 275–288. [regions]

357. [Kauf83] A. Kaufman, D. Forgash, and Y. Ginsburg, Hidden surface removal using a forest of quadtrees, *Proceedings of the First IPA Conference on Image Processing, Computer Graphics, and Pattern Recognition*, A. Kaufman, ed., Information Processing Association of Israel, Jerusalem, 1983, 85–89. [volumes] A.7.1.1

358. [Kawa80a] E. Kawaguchi and T. Endo, On a method of binary picture representation and its application to data compression, *IEEE Transactions on Pattern Analysis and Machine Intelligence 2*, 1(January 1980), 27–35. [regions] D.1.3 D.1.5 D.5.4 A.1.4 A.2.2 A.3.4.4 A.5.1.3

359. [Kawa83] E. Kawaguchi, T. Endo, and J. Matsunaga, Depth-first expression viewed from digital picture processing, *IEEE Transactions on Pattern Analysis and Machine Intelligence 5*, 4(July 1983), 373–384. [regions] D.1.2 A.1.3 A.2.2 A.6.3 A.8

360. [Kawa80b] E. Kawaguchi, T. Endo, and M. Yokota, DF-expression of binary-valued picture and its relation to other pyramidal representations, *Proceedings of the Fifth International Conference on Pattern Recognition*, Miami Beach, December 1980, 822–827. [regions] D.1.2 D.1.3 A.1.3 A.1.4

361. [Kawa88] E. Kawaguchi and R. I. Taniguchi, Coded DF-expression for binary and multi-valued picture, *Proceedings of the Ninth International Conference on Pattern Recognition*, Rome, November 1988, 1159–1163. [regions]

362. [Kede82] G. Kedem, The quad-CIF tree: a data structure for hierarchical on-line algorithms, *Proceedings of the Nineteenth Design Automation Conference*, Las Vegas, June 1982, 352–357. [rectangles] D.3.5 D.3.5.1

363. [Kela84a] A. Kela, Programmers guide to the PADL-2 octree processor output system, Production Automation Project Input/Output Group Memo 15, University of Rochester, Rochester, NY, January 1984. [finite element]

364. [Kela86] A. Kela, R. Perucchio, and H. Voelcker, Toward automatic finite element analysis, *Computers in Mechanical Engineering 5*, 1(July 1986), 57–71. [finite element] D.1.3 D.5.6 A.P A.1.4 A.7.1.6

365. [Kela84b] A. Kela, H. Voelcker, and J. Goldak, Automatic generation of hierarchical, spatially addressable finite-element meshes from CSG representations of solids, *International Conference on Accuracy Estimates and Adaptive Refinements in Finite Element Computations*, Lisbon, Portugal, June 1984, 221–234. [finite element] D.1.3 A.1.4

366. [Kell71] M. D. Kelly, Edge detection in pictures by computer using planning, in *Machine Intelligence 6*, B. Meltzer and D. Michie, eds., American Elsevier, New York, 1971, 397–409. [regions] D.1.3 A.1.4

367. [Kent86] E. W. Kent, M. O. Shneier, and T. H. Hong, Building representations from fusions of multiple views, *Proceedings of the IEEE International Conference on Robotics and Automation*, San Francisco, April 1986, 1634–1639. [volumes]

368. [Kern78] B. W. Kernighan and D. M. Ritchie, *The C Programming Language*, Prentice-Hall, Englewood Cliffs, NJ, 1978. [general] D.P A.P L

369. [Kers79] M. L. Kersten and P. van Emde Boas, Local optimizations of QUAD trees, Technical Report IR-51, Free University of Amsterdam, Amsterdam, The Netherlands, June 1979. [points] D.2.3.1

370. [Kim83] Y. C. Kim and J. K. Aggarwal, Rectangular coding for binary images, *Proceedings of Computer Vision and Pattern Recognition 83*, Washington, DC, June 1983, 108–113. [regions] D.1.2 A.1.3 A.9.3.4

371. [Kim86] Y. C. Kim and J. K. Aggarwal, Rectangular parallelepiped coding: a volumetric representation of three-dimensional objects, *IEEE Journal of Robotics and Automation 2*, 3(September 1986), 127–134. [regions] D.1.2 A.1.3 A.9.3.4

372. [Kirk83] D. Kirkpatrick, Optimal search in planar subdivisions, *SIAM Journal on Computing 12*, 1(February 1983), 28–35. [regions] D.P D.4.3

373. [Kits89] M. Kitsuregwa, L. Harada, and M. Takagi, Join strategies on kd-tree indexed relations, *Proceedings of the Fifth IEEE International Conference on Data Engineering*, Los Angeles, February 1989, 85–93. [points]

374. [Klee77] V. Klee, Can the measure of $\cup[a_i,b_i]$ be computed in less than $O(n\log n)$ steps? *American Mathematical Monthly 84*, 4(April 1977), 284–285. [rectangles] D.3.3

375. [Klei86] A. Kleiner and K. E. Brassel, Hierarchical grid structures for static geographic data bases, *Proceedings of Auto-Carto London*, vol. 1, London, September 1986, 485–496. [regions]

376. [Klin71] A. Klinger, Patterns and search statistics, in *Optimizing Methods in Statistics*, J. S. Rustagi, ed., Academic Press, New York, 1971, 303–337. [regions] D.1.2 D.1.3 A.1.3 A.1.4

377. [Klin76] A. Klinger and C. R. Dyer, Experiments in picture representation using regular decomposition, *Computer Graphics and Image Processing 5*, 1(March 1976), 68–105. [regions] D.1.2 D.1.3 A.1.3 A.1.4 A.2.1.1

378. [Klin79] A. Klinger and M. L. Rhodes, Organization and access of image data by areas, *IEEE Transactions on Pattern Analysis and Machine Intelligence 1*, 1(January 1979), 50–60. [regions] A.2.1.1 A.3.2.2

379. [Knot71] G. D. Knott, Expandable open addressing hash table storage and retrieval, *Proceedings of SIGFIDET Workshop on Data Description, Access, and Control*, San Diego, November 1971, 187–206. [points] D.2.8.1 D.2.8.2.1

380. [Know80] K. Knowlton, Progressive transmission of grey-scale and binary pictures by simple, efficient, and lossless encoding schemes, *Proceedings of the IEEE 68*, 7(July 1980), 885–896. [regions] D.1.4.1 A.1.3 A.8 A.8.1 A.8.3

381. [Knut73a] D. E. Knuth, *The Art of Computer Programming*, vol. 1, *Fundamental Algorithms*, Second Edition, Addison-Wesley, Reading, MA, 1973. [general] D.P D.1.3 D.2.3.1 D.2.8.2.1 D.2.8.2.3 D.4.3.2 A.P A.1.4 A.2.1.4 A.3.2.1.2

382. [Knut73b] D. E. Knuth, *The Art of Computer Programming*, vol. 3, *Sorting and Searching*, Addison-Wesley, Reading, MA, 1973. [general] D.P D.1.2 D.2.1 D.2.2 D.2.3.1 D.2.3.3 D.2.4.1 D.2.4.3 D.2.5 D.2.6.2 D.2.8.2.1 D.2.8.2.2 A.P A.1.3

383. [Knut76] D. E. Knuth, Big Omicron and big omega and big theta, *SIGACT News 8*, 2(April-June 1976), 18–24. [general] D.P A.P

384. [Koba87] H. Kobayashi, T. Nakamura, and Y. Shigei, Parallel processing of an object space for image synthesis, *Visual Computer 3*, 1(February 1987), 13–22. [volumes] A.3.3

385. [Koba88] H. Kobayashi, S. Nishimura, H. Kubota, T. Nakamura, and Y. Shigei, Load balancing strategies for a parallel ray-tracing system based on constant subdivision, *Visual Computer 4*, 4(October 1988), 197–209. [volumes]

386. [Kois88] P. Koistinen, Interval methods for constructive solid geometry: display via block model conversion, Master's Thesis, Laboratory for Information Processing, Helsinki University of Technology, Helsinki, Finland, May 1988. [volumes] D.5.5.1.3

387.   [Kois85] P. Koistinen, M. Tamminen, and H. Samet, Viewing solid models by bintree conversion, in *Proceedings of the EUROGRAPHICS'85 Conference*, C. E. Vandoni, ed., North-Holland, Amsterdam, 1985, 147–157. [volumes] A.7.1.4

388.   [Korn85] M. R. Korn and C. R. Dyer, 3–d multiview object representation for model based object recognition, TR 602, Computer Science Department, University of Wisconsin, Madison, WI, June 1985. [surfaces]

389.   [Krie84] H. P. Kriegel, Performance comparison of index structures for multikey retrieval, *Proceedings of the SIGMOD Conference*, Boston, June 1984, 186–196. [points] D.2.8.2.3

390.   [Krie86] H. P. Kriegel and B. Seeger, Multidimensional order preserving linear hashing with partial expansions, *Proceedings of the International Conference on Database Theory*, Rome, September 1986, 203–220 (Lecture Notes in Computer Science 243, Springer-Verlag, New York, 1986). [points]

391.   [Krie87] H. P. Kriegel and B. Seeger, Multidimensional dynamic quantile hashing is very efficient for non-uniform record distributions, *Proceedings of the Third IEEE International Conference on Data Engineering*, Los Angeles, February 1987, 10–17. [points]

392.   [Krie88] H. P. Kriegel and B. Seeger, PLOP-hashing: a grid file without directory, *Proceedings of the Fourth IEEE International Conference on Data Engineering*, Los Angeles, February 1988, 369–376. [points]

393.   [Kris85] R. Krishnamurthy and K. Y. Whang, Multilevel grid files, IBM T. J. Watson Research Center Report, Yorktown Heights, NY, 1985. [points]

394.   [Krol85] K. Krolof and M. Tamminen, A viewing pipeline for discrete solid modeling, *Visual Computer 1*, 1(July 1985), 24–36. [volumes]

395.   [Krop86] W. G. Kropatsch, Curve representations in multiple resolutions, *Proceedings of the Eighth International Conference on Pattern Recognition*, Paris, October 1986, 1283–1285. [lines] D.1.3 A.1.4

396.   [Kuma86] P. S. Kumar and M. Manohar, On probability of forest of quadtrees reducing to quadtrees, *Information Processing Letters 22*, 3(March 1986), 109–111. [regions]

397.   [Kuni86] T. L. Kunii, I. Fujishiro, and X. Mao, G-quadtree: a hierarchical representation of gray-scale digital images, *Visual Computer 2*, 4(August 1986), 219–226. [regions]

398.   [Kuni85] T. L. Kunii, T. Satoh, and K. Yamaguchi, Generation of topological boundary representations from octree encoding, *IEEE Computer Graphics and Applications 5*, 3(March 1985), 29–38. [volumes] D.5.4

399.   [Kurl88] D. Kurlander and E. A. Bier, Graphical search and replace, *Computer Graphics 22*, 4(August 1988), 85–92 (also *Proceedings of the SIGGRAPH'88 Conference*, Atlanta, August 1988). [regions] D.3.4

400.   [Kush82] T. Kushner, A. Wu, and A. Rosenfeld, Image processing on ZMOB, *IEEE Transactions on Computers 31*, 10(October 1982), 943–951. [regions]

401.   [Lane80] J. M. Lane, L. C. Carpenter, T. Whitted, J. F. Blinn, Scan line methods for displaying parametrically defined surfaces, *Communications of the ACM 23*, 1(January 1980), 23–34. [surfaces] A.7.1.6

402.   [Lars80] P.Å. Larson, Linear hashing with partial expansions, *Proceedings of the Sixth International Conference on Very Large Data Bases*, Montreal, October 1980, 224–232. [points] D.2.8.2.1

403.   [Lars88] P.Å. Larson, Dynamic hash tables, *Communications of the ACM 31*, 4(April 1988), 446–457. [points] D.2.8.2.1 D.2.8.2.2

404. [Laur85] R. Laurini, Graphical data bases built on Peano space-filling curves, in *Proceedings of the EUROGRAPHICS'85 Conference*, C. E. Vandoni, ed., North-Holland, Amsterdam, 1985, 327–338. [regions] D.1.3 A.1.4

405. [Laur87] R. Laurini, Manipulation of spatial objects by a Peano tuple algebra, Computer Science TR-1893, University of Maryland, College Park, MD, July 1987. [regions]

406. [Laut78] U. Lauther, 4–dimensional binary search trees as a means to speed up associative searches in design rule verification of integrated circuits, *Journal of Design Automation and Fault-Tolerant Computing 2*, 3(July 1978), 241–247. [rectangles] D.3.4

407. [Lauz85] J. P. Lauzon, D. M. Mark, L. Kikuchi, and J. A. Guevara, Two-dimensional run-encoding for quadtree representation, *Computer Vision, Graphics, and Image Processing 30*, 1(April 1985), 56–69. [regions] A.2.1.3 A.3.4.1 A.5.1.3

408. [Lava89] Lavakusha, A. K. Pujari, and P. G. Reddy, Linear octrees by volume intersection, *Computer Vision, Graphics, and Image Processing 45*, 3(March 1989), 371–379. [volumes]

409. [Lawl76] E. Lawler, *Combinatorial Optimization: Networks and Matroids*, Holt, Rinehart and Winston, New York, 1976. [general] D.2.9

410. [Lawl85] E. L. Lawler, J. K. Lenstra, A. H. G. Rinnooy-Kan, and D. B. Shmoys, *The Traveling Salesman Problem*, John Wiley & Sons, New York, 1985. [general] D.1.3 A.1.4

411. [Lea88] D. Lea, Digital and Hilbert k-d trees, *Information Processing Letters 27*, 1(February 1988), 35–41. [points]

412. [Lee83] D. T. Lee, Maximum clique problem of rectangle graphs, in *Advances in Computing Research*, vol. 1, *Computational Geometry*, F. P. Preparata, ed., JAI Press, Greenwich, CT, 1983, 91–107. [rectangles] D.2.9 D.3.3

413. [Lee77a] D. T. Lee and F. P. Preparata, Location of a point in a planar subdivision and its applications, *SIAM Journal on Computing 6*, 3(July 1977), 594–606. [regions] D.4.3 D.4.3.2

414. [Lee82a] D. T. Lee and F. P. Preparata, An improved algorithm for the rectangle enclosure problem, *Journal of Algorithms 3*, 3(September 1982), 218–224. [rectangles] D.3.2.4

415. [Lee80a] D. T. Lee and B. J. Shacter, Two algorithms for constructing a Delaunay triangulation, *International Journal of Computer and Information Sciences 9*, 3(June 1980), 219–242. [regions] D.2.4.3

416. [Lee77b] D. T. Lee and C. K. Wong, Worst-case analysis for region and partial region searches in multidimensional binary search trees and quad trees, *Acta Informatica 9*, 1(1977), 23–29. [points] D.2.3 D.2.3.2 D.2.3.3 D.2.4.3

417. [Lee80b] D. T. Lee and C. K. Wong, Quintary trees: a file structure for multidimensional database systems, *ACM Transactions on Database Systems 5*, 4(September 1980), 339–353. [points]

418. [Lee82b] Y. T. Lee and A. A. G. Requicha, Algorithms for computing the volume and other integral properties of solids. I. Known methods and open issues, *Communications of the ACM 25*, 9(September 1982), 635–641. [volumes] D.5.5

419. [Lee82c] Y. T. Lee and A. A. G. Requicha, Algorithms for computing the volume and other integral properties of solids. II. A family of algorithms based on representation conversion and cellular approximation, *Communications of the ACM 25*, 9(September 1982), 642–650. [volumes] D.5.5 D.5.5.1.1

420. [Lele87] D. A. Lelewer and D. S. Hirschberg, Data compression, *ACM Computing Surveys 19*, 3(September 1987), 261–296. [regions] A.8

421. [Lete83] P. Letelier, Transmission d'images à bas débit pour un système de communication téléphonique adapté aux sourds, Thèse de docteur-ingénieur, Université de Paris-Sud, Paris, September 1983. [regions] D.2.6.1

422. [Li86] H. Li, M. A. Lavin, and R. J. LeMaster, Fast Hough transform: a hierarchical approach, *Computer Vision, Graphics, and Image Processing 36*, 2/3(November / December 1986), 139–161. [regions]

423. [Li82] M. Li, W. I. Grosky, and R. Jain, Normalized quadtrees with respect to translations, *Computer Graphics and Image Processing 20*, 1(September 1982), 72–81. [regions] D.1.5 A.1.2 A.4.3.1 A.9.3.4

424. [Li87a] S. X. Li and M. H. Loew, The quadcode and its arithmetic, *Communications of the ACM 30*, 7(July 1987), 621–626. [regions]

425. [Li87b] S. X. Li and M. H. Loew, Adjacency detection using quadcodes, *Communications of the ACM 30*, 7(July 1987), 627–631. [regions]

426. [Libe86] F. D. Libera and F. Gosen, Using B-trees to solve geographic range queries, *Computer Journal 29*, 2(April 1986), 176–181. [regions]

427. [Ling82] A. Lingas, The power of non-rectilinear holes, *Proceedings of the Ninth International Colloquium on Automata, Languages, and Programming*, Aarhus, Denmark, July 1982, 369–383 (Lecture Notes in Computer Science 140, Springer-Verlag, New York, 1982). [regions] D.1.2 A.1.3

428. [Linn73] J. Linn, General methods for parallel searching, Technical Report 81, Digital Systems Laboratory, Stanford University, Stanford, CA, May 1973. [points] D.2.4.4

429. [Lipt77] R. J. Lipton and R. E. Tarjan, Application of a planar separator theorem, *Proceedings of the Eighteenth Annual IEEE Symposium on the Foundations of Computer Science*, Providence, RI, October 1977, 162–170. [regions] D.4.3

430. [Litt79] J. J. Little and T. K. Peucker, A recursive procedure for finding the intersection of two digital curves, *Computer Graphics and Image Processing 10*, 2(June 1980), 159–171. [lines] D.4.1

431. [Litw80] W. Litwin, Linear hashing: a new tool for file and table addressing, *Proceedings of the Sixth International Conference on Very Large Data Bases*, Montreal, October 1980, 212–223. [points] D.2.7 D.2.8.2.1

432. [Lome89a] D. Lomet and B. Salzberg, A robust multi-attribute search structure, *Proceedings of the Fifth IEEE International Conference on Data Engineering*, Los Angeles, February 1989, 296–304. [points] D.2.6.2

433. [Lome89b] D. Lomet and B. Salzberg, The hB-Tree: a robust multi-attribute indexing method, *ACM Transactions on Database Systems 14*, 1989 (also Northeastern University Technical Report NU-CCS-87–24). [points] D.2.6.2

434. [Loza81] T. Lozano-Perez, Automatic planning of manipulator transfer movements, *IEEE Transactions on Systems, Man, and Cybernetics 11*, 10(October 1981), 681–698. [regions] D.1.3 A.1.4

435. [Luek78] G. Lueker, A data structure for orthogonal range queries, *Proceedings of the Nineteenth Annual IEEE Symposium on the Foundations of Computer Science*, Ann Arbor, MI, October 1978, 28–34. [points] D.2.3

436. [Lum70] V. Y. Lum, Multi-attribute retrieval with combined indexes, *Communications of the ACM 13*, 11(November 1970), 660–665. [points]

437. [Lumi83a] R. Lumia, A new three-dimensional connected components algorithm, *Computer Vision, Graphics, and Image Processing 23*, 2(August 1983), 207–217. [volumes] A.5.1.1 A.5.1.2 A.5.1.3

438. [Lumi86] R. Lumia, Rapid hidden feature elimination using an octree, *Proceedings of the IEEE International Conference on Robotics and Automation*, San Francisco, April 1986, 460–464. [volumes]

439. [Lumi83b] R. Lumia, L. Shapiro, and O. Zuniga, A new connected components algorithm for virtual memory computers, *Computer Vision, Graphics, and Image Processing 22*, 2(May 1983), 287–300. [regions] A.5.1 A.5.1.1 A.5.1.2 A.5.1.3

440. [Mair88] H. G. Mairson and J. Stolfi, Reporting and counting intersections between two sets of line segments, in *Theoretical Foundations of Computer Graphics and CAD*, R. A. Earnshaw, ed., Springer-Verlag, Berlin, 1988, 307–325. [lines] D.4.3.3

441. [Mano88] M. Manohar, P. S. Rao, and S. S. Iyengar, Template quadtrees for representing region and line data present in binary images, NASA Goddard Flight Center, Greenbelt, MD, 1988. [regions] D.4.2.1

442. [Mänt87] M. Mäntylä, *An Introduction to Solid Modeling*, Computer Science Press, Rockville, MD, 1987. [general] D.P D.5.1 D.5.4 A.P

443. [Mänt82] M. Mäntylä and R. Sulonen, GWB: A solid modeler with Euler operators, *IEEE Computer Graphics and Applications 2*, 7(September 1982), 17–31. [volumes] D.5.4

444. [Mänt83] M. Mäntylä and M. Tamminen, Localized set operations for solid modeling, *Computer Graphics 17*, 3(July 1983), 279–288 (also *Proceedings of the SIGGRAPH'83 Conference*, Detroit, July 1983). [volumes]

445. [Mao87] X. Mao, T. L. Kunii, I. Fujishiro, and T. Noma, Hierarchical representations of 2d/3d gray-scale images and 2d/3d two-way conversion, *IEEE Computer Graphics and Applications 7*, 12(December 1987), 37–44. [regions]

446. [Marb84] D. Marble, H. Calkins, and D. Peuquet, eds., *Basic Readings in Geographic Information Systems*, SPAD Systems, Williamsville, NY, 1984, 2:57–78. [general] D.4.4

447. [Marg88] A. Margalit and G. D. Knott, An algorithm for computing the union, intersection or difference of two polygons, *Computers & Graphics*, 1989 (also University of Maryland Computer Science TR-1995). [regions] D.5.2 A.4.6

448. [Mark86a] D. M. Mark, The use of quadtrees in geographic information systems and spatial data handling, *Proceedings of Auto-Carto London*, vol. 1, London, September 1986, 517–526. [regions]

449. [Mark85a] D. M. Mark and D. J. Abel, Linear quadtrees from vector representations of polygons, *IEEE Transactions on Pattern Analysis and Machine Intelligence 7*, 3(May 1985), 344–349. [regions] A.4.3.1

450. [Mark86b] D. M. Mark and J. A. Cebrian, Octtrees: a useful data-structure for the processing of topographic and sub-surface area, *Proceedings of the 1986 ACSM-ASPRS Annual Convention*, vol. 1, *Cartography and Education*, Washington, DC, March 1986, 104–113. [surfaces]

451. [Mark85b] D. M. Mark and J. P. Lauzon, The space efficiency of quadtrees: an empirical examination including the effects of 2–dimensional run-encoding, *Geo-Processing 2*, 1985, 367–383. [regions] A.2.1.3

452. [Mars88] S. C. Marsh, Fine grain parallel architectures and creation of high-quality images, in *Theoretical Foundations of Computer Graphics and CAD*, R. A. Earnshaw, ed., Springer-Verlag, Berlin, 1988, 728–753. [hardware]

453. [Mart79] G. N. N. Martin, Spiral storage: incrementally augmentable hash addressed storage, Theory of Computation Report No. 27, Department of Computer Science, University of Warwick, Coventry, Great Britain, March 1979. [points] D.2.8.2.2

454. [Mart82] J. J. Martin, Organization of geographical data with quad trees and least square approximation, *Proceedings of the IEEE Conference on Pattern Recognition and Image Processing*, Las Vegas, June 1982, 458–463. [lines] D.4.2.1

455. [Mart86] M. Martin, D. M. Chiarulli, and S. S. Iyengar, Parallel processing of quadtrees on a horizontally reconfigurable architecture computing system, *Proceedings of the IEEE International Conference on Parallel Processing*, St. Charles, IL, August 1986, 895–902. [regions]

456. [Mart83] W. N. Martin and J. K. Aggarwal, Volumetric descriptions of objects from multiple views, *IEEE Transactions on Pattern Analysis and Machine Intelligence 5*, 2(March 1983), 150–158. [volumes] D.5.2 A.4.6

457. [Maso87] D. C. Mason, Dilation algorithm for a linear quadtree, *Image and Vision Computing 5*, 1(February 1987), 11–20. [regions] A.6.6

458. [Maso88] D. C. Mason and M. J. Callen, Comparison of two dilation algorithms for linear quadtrees, *Image and Vision Computing 6*, 3(August 1988), 169–175. [regions]

459. [Math87] C. Mathieu, C. Puech, and H. Yahia, Average efficiency of data structures for binary image processing, *Information Processing Letters 26*, 2(October 1987), 89–93. [regions]

460. [Mats84] T. Matsuyama, L. V. Hao, and M. Nagao, A file organization for geographic information systems based on spatial proximity, *Computer Vision, Graphics, and Image Processing 26*, 3(June 1984), 303–318. [points] D.2.8.1 D.3

461. [Mazu87] P. Mazumder, Planar decomposition for quadtree data structure, *Computer Vision, Graphics, and Image Processing 38*, 3(June 1987), 258–274. [regions]

462. [Mazu88] P. Mazumder, A new strategy for octtree representation of three-dimensional objects, *Proceedings of Computer Vision and Pattern Recognition 88*, Ann Arbor, MI, June 1988, 270–275. [regions]

463. [McCa60] J. McCarthy, Recursive functions of symbolic expressions, *Communications of the ACM 3*, 4(April 1960), 184–195. [general] L

464. [McCl65] E. J. McCluskey, *Introduction to the Theory of Switching Circuits*, McGraw-Hill, New York, 1965, 60–61. [general] D.1.2 A.1.3

465. [McCr80] E. M. McCreight, Efficient algorithms for enumerating intersecting intervals and rectangles, Xerox Palo Alto Research Center Report CSL-80–09, Palo Alto, CA, June 1980. [rectangles] D.3.2.2 D.3.4

466. [McCr85] E. M. McCreight, Priority search trees, *SIAM Journal on Computing 14*, 2(May 1985), 257–276. [rectangles] D.2.5 D.3.2.3

467. [McKe84] D. M. McKeown Jr. and J. L. Denlinger, Map-guided feature extraction from aerial imagery, *Proceedings of the Workshop on Computer Vision: Representation and Control*, Annapolis, MD, April 1984, 205–213. [regions]

468. [Meag80] D. Meagher, Octree encoding: a new technique for the representation, the manipulation, and display of arbitrary 3–d objects by computer, Electrical and Systems Engineering Technical Report IPL-TR-80–111, Rensselaer Polytechnic Institute, Troy, NY, October 1980. [volumes] D.1.5 D.5.5.1.2 A.1.2

469. [Meag82a] D. Meagher, Geometric modeling using octree encoding, *Computer Graphics and Image Processing 19*, 2(June 1982), 129–147. [volumes] D.1.3 A.1.4 A.5.1.3 A.6.5.2 A.6.5.3 A.7.1.4

470. [Meag82b] D. Meagher, Octree generation, analysis and manipulation, Electrical and Systems Engineering Report IPL-TR-027, Rensselaer Polytechnic Institute, Troy, NY, 1982. [volumes] D.5.1 D.5.5.1.1 D.5.5.1.3

471. [Meag82c] D. Meagher, Efficient synthetic image generation of arbitrary 3–d objects, *Proceedings of the IEEE Conference on Pattern Recognition and Image Processing*, Las Vegas, June 1982, 473–478. [volumes]

472. [Meag82d] D. Meagher, The octree encoding method for efficient solid modeling, Electrical and Systems Engineering Report IPL-TR-032, Rensselaer Polytechnic Institute, Troy, NY, August 1982. [volumes] A.2.1.2

473. [Meag82e] D. Meagher, Computer software for robotic vision, *Proceedings of SPIE— Robotics and Industrial Inspection 360*, San Diego, August 1982, 318–325. [volumes]

474. [Meag84] D. Meagher, The Solids Engine℠: a processor for interactive solid modeling, *Proceedings of the NICOGRAPH '84 Conference*, Tokyo, November 1984, A-2, 1–11. [volumes] D.5.3 D.5.5 A.7.1.4

475. [Mehl84] K. Mehlhorn, *Multi-dimensional Searching and Computational Geometry*, Springer-Verlag, Berlin, 1984. [general] D.P D.4.3.1

476. [Mei86] G. G. Mei and W. Liu, Parallel processing for quadtree problems, *Proceedings of the IEEE International Conference on Parallel Processing*, St. Charles, IL, August 1986, 452–454. [regions]

477. [Meno87a] S. Menon, P. Gao, and T. R. Smith, Multi-colored quadtrees for GIS: exploiting bit-parallelism for rapid Boolean overlay, *Proceedings of the International Symposium on Geographic Information Systems*, vol. 2, Arlington, VA, November 1987, 371–383. [regions]

478. [Meno87b] S. Menon and T. R. Smith, Multi-component object search using spatial constraint propagation, *Proceedings of the International Symposium on Geographic Information Systems*, vol. 2, Arlington, VA, November 1987, 281–293. [regions]

479. [Merr78] T. H. Merrett, Multidimensional paging for efficient database querying, *Proceedings of the International Conference on Management of Data*, Milan, June 1978, 277–289. [points] D.2.8.2.3

480. [Merr82] T. H. Merrett and E. J. Otoo, Dynamic multipaging: a storage structure for large shared data banks, in *Improving Database Usability and Responsiveness*, P. Scheuermann, ed., Academic Press, New York, 1982, 237–254. [points] D.2.8.2.3

481. [Merr73] R. D. Merrill, Representations of contours and regions for efficient computer search, *Communications of the ACM 16*, 2(February 1973), 69–82. [lines] D.4.4

482. [Mich80] J. Michener, personal communication, 1980. [regions] A.4.3.1

483. [Milf84] D. J. Milford and P. J. Willis, Quad encoded display, *IEE Proceedings 131*, Part E, 3(May 1984), 70–75. [hardware]

484. [Milf81] D. J. Milford, P. J. Willis, and J. R. Woodwark, Exploiting area coherence in raster scan displays, *Proceedings of Electronic Displays 81*, London, 1981, 34–46. [hardware]

485. [Mill85] R. Miller and Q. F. Stout, Pyramid computer algorithms for determining geometric properties of images, *Proceedings of the Symposium on Computational Geometry*, Baltimore, June 1985, 263–269. [regions]

486. [Mins69] M. Minsky and S. Papert, *Perceptrons: An Introduction to Computational Geometry*, MIT Press, Cambridge, MA, 1969. [general] A.5.3

487. [Moba88] B. G. Mobasseri, Soft-linked quadtree: a cascaded ring structure using flexible linkage concept, *Proceedings of Computer Vision and Pattern Recognition 88*, Ann Arbor, MI, June 1988, 622–627. [regions]

488. [Moor79] R. E. Moore, *Methods and Applications of Interval Analysis*, Philadelphia, SIAM, 1979. [general] D.5.5.1.3

489. [Mort85] M. E. Mortenson, *Geometric Modeling*, John Wiley and Sons, New York, 1985. [general] A.7.1.6

490. [Mort66] G. M. Morton, A computer oriented geodetic data base and a new technique in file sequencing, IBM Ltd., Ottawa, Canada, 1966. [regions] D.1.2 D.1.3 D.2.7 A.1.4 A.2.1.1 A.4.1

491. [Mudu84] S. P. Mudur and P. A. Koparkar, Interval methods for processing geometric objects, *IEEE Computer Graphics and Applications 4*, 2(February 1984), 7–17. [surfaces] D.5.5.1.3 D.5.6

492. [Mull85] J. K. Mullin, Spiral storage: efficient dynamic hashing with constant performance, *Computer Journal 28*, 3(August 1985), 330–334. [points] D.2.8.2.2

493. [Mura88] M. Muralikrishna and D. J. DeWitt, Equi-depth histograms for estimating selectivity factors for multi-dimensional queries, *Proceedings of the SIGMOD Conference*, Chicago, June 1988, 28–36. [points]

494. [Nagy79] G. Nagy and S. Wagle, Geographic data processing, *ACM Computing Surveys 11*, 2(June 1979), 139–181. [lines] D.P D.4 D.4.4 A.P

495. [Nair87] K. N. R. Nair and R. Sankar, An approach to geometric modeling of solids bounded by sculptured surfaces, *Computers & Graphics 11*, 2(1987), 113–120. [volumes]

496. [Naka88] Y. Nakamura, S. Abe, Y. Ohsawa, and M. Sakauchi, MD-tree: a balanced hierarchical data structure for multi-dimensional data with highly efficient dynamic characteristics, *Proceedings of the Ninth International Conference on Pattern Recognition*, Rome, November 1988, 375–378. [regions]

497. [Nand86a] S. K. Nandy and L. M. Patnaik, Linear time geometrical design rule checker based on quadtree representation of VLSI mask layouts, *Computer-Aided Design 18*, 7(September 1986), 380–388. [regions]

498. [Nand87] S. K. Nandy and L. M. Patnaik, Algorithm for incremental compaction of geometrical layouts, *Computer-Aided Design 19*, 5(June 1987), 257–265. [regions]

499. [Nand86b] S. K. Nandy and I. V. Ramakrishnan, Dual quadtree representation for VLSI designs, *Proceedings of the Twenty-third Design Automation Conference*, Las Vegas, June 1986, 663–666. [regions]

500. [Naur60] P. Naur, ed., Revised report on the algorithmic language ALGOL 60, *Communications of the ACM 3*, 5(May 1960), 299–314. [general] D.P A.P L

501. [Nava86a] I. Navazo, Contribucío a les tècniques de modelat geomètric d'objectes polièdrics usant la codificacío amb arbres octals, Ph.D. dissertation, Escola Tecnica Superior d'Enginyers Industrials, Department de Metodes Informatics, Universitat Politèchnica de Catalunya, Barcelona, Spain, January 1986. [volumes] D.5.3 A.1.3

502. [Nava89] I. Navazo, Extended octree representation of general solids with plane faces: model structure and algorithms, *Computers & Graphics 13*, 1 (1989), 5–16. [volumes] D.5.3

503. [Nava86b] I. Navazo, D. Ayala, and P. Brunet, A geometric modeller based on the exact octree representation of polyhedra, *Computer Graphics Forum 5*, 2 (June 1986), 91–104. [volumes] D.5.3 A.7.1.6 A.7.2.2 A.7.4

504. [Nava87] I. Navazo, J. Fontdecaba, and P. Brunet, Extended octrees, between CSG trees and boundary representations, *Proceedings of the EUROGRAPHICS'87 Conference*, G. Marechal, ed., North-Holland, Amsterdam, 1987, 239–247. [volumes] D.5.3

505. [Nels86a] R. C. Nelson and H. Samet, A consistent hierarchical representation for vector data, *Computer Graphics 20*, 4(August 1986), 197–206 (also *Proceedings of the SIGGRAPH'86 Conference*, Dallas, August 1986). [lines] D.4.2.3 D.4.2.3.4 D.4.2.3.5 D.5.5.2 A.1.3

506. [Nels86b] R. C. Nelson and H. Samet, A population analysis of quadtrees with variable node size Computer Science TR-1740, University of Maryland, College Park, MD, December 1986. [points] D.2.8.1 D.4.2.3.4 D.5.5.2

507. [Nels87] R. C. Nelson and H. Samet, A population analysis for hierarchical data structures, *Proceedings of the SIGMOD Conference*, San Francisco, May 1987, 270–277. [points] D.2.8.1

508. [Nemo86] K. Nemoto and T. Omachi, An adaptive subdivision by sliding boundary surfaces for fast ray tracing, *Proceedings of Graphics Interface '86*, Vancouver, May 1986, 43–48. [surfaces]

509. [Newe75] M. E. Newell, The utilization of procedure models in digital image synthesis, Computer Science Department UTEC-CSc-76–218, University of Utah, Salt Lake City, Summer 1975. [volumes] A.7.2.2

510. [Niev84] J. Nievergelt, H. Hinterberger, and K. C. Sevcik, The grid file: an adaptable, symmetric multikey file structure, *ACM Transactions on Database Systems 9*, 1(March 1984), 38–71. [points] D.2.1 D.2.8.2.3

511. [Niev82] J. Nievergelt and F. P. Preparata, Plane-sweep algorithms for intersecting geometric figures, *Communications of the ACM 25*, 10(October 1982), 739–746. [general] D.4.3.3

512. [Nils69] N. J. Nilsson, A mobile automaton: an application of artificial intelligence techniques, *Proceedings of the First International Joint Conference on Artificial Intelligence*, Washington, DC, 1969, 509–520. [regions] D.1.3 A.1.4

513. [Nish85] T. Nishita and E. Nakamae, Continuous tone representation of three-dimensional objects taking account of shadows and interreflection, *Computer Graphics 19*, 3(July 1985), 23–30 (also *Proceedings of the SIGGRAPH'85 Conference*, San Francisco, July 1985). [general] A.7.2.1

514. [Nobo88] H. Noborio, S. Fukuda, and S. Arimoto, Construction of the octree approximating three-dimensional objects by using multiple views, *IEEE Transactions on Pattern Analysis and Machine Intelligence 10*, 6(November 1988), 769–782. [volumes] D.5.2 A.4.6

515. [Noro88] V. T. Noronha, A survey of hierarchical partitioning methods for vector images, *Proceedings of the Third International Symposium on Spatial Data Handling*, Sydney, Australia, August 1988, 185–200. [rectangles]

516. [Ohsa83a] Y. Ohsawa and M. Sakauchi, The BD-tree—a new n-dimensional data structure with highly efficient dynamic characteristics, *Information Processing 83*, R. E. A. Mason, ed., North-Holland, Amsterdam, 1983, 539–544. [points] D.2.6.2

517. [Ohsa83b] Y. Ohsawa and M. Sakauchi, Multidimensional data management structure with efficient dynamic characteristics, *Systems, Computers, Controls 14*, 5(1983), 77–87 (translated from *Denshi Tsushin Gakkai Ronbunshi 66–D*, 10(October 1983), 1193–1200. [points] D.2.6.2

518. [Ohya84] T. Ohya, M. Iri, and K. Murota, Improvements of the incremental method for the Voronoi diagram with computational comparison of various algorithms, *Journal of the Operations Research Society of Japan 27*, 4(December 1984), 306–337. [regions]

519. [Okaw88] F. Okawara, K. Shimizu, and Y. Nishitani, Data compression of the region quadtree and algorithms for set operations, Department of Computer Science Report CS-88–6, Gunma University, Gunma, Japan, July 1988 (translated from *Proceedings of the 36th All-Japan Conference on Information Processing*, Information Processing Society of Japan, Tokyo, Japan, March 1988, 73–74). [regions] A.2.1.2

520. [Okin73] N. Okino, Y. Kakazu, and H. Kubo, TIPS-1: Technical information processing system for computer aided design, drawing and manufacturing, in *Computer Languages for Numerical Control*, J. Hatvany, ed., North Holland, Amsterdam, 1973, 141–150. [volumes] D.5.5

521. [Oliv84a] M. A. Oliver, Two display algorithms for octrees, in *Proceedings of the EUROGRAPHICS'84 Conference*, K. Bo and H. A. Tucker, eds., North-Holland, Amsterdam, 1984, 251–264. [volumes]

522. [Oliv86] M. A. Oliver, Display algorithms for quadtrees and octtrees and their hardware realisation *Data Structures for Raster Graphics*, F. J. Peters, L. R. A. Kessener, and M. L. P. van Lierop, eds., Springer Verlag, Berlin, 1986, 9–37. [regions]

523. [Oliv84b] M. A. Oliver, T. R. King, and N. E. Wiseman, Quadtree scan conversion, in *Proceedings of the EUROGRAPHICS'84 Conference*, K. Bo and H. A. Tucker, eds., North-Holland, Amsterdam, 1984, 265–276. [regions] A.4.2.2

524. [Oliv83a] M. A. Oliver and N. E. Wiseman, Operations on quadtree-encoded images, *Computer Journal 26*, 1(February 1983), 83–91. [regions] A.2.1.1 A.2.2

525. [Oliv83b] M. A. Oliver and N. E. Wiseman, Operations on quadtree leaves and related image areas, *Computer Journal 26*, 4(November 1983), 375–380. [regions] A.6.4 A.9.3.4

526. [Olse85] D. R. Olsen, Jr., and C. N. Cooper, Spatial trees: a fast access method for unstructured graphical data, *Proceedings of Graphics Interface '85*, Montreal, May 1985, 69–74. [regions]

527. [Omol80] J. O. Omolayole and A. Klinger, A hierarchical data structure scheme for storing pictures, in *Pictorial Information Systems*, S. K. Chang and K. S. Fu, eds., Springer-Verlag, Berlin, 1980, 1–38 (Lecture Notes in Computer Science 80). [regions] D.4.2.1

528. [Ooi87] B. C. Ooi, K. J. McDonell, and R. Sacks-Davis, Spatial k-d tree: an indexing mechanism for spatial database, *Proceedings of the Eleventh International Computer Software and Applications Conference (COMPSAC)*, Tokyo, October 1987, 433–438. [rectangles] D.2.8.1 D.3.4

529. [Ooi89] B. C. Ooi, R. Sacks-Davis, and K. J. McDonell, Extending a dbms for geographic applications, *Proceedings of the Fifth IEEE International Conference on Data Engineering*, Los Angeles, February 1989, 590–597. [rectangles]

530. [Oren82] J. A. Orenstein, Multidimensional tries used for associative searching, *Information Processing Letters 14*, 4(June 1982), 150–157. [points] D.2.6.2 D.2.7 D.2.8.1 D.2.8.2.4 A.1.3

531. [Oren83] J. A. Orenstein, A dynamic hash file for random and sequential accessing, *Proceedings of the Sixth International Conference on Very Large Data Bases*, Florence, October 1983, 132–141. [points] D.2.7 D.2.8.2.1

532. [Oren86] J. A. Orenstein, Spatial query processing in an object-oriented database system, *Proceedings of the SIGMOD Conference*, Washington, DC, May 1986, 326–336. [points]

533. [Oren84] J. A. Orenstein and T. H. Merrett, A class of data structures for associative searching, *Proceedings of the Third ACM SIGACT-SIGMOD Symposium on Principles of Database Systems*, Waterloo, April 1984, 181–190. [points] D.1.3 D.2.7 D.2.8.2.1 A.1.4

534. [ORou81] J. O'Rourke, Dynamically quantized spaces for focusing the Hough Transform, *Proceedings of the Sixth International Joint Conference on Artificial Intelligence*, Vancouver, August 1981, 737–739. [points] D.2.8.1

535. [ORou88] J. O'Rourke, Computational geometry, in *Annual Reviews in Computer Science 3*, Annual Reviews, Palo Alto, CA, 1988, 389–411. [general] D.P

536. [ORou84] J. O'Rourke and K. R. Sloan Jr., Dynamic quantization: two adaptive data structures for multidimensional squares, *IEEE Transactions on Pattern Analysis and Machine Intelligence 6*, 3(May 1984), 266–280. [points] D.2.8.1

537. [Oska88] D. N. Oskard, T. H. Hong, and C. A. Shaffer, Real-time algorithms and data structures for underwater mapping, *SPIE Symposium on Sensor Fusion: Spatial Reasoning and Scene Interpretation*, Cambridge, MA, November 1988. [regions]

538. [Osse84] W. Osse and N. Ahuja, Efficient octree representation of moving objects, *Proceedings of the Seventh International Conference on Pattern Recognition*, Montreal, August 1984, 821–823. [volumes] A.6.5.3

539. [Ottm80] T. Ottmann and D. Wood, 1–2 brother trees or AVL trees revisited, *Computer Journal 23*, 3(August 1980), 248–255. [general] D.2.7

540. [Ouks85] M. Ouksel, The interpolation-based grid file, *Proceedings of the Fourth ACM SIGACT-SIGMOD Symposium on Principles of Database Systems*, Portland, OR, March 1985, 20–27. [points]

541. [Ouks83] M. Ouksel and P. Scheuermann, Storage mappings for multidimensional linear dynamic hashing, *Proceedings of the Second ACM SIGACT-SIGMOD Symposium on Principles of Database Systems*, Atlanta, March 1983, 90–105. [points] D.2.7 D.2.8.2.1

542. [Oust84] J. K. Ousterhout, Corner-stitching: a data structuring technique for VLSI layout tools, *IEEE Transactions on Computer-Aided Design 3*, 1(January 1984), 87–100. [rectangles] D.3.1 D.3.4

543. [Over83] M. H. Overmars, *The Design of Dynamic Data Structures*, Lecture Notes in Computer Science 156, Springer-Verlag, New York, 1983. [general] D.P D.2.1

544. [Over85] M. H. Overmars, Range searching in a set of line segments, *Proceedings of the Symposium on Computational Geometry*, Baltimore, June 1985, 177–185. [rectangles] D.3.2.4

545. [Over88a] M. H. Overmars, Geometric data structures for computer graphics: an overview, in *Theoretical Foundations of Computer Graphics and CAD*, R. A. Earnshaw, ed., Springer-Verlag, Berlin, 1988, 21–49. [rectangles] D.P D.2.1 D.2.5 D.2.6.2 D.3.2.4

546. [Over82] M. H. Overmars and J. van Leeuwen, Dynamic multi-dimensional data structures based on quad- and k-d trees, *Acta Informatica 17*, 3(1982), 267–285. [points] D.2.3.1 D.2.3.2 D.2.4.1

547. [Over88b] M. H. Overmars and C. K. Yap, New upper bounds in Klee's measure problem, *Proceedings of the Twenty-ninth Annual IEEE Symposium on the Foundations of Computer Science*, White Plains, NY, October 1988, 550–556. [rectangles] D.3.3

548. [Ozka85] E. A. Ozkarahan and M. Ouksel, Dynamic and order preserving data partitioning for database machines, *Proceedings of the Eleventh International Conference on Very Large Data Bases*, Stockholm, August 1985, 358–368. [points]

549. [Pali86] J. Palimaka, O. Halustchak, and W. Walker, Integration of a spatial and relational database within a geographic information system, *Proceedings of the 1986 ACSM-ASPRS Annual Convention*, vol. 3, *Geographic Information Systems*, Washington, DC, March 1986, 131–140. [regions]

550. [Park71] C. M. Park and A. Rosenfeld, Connectivity and genus in three dimensions, Computer Science TR-156, University of Maryland, College Park, MD, May 1971. [volumes] A.5.1 A.5.1.1

551. [Patr68] E. A. Patrick, D. R. Anderson, and F. K. Bechtel, Mapping multidimensional space to one dimension for computer output display, *IEEE Transactions on Computers 17*, 10(October 1968), 949–953. [points] D.1.3 A.1.4

552. [Pean90] G. Peano, Sur une courbe qui remplit toute une aire plaine, *Mathematische Annalen 36*, 1890, 157–160. [regions] D.1.3 D.2.7 A.1.4

553. [Pete85] F. Peters, An algorithm for transformations of pictures represented by quadtrees, *Computer Vision, Graphics, and Image Processing 32*, 3(December 1985), 397–403. [regions] A.6.5.1

554. [Peuc76] T. Peucker, A theory of the cartographic line, *International Yearbook of Cartography 16*, 1976, 134–143. [lines] D.4.1

555. [Peuc75] T. Peucker and N. Chrisman, Cartographic data structures, *American Cartographer 2*, 2(April 1975), 55–69. [general] D.4.4 D.5.6

556. [Peuq79] D. J. Peuquet, Raster processing: an alternative approach to automated cartographic data handling, *American Cartographer 6*, 2(April 1979), 129–139. [regions] D.4.4

557. [Peuq83] D. J. Peuquet, A hybrid data structure for the storage and manipulation of very large spatial data sets, *Computer Vision, Graphics, and Image Processing 24*, 1(October 1983), 14–27. [regions] D.4.4

558. [Peuq84] D. J. Peuquet, A conceptual framework and comparison of spatial data models, *Cartographica 21*, 4(1984), 66–113. [general] D.P D.1.4.1 A.P

559. [Pfal67] J. L. Pfaltz and A. Rosenfeld, Computer representation of planar regions by their skeletons, *Communications of the ACM 10*, 2(February 1967), 119–122. [regions]

560. [Phon75] B. T. Phong, Illumination for computer generated images, *Communications of the ACM 18*, 6(June 1975), 311–317. [general] A.7.1.4 A.7.2.1

561. [Piet82] M. Pietikainen, A. Rosenfeld, and I. Walter, Split-and-link algorithms for image segmentation, *Pattern Recognition 15*, 4(1982), 287–298. [regions] D.1.3 A.1.4

562. [Ponc85] J. Ponce, Prism trees: an efficient representation for manipulating and displaying polyhedra with many faces, Artificial Intelligence Memo 838, Massachusetts Institute of Technology, Cambridge, MA, April 1985. [surfaces] D.4.1

563. [Ponc87a] J. Ponce and D. Chelberg, Localized intersections computation for solid modelling with straight homogeneous generalized cylinders, *Proceedings of the IEEE International Conference on Robotics and Automation*, Raleigh, NC, March 1987, 1481–1486. [volumes]

564. [Ponc87b] J. Ponce and O. Faugeras, An object centered hierarchical representation for 3d objects: the prism tree, *Computer Vision, Graphics, and Image Processing 38*, 1(April 1987), 1–28. [surfaces] D.4.1 D.5.6 D.5.7

565. [Port84] T. Porter and T. Duff, Compositing digital images, *Computer Graphics 18*, 3(July 1984), 253–259 (also *Proceedings of the SIGGRAPH'84 Conference*, Minneapolis, July 1984). [general] A.7.1.1

566. [Posd82] J. L. Posdamer, Spatial sorting for sampled surface geometries, *Proceedings of SPIE—Biostereometrics'82 361*, San Diego, August 1982. [surfaces] D.5.2 A.4.6 A.7.1.6

567. [Potm87] M. Potmesil, Generating octree models of 3d objects from their silhouettes in a sequence of images, *Computer Vision, Graphics, and Image Processing 40*, 1(October 1987), 1–29. [volumes] D.5.2 A.4.6

568. [Prat78] W. K. Pratt, *Digital Image Processing*, Wiley-Interscience, New York, 1978. [general] D.1.2 A.1.3

569. [Prep83] F. P. Preparata, ed., *Advances in Computing Research*, vol. 1, *Computational Geometry*, JAI Press, Greenwich, CT, 1983. [general] D.P

570. [Prep77] F. P. Preparata and S. J. Hong, Convex hulls of finite sets of points in two and three dimensions, *Communications of the ACM 20*, 2(February 1977), 87–93. [regions] A.7.3

571. [Prep85] F. P. Preparata and M. I. Shamos, *Computational Geometry: An Introduction*, Springer-Verlag, New York, 1985. [general] D.P D.3 D.3.2 D.3.4 D.4.3 D.5.6

572. [Prio88] T. Priol and K. Bouatouch, Experimenting with a parallel ray-tracing algorithm on a hypercube machine, INRIA Report No. 843, IRISA, Campus de Beaulieu, Rennes, France. [volumes]

573. [Puec85] C. Puech and H. Yahia, Quadtrees, octrees, hyperoctrees: a unified analytical approach to tree data structures used in graphics, geometric modeling, and image processing, *Proceedings of the Symposium on Computational Geometry*, Baltimore, June 1985, 272–280. [regions] A.3.2.1.2

574. [Pull87] R. Pulleyblank and J. Kapenga, The feasibility of a VLSI chip for ray tracing bicubic patches, *IEEE Computer Graphics and Applications 7*, 3(March 1987), 33–44. [hardware] A.7.2.5

575. [Quar84] P. Quarendon, A general approach to surface modelling applied to molecular graphics, *Journal of Molecular Graphics 2*, 3(September 1984), 91–95. [surfaces]

576. [Quin82] K. M. Quinlan and J. R. Woodwark, A spatially-segmented solids database — justification and design, *Proceedings of CAD'82 Conference*, Butterworth, Guildford, Great Britain, 1982, 126–132. [volumes] D.5.3 A.1.3

577. [Ragh77] V. V. Raghvan and C. T. Yu, A note on a multidimensional searching problem, *Information Processing Letters 6*, 4(August 1977), 133–135. [points]

578. [Rama82] K. Ramamohanarao and J. W. Lloyd, Dynamic hashing schemes, *Computer Journal 25*, 4(November 1982), 478–485. [points] D.2.8.2.1

579. [Rama84] K. Ramamohanarao and R. Sacks-Davis, Recursive linear hashing, *ACM Transactions on Database Systems 9*, 3(September 1984), 369–391. [points] D.2.8.2.1

580. [Rama85] K. Ramamohanarao and R. Sacks-Davis, Partial match retrieval using recursive linear hashing, *BIT 25*, 3(1985), 477–484. [points] D.2.8.2.1

581. [Rama83] V. Raman and S. S. Iyengar, Properties and applications of forests of quadtrees for pictorial data representation, *BIT 23*, 4(1983), 472–486. [regions] A.2.1.4

582. [Rana81a] S. Ranade, Use of quadtrees for edge enhancement, *IEEE Transactions on Systems, Man, and Cybernetics 11*, 5(May 1981), 370–373. [regions]

583. [Rana80] S. Ranade, A. Rosenfeld, and J. M. S. Prewitt, Use of quadtrees for image segmentation, Computer Science TR-878, University of Maryland, College Park, MD, February 1980. [regions]

584. [Rana82] S. Ranade, A. Rosenfeld, and H. Samet, Shape approximation using quadtrees, *Pattern Recognition 15*, 1(1982), 31–40. [regions] A.8.1 A.8.2.1

585. [Rana81b] S. Ranade and M. Shneier, Using quadtrees to smooth images, *IEEE Transactions on Systems, Man, and Cybernetics 11*, 5(May 1981), 373–376. [regions]

586. [Rats84] H. Ratschek and J. Rokne, *Computer Methods for the Range of Functions*, Ellis Horwood, Chichester, 1984. [general] D.5.5.1.3

587. [Ravi87] S. Ravindran and M. Manohar, An algorithm for converting a forest of quadtrees to a binary array, *Image and Vision Computing 5*, 4(November 1987), 297–300. [regions]

588. [Redd78] D. R. Reddy and S. Rubin, Representation of three-dimensional objects, CMU-CS-78-113, Computer Science Department, Carnegie-Mellon University, Pittsburgh, April 1978. [volumes] D.1.3 A.1.4

589. [Regn85] M. Regnier, Analysis of grid file algorithms, *BIT 25*, 2(1985), 335–357. [points] D.2.8.1 D.2.8.2.3 D.3.4

590. [Rein77] E. M. Reingold, J. Nievergelt, and N. Deo, *Combinatorial Algorithms: Theory and Practice*, Prentice-Hall, Englewood Cliffs, NJ, 1977. [general] D.2.7

591. [Rein81] E. M. Reingold and R. E. Tarjan, On the greedy heuristic for complete matching, *SIAM Journal on Computing 10*, 4(November 1981), 676–681. [points] D.2.9

592. [Reis76] J. F. Reiser (ed.), SAIL, Stanford Artificial Intelligence Laboratory Memo AIM-289, Stanford University, Stanford, CA, August 1976. [general] D.P A.P L

593. [Requ80] A. A. G. Requicha, Representations of rigid solids: theory, methods, and systems, *ACM Computing Surveys 12*, 4(December 1980), 437–464. [volumes] D.P D.3.4 D.5.1 D.5.5 D.5.5.1 A.P A.7.1.4

594. [Requ82] A. A. G. Requicha and H. B. Voelcker, Solid modeling: a historical summary and contemporary assessment, *IEEE Computer Graphics and Applications 2*, 2(March 1982), 9–24. [volumes] D.5.5

595. [Requ83] A. A. G. Requicha and H. B. Voelcker, Solid modeling: current status and research directions, *IEEE Computer Graphics and Applications 3*, 7(October 1983), 25–37. [volumes] D.5.5

596. [Rhei80] W. C. Rheinboldt and C. K. Mesztenyi, On a data structure for adaptive finite element mesh refinements, *ACM Transactions on Mathematical Software 6*, 2(June 1980), 166–187. [finite element] D.1.3 A.1.4

597. [Rise77] E. M. Riseman and M. A. Arbib, Computational techniques in the visual segmentation of static scenes, *Computer Graphics and Image Processing 6*, 3(June 1977), 221–276. [regions] D.1.3 A.1.4

598. [Robi81] J. T. Robinson, The k-d-B-tree: a search structure for large multidimensional dynamic indexes, *Proceedings of the SIGMOD Conference*, Ann Arbor, MI, April 1981, 10–18. [points] D.2.7 D.2.8.1 D.3.5.3

599. [Roge85] D. F. Rogers, *Procedural Elements for Computer Graphics*, McGraw-Hill, New York, 1985. [general] D.4.2.3.1 D.5.2 D.5.6 A.1.3 A.4.5 A.4.6 A.5.1.1 A.6 A.6.4 A.7.1.2 A.7.1.4 A.7.2.3 A.7.2.4

600. [Rons88] C. Ronse, Codage en liste d'arbres quaternaires, *Technique et Science Informatiques 7*, 2(1988), 235–245. [regions]

601. [Rose85] J. B. Rosenberg, Geographical data structures compared: a study of data structures supporting region queries, *IEEE Transactions on Computer-Aided Design 4*, 1(January 1985), 53–67. [rectangles] D.3.4

602. [Rose74] A. Rosenfeld, Digital straight line segments, *IEEE Transactions on Computers 23*, 12(December 1974), 1264–1269. [lines]

603. [Rose83a] A. Rosenfeld, ed., *Multiresolution Image Processing and Analysis*, Springer-Verlag, Berlin, 1983. [general] D.P A.P A.4.2.3

604. [Rose88] A. Rosenfeld, Image analysis and computer vision: 1987, *Computer Vision, Graphics, and Image Processing 42*, 2(May 1988), 234–293. [general] D.P A.P

605. [Rose82a] A. Rosenfeld and A. C. Kak, *Digital Picture Processing*, Second Edition, Academic Press, New York, 1982. [general] D.P D.3.2.1 A.P A.5.2 A.7.4 A.8.1 A.9.1 A.9.3.4

606. [Rose66] A. Rosenfeld and J. L. Pfaltz, Sequential operations in digital image processing, *Journal of the ACM 13*, 4(October 1966), 471–494. [regions] D.1.2 A.1.3 A.5.1 A.5.1.1 A.5.1.2 A.9

607. [Rose82b] A. Rosenfeld, H. Samet, C. Shaffer, and R. E. Webber, Application of hierarchical data structures to geographical information systems, Computer Science TR-1197, University of Maryland, College Park, MD, June 1982. [general] D.1.5 A.1.2 A.3.2.3 A.6.4 A.6.5.2

608. [Rose83b] A. Rosenfeld, H. Samet, C. Shaffer, and R. E. Webber, Application of hierarchical data structures to geographical information systems: phase II, Computer Science TR-1327, University of Maryland, College Park, MD, September 1983. [general] D.2.6.2 A.2.1 A.2.1.1

609. [Ross86] J. R. Rossignac and A. A. G. Requicha, Depth-buffering display techniques for constructive solid geometry, *IEEE Computer Graphics and Applications 6*, 9(September 1986), 29–39. [volumes] D.5.5

610. [Roth82] S. D. Roth, Ray casting for modeling solids, *Computer Graphics and Image Processing 18*, 2(February 1982), 109–144. [volumes] D.5.2 D.5.5 A.4.6 A.7.2.2 A.7.2.5

611. [Rous85] N. Roussopoulos and D. Leifker, Direct spatial search on pictorial databases using packed R-trees, *Proceedings of the SIGMOD Conference*, Austin, TX, May 1985, 17–31. [points] D.2.8.1 D.3.5.3

612. [Rubi80] S. M. Rubin and T. Whitted, A 3-dimensional representation for fast rendering of complex scenes, *Computer Graphics 14*, 3(July 1980), 110–116 (also *Proceedings of the SIGGRAPH'80 Conference*, Seattle, July 1980). [volumes] A.7.2.2

613. [Ruff84] R. Ruff and N. Ahuja, Path planning in a three-dimensional environment, *Proceedings of the Seventh International Conference on Pattern Recognition*, Montreal, August 1984, 188–191. [volumes]

614. [Ruto68] D. Rutovitz, Data structures for operations on digital images, in *Pictorial Pattern Recognition*, G. C. Cheng et al., eds., Thompson Book Co., Washington, DC, 1968, 105–133. [regions] D.1.2 A.1.3 A.2.1.3 A.4.2 A.9

615. [Saal87] A. Saalfeld, Triangulated data structures for map merging and other applications in geographic information systems, *Proceedings of the International Symposium on Geographic Information Systems*, vol. 3, Arlington, VA, November 1987, 3–13. [regions] D.4.3.1 D.5.2 A.4.6

616. [Saka84] M. Sakauchi and Y. Ohsawa, General framework for n-dimensional pattern data management, in *Proceedings of the International Symposium on Image Processing and its Applications*, M. Onoe, ed., Institute of Industrial Science, University of Tokyo, 1984, 306–316. [points]

617. [Salz86] B. Salzberg, Grid file concurrency, *Information Systems 11*, 3(1986), 235–244. [points]

618. [Salz88] B. Salzberg, *File Structures: An Analytic Approach*, Prentice-Hall, Englewood Cliffs, NJ, 1988. [general] D.2.6.2

619. [Same77] H. Samet, Deletion in k-dimensional quadtrees, unpublished manuscript, 1977. [points] D.2.3.2

620. [Same80a] H. Samet, Region representation: quadtrees from boundary codes, *Communications of the ACM 23*, 3(March 1980), 163–170. [regions] A.4.3.1

621. [Same80b] H. Samet, Region representation: quadtrees from binary arrays, *Computer Graphics and Image Processing 13*, 1(May 1980), 88–93. [regions] D.1.2 A.4.1

622. [Same80c] H. Samet, Deletion in two-dimensional quad trees, *Communications of the ACM 23*, 12(December 1980), 703–710. [points] D.2.3.2 A.7.1.5

623. [Same81a] H. Samet, An algorithm for converting rasters to quadtrees, *IEEE Transactions on Pattern Analysis and Machine Intelligence 3*, 1(January 1981), 93–95. [regions] D.1.2 A.4.2.1

624. [Same81b] H. Samet, Connected component labeling using quadtrees, *Journal of the ACM 28*, 3(July 1981), 487–501. [regions] A.5.1.2 A.5.1.3 A.9.2

625. [Same81c] H. Samet, Computing perimeters of images represented by quadtrees, *IEEE Transactions on Pattern Analysis and Machine Intelligence 3*, 6(November 1981), 683–687. [regions] A.5.2 A.9.2 A.9.3.3

626. [Same82a] H. Samet, Neighbor finding techniques for images represented by quadtrees, *Computer Graphics and Image Processing 18*, 1(January 1982), 37–57. [regions] A.3.2.1.1 A.3.2.1.2 A.3.2.3 A.5.1.2

627. [Same82b] H. Samet, Distance transform for images represented by quadtrees, *IEEE Transactions on Pattern Analysis and Machine Intelligence 4*, 3(May 1982), 298–303 (also University of Maryland Computer Science TR-780). [regions] A.9.2

628. [Same83a] H. Samet, A quadtree medial axis transform, *Communications of the ACM 26*, 9(September 1983), 680–693 (also corrigendum, *Communications of the ACM 27*, 2(February 1984), 151). [regions] A.8 A.9.3

629. [Same84a] H. Samet, Algorithms for the conversion of quadtrees to rasters, *Computer Vision, Graphics, and Image Processing 26*, 1(April 1984), 1–16. [regions] A.4.2.2

630. [Same84b] H. Samet, The quadtree and related hierarchical data structures, *ACM Computing Surveys 16*, 2(June 1984), 187–260. [general] D.P A.P

631. [Same85a] H. Samet, A top-down quadtree traversal algorithm, *IEEE Transactions on Pattern Analysis and Machine Intelligence 7*, 1(January 1985), 94–98. [regions] A.3.2.3 A.4.3.1 A.5.1.2 A.5.1.3 A.5.2 A.9.2

632. [Same85b] H. Samet, Reconstruction of quadtrees from quadtree medial axis transforms, *Computer Vision, Graphics, and Image Processing 29*, 3(March 1985), 311–328. [regions] A.9.3.3

633. [Same85c] H. Samet, Data structures for quadtree approximation and compression, *Communications of the ACM 28*, 9(September 1985), 973–993. [regions] A.8 A.8.2.2

634. [Same88a] H. Samet, Hierarchical representations of collections of small rectangles, *ACM Computing Surveys 20*, 4(December 1988), 271–309. [rectangles] D.P D.3.5.1.3

635. [Same90a] H. Samet, *The Design and Analysis of Spatial Data Structures*, Addison-Wesley, Reading, MA, 1990. [general] A.P A.1

636. [Same90b] H. Samet, *Applications of Spatial Data Structures: Computer Graphics, Image Processing, and GIS*, Addison-Wesley, Reading, MA, 1990. [general] D.P

637. [Same89a] H. Samet, Neighbor finding in images represented by octrees, *Computer Vision, Graphics, and Image Processing 46*, 3(June 1989), 367–386. [volumes] A.3.3 A.3.4

638. [Same89b] H. Samet, Implementing ray tracing with octrees and neighbor finding, Computer Science TR-2204, University of Maryland, College Park, MD, February 1989. [volumes] A.7.2

639. [Same80d] H. Samet and A. Rosenfeld, Quadtree structures for image processing, *Proceedings of the Fifth International Conference on Pattern Recognition*, Miami Beach, December 1980, 815–818. [regions] D.P A.P

640. [Same84c] H. Samet, A. Rosenfeld, C. A. Shaffer, R. C. Nelson, and Y. G. Huang, Application of hierarchical data structures to geographical information systems: phase III, Computer Science TR-1457, University of Maryland, College Park, MD, November 1984. [general] D.1.5 D.4.2.4 A.1.2 A.6.6

641. [Same85d] H. Samet, A. Rosenfeld, C. A. Shaffer, R. C. Nelson, Y. G. Huang, and K. Fujimura, Application of hierarchical data structures to geographic information systems: phase IV, Computer Science TR-1578, University of Maryland, College Park, MD, December 1985. [general] A.4.2.3 A.6.3.3 A.6.5.3

642. [Same83b] H. Samet, A. Rosenfeld, C. A. Shaffer, and R. E. Webber, Quadtree region representation in cartography: experimental results, *IEEE Transactions on Systems, Man, and Cybernetics 13*, 6(November/December 1983), 1148–1154. [general]

643. [Same84d] H. Samet, A. Rosenfeld, C. A. Shaffer, and R. E. Webber, A geographic information system using quadtrees, *Pattern Recognition 17*, 6(November/December 1984), 647–656. [general] D.4.2.4 A.2.1.2 A.3.4.1 A.8.2.1

644. [Same85e] H. Samet and C. A. Shaffer, A model for the analysis of neighbor finding in pointer-based quadtrees, *IEEE Transactions on Pattern Analysis and Machine Intelligence 7*, 6(November 1985), 717–720. [regions] A.3.2.1.2

645. [Same87a] H. Samet, C. A. Shaffer, R. C. Nelson, Y. G. Huang, K. Fujimura, and A. Rosenfeld, Recent developments in linear quadtree-based geographic information systems, *Image and Vision Computing 5*, 3(August 1987), 187–197. [general] D.1.2 D.4.2.4 A.1.3 A.2.1.2 A.3.2.1.3 A.3.4.1 A.8.2.1

646. [Same86a] H. Samet, C. A. Shaffer, and R. E. Webber, The segment quadtree: a linear quadtree-based representation for linear features, in *Data Structures for Raster Graphics*, F. J. Peters, L. R. A. Kessener, and M. L. P. van Lierop, eds., Springer Verlag, Berlin, 1986, 91–123 (also *Proceedings of Computer Vision and Pattern Recognition 85*, San Francisco, June 1985, 385–389). [lines]

647. [Same86b] H. Samet, C. A. Shaffer, and R. E. Webber, Digitizing the plane with cells of non-uniform size, Computer Science TR-1619, University of Maryland, College Park, MD, January 1986. [lines] D.4.2.3.1 A.1.3

648. [Same87b] H. Samet, C. A. Shaffer, and R. E. Webber, Digitizing the plane with cells of non-uniform size, *Information Processing Letters 24*, 6(April 1987), 369–375. [lines] D.4.2.3.1 A.1.3

649. [Same84e] H. Samet and M. Tamminen, Experiences with new image component algorithms, *Proceedings of the EUROGRAPHICS'84 Conference*, K. Bo and H. A. Tucker, eds., North-Holland, Copenhagen, 1984, 239–249. [volumes]

650. [Same85f] H. Samet and M. Tamminen, Computing geometric properties of images represented by linear quadtrees, *IEEE Transactions on Pattern Analysis and Machine Intelligence 7*, 2(March 1985), 229–240 (also University of Maryland Computer Science TR-1359). [regions] D.3.5.1.3 A.3.4.4 A.5.1.3 A.5.3 A.6.3.3

651. [Same85g] H. Samet and M. Tamminen, Bintrees, CSG trees, and time, *Computer Graphics 19*, 3(July 1985), 121–130 (also *Proceedings of the SIGGRAPH'85 Conference*, San Francisco, July 1985). [volumes] D.1.3 D.5.3 D.5.5 D.5.5.1.3 A.1.4 A.7.2.4

652. [Same85h] H. Samet and M. Tamminen, Approximating CSG trees of moving objects, Computer Science TR-1472, University of Maryland, College Park, MD, January 1985. [volumes] D.5.3 D.5.5 D.5.5.1.2 D.5.5.1.3

653. [Same86c] H. Samet and M. Tamminen, A general approach to connected component labeling of images, Computer Science TR-1649, University of Maryland, College Park, MD, August 1986 (also *Proceedings of Computer Vision and Pattern Recognition 86*, Miami Beach, June 1986, 312–318). [regions] A.5.1.1 A.5.1.3

654. [Same88b] H. Samet and M. Tamminen, Efficient component labeling of images of arbitrary dimension represented by linear bintrees, *IEEE Transactions on Pattern Analysis and Machine Intelligence 10*, 4(July 1988), 579–586. [volumes] D.1.4.1 D.3.5.1.3 D.5.2 A.1.3 A.3.4.4 A.4.2.3 A.4.6 A.5.1.2 A.5.1.3 A.6.3.3 A.9.2

655. [Same82c] H. Samet and R. E. Webber, On encoding boundaries with quadtrees, Computer Science TR-1162, University of Maryland, College Park, MD, February 1982. [lines] D.4.2.2 A.3.2.3

656. [Same84f] H. Samet and R. E. Webber, On encoding boundaries with quadtrees, *IEEE Transactions on Pattern Analysis and Machine Intelligence 6*, 3(May 1984), 365–369. [lines] D.4.2.2

657. [Same85i] H. Samet and R. E. Webber, Storing a collection of polygons using quadtrees, *ACM Transactions on Graphics 4*, 3(July 1985), 182–222 (also *Proceedings of Computer Vision and Pattern Recognition 83*, Washington, DC, June 1983, 127–132; and University of Maryland Computer Science TR-1372). [lines] D.4.2.3 D.4.3.3 A.1.3 A.7.2.2

658. [Same88c] H. Samet and R. E. Webber, Hierarchical data structures and algorithms for computer graphics. Part I. Fundamentals, *IEEE Computer Graphics and Applications 8*, 3(May 1988), 48–68. [general] D.P A.P A.6.3.3

659. [Same88d] H. Samet and R. E. Webber, Hierarchical data structures and algorithms for computer graphics. Part II. Applications, *IEEE Computer Graphics and Applications 8*, 4(July 1988), 59–75. [general] D.P A.P

660. [Same89c] H. Samet and R. E. Webber, A comparison of the space requirements of multi-dimensional quadtree-based file structures, *Visual Computer*, 1989 (also University of Maryland Computer Science TR-1711). [regions] A.2.1.2

661. [Sand86] J. Sandor, Octree data structures and perspective imagery, *Computers & Graphics 9*, 4(1985), 351–363. [volumes]

662. [Sarn86] N. Sarnak and R. E. Tarjan, Planar point location using persistent search trees, *Communications of the ACM 29*, 7(July 1986), 669–679. [regions] D.3.2.4

663. [Saxe79] J. B. Saxe, On the number of range queries in k-space, *Discrete Applied Math 1*, 3(November 1979), 217–225. [points]

664. [Sche87] I. D. Scherson and E. Caspary, Data structures and the time complexity of ray tracing, *Visual Computer 3*, 4(December 1987), 201–213. [volumes] A.7.2.5

665. [Sche88] I. D. Scherson and E. Caspary, Multiprocessing for ray tracing: a hierarchical self-balancing approach, *Visual Computer 4*, 4(October 1988), 188–196. [volumes]

666. [Sche82] P. Scheuermann and M. Ouksel, Multidimensional B-trees for associative searching in database systems, *Information Systems 7*, 2(1982), 123–137. [points] D.2.8.2.3

667. [Schm86] F. J. M. Schmitt, B. A. Barsky, and W. H. Du, An adaptive subdivision method for surface-fitting from sampled data, *Computer Graphics 20*, 4(August 1986), 179–188 (also *Proceedings of the SIGGRAPH'86 Conference*, Dallas, August 1986). [surfaces] D.5.6

668. [Schm85] F. Schmitt and B. Gholzadeh, Adaptive polyhedral approximation of digitized surfaces, *Proceedings of SPIE—Computer Vision for Robots 595*, Cannes, France, December 1985, 101–108. [surfaces]

669. [Schw86] J. T. Schwartz and M. Sharir, Motion planning and related geometric algorithms in robotics, Courant Institute of Mathematical Sciences Report TR-241, New York University, New York, August 1986. [regions] D.1.3 A.1.4

670. [Schw85] J. T. Schwartz, M. Sharir, and A. Siegel, An efficient algorithm for finding connected components in a binary image, Robotics Research Technical Report No. 38, New York University, New York, February 1985 (Revised July 1985). [regions] A.5.1.1

671. [Scot85] D. S. Scott and S. S. Iyengar, A new data structure for efficient storing of images, *Pattern Recognition Letters 3*, 3(May 1985), 211–214. [regions] D.1.2 A.1.3 A.9.3.4

672. [Scot86] D. S. Scott and S. S. Iyengar, TID — a translation invariant data structure for storing images, *Communications of the ACM 29*, 5(May 1985), 418–429. [regions] D.1.2 A.1.3 A.9.3.4

673. [Sedg83] R. Sedgewick, *Algorithms*, Addison-Wesley, Reading, MA, 1983. [general] A.5.1.1

674. [Seeg88] B. Seeger and H. P. Kriegel, Techniques for design and implementation of efficient spatial access methods, *Proceedings of the Fourteenth International Conference on Very Large Data Bases*, F. Bachillon and D. J. DeWitt, eds., Los Angeles, August 1988, 360–372. [points]

675. [Sell87] T. Sellis, N. Roussopoulos, and C. Faloutsos, The R^+-tree: a dynamic index for multi-dimensional objects, Computer Science TR-1795, University of Maryland, College Park, MD, February 1987. [rectangles] D.3.5.3

676. [Shaf85] C. A. Shaffer, personal communication, 1985. [regions] A.5.2

677. [Shaf86a] C. A. Shaffer, Application of alternative quadtree representations, Ph.D. dissertation, TR-1672, Computer Science Department, University of Maryland, College Park, MD, June 1986. [regions] D.1.2 D.3.5.2 D.5.2 A.4.2.3 A.6.3.3 A.8.2.3 A.9.3.1 A.9.3.4

678. [Shaf86b] C. A. Shaffer, An empirical comparison of vectors, arrays, and quadtrees for representing geographic data, *Proceedings of the International Colloquium on the Construction and Display of Geoscientific Maps Derived from Databases*, Dinkelsbühl, West Germany, December 1986, 99–115. [general]

679. [Shaf88a] C. A. Shaffer, A formula for computing the number of quadtree node fragments created by a shift, *Pattern Recognition Letters 7*, 1(January 1988), 45–49. [regions] A.6.5.3

680. [Shaf87a] C. A. Shaffer and H. Samet, Optimal quadtree construction algorithms, *Computer Vision, Graphics, and Image Processing 37*, 3(March 1987), 402–419. [regions] D.1.2 D.5.2 A.4.2.3 A.6.3.3

681. [Shaf87b] C. A. Shaffer and H. Samet, An in-core hierarchical data structure organization for a geographic database, Computer Science TR 1886, University of Maryland, College Park, MD, July 1987. [regions] A.2.2

682. [Shaf87c] C. A. Shaffer, H. Samet, and R. C. Nelson, QUILT: a geographic information system based on quadtrees, Computer Science TR-1885.1, University of Maryland, College Park, MD, July 1987. [general] D.4.2.4 A.2.1.2 A.3.4.1 A.6.6 A.8.2.1

683. [Shaf88b] C. A. Shaffer and H. Samet, An algorithm to expand regions represented by linear quadtrees, *Image and Vision Computing 6*, 3(August 1988), 162–168. [regions] A.6.6

684. [Shaf88c] C. A. Shaffer and H. Samet, Set operations for unaligned linear quadtrees, Department of Computer Science TR 88–31, Virginia Polytechnic Institute and State University, Blacksburg, VA, September 1988 (also *Computer Vision, Graphics, and Image Processing*). [regions] A.6.3.3 A.6.5.3

685. [Shaf89] C. A. Shaffer and Q. F. Stout, Linear time distance transforms for quadtrees, Department of Computer Science TR 89–7, Virginia Polytechnic Institute and State University, Blacksburg, VA, 1989. [regions] A.9.2

686. [Sham78] M. I. Shamos, Computational geometry, Ph.D. dissertation, Department of Computer Science, Yale University, New Haven, CT, 1978. [general] D.4.3

687. [Sham75] M. I. Shamos and D. Hoey, Closest-point problems, *Proceedings of the Sixteenth Annual IEEE Symposium on the Foundations of Computer Science*, Berkeley, October 1975, 151–162. [points] D.4.3 A.6.3.2

688. [Sham76] M. I. Shamos and D. Hoey, Geometric intersection problems, *Proceedings of the Seventeenth Annual IEEE Symposium on the Foundations of Computer Science*, Houston, October 1976, 208–215. [points] D.3 D.3.2.4

689. [Shan87] M. A. Shand, Algorithms for corner stitched data-structures, *Algorithmica 2*, 1(1987), 61–80. [rectangles] D.3.4

690. [Shne81a] M. Shneier, Path-length distances for quadtrees, *Information Sciences 23*, 1(February 1981), 49–67. [regions] D.3.5.1.3 A.9.2

691. [Shne81b] M. Shneier, Calculations of geometric properties using quadtrees, *Computer Graphics and Image Processing 16*, 3(July 1981), 296–302. [regions] A.5.2 A.6.3.2

692. [Shne81c] M. Shneier, Two hierarchical linear feature representations: edge pyramids and edge quadtrees, *Computer Graphics and Image Processing 17*, 3(November 1981), 211–224. [lines] D.1.3 D.4.2.1 A.1.4 A.7.1.2

693. [Shne87] M. O. Shneier, R. Lumia, and M. Herman, Prediction-based vision for robot control, *Computer 20*, 8(August 1987), 46–55. [volumes]

694. [Shpi87] M. Shpitalni, Relations and transformations between quadtree encoding and switching function representation, *Computer-Aided Design 19*, 5(June 1987), 266–272. [regions]

695. [Silv81a] C. Silva, Alternative definitions of faces in boundary representation of solid objects, Technical Memorandum 36, Production Automation Project, University of Rochester, N.Y., 1981. [volumes] D.5.4

696. [Silv79] Y. V. Silva Filho, Average case analysis of region search in balanced k-d trees, *Information Processing Letters 8*, 5(June 1979), 219–223. [points]

697. [Silv81b] Y. V. Silva Filho, Optimal choice of discriminators in a balanced k-d binary search tree, *Information Processing Letters 13*, 2(November 1981), 67–70. [points]

698. [Six88] H. W. Six and P. Widmayer, Spatial searching in geometric databases, *Proceedings of the Fourth IEEE International Conference on Data Engineering*, Los Angeles, February 1988, 496–503. [rectangles]

699. [Six80] H. W. Six and D. Wood, The rectangle intersection problem revisited, *BIT 20*, 4(1980), 426–433. [rectangles] D.3.2.1

700. [Six82] H. W. Six and D. Wood, Counting and reporting intersections of *d*-ranges, *IEEE Transactions on Computers 31*, 3(March 1982), 181–187. [rectangles] D.3.2.1

701. [Sloa81] K. R. Sloan Jr., Dynamically quantized pyramids, *Proceedings of the Sixth International Joint Conference on Artificial Intelligence*, Vancouver, August 1981, 734–736. [points] D.2.8.1

702. [Sloa79] K. R. Sloan Jr. and S. L. Tanimoto, Progressive refinement of raster images, *IEEE Transactions on Computers 28*, 11(November 1979), 871–874. [regions] A.8.3

703. [Smit87] T. Smith, D. Peuquet, S. Menon, and P. Agarwal, A knowledge-based geographical information system, *International Journal of Geographical Information Systems 1*, 2(April-June 1987), 149–172. [regions]

704. [Snyd87] J. M. Snyder and A. H. Barr, Ray tracing complex models containing surface tessellations, *Computer Graphics 21*, 4(July 1987), 119–128 (also *Proceedings of the SIGGRAPH'87 Conference*, Anaheim, July 1987). [volumes]

705. [Sobh86] C. Sobhanpanah and I. O. Angell, Polygonal mesh and quad-tree display algorithms for nonconvex crystal structures, *Computers & Graphics 10*, 4(1986), 341–349. [regions]

706. [Soln77] N. Solntseff and D. Wood, Pyramids: A data type for matrix representation in PASCAL, *BIT 17*, 3(1977), 344–350. [matrices]

707. [Somm29] D. M. Y. Sommerville, *An Introduction to the Geometry of N Dimensions*, Methuen, London, 1929. [general]

708. [Soto78] D. L. G. Sotomayor, Tessellation of triangles of variable precision as an economical representation for DTM's, *Proceedings of the Digital Terrain Models (DTM) Symposium*, St. Louis, May 1978, 506–515. [surfaces] D.5.6

709. [Spee85] L. R. Speer, T. D. DeRose, and B. A. Barsky, A theoretical and empirical analysis of coherent ray tracing, in *Computer-Generated Images—The State of the Art*, N. Magnenat-Thalmann and D. Thalmann, eds., Springer-Verlag, Tokyo, 1985, 11–25 (also *Proceedings of Graphics Interface '85*, Montreal, May 1985, 1–8). [volumes] A.7.3

710. [Sper85] G. Sperling, M. Landy, Y. Cohen, and M. Pavel, Intelligible encoding of ASL image sequences at extremely low information rates, *Computer Vision, Graphics, and Image Processing 31*, 3(September 1985), 335–391. [regions]

711. [Srih81] S. N. Srihari, Representation of three-dimensional digital images, *ACM Computing Surveys 13*, 1(December 1981), 399–424. [volumes] D.P A.P

712. [Sriv87] S. K. Srivastava and N. Ahuja, An algorithm for generating octrees from object silhouettes in perspective views, *Proceedings of the IEEE Computer Society Workshop on Computer Vision*, Miami Beach, November 1987, 363–365. [volumes] D.5.2 A.4.6

713. [Sten86] J. R. Stenstrom and C. I. Connolly, Building wire frames from multiple range views, *Proceedings of the IEEE International Conference on Robotics and Automation*, San Francisco, April 1986, 615–620. [volumes]

714. [Ston86] M. Stonebraker, T. Sellis, and E. Hanson, An analysis of rule indexing implementations in data base systems, *Proceedings of the First International Conference on Expert Database Systems*, Charleston, SC, April 1986, 353–364. [rectangles] D.3.5.3

715. [Stra69] V. Strassen, Gaussian elimination is not optimal, *Numerische Mathematik 13*, 4(August 1969), 354–356. [matrices] D.2.6.1

716. [Suth74] I. E. Sutherland, R. F. Sproull, and R. A. Schumacker, A characterization of ten hidden-surface algorithms, *ACM Computing Surveys 6*, 1(March 1974), 1–55. [surfaces] D.1.2 D.2.1 A.1.2 A.7 A.7.1

717. [Tamm81a] M. Tamminen, The EXCELL method for efficient geometric access to data, *Acta Polytechnica Scandinavica*, Mathematics and Computer Science Series No. 34, Helsinki, Finland, 1981. [regions] D.2.8.2.3 D.2.8.2.4 D.4.2.3.4 D.5.3 A.1.3

718. [Tamm81b] M. Tamminen, Order preserving extendible hashing and bucket tries, *BIT 21*, 4(1981), 419–435. [points] D.2.7

719. [Tamm82a] M. Tamminen, The extendible cell method for closest point problems, *BIT 22*, 1(1982), 27–41. [points]

720. [Tamm82b] M. Tamminen, Efficient spatial access to a data base, *Proceedings of the SIGMOD Conference*, Orlando, June 1982, 47–57. [lines] D.5.3

721. [Tamm82c] M. Tamminen and R. Sulonen, The EXCELL method for efficient geometric access to data, *Proceedings of the Nineteenth Design Automation Conference*, Las Vegas, June 1982, 345–351. [general]

722. [Tamm82d] M. Tamminen, Hidden lines using the EXCELL method, *Computer Graphics Forum 1*, 3(September 1982), 96–105. [lines]

723. [Tamm83] M. Tamminen, Performance analysis of cell based geometric file organizations, *Computer Vision, Graphics, and Image Processing 24*, 2(November 1983), 168–181. [regions] D.2.8.1

724. [Tamm84a] M. Tamminen, Comment on quad- and octtrees, *Communications of the ACM 27*, 3(March 1984), 248–249. [regions] D.1.4.1 A.1.3 A.2.1.2

725. [Tamm84b] M. Tamminen, Efficient geometric access to a multirepresentation geodatabase, *Geo-Processing 2*, 1984, 177–196. [lines] D.2.8.2.1

726. [Tamm84c] M. Tamminen, Encoding pixel trees, *Computer Vision, Graphics, and Image Processing 28*, 1(October 1984), 44–57. [regions] D.5.4 A.2.2

727. [Tamm84d] M. Tamminen, Metric data structures — an overview, Report-HTKK-TKO-A25, Helsinki University of Technology, Espoo, Finland, 1984. [points]

728. [Tamm85a] M. Tamminen, On search by address computation, *BIT 25*, 1(1985), 135–147. [points] D.2.6.2

729. [Tamm85b] M. Tamminen and F. W. Jansen, An integrity filter for recursive subdivision meshes, *Computers & Graphics 9*, 4(1985), 351–363. [surfaces] A.7.1.6

730. [Tamm84e] M. Tamminen, O. Karonen, and M. Mäntylä, Ray-casting and block model conversion using a spatial index, *Computer-Aided Design 16*, 4(July 1984), 203–208. [volumes] A.7.2.2 A.7.2.3

731. [Tamm84f] M. Tamminen, P. Koistinen, J. Hamalainen, O. Karonen, P. Korhonen, R. Raunio, and P. Rekola, Bintree: a dimension independent image processing system, Report-HTKK-TKO-C9, Helsinki University of Technology, Espoo, Finland, 1984. [volumes] D.5.5.1.1

732. [Tamm84g] M. Tamminen and H. Samet, Efficient octree conversion by connectivity labeling, *Computer Graphics 18*, 3(July 1984), 43–51 (also *Proceedings of the SIG-GRAPH'84 Conference*, Minneapolis, July 1984). [volumes] D.5.4

733. [Tang88] Z. Tang and S. Lu, A new algorithm for converting boundary representation to octree, in *Proceedings of the EUROGRAPHICS'88 Conference*, D. Duce, ed., North-Holland, Amsterdam, 1988, 105–116. [volumes]

734. [Tani76] S. Tanimoto, Pictorial feature distortion in a pyramid, *Computer Graphics and Image Processing 5*, 3(September 1976), 333–352. [regions] D.1.3 A.1.4

735. [Tani80] S. Tanimoto and A. Klinger (eds.), *Structured Computer Vision*, Academic Press, New York, 1980. [general] D.P A.P

736. [Tani75] S. Tanimoto and T. Pavlidis, A hierarchical data structure for picture processing, *Computer Graphics and Image Processing 4*, 2(June 1975), 104–119. [regions] D.1.3 D.2.8.1 A.1.4 A.8.3

737. [Tani79] S. L. Tanimoto, Image transmission with gross information first, *Computer Graphics and Image Processing 9*, 1(January 1979), 72–76. [regions] A.8.3

738. [Tarj75] R. E. Tarjan, Efficiency of a good but not linear set union algorithm, *Journal of the ACM 22*, 2(April 1975), 215–225. [general] A.5.1.1

739. [Tarj83] R. E. Tarjan, Updating a balanced search tree in $O(1)$ rotations, *Information Processing Letters 16*, 5(June 1983), 253–257. [general] D.3.2.3

740. [Tarj84a] R. E. Tarjan, *Data Structures and Network Algorithms*, SIAM, Philadelphia, 1984. [general] D.2.9

741. [Tarj84b] R. E. Tarjan and J. van Leeuwen, Worst-case analysis of set union algorithms, *Journal of the ACM 31*, 2(April 1984), 245–281. [general] A.5.1.1

742. [Thib87] W. C. Thibault and B. F. Naylor, Set operations on polyhedra using binary space partitioning trees, *Computer Graphics 21*, 4(July 1987), 153–162 (also *Proceedings of the SIGGRAPH'87 Conference*, Anaheim, July 1987). [volumes]

743. [Thom83] A. L. Thomas, Geometric modeling and display primitives towards specialized hardware, *Computer Graphics 17*, 3(July 1983), 299–310 (also *Proceedings of the SIGGRAPH'83 Conference*, Detroit, July 1983). [hardware] D.5.5

744. [Tikk83] M. Tikkanen, M. Mäntylä, and M. Tamminen, GWB/DMS: a geometric data manager, in *Proceedings of the EUROGRAPHICS'83 Conference*, P. J. W. ten Hagen, ed., North-Holland, Amsterdam, 1983, 99–111. [volumes]

745. [Tilo81] R. B. Tilove, Exploiting spatial and structural locality in geometric modeling, TM-38, Production Automation project, University of Rochester, N.Y., 1981. [volumes] D.5.5.1.2

746. [Tilo84] R. B. Tilove, A null-object detection algorithm for constructive solid geometry, *Communications of the ACM 27*, 7(July 1984), 684–694. [volumes] D.5.5.1.2 D.5.5.2

747. [Tobl86] W. Tobler and Z. T. Chen, A quadtree for global information storage, *Geographical Analysis 18*, 4(October 1986), 360–371. [surfaces] D.1.4.1

748. [Torr67] K. E. Torrance and E. M. Sparrow, Theory for off-specular reflection from roughened surfaces, *Journal of the Optical Society of America 57*, (September 1967), 1105–1114. [general] A.7.2.1

749. [Tous80] G. T. Toussaint, Pattern recognition and geometrical complexity, *Proceedings of the Fifth International Conference on Pattern Recognition*, Miami Beach, December 1980, 1324–1346. [points] D.P D.4 D.4.2.3.6 D.4.3

750. [Tous82] G. T. Toussaint and D. Avis, On a convex hull algorithm for polygons and its application to triangulation problems, *Pattern Recognition 15*, 1(1982), 23–29. [regions]

751. [Trop81] H. Tropf and H. Herzog, Multidimensional range search in dynamically balanced trees, *Angewandte Informatik 23*, 2(February 1981), 71–77. [points] D.2.7

752. [Tuck84a] L. W. Tucker, Control strategy for an expert vision system using quadtree refinement, *Proceedings of the Workshop on Computer Vision: Representation and Control*, Annapolis, MD, April 1984, 214–218. [regions] D.1.3 A.1.4

753. [Tuck84b] L. W. Tucker, Computer vision using quadtree refinement, Ph.D. dissertation, Department of Electrical Engineering and Computer Science, Polytechnic Institute of New York, Brooklyn, May 1984. [regions] A.3.2.3

754. [Uhr72] L. Uhr, Layered "recognition cone" networks that preprocess, classify, and describe, *IEEE Transactions on Computers 21*, 7(July 1972), 758–768. [regions] D.1.3 A.1.4

755. [Ullm82] J. D. Ullman, *Principles of Database Systems*, Second Edition, Computer Science Press, Rockville, MD, 1982. [general] D.3.1

756. [Unni88] A. Unnikrishnan, P. Shankar, and Y. V. Venkatesh, Threaded linear hierarchical quadtrees for computation of geometric properties of binary images, *IEEE Transactions on Software Engineering 14*, 5(May 1988), 659–665. [regions]

757. [Unni84] A. Unnikrishnan and Y. V. Venkatesh, On the conversion of raster to linear quadtrees, Department of Electrical Engineering, Indian Institute of Science, Bangalore, India, May 1984. [regions] A.4.2.1

758. [Unni87a] A. Unnikrishnan, Y. V. Venkatesh, and P. Shankar, Connected component labelling using quadtrees — a bottom-up approach, *Computer Journal 30*, 2(April 1987), 176–182. [regions]

759. [Unni87b] A. Unnikrishnan, Y. V. Venkatesh, and P. Shankar, Distribution of black nodes at various levels in a linear quadtree, *Pattern Recognition Letters 6*, 5(December 1987), 341–342. [regions]

760. [Vaid88] P. M. Vaidya, Geometry helps in matching, *Proceedings of the Twentieth Annual ACM Symposium on the Theory of Computing*, Chicago, May 1988, 422–425. [points] D.2.9

761. [Vais84] V. K. Vaishnavi, Multidimensional height-balanced trees, *IEEE Transactions on Computers 33*, 4(April 1984), 334–343. [points] D.2.4.1

762. [Vais80] V. Vaishnavi and D. Wood, Data structures for the rectangle containment and enclosure problems, *Computer Graphics and Image Processing 13*, 4(August 1980), 372–384. [rectangles] D.3.2.4

763. [Vais82] V. Vaishnavi and D. Wood, Rectilinear line segment intersection, layered segment trees and dynamization, *Journal of Algorithms 3*, 2(June 1982), 160–176. [rectangles] D.3.2.4

764. [Vand84] D. J. Vanderschel, Divided leaf octal trees, Research Note, Schlumberger-Doll Research, Ridgefield, CT, March 1984. [volumes] D.5.3 A.1.3

765. [vanL81] J. van Leeuwen and D. Wood, The measure problem for rectangular ranges in d-space, *Journal of Algorithms 2*, 3(September 1981), 282–300. [rectangles] D.3.3

766. [vanL86a] M. L. P. van Lierop, Geometrical transformations on pictures represented by leafcodes, *Computer Vision, Graphics, and Image Processing 33*, 1(January 1986), 81–98. [regions] A.6.3.3 A.6.5.2

767. [vanL86b] M. L. P. van Lierop, Intermediate data structures for display algorithms, *Data Structures for Raster Graphics*, F. J. Peters, L. R. A. Kessener, and M. L. P. van Lierop, eds., Springer Verlag, Berlin, 1986, 39–55. [regions]

768. [Vara84] T. Varady and M. J. Pratt, Design techniques for the definition of solid objects with free-form geometry, *Computer Aided Geometric Design 1* (1984), 207–225. [surfaces]

769. [Veen85] J. Veenstra and N. Ahuja, Octree generation from silhouette views of an object, *Proceedings of the International Conference on Robotics*, St. Louis, March 1985, 843–848. [volumes] D.5.2 A.4.6

770. [Veen86] J. Veenstra and N. Ahuja, Efficient octree generation from silhouettes, *Proceedings of Computer Vision and Pattern Recognition 86*, Miami Beach, June 1986, 537–542. [volumes] D.5.2 A.4.6

771. [Veen88] J. Veenstra and N. Ahuja, Line drawings of octree-represented objects, *ACM Transactions on Graphics 7*, 1(January 1988), 61–75. [volumes] D.5.4

772. [Voel77] H. B. Voelcker and A. A. G. Requicha, Geometric modeling of mechanical parts and processes, *IEEE Computer 10*, 12(December 1977), 48–57. [volumes] D.3.4 D.5.5

773. [VonH88] B. Von Herzen, Applications of surface networks to sampling problems in computer graphics, Ph.D. dissertation, Technical Report Caltech-CS-TR-88–15, Computer Science Department, California Institute of Technology, Pasadena, CA, 1988. [surfaces] D.5.6 D.5.8 A.7.1.6

774. [VonH87] B. Von Herzen and A. H. Barr, Accurate triangulations of deformed, intersecting surfaces, *Computer Graphics 21*, 4(July 1987), 103–110 (also *Proceedings of the SIGGRAPH'87 Conference*, Anaheim, July 1987). [surfaces] D.5.6 D.5.8 A.7.1.6

775. [Walk88] M. Walker, R. S. Lo, and S. F. Cheng, Hidden line detection in polytree representations, *Computers & Graphics 12*, 1(1988), 65–69. [volumes]

776. [Wall84] A. F. Wallis and J. R. Woodwark, Creating large solid models for NC toolpath verification, *Proceedings of CAD'84 Conference*, Butterworth, Guildford, Great Britain, 1984, 455–460. [volumes] D.5.5

777. [Wals85] T. R. Walsh, On the size of quadtrees generalized to d-dimensional binary pictures, *Computers and Mathematics with Applications 11*, 11(November 1985), 1089–1097. [volumes] D.1.5 A.1.2

778. [Wals88] T. R. Walsh, Efficient axis-translation of binary digital pictures by blocks in linear quadtree representation, *Computer Vision, Graphics, and Image Processing 41*, 3(March 1988), 282–292. [volumes] A.6.5.3

779. [Ward88] G. J. Ward, F. M. Rubinstein, and R. D. Clear, A ray tracing solution for diffuse interreflection, *Computer Graphics 22*, 4(August 1988), 85–92 (also *Proceedings of the SIGGRAPH'88 Conference*, Atlanta, August 1988). [volumes]

780. [Warn68] J. E. Warnock, A hidden line algorithm for halftone picture representation, Computer Science Department TR 4–5, University of Utah, Salt Lake City, May 1968. [regions] D.1.3 A.1.4 A.7.1 A.7.1.2

781. [Warn69a] J. E. Warnock, The hidden line problem and the use of halftone displays, in *Pertinent Concepts in Computer Graphics—Proceedings of the Second University of Illinois Conference on Computer Graphics*, M. Faiman and J. Nievergelt, eds., University of Illinois Press, Urbana, IL, March 1969, 154–163. [regions] A.7.1

782. [Warn69b] J. E. Warnock, A hidden surface algorithm for computer generated half tone pictures, Computer Science Department TR 4–15, University of Utah, Salt Lake City, June 1969. [regions] D.1.3 D.4.2.1 A.1.4 A.7.1.2

783. [Wats84] D. F. Watson, and G. M. Philip, Systematic triangulations, *Computer Vision, Graphics, and Image Processing 26*, 2(May 1984), 217–223. [regions] D.4.3.1 D.5.2 A.4.6

784. [Webb84] R. E. Webber, Analysis of quadtree algorithms, Ph.D. dissertation, TR-1376, Computer Science Department, University of Maryland, College Park, MD, March 1984. [lines] D.4.2.3 A.3.3.4 A.4.3.1 A.4.3.2 A.5.1.2

785. [Webb85] R. E. Webber, personal communication, 1985. [regions] A.3.2.1.2

786. [Webb89] R. E. Webber and M. B. Dillencourt, Compressing quadtrees via common subtree merging, *Pattern Recognition Letters*, 1989 (also University of Maryland Computer Science TR-2137). [regions]

787. [Webe78] W. Weber, Three types of map data structures, their ANDs and NOTs, and a possible OR, in *Proceedings of the First International Advanced Study Symposium on Topological Data Structures for Geographic Information Systems*, G. Dutton, ed., Harvard Papers on Geographic Information Systems, 1978. [regions] A.2.1.1

788. [Wegh84] H. Weghorst, G. Hooper, and D. P. Greenberg, Improved computational methods for ray tracing, *ACM Transactions on Graphics 3*, 1(January 1984), 547–554 [volumes] A.7.2.1 A.7.2.2

789. [Weid78] B. W. Weide, Statistical methods in algorithm design and analysis, CMU-CS-78-142, Computer Science Department, Carnegie-Mellon University, Pittsburgh, August 1978. [general] D.3.2.2 D.3.2.4

790. [Weil85] K. Weiler, Edge-based data structures for solid modeling in a curved-surface environment, *IEEE Computer Graphics and Applications 5*, 1(January 1985), 21–40. [volumes] D.5.4

791. [Weil86] K. Weiler, Topological structures for geometric modeling, Ph.D. dissertation, Department of Computer and Systems Engineering, Rensselaer Polytechnic Institute, Troy, NY, August 1986. [volumes] D.5.4

792. [Weil77] K. Weiler and P. Atherton, Hidden surface removal using polygon area sorting, *Computer Graphics 11*, 2(Summer 1977), 214–222 (also *Proceedings of the SIGGRAPH'77 Conference*, San Jose, CA, July 1977). [volumes] A.7.1 A.7.1.3 A.7.3

793. [Weng87] J. Weng and N. Ahuja, Octrees of objects in arbitrary motion: representation and efficiency, *Computer Vision, Graphics, and Image Processing 39*, 2(August 1987), 167–185. [volumes] D.5.5.1.3 A.6.5.1

794. [Wern87] K. H. Werner, S. Yie, F. M. Ottliczky, H. B. Prince, and H. Diebel, ME CAD geometry construction, dimensioning, hatching, and part structuring, *Hewlett-Packard Journal 38*, 5(May 1987), 16–29. [points]

795. [Whit82] M. White, N-trees: large ordered indexes for multi-dimensional space, US Bureau of the Census, Statistical Research Division, Washington, DC, 1982. [points] D.1.3 D.2.7 A.1.4

796. [Whit80] T. Whitted, An improved illumination model for shaded display. *Communications of the ACM 23*, 6(June 1980), 343–349. [surfaces] A.7.2 A.7.2.1 A.7.2.2 A.7.2.5 A.7.3

797. [Will78] D. E. Willard, Balanced forests of k–d* trees as a dynamic data structure, Aiken Computation Lab TR-23–78, Harvard University, Cambridge, 1978. [points] D.2.4.1

798. [Will82] D. E. Willard, Polygon retrieval, *SIAM Journal on Computing 11*, 1(February 1982), 149–165. [points] D.2.3 D.2.3.3

799. [Will85a] D. E. Willard, New data structures for orthogonal range queries, *SIAM Journal on Computing 14*, 1(February 1985), 232–253. [points]

800. [Will85b] P. Willis and D. Milford, Browsing high definition colour pictures, *Computer Graphics Forum 4*, 3(September 1985), 203–208. [hardware]

801. [Wise84] D. S. Wise, Representing matrices as quadtrees for parallel processors (extended abstract), *ACM SIGSAM Bulletin 18*, 3(August 1984), 24–25. [matrices]

802. [Wise85] D. S. Wise, Representing matrices as quadtrees for parallel processors, *Information Processing Letters 20*, 4(May 1985), 195–199. [matrices] D.2.6.1

803. [Wise86] D. S. Wise, Parallel decomposition of matrix inversion using quadtrees, *Proceedings of the IEEE International Conference on Parallel Processing*, St. Charles, IL, August 1986, 92–99. [matrices]

804. [Wise87a] D. S. Wise, Matrix algebra and applicative programming, in *Functional Programming Languages and Computer Architecture Theoretical Aspects of Computer Science*, G. Kahn, ed., Portland, OR, 1987, 134–153 (Lecture Notes in Computer Science 274, Springer-Verlag, Berlin, 1987). [matrices] D.2.6.1

805. [Wise87b] D. S. Wise and J. Franco, Costs of quadtree representation of non-dense matrices, Technical Report No. 229, Computer Science Department, University of Indiana, Bloomington, Indiana, October 1987. [matrices] D.2.6.1

806. [Witt83] I. H. Witten and B. Wyvill, On the generation and use of space-filling curves, *Software—Practice and Experience 13*, 6(June 1983), 519–525. [regions] D.1.3 D.2.7 A.1.4

807. [Wong85] E. K. Wong and K. S. Fu, A hierarchical-orthogonal-space approach to collision-free path planning, *IEEE Journal of Robotics and Automation 2*, 1(March 1986), 42–53. [volumes]

808. [Woo85] T. C. Woo, A combinatorial analysis of boundary data structure schemata, *IEEE Computer Graphics and Applications 5*, 3(March 1985), 19–27. [volumes] D.5.4

809. [Wood82a] J. R. Woodwark, The explicit quad tree as a structure for computer graphics, *Computer Journal 25*, 2(May 1982), 235–238. [regions] A.2.1.1

810. [Wood84] J. R. Woodwark, Compressed quad trees, *Computer Journal 27*, 3(August 1984), 225–229. [regions]

811. [Wood86] J. R. Woodwark, Generating wireframes from set-theoretic solid models by spatial division, *Computer-Aided Design 18*, 6(July/August 1986), 307–315. [volumes] D.5.5

812. [Wood80] J. R. Woodwark and K. M. Quinlan, The derivation of graphics from volume models by recursive subdivision of the object space, *Proceedings Computer Graphics 80 Conference*, Online Publishers, London, 1980, 335–343. [volumes] D.5.5 D.5.5.1.2

813. [Wood82b] J. R. Woodwark and K. M. Quinlan, Reducing the effect of complexity on volume model evaluation, *Computer-aided Design 14*, 2(March 1982), 89–95. [volumes] D.5.5 D.5.5.1.2

814. [Wu82] A. Y. Wu, T. H. Hong, and A. Rosenfeld, Threshold selection using quadtrees, *IEEE Transactions on Pattern Analysis and Machine Intelligence 4*, 1(January 1982), 90–94. [regions]

815. [Wulf71] W. A. Wulf, D. B. Russell, and A. N. Habermann, BLISS: a language for systems programming, *Communications of the ACM 14*, 12(December 1971), 780–790. [general] L

816. [Wyvi85] G. Wyvill and T. L. Kunii, A functional model for constructive solid geometry, *Visual Computer 1*, 1(July 1985), 3–14. [volumes] D.5.3 D.5.5 D.5.5.2 A.7.2.2 A.7.2.3 A.7.2.4

817. [Wyvi86] G. Wyvill, T. L. Kunii, and Y. Shirai, Space division for ray tracing in CSG, *IEEE Computer Graphics and Applications 6*, 4(April 1986), 28–34. [volumes] D.5.5.2 A.7.2.2

818. [Yahi86] H. Yahia, Analyse des structures de donné arborescentes représentant des images, Thèse de docteur de troisième cycle, Université de Paris-Sud, Paris, December 1986. [regions]

819. [Yama84] K. Yamaguchi, T. L. Kunii, K. Fujimura, and H. Toriya, Octree-related data structures and algorithms, *IEEE Computer Graphics and Applications 4*, 1(January 1984), 53–59. [volumes] D.1.4.1 D.5.2 A.4.6 A.6.5.3 A.7.1.4

820. [Yau84] M. Yau, Generating quadtrees of cross-sections from octrees, *Computer Vision, Graphics, and Image Processing 27*, 2(August 1984), 211–238. [volumes] A.7.1.4

821. [Yau83] M. Yau and S. N. Srihari, A hierarchical data structure for multidimensional digital images, *Communications of the ACM 26*, 7(July 1983), 504–515. [volumes] D.1.3 D.5.2 D.5.3 A.1.4 A.2.1.2 A.4.2.3 A.4.6

822. [Yerr83] M. A. Yerry and M. S. Shephard, A modified quadtree approach to finite element mesh generation, *IEEE Computer Graphics and Applications 3*, 1(January/February 1983), 39–46. [finite element] D.1.3 A.1.4

823. [Ziav88] S. G. Ziavras and N. A. Alexandridis, Improved algorithms for translation of pictures represented by leaf codes, *Image and Vision Computing 6*, 1(February 1988), 13–20. [regions]

NAME AND CREDIT INDEX

Abdali, S. K., 429
Abe, S., 458
Abel, D. J., 30–31, 37, 136, 154, 199, 429, 455
Abram, G. D., 13, 283–284, 443
Adams, O., 429
Adel'son–Velskii, G. M., 429
Agarwal, P., 470
Aggarwal, J. K., 10, 176–177, 180–181, 218, 281, 393, 410, 436, 451, 456
Aho, A. V., vii, 166, 430
Ahuja, N., 176–179, 181, 247–248, 253–256, 259–260, 410, 415–416, 430, 461, 465, 471, 474–475
Akman, V., 14, 174, 410, 442
Alander, J., 430
Alexandridis, N., 430, 434, 477
Alexandrov, V. V., 26, 430
Allen, L., xi
Altenhofen, M., 430
Amanatides, J., 296, 316, 420, 430
Anderson, D. P., 228, 430
Anderson, D. R., 26, 461
Andresen, F. P., 422, 430
Ang, C. H., xi, 261, 416, 430
Angell, I. O., 470
Ansaldi, S., 430
Antony, R., xi, 431

Antoy, M., xi
Antoy, S., xi
Appel, A. A., 296, 431
Arbib, M. A., 24, 464
Aref, W., xi
Arimoto, S., 176, 459
Arnaldi, B., 315, 431
Artzy, E., 431
Arvo, J., xi, 319–321, 431
Asano, T., 440
Atherton, P., 270, 275–276, 318–319, 431, 475
Atkinson, H. H., 431
Avis, D., 431, 473
Ayala, D., 20, 289, 298, 324, 431, 434, 458
Aziz, N. M., 431

Ballard, D. H., 431
Barnes, J., 431
Barr, A. H., 290–291, 470, 474
Barrera, R., 431
Barsky, B. A., 319, 468, 470
Bartholdi, J. J. III, 432
Baskett, F., 443
Battaile, B., 294, 321, 445
Bauer, H., ix, 425, 432

Bauer, M. A., 432
Baumgart, B. G., 270, 432
Beaulieu, J. M., 432
Bechtel, F. K., 26, 461
Beck, J., 301, 304, 438
Becker, S., ix, 425, 432
Bcckley, D. A., 432
Beer, M., 432
Bell, S. B. M., 5, 432
Bent, S. W., 432
Bentley, J. L., 14–15, 23, 26, 432–433,
    442–443
Bern, M., 433
Berra, P. B., 446
Besslich, P. W., 433
Bestul, T., xi
Bhaskar, S. K., 433
Bhetanabhotla, M. N., 449
Bier, E. A., 452
Bieri, H., 219, 433
Bilmes, J., 446
Blinn, J. F., 289, 452
Bloomenthal, J., 433
Blum, H., 10, 357, 433
Boissonnat, J. D., 174, 442
Bolour, A., 433
Bonfatti, F., 433
Borgefors, G., 360, 369, 433
Bouatouch, K., 315, 431, 462
Bowyer, A., 434
Braid, I. C., 434
Brassel, K. E., 451
Bresenham, J. E., 315, 419, 434
Bright, S., 281, 434
Brock, P. J., 322–324, 437
Brodatz, P., 78, 434
Brooks, J., 297, 434
Brooks, R. A., 23, 434
Brown, R. L., 434
Brunet, P., 20, 289, 298, 324, 431, 434, 458
Bucher, W., 434
Burkhard, W. A., 434
Burnett, B., xi
Burrough, P. A., ix, 434
Burt, P. J., 434
Burton, F. W., 31, 434–435

Butz, A. R., 26, 435

Calkins, H., 455
Callen, M. J., 456
Cameron, S. A., 435
Carlbom, I., 20, 435
Carlson, W. E., 289, 435
Carpenter, L., 289, 294, 316, 437, 452
Carson, S., xi
Caspary, E., 315, 435, 468
Catmull, E., 287–289, 291, 322, 435
Cavazza, L., 433
Cebrian, J. A., 455
Chakravarty, I., 20, 435
Chan, K. C., 435
Chandran, S., xi
Chang, J. M., 435
Chaudhuri, B. B., 435
Chazelle, B., 420, 435
Chelberg, D., 436, 462
Chen, C., 435
Chen, H. H., 435
Chen, L. S., 281, 436
Chen, S. S., xi
Chen, Y. C., 436
Chen, Z. T., 436, 472
Cheng, S. F., 474
Chestek, R., 436
Chiarulli, D. M., 456
Chien, C. H., xi, 176–177, 180–181, 218,
    281, 410, 436
Chien, Y. T., xi
Chrisman, N., 462
Chu, J. H., xi, 347, 399, 436
Clark, J. H., 297, 436
Clay, R. D., 436
Clear, R. D., 474
Cleary, J. G., 315, 436
Clemmesen, M., 437
Cohen, E., 437
Cohen, J., 437
Cohen, M. F., 321–324, 437, 448
Cohen, Y., 13, 55, 325, 403–404, 437, 471
Cole, A. J., 437
Comer, D., 30, 37, 53, 136, 437
Connolly, C. I., 180, 437, 471

Cook, B. G., 30, 437
Cook, H., xi
Cook, R. L., 294–295, 316, 437
Cooper, C. N., 460
Cottingham, M. S., 437
Coxeter, H. S. M., 9, 437
Creutzburg, E., 437
Crow, F. C., 282, 437
Cutlip, M. W., 438
Cyrus, M., 301, 304, 438

Dadoun, N., 296–297, 317–318, 420, 438
Dandamudi, S. P., 438
Darbari, H., 449
Davis, E., 438
Davis, L. S., 24, 422, 430, 438, 442, 449
Davis, W. A., 276, 438, 444
De Coulon, F., 55, 438
De Floriani, L., xi, 430, 438
Delaunay, B., 438
DeMillo, R. A., 74, 131, 404, 438
Denlinger, J. L., 456
Deo, N., 463
DeRose, T. D., 319, 470
Dew, P. M., 438
DeWitt, D. J., 458
Diaz, B. M., 5, 432
Diebel, H., 475
Diehl, R., 430
Dijkstra, E. W., 22
Dillencourt, M. B., x–xi, 400, 408, 439, 475
Dinstein, I., 189, 439
Dippe, M., 316, 439
Dobkin, D., 319, 420, 435, 439
Doctor, L. J., 42, 276, 281, 439
Dodsworth, J., 438
Dorst, L., 439
Driscoll, J. R., 439
Du, H. C., 441
Du, W. H., 468
Dubitzki, T., 439
Duda, R. O., 439
Duff, T., 272, 289, 417, 439, 462
Duin, R. P. W., 439
Dürst, M. J., 48, 439

Dutton, G., 439
Dyer, C. R., x, 5–6, 14, 23, 30, 156, 219,
    221–222, 265, 352, 397, 399, 415,
    439–440, 451–452

Eastman, C. M., 23, 440
Eastman, R. D., xi, 422, 430
Edahiro, M., 440
Edelman, S., 440
Edelsbrunner, H., xi, 434, 440–441
Egenhofer, M. J., 441
Eisenstat, S. C., 74, 131, 404, 438
Elber, G., 441
Elcock, E. W., 441
Elmes, G. A., 441
Emmer, M., 9, 437
Emmerman, P. J., xi, 431
Enbody, R. J., 441
Endo, T., 12, 23, 53–54, 110, 200, 229, 326,
    450
Escher, M. C., 9
Esterling, D. M., 441
Estrin, G., xi
Evens, M. W., 432

Fabbrini, F., 441
Faddeeva, V. N., 441
Fagin, R., 441
Falcidieno, B., 430, 438
Faloutsos, C., xi, 441, 469
Fan, N. P., 442
Faugeras, O., 174, 442, 462
Faverjon, B., 23, 442
Fekete, G., xi, 442
Feynman, R. P., 281, 442
Finkel, R. A., 14, 23, 442–443
Flajolet, P., 442
Flickner, M. D., 189, 439
Foley, J. D., 176, 442
Fong, A. C., 189, 442
Fontdecaba, J., 458
Forgash, D., 271, 450
Forrest, A. R., 442

Franco, J., 476
Frank, A., 441, 442
Franklin, W. R., 14, 174, 410, 442
Fredkin, E., 14, 443
Fredman, M. L., 443
Freeman, H., 144, 443
Freeston, M., 443
Frieder, G., 431
Friedman, J. H., 14, 432, 443
Fu, K. S., 435, 476
Fuchs, H., 13, 270, 283–284, 286, 318, 443
Fuhrmann, D. R., 443
Fujimoto, A., 297, 304, 315, 419, 443
Fujimura, K., xi, 12, 20, 23, 45, 78, 99, 177,
        179, 254, 259, 278, 282, 314, 339,
        416–417, 443, 466–467, 477
Fujishiro, I., 452, 455
Fukuda, S., 176, 459

Gannon, J. D., xi
Gao, P., 443, 457
Garcia, G., 444
Garey, M. R., 11–12, 26, 444
Gargantini, I., 30, 37–38, 40, 50, 85, 105,
        199, 229, 253–254, 259, 431, 435,
        441, 444
Gaston, P. C., 444
Gautier, N. K., 444
German, S., xi
Gervautz, M., 444
Gholzadeh, B., 468
Gibson, L., 444
Gillespie, R., 276, 444
Ginsburg, Y., 271, 450
Glassner, A. S., 297–298, 300–302, 315,
        444
Goel, S., 449
Goldak, J., xi, 23, 450
Goldberg, M., 432
Goldschlager, L. M., 25, 444
Goldstein, R. A., 420, 444
Gomez, D., 445
Goodchild, M. F., 25, 401, 445
Goral, C. M., 294, 321, 445
Gordon, D., 281, 445
Gordon, P., xi

Gorsky, N. D., 445
Gosen, F., 454
Gouraud, H., 281, 445
Gouzènes, L., 445
Gowda, I. G., 445
Graham, S., ix, 425, 432
Grandfield, A. W., 25, 401, 445
Grant, E. D., 13, 283–284, 443
Greenberg, D. P., 293–294, 297, 321–324,
        437, 445, 448, 475
Greene, D., 445
Grosky, N. D., 26, 430
Grosky, W. I., 8, 116, 391, 400, 407, 445,
        454
Grünbaum, B., 445
Guevara, J. A., 48, 105, 213, 453
Guibas, L. J., 435, 441, 445
Günther, O., 445–446
Güting, H., 446
Guttman, A., 446
Guzman, A., 445

Habermann, A. N., 426, 476
Hachem, N. I., 446
Haken, D., 433
Halustchak, O., 461
Hamalainen, J., 430, 472
Hamilton, J. W., xi
Hanrahan, P., 296, 318, 420, 446
Hanson, E., 471
Hao, L. V., 456
Harada, L., 451
Haralick, R. M., 188, 190, 446
Harary, F., 219, 446
Hardas, D. M., 354, 421, 446
Hart, P. E., 439
Hayward, V., 446
Hebert, M., 174, 442
Hecht, M. S., 162, 446
Heckbert, P. S., 296, 318, 420, 446
Henderson, P., 319, 446
Henderson, T. C., 447
Herbert, F., 447
Herman, G. T., 281, 431, 436
Herman, M., 447, 470

Hertel, S., 447
Herzog, H., 473
Hickey, T., 437
Hilbert, D., 25, 116, 447
Hillier, F. S., 400, 447
Hillyard, R. C., 434
Hinojosa, A., 431
Hinrichs, K., 447
Hinterberger, H., 459
Hirschberg, D. S., 325, 447, 453
Hoare, C. A. R., 22, 447
Hoel, E., xi
Hoey, D., 234, 469
Holroyd, F., 5, 432
Hon, R. W., 433
Hong, S. J., 420, 462
Hong, T. H., 176, 434, 447, 450, 461, 476
Hooper, G., 293, 297, 475
Hopcroft, J. E., vii, 166, 430
Horowitz, S. L., 10, 447
Hoshi, M., 447
Houthuys, P., 447
Huang, L., xi
Huang, T. S., 435
Huang, Y. G., 8, 12, 45, 78, 99, 142, 236,
    259, 261, 339, 466–467
Huffman, D. A., 325, 355, 447
Hunter, G. M., 6, 14, 20, 23, 81, 153, 162,
    191, 197–198, 218, 222, 229, 231,
    247–248, 271, 273, 291, 367–368,
    404, 408, 411, 413, 448
Hut, P., 431
Hutflesz, A., 448
Hyytia, K., 430

Ibbs, T. J., 448
Ibrahim, H. A. H., 448
Ichikawa, T., 448
Immel, D. S., 321–324, 437, 448
Iri, M., 448, 459
Ismail, M. G. B., 353, 448
Iwata, K., 297, 304, 315, 419, 443
Iyengar, S. S., xi, 10, 51, 393, 424, 444, 449,
    455–456, 463, 468

Jaatinen, A., 430
Jackins, C. L., 23, 85, 197, 210, 217,
    248–250, 252, 260, 415, 448
Jackson, M. J., 5, 432
Jain, R., 8, 116, 391, 400, 407, 445, 454
Jansen, F. W., xi, 290, 299, 316, 449, 471
Jared, G. E. M., 449
Javis, J. F., 229–230, 449
Jensen, K., ix, 425, 449
Johnsen, O., 55, 438
Johnson, D. S., 11–12, 26, 444
Jones, L., 51, 449
Joshi, R. C., 449
Jou, E., xi
Joy, K. I., 449
Juan, R., 20, 431
Judice, C. N., 229–230, 449

Kajia, J. T., 294, 449
Kak, A. C., ix, 213, 328, 360, 396, 420, 464
Kakazu, Y., 459
Kambhampati, S., 422, 430, 449
Kanatani, K., 449
Kapenga, J., 316, 463
Kaplan, M. R., 297–298, 302, 315, 449
Karlsson, R. G., 449
Karonen, O., 297–300, 302, 430, 449, 472
Kasif, S., 450
Katajainen, J., 450
Kaufman, A., 271, 450
Kawaguchi, E., 12, 23, 53–54, 110, 200,
    229, 326, 450
Kedem, G., 450
Kedem, Z. M., 13, 270, 283–284, 286, 318,
    443
Kela, A., viii, xi, 23, 291, 450
Kelly, M. D., 24, 450
Kent, E. W., 450
Kernighan, B. W., ix, 425, 450
Kerola, P., 449
Kersten, M. L., 450
Kikuchi, L., 48, 105, 213, 453
Kim, Y. C., 10, 393, 451
King, T. R., 135, 460

Kirk, D., xi, 319–321, 431
Kirkpatrick, D., 296–297, 317–319, 420, 438–439, 445, 451
Kitsuregwa, M., 451
Klee, V., 451
Kleiner, A., 451
Klinger, A., viii, 14, 23, 30, 81, 430, 451, 460, 472
Knott, G. D., x, 410, 436, 451, 455
Knowlton, K., 12, 325, 328, 354, 356, 451
Knuth, D. E., ix–x, 14, 24, 51–52, 70, 78, 451
Kobayashi, H., 85, 451
Koistinen, P., 281, 451–452, 472
Kokubo, I., 440
Kollias, J. G., 31, 434–435
Kollias, V. J., 434–435
Koparkar, P. A., 458
Koppinen, M., 450
Korhonen, P., 472
Korn, M. R., 452
Kriegel, H. P., 446, 452, 468
Krishnamurthy, R., 452
Krolof, K., 452
Kropatsch, W. G., 25, 452
Kubo, H., 459
Kubota, H., 451
Kumar, P. S., 452
Kunii, T. L., 20, 177, 179, 254, 259, 278, 282, 297–298, 301–302, 304, 313–314, 417, 419, 439, 443, 452, 455, 476–477
Kurlander, D., 452
Kushner, T., 452
Kusuma, N., xi

Laflin, S., 281, 434
Lakhani, N. B., 444
Landis, Y. M., 429
Landy, M., 13, 55, 325, 403–404, 437, 471
Lane, J. M., 289, 452
Larson, P.Å., xi, 452
Laurini, R., 26, 453
Lauther, U., 453
Lauzon, J. P., 48, 50, 105, 213, 453, 455

Lavakusha, 453
Lavin, M. A., 454
Lawler, E., 26, 453
Lea, D., 453
Le Corre, J. F., 444
Lee, D. T., 445, 453
Lee, Y. T., 453
Leifker, D., 465
Leighton, R. B., 281, 442
Lelewer, D. A., 325, 453
LeMaster, R. J., 454
Lenstra, J. K., 26, 453
Letelier, P., 454
Li, C. C., 442
Li, H., 454
Li, M., 8, 116, 391, 400, 407, 445, 454
Li, S. X., 454
Libera, F. D., 454
Lieberman, G. J., 400, 447
Lingas, A., 11, 454
Linn, J., 454
Lipton, R. J., 74, 131, 404, 438–439, 454
Lischinski, D., xi
Little, J. J., 454
Litwin, W., 454
Liu, W., 457
Lloyd, J. W., 463
Lo, R. S., 474
Loew, M. H., 454
Lomet, D., 454
Lozano–Perez, T., 23, 434, 444, 454
Lu, S., 472
Lucas, D., 444
Lueker, G., 454
Lum, V. Y., 454
Lumia, R., 184, 188–189, 198, 212–213, 411, 454–455, 470
Lyche, T., 437

Mairson, H. G., 455
Manohar, M., 444, 452, 455, 463
Mäntylä, M., ix, 297–300, 302, 455, 472
Mao, X., 452, 455
Marble, D., xi, 455

Margalit, A., 410, 455
Mark, D. M., 48, 50, 105, 154, 213, 453, 455
Marsh, S. C., 455
Martin, G. N. N., 455
Martin, J. J., 456
Martin, M., 456
Martin, W. N., 176, 456
Mason, D. C., 265, 456
Mathieu, C., 456
Matsui, S., 448
Matsunaga, J., 12, 54, 229, 326, 450
Matsuyama, T., 456
Maurer, H. A., 433, 441
Mazumder, P., 456
McCarthy, J., 426, 456
McCluskey, E. J., 12, 456
McCreight, E. M., 456
McDonald, R., xi
McDonell, K. J., 460
McKeown, D. M. Jr., 456
Meagher, D., xi, 7, 23, 42, 211, 249–250, 252, 280–281, 399, 415, 417, 456–457
Mehlhorn, K., 447, 457
Mehrotra, R., 445
Mei, G. G., 457
Menon, S., 457, 470
Merrett, T. H., 25, 457, 460
Merrill, R. D., 457
Mesztenyi, C. K., 23, 464
Michener, J., 407, 457
Milford, D., 457, 476
Miller, R., 457
Minsky, M., 219, 457
Mitjonen, M., 449
Mobasseri, B. G., 457
Montani, C., 441
Moore, R. E., 457
Moreton, H. P., 436
Morris, D. T., 438
Morrison, R., 437
Mortenson, M. E., 286, 288, 290, 457
Morton, G. M., 22, 25, 30, 113, 458
Mount, D., xi, 281, 286, 291, 400, 439
Mudur, S. P., 458
Muller, H., 436

Mullin, J. K., 458
Muntz, R., xi
Muraka, R., 297, 434
Muralikrishna, M., 458
Murota, K., 448, 459
Mussi, P., 174, 442

Naamad, A., 445
Nagao, M., 456
Nagel, R., 420, 444
Nagy, G., ix, xi, 438, 458
Nair, K. N. R., 458
Nakamae, E., 295, 459
Nakamura, T., 85, 451
Nakamura, Y., 458
Nandy, S. K., 458
Nash, C., 253–255, 259–260, 415, 430
Naur, P., ix, 425, 458
Navazo, I., 20, 289, 298, 324, 431, 434, 458
Naylor, B. F., 13, 270, 283, 286, 318, 443, 472
Nelson, G., xi
Nelson, R. C., xi, 8, 12, 21, 45, 78, 99, 142, 236, 259, 261, 263, 339, 458–459, 466–467, 469
Nemoto, K., 459
Newell, M. E., 296, 459
Nievergelt, J., 441, 447, 459, 463
Nilsson, N. J., 23, 459
Ninke, W. H., 229–230, 449
Nishimura, S., 451
Nishita, T., 295, 459
Nishitani, Y., 42, 459
Noborio, H., 176, 459
Noma, T., 455
Noronha, V. T., 459

Ohsawa, Y., 458–459, 465
Ohya, T., 459
Okawara, F., 42, 459
Okino, N., 459
Oliver, M. A., 31, 55, 135, 245, 393, 460
Olsen, D. R. Jr., 460
Omachi, T., 459

Omolayole, J. O., 460
Onuoha, D., 297, 434
Ooi, B. C., 460
Orenstein, J. A., 18, 25, 460
Orivouri, E., 449
O'Rourke, J., 441, 460
Oskard, D. N., 461
Osse, W., 255–256, 260, 415–416, 461
Otoo, E. J., 457
Ottliczky, F. M., 475
Ottmann, T. A., 433, 461
Ouksel, M., 461, 468
Ousterhout, J. K., 461
Overmars, M. H., 441, 461
Ozkarahan, E. A., 461

Palimaka, J., 461
Papert, S., 219, 457
Park, C. M., 184, 189, 461
Patnaik, L. M., 458
Patrick, E. A., 26, 461
Pavel, M., 13, 55, 325, 403–404, 437, 471
Pavlidis, T., 10, 24, 354, 447, 472
Peano, G., 25, 461
Pearson, G., xi
Penrose, R., 9, 437
Perucchio, R., viii, 23, 291, 450
Peters, F., 247, 461
Peucker, T., 454, 462
Peuquet, D., ix, 455, 462, 470
Pfaltz, J. L., 10, 184, 188–190, 197, 357,
    462, 464
Philip, G. M., 174, 475
Phong, B. T., 281, 294–295, 462
Pienovi, C., 438
Pietikainen, M., 25, 462
Pippenger, N., 441
Platzman, L. K., 432
Polyakov, A. O., 26, 430
Ponce, J., 442, 462
Porter, T., 272, 294, 316, 417, 437, 462
Posdamer, J. L., 174–175, 181, 289, 462
Potmesil, M., 176, 462
Pratt, M. J., 474
Pratt, W. K., 12, 462
Preparata, F. P., 420, 453, 459, 462
Prewitt, J. M. S., 463

Prince, H. B., 475
Priol, T., 315, 431, 462
Puech, C., 77, 442, 456, 463
Pujari, A. K., 453
Pulleyblank, R., 316, 463
Purtilo, J., xi

Quarendon, P., 463
Quinlan, K. M., 20, 463, 476

Raghvan, V. V., 463
Rahn, F., 297, 434
Ramakrishnan, I. V., 458
Ramamohanarao, K., 463
Raman, V., 51, 463
Raman, V. K., 432
Ramanath, M. V. S., 431, 444
Ranade, S., 326, 328, 345–346, 420, 463
Rao, P. S., 455
Rastatter, J., xi
Ratschek, H., 463
Raunio, R., 472
Ravindran, S., 463
Reddy, D. R., 23, 463
Reddy, P. G., 453
Regnier, M., 463
Reingold, E. M., 463
Reiser, J. F., xi, 425, 463
Rekola, P., 430, 472
Remington, J., xi
Requicha, A. A. G., ix, 281, 453, 464, 474
Reynolds, R. A., 281, 436, 445
Rheinboldt, W. C., 23, 464
Rhodes, M. L., 30, 81, 451
Riesenfeld, R., 437
Rinnooy–Kan, A. H. G., 26, 453
Riseman, E. M., 24, 464
Ritchie, D. M., ix, 425, 450
Robinson, J. T., 464
Rogers, D. F., 21, 165, 176, 185, 225, 243,
    274, 281, 301, 304, 315, 410, 464
Rokne, J., 463
Ronse, C., 464
Rosenberg, J. B., 464

Rosenfeld, A., viii–x, 6, 8, 10, 25, 30, 40, 45, 84–85, 99, 136, 142, 156, 184, 188–190, 197, 213, 236, 243, 245, 248, 259, 261, 326, 328, 339, 345–346, 357, 360, 396, 420, 433–434, 439–440, 452, 461–464, 466–467, 476
Rossignac, J. R., 464
Roth, S. D., 174, 297, 420, 465
Roussopoulos, N., 24, 438, 441, 465, 469
Rubin, S., 23, 297, 463, 465
Rubinstein, F. M., 474
Ruff, R., 465
Russell, D. B., 426, 476
Rutovitz, D., 10, 49, 116, 357, 465

Saalfeld, A., xi, 174, 465
Sacks–Davis, R., xi, 460, 463
Sakauchi, M., 458–459, 465
Salzberg, B., 454, 465
Salzman, J., xi
Samet, H., vii–ix, 8, 12, 18, 21, 23, 30, 40, 42, 45, 55, 63–64, 70, 72, 74, 78, 84–85, 98–99, 110, 113, 117, 125, 136, 142–144, 155–156, 174, 187–189, 191, 195, 197, 199–200, 210–213, 215, 217, 222, 235–236, 238, 242–243, 245, 248, 259, 261, 263, 284, 298, 314, 326, 328, 339, 345–346, 348, 363, 366–367, 370, 381, 389, 400, 404, 408, 411, 414, 416, 420, 430, 439–440, 443, 452, 458–459, 463, 464–469, 472
Sandor, J., 468
Sands, M., 281, 442
Sankar, R., 458
Sarnak, N., 439, 468
Sasikumaran, S., 449
Satoh, T., 452
Satterthwaite, E., ix, 425, 432
Saxe, J., 433, 468
Scherson, I. D., 315, 468
Scheuermann, P., 461, 468
Schilling, W., 446
Schmitt, F., 468
Schumacker, R. A., 2, 267–269, 471
Schwartz, J. T., 23, 189, 468

Scott, D. S., 10, 393, 424, 468
Sedgewick, R., 190, 445, 468
Seeger, B., 452, 468
Seidel, R., 441
Sellis, T., xi, 441, 469, 471
Sevcik, K. C., 459
Shacter, B. J., 453
Shaffer, C. A., xi, 6, 8, 12, 30, 40, 45, 55, 70, 74, 78, 84–85, 99, 136, 142, 216, 236, 243, 245, 248, 259, 261, 263, 339, 353, 367, 369, 392, 395, 397, 400, 414–416, 422–424, 430, 461, 464, 466–467, 469
Shamos, M. I., 234, 462, 469
Shand, M. A., 469
Shankar, P., 473
Shapira, R., 443
Shapiro, E., 440
Shapiro, L., 184, 188–189, 198, 212–213, 411, 455
Sharir, M., 23, 189, 468
Shephard, G. C., 445
Shephard, M. S., 23, 477
Sherlekar, D., xi
Shigei, Y., 85, 451
Shimizu, K., 42, 459
Shirai, Y., 298, 476
Shmoys, D. B., 26, 453
Shneier, M., 25, 176, 218, 231, 274, 363, 368, 447, 450, 463, 469–470
Shpitalni, M., 441, 470
Shustek, L. J., 443
Siegel, A., 189, 468
Silva, C., 470
Silva Filho, Y. V., 470
Sim, Y. B., 180–181, 410, 436
Six, H. W., 448, 470
Sleator, D. D., 432, 439
Sloan, K. R. Jr., 354, 356, 460, 470
Smeulders, A. W. M., 439
Smith, J. L., 31, 37, 429
Smith, T., xi, 443, 457, 470
Snyder, J. M., 470
Sobhanpanah, C., 470
Solntseff, N., 470
Sommerville, D. M. Y., 470
Sorenson, P. G., 438
Sotomayor, D. L. G., 470

Sparrow, E. M., 295, 472
Speer, L. R., 319, 470
Sperling, G., 471
Sproull, R. F., 2, 267–269, 471
Srihari, S. N., ix, 23, 42, 143, 175, 354, 410,
    421, 446, 471, 477
Srivastava, S. K., 176, 471
Stanat, D. F., 433
Stanley, M., xi
Steele, R., 353, 448
Steiglitz, K., 6, 23, 81, 153, 162, 191,
    197–198, 218, 222, 229, 231,
    247–248, 271, 273, 291, 367–368,
    404, 408, 411, 448
Steinberg, H. A., 297, 434
Stenstrom, J. R., 471
Stevens, A., 448
Stolfi, J., 441, 455
Stonebraker, M., 471
Stout, Q. F., 367, 369, 457, 469
Strassen, V., 471
Strong, H. R., 441
Stroud, I. A., 434
Sulonen, R., 455
Sutherland, I. E., 2, 267–269, 471
Sutherland, R. J., 449
Swensen, J., 316, 439

Tabakman, Z., 444
Takagi, M., 451
Tamminen, M., x, 12, 20–21, 23, 55, 110,
    143, 174, 187–189, 191, 199–200,
    210–213, 222, 238, 242, 281, 290,
    297–300, 302, 314, 367, 403, 411,
    449, 452, 455, 467, 471–472
Tanaka, T., 297, 304, 315, 419, 443
Tang, Z., 472
Taniguchi, R. I., 450
Tanimoto, S., viii, 23–25, 85, 197, 210, 217,
    248–250, 252, 260, 354, 356, 415,
    448, 470, 472
Tarjan, R. E., 186–187, 432, 439, 454, 463,
    468, 472
Teuber, M. L., 9, 438
Thibault, W. C., 472
Thomas, A. L., 472
Tikkanen, M., 430, 473

Tilove, R. B., 472
Tobler, W., 436, 472
Tokarcik, L., xi
Tong, L., xi
Torborg, J. G., 42, 276, 281, 439
Toriya, H., 177, 179, 254, 259, 278, 282,
    417, 443, 477
Torrance, K. E., 294–295, 321, 437, 445,
    472
Toussaint, G. T., 473
Triendl, E., 447
Tropf, H., 473
Tucker, L. W., 23, 84, 473

Udupa, J. K., 281, 436
Uhr, L., 24, 473
Ullman, J. D., vii, 166, 430, 473
Unnikrishnan, A., 405, 473

Vaidya, P. M., 473
Vaishnavi, V., 473
van Dam, A., 176, 442
van Emde Boas, P., 450
van Leeuwen, J., 187, 441, 461, 472–473
van Lierop, M. L. P., 241, 249–250, 252,
    260, 415, 473–474
van Rosedale, J., 441
van Wijk, J. J., 316, 449
Vanderschel, D., 20, 435, 473
Varady, T., 449, 474
Vazquez, A. M., 431
Veenstra, J., 176–179, 181, 410, 430, 474
Venkatesh, Y. V., 405, 473
Voelcker, H., viii, 23, 291, 450, 464, 474
Von Herzen, B., xi, 290–291, 474

Wagle, S., ix, 458
Walker, M., 474
Walker, W., 461
Wallis, A. F., 474
Walsh, J. P., 296–297, 317–318, 420, 438
Walsh, T. R. S., 8, 256, 258–260, 399–400,
    415–416, 431, 435, 441, 444, 474

Walter, I., 25, 462
Wang, X., 438
Ward, G. J., 474
Warnock, J. E., 22, 270, 272–274, 289, 474
Watson, D. F., 174, 475
Webber, R. E., ix–x, 6, 18, 30, 40, 42, 45,
      78, 84–85, 98–99, 144, 154–155,
      197–198, 235, 243, 245, 248, 282,
      298, 339, 400, 404, 407–408, 411,
      464, 466–468, 475
Weber, J., xi
Weber, W., 30, 475
Weghorst, H., 293, 297, 475
Weide, B., 443, 475
Weiler, K., 270, 275–276, 318–319, 440,
      475
Weng, J., 247–248, 475
Werner, K. H., 475
Whang, K. Y., 452
White, M., 25, 475
Whitted, T., 289, 292, 295–297, 316–318,
      452, 465, 475
Widmayer, P., xi, 448, 470
Willard, D. E., 475
Williams, E. H. Jr., 433
Willis, P., 434, 457, 476
Wirth, N., ix, 425, 449
Wise, D. S., xi, 429, 476
Wiseman, N. E., 31, 55, 135, 245, 393, 460
Witten, I. H., 25, 476
Wollman, K., xi
Wong, C. K., 453
Wong, E. K., 476

Woo, T. C., 476
Wood, D., 433, 461, 470, 473
Woodwark, J. R., 20, 30, 434, 457, 463, 474,
      476
Wu, A. Y., 433, 439, 452, 476
Wu, O. L., 444
Wulf, W. A., 426, 477
Wyvill, B., 25, 476
Wyvill, G., 297–298, 301–302, 304,
      313–315, 419, 436, 476

Yahia, H., 77, 456, 463, 477
Yamaguchi, K., 177, 179, 254, 259, 278,
      282, 417, 443, 452, 477
Yap, C. K., 461
Yau, M., 23, 42, 143, 175, 280, 410, 417,
      477
Yen, D. W. L., 189, 439
Yerry, M. A., 23, 477
Yie, S., 475
Yokota, M., 12, 23, 450
Yu, C. T., 463
Yuba, T., 447

Zemankova, M., 440
Ziavras, S. G., 477
Zou, H., 435
Zuniga, O., 184, 188–189, 198, 212–213,
      411, 455

SUBJECT INDEX

Ω, *ix*

O, *ix*

2–3 tree, 166

2.5–dimensional hidden–surface elimination, 270–272, 276–277

2DRE (two–dimensional run encoding), 48–51, *49*, 105
  rotation (also see linear image transformation), 50
  translation (also see linear image transformation), 50

3DDDA (also see three–dimensional digital differential analyzer), 419

3DRE (three–dimensional run encoding), *105*

4–adjacent,
  blocks, *2*
  image elements, *184*
  pixels, *2*

8–adjacent,
  blocks, *2*
  image elements, *184*
  pixels, *2*

ACC, 262

ACCESS, 33

access array, *138*

Ackermann function, 187

acoustics, 317

active border, *199*, 221, *238*, 259, 265, 367, 414

active border element, *199*

active corner, *221*, 223, 422

active edge, *199*

active equivalence class, *188*

active image element, *188*

active node, *136*

active node table, *137*

active output quadtree block, 237

active region, 408

active unaligned quadtree block, *238*

adaptive hierarchical coding (see AHC)

adaptive uniform grid, 14

adaptive–grid method, *297*

ADD_EDGE_NEIGHBOR, 123

ADD_NODE, 35

ADD_TO_LINK_LIST, 159

ADJ, 61, 88

adjacency graph, 10

adjacency tree, *82*, 156, 198, 218, 222, 368, 404, 406, 410, 421

adjacent,
  blocks, *59*
  pixels, *58*

admissible scanning order, *190*, 190–191

AHC (adaptive hierarchical coding), *13*, 22

ALG1, 128

ALG2, 129

ALGOL, ix, 425

ALGOL W, ix, 425

algorithm A to construct a QMAT from a region quadtree, 375

algorithm B to construct a QMAT from a region quadtree, 375–376

aliasing, *274*, 289, 316–318

ALIGNED, 69

aligned quadtree, *229*
  intersection, 231–233
  set–theoretic operations, 231–234
  union, 233

alignment problem, 290–291

animation, 23

antialiasing, *274*, 316–317

aplc approximation, *353*

approximation,
  aplc (see aplc approximation)
  black forest (see black forest approximation, FBB)
  forest–based (see forest–based approximation)
  inner (see inner approximation, IB)
  inner black (see inner approximation, IB)
  inner white (see IW)
  outer (see outer approximation, OB)
  outer black (see outer approximation, OB)
  outer white (see OW)
  progressive (see progressive approximation)
  pyramid–based (see pyramid–based approximation)
  quadtree–based (see quadtree–based approximation)
  shape (see shape approximation)
  truncation–based (see truncation–based approximation)
  white forest (see white forest approximation, FWW)

approximation quality, 339–345

architecture, 23

area computation, 218

ARRAY_TO_QUADTREE, 114

ASSIGN_COLOR, 150

auto–adaptive block coding, 55

B face, *86*

B–tree, 30, 53, 99, 136, 142, 241

B⁺–tree, 37

back–to–front algorithm (painter's algorithm), 271–272, 276, 282, 285–286

beam tracing, 268, 296, 316–321

beam tree, *318*

begin, 426

Bezier curve, 287

bicubic surface patches, 286, 289, 292

big *O* notation, ix

binary array,
  conversion to a region quadtree, 112–116
  image representation, 55

binary image, *1*

binary image tree (see bintree), 12

binary pyramid, 354, 356

binary space partition tree (see BSP tree)

binary tree (also binary search tree), extended, 404, 406

bintree, *12*, 47, 55–56, 116, 125, 135, 200, 222–223, 298, 315, 328, 354, 370, 375, 419
  bucket PR (see bucket PR bintree)
  DF–expression, 55–56, 200–201
  FD linear (see FD linear bintree)
  PR (see PR bintree)

biquadratic surface patches, 324

bit interleaving, 174–175

bit manipulation, 136, 199, 405

BLACK, 149

black forest (FB), *51*, 329

black forest approximation (FBB), *329*

BLISS, 426

BMAT, *375*

border, *2*, *183*

border code (see chain code)

borderelement, 202

borderlist, 202

bottom–up neighbor finding, *85*

bottom–up quadtree algorithms, *85*

bottom–up ray tracing, 299–305
  implementation, 305–315

boundary, *2*, 2–3, *58*

BOUNDARY, 149

boundary code (see chain code)

boundary model (BRep), *270*, 297, 316

boundary node, *6*

bounding box,
    minimum volume (see minimum volume
        bounding box)
bounding volume, 297, 299
branching process, 77
breadth–first traversal, 39
BSP tree (binary space partition tree), *13*,
    270, 318–320, 420
    hidden–surface elimination, *283–286*
B–tree, 30, 53, 99, 136, 142, 241
bucket, *14*, 21
bucket PM octree, 315
bucket PR bintree, 319
bucket PR quadtree, 175
buffer computation (see region expansion)
BUILD_DF, 53
BUILD_TREE, 35, 335

C programming language, ix, 142, 210, 425,
    427
Catmull algorithm, 287–289, 322
CC, 148
CCEDGE, 111
cclist, 148
CCQUAD, 112
CCSIDE, 216
CEDGE, 111
cel, *271*
cell, 305
cell method (also see fixed–grid method), *14*
CENTER, 166
center image, 142
centroid computation,
    DF–expression, 54
chain code, *144*, 144–162, 233, 353
    construction from a region quadtree,
        156–162
    conversion to a region quadtree, 144–156
CHAINCODE_TO_QUADTREE, 149
Chamfer metric, *360*, 368, 381
CHANGE, 312
checkerboard, 5, 55, 70, 210, 352, 410
Chessboard distance function (also see
    Chessboard metric), 261, 265
Chessboard distance transform, 361–370
Chessboard metric, 358–360, 363

CHESSBOARD_DIST, 364
city block distance function (also see city
    block metric), 261
city block distance transform, 361–363
city block metric, 358–360, 363
CLIP_LINES, 168
CLIP_SQUARE, 167
clipping, 21, 165, 243, 317–318
CODE, 146
CODE1, 31
CODE2, 34
coherence, *269*
    image–space (see image–space coher-
        ence)
    object–space (see object–space coher-
        ence)
    scene (see scene coherence)
COL, 99, 106, 113, 202
color, 113
colored pixel, *273*
coloring algorithm, 163, 197
COMMON_EDGE, 62, 90
COMMON_FACE, 90
COMPARE, 149
COMPARE_T, 311
complete quadtree, 24, 131
component, *2, 186*
component counting (also see Euler number,
    genus), 5, 219–223, 422
COMPONENTS, 205
composite value (v_c), *355*, 355–356
compression, 55, 346–352
computational geometry, 317
computed tomography, 175
computer graphics, vii, viii
computer vision, vii, 23
COND, 426
cone tracing, 296, 316, 320
CONFLICT, 286
connected component labeling, 2, 5, 174,
    183, 215, 221, 366
    depth–first approach, *185*, 191, 199
    explicit quadtree (also see pointer quad-
        tree), 191–198
    pointerless quadtree, 199–213
    predetermined approach, *185*, 191, 199,
        201

three–dimensional data, 189, 204–205
connected graph, *219*
connection graph, *185*
connectivity destruction, 341–343
CONSTRUCT, 114
constructive solid geometry (CSG), *281*
convex hull, *288*, 318, 320, 398
coplanarity problem, 290–291
COPY_TREE, 231
core (also see main memory), 29, 241
corner, *58*, *184*
CORNER, 305
corridor computation (see region expansion)
covered, *248*
CQUAD, 112
crack, 291
crack perimeter, *213*
create, 426
CREATE_QNODE, 115
cross–sectional images, 175
CSG (see constructive solid geometry)
CSG tree (constructive solid geometry tree), 281
CSIDE, 216
curved surfaces,
    display of, 286–292
cutoff value, *42*
cycle, *220*
Cyrus–Beck clipping algorithm, 301, 304

D face, *86*
D–Euclidean metric, 360
d_A (also see city block metric), *358*
DATA, 166, 202
DB edge, *87*
DDA algorithm (see digital differential
    analyzer algorithm)
d_E (also see Euclidean metric), *358*
De Morgan's law, 233
DECODE_2DRE, 50
degree, *3*
DEN, 306
depth, *31*
depth–first connected component labeling,
    185, 191, 199, 367
DEPTH_FIRST, 185

DF edge, *87*
DF–expression,
    bintree, 55–56, 200–201
    centroid computation, 54
    neighbor finding, 110
    quadtree, 23, *53*, 53–54, 116, 125, 135,
        156, 234, 345
    rotation (also see linear image transfor-
        mation), 54
    scaling (also see linear image transfor-
        mation), 54
    set–theoretic operations, 54
    translation (also see linear image
        transformation), 54
DF_TO_QT, 54
DF_TO_QUADTREE, 54
DICTIONARY, 166
differentiator (v_d), *355*, 355–356
diffuse reflection, 292
digital differential analyzer (DDA) algorithm,
    315
digital tree, *14*
digitization, 164, 245
DIR, 33
DIRECT, 305
direction cube, *319*
directional code, *30*
disk,
    access, 135, 241
    memory device, 26, 47, 161, 241
display quadtree, *277*
DIST (also see distance transform), 364
DIST_EDGE, 365
DIST_VERTEX, 366
distance function (also see metric), *358*,
    358–360
    Chessboard (see Chessboard distance
        function)
    city block (see city block distance func-
        tion)
    Euclidean (see Euclidean distance func-
        tion)
    quadtree (see quadtree distance)
distance transform (DIST), *361*
    Chessboard (see Chessboard distance
        transform)
    city block (see city block distance
        transform)

Euclidean (see Euclidean distance
   transform)
path–length (see path–length distance
   transform)
distributed ray tracing, 294, 316
dithering, 229–231, *230*
divide and conquer, vii, 320, 420
d_M (also see Chessboard metric), *358*
don't care, *37*
dope vector, *78*
dynamic interference detection, 314
dynamic programming, *400*

E side (also boundary, edge), *58*
edge, *58*, *184*
edge quadtree, 273–274
edge view, 177
edge–neighbor, *58*
EDGE_DIR, 313
edgelist, 166
eight triangle rule, *291*, 418
eight–connected, 2, 162, 213
else, 426
emit, *321*
ENCODE_FBW, 333
ENCODE_FWB, 338
end, 426
ENDROW, 135
eq_class, 193
equivalence class, *186*
equivalence table, *188*, 212
Escher staircase, 9
Euclidean distance function (also see
   Euclidean metric), 26, 261
Euclidean distance transform, 361–363
Euclidean metric, 358–360, 363
Euler number (also see genus), 200,
   219
Euler's formula, *219*, 222
EVENROW, 122
EXCELL, 21, 299–300, 302
EXP_CCL, 193
EXP_PERIMETER, 216
EXPAND, 261
EXPAND1, 261
EXPAND2, 261

EXPAND3, 261
explicit quadtree (also see pointer quadtree),
   26
extended binary tree, 404, 406
exterior node, *6*
external face, *219*

F face, *86*
face, *219*
   external, *219*
   internal, *219*
face view, 177
face–neighbor, *85*
FACE_DIR, 312
facsimile transmission, 325
FATHER, 26
FB (also see black forest), *329*
FB′, *338*
FBB (also see black forest approximation),
   330
FBB′, *338*
FBW, *332*
FBW′, *339*
FD linear bintree, *48*
FD linear octree, 227, 305
FD linear quadtree, *40*, 42–48, 116, 125, 135,
   156, 161–162, 212, 263
   neighbor finding, 98–105
FD locational code, *40*, 40–41, 49, 136, 234,
   260, 303, 413
FD_OT_GTEQ_NEIGHBOR, 102
FD_QT_GTEQ_NEIGHBOR, 100
FDL_OT_EQ_EDGE_NEIGHBOR, 103
FDL_OT_EQ_FACE_NEIGHBOR, 103
FDL_OT_EQ_VERTEX_NEIGHBOR, 104
FDL_QT_EQ_EDGE_NEIGHBOR, 101
FDL_QT_EQ_VERTEX_NEIGHBOR, 101
feature detection, 24
feature extraction, 24
FIND, *186*, 195, 237
FIND_2D_BLOCK, 128
FIND_3D_BLOCK, 227
findpath problem, 23
finite element analysis, viii, 23, 291
FIRST_POINT, 309
five–dimensional space, 319–320

fixed–grid method (also see cell method), *14*, 297, 304
FL linear quadtree, *38*
    construction from a vector representation, 154
    neighbor finding, 105–108
FL locational code, *37*, 37–40, 48, 329
FL_QT_GTEQ_NEIGHBOR, 107
floodplain image, 45–46, 71, 78–81, 142, 262, 339, 350
forest,
    black (see black forest, FB)
    white (see white forest, FW)
forest of quadtrees, 51–53, 270
forest–based approximation, 329–354
FOREST_BLACK, 52
FOREST_BLACK2, 334
FOREST_GB, 52
FOREST_WHITE2, 334
four triangle rule, *291*, 418
four–connected, *2*, 158, 162, 213
four–dimensional scene, 314
fragment, 21
front–to–back algorithm, 272, 278–279, 282, 285, 319
full node, *4*
FW (also see white forest), *331*
FW′, *338*
FWB, *338*
FWB′, *338*
FWW (also see white forest approximation), *331*
FWW′, *338*

GAMMA, 81
GB, *51*
GB′, *331*
GEN, *59*
general unaligned–quadtree intersection, *235*
    linear quadtree, 236
    pointer quadtree, 236
generalized octree, 176
genus (also see Euler number), 200, *219*, 220–223
GENUS, 220
geographic information systems (GIS), vii,

    ix, 40, 45
GET_QUADRANT, 129
GIS (see geographic information systems)
GL coding, *55*
global, 425
Gouraud shading, *281*, 291
graphic tablet, 228
Gray code, *12*, 22
gray level, 10
gray node, *4*
gray–scale image, *2*, 354–356
grouping step, 11
GVN, *59*
GW, *51*
GW coding, *55*
GW′, *331*
h–refinement, 291
halfspace,
    linear (see linear halfspace)
halftoning (see dithering)
hardware, 281, 316
hash table, 298
hashing, 302
heap, 426
hexagonal silhouette, 179, 277
hexagonal tessellation (see hexagonal tiling)
hexagonal tiling, 4
hidden–line elimination, 22, 268, 273–274
hidden–surface elimination, 22, *267*, 267–270, 273–276, 293, 320
    2.5–dimensional (see 2.5–dimensional hidden–surface elimination)
    BSP tree (binary space partition tree), *283*–286
    image–space algorithms, 269
    object–space algorithms, 269
Hierarchical Scene Representation (see HSR)
hole, *2*, 6, 155, 218
hole creation, 341–342, 344–345
homogeneous image, *10*
HSR (Hierarchical Scene Representation), 318–320
Huffman code, 325, 355

IB (inner black approximation, also see inner approximation), *326*

ideal Lambertian reflector, *295*
illumination model, 294
    Phong (see Phong model)
    Whitted (see Whitted model)
image, *1*
    binary, *1*
    border, *2*
    gray–scale, *2*
    homogeneous, *10*
image coding, ix
image compression, ix
image dilation (see region expansion)
image element, *183*
image graph, *184*
image processing, vii–ix, 23
image understanding , 24
image–rendering task, *268*
image–space coherence, 269–270, 273, 275,
    296, 316–317
image–space hierarchies, *2*
in core (see core, main memory)
incomplete edge (also see active edge), 199
INCREMENT, 208
inner approximation (IB), *326*, 328–329
inner black approximation (see inner
    approximation, IB)
inner perimeter, *213*
inner set, *275*
inner white approximation (see IW)
interference detection,
    dynamic (see dynamic interference
    detection)
interior, 3
INTERIOR, 151
interior node, 6
intermediate quadtree, 272
internal face, *219*
intersection,
    aligned quadtree, 231–233
    unaligned quadtree, 234–242
INTERSECTION, 232
invisibility,
    mutual (see mutual invisibility)
isolated point, 166
isometric projection, *277*, 277–280,
    282
isometric view, 179
IW (inner white approximation), *328*

joining triangulation, 175

k–d tree, *15*–16, 286
    PR (see PR k–d tree)
k–d trie, *18*
key, *25*

L face, *86*
LAB, 202
LABEL, 193
LABEL_ADJACENT, 194
LABEL_GBGW, 51
Lambertian reflector,
    ideal (see ideal Lambertian reflector)
Lambertian surface, *294*, 294–295
Lambert's cosine law, *294*
landuse image, 71, 78–81, 142, 262
lazy evaluation, 319
LB edge, *87*
LBR (largest block representation), *353*,
    353–354
LD edge, *87*
LDB vertex (also octant), *87*
LDF vertex (also octant), *87*
leaf node, *4*
LEFT, 166
LEN, 166
LESS, 81
LEV, 99, 333
level, *4*
LF edge, *87*
light source, 293–294
lightpen, 228
line, 166
line of projection, *276*
linear bintree,
    FD (see FD linear bintree)
linear halfspace, *14*
linear image transformation, 245–260
    address computation, 253–260
    inverse transformation, 248–252
    transforming the source tree, 246–248
linear octree,
    FD (see FD linear octree)

linear quadtree, *37*
    FD (see FD linear quadtree)
    FL (see FL linear quadtree)
    general unaligned–quadtree intersection, 236
    predictive construction from a raster representation, 135–143
    rectilinear unaligned–quadtree intersection, 236–242
    VL (see VL linear quadtree)
linear sextree, *135*
LINK, 159
LISP, 426
list, 332
list, 426
LIST, 138
locational code, *30*
    FD (see FD locational code)
    FL (see FL locational code)
    VL (see VL locational code)
LU edge, *87*
LUB vertex (also octant), *87*
LUF vertex (also octant), *87*

main memory (also see core), 29–30, 47, 78, 99, 112, 116, 125, 135, 188, 305
major axis, *277*
MAKE_EQ_EDGE_NEIGHBOR, 386
MAKE_EQ_VERTEX_NEIGHBOR, 386
MAKESET, *186*
Manhattan distance function (also see Manhattan metric), 261
Manhattan metric (see city block metric)
MARK, 159
MARKED, 159
MAT (see medial axis transformation)
matching, 218
maximal block, 51, *360*
maximal block representation, 10
maximal quadtree skeleton block, *374*
maximal square, 330
maximum value metric (see Chessboard metric)
MAXLEQ, 100
MAXLESS, 106
mean gray level, 10

medial axis transformation (MAT), *10*
medical image processing, 23
memory (see main memory, core)
MERGE, 123
merge step, 11
merging cluster, *262*, 264–265, 416
merging triangulation, 175
mesh generation, 23
metric (also see distance function), *358*
    Chamfer (see Chamfer metric)
    Chessboard (see Chessboard metric)
    city block (see city block metric)
    D–Euclidean (see D–Euclidean metric)
    Euclidean (see Euclidean metric)
    Manhattan (see city block metric)
    maximum value (see Chessboard metric)
    Octagonal (see Octagonal metric)
MINGEQ, 106
minimum volume bounding box, 318, 320
mixed node, *328*
model A of neighbor distribution, *74*
model B of neighbor distribution, *74*
moment computation, 218
monotone regions, 356
Monte Carlo methods, 294, 316
MORE, 81
Morton matrix, *30*, 49–51
Morton order, *25*, 113, 116, 237–238, 241–242, 259, 401, 414
motion blur, 314, 316
mouse, 228
MOVE_DOWN, 81
MOVE_LEFT, 81
MOVE_RIGHT, 81
MOVE_UP, 81
multicolored image, 375
multicolored quadtree, 12
multiresolution, viii, 24
mutual invisibility, 322
mutual occlusion, 276
MX quadtree, 6, *16–17*, 162, 164, 234, 273
    construction from a polygon, 162–163, 247
MX quadtrie, *17*

N order, *25*

N side (also boundary, edge), *58*

naive algorithm for conversion from a raster representation to a quadtree, *142*

NE (also corner, vertex), *4*

nearest common ancestor (nca),
    octree, *91*
    quadtree, *63*

nearest neighbor problem (see neighboring object problem)

neighbor, *60*

neighbor finding,
    analysis for an octree, 95–97
    analysis for a quadtree, 70–78
    bottom–up, *85*
    DF–expression, 110
    FD linear quadtree, 98–105
    FL linear quadtree, 105–108
    pointerless quadtree and octree, 98–110
    pointer octree, 85–98
    pointer quadtree, 61–85
    stage one, *70*
    stage two, *70*
    top–down, *85*, 197, 217, 366
    use in ray tracing, 300–305
    VL linear quadtree, 108–109

neighboring object location, 228–229

net, *83*–84, 163, 197, 411

NET, 84

networks,
    road, 164

NEXT, 118, 148, 166, 202, 333

NEXT_CELL_DIRECTION, 310

NEXT_LINK, 160

NEXTROW, 135

NOCOLOR, 145

node,
    active, *136*
    full, *4*
    gray, *4*
    leaf, *4*
    mixed, *328*
    nonleaf, *4*
    opaque, *277*
    root, *4*
    transparent, *277*
    void, *4*

node, 111, 166, 193, 364

NODETYPE, 26, 166

nonleaf node, *4*

normalized quadtree, *218*

NP–completeness, *11*, 26

NUM, 306

NW (also corner, vertex), *4*

OB (outer black approximation, also see outer approximation), *326*

obel, *4*

object–space coherence, 269–270, 275, 296

object–space hierarchies, *2*

oblique parallel projection, *176*

occlusion, 271
    mutual, 276

Octagonal metric, 360

octant, *4*

octree,
    bucket PM (see bucket PM octree)
    FD linear (see FD linear octree)
    generalized (see generalized octree)
    PM (see PM octree)
    range (see range octree)
    region (see region octree)

ODDROW, 121

OFFSET, 226

OMEGA (Ω), *ix*

opaque, *298*

opaque node, *277*

OPEDGE, 111

OPQUAD, 112

OPSIDE, 216

optimal algorithm for conversion from a raster representation to a quadtree, *136*

optimal grid resolution, 407

optimal position of a region quadtree, 8

OPTIMAL_BUILD, 138

orthographic parallel projection, *176*

OT_EQ_EDGE_NEIGHBOR, 92

OT_EQ_FACE_NEIGHBOR, 91

OT_EQ_VERTEX_NEIGHBOR, 93

OT_GETQ_EDGE_NEIGHBOR, 94

OT_GTEQ_EDGE_NEIGHBOR2, 94, 306

OT_GTEQ_FACE_NEIGHBOR, 93

OT_GTEQ_FACE_NEIGHBOR2, 94, 306

OT_GTEQ_NEIGHBOR, 311

OT_GTEQ_VERTEX_NEIGHBOR, 94

OT_GTEQ_VERTEX_NEIGHBOR2, 94, 306
OUT_ROW, 129
OUT_TAB, 237
outer approximation (OB), *326*, 328–329
outer black approximation (see outer
    approximation, OB)
outer perimeter, *213*
outer set, *275*
outer white approximation (see OW)
outline algorithm, 163
outline–and–color algorithm, *163*, 247, 367
   color step (see coloring algorithm)
   outline step (see outline algorithm)
OUTPUT, 237
OUTPUT_END_OF_ROW, 127
OUTPUT_RUN, 127
overlay (see union)
OW (outer white approximation), *328*

P1, 166
P2, 166
page fault, 161, 186
painter's algorithm (see back–to–front algo-
    rithm)
panhandle–like objects, 345–346
parallel architectures, 316
parallel processing,
   quadtree medial axis transform (QMAT),
    395–397, 424
parallel projection, *276*, 276–280, 282, 292
   oblique, *176*
   orthographic, *176*
partial edge (also see active edge), 199
partial ordering, 329
PASCAL, ix, 425–426
patch, 286–290, 298, *321*
PATH, 99, 106, 333
path compression, *190*
path planning, 314, 369
path–length distance transform, *363*, 368
pathlength balancing transformation, *198*
pattern matching, 24
pattern recognition, vii, 23
Peano–Hilbert order, *25*, 116, 401
pebble image, 71, 78–81, 142
perimeter, 5–8

computation, 68, 200, 213–219, 366, 389
   crack, *213*
   inner, *213*
   outer, *213*
PERIMETER, 215
perspective projection, *276*, 280, 292
PHASEII, 209
Phong model, 294–295
Phong shading, *281*
piano movers problem, 23
pixel, *1*
pixel, 113
plan, 24
planar graph, *219*
plane–sweep techniques, 143
PM octree, *20*, 228, 245, 270, 303
   bucket (see bucket PM octree)
   curved surface, 289, 298, 324
   radiosity, 324
PM quadtree, *18*, 228, 245, 303
PM_DELETE, 171
PM_INSERT, 168
PM$_1$ quadtree, 18–20, 163–174, *165*, 298,
    303–304
   deletion, 170–172
   insertion, 167–170
PM1_CHECK, 168
point, 166
point location,
   five–dimensional space, 320
   quadtree, 225–227
point quadtree, *15*
point–in–polygon determination, 408
point–in–region determination,
   quadtree medial axis transform (QMAT),
    393–395
pointer, 426
pointer quadtree, *42*
   construction from a raster representation,
    117–125
   general unaligned–quadtree intersection,
    236
   rectilinear unaligned–quadtree intersec-
    tion, 235–236
pointerless quadtree, *30*
   connected component labeling, 199–213
pointing device, 228
polygon,

conversion to an MX quadtree, 162–163, 247
polygon coloring, *183*
   seed–filling algorithm (see seed–filling polygon coloring algorithm)
polygon expansion (see region expansion)
polygon intersection problem, 234
polygonal map, *18*
positive definiteness property, 358
POSSIBLE_PM1_MERGE, 171
PR bintree, *18*
   bucket (see bucket PR bintree)
PR k–d tree, *18*
PR quadtree, *17*–18, 164–165, 172
   bucket (see bucket PR quadtree)
PR quadtrie, *18*
PREDETERMINED, 187
predetermined connected component labeling, *185*, 191, 199, 201
predictive quadtree construction, 174
preload, 425
preorder traversal, 53
preprocessing cone, 24
primary ray, *292*, 294, 306
progressive approximation, 40, 325
progressive transmission, 325
projection,
   isometric (see isometric projection)
   oblique parallel, *176*
   orthographic parallel, *176*
   parallel (see parallel projection)
   perspective (see perspective projection)
projection image, 176
projection methods, 293
   region octree, 276–283
PROPAGATE_EDGE, 387
PROPAGATE_VERTEX, 387
PT_IN_SQUARE, 167
PTR, 305, 333
pyramid, viii, *24*–25, 354, 356
   binary (see binary pyramid)
   viewing, 267
pyramid–based approximation, 354–356

q–edge, *20*, *165*
Q–tree, 14

QCAT, *380*
QCODE, 52
QMAT (see quadtree medial axis transform)
QMAT_TO_QUADTREE, 385
QRAT, *380*
QT_EQ_EDGE_NEIGHBOR, 63
QT_EQ_VERTEX_NEIGHBOR, 65
QT_GTEQ_EDGE_NEIGHBOR, 64
QT_GTEQ_EDGE_NEIGHBOR2, 66
QT_GTEQ_VERTEX_NEIGHBOR, 65
QT_GTEQ_VERTEX_NEIGHBOR2, 66
QT_VERTEX_EDGE_NEIGHBOR, 67
QT_VERTEX_VERTEX_NEIGHBOR, 68
QUAD, 112
quadrant, *4*
quadrant, 426
quadtree, *2*
   aligned (see aligned quadtree)
   complete (see complete quadtree)
   display (see display quadtree)
   edge (see edge quadtree)
   explicit (see explicit quadtree)
   FD linear (see FD linear quadtree)
   FL linear (see FL linear quadtree)
   intermediate (see intermediate quadtree)
   multicolored (see multicolored quadtree)
   MX (see MX quadtree)
   normalized (see normalized quadtree)
   PM (see PM quadtree)
   PM$_1$ (see PM$_1$ quadtree)
   point (see point quadtree)
   pointer (see pointer quadtree)
   pointerless (see pointerless quadtree)
   PR (see PR quadtree)
   region (see region quadtree)
   restricted (see restricted quadtree)
   roped (see roped quadtree)
   semi (see semi–quadtree)
   triangular (see triangular quadtree)
   unaligned (see unaligned quadtree)
   VL linear (see VL linear quadtree)
quadtree distance, 68, 361–370
quadtree medial axis transform (QMAT), 68, 326, 370–398, *372*
   algorithm A to construct from a region quadtree, 375
   algorithm B to construct from a region quadtree, 375–376

construction from a region quadtree, 375–381

conversion to a region quadtree, 381–389

parallel processing, 395–397, 424

point–in–region determination, 393–395

sensitivity to shifts, 390–392, 397, 424

space requirements, 390–392, 396–397, 423–424

use as an image representation, 390–398

quadtree skeleton, *370*, 370–398

quadtree truncation, 328

quadtree–based approximation, 35, 39

QUADTREE_TO_CHAINCODE, 159

QUADTREE_TO_QMAT, 378

quadtrie, 14

MX (see MX quadtrie)

PR (see PR quadtrie)

quaternary code, *37*

QUILT system, 263

quinary code, 37

R face, *86*

radiate, *321*

radiosity, 268, 294, 321–324

random image model, 70, 197

range data, 179

range image, 180

range octree, *181*

ranging device, 179–180

raster representation, *116*

construction from a region quadtree, 125–135

conversion to a pointer quadtree, 117–125

predictive conversion to a linear quad-tree, 135–143

raster–scan order, *188*

RASTER_TO_QUADTREE, 120

rational, 306

rational arithmetic, 301

ray,

primary (see primary ray)

reflected (see reflected ray)

refracted (see refracted ray)

secondary (see secondary ray)

ray casting (see ray tracing)

ray coherence, 320

ray space, 319

ray tracing, 268, 292–315

bottom–up (see bottom–up ray tracing)

distributed (see distributed ray tracing)

neighbor finding, 300–305

top–down (see top–down ray tracing)

ray tree, *296*, 318

ray–object intersection, 296–297, 303–304, 315

RAY_INTERSECTS_OBJECT_IN_CELL, 305

RAY_TRACER, 308

RB edge, *87*

RD edge, *87*

RDB vertex (also octant), *87*

RDF vertex (also octant), *87*

recognition cone, 24

recoloring (see dithering)

rectangle representation, 374

rectangular coding, 10, 393

rectilinear unaligned–quadtree intersection, *235*, 244

linear quadtree, 236–242

pointer quadtree, 235–236

recurrence relations, 131

reference, 425

reflect, *321*

REFLECT, 62, 89

reflected ray, 293–294

reflection,

diffuse (see diffuse reflection)

specular (see specular reflection)

refracted ray, 293

refraction, 292

region,

black, *2*

boundary, *2*

eight–connected, *2*

four–connected, *2*

white, *2*

region expansion, 260–266, 375, 397

region graph, *222*

region octree, *4*, 204, 270

construction from multiple views, 174–181

projection methods, 276–283

radiosity, 322

region quadtree, *3*

bottom–up construction from a raster representation, 117–125
construction from a binary array, 112–116
construction from a chain code, 144–156
conversion to a chain code, 156–162
conversion to a raster representation, 125–135
optimal position, 8
predictive construction from a raster representation, 135–143
space requirements, 6–8
top–down construction from a raster representation, 125
regular decomposition, 2
relaxation, 420
resolution, viii, 2, 40
   multiresolution, viii, 24
   variable, viii, 3
restricted quadtree, 290, 290–291
RETURN_TREE_TO_AVAIL, 172
RF edge, 87
rgb–α–z approach, 289
RIGHT, 166
robotics, vii, 23
root node, 4
rope, 82, 134, 163, 197, 242
ROPE, 82
ROPE_QT_GTEQ_EDGE_NEIGHBOR, 82
roped quadtree, 82–84
rotation (also see linear image transformation), 246
   2DRE, 50
   90 degrees, 246–247
   arbitrary, 249–252
   DF–expression, 54
round off error, 419
ROW, 118
rowlist, 118
RU edge, 87
RUB vertex (also octant), 87
RUF vertex (also octant), 87
run representation (also see runlength representation), 10
runlength representation, 10, 111, 325, 353, 357
runs, 116

S side (also boundary, edge), 58
SAIL, ix, 425
SBW, 345
scaling (also see linear image transformation), 247, 249
   DF–expression, 54
scene, 271
scene coherence, 269–270, 296–297, 315–316, 418
SE (also corner, vertex), 4
secondary ray, 293, 293–294, 306
seed–filling polygon coloring algorithm, 185
segment tree, 180–181
segmentation, 10
semi–quadtree, 241
set–theoretic operations, vii, 229–243
   aligned quadtree, 231–234
   DF–expression, 54
   unaligned quadtree (also see rectilinear unaligned–quadtree intersection, general unaligned–quadtree intersection), 234–242
sextree, 135, 406
   linear (see linear sextree)
shading, 281, 291, 418
   Gouraud (see Gouraud shading)
   model (see illumination model)
   Phong (see Phong shading)
shape approximation, 328
shape recognition, 396
SHARE_PM1_VERTEX, 169
shift sensitivity of quadtree medial axis transform (QMAT), 390–392, 397, 424
shifting (see translation)
short–circuit evaluation, 425
side, 58, 184
silhouette, 176–177, 179, 277
simple polygon, 6
simultaneous linear equations, 321
SIZ, 202, 305
skeleton, 358–360, 359
   quadtree (see quadtree skeleton)
Snell's law, 295
solid modeling, vii, ix, 23
SON, 26, 166
SONTYPE, 26

SONTYPE4, 31
SONTYPE5, 33
space planning, 23
space tracing, *297–299*, 315
space–filling curve, *25*, 116
space–ordering methods, 25–26
spatial databases, vii
spatial index, vii, 22
specular exponent, *295*
specular reflection, 292, *294–295*
split step, 11
split–and–merge segmentation algorithm, 10, 25
SPLIT_PM_NODE, 169
spurious holes (see hole creation)
square, 166
SQUARE, 166
squarecode, *245*, 393
stack, 426
stage one of neighbor finding, *70*
stage two of neighbor finding, *70*
staircase, 199, 201, 205, 213, 411
staircase–like objects, 345
standard deviation, 10
stone image, 142
stopping points for thinning, 396
subsumed, *371*
subsuming element, *389*
subsumption property, *371*
SUM_ADJACENT, 217
surface area, 7
surface interpolation, 174
surface triangulation, 174
SW (also corner, vertex), *4*
sweep, 176
symmetry property, 358

T_IN, 305
T_OUT, 305
TABLE, 137
tail recursion, *162*
tessellation, *286*
tetrahedralization, 291
then, 426
thinning, 396–397

stopping points, 396
three–dimensional digital differential analyzer (3DDDA), 419
three–dimensional run encoding (also see 3DRE), *105*
threshold, 10
thresholding, *183*
TID, 10, 393
top–down neighbor finding, *85*, 197, 217, 366
top–down quadtree algorithms, *85*
top–down ray tracing, 299
TOP_DOWN_ACTIVE_BORDER_DIST, 367
TOP_DOWN_NEIGHBOR_DIST, 367
topography image, 71, 78–81, 142
total path length (TPL), 409
TPL (see total path length)
translation (also see linear image transformation),
  2DRE, 50
  DF–expression, 54
  linear quadtree, 256–259
  pointer quadtree, 253–256
  power of two, 247
  region quadtree, 6, 8, 244
translucence, *293*
transmit, 335
transparence, *293*
transparent node, *277*
traveling salesman problem, *26*
TRAVERSE, 207
triangle inequality property, 358
triangular decomposition, 278–279
triangular quadtree, 179, 279
triangular tessellation (see triangular tiling)
triangular tiling, 4
triangulation, 174, 290
trie, *14*
  k–d (see k–d trie)
truncation error, 419
truncation–based approximation, 326–329
TRY_TO_MERGE_PM1, 171
two triangle rule, *291*
two–dimensional run encoding (also see 2DRE), *49*, 213
TYPE, 100, 305

U face, *86*
UB edge, *87*
UF edge, *87*
unaligned quadtree, *229*
    set–theoretic operations (also see rectil-
        inear unaligned–quadtree intersection,
        general unaligned–quadtree intersec-
        tion), 234–242
uncolored, *117*
uniform orientation, *4*
union,
    aligned quadtree, 233
    DF–expression, 413
UNION, *186*, 194
UNION_FIND, *186*
UNIX,
    4,2BSD version , 210
    4.3BSD version, 142, 263

value, 425
variable resolution, viii, 3
VAX11/750, 210
VAX11/785, 142, 263
v_c (also see composite value), *355*
v_d (also see differentiator), *356*
VEN, *59*
vertex, *184*
VERTEX, 112
vertex set, *262*, 265, 416
vertex view, 177
vertex–neighbor, *58*
VERTEX_DIR, 313
very large–scale integration (see VLSI)
view,
    edge (see edge view)
    face (see face view)
    isometric (see isometric view)
    vertex (see vertex view)

viewing pyramid, 267
viewpoint, *276*
visibility number, 285
VL linear quadtree, *34*, 48, 116
    neighbor finding, 108–109
VL locational code, *34*, 34–35, 39–40, 48,
        52, 298, 329, 333
VLSI (very large–scale integration), 296
void node, *4*
voxel, *4*
VVN, *59*

W side (also boundary, edge), *58*
Warnock algorithm, 270, 272–275, 289
Weiler–Atherton algorithm, 270, 275–276,
        318
white forest (FW), *330*
white forest approximation (FWW), *331*
WHITEBLOCKS, 38, 256
Whitted model, 295–296
windowing, 243–245
winged–edge representation, 270
wireframe representation, 268

X_EDGE, 239
XCOORD, 166

Y_EDGE, 239
YCOORD, 166

Z order, *25*
z–buffer, 289